SOUTHERN UTAH UNIVERSITY:
The First Hundred Years
A HERITAGE HISTORY

By Anne Okerlund Leavitt

Congratulations
2005 Graduate!!!

 SUU Press
Complimentary Copy

Presidential illustrations by Rohn Solomon

SOUTHERN UTAH UNIVERSITY PRESS
CEDAR CITY, UTAH

Library of Congress Catalog Card Number: 97-66545

ISBN Number: 0-935615-10-5

Printed in the United States of America

10   9   8   7   6   5   4   3   2   1

To Dixie

Contents

Part One: The Evolving Entity

Part Two: The Developing Disciplines

The College of Education

The College of Arts, Letters and Humanities

The College of Business, Communication and Technology

The College of Science

Preface

In September 1949, my father loaded his family into our aging Oldsmobile and set off over the mountains from Loa, Utah, to bring me, the eldest child, to school at the Branch Agricultural College in Cedar City. The trip signaled a transition from childhood, and carried the exhilaration of seeing "new country," for none of us had seen Cedar City. However, our excitement was tempered by a view of the sacrifice required. My suitcase was filled with dresses my mother had made for me. Both parents took extra jobs. The family got by on less. Mindful of the price being paid for my privilege, I did all I could by working on campus. Nonetheless, I knew then and know now that without my parents' sacrifice, my life would not have been enriched by a college education.

Thousands of variations of the same story accrete to form the bedrock beneath the founding and flowering of Southern Utah University—one generation seeking to provide the next with better.

With my 17-year-old perspective I saw little generational bedrock, but from the beginning I knew this was a wondrous place. It offered me a new world, filled with the exhilaration of discovery. I had dreamed of learning to be an opera diva, or an actress of renown, or possibly a writer of stories warm, elevating, dramatic and inspiring.

Five decades, six sons, and a multitude of adventures later, the opera and the acting aspirations are amusing memories. But the dream of writing never wilted and finds expression here in telling the warm, elevating, dramatic and inspiring story of the institution which enhanced my vision of the world and of my possibilities. I rejoice in the privilege.

The story of Southern Utah University is a story of people. It is a saga, filled with struggle and striving and miracles—always occurring at just the right moment, always after the striving. It is the continuing story of people willing to extend themselves far beyond their personal comforts and concerns, in building the institution that would bless many thousands of lives.

A clear theme has emerged in the writing: the inextricable connection between the school and the community—the remarkable dedication of the citizens of the town, as well as the people who became the faculty and staff, in whatever era they came. The University is an extraordinary institution, that lives because of the people who have loved it and sacrificed for it.

I have gained an expanded view of the cumulative effects of the sacrifices of generations past upon generations present and future, and often have pondered whether or not the builders, in any age, have had an inkling of what would eventually emerge from their efforts. The unity of purpose and willingness of heart that encompassed Cedar City in 1897 was no small thing. Neither has been the devotion that has continued over the hundred years, as individuals and groups, faculty and staff, have worked untiringly to build, to fight uneven odds, to extract from themselves heroic endeavor. I return again and again to a scriptural phrase: "Let no man count these as small things; for there is much that lieth in futurity...which depends upon these things."

This history has a two-part structure. The first is a narrative chronology, which is entitled "The Evolving Entity." The second part, entitled "The Developing Disciplines," arose because I recognized the narrative chronology could contain only a meager mention of the people involved in the various departments. I was unwilling to accept that reality, and hence invited more than 30 individuals whose lives had been intertwined with the different departments to write the history of their particular discipline. Most responded with wonderful willingness. Some produced complete histories with extensive biographies and wonderful details. Dr. Blaine Johnson and Dr. Kent Myers, for example, each worked for more than a year to produce works of significant size. Some wrote only small, personal remembrances. Some department histories are the work of one contributor and some are team efforts. Far more material flowed forth than could be contained in this book, but all of it is appreciated and will be preserved in the special collections area of the SUU library.

Some of the chapter comprising "The

Developing Disciplines" are a bit ragged, reflecting the multiplicity of contributors, their widely varying styles and perspectives. An additional year of polishing would have brought additional unity to this part of the book, but at the expense of obscuring the patchwork personalities which have brought this institution into being. I am grateful to these dozens of contributors to "The Developing Disciplines." They are carefully noted in the endnotes. The reader is encouraged to not only enjoy their work, but to acknowledge their effort.

The appendix includes the complete text of a wonderful document, *The Founders Speak*, by Rhoda Matheson Wood. It is fascinating reading and I have used it extensively in writing the story of the building of the first Branch Normal School building. It has not been published before and I am glad that it will now be preserved and available. The Founding of BAC, written by Fae Decker Dix from recollections of Randall W. Lunt and published previously as a leaflet, is also included as a key historical resource.

I have not attempted to focus upon the many accomplishments of distinguished graduates, though the school has produced excellent educators, corporate heads, artists of renown and significant political leaders. It seems to me that the most profound effects have resulted as the school has nourished and expanded young people who came, primarily, from the small communities of the region, and who then returned to their towns to become the mothers and fathers, plumbers and build-

ing contractors, teachers and businesspeople, servants of church and community that make up the fabric of a solid society.

My desire to be inclusive was a bit naive. There will be many important events and people that I did not discover or hadn't space to mention, and I suffer some pangs about that. Sometimes the captions on the photographs do not identify the subjects, but they seemed important to include, even when specifics were unavailable, because the delightful images convey the feel of the time. I had hoped to include photographs of all long-term faculty and staff. That became an issue of both time and space, and in the end I could only include some, who are representative of many, many others.

I have tried to write with accuracy and have been careful to research and verify. I have not tried so diligently to be objective, for learning and pondering the breadth of the subject magnified my passion for the place and the people. My writing reflects my partiality and for that I offer no apology.

There is here preserved a history of the first 100 years of an extraordinary institution founded to forward the dreams of succeeding generations. It is my fondest hope that the story will engender in those generations some of the fervor that I feel toward Southern Utah University and those who have fostered its progress.

Anne Okerlund Leavitt
Cedar City, Utah
March, 1997

Acknowledgments

As I began to research and write, our fourth son, Eric, suggested I dedicate this history to those whose names were inadvertently omitted. I do worry about those people, but my most compelling concern is that the scores who contributed real and significant assistance be acknowledged and feel my deep gratitude. I am profoundly grateful for:

Dixie L. Leavitt, beloved husband and friend, who taught me, through his own devotion and long service, to cherish the school; who believed that the history should be written; and that I could do it. He sacrificed order, time, and comfort for the project. Dixie's strengthening influence, encouragement and prayers were constant. He never complained.

My 87-year-old widowed mother, Phyllis Meeks Okerlund, who, with my father, sacrificed to send five children through the school. She cheerfully relinquished my attention and company during a tender time in her life, moved by a mother's belief that her daughter was the only person with the talent to accomplish the task.

My children and grandchildren, sisters, brothers and friends, who carefully measured their contacts with me because of " the book." I will enjoy giving them a more complete measure of attention.

President Gerald R. Sherratt, a friend who had the audacity to enlist a housewife to write history; who read and re-read, endlessly excised commas and capitals and straightened skewed perceptions. Jerry cheered, praised and encouraged. He watched over the details. He added much, but resisted being acknowledged. Coupled with President Sherratt's efforts were those of his administrative assistant Ruth Challis, who fielded countless phone calls and ran the resultant errands, always cheerfully.

Jan Nelson, who bestowed wondrous friendship in the form of weeks of watch care, tedious tasks, constant concern and tangible help. She distilled histories into chapters, corrected, and counseled, and in the process learned to love the school, the place and the people. My debt surely extends to Jan's husband, Norm Nelson, who encouraged and supported Jan's participation from the beginning to the marathon end.

Maralyn Dotson, who called to say, "I want to help. I'm a fast typist and I will do anything you want me to do." And she did. Her gift included countless hours deciphering the hand-written manuscripts of departmental histories and old documents, delivered to me on tidy computer disks. She loved and encouraged the writers of departmental histories, sometimes urging them, sometimes soothing them. I relied heavily upon Maralyn. My reliance was well-placed.

More than 30 people who wrote histories of their departments—contributing their own adventures and perceptions. I cannot mention each, for fear of forgetting one, but I am indebted to all, for they were my sources for part two, "The Developing Disciplines." They are carefully noted in the endnotes, and their work, collectively voluminous, is preserved in the Special Collections area of the SUU Library. It is my hope that readers will be diligent in following the endnotes, for I deeply desire that these willing and able friends be clearly acknowledged for their contributions.

Those who wrote in years past, for without them there would be no preservation of this history. John Urie, Henry Lunt, Caroline Keturrah Parry, William R. Palmer, Inez Cooper, Rhoda Matheson Wood, Fae Decker Dix, Gladys McConnell, George Croft and Morgan Rollo: I have learned to love them all.

Photographers, mostly unknown, who captured the spirit of the place and preserved it in delightful forms. Some are known, including Richard Rowley, Boyd Redington, Larry Baker, Richard Engleman, Lynn S. Dennett, Jeff Dower, James Howells, Lonnie Behunin, Rohn Solomon, John Guertler, Richard Dotson and Dave Meanea. They are appreciated, as is Amy Skelton who searched, sorted and scanned stacks of photographs.

Blanche Cox Clegg, Tim Muir and others of the staff of Special Collections who cheerfully searched and endlessly provided materials, photographs and documents. The library media staff poured over miles of microfilm and extracted stacks of research resource from a hundred years of newspapers.

Larry Baker, who, working through the nights on far more projects than anyone ought to attempt, added this one, creating the book's design, effecting much of its layout, and directing the project to completion.

Rohn Solomon, who was a quiet hero at the end, when the duress of the deadline became acute, resolutely comforting, pressing forward with patient persistence, and working with astonishing skill through long days and longer nights. Daphne Solomon, whose quickness at learning and applying new skills helped pull the project through.

Doris Williamson and Kathy Cloward, each ingenious at offering the right expertise at precisely the right moment.

Phillip Chidester, gentle and gifted man, who read and corrected, legitimized my formless footnotes and did not disdain.

And Marsha Lundgren, who with radiant face and resolute manner said, "I'm just like those pioneers. I'm the most likely person to do the index. I've had experience, I know how to do it. I'll step up to the line." And she did!

To all of these, and to innumerable people whose interest and encouragement spurred me on, I extend my deeply felt thanks.

PART 1

The Evolving Entity

EARLY CEDAR CITY SCENES, ABOVE: MAIN STREET,   BELOW: LOOKING WEST ON CENTER STREET.

CHAPTER I

The Place and The People

The story of Southern Utah University began long before its beginning, in the drama of the people who built it, in the place they had come to settle. The place reshaped the people by the hardships it imposed upon them. The place was wilderness. The earliest passersby had passed by without lingering, for the journey ahead was harsh and arduous. Fray Silvestre Vélez de Escalante, to describe the area, used words like "abundant" and "very good" in his journal entries, but all saw that it was country that would require much taming to make it truly habitable. The people who came to stay were tamers. They were individuals, intelligent and hardy, whose absolute commitment to a common cause welded them into an instrument equal to the task.

In 1854 Solomon M. Carvalho retraced the trail through the Cedar Valley, now ringing with the clang of axe and hammer, that he had helped to blaze 10 years earlier as a member of John C. Fremont's exploration party. This time he recorded "The persevering industry of these people is unsurpassed." [1]

Persevering industry was the reason that the people he now found striving to settle the harsh southern Utah country, were surmounting their extraordinary challenges. His observation has deep significance in the story of Southern Utah University.

In 1776, the year the colonists in the east were battling the British for their freedom, Fray Escalante and Fray Francisco Atanasio Dominguez, Catholic priests and explorers, entered the Cedar Valley as the first recorded white men. They were returning from an unsuccessful journey in search of a new route from Santa Fe, New Mexico to California. He named the place the Valley of Señor San Jose. On October 12, 1776, Father Escalante wrote in his journal:

The Valley of Senor San Jose, through which we have just passed, in its northern part is in 37 degrees of latitude...From north to south it is about 12 leagues long...it has very abundant pasturage, large meadows, fair sized marshes, and plenty of very good land for settlement with seasonal crops, although there is not enough water, even the high places at this

season had green and fresh pasturage. The Indians who live in this valley dress very scantily, and eat grass seeds, hares, pinon nuts in season...They do not plant corn...They are very cowardly. [2]

THE NATIVES OF SOUTHERN UTAH, CIRCA 1880

The natives so unkindly assessed as cowardly, had little reason to be brave. They had survived in the sagebrush covered land for generations, living on roots and berries, rabbits and rodents, and an occasional deer. They had existed there, probably for centuries, in destitution. Little wonder that the passing train of white-skinned visitors startled them and caused them to appear fainthearted. They were already terrorized by the neighboring Ute tribe of Chief Walkara who captured their women and children, then sold them to unscrupulous traders who carried them away to the coast, where they brought a good price on the slave market. The native population was rapidly dwindling. [3]

In 1847, the settlement of the western wilderness began in earnest as endless wagon trains and handcart companies streamed into the Great Basin. These were the Mormon pioneers, a people so determined to establish themselves in a place far enough away from the rejection and persecution with which their early history is replete that they were willing to brave every obstacle. These were not passersby. They came to build upon the land.

A small group of Mormon men, formed into a military contingent called the Mormon Battalion, had made an heroic march to San Bernardino, California, in the cause of the union in the Mexican War. Marching to join their people in the northern reaches of the territory, they passed through Cedar Valley on their way back to the Salt Lake Valley and made mental notes of the resources of the area. Their report to Brigham Young, the leader of the Mormons, kindled an interest acted upon two years later, when the general assembly of the provisional government of the State of Deseret at its September 1849 session, commissioned the honorable Parley P. Pratt to raise a company of 50 men with the necessary teams and equipment to explore the unknown region of Southern Utah. [4]

Parley P. Pratt, never one to hang back, quickly organized 50 strong men who had agreed to go south. On November 24, 1949, Elder Pratt gave the signal to "move em out." It was a promising parade: 12 wagons, one carriage, 24 yokes of oxen, seven beeves, 38 horses and mules, and average of 150 pound of flour to a man, some hard bread and corn meal, one brass field piece, firearms, ammunition in proportion. [5]

The Pratt journey proved to be among the most grueling explorations of the settling of the territory. Extreme hardship of weather plagued the party. But their sense of mission drove them to legendary determination. This expedition differed in purpose from all the previous visitors to the southern end of the Utah territory. They were to assess the place in terms of its potential in the building of the kingdom. They were to discern and recommend whether the saints could succeed in establishing settlements in the wilderness.

A telling entry from Parley P. Pratt's diary describes the hazards of the journey:

During our exploring expedition we encountered severe weather, deep snows and many hardships and toils incident to such an undertaking. We explored the best portions of the country south from Salt Lake City to the mouth of the Santa Clara on the Rio Virgin, which is a principal branch of the Colorado. Our distance in going and returning (counting the direct traveled route as afterward opened) was between 700 or 800 miles. In much of this distance we made the first track; and even the portion which had before been penetrated by wagons was so completely snowed under that we seldom found the trail. [6]

By March, 1850 all of Pratt's expedition had returned to Salt Lake and had given Brigham Young and the legislature a report both positive and persuasive. He described "...a handsome expansive plain of very rich land consisting partly of overflowed wire-grass meadows all of which might be drained and cultivated, using the water from the higher levels. Other portions of the plain are dry and level, delightful for the plow and clothed with rich meadow grass." But most wonderful of all, "On the south western border of this valley arc thousands of acres of cedar, constituting an almost inexhaustible supply of fuel, which makes excellent coal. In the center of these forests rises a hill of the richest iron ore. The water, soil, fuel, timber and mineral wealth of this valley...are judged capable of sustaining and employing from 50,000 to 100,000 inhabitants, all of which would have these resources more conveniently situated than any other settlements the company has seen west of the States." [7] Elder Pratt's company had completed its assignment to explore and evaluate the prospects of the region.

On July 27, 1850 The *Deseret News* published a call for volunteers to settle in southern Utah:

Brethren of Great Salt Lake City and vicin-

ity, who are full of faith and good works, who have been blessed with means;...are informed by the Presidency of the Church that a colony is wanted at Little Salt Lake this fall; that 50 or more good effective men with teams and wagons, provisions and clothing, are wanted for one year. Seed grain in abundance and tools in all their variety for a new colony are wanted to start from this place immediately after the fall conference, to repair to the Valley of the Little Salt Lake without delay. There to sow, build and fence; erect a saw and grist mill, establish an iron foundry as speedily as possible and do all other acts and things necessary for the preservation and safety of an infant settlement. [8]

With a clear vision that the assignment to create an iron industry would require specialized talents as well as considerable financial resources, Church leaders dispatched missionaries to the British Isles, where people with such skills were plentiful, with the express purpose of converting people who could help, and persuading them to haste to Zion. The phrase, "...who have been blessed with means," was an important aspect of the need, for money was sorely needed in the establishment of the new enterprise.

The list of the people who came from England and Wales reveals astonishing success in finding people who would fulfill the need. Many were wealthy and brought their wealth along with their talents, their skills and their devotion. Many were refined, having taken advantage of the cultural opportunities provided by fortunate circumstances. From them flowed the rich cultural tradition that helped to sustain them through extraordinary trials and formed the unique ambience of their communities. This was no chance assemblage. It was a carefully selected group, bound together by their shared fervor for the religion they had embraced. [9]

Huge, genial George A. Smith, beloved Mormon "apostle" of great

GEORGE A. SMITH

energy and ability, was given command of the "Iron Mission" as it later became known. Calls for volunteers swelled his company to 169, including 120 men, 30 of whom were accompanied by their families. It was a formidable company, larger than any earlier colonizing group, organized on a military basis and well equipped and provisioned for its distant frontier assignment.

George A. Smith appointed Henry Lunt, a member of his company who had emigrated from England, to be his personal secretary and to assist John D. Lee, as clerk. Lunt was true to his trust. He made careful lists of the people who embarked on this adventure into new country, and a wonderfully detailed account of the provisions they gathered to carry with them over the long, laborious miles from Salt Lake City.

A glance at the list reveals that they were prepared for their task: plenty of axes and shovels, plows and pistols, seed and sickles. Here were a people determined to dedicate their lives to the new settlement and to produce and provide iron for the building of Zion. They were a well-balanced group, including artisans and craftsmen chosen for the skills needed in the effort.

HENRY LUNT

There were several farmers, two blacksmiths, five carpenters and joiners, two shoemakers, two surveyors, one millwright, each with tools. There were four top and pit sawyers with saw, one stone cutter, two stone masons, one gunsmith, one tailor, moulders, smelters, bricklayers, teachers, one pottery maker, tanners, millers, saddle and harness makers, two doctors, midwives, weavers, spinners, glove and hat makers, soap makers. [10]

It is noteworthy that despite the glowing report of the 50 men in the Pratt party of explorers, only three of their number were among those who now volunteered to join the company and to make their permanent homes in the Little Salt Lake Valley. These included William R. Vance, James Farrer and Joseph Horne. Horne became the pilot for the group.

Since they came from different parts of the Salt Lake Valley, their general rendezvous point was Provo. By 4 o'clock on Sunday afternoon, December 15, 1850, the company had gathered from their various directions. George A. Smith conducted a meeting that evening.

He appointed captains of 50s and 10s for orderly travel, promised them safety on condition of diligence, and then dismissed them with prayer.

That night wolves killed one of their horses. The next morning at 9 a.m., the wagons rolled resolutely out under clear skies, over muddy terrain. By evening a high wind buffeted the train and snow began to fall. Henry Lunt's meticulous record affords a close-up view of the hardships of the trek from the first day. He records the temperature every day at 6 a.m., 12 noon and 6 p.m. The daytime temperatures ranged from 16 below zero to the 40s on "fine, clear days." Always the nights dropped below freezing. He records snow depths to four feet, but every day they made some progress—some days six miles, some seven, and on a rare good day, usually when they encountered hard frozen ground, 15 or 16 miles.

By December 18 they had left all vestiges of civilization. That day they camped at Peteetneet Creek (now Payson), where they had found Captain James Pace, an old friend of President Smith, working with a few men to construct a fort. Lunt recorded, "These were the last white men we saw on the journey." [11]

On Christmas Day, Lunt wrote: "Morning intensely cold, thermometer 12 degrees below zero. Began to cross the river at 11 o'clock a.m., all but two wagons were crossed this day; no accident occurred. Had a very steep bluff to ascend on coming out of the river. Camped by the river side below the ford. Feed poor for the animals." [12]

We may wonder at the wisdom of beginning a journey of 250 miles in the dead of winter, until we remember that they had to be ready for spring. The seeds they carried with them were their hope for sustenance. Their axes and shovels would be well-used in clearing brush and bringing water onto the land. But before they could begin to clear and plant, they would have to find materials to construct shelters for themselves. Hands and feet nearly frozen, they trudged resolutely on, over the unyielding rocks and ruts, fueled by an incredible sense of mission.

On January 13, 1851 the weary party reached Center Creek (Parowan). This was their destination, for they intended to form the first settlement there as an agricultural base before moving on to their assigned mission to produce iron. Within a week of arrival they had held elections, organized the

settlement, and begun the construction of a canyon road for the bringing of timber to build a fort and a meeting house.

A marvelous spirit of community evolved. While they lived in wagon boxes, the building of the fort, the clearing of the fields, the building of the meeting house all progressed with amazing dispatch. One entry from the journal of Henry Lunt reads, "Monday, January 27: About 26 teams went to haul logs for the meeting house, while others worked on the foundation, hauling and laying rock etc." For the next few days he reports work and progress on the meeting house. Then on Thursday, January 30, "Prest. Smith[13] informed the brethren that there was no public work for today, so everybody went to work to get logs and materials for their own buildings."

John Urie, remarked upon such early instances and the phenomenon of a group of people who intuitively placed the public good ahead of private interests. In an 1880 history of Cedar City, he wrote: "Everything of a public nature was heartily taken hold of and pushed through as fast as circumstances would permit."

When, a generation later, the most rigorous demands were exacted from the descendants of these settlers, in order to fulfill their dreams of education for their children, they were prepared and strengthened by their pre-established tradition of optimum cooperative effort for the good of the whole.

Their dreams, from the beginning, were focused upon providing opportunities for their children and upon building for themselves better lives. They were primarily people from England and Ireland, from Scotland and Wales, who had relinquished their opportunity for education, as well as the security of family, home and nation. They came because of their religious faith, of which the most basic doctrines taught that the glory of God is intelligence. Their scriptures repeatedly admonished them to, "...seek ye out of the best books words of wisdom; seek learning, even by study and by faith...become acquainted with good books, and with languages, tongues and peoples..."[14] How could they obey such mandates if they had no access to books or if they could not read?

That learning was of primary concern is demonstrated by a delightful first hand account of the first school, taught by George A. Smith himself, in a lean-to of sagebrush branches, built at the side of his wagons that first winter of 1850-51 at Center Creek. "My wicky-up is a very important establishment," he wrote, early in March, "composed of brush, a few slabs and three wagons, a fire in the center and a lot of milking stools, benches and logs placed around, two of which are cushioned with buffalo robes. Folks at home would be surprised to see my school some of the cold nights of February, scholars standing around my huge campfire, the wind broken off by the brush and the whole canopy of heaven for a covering. Thermometer standing at seven degrees, one side roasting while the other freezing, requiring a continual turning to keep as near as possible an equilibrium of temperature. I would stand with my grammar book, the only one in school, would give out a sentence at a time, and pass it round. Notwithstanding these circumstances, I never saw a grammar class learn faster for the time." [15]

Grammar mattered to them, because their languages and their dialects were so disparate. They were melding themselves into a society. The common need to communicate quickened their interest in learning from this single grammar text. Several journal entries in each week conclude with "School in the evening."

By the time Brigham Young arrived for a visit on May 10, 1851, there were buildings in progress, and 1,000 acres of cleared and planted fields. It was, in fact, an incorporated town, which President Young officially christened Parowan.

As soon as the harvest was completed in the fall and the pioneers were assured of food to survive the winter ahead, they turned to their iron manufacturing assignment. A fort site was selected on Coal Creek, and George A. Smith called Henry Lunt to lead a colonizing company of 30 carefully chosen English, Scottish, and Welsh iron miners and manufacturers to travel from Parowan to the proposed site of the new fort some 20 miles south. They arrived on November 11, 1851, with 11 wagons, and were reinforced by an additional company a few weeks later. The iron workers established winter quarters by setting the wagon boxes in a straight line facing south. They built, as well, a 300-foot square enclosure of brush reinforced with cottonwoods and adobes which served as a fort as well as a corral for the animals. The temporary location was north of the present Cedar City cemetery. Soon the company moved further west and their priority became clearing a field of 500 acres and digging an irrigation canal for bringing precious water to it. Each man acquired ownership of a 10-acre block by the drawing of lots, and was also entitled to a garden plot near the fort. [16]

Christina Bulloch was only 14 years old when she arrived at the site of the new city with her Scottish immigrant parents. Her diary gives an intimate view of the adventure:

There were but two wagon boxes there when we arrived. Some men had started to build a stockade corral there from driftwood. There was plenty of that along the creek banks. Upon arriving we put our wagons in line, each one facing south. A cedar branch wickiup was made for each wagon where the campfires were built...One of our biggest problems was keeping warm at night. Bedding had become so scarce that most families had barely enough to be comfortable when the weather was mild. That winter we had lots of real cold weather. The problem was solved by having the musicians tune up and we'd have a dance. The people danced until they were warm before going to bed. There really was no room big enough for everyone to dance in, so it was decided to have half the people go to bed early when the nights were icy. They slept until midnight while the other half enjoyed a lively dance time. Then they awakened the sleeping folks who got up and had their turn to the music and the first group slipped into their warmed beds. It was quite jolly, sometimes I could have danced all night. [17]

Again the arduous work of clearing and fort-building fully occupied this small company of 30, and many of them were specifically assigned to commence the work of iron production. Fortunately Brigham Young soon sent an additional group of Scottish, English and Welch converts, all of them emigrant iron workers, augmenting their numbers. With this group came Bullochs, Bladens, Adams, Eastons and Woods—all names that would later figure prominently in the dramatic stories of the founding of their school.

Although the next two years exacted a heavy toll upon the Cedar City settlers, their agricultural and municipal endeavors moved inexorably forward. We can only imagine how their patience was tested when it was determined, after they had cleared and planted the fields and constructed cabins, that the location was unsafe. What a set-back to have to abandon the fruits of their labors and begin to build again. The iron industry consumed much of their talent, their pooled manpower and resources. They struggled always with the obstacles of insufficient water, poor coal, floods and indian troubles. Yet the people continued resolute and at the end of the year one wrote: "...in the midst of semi-hostile savages, guarding, fencing, farming, exploring and building houses, mills etc, we have had our prayers answered in the preservation of our lives and property." [18]

Sometimes their prayers were answered with astonishing ideas. From Christina Bulloch's diary comes this tale of inventiveness and adaptability:

The time of the Black Canker was the worse time we had. We had no sugar for a long time. Our mouths started swelling and turning dark. It was found that in the mornings the dew on the willow and the cottonwood leaves tasted sweet. We shook and washed these drippings off and boiled them down for syrup. It was like a miracle, but after we got fruits and root vegetables and sorgham, the dew no longer tasted sweet.[19]

During the winter of 1852-53 they established a school in the Old Fort. In December George A. Smith reported to his LDS Church brethren in Salt Lake City that Matthew Carruthers, a graduate of Edinburgh University, was running a large school, well attended. He taught, under call from the Church, day school for the children and night school attended mostly by adult members of the community. [20] Apostle Smith reported that they were hampered by a shortage of schoolbooks, a chronic problem in grammar schools at the time. Eager to give support to the infant settlement, Church leaders responded with a shipment of 238 schoolbooks, including 1st, 2nd, 3rd readers, grammars, arithmetics, dictionaries, spellers, and for older pupils, texts on hygiene, chemistry and philosophy.

After they abandoned the Old Fort and the people moved to their second location, they held school in private homes or in their humble meeting houses. It is evident that despite all the distracting difficulties, education was an over-riding priority.

Finally, by 1857, the burdens became unbearably heavy. Their iron-making efforts were thwarted by fuel problems, failure of water power, destructive floods. There were Indian troubles when the settlers interfered with Chief Walkara's lucrative slave trade. Protective fortifications became a more compelling need than ironmaking.

At that point even more weighty concerns darkened the horizon. The nation's government, considering the Mormons an upstart group in the western reaches of the territory, had sent an army to bring the people under submission. Through the entire territory there arose a determination to resist the threat of intrusion, and to never again endure displacement. In this atmosphere there occurred at Mountain Meadow, near Cedar City, a withering tragedy in which a passing company of immigrants were killed. In the wake of the unspeakable calamity, many disheartened people simply left. Cedar City was reduced from a community of nearly a thousand people to less than four hundred. Iron manufacturing closed down. For a time there was a real question whether or not the town would endure.

But the roots of survival were firmly embedded in the soil of Cedar City...the cloud of failure which shadowed them mercifully watered new industry. [21] The same threat of Johnston's Army which had stopped iron operations in 1857 resulted in the abandonment of outlying Mormon settlements and sent many San Bernardino colonists to Cedar City, augmenting their numbers. The iron workers turned to agriculture and home industry for survival. Cattle and sheep proved vital

THRESHING
CREW,
1880s

to their economy. Alfalfa seed brought by Australian converts to San Bernardino and relayed to Iron County proved to be vitally important as did the a quart of cotton seed carried from Parowan to the Mormon Indian Mission on the Santa Clara. When the latter materialized into thirty yards of good cotton cloth, of which a sample reached Brigham Young's office, the resulting "Cotton Mission," established 50 miles to the south in the Dixie country, helped to revitalize the whole area.

John Urie, in his *History of Cedar City*, of 1880, looks back upon the period of revitalization of Cedar City with exuberant personal pride. [22] His arrival as a young man of 20 had coincided with the darkest of times. But when he writes as a mature man of 45, his memories are filled with elation that they had triumphed in the face of overwhelming difficulty:

The year 1856 is marked for scarcity of bread...The iron works had become a failure and were now at a standstill. Notwithstanding all our efforts to make iron successfully...Our ingenuity was put to the test and our inventive skill was brightened up by necessity. We began to turn our attention to home manufacturing to supply our local wants. Tanneries, shoe shops, furniture, the making of combs, threshing machines, blacksmiths, wagon makers, nail machinery, etc. and last, though not least, a woolen factory was established and made from the raw material in our vicinity. Sheep

were becoming more plentiful and they were certainly needed. Our clothing was scant, indeed many of us going barefoot to work, to meeting and even the dance. The year 1857 gave us a new wool carding machine, home made in all of its parts with the exception of the cards. The iron was furnished by our furnaces. Looms, spinning machine, carder etc were all made here, and by as good mechanics as are to be found anyplace in the world. In these years of scarcity and disappointment, the domestic spinning wheel and hand loom were not neglected. Many of our wives and daughters could take the wool from the sheep's back, wash, card, spin, color, weave and make it up for their husbands, brothers and sisters. Cotton grown 60 miles south of us was taken and carded by the hand for warping

CEDAR CO-OPERATIVE SHEEP ASSOCIATION

are numerously attended. Several societies for the diffusion of useful knowledge to the young are well-patronized and taken advantage of. The ladies have a Relief Society for the purpose of mutual instruction and to relieve the wants of the needy, the sick and afflicted. Take us altogether, we are a happy family on the rim of the Great American Basin. Our past experience has made us sober and grave, clever and ingenious, dignified and independent.[22]

Past experience had also taught the settlers of Cedar City that whatever they needed to accomplish could be done with honest cooperative effort. If they had failed in the iron industry, they had succeeded in the establishment of a pattern of living together and working together for the common benefit of the community.

A look at the next three decades reveals that this theme of united effort carried through every undertaking. Agriculture could thrive because they worked together to create canals to convey water to irrigate the land. When floods washed away their system, they began again, resigned to the fact that irrigation farming was an eternal struggle.

L ivestock enterprises grew and prospered because they linked themselves into cooperative alliances. Livestock cooperatives included the Cedar Cattle Company and the Cedar City Cooperative Sheep Association, which became a bulwark of the economy for over fifty years. Incorporated in 1861, the Cedar City Cooperative Sheep Association was a preferred depository for individuals, school boards, bands, the City Corporation and the Perpetual Emigration Fund.

A most amazing example of cooperative collaboration, throughout the larger community and the entire L.D.S. Church, was the Perpetual Emigration Fund. In 1868 a correspondent for the *Deseret News* sent the following item from Cedar City:

February 6, 1868. Our bishop is still busy and persevering in raising money to gather the poor Saints from the old countries...He is full of the spirit of emigration and has already had the pleasure of remitting to President Young $700.00 in money besides contributions in wheat, etc. Even our Sunday School scholars brought in their five

and sewing thread.

Fairs were frequent. The exhibition of skill, and enterprise was unique and marvelous. We were rich although sometimes we felt poor. The luxuries of life were scarce and expensive. Itinerant merchants with elastic conscience would sell us sugar at $1.00 per lb., tea $5.00 per lb., domestic Calico $1.00 per yard, prints 75 cents per yd., coffee $1.00 per lb., tobacco $1.00 per six-inch plug, and allow us but $1.00 per bushel for grain. A hundred other little necessities were sold at from 100 percent to 5,000 percent above cash. Grain was plentiful during these years and no market. Our living was plain and simple and our health excellent, but few deaths having occurred since 1851 to '60. We are fond of domestic enjoyment. We can and have enjoyed our home dramatic talent, our bands of music, the dance and the different outdoor games common to a country community. The social gathering of families and friends were and are at this day of frequent occurrence and bring much pleasure.

The year 1880 gives us 740 inhabitants, 135 houses, 2000 acres of land enclosed, 12,000 sheep of superior quality, 3000 cattle, 1000 horses, a superior grist mill, steam saw mill, tannery, shoe shop, furniture shop, two mercantile stores and a beautiful little village with its orchards and shade trees, the envy of many passersby.

Our condition in 1880 is vastly superior in intelligence and wealth to what it was in 1851. Our means of livelihood are of easier access. Markets are on our borders for all our surplus produce. Schools and churches

and 10 cent bills to swell the fund and still the noble work goes on with unabated vigor.

In 1870 Cedar City's bishop spoke again through the *Deseret News:*

The average yield to the acre for the entire settlement has greatly increased within the past 10 years. Altogether Cedar seems to be a thrifty settlement and a good place for men to go who wish to get a start. Bp. Lunt informs us that they desire more population and they are willing to give settlers land to cultivate and water to irrigate it. They lack men of capital but they themselves are hard working men whose only capital is labor and they know how to appreciate that class."

It is telling that even the children understood the spirit of building their community. They learned first-hand the necessity as they took their turns at herding the cooperative dairy herd on the hillsides and gave their small personal savings to help bring other families to their midst.

On every hand was evidence of cooperative effort for the common good of the citizens of Cedar City. People brought their surplus garden produce to the Cedar City Cooperative Mercantile, where it was received and sold to peddlers who took it to mining camps for some cash. The coopera-

tive flour mill ground the wheat, the cooperative woolen mill spun their wool into yarn.

Mormon bishops preached the articles of unity from the Sabbath pulpit: (1) abstinence from profanity (2) family prayer, (3) observance of the health code called the Word of Wisdom, (4) love, affection and unselfishness in the family, (5) personal cleanliness and chastity, (6) Sabbath observance, (7) avoidance of "foolish and extravagant fashions" and patronage of home manufacture, (8) combined labor for mutual benefit, (9) the return of borrowed property,and seeking owners of that found, (10) devotion to the upbuilding of the Kingdom of God. Faithful Mormons heard these tenets on Sunday and lived by them every day of the week.

As the first of their number had trudged southward in 1851, they undoubtedly sang again the familiar hymn of their earlier westward journey, *"...We'll find a place which God for us prepared..."* [23] What they had found was a place that would demand of them every last vestige of their creative energy. And in the process of their triumph over the first four decades, they had established a pattern of harmonious cooperation that made them a people uniquely fitted for the grand cooperative accomplishment that would shape the destiny of their town. They were prepared to meet the challenge just appearing on the horizon.

THE ROAD
INTO CEDAR
CITY

The laying of the cornerstone, March 14, 1898

Old Main dedication, October 28, 1898

CHAPTER II

The Founding

"We're not going to quit and don't get it into your heads that we are. We're going to go down and get bobsleds and then come back in here and get that lumber out!"

Cornelius Bladen, captain of the 1898 lumbering expedition.

On August 2, 1852, Henry Lunt called all the "brethren" of the fledgling community of Cedar City together to attend to some crucial business. They were to elect a justice of the peace, a constable, a poundkeeper, two fence viewers and three school trustees. All nominated were duly elected (unanimously). [1]

Richard Harrison, James Boswell and George Wood were the newly elected school trustees. They faced a seemingly impossible challenge. Total tax revenue for Iron County in 1852 was $198.94. Because that sum had to be divided to cover all community needs, including the building of roads where none had ever been, and the very real requirement for police protection in a time of frequent indian attacks, the ready funds and more would be quickly depleted. Simply stated, there were no public funds for schools. But these trustees served a people who shared a driving dream of education for their children and even for themselves. Their constituency included some, recently arrived from England, who had enjoyed a level of education and refinement. They considered schools for their children a compelling priority.

From the wintry nights of learning grammar by the light of George A. Smith's campfire, through their days in the newly formed fort at Cedar City, these settlers had always found ways and means to provide schooling, however informal. Finding qualified teachers was an ever-present problem. Many of their number were sufficiently educated to teach, but they had families to provide for and could not leave their pressing work. The trustees had no money to import trained educators, so they selected for teachers younger members of the local families, who were paid by the parents of the students. The salary for these home teachers was $2 to $5 per quarter per scholar. It could be paid one-third in wheat, one-third in produce and one-third in cash, if it were available.

One charge of the trustees was to examine the qualifications of prospective teachers. Whether these appointed examiners had the scholarship to judge the pedagogical qualifications of applicants we cannot judge, but the record makes it crystal clear that they were united in their determination to exclude from the schools the morally or spiritually unfit. [2]

And for people whose religious doctrines included the concept, "...A man is saved no faster than he gains knowledge," education was a serious concern. [3]

In the spring of 1853 two "gentile" [4] brothers, surnamed Ross, arrived in Cedar City on their way to the California gold fields. Beguiled by the idea that they could perhaps make their fortunes in the budding iron indus-

JOHN CHATTERLEY AND FAMILY
IN FRONT OF THEIR HOME.

try, the brothers obtained a lot and put up a house, each building for himself a large log room with a fireplace and a window. But as winter came, California and gold beckoned the brothers Ross again, and they advertised their house for sale. Joseph Chatterley quickly purchased the house and offered it as a site for a community center.

*T*he citizenry proudly dressed the log structure with stucco and began calling it "Chatterley Hall." In January of 1854 Chatterley Hall became Cedar City's first school house. One of the spacious fireplace rooms housed the upper grades and the other the lower grades. [5]

Mary Ann Corlett, a stepdaughter of Joseph Chatterley and a graduate of the Liverpool Finishing School, was hired to teach the lower grades, while Matthew Carruthers, a graduate of the University of Edinburgh, taught the upper grades. As impressive as their credentials were, their pay was usually received as a bucket of milk, a pat of butter, a sack of wheat, or whatever produce the parents could supply. A Mrs. Chaffin taught students in her own home, where she was noted for positioning herself to see several rooms and every child all at once.

When the Cedar Cooperative Mercantile was established, an ingenious pattern of commerce emerged that made payment of tuition a more formal transaction. Parents bought "admits" which were certificates of credit they purchased with their produce or other goods. The children presented the admit at the begin-

ning of each quarter of school. Teachers were paid by the trustees in store orders, redeemable at the "Co-op" for merchandise over the counter. Occasionally teachers sold their store orders for a little cash, usually at a considerable reduction.

During 1874-1875, the United Order flourished. The "order" was a system of equality wherein people received an equal share of the community goods, regardless of their work assignment. Schools improved because leaders had the authority to assign the most qualified people to teach, and pay them at the same scale, no matter what their assigned work. But the greatest leap forward in education in rural Utah was the establishment of a system of Stake Academies, sponsored by the L.D.S. Church.

Now at last there flowed into Cedar City and other outlying areas, highly competent and educated teachers. Most had been trained at Brigham Young Academy. Historian William R. Palmer, writing from his own experience with the schools, "The men were protegees of Dr. Karl G. Maesar, a renowned early educator and president of Brigham Young Academy, and their community attitude and example was as much a factor for uplift as their advanced scholarship." [6]

In Cedar City the Parowan Stake Academy was established in the fall of 1886. First held on the top floor of the Knell Block Building on Cedar City's Main Street, it was a fine school, offering courses equivalent to high schools of today. The Academy was later moved to a building at the north of Main Street, on the block that became the city park.

For the first time the curriculum included chemistry, botany, zoology, algebra, physical geography and the rudiments of domestic science. Students paid tuition, but the Academy was also supported by private donations from public spirited citizens. The Mormon Church trained, provided and paid the teachers; the local community provided classrooms, equipment and maintenance costs. The classrooms were humble and the equipment inadequate, but the expertise of the teachers far exceeded those of former years.

The fame of the school spread over Southern Utah, attracting students from many surrounding counties. Local citizens were so hopeful that it

THE KNELL BLOCK IN 1904, SITE OF PAROWAN ACADEMY

would become a permanent institution that they purchased five acres in the center of town, which they named "Academy Hill," intending that permanent buildings should be constructed at the first feasible instance.

Learning whetted the appetite for more. Parents longed for higher education opportunities for their children. Only a few could send their youngsters, upon graduation from the Academy, north to one of the state universities. All of the people saw the need for better teacher training; each community aspired to have a normal school close at hand to accomplish that training.

Beaver County's representatives were ahead of the others in their efforts to have a school located in their county. While other counties hoped, Beaver County had been working since 1892 to influence the Territorial Legislature, the state superintendent of public instruction and the principal of the Normal School at the University of Utah, to establish a branch of the Normal School just outside Beaver City, where the abandoned Fort Cameron stood nearby, vacant and ready to be remodeled into a normal school campus. J.F. Tolton and R. F. Tanner had been active in the territorial legislatures and continued to lead in the effort to lobby for the school to be established in their county. [7]

When the Legislature of 1897 convened, Beaver County's Representative William L.H. Dotson had prepared an act calling for the establishment of a branch of the University of Utah at Fort Cameron. Called House Bill 52, it was accompanied by House Petition #7, which contained the signatures of 146 citizens of Beaver City, urging the legislators to authorize the purchase of Fort Cameron and establish the school. Both of these documents were read

REP. JOHN PARRY

in the House of Representatives and referred to the committee on education on February 4, 1897.

Sen. Edward H. Snow was enlisted in the cause and on February 19, 1997, he introduced Senate Bill 44, which read:

> *An act providing for the establishment of a Branch of the State Normal School at Beaver City as a part of the Normal Department of the University of Utah, under the direction and control of the Regents thereof.*

The bill was referred to the Committee on Education which, on February 24, recommended passage. Proceeding to the floor of the Senate, the bill was read for first and second readings and was held over for one day.

Backstage there was a lot of action. Legislators from the southern counties were scrambling. There would be a great advantage to the town graced by a college.

REP. WILLIAM L.H. DOTSON

SEN. EDWARD H. SNOW

Every member of the legislature realized that. Sen. Snow wrote of the activity:

When I was the state senator at the legislative session, J.F. Tolton and R.L. Tanner came up to Salt Lake from Beaver to lobby for a branch of the university to be located at Beaver. I was asked to introduce a bill for this purpose. No sooner was it mooted than all the communities of the south wanted it in their counties. As I represented four counties I decided to introduce the bill establishing the school but appointing a commission consisting of Dr. Karl G. Maesar, Dr. Jas. E. Talmage and Dr. J. R. Park to investigate and locate the school. [8]

Young John Parry of Cedar City, serving his first term in the Legislature, was a self-educated man. His classroom education had consisted of only three weeks in the school room in his entire life. He was, nevertheless, equal to his stewardship as a legislator. With action both precipitous and prompt, Parry labored to persuade Sen. Snow to amend Senate Bill 44.

It would have been awkward for Sen. Snow to have refused. His district included Iron, Washington, Beaver and Kane counties, and he had to respond to the citizens of each of those areas. So, as distressing as it must have been to the Beaver County contingent, the bill was re-written and re-introduced as Senate Bill 50, which read:

An Act providing for the establishment of a Branch of the State Normal School, the appointment of a commission to select the site, and making an appropriation for the maintenance and furnishing thereof.

Much of the action was centered in the education committee. The agreement must have been reached in committee on February 24, 1897, because Rep. John Parry, on that date, went to the Deseret Telegraph Company and wired Charles Adams, bishop of the Parowan Ward, and Uriah T. Jones, president of the Parowan Stake in Cedar City, this message:

Salt Lake City, Utah, February 24, 1897

The state contemplates locating a branch of the University in southern part of the state. What has Iron County got to offer?

(Signed) John Parry, Representative [9]

On February 25, the amended bill, now titled SB 50, came out of committee to the senate floor, where on motion of Senator Snow the rules were suspended, the bill was read the first, second and third times, voted upon and passed.

The telegram arrived in both towns. Bishop Adams in Parowan did not realize that it was urgent and planned to answer it by letter. That same day in Cedar City, President Jones organized a mass meeting of all the citizens of the town. He read the telegram from John Parry, extracted a commitment from the people and then sent the following reply:

Cedar City, Utah
February 26, 1897
Honorable John Parry,
Representative:

If the amount of the contribution is the consideration in locating of site for Branch School, sentiment of mass meeting held last night was to offer equal inducement to any other locality. Temple Knoll, six acres within one quarter of mile of Main Street, and $8000 in labor and material, more if necessary, and use of present Ward Building.

(Signed) Uriah T. Jones

The message reached John

THE DESERET TELEGRAPH COMPANY.

This Company TRANSMITS and DELIVERS messages only on conditions limiting its liability, which have been assented to by the sender of the following message.
Errors can be guarded against only by repeating a message back to the sending station for comparison, and the Company will not hold itself liable for errors or delays in transmission or delivery of UNREPEATED MESSAGES beyond the amount of tolls paid thereon, nor in any case where the claim is not presented in writing within sixty days after sending the message.

SENT BY | REC'D BY | CHECK.
C3 Paid

QUICK SERVICE.

Received at 73 Main St., next Deseret Bank, Salt Lake City, at 11 35 A m. FEB 26 1897

Dated, Cedar City, Ut 26

To Hon. John Parry. Repr.

amount of contribution is the consideration in location of site for
School. sentiment of mass meeting held last night was to offer
cements to any other locallity. The following is at your disposal
Knoll 6 acres within one quarter mile Main St and eight thousand
ars in labor and material. more if necessary. and use of present ward

T. Jones.

BE SURE YOU ANSWER BY THIS LINE.

SEE OFFICE ADDRESS ON THIS MESSAGE.

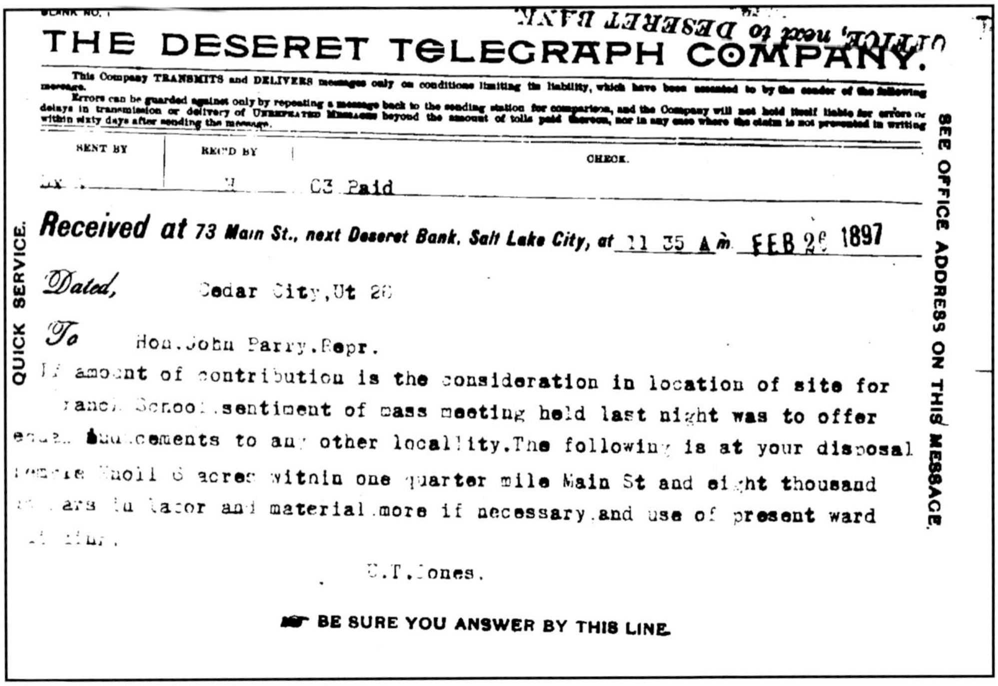

Parry at 11:35 a.m. almost simultaneous to the moment the amended SB 50 passed in the House. He was now assured that his home people were firmly behind him and that he had something tangible to offer as an alternative to the impressive Beaver County proposal offering Fort Cameron.

Fort Cameron was an extensive military installation that had housed 250 United States troops, from 1873 to 1882. The camp included 10 sturdy buildings, built of black volcanic stone, surrounding a large grassy parade ground. It was set in a grove of cottonwood trees with the Beaver River running through it. [10] With very little effort, it would have made a most picturesque campus. On March 3, the House committee on education reported the respectful rejection of House Bill #52 and House Petition #7 from the citizens of Beaver. The contest was on.

The cause and the competition captured the interest of the *Deseret News*. The March 6 issue included this editorial:

...There is substantial justice in the claim that the southern counties of the state should receive relief in this regard. Their young men and women, who desire to become teachers, have a right to ask that some of the facilities for normal training, paid for by the state, be placed within their reach....The News *is in favor of giving the southern counties a good normal school, whether or not Fort Cameron be chosen for its site.* [11]

The bill, which reached the desk of Gov. Heber M. Wells, on March 11, 1897, read as follows:

Be it enacted by the Legislature of the State of Utah:

SECTION 1. A branch of the State Normal School is hereby established in the southern part of this State, the same to be located as hereinafter provided.

Sec. 2. A Commission of three persons is hereby created consisting of the Superintendent of Public Instruction, the president of the University of Utah, and one other to be appointed by the Governor by and with the consent of the Senate; and whose duty it shall be, within four months after the passage of this act, to visit the counties of Beaver and Iron and determine upon a site within said counties for the location of said school. Said Commission shall serve without compensation but their expenses shall be paid, when audited and approved by the State Board of Examiners.

Sec. 3. The said Commission, or a majority thereof, shall have full power to determine the site for said school and when so determined, shall certify the same to the Secretary of State. The Governor shall fill any vacancy that may occur in said Commission.

Sec. 4. As a condition to the location of said school the city or county in which said Commission shall decide to locate the same, shall vest in the State a good and sufficient title to suitable grounds and buildings, for the accommodation of said school, or guarantee the same within such reasonable time as said Commission shall designate, but said school shall not be commenced until such a title is so vested. Upon the acceptance by the Secretary of State of the title to said grounds and building, the State shall maintain at such place a branch of the State Normal School to be under the control and management of the board of regents of the University of Utah.

Sec. 5. Whenever the State shall fail to maintain said school for a period of two years the title to the building and grounds as contemplated in section 4, shall revert to the donors.

Sec 6. For the purpose of maintaining and furnishing said school for the academic years of 1897-98 and 1898-99 the sum of fifteen thousand dollars, or so much thereof as may be necessary, is hereby appropriated out of any moneys in the treasury not otherwise appropriated.

Approved March 11, 1897 [12]

Gov. Wells, who had already shown enthusiasm for the project, signed the bill into law without hesitation. He appointed Dr. James E. Talmage, a prominent educator and church leader, to serve with Dr. Karl G. Maesar, superintendent of public instruction, and Dr. John R. Park, president of the University of Utah. He instructed them to visit the communities vying for the school and awarded them $200 to fund their journeys.

A flurry of preparation ensued in each of the towns. The citizens of Beaver, Parowan, Paragonah and Cedar City, prepared their best possible offer to win the nod of favor from the Commission.

Within 10 days Cedar City had marshalled its troops. A mass meeting was called on March 21, 1897. A general committee was appointed to head the effort that consisted of Lehi W.

Jones, chairman, John S. Woodbury, and Edward J. Palmer, who were to serve as secretary and treasurer, respectively. They served without respite during the entire founding period. They called mass meetings often to discuss various plans and appoint subcommittees.

The committee asked Representative John Parry, just returned from his legislative session, and Mayhew H. Dalley, a prominent Cedar City citizen, to draft the formal petition setting forth the advantages of locating the school in their town. As they began working to extol the merits of their community, they became aware that rival towns, in a spirit of fierce competition, were exerting some energy in perpetrating a perception of the disadvantages of placing the school in Cedar City. The resultant petition is positive and persuasive, exuding pride in their town. It also contains defensive passages designed to clear up any misconception about Cedar City's merit as an educational center. It was completed May 8, 1897 and forwarded to the state selection committee. It read:

To the Hons. John R. Park, James E. Talmage, and Karl G. Maesar, Commissioners to Locate State Branch Normal School.

Gentlemen:

For your consideration in determining the location of the State Branch Normal School, we submit the following:

CEDAR CITY is centrally located in the Southern Utah Educational District, embracing the following counties, viz: Kane with a population of 1968, Washington with a population of 4619, Iron 3123, Garfield 2888, Wayne 1520, Piute 1727, and Beaver 3791; its distance from the principal towns in said counties being as follows: Kanab 120 miles, St. George 55 miles, Virgin City 45 miles, Hebron 50 miles, Pine Valley 40 miles, Pinto 30 miles, Junction 55 miles, Panguitch 50 miles, Beaver 55 miles, Milford 54 miles, Minersville 40 miles. (Wayne and Piute Counties, however, will naturally in the future be attached to some other school district.)

We know of no city or town in Utah where the percent of mortality is less. Diphtheria and other dread contagious diseases are unknown. While our water at certain periods of the year is not the most desirable, yet we are favored with pure mountain streams near the city, which our City Council contem-

plate utilizing in the near future for culinary purposes.

It is claimed by some that Cedar City is destined to be a manufacturing town and that the results of the erection of Iron Works will be a smoky, unhealthy atmosphere. We have no fears of such unfavorable results, as our iron mines are from 10 to 15 miles distant and on lower levels than the coal beds from which the furnaces are to be supplied. This naturally places the works at 10 miles or more from the town; for the idea of hauling ores on an uphill grade, when the fuel to supply the furnaces can be hauled to the mines across the valley without exhausting a pound of steam is an absurdity.

The establishment of such manufactories, however, near the city will increase the patronage and support of the Normal school and thereby prove a benefit.

Right at our doors we have an abundance of building rock, limestone, beds of brick and fire clay, mountains of gypsum, inexhaustible veins of coal in variety, groves of pulp material, and forests of saw-timber. Fertile valleys surround us and broad mountain plateaus overlook our City, which in turn yield an abundance of farm and dairy products noted for excellent quality.

Our mountains and canyons are dotted with pure springs and lakes furnishing unsurpassed summer resorts.

No other city in Southern Utah has manifested a greater interest in educational matters. The Parowan Stake Academy, located at this place, having been supported and upheld by the energy of our citizens, under adverse circumstances has outlived all similar institutions established in Southern Utah. Since the establishment of this institution the average attendance has been upward of 100 pupils. By entering into personal obligation and signing notes to secure the teachers employed, to make any deficiency that might arise, also furnishing fuel and light for a number of years, it was possible to keep this academy going. This has been done by the local board and such members of the Stake Board as reside in Cedar City.

The interest manifested in our District Schools is very commendable. Special school taxes have been voted by the people each year. Our school buildings, furniture, and apparatus is unequalled in Southern Utah. During the present school year seven teachers have been employed in the district schools for three terms of 10 weeks each, and four teach-

ers are now engaged in a further session of five weeks. With a school population of 404, the attendance at the present school year numbers 385. This year's expenditures amount to over $3700.00, of which nearly $1900.00 has been raised by local taxation. Our school district is free from debt. (This District pays 49 percent of the entire taxes in this County for State and County purposes.)

Nature has designed for us the most suitable site in Southern Utah for the establishment of the State Branch Normal School.

In conclusion, these, with other innumerable advantages, we claim Cedar City foremost among the competitors for the State Branch Normal School, in location, in patronage, healthfulness, natural resources, and local and general support

Respectfully submitted by the Citizens of Cedar City,

Signed: John Parry and Mayhew H. Dalley [13]

*T*he city fathers designated Lehi W. Jones and John Woodbury to draft a document describing the specific spot of land they would deed to the state and promising to deed the Ward Hall, having it ready for school to start on August 15th, just three months away.

The people prepared to do all in their power to make a positive impression when the Commission visited. Elias Morris proved to be an effective advocate for Cedar City from his home in Salt Lake City. Mr. Morris and his wife, Mary Parry Morris (sister of John Parry), were former Cedar City residents and fervent supporters. In a discreet letter to his young legislator brother-in-law, Elias Morris advised dignified restraint:

Salt Lake City, Utah
April 27, 1897

Dear Brother,

The Commission selected and appointed to locate the Normal School in the southern part of Utah will leave here next Monday (May 3rd.) Will commence their investigation at Beaver. Excuse me the liberty of advising you at Cedar. I had a little talk with one of the three yesterday. He told me that some of the counties have written to them offering favors by furnishing them with carriages, hotel accommodations, and to meet them with

brass bands, etc. I know their feelings, and allow me to suggest—make no demonstration whatever, have your committee selected and meet them when they come to Cedar City, but no demonstration whatever. Don't even offer to pay their hotel bill for they do not want to be under obligation to any city or county. They go prepared to pay their own expenses, for the state has to foot the bill. Cedar will get the Normal School, and don't you forget it.

Keep this confidential. Kind regards to all.

Your brother,
Elias [14]

Nevertheless, the people were prepared to make them welcome and to make as favorable an impression as possible.

The Commission arrived in Iron County on May 6, 1897. The first two days were spent in Parowan, where Elder James A. Talmage records they were treated to an "elaborate reception." [15] On May 9, Saturday, they proceeded to Cedar City where they visited the proposed school site.

Immediately they declared that the "Temple Knoll" was not a large enough piece for a campus of the state school. They advised John Parry, Henry Leigh and Mayhew H. Dalley that they would have to secure at least nine acres more land, to make their bid acceptable.

While prominent citizens took the members of the Commission to see the Iron deposits west of town, the Cedar Committee negotiated furiously to acquire sufficient land to fill the requirements of the Commission:

Academy Hill, also called Temple Knoll, which the community owned, was only six acres. They needed 15. John Chatterley and Uriah T. Jones were appointed to secure the needed acreage. They purchased in behalf of the committee, six city lots from Joseph Wilkinson for $400 and one lot from Eliza Pucell for $100, with some added land from Peter Fife.

A mass meeting was called for the next evening, May 10, a Sunday night.

The committee was ready to present its recommendations to the people of the community and the Commission. Elder Talmage records:

JOHN R. PARK

KARL G. MAESAR

JAMES E. TALMAGE

Evening of May 10: Large mass meeting. Citizens Committee presented recommendations. After a discussion and acceptance of their committee's plans, mass meeting was adjourned and the people met in their religious service. Dr. Maesar and I addressed the congregation. [16]

After another day of inspecting the natural resources around Cedar City, the Commission started their homeward journey. They visited Parowan again, visited Paragonah and met again with the Beaver committee, then on May 13, took the train from Milford to Salt Lake City.

*L*ittle had been spoken about the visit of the Commission to the other counties, but it is reasonable to assume that the existence of a thriving mining industry in western Beaver County could not have escaped their notice. The Horn Silver Mines, the Newhouse Mines

and others were producing copper, gold and silver at such an abundant rate that the revenue would have astonished the simple folks in neighboring Iron County. The prosperity had also given rise to the town of Frisco, known as the wildest camp in Utah. It boasted a dance hall, 23 saloons, which apart from dealing in liquor, had every conceivable gambling device then known. It was reputed by one Walter James that without exception after every payday there were fresh graves to be dug.

*W*hile it is natural to assume that these factors influenced the decision of the Commission in disfavoring the Beaver petition, the evidence does not bear out that assumption. The following year a branch of Brigham Young University, whose president was Karl G. Maesar, a member of the Commission, was established at Fort Cameron. Called The Murdoch Academy, the school operated success-

FROM THE JOURNAL OF JAMES E. TALMAGE

Complying with the law, the Governor's Commission started the inspection of Beaver and Iron Counties. We may follow them through the carefully recorded notes from the journal of Dr. James E. Talmage. (By courtesy of his son, Dr. Sterling B. Talmage.)

May 3, 1897. Left Salt Lake City for Beaver and Iron Counties.
May 4. Arrived in Milford. Took short trip on horse back to view geological deposits in nearby country.
May 5. Beaver. Met Citizens Committee.
May 6. Parowan. Elaborate reception.
May 7. Met Citizens Committee. After discussion was taken to see location of school site; also went on geological trip into canyon.
May 8. At 9:30 a.m. Saturday, left Parowan for Cedar City. Stayed at the Corry House. Met Citizens Committee. Representatives from Washington County were in Cedar City to support Cedar people's request for the Branch of the State Normal School to be located in Cedar City.
May 9. Visited school site. Commission felt that there was not enough land. The Citizens Committee proceeded to secure more land and spent the day in that effort. Mass meeting to be called for evening of May 10.
May 10. Sunday. Was taken by a man named

[Thomas] Taylor to visit the great iron ore deposits west of Cedar City.
Evening of May 10. Large mass meeting. Citizens Committee presented recommendations after a discussion and acceptance of their Committee's plans. Mass meeting was adjourned and the people met in their religious service. Dr. Maeser and I addressed the congregation.
May 11. Was taken up Cedar Canyon by Brother John Parry, Mayhew Dalley and Andrew Corry, to inspect the coal deposits, the gypsum deposits and the sandstone quarries. We had excellent horses and the trip was very pleasant.
May 11. 3:30 p.m. we started on our return trip.
May 12. Met the Citizens Committee of Parowan again, and then went on to Paragonah and met a delegation of citizens there. Stayed at the home of a Brother Robinson.
May 13. Went on to Beaver. Met the Committee of Beaver again. Was taken to Milford. Accompanying us to Milford was Mr. Hurst [William R. Hurst] a member of the Beaver Committee.
May 14. Arrived in Salt Lake City.
May 17. First meeting of the Commission was held in the Board of Education Office. [Dr. John R. Park, Superintendent of Public Instruction, was Chairman of Commission.]
May 19. Decision to locate Branch of State Normal School in Cedar City. Knowing that our decision would cause much dissatisfaction, yet we had to do what we thought was best for the greatest number of prospective students.

HENRY LEIGH   MAYHEW DALLEY   EDWARD PALMER

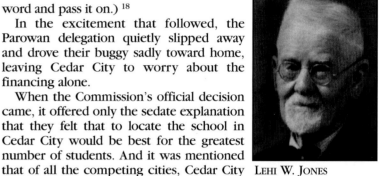

LEHI W. JONES

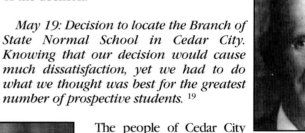

JOHN S. WOODBURY

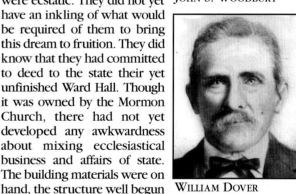

WILLIAM DOVER

THOMAS BLADEN

fully for nearly 10 years and became genuine competition for the Cedar City school.

Rep. Parry had received a letter, hand-carried to Salt Lake City, from some of his Parowan constituents, expressing their resentment. The letter indicated that they thought he had favored Cedar City in his presentation. In a handwritten reply, dated March 2, 1897, he declares his honest striving to be fair with both communities. He writes:

I beg to state that I treated both settlements on a par, telegraphing to both places—to Bishop Adams and U.T. Jones...and I have not had a reply, nor read anything in the Iron County Record to let me know what Parowan has to offer. [17]

The rift must have healed somewhat, for negotiations between the two towns had resulted in a tentative agreement that whichever community was awarded the school, the other would contribute $2,400 and some labor. On the morning of May 19, a group of leading citizens from each of the two towns stood in front of the Co-op Store, awaiting the arrival of a few others. In the imminent meeting they were to discuss the terms of cooperation between their communities and sign the contract binding each to the $2,400, regardless of which might be chosen as the site...At this moment a boy dashed through the crowd and handed John Parry a telegram which read:

FRANCIS WEBSTER, THOMAS JEDEDIAH JONES, JOHN PARRY.

"Unanimous vote in favor of Cedar City for Normal School. (signed) Elias Morris" (Morris had been waiting outside the door where the Commission met, so as be to the first to get the

word and pass it on.) [18]

In the excitement that followed, the Parowan delegation quietly slipped away and drove their buggy sadly toward home, leaving Cedar City to worry about the financing alone.

When the Commission's official decision came, it offered only the sedate explanation that they felt that to locate the school in Cedar City would be best for the greatest number of students. And it was mentioned that of all the competing cities, Cedar City was the only one which had no saloons. James E. Talmage wrote in his personal diary of the decision:

May 19: Decision to locate the Branch of State Normal School in Cedar City. Knowing that our decision would cause much dissatisfaction, yet we had to do what we thought was best for the greatest number of prospective students. [19]

The people of Cedar City were ecstatic. They did not yet have an inkling of what would be required of them to bring this dream to fruition. They did know that they had committed to deed to the state their yet unfinished Ward Hall. Though it was owned by the Mormon Church, there had not yet developed any awkwardness about mixing ecclesiastical business and affairs of state. The building materials were on hand, the structure well begun and the people were committed to the task. But it was also springtime. Crops had to be planted and sheep and cattle cared for in the valley and on the mountain ranges. It would take extraordinary effort to complete the building in time for a fall, 1897, opening of the Branch Normal School.

The men worked all day in their fields, then with their wives and older children, attended mass meetings at night. There was much community planning to be done. Everyone considered it his privilege to offer his time, his team and his materials, that the work might be speeded up. There was a bond of loyalty and love that permeated the village, as if there was one heart, one mind, one pair of hands. [20]

The amazing cooperation of all the people of Cedar City did not just happen. Such an effort requires remarkable leadership. The general committee still consisted of Edward Palmer, Lehi W. Jones and John S. Woodbury. Many community leaders shouldered heavy responsibility in the months that followed.

The chairman of the building committee was Thomas Jedediah Jones. He was a skilled builder and well suited to oversee the project. John Parry, serving as a counselor, was still Iron County representative and liaison with Salt Lake City. Francis Webster, a well established, educated member of the committee, seems to have been the human relations specialist, for he was noted for listening to complaints with fairness, and then persuading all people to do their share and to keep giving when they had already given all they thought they could. William Dover, an able mason and a splendid craftsman, was the member of the committee who supervised the masonry work on the permanent Branch Normal School building. Thomas Bladen also served as a member of the committee, supervising a large crew of men in the quarrying, hauling, dressing and placing of the stone in the building. Henry Leigh kept the accounts and made the disbursements. Mayhew Dalley served until November, when he was elected superintendent of Iron County schools. The men of the town made the accomplishment of the school their highest priority.

By August the almost-impossible had been accomplished. Well organized crews had worked at a feverish pace throughout the summer. The completed Ward Hall opened its doors to receive the first class of students of the southern Branch of the State Normal School.

The building had been designed for use as a social hall, with a stage, a ballroom and classrooms for the auxiliary organizations of the

THE WARD HALL, 1897

Church. It was not designed to house laboratories, classrooms nor an auditorium for a school, but it could be modified to serve this purpose, and the people of the town thought it would do nicely until they could, at a logical pace, build a permanent building on the designated spot.

While the people of Cedar City were exerting their energies toward the final touches on the Ward Hall, the Board of Regents of the University of Utah had more carefully read the enabling legislation. They now realized that they had a problem.

On June 21, 1897 a special meeting was held in the office of the president of the Deseret National Bank at 12 noon. Present were James Sharp, president of the Board of Regents of the University of Utah and members of the board, Waldemar Van Cott, Frank Pierce, Rebecca E. Little and Dr. Joseph Kingsbury, president of the University of Utah. Also present by special invitation were J.T. Hammond, secretary of state, and Dr. John R. Park, state superintendent of public instruction, who had also served as chairman of the Commission on location of the Branch Normal School, and the state auditor, Morgan Richards. The sole subject for consideration at the meeting was the Branch Normal School.

Someone had discovered that by a close interpretation of the law, it was not possible to spend the $15,000 appropriation for the academic year of 1897-98 until, "...a good and sufficient title to suitable grounds and building shall be so vested in the State." This presented a serious problem. The State Branch Normal School was to be under the control and management of the Board of Regents of the University of Utah, who at this time had no money at their disposal to pay teacher's salaries, buy books or furniture. They had no money even to advertise the opening of the school. They met now to consider what could be done.

*T*he regents appointed Waldemar Van Cott, Rebecca Little, Frank Pierce and John R. Park as a special committee to devise some means by which the school could begin in September as planned. They drew up a suggested solution, outlined in a lengthy letter, then sent a telegram to alert the committee in Cedar City. The telegram rattled into the Lunt Telegraph Office at 10 a.m. on June 22, 1897. Dan Matheson delivered the wire to John Parry's home. Telegrams always were associated with disturbing news. This one was no exception. It read:

Salt Lake City, Utah, June 22, 1897,
To: Parry, Leigh and Dalley, Committee, Cedar City

University mailed important letter today about Branch Normal School. See Promptly

Waldemar Van Cott, Chairman, Special Committee for Board of Regents, University of Utah

John Parry read the alert to his wife and eldest son. We can well imagine his feelings of suspense and anxiety as he left the house and walked up Main Street to the Co-op Store, where he shared the contents of the telegram with Henry Leigh and several other men. Then the two committee members, Leigh and Parry, walked over to Mayhew Dalley's office to show him the missive that brought such sudden uncertainty. To this point they had been confident that everything was going well in the progress of their school.

June 22 was a Tuesday. The letter should arrive in Saturday's mail. They must call together the people of the town and inform them of the contents of the anticipated letter. They posted notices written on wrapping paper in the windows of all the public build-ings. The principal, Mr. Hubbard, read this message to the school children: "Mass Meeting in City Hall, Saturday night. Everybody come." Mass meeting could mean only one thing, something about the Branch Normal School. The whole town attended—men, women and children.

Most of the prominent men of the community were waiting for the arrival of the mail coach on Saturday. President U. T. Jones, postmaster, carried the mail bags into the post office where he searched the contents, found the letter and delivered it into John Parry's hands. It was a thick letter that would take time to read, so John Parry invited the group to come to his home where they could sit together to read and discuss its contents." [21]

The letter outlined both the problem and a suggested solution. [22] *(See box on following page.)* The problem was that the legislation was worded in such a manner that the $15,000 appropriation for funding the school year 1897-98 could not be released until the permanent building, built on the designated property, was deeded to the State. Both the Secretary of State and the State Auditor had ruled that the law did not authorize the release of the funds until these requirements were met. The regents regretfully informed the committee that they had no money to pay the four teachers they had already engaged to come to Cedar City. They had no money for books or equipment. So much for the problem. As to the solution, the regents had no choice but to ask the people of Cedar City to advance the needed money so that they could proceed to buy the necessary items, pay the hired teachers, and prepare for school to open in September. They noted also that most of the items had to be ordered from the east, so the money would have to be advanced forthwith. Without the advance, school for that year would have to be cancelled. The regents also included a copy of the law, in case the people of Cedar City did not have access to it. There should be no question about the validity of their difficulty.

*T*he regents were careful to assure the committee that should they be able to advance the funds, reimbursement would be no problem. The appropriation could be released as soon as the building was completed. And if there were any difficulties with that, the regents themselves would have no hesitation going to the Legislature for the return of the money.

Salt Lake City, Utah
June 22, 1897

John Parry, Henry Leigh, M. H. Dalley,
Committee, Cedar City, Utah

Dear Sirs:

Dr. John R. Park informs us that you constitute the Committee at Cedar City that was delegated to see to the establishment of the Branch State Normal School at your place, and therefore the special committee of the Board of Regents of the University of Utah writes to you.

The last Legislature, according to an Act found on page 41-2 of the laws of 1897, provides for the establishment of a State Normal School at a place to be selected by a Commission. This Commission has selected Cedar City, as appears by report on file with Secretary of State. By looking carefully into Section 4 of such Act, it appears that the Secretary of State is not authorized to accept a deed until the title to the land and buildings is vested in the state.

The Commission describes this land selected, but states that there are no buildings on the same sufficient for school purposes; the Commission also in its report expresses the hope that a school may be conducted at Cedar City the present year in temporary quarters as Cedar City has until August 1st, 1898 to complete the buildings.

The Legislature has made sufficient appropriation in order to carry on the school for the years of 1897-8 and 1898-9.

Heretofore the Board of Regents of the University of Utah has engaged a corps of instructors for this school and was preparing to vigorously and successfully carry on this branch school, but the Regents are now confronted with this problem:

The Secretary of State and the State Auditor decline to issue warrants for any part of the appropriation until the title is vested in the State for the land described in the Commission's report, and also refuse to issue a warrant until the buildings are completed as contemplated by Section 4 of the law before mentioned.

The Board of Regents is unable to solve this difficulty in any way so as to make immediate use of the appropriation of any part of the same for the purpose of carrying on this school this year. Nevertheless, the Regents are very solicitous to have this school in operation this year, and with this end in view they have delegated the matter to a special committee which suggests the following proposition:

If this school can be carried on in Cedar City this year in temporary quarters it will be necessary for your committee to advance money to the Board of Regents to pay the monthly salaries of the instructors. We understand you will supply school furniture; money will also have to be advanced to the Board of Regents to purchase school apparatus and books in order to make the school efficient. If your committee will take immediate steps and advance these expenditures, the Regents will send these instructors to Cedar City and proceed with the school for the year 1897-8; and if Cedar City deeds the property mentioned in the report of the commission to the state and constructs the buildings as contemplated and if the implied contract with the citizens of Cedar City is carried out according to its letter and spirit, the Board of Regents will most cheerfully endeavor to reimburse all who advance money and if for any reason such money should not be obtained from the Secretary of State and Auditor, the Board of Regents will cheerfully recommend to the next Legislature your reimbursement and we have no doubt but what warrants will be issued to you by August 1st, 1898 (the time when the buildings are to be completed) and that no question will be made either by the Secretary of State or the Auditor; in fact the Secretary of State has so expressed himself; but in any event we feel fully convinced that the Legislature will reimburse you. You must remember that the money is already appropriated for two years of school and if the school is actually carried on the two years there is no reasonable doubt but what the appropriation will be used for that purpose and the only inconvenience in advancing this money will be to wait for the issuance of warrants until August 1, 1898, at which time we are satisfied warrants will be issued. We say that the money must be advanced to the Board of Regents, as such Board is designated by law to disburse the money and we would not be authorized to delegate other persons to make such disbursement. The Board of Regents has made a very careful and economical estimate amounting to $4,422 for the first year, a copy of which estimate is herewith enclosed.

We suggest that within 30 days you advance us $872.00, which is made up of the following items contained in the estimate, to wit:

Circulars, etc.	$50.00
Advertising in newspapers	40.00
Stationery and stamps	20.00
Traveling expenses	75.00
General apparatus	647.00
Physical apparatus	40.00
Total..........................	872.00

Within 30 days it will be necessary to send East for some of this apparatus, as it can thus be procured much cheaper than it could here, and in order to get the apparatus to Cedar City in time for the opening of school it will not be wise to delay beyond 30 days. ➡

The papers are already publishing here that there will be no school in Cedar City this coming year, hence you can see the importance of publishing circulars immediately and advertising in newspapers in order to correct this erroneous impression.

The item of traveling expenses is necessary, as the President of the University, Dr. Kingsbury, will be compelled to make at least one trip to Cedar City to see the school. It will also be necessary for Professor Stewart, member of the Normal Department, to make one or two such trips and probably some of these trips will be made before the opening of school. The other items we think explain themselves. This leaves a balance of $3,550, and we suggest that it be divided into 10 monthly payments amount of $355 each, and that these payments be made monthly, in advance, commencing September 1st, 1897, as it is expected the school will open about September 20, 1897, if opened at all.

The instructors that we have engaged are anxious to procure other positions if they are not going to Cedar City, and it is but just and right that we should notify them whether we are going to terminate their contracts or not hence you can see the necessity of prompt action on your part. If your committee concludes it can do nothing in the premises until August 1st, 1898, we shall immediately terminate all contracts with such instructors and the school will not be held this year.

We send you herewith a leaf containing the law on this Branch State Normal School for fear you may not have a copy in Cedar City. Please answer promptly as to what you will do in the premises, and if your reply is that you will make the advances we will draw up contract immediately and send it to you.

The Board of Regents realizes that the southern part of the state is desirous of having this school in operation this year and that many students are looking forward to its opening and that it is of great importance that the school should be in session this year as was contemplated by the Legislature.

The Regents also have a pride in this matter, and if you will cooperate with us we will do everything possible to make the school a success this present year.

In case we do not hear from you promptly we will be compelled to cancel the contracts with our instructors as they will desire to seek other positions.

Respectfully

Waldemar Van Cott

That afternoon, as the Cedar City Citizens Committee met to read the letter and discuss the dilemma, they determined that they would not lose their school. Whatever was required, school would open in Cedar City that year. Eight public-spirited men stepped up to the line and agreed to mortgage their homes to obtain the required amount. They were willing to sign the contract, proposed by the regents, to that effect.

That night the City hall was crowded with folks who anxiously awaited disclosure of the contents of the letter. The letter was read, the problem thoroughly discussed, and the offer of the eight men, made earlier that afternoon, presented to the general citizenry. The crowd raised their voices in enthusiastic response. Other men offered collateral in case of future needs. The meeting that historic night guaranteed not only financial security, but even more importantly, the spiritual guarantee of united effort until the task was completed. The people voted unanimously for the Citizens Committee to inform the Board of Regents of their decisions. Sunday's mail carried a letter to Waldemar Van Cott, and through him to the regents. The finances for the expenses of the school would be forthcoming. [23] The Branch Normal School would open the coming September.

JOHN PARRY

FRANCIS WEBSTER

HENRY LEIGH

JOSEPH S. HUNTER

ROBERT BULLOCH

THOMAS JED JONES

L.W. JONES

JOHN CHATTERLEY

*U*pon receiving the news of the commitment made by the Cedar City townspeople, the regents summarily forwarded a contract binding them to the expenses that would be incurred. The contract, dated July 19, 1897, carried the signatures of John Parry, Francis Webster, Henry Leigh, Joseph S. Hunter, Robert Bulloch, Thomas Jed Jones, L. W. Jones and John Chatterley. [24]

Though all eight men had agreed that their homes could be used as collateral for the loan, the Zion's Savings Bank took mortgages on the homes of three of them: John Chatterley, Lehi Jones and Robert Bulloch. Plans for the opening of school commenced. True to the provisions of the contract, the mortgages on the three homes were redeemed when the funds were released.

In April, even before the site was selected, at the recommendation of Dr. Joseph T. Kingsbury, president of the University of Utah, the Board of Regents had hired four excellent teachers to send to the southern Branch Normal School. Milton Bennion was engaged as princi-

pal at a salary of $1,100 for the year. Two male teachers, George W. Decker and Howard R. Driggs, both graduates of the University of Utah, were hired at salaries of $800 each, and Annie Spencer had agreed to come to teach elocution and physical culture for $500 for the year.

School began that September in the newly completed Ward Hall, with 46 girls and 72 boys. It boasted a superb faculty, who established a remarkable tradition of educational quality. The curriculum included two courses of study. One comprised the first three years of the regular four-year course leading to a normal certificate. The second was a preparatory course for students over 18 years of age, not prepared to do the work of the Normal course. It was a wonderful realization of the hopes of the community.

But the little town still faced the requirement

A CONTRACT BETWEEN THE BOARD OF REGENTS AND THE UNDERSIGNED CITIZENS OF CEDAR CITY, UTAH

WHEREAS, the State Legislature of Utah, in 1897, contemplated that a Branch Normal School would be conducted in the Southern part of the State and money was appropriated for that purpose; and

WHEREAS, Cedar City has been selected as the place for the establishment of such school; and,

WHEREAS, such money is not available for the school year of 1897-98; and,

WHEREAS, it is desired by all the undersigned parties that such school should be conducted during such school year; and,

WHEREAS, the second party hereinafter mentioned has engaged instructors and will engage other instructors and is to procure general school apparatus and purchase school furniture and other necessaries to conduct such school;

NOW THEREFORE, in consideration of the premises and of one dollar in hand paid to each of the undersigned, the receipt whereof is hereby acknowledged, all the undersigned, the first parties, jointly and severally, and the University of Utah, the second party;

WITNESSETH: That said first parties hereby agree to pay to the second party on or before September 1, 1897, $872.00, and the further sum of $1,343.50, the first sum to be used for the general purposes of advertising, stationery, stamps, expenses and school apparatus, and the second sum or so much thereof as may be necessary for the purchase of school furniture and school supplies.

Said first parties further agree to pay to the second party $355.00 per month, the first payment to be made September 1, 1897, and thereafter to pay a like sum on the first day of each month for the next succeeding nine months.

The second party pledges itself to do its best to have the proper State officers and the next State Legislature reimburse the first parties for all such, or other advances and payments, together with interest; provided the permanent school site and buildings at Cedar City, Utah, are vested and accepted as contemplated by law and by all the parties hereto.

A letter of said second party's committee, dated June 22, 1897, and an answer thereto from John Parry, et al, dated June 29, 1897, are hereby referred to and hereby made a part hereof.

WITNESS the hands of said first parties this July 19th, 1897.

John Parry
Francis Webster
Henry Leigh
Joseph S Hunter
Robert Bulloch
Thomas Jed. Jones
L. W. Jones
John Chatterley

to create a campus. They had promised that there would be a building upon the land they had committed to deed to the state. The building specifications were explicit, designed to conform to the standards of buildings at the University of Utah, at an estimated cost of $35,000, and no one, at this point, had a really clear idea of where the money would come from.

The committee had placed orders for building materials in June. The Rollo family had begun to produce the brick during the summer and early autumn. The Jensens, who had the contract to provide the lumber, had sawed and hauled some of it to town before an early fall storm forced them to shut down their operation. Some red sandstone had been quarried and dressed and the excavation work begun. But this prepared material had been used up in the completion of the Ward Hall. The Citizens Committee hoped that they could prevail upon the state officials to be lenient and extend the deadline for the permanent building.

Just before the Christmas vacation, Henry Leigh, John Parry and Francis Webster called upon Principal Bennion to enlist his aid. They explained that the shortage of materials, the unusual extremity of the winter, and the unlikely prospect of their obtaining the needed lumber rendered the accomplishment of the construction virtually impossible. They asked Mr. Bennion to call upon President Kingsbury and the Board of Regents during his Christmas holiday in Salt Lake City, to explain the situation and then to ask for an extension of time for the completion of the school building.

Bennion made an appointment for a meeting to be held immediately upon his arrival in Salt Lake. In addition to the Board of Regents, the Secretary of State and the State Auditor were also present. The officials listened with sympathetic attention and then deliberated on the matter. Their decision was firm.

To Milton Bennion would fall the regrettable task of reporting to the Citizens Committee the decree of the regents. As much as they regretted the conditions, and as sincerely as they sympathized with the people of Cedar City, "...if the law could not be complied with, the school would be closed at the completion of the first year." They did not have the authority to change the law.

The principal returned from his holiday, met with the committee and delivered the dreaded message. The town convened en masse yet again. On January 1, 1898, the citizenry heard the grim details. All agreed there was little question that the future of the southern Branch

Normal School was in crisis. Work would have to begin immediately, if there were to be any hope of meeting the September 1 deadline. But not everyone agreed that it was possible.

It was a spirited gathering, with some denouncing the state for their unreasonable stand. Others, though understanding the requirement of the law, felt the challenge was impossible. There were those whose intense passion for the project lifted them to persuasive eloquence, "We should be proud we were so chosen! We have but nine months in which to build the building worthy to house the Branch Normal School. If we wait until snow begins to melt before we start getting out the necessary lumber, mud will hinder us and it might be late June before we can get into the mountain, and then farm and ranch work will take every available team. We are doing very little except choring through the winter. Will anyone volunteer to make a start ?" [24]

Cornelius Bladen, who in the days that followed would often use rough rhetoric to inspire the reticent, said he'd be willing to try. Others expressed a tenuous willingness. In the end, the people of the town united in their determination not to lose their cherished school. They determined that they would commit themselves to the task, however grueling. At the conclusion of the meeting, a group of men had agreed to embark upon a journey that they felt in their hearts was beyond the realm of the feasible. They had agreed to venture into the snow-filled mountains, where no one ever had gone in winter. And every family in town had pledged all their resources to the cause.

Before the meeting concluded, committees were formed to assemble food, bedding and warm clothing for the men. The home of Mr. and Mrs. James Corlett was to receive bedding, jams, jellies, dried fruit, beans, peas and dried corn, five-gallon cans of honey and the left-over Christmas fruitcakes.

Christopher Arthur at the Co-op store received such foods as eggs, graham flour, cracked wheat for mush, flour for bread and grain for the horses. The eggs were wrapped in newspaper and stored in strongboxes filled with grain. The store donated sugar, tea, coffee, plug smoking tobacco, spices and raisins. The Co-op was also to provide tin plates and cups, knives, forks, spoons and matches.

Caroline Parry remembered her parents' home as designated to receive cheese and brined or salt-cured meats:

I remember an incident so typical of the people of Cedar City. The blocks are long for a child or an elderly person to walk. All food donations were supposed to be deposited the night before the lumber crews were to start for the sawmill, but dear crippled Sister Harris decided that her dried fruit, corn and beans were not enough, they would donate a ham. She went to the basement and lugged a large ham, tied it in a clean kitchen apron, put it in her little boy's wagon and sent her two small sons with this ham and a note. My mother kept the note, but hurried my brother Ed off up the street to the Co-op where she hoped it was not too late for Sister Harris's ham to be loaded on one of the wagons. She was so determined to help bring education to southern Utah. [25]

January 5, 1898, a crowd gathered at the Cedar Flour Mill, at the mouth of Cedar Canyon, to wish well the first crew of the expedition. Eleven men were ready for departure, in four wagons and one bob-sleigh, each drawn by two spans of horses. The group was led by Heber Jensen, the owner of the sawmill, riding a good saddle horse. Their mission was to reach Jensen's sawmill on the east slope of the mountain beyond Brian Head, 30 to 35 miles from town, to bring out 15,000 board feet of lumber left there in the fall. They were also to determine whether or not it was possible to cut, saw and haul enough lumber to erect their building, under conditions that had never been tried before.

ROADS OF THE 1890s

As I said, the Jensen mill on the Mammoth is about 35 miles from Cedar City. Then, even in summertime, it took three days to make a return trip from Cedar to the mill; so you can imagine what travel was like over winter roads. And what roads! Steep, sidling and narrow, with switch backs and close timber, hardly wide enough any place for two teams to pass each other, rough with imbedded rocks and roots over which a vehicle lurched and twisted, up and down and around every little hill and hummock—no such thing then as slicing through a hill to make a straight, smooth road as they do nowadays. Of course, in winter the snow did cover roots and rocks; but it added other dangers. Today, when I think of our four-horsepower inching along, then compare it with a modern vehicle of 230 H.P. that leaps that distance over our modern roads, smooth as carpet, in less than an hour, I just want to laugh out loud.

MOUNTAIN ROUTE

Furthermore, the road didn't run where it does now. It went up Cedar Canyon to Martin's Flat, a distance of seven miles, whence it turned left, or northeast, out of the main canyon into a smaller one known as Log Road, or Little Canyon, up onto a big flat covered with cedar trees, known as Top of the Cedars, a further distance of three miles. From there, still traveling northeast, the road led into another canyon known as Maple Canyon, or Sheep Hollow. It mounted out of that to come upon a dangerous twisting dugway, called S Dugway, that lay at the foot of a high hill called Sugar Loaf. The road skirted around the north side of Sugar Loaf to come upon a little stream called Little Red Creek. It was six miles from Top of the Cedars to that stream. From that point up over a very sharp hill that we called Steep Hill down into a hollow to Old Settin' was two more miles. Old Settin' was the original site of the sawmill before they moved to Mammoth, and it was to be one of the permanent camp sites and way stations of the expedition. For the next six miles, from Old Settin' to Mammoth Summit, the road climbed through a forest across Navajo Ridge up Lightning Hill to emerge upon a long bare knoll lying at the foot of Brian Head peak. It continued south-east along this knoll, over hill and down dale, beyond Brian Head for perhaps two miles until it reached the highest point on the road, Mammoth Summit. The altitude of Cedar City is 5,833 feet. Brian Head, itself, is 11,315 feet. The road at Mammoth Summit is approximately 10,800 feet in altitude. Brian Head looks down over Cedar Breaks. The road skirted along part of the north rim of Cedar Breaks, perhaps a hundred yards away, but always we were too busy clinging to the road to be gazing at scenic grandeur. From Mammoth Summit the road gradually dropped down a ridge to the mill site, another 11 miles, making a total distance of 35 miles.

From *For Sweet Learning's Sake*, by Rob Will Bulloch as told to Gladys McConnell.

It was a warm January day. The men were paired as follows: Neil Bladen and Sim Simkins, each with a good team on the bob-sleigh; Randall Lunt and Daniel G. Perkins, each with a team on Lunt's wagon; J.J.G. Webster and Richard Bryant with Francis Webster's two teams and wagon; Jim Hunter's two teams and new wagon, with John Perry; and Renz Adams and Orson Tyler driving a wagon with Adam's three good horses and a strong mare named Doll, which belonged to the George Wood family. [26] They carried feed for 21 horses, as well as the bedding and grub boxes for the 11 men.

The first day's journey brought them approximately ten miles to the Summit Sheep Corral at the head of Maple Canyon, pushing through a foot of old snow all the way. The route leaves the present-day canyon road at Martin's Flat, seven miles from Cedar City, and veers north. [27] At the Summit Sheep Corral, with only a pole fence for shelter, they spent the night. As they gathered round their campfire that night, the men unanimously elected Neil Bladen to be the captain of the expedition, accepting him as the leader of their group. It was a good choice, for as the trials deepened, he kept fast the vision of their purpose, never slackening in his determination, never faltering in encouraging his fellows.

The second day they traveled more slowly as they climbed through increasingly deep snow. By nightfall they reached the old Jensen mill setting.

This place had been the original mill site, and there were still old sheds and cabins abandoned only the summer before by the Jensens when they had moved to the high mountain site where the lumber and equipment now lay. They referred to the place as "Old Settin'." The largest cabin boasted a huge fireplace, which to cold and weary men would be a most welcome luxury. It was to be one of four permanent campsites during the whole winter's job of getting out the lumber. It

had been a slow and arduous day, that second day, battling through snow as deep as three feet in some places. The distance they had covered amounted to only about eight miles, for the cumbersome wagons were proving to be slow and hazardous.

NEIL BLADEN

When morning came they unloaded some of the hay and grain, leaving it to make their loads lighter, and pressed on.

The third day out the snow was still three feet deep but the weather was still calm, and there were few drifts. Progress was painfully slow. They finally camped that night after making six miles. They were just short of Mammoth Summit, at a place later to be called Lightning Hill, near the intersection of the present day road down Parowan Canyon. Here, they knew, was a stream of water down a small ravine. They determined to tramp a trail through the snow, so they could lead their horses to water, rather than go through the tedious process of melting snow for them. So, pushing with their hands, kicking, tramping and beating with their feet, they managed to form a narrow trail, through which they could lead their 21 horses, one by one, to the creek for water. That done, they scraped down the snow, laid hay for their mattresses and unrolled their bedding to finally sleep, after a grueling day.

CEDAR CITY
CO-OP STORE

*T*he following morning, noting again the depth of the snow and still weary from their struggles of yesterday, they decided to leave one wagon on the hill so as to have four unencumbered horses to help break the road across to the timberline. Stretching before them lay the broad plain known as "The Mammoth." Yawning out from their right was a strangely formed amphitheatre of brightly hued bluffs. They could not know that it would one day be a National Monument called Cedar Breaks, nor that the world would come to gaze at it. They glanced at its majestic pinnacles wearing robes of snowdrifts, and the great pines on its rim bending with the weight

THE AREA OF
THE LUMBER
EXPEDITION, IN
A SPRINGTIME
SETTING.

PHOTO
RICHARD
DOTSON

of the snow, but they did not have time for saluting beauty. They were grimly bent upon achieving the mill without delay. [28]

Now they encountered heavy drifts across the plain that spread between them and the timberline. By driving before them the horses they had loosed from the abandoned wagon to break the trail, they reached the timberline by noon. From there, their descent to the mill site would be faster. But as they descended to the mill, that afternoon of January 8, it began to snow. In spite of the snow, they reached their destination by nightfall, having traveled a greater distance than on any of the previous days. The men were especially grateful to Heber Jensen for his uncanny sense of direction, his ability to find the road under its snowy cover.

At camp, the realization of their grim situation began to sink in. They now understood some things of great significance. First, that wagons were not good conveyances for their purpose. Second, that the storm now beginning could obliterate the road they had struggled to make, and could prevent the follow-up contingent they were counting on to bring food and supplies from getting to them with their vital cargo. They silently took in the gravity of their situation.

With little food for men or animals, they spent a restless night and woke to find, "...a steady, quiet snowstorm pouring itself relentlessly down in flakes so large it appeared as if they were looking out into a wall of great white sheets, flapping in their faces." [29]

They knew they had to get out. They loaded as much lumber as they thought they could carry and headed back up the slope they had descended the night before. In the words of Jim Hunter, "We all agreed the only thing to do was to get out while we could, so we turned right around and began pulling back up the road..

Neil had 600 feet or so of lumber on his sleigh and I had 840 feet on my wagon. The rest of the wagons were empty except for beds and grub boxes. There was not even a trace of the road we made the day before, and it kept on snowing. At night we pulled into a thick grove of pines on the Mammoth to make camp. I had to unhitch my leaders so I could swing the wagon into position where I wanted it for the front was dragging snow. [30]

John Perry, who shared Jim's wagon, remembered the day in equally dramatic terms. "After all day of struggling through snow that kept falling and getting deeper by the minute, we pulled into a heavy grove of pines up on the Mammoth to try to make a camp. The snow was dragging across the tongue and against the front standard of Jim's wagon as he swung into place. When morning came we put our bedding and a little food on the horses and took off, leaving the rest of our wagons sitting there in the trees. As we strung out single file, 21 horses and 11 men, Neil on lead, he stopped suddenly and yelled, his voice drifting back to the hindmost, 'We're not going to quit and don't get it into your heads that we are. We're going to go down and get bobsleds and then come back in here and get that lumber out!'

"I have often thought of that picture and felt that the man was inspired." [31]

On the morning of January 8, while the first party was making its last push into the mill site, the promised second party left Cedar City. There were four men: Rob Will Bulloch, driving two of his father's teams harnessed to his father's wagon; Byron Carrigan, who had been hired by Jed Jones, was driving two of Jones' teams hooked to a sleigh; Oriah Leigh riding a saddle horse; and Spencer Covert riding with Carrigan on the sleigh. Their mission was to carry feed for the horses and food and supplies to sustain the trail-breakers, who could only carry enough feed for the three days they had already been out.

Most of the cargo was loaded on the wagon, because the sleigh runner dragged mud in the shallow snow of the lower canyons and the south slopes.

Rob Will Bulloch was the youngest man of the lumbering expedition. His

HEBER JENSEN

first-hand account provides an intimate picture of the trials of this contingent. It is a guileless picture in which he reveals his own inexperience, his fears and his respect for the men and animals that were his companions. [32]

On January 8, we got a late start out of town, my outfit going first, Carrigan following with the sleigh. We rolled right along for the road was well marked by the first party, our speed measured by the stride of our patient, toiling horses. As the day wore on, the sky became so leaden and heavy it almost seemed to be resting on our heads. Everything looked pretty gloomy and forbidding as we gazed at the white hills marked by dark evergreens. The world was a vast silence except for the sounds made by our own horses as they snorted and puffed and rattled the chains on the singletrees connecting the teams. By 5:30 p.m. we reached the bottom of Maple Canyon, about 13 miles from town, where we camped for the night. We found water in a little stream only partly frozen over, and we fed them all from my wagon to save unbinding both loads. The horses fed and blanketed, we made a campfire to warm our supper and spread our beds in the open, on the south side of a little hillock covered with manzanita bushes, but bare of snow. [32]

When we awoke at dawn, the threat of storm had become a reality. Big snowflakes were falling with deadly relentlessness. We jumped out, rolled and loaded our bedding, bound my wagon, hitched the horses, and without stopping to eat breakfast, pulled out of camp. The marks of the ongoing road were rapidly becoming obliterated...The snowfall increased every minute until it became a solid curtain that we could scarcely see through; and it kept on like that all that day and night, to become one of the worst storms this country has ever known. The horses inched along, feeling and testing the ground ahead before stepping onto uncertain road. Slowly we crept out of Maple Canyon toward the dangerous S Dugway. Here we stopped to eat a cold breakfast from our grub boxes, every man looking like a snow man, as he climbed off his wagon.

We anxiously discussed the worsening situation, and decided to unload part of my cargo to speed us up. We left ten bales of hay and two sacks of grain beside the road and when we were ready to start...Spence [32] *mounted Leigh's saddle horse and rode ahead to guide us and break the trail wherever he could.*

Hour after hour we toiled along, the going steadily becoming worse. Any misstep might send us hurtling off the road into a ravine from which we could never extricate ourselves. Wet, cold and hungry, we longed to reach the shelter and warmth of Old Settin' where we hoped some of the first party would be camped. By early afternoon, we finally reached Little Red Creek, having traveled about three miles in eight hours time.

We started on toward Steep Hill where the road wound up the north side of a very precipitous incline, and here we really ran into trouble. Every sign of the road had vanished, and the new snow on top of the old came well over the horses' backs. When my span of gray mares found they couldn't hold their heads above the snow and got their nostrils full of the cold smothery stuff, they became so panic stricken they were uncontrollable. They plunged and floundered until we decided to unhitch them and ride two and lead two, leaving my load where it stood. We loaded my grub box and bedding onto Carrigan's sleigh; and with Spence leading on the saddle horse, Leigh and I tried to go next, with the sleigh to follow us. But even then my horses would not buck the snow. We finally had to follow the sleigh as it broke trail for my stubborn animals.

*W*e groped for the road, the horses on the sleigh pushing and tugging and floundering up Steep Hill. It took us more than an hour to pull up one particularly sharp pitch only 200 yards long. At last we reached the top and after a short distance came to a hollow, down which we could see Old Settin'. How overjoyed we were to be in sight of our destination. We were numb with cold, our faces, hands and feet like chunks of ice. We drew up at Old Settin' about 5 o'clock, having traveled that day a little over five miles in 11 hours.*

But what a cold, bleak reception we found. No one was there; in fact, we could not tell if the first party had ever camped there. It was utterly quiet and deserted, almost buried in snow. The low buildings, all more or less tumbled down, consisted of a log cabin of two rooms, separated by a breeze-way, two log stables, a half caved-in shed, and a boiler house with the east wall knocked out to let the boiler through when the mill was moved to Mammoth.

Spence took charge at once, showing us

where to get water, while he went to the cabin to make a fire. At the bottom of a little wash, reached by a short ladder, was a boxed-in spring that flowed into a wooden flume, once used to carry away sawdust from the mill. We found an old tub there; so one man climbed down to the spring with the buckets we carried, passing the pails up to a man on top, and we filled the tub time after time. The water was warm; so the nine thirsty, exhausted horses really enjoyed that drink. We blanketed and grained them and put them into the stables, from which we scooped the snow drifts, to give them their hay.

Spence, meantime, had swept some of the drifted snow out of the cabin with an old broom left there. Only one of the rooms was habitable, the one with the fireplace; and even then much of the caulking between the logs had fallen out, letting the wind and snow blow through. Even though we were in a forest, the snow had buried all the wood, but Spence knew where an old slab pile lay and he had dug several ice-encrusted slabs out, broken them up for firewood, and had a good fire going when at dusk the other three of us got into the house out of the heavy storm. How cheerful that fire seemed, and how good our hot supper tasted—the first warm food or drink we had had all day.

After supper we swept our cabin as clean as we could of snow, cut wedge shaped blocks from the slabs to fill the cracks in the walls, and pulled up scraps off an old thread-bare rag carpet left on the floor to stuff the smaller holes. The roaring fire began to dry the room; so by the time we spread our bedrolls down, we were fairly warm and comfortable.

It was then our anxiety over the first party pushed to the surface. Where were our fellow workers? Why were they not at Old Settin'? Had they run into heavier storm than we had? Were they stranded without shelter? These, or even uglier possibilities were unpleasant bedtime thoughts; but we were too tired to stay awake very long. [33]

That night of January 9, while the four exhausted men of the second party slept on the cabin floor before their woodslab fire, the 11 men of the first party were not nearly so comfortable. Struggling all day through the historic blizzard, they had by nightfall covered less than six miles. They pulled their wagons into the pine forest and dug through three to six feet of new snow, carving caves to lay their bedding down.

They awakened under a thick blanket of snow, and found the loaded wagons deeply buried. It was clear they would have to abandon them. They piled their quilts and horse blankets onto the horses, under the harnesses, tied grub sacks onto the hames, then with each man riding one horse and leading another, they started single file toward home, Heber Jensen, with his unfailing sense of direction, in the lead. From that time forward the place was known as "The Wagons."

As they climbed toward Mammoth Summit, there was not a trace of the road they had made. Then howling winds struck with a force that formed loose snow into drifts 10 to 15 feet deep and 75 to 100 yards across. Their planned approach was for each man to take his turn at the front, riding one horse, leading another. He should push into the drifts until his horses gave out, then let the next team step forward to head the line. It worked well as long as the horses could keep their heads above the snow. Each animal could make about 200 yards progress, but when the loose snow fell in on them, threatening to smother them, they reared and vaulted and refused to breast the snow any longer.

The hazard was great, not only in the lack of progress, but when the panicky animals became unmanageable, plunging, backing, fighting to get out, there was the unthinkable danger that they would push the whole string off the high, icy dugways.

It is at this point in the story that the heroic horse, "Old Sorrel", came to the fore—a big, rangy, eight year old draft horse, called Sorrel because of his color. He was from a Percheron grandsire, strong and steady. Described as "long-legged, long-necked and long-faced," he weighed about 1,600 pounds. Sorrel had been raised from a colt by the family of Lorenzo (Renz) Adams. His reaction to this crisis was markedly differently from the other horses. [34]

Sim Simkins later described the episode, "That horse is the greatest trail blazer I've ever seen! He's almost human. We owe our lives to him. Renz didn't ride him; he guided him with the lines to the head of the file, and when Renz spoke calmly to him, he seemed to sense the crisis. He would plunge against the white barriers, rearing up and pawing at them with his front feet, pushing and straining against them until they gave way. Then when the snow would slide in on him, he would rear again, shake the loose snow off his head, blow his nostrils free, then pause for rest, sitting down on his haunches as a dog does. After panting, heaving his sides in and out in long quivering breaths, the while Renz talked to him just like he was another human being, he would look around as if to say, 'Well, I'll try it again, Brothers,' then he would rise and go at it once more. How long could he keep that up, we wondered, as we anxiously watched, knowing our fate rested with him, for there was no retracing our steps, only the desperate hope of going ahead. Time and time again he got through drifts, the worst one over a hundred yards long! It's hard to imagine the effort that animal put forth. Thanks to him, we're here." [34]

The men of the second party had awakened early on this day, grateful to discover that the storm had passed; the snow had stopped. Still they worried about the men of the first party, and realized that their mission to provide feed for their horses and provisions for the men was crucial and that they would have to return for the supplies left at two different points along the route of yesterday's journey. Now, with only the sleigh, it would take two trips. First they returned to the wagon and brought all that remained there. When they returned to Old Settin' there was still no sign of the 11 men. Their concern deepened, but they hitched up two fresh teams and made the eight-mile round trip to pick up the hay and grain left beside the road. The job took all day.

Just at sundown, they crept over the crest of Steep Hill and dropped down toward Old Settin'. There, across the hollow, they could see the men of the first party, riding their horses down the hill through the trees. Both parties sighted each other at the same time, and the mountain echoed with their joyous shouting. The four noted quickly that the count of both men and horses was correct. There was immediate relief; there had been no loss of life.

That night, the men who crowded into the ramshackle buildings were a somber group. When Neil Bladen and Heber Jensen tried to broach the subject of a plan to move forward with the lumbering effort, there was no positive response. Most of the men agreed that their only motion should be homeward. Fifteen men, crowded into a cabin and a shed

to sleep, talked quietly about their narrow escapes from disaster. They were reverent about the horse they knew had saved them, but not inclined at that point to face any more challenges.

OLD SORREL, AS HE WOULD LATER BE IMMORTALIZED IN BRONZE.

The next morning Bladen and Jensen were still filled with fervor for the cause. They pleaded and argued that the work must go on. "Go to town and tell them that we must have sleighs, not wagons, for this work. And tell them we know now that we must have warmer clothes for this weather." When he could sense that their pleas were not penetrating the weary hearers, Neil Bladen leaped up onto the sleigh, using it for a rostrum as he continued his persuasive speech. Seeing they were determined to give up, he cried, "Well, go home all you damn tenderfeet; we'll get along without you. We'll get the lumber out ourselves!"

At the height of his oratory, unexpected reinforcement arrived. Two men, Samuel Heyborne and David Urie, rode into camp. From the two-foot snowfall down in town, the committee knew that the men were having trouble. They had sent these two to urge them to stay on the job and to assure them that plenty of supplies were already on the way.

Five men stayed, determined to return for the wagons they had left buried in the snow on the Mammoth. All the others made their way down the canyon into town.

The Committee called another emergency town meeting the next night. There was to be yet another discussion whether they should go through with the project. Rob Will Bulloch recalls the proceedings:

That meeting is a matter of history now. We younger fellows were loitering around and wondering what they might say or do that could make us face that deep snow and cold again, rather sure that they couldn't put it over. One and another of us drifted in and out, listening, arguing among ourselves. Who said it, when or how it was said I couldn't say, but something stirred us to a determination to go back, get to work and see the thing through. [35]

On the second day the five men who'd stayed on the mountain rolled into town with the load of lumber they had recovered. Moved by this infusion of encouragement, many men volunteered to go, including most of those who had endured the grueling first venture. The Committee resolved that the effort could be extended. The expedition must make whatever effort would be required.

For the next three or four days, J.H. Walker, Fred Ashdown and George Urie, the blacksmiths, worked around the clock fashioning home-made bobsleds. They commandeered every piece of scrap iron in town. The iron with which the smiths shod hand-sawn plank runners came from Thomas Taylor's railroad material and Frank Adams' accumulated hoard. A few miles of icy road brightened the rusty iron, and the runners ran as efficiently as much more pretentious-looking outfits. [36]

When the lumber crew left town again, they were much better prepared for the job ahead. The women began working at a frenzied pace to make warmer clothing suited to the extremity of weather the men faced. A constant supply of good, nourishing food streamed from the kitchens of the town. The wagons that brought the lumber, returned to the mountain loaded with the contributions of the townswomen—hams, bacons, home-made bread and butter, jams and preserves, cakes, pies. Every woman sent the specialty of her home to the men laboring in the mountains.

The work on the mountain settled into a routine, each man working at the task that best suited him, according to the wisdom of their leader, Neil Bladen. Bladen served as the captain of the expedition through to the finish. [37]

The lumber began to filter down from the mountain in four-section relays, across the icy

THE STORY OF OLD SORREL

From an interview with Charlie Adams by Rhoda Wood. Conducted on March 16, 1952. Mr. Adams died the following July.

Sorrel was Sneak's colt. Sneak was a well bred mare owned by my father, Timothy Adams. Sneak's sire was Robin, a gray Percheron stallion owned by John Parry. As a filly Sneak ran with her band out on the Cedar Bottoms and got with foal by a horse owned by Bengt Nelson. When Sorrel was born, Sneak refused to mother him and I became his mother. As regularly as the cows were milked, the little sorrel colt drank his ration from a pan; never enough to suit him, but enough to let him grow and thrive.

Now, as everyone who has ever raised a baby colt in this way knows, they develop a special keenness and an almost human-like characteristic if they are intelligent at all. Although I always claimed him as mine, Old Sorrel was used by the whole family through all of his 23 years. That is old for any horse. He was not a pretty horse, but I was riding him when very young. He took me wherever I wanted to go, which is what counts with any boy.

We lived across lower Main Street from the George Wood family. I always wanted to be with and go wherever the Wood boys went; driving cattle, to the farm, their mountain ranch and any trips. When their Doll or Dan emerged from their drive on winter mornings, hitched to and dragging the "frog" with a barrel on it and buckets banging, I would come from our yard, ready to race for the creek where a hole cut in the ice allowed us to dip up the day's supply of water for our respective homes.

In March 1896, George sent two of his boys, John, who was about my age, and Will, just a youngster, and of course, me, to drive some cattle from the farm up into Dry Creek where they could feed on south hillsides and gradually drift into Cedar Canyon and on up to their mountain ranch by the time the snow would be melted. We drove them up to the head of the canyon and then decided to come back by way of Fiddlers rather than retracing the route we went up.

When we came to the Dugway, instead of a road, a slanting hill of snow was ahead with no sign of a path to hold us. We debated whether we should go back around the way we had come, or take a chance, finally deciding to walk and lead the horses. I was at the rear. Suddenly Old Sorrel's reins jerked out of my hand and the horse with the whole hillside of snow was sliding down the slope. John and Will with their horses and myself stood there watching it go; never expecting to the see horse again, except as bones when the snow melted in the spring.

Suddenly there was movement in the snow below. First a leg kicked free, then his haunches, then a mighty heave, a powerful shake, and he was scrambling back up through the snow to us apparently none the worse for his burial, but having learned a lesson about snow which later helped him to become what Rob Will Bulloch called him, "the savior of the Founders' lumbering expedition."

roadbed, hard-packed by the inexorable passing of the loaded sleighs: the first stretch from the mill to the place they called Bryant's Hotel, just beyond Mammoth Summit; the second from "the hotel" to Old Settin'; the third stretch from there to the Summit Sheep Corral, and the fourth from there to Cedar City. It was at the Corral that they stacked the precious lumber on wagons for the triumphant trip to town. Hair-raising difficulties threatened the delivery of every load. [38]

Harnesses broke in the strain and intense cold. Snow and ice balled up on horseshoes until the animals walked on stilts of ice and the shoes had to be pried off. Wind whipped the snow back and forth until the road vanished, causing the teams to flounder off the beaten track into soft snow, sometimes falling into deep holes. After one particularly trying day, the crew reached the mill with their tales of trouble. Heber Jensen came up with a solution. By lantern light he cut a load of slab edgings into stakes and piled them onto sleighs. Next day as they located the road along the barren stretches, they drove stakes every thirty yards along the north side of the way. The rest of the winter the road was plainly marked.

The experiences of the lumber crew were high drama, but quiet drama was playing out in small vignettes down in town. The Committee, who became known as "the beggars," had a firm pledge from their fellow townspeople to give "all our public and private resources that are necessary for the building of this school house." They worked unceasingly, visiting homes to ask for what they needed.

Thomas Jed Jones was made chairman of the building committee, perhaps because of his gift for getting people to respond to a need. Heber Jensen recalled his effectiveness:

Great Scott! I can remember as if it were yesterday how T.J. Jones rode all over town on horseback asking men to work, gathering supplies for those who were already working, raising everybody's spirits and making them look ahead. I remember one young fellow who had been called upon to give a few days labor when the brick layers were almost to the top of the building. Jed Jones told the youth that he wouldn't have any work to do, if he would just mix the mud and carry it to the top of those walls,

the brick layers would do the work. He made it sound right easy." [39]

William R. Palmer, whose memories of childhood included these days, wrote of the process developed by the "home front" organization.

The organization in Cedar City reached down to every home and called for unselfish, devoted service from every man, woman and child...The furnishing of supplies was allotted by streets and each street had to have it's contingent of necessities in, to a central point, at the stipulated time...The men in town gathered up hay and grain, teams, harnesses, wagons, sleds and all the equipment that was needed for the logging, sawing and hauling operation. The home of Mrs. Mary Corlett on Main Street was the place to which all supplies for the mountain crews were gathered. Each family took their offerings to her on the appointed day, and hers was the great responsibility of receiving and receipting for them and dispatching them to the men at the saw mill. The fact that men were willing to let good teams and outfits go in the hands of strange drivers to work under such unprecedented conditions reveals the earnestness and the united purpose of Cedar City citizens to succeed. It was an unusually severe winter with much snow even in town, and the absence of men imposed upon women, in a great many homes, the responsibility of doing the outside chores...The Committee gave to the description, "All public and private resources," the most literal application. They went after the people with all the assurance of ownership and both the weak willed and the willing ones surrendered without argument. "Brother" Webster was "Front" in gathering up the resources, and he became the "nut cracker" for the committee. He was sent after the selfish, unwilling men and he was blind and deaf to the word "no."

"Tut, tut" was his laconic reply to every argument or protest and there is no case on record where he ever came away empty-handed. [40]

An aged founder remembered Francis Webster warmly,

Francis Webster was more than attentive to duty. His sudden appearance spelled failure to one's own plans, or the fulfillment of one's own personal desires. If he asked for some donation of material, and he seemed to always know if you had anything to spare, you might as well say "Yes" immediately, for he always got what he went for. We all gave him credit for not asking something unless you were able to spare. [41]

The harshness of the winter added to the difficulty of the myriad tasks of building. Stone cutters and brick makers worked in below zero weather through the frigid months to prepare the stone for the foundation and the brick for the walls. Their tasks, though less dramatic, and less frequently extolled than the lumbering crew, were tedious and their methods primitive.

The details of brickmaking are illustrative of the intensity of effort required in every part of the process. The brick yards were located on the southeastern edge of town. Piles of fine white sand and clay soil ringed the perimeter and had to be constantly replenished. The dry soils were mixed and sieved by being shoveled through large metal strainers, to remove rocks or bits of vegetation. The strained material was then carried to the mixer near the center of the yard. The mixer was a large wooden container which held the mixed sand, soil and water. At the center of the mixer was a pole with spikes attached and a shaft extending outward. A mule pulled the shaft, causing the spiked pole to rotate, mixing the contents into mud. The mud was drawn from the bottom of the mixer onto hods and carried on the shoulders of the "mud men" to be dumped on tables and allowed to dry until it was just right to be scooped, by bare hands, into molds that had been coated with white sand.

After a little drying in the sun, the molds were emptied, each brick turned several times, then stacked in the kiln and fired. Then the kiln was unloaded, the bricks stacked into wagons and carried to the building site. Every part of the process required a pair of hands. Thousands and thousands of times, the process was repeated until there were sufficient bricks for the construction of the outside and inside walls of the building. The brick-making crew included Alex Rollo and Harry Hunter, Andrew Rollo, Richard Bryant, William, Tom and John Walker, Al, Dave, and John Connell, Dick Palmer, Will Sawyer, Bill and Lafe McConnell and Dave and Bill Dix. Day and night the kiln fires had to be watched, so that it would not go out during a firing.

The cold weather continued through the entire winter, but the pace of the work did not slacken. Then on March 14th the town paused and came together for the ceremonial laying of the cornerstone.

It was cold. Eight inches of snow lay on the great stacks of lumber, the piles of dressed sandstone and thousands of brick. The townspeople stood on the stacked materials in order to see the proceedings and hear the words of the prayer and speeches. After the prayer, Principal Milton Bennion laid the cornerstone. At his side were George W. Decker, Howard R. Driggs and Annie Spencer, the faculty. The men of the Citizens Committee stood prominently by. The whole town was there, the women wrapped in large three-cornered woolen shawls, the men bundled against the biting cold.

Records document the presence of...the Adams, the Ashdowns, the Arthurs, the Armstrongs and Ahlstroms. The Bauers, the Bensons, the Besses, the Bladens, the Browns, the Bullochs, the Bryants, the Burbecks, the Bergstroms. The Chatterleys, the Corrys, the Corletts, the Cossletts, the Carrigans, the Condies, the Chaffins and the Clarks. There were the Dalleys, the Dixes, the Dovers, the Duttons, the Deckers, the Driggs, and the Daughertys. The Elikers, the Fifes and the Fretwells. The Gowers and the Goulds. The Haights, the Hansens, the Harrises, the Heybornes, the Higbees, the Houchens, the Hunters, the Humphries, the Haulmans and the Hollands. The Jensens, Heber and John, who operated the lumber mill. The Jones, the Jacobsens, and the Krumans. The Leighs, the Lunts, and the Lamberts. The Macfarlanes, the Mackelprangs, the Mathesons, the Muries, the McConnells, the Middletons and the Nelsons. There were the Palmers, the Parrys, the Perrys, the Pendeltons, the Perkins, the Poynors, the Pryors, and the Pucells. There were the Rollos, who made the brick, and the Roots, the Roches, and the Rosenbergs. The Sandines, the Sawyers, the Sherratts, the Schoppmans, the Spencers. The Taits, the Tailors, the Taylors, the Thorleys, and the Tuckers. There were the Unthanks and the Uries. The Walkers, the Websters, the Wilkensons, the Williamses, the Woods. All were there, happy, determined and resolute." [42]

Spring brought a heightened pitch to the activity. Carpenters, bricklayers and stonemasons worked feverishly on the building itself with hand-operated hammers, saws, and wheelbarrows. Ten-year-old boys played horse for the hod carriers, helping to get the heavy barrow loads of lime-cement to the masons on the walls. Little girls carried lunches to fathers and brothers. Mothers added to their regular duties the onerous chores of farming, aided by their boys and by the older girls, who also kept the house, gardened and looked after the children. [43]

In April the celebrant lumbering crews brought down the last historic load. It was a dramatic finale. They had to haul their cargo down through Panguitch, over Bear Valley, through Parowan and home, because the load consisted of great support timbers, too long for the twisting route and too heavy for the increasingly softening snow. What a success their gargantuan effort had been! Stockpiled at the building site were 130,000 feet of lumber, 75,000 shingles and huge stacks of lath. The men came home from the mountain, but work for the school went on. The heroes of the expedition took up less dramatic tasks related to the building, for the goal was never far from the consciousness of the citizens of the town.

*T*he people had worked relentlessly for a full year since the mass meeting of the June before had startled them into high gear. This year the Board of Regents fired a second volley of shattering news. President Kingsbury had reported to the Regents that the building in Cedar City was progressing well, but that there had been an inadvertent deletion in the plans sent by the architect for the building. No provision for heating had been made! A basic omission. Dr. John R. Park, a member of the selection commission, had been assigned to keep an eye on the progress of the school. Immediately he made an "inspection" journey to Cedar City. After many laudatory comments about the amazing accomplishments of the Cedar City citizens, Dr. Park delivered the message to the committee with this question: could the people accept the additional burden of providing a heating and ventilating plant of the quality of those used in the buildings at the University of Utah?

The stalwarts called another mass meeting to relay the reeling blow. The people were already pressing with all their might and strength to be ready for school to open in September. There were those who spoke hotly of the unfairness. But in the end it was clear that school could not open without a means to heat the building. They must regroup to bring their building to the standard of like structures on the University of Utah campus. This time the money crisis was met by different dedicated citizens, who offered to obtain the funds by pledging their sheep against the loan. Mrs. Catherine Bell, Richard Aldrich Thorley, Francis Webster and David Bulloch mortgaged their sheep to guarantee the loan. Henry Leigh was dispatched to Salt Lake City to collect bids for the heating plant.

*M*eticulously kept accounts show that Henry Leigh was allowed $25 for his 10-day trip. His train fare was $9.00, his expenses $7.50, which did not include $15.00 to the stables for his rented team and buggy. When Henry returned home he had contracted with David James Company to furnish the plant for $4,547.05. It was shipped by rail to Modena at a freighting cost of $40.00.

When the heating and ventilating equipment arrived in Modena, Gus Mackleprang, Neil Bladen and John Adams were waiting with their wagons, ready to bring it home. The crates were bulky and heavy and required derricks and hand gear on wheels to unload them.

The railroad man was concerned. "How're you going to unload these crates when you get them to the Normal School Building?" he asked. The men had been wondering the same thing.

"I'd like to do something to help a little with that school. I'll let you take the derrick and the wheeler with you, Gus. You can return it with the first team that comes from Cedar City."

So they gladly accepted his offer and borrowed the derrick, thus enabling them to place the heating and ventilating apparatus in the building with much greater ease than they had expected. Better still, in this simple gesture the spirit of supportive interest of all the people in the south warmed their hearts and supplemented their courage.

Nonetheless, the addition of the heat plant required a good deal of dedicated labor, and when September came, the system was not quite complete. A few other finishing touches also remained. However, in acknowledgement of their heroic efforts, the Board of Regents petitioned the state to consider the contract fulfilled. The state accepted the building and the land upon which it stood. School, at last, was ready to begin at the new site on Academy Hill.

THE CLASS OF 1909 PREPARES FOR A 'GRAND PARADE.'

A SOCIAL GATHERING, CIRCA 1904

CHAPTER III

Branch Normal School, 1897-1913

" *We have as good a body of students so far as earnestness and zeal are concerned as there are in the state. And the people are all enthusiastic for the school.*"

J. Reuben Clark, Jr.

The ring of hammers and the sound of saws still reverberated through the halls of the not-quite-completed Branch Normal School building the second week of September, 1898. Nevertheless, committee members, faculty and helpful townspeople began to haul furniture, school apparatus and books from the Ward Hall, setting of the first year school, to their new and permanent home.

The place did not appear to be ready. The rocky hillside still bore ample evidence of the frantic construction adventure. Bits of brick and shards of stone lay scattered about. Dust was everywhere, and calcimined walls were scarcely dry. But so heroic had been the effort of the entire community, that the state had been persuaded to overlook some inadequacies, and to allow school to begin, confident that the rough spots would be smoothed in time for the formal acceptance ceremony, scheduled for October 28th.

The excitement was tangible. After so many years of struggle for rudimentary education, there was now to be a superb source of learning for the young people of the area. The faculty chosen by President Kingsbury and the regents could not have been better. Their year of teaching in the Ward Hall had endeared them to the community. They had established a high standard of excellence, while at the same time they had approached the curriculum with clear understanding of the need of their pupils.

In addition to the regular normal course, they taught what was called, "The Preparatory Course." The description of that course stated:

As there are in the more remote settlements many young men and women who have not had the advantages of a complete common school education, this course is designed to offer for students over 18 years of age, special instruction in the subjects required for entrance. [1]

Certainly the students came from the "more remote settlements." The first list includes young people from such widely disparate places as Hebron, Hatchtown and Hilldale; Panguitch, "Paragoonah" and Pinto; Kanab, Kanarra and Bunkerville, Nevada, as well as St. George and Cedar City. They arrived in wagons and buggies, with a few household necessities and food from home.

They came to a town barely able to qualify as a city. Cedar City consisted of one block of business buildings scattered irregularly along both sides of Main Street. At the south end, or head, of this street stood the Tabernacle. The rest of the town was sprawlingly laid out in the north-south east-west grid fashion that characterized Mormon settlements. Houses were spaced far apart, generously surrounded by gardens and

LIBRARY BUILDING, 1900

CEDAR CITY,
1900

thing was needed to further the cause of the school, no one hesitated to ask, and few were inclined to refuse.

Applicants for admission to the first year of the normal school were required to be at least 15 years of age, and must be able to pass tests in arithmetic, United States history, reading and spelling. The entrance examination was extensive, but could be waived if the student carried a certificate of completion of the public school course, signed by the principal, or a certificate signed by the superintendent verifying that he could pass the examination for graduation from the district schools. [3] In short, admission requirements were liberal.

Under the heading, "Apparatus and Books" the circular boasts, "Several hundred dollars have been appropriated for apparatus and books, which will be purchased and ready for use on the opening of school." On the subject of Physical Education: "All needful provision has been made for the proper development of the body. The students have the advantage of a variety of apparatus...appliances for out-door exercises, for football, baseball, basketball and croquet have been provided."

Each day began with a devotional in the chapel, public lectures were frequent, and all students were invited to become members of student organizations to promote literary and general culture.

The persuasive pamphlet does not mention the most remarkable advantage that awaited students at the Southern Branch of the State Normal School. The team of four bright, young educators that made up the first faculty created a palpable atmosphere of excitement. Each of the four was perfectly suited for his or

orchards. Each house also had its corrals and barnyards. Except for a few large cottonwood trees, shade was scanty. At the new school there was as yet no shade whatever. [2] The streets were dusty in dry season and muddy when wet. There were only a few board side walks, and the citizenry still obtained their drinking water from the ditches that ran in front of the houses.

What the town lacked in stature it made up in heart. Cedar City was wholly dedicated to making a success of the new school. Inbound students needed housing so folks were urged to open their homes. People crowded their families to make room, receiving relatives and often strangers to lodge with them.

One of the first expenditures made by the Board of Trustees from the money advanced by the people of Cedar City in June, 1897, was the printing of a "circular" that extolled the virtues of the town and the new school. The circular suggested that $2.00 to $2.50 a week would pay for room and board. Mr. Edward Palmer could be contacted for information about room and board. Mr. Palmer, who undoubtedly performed this labor as a service to his community and the school, was busily engaged in a continuing search for a vacant nook or cranny which might be conscripted to house a scholar. The same spirit drove both the method and the response. If any-

MAIN STREET, 1900

her responsibility and each brought to the school unique qualities of competence, dedication, vitality and strength of character. That such a cadre had been assembled to launch this new school was the best of good fortune, for they established from the beginning a grand tradition of excellence. This faculty was largely responsible for generating an essence, unique to this place, that continues to this day. Students arriving from the farms and villages of southern Utah, chafing from inherent insecurity, quickly discovered that these extraordinary teachers expected them to stretch beyond their natural and acquired capabilities. The remarkable personalities of their faculty inspired them. Both academics and extracurricular activities expanded them.

Milton Bennion was 27 years old when he arrived in Cedar City to become the first principal of the Branch Normal School. He was also the teacher of pedagogy and history. A young man of superb good humor, he had grown to young manhood in Taylorsville, Utah, the youngest son of a widowed mother. Having first combined a vigorous interest in horses with a precocious teaching career, Milton had just enrolled in LDS College in Salt Lake City under the tutelage of James E. Talmage when an unexpected letter had arrived from the Church of Jesus Christ of Latter-day Saints, calling him to serve a three-year mission in New Zealand. He had fulfilled that assignment, which included great adventures, the learning of languages and dialects and ended with travels almost circling the globe. Greatly matured, he returned to his studies with Dr. Talmage and others, completed requirements for his degree and

obtained his first teaching position as principal of the Branch Normal School in Cedar City.

Bennion was a highly regarded personal friend of Dr. Joseph Kingsbury, then president of the mother institution. His being hired to serve in a rural community is evidence of the sincere commitment of the trustees to the new school. He brought to the fledgling institution cosmopolitan experience, a code of personal integrity and honor, a commitment to the enhancement of his students' character as well as to expansion of their intellect. And he established the expectation that students would conform to this standard. He began his first year of teaching as a bachelor, betrothed to Miss Cora Lindsay, to whom he was married before the beginning of his second year at Branch Normal School. [4]

George William Decker was the only member of the first faculty with southern Utah roots. He was born in Parowan to Zachariah Bruyn Decker and Nancy Bean Decker, who had come to the valley with the first settlers. George Decker had been born only 14 years after the settlement, which brought him into the rugged environment that was formative to his character and his wonderfully adventuresome personality. The 10th of 12 children, George burned with insatiable curiosity and hungered for information. When the Presbyterians opened a library in Parowan he brought home every book he could borrow. Then with characteristic reckless vitality, he hauled great loads of wood from the canyons, to keep a fire burning all night long, while he feasted upon

GEORGE W.
DECKER

history, biography and such snatches of science as were available. [5]

One of the real "cowboys" of the early West, George Decker was among the original "Hole In The Rock" pioneers at age 14. The Hole In the Rock trek was a pioneering enterprise that took southern Utah settlers into the deserts of the San Juan. It is famed for the seemingly impossible feat of lowering wagons through a small opening in the sandstone mountain to the Colorado riverbed, many treacherous feet below. He made the trek even more dramatic, by making the return trip from Bluff to Parowan through the snowy mountains alone. In 1893 he received a degree in pedagogy from the University of Deseret. It may have been an even more striking example of his courage and confidence that he was one of the first to pursue an advanced education after he was married. He and his wife, Orpha Bayles, were the parents of a baby daughter. He took his young family to Salt Lake City so that he could attend the University of Utah. After his

graduation he returned to serve as principal of Parowan schools until 1897, when he came to teach mathematics and natural science at Branch Normal School. He also served as librarian at the new school. He quickly became a favorite with the students for his capacity to impart information with vitality and excitement, but also for his genuine concern for each student.

He became known for taking youngsters home for food and nourishment, and for quietly paying tuition for those whose education was jeopardized by family financial limitations. George Decker gave himself to the school for the full period in which the institution was known as Branch Normal School, serving the last eight years as principal.

Howard R. Driggs, the third member of the first faculty, was born in Mt. Pleasant, Utah. His Mormon pioneer family had settled in Sanpete County but their early American history connects to the Dutch settlers of the late 1600s. He graduated from the University

MILTON BENNION
1870-1953

Education of the *character* of the student was the central theme of Milton Bennion's administration at Branch Normal School and of the rest of his splendid life. He came to Cedar City, as an earnest 27-year-old, to be the founding principal of the fledgling branch of the University of Utah. During his three years at BNS his watchword was integrity; he exemplified cleanliness in thought and deed for his earnest, even younger students.

Principal Bennion's duties did not preclude the opportunity, or even necessity, of his being a teacher. Even at this early point in his career, his teaching was a keen combination of wisdom and wit. Without benefit of good visual aids he taught a lively course in United States history, bringing the Constitution to life by having his class reenact the scenes in the Constitutional Convention, where the great document was framed. As teacher and administrator he urged upon his charges, not only nobleness but independence of thought. One of his first efforts was to establish a self-governing student body and to allow the students an opportunity to develop their own initiatives.

Milton Bennion had garnered an amazing preparation for his lifelong career in education in those 27 years before his assignment at BNS—teaching in the Taylorsville public school, spending three years in New Zealand as a missionary and virtually traveling the world—but sophistication never took the farm out of the farm boy from Taylorsville.

That Bennion became the mainstay of the faculty at the University of Utah,

where he had received his undergraduate degree, indicates a great deal about his extraordinary gifts. While he remained an anchor for that faculty for more than 40 years—either in service as a teacher, on leave of absence for advanced degrees and honors, or as dean of education and ultimately vice president—he had the energy and expansiveness to serve in many other positions of trust. These included a chairmanship of state and national associations and president of both the Utah Academy of Science and Arts and Letters. He also chaired the Utah State Welfare League and was active in of the Church of Jesus Christ of Latter-day Saints all of his life, especially in connection with the Sunday Schools, over which he served as general president for 40 years.

Milton Bennion was productive and congenial all the 82 years of his life. He was an educator, but there was nothing pedantic in his nature. He liked people, was an exemplary husband to Cora Lindsay Bennion and father of 10 children. His influence lived on through the lives of thousands of students and peers who were inspired and enriched by his teaching, his books, his friendship and his example.

family background had fitted her for an adventurous life on the frontier. Thomas Spencer and Sarah Ann Tomalin had joined the Church of Jesus Christ of Latter-day Saints in England and emigrated to Virginia in 1871, moving later to Michigan where Annie was born in May of 1874. Thomas had taken up river-front land, and with the help of his three children, cleared away the trees and stumps and planted his 20 acres. Thomas and Sarah planned to go West, as soon as their circumstances would allow. The years in Michigan provided Annie with opportunities that might not have come to her had her parents accomplished their dream earlier. Sarah worked at nursing using her earnings to provide educational advantages for her three children. Annie was able to study music and elocution. The family purchased a small organ, upon which Annie gained some skill. She earned a small salary by playing for the nearby Presbyterian Church. Young Annie Spencer showed at an early age her inclination in the subjects that were later to qualify her for her position at Branch Normal School. As a very small child, as her father recorded, she climbed upon stumps in the dooryard and made up and delivered spirited speeches. Speaking contests were popular in the region of their home, and Annie regularly won medals for her orations.

In 1891 the Spencers finally had a good crop; 1,000 bushels of potatoes, for which they received $1 a bushel. This good fortune helped them to realize their long held dream to go West. They sold all their belongings, except the organ and sewing machine, and on May 1, 1892, boarded the Denver and Rio Grande Railroad for the trip to Salt Lake City.

of Utah's department of education and began to teach in the Pleasant Grove public schools. He was then appointed to the first faculty of the Branch Normal School. On September 8, 1897, Howard took Miss Eva Frampton as his bride. Cedar City must have been their honeymoon destination, for the first examinations for the term were held on September 15th, and young Mr. Driggs would have been expected to be at his post at the new Branch Normal School.

He came with the title of secretary and registrar, but also headed the department of English language and literature.

The young faculty quickly became integrated into Cedar City society, but they also formed a tightly knit society of their own. In the early summer of 1898, after the first year of teaching at Cedar City, Howard and Eva Driggs joined the newly wedded Milton and Cora Bennion aboard a train bound for Chicago. They spent the summer together in a five-room furnished apartment, while all four studied at the University of Chicago. The two young women studied music while their husbands took full educational courses to better prepare themselves to conduct their stewardships at Branch Normal School.

Howard Driggs taught for six years at BNS. In later years he became a renowned historian, author of a number of volumes of western history and a nationally known educator. For 20 years he was a professor of English education at New York University. His influence as a member of the first faculty was formative for the school.

Miss Annie Spencer arrived in Cedar City in the fall of 1897 to complete the roster of faculty hired to establish the first-year Branch Normal School. [6] Miss Spencer was young, just 23 years old. Her

ANNIE SPENCER, 1897

Arriving in Utah, they began life on the frontier. For $900 they purchased a homestead at the mouth of Little Cottonwood Canyon which needed clearing and cultivating. And they found that farming in the West was nothing like farming in the East. They knew nothing about irrigation and were thankful for their only success, a crop of squash which kept them alive until they became more proficient. Annie taught piano lessons for 25 cents a lesson. Eleanor and John, her brother and sister, found schools in which they could teach.

The second summer in Utah, Annie Spencer and her siblings took a course in physical education, which had just been introduced in Utah by Maude Mae Babcock. Miss Babcock was also a newcomer to Utah. After having been converted to the Mormon Church, while living in New York City, she had come West and had begun to teach at the University of Utah and the LDS College. After this summer Annie knew that she wanted to teach physical education and elocution.

Continuing her study with Miss Babcock, Annie reveled in the opportunity to study with other remarkable educators. She took fundamentals of music from Evan Stephens and education classes from James E. Talmage. She studied art with James Taylor Harwood, Edwin Evans and John Hafen, all of whom became renowned western artists. She performed recitations at the Social Hall and the Salt Lake Tabernacle, being coached for her performances by Evan Stephens and Miss Babcock. At length she was judged qualified to accept a position as Miss Babcock's assistant.

Annie applied to teach music, physical education and reading at the new school being formed in southern Utah. She then went East with Miss Babcock for a summer of study at Harvard University at Cambridge, Mass. Upon her return she was delighted to find that her position was assured. Boarding a train for Milford, Annie was admittedly nervous to be on her own. She was met in a white topped wagon and and taken the 65 miles to Cedar City where she began her teaching career, of which she was later to say, "My years of teaching and mingling with the young people and my association with the stalwart pioneers of Cedar City and surrounding towns were the richest and happiest of my life." One is led to contemplate the educational dimension she brought to the lives of young men and women of rural southern Utah as she embarked upon the Branch Normal School adventure.

The success of the first year of school, even though held in makeshift quarters at the Ward Hall, only sharpened the enthusiasm of the people of Cedar City for the Branch Normal School. That, coupled with the year-long labor of the entire town to complete the building, created an atmosphere of exhilaration now as they moved from the Ward Hall to their beautiful new quarters and prepared for the celebration attending its acceptance by the State of Utah.

The governor was coming! Utah had not long had a governor, for it had not long been a state and the Territorial leaders sent from the nation's capitol had been tolerated rather than beloved. But now their own first governor, the 36-year-old Heber M. Wells, had accepted the invitation to come in person to accept the proud offering of their herculean exertions.

No detail was overlooked. Committees were formed for the program, the reception and the banquet. The general committee was chaired by John Parry and included Principal Milton Bennion, Stake President U.T. Jones, Henry Leigh, Francis Webster, George W. Middleton, T. J. Jones, L.W. Jones, Mayor Robert Heyborne, Charles Dover, Robert Bulloch and Thomas Bladen. The women planned food befitting such an occasion and the school children practiced special music and drills, for they were to line the way to the building. The dignitaries accompanying the governor, as well as the townspeople, would pass through the double rows of children.

The invitations were prepared and made to look fittingly fancy. [7] They read:

Yourself and Lady

are cordially invited to be present at the ceremonies incident upon the transfer of title to the Southern Branch Normal School Building and Grounds from the Building Committee to the State of Utah, which will take place at the school building. Friday. October 28, at one o'clock. P. M.

INVITATION COMMITTEE

The *Deseret Evening News* of October 29, 1898, reported the details of the day :

TITLE TO HANDSOME BUILDING AND SPACIOUS GROUNDS TRANS- FERRED TO THE STATE; THE GIFT WAS ACCEPTED BY GOVERNOR WELLS; PROFESSOR STEWART OF THE STATE NORMAL WAS ALSO PRESENT; THE OCCASION WAS A MEMORABLE ONE.

Cedar City, October 29. Cedar was all animation yesterday, according to a dispatch to the Herald, *due to a number of events of more than ordinary importance. At 2 o'clock the exercise incident to the transfer of title to the Branch Normal School building and grounds commenced at the school building, and an interesting program was carried out.*

Following this was a sumptuous repast served for the old people at the spacious ward hall, to which all visiting friends were invited, and the day closed with a grand ball in the evening, also for the old folks. [8]

Gov. Wells and Professor Stewart of the State Normal School were present and took part in the exercise at the Branch Normal, arriving here shortly after noon. (From Milford, the railroad terminal, these gentlemen traveled by horse and buggy.) Between 250 and 300 school children, ranging from the primary to the intermediate grades, were drawn up in double file at the approach to the building, between which the distinguished visitors passed, giving them a good opportunity to judge as to the need of the people in this section in educational matters, and whether or not the State had made a mistake in locating a school here.

Dr. George Middleton was made master of ceremonies, and the meeting opened by the choir and congregation singing "America." After the invocation by Joseph S. Armstrong, Stake President U.T. Jones delivered an address of welcome to the visitors.

Gov. Wells then delivered a brief, business-like address, eulogizing the people of Cedar City in the strongest terms for the marvelous work they had accomplished in so short a time. He expressed an interest in the southern part of the state and said he believed there was an era of prosperity drawing upon us. He referred to the prospect of railroad communication with the outside world and said he had faith that at last one of the two lines pointing in this direction would be immediately built.

Principal Bennion of the Branch Normal related the history of the location and the commencement of the school. [9]

Professor Stewart expressed deep interest in the southern wing of the State Normal School. He said he could not find words to express his appreciation of the wonderful work that had been accomplished by the people of Cedar City by erecting the commodious and spacious normal building in so short a time, besides preparing the temporary quarters for the accommodation of the school during the first year of its existence. He reviewed with interest the growth of the institution and said all that should be said in praise of the Cedar people. Other speakers followed, among them Rep. James Duffin of Toquerville, Washington County, who also reviewed the history of the institution from its earliest conception, being a member of the State Legislature when the bill was passed establishing a Branch of the State Normal in the southern end of the state.

The address, finally bequeathing to the State the title and ownership of the building and grounds, was delivered by the Honorable John Parry, Iron County's representative. The hard-

REP. JAMES G. DUFFIN

REP. JOSEPH E.
ROBINSON

ships and privations endured in the construction and procuring of the school were gone over and explained. The Governor graciously received the deeds and abstracts.

The dedicatory prayer was offered by Bishop William H. Corry. The choir sang an anthem and the meeting adjourned.

The Normal School building is substantial and commodious, and equipped with every modern sanitary device calculated to promote the health and comfort of the Normal students. Including the heating and ventilating apparatus, the cost of the building will be nearly $25,000. A tract of 15 acres of land surrounds the structure. The building and grounds are a gift of the enterprising people of Iron County to the State of Utah, the only condition being that as soon as the property title vests in and is accepted by the State, it will suitably maintain and foster the institution which will be of great benefit to the people of Southern Utah. The land is ornamented and embellished with trees and shrubbery and the State Normal School will be picturesque and attractively established.
[10]

*I*t must have been quite an afternoon. Local journal accounts detail other speeches not included in the newspaper account. Rep. William L. H. Dotson was extolled by Rep. Duffin for having made an early and relentless effort to get a school for the south. Sen. Edward Snow said a few words about his own enthusiasm for the school and his support of it in the legislature, as did Rep. Robinson of Kane County. By the time speeches had finished and the people ready to stroll back to the Ward Hall for the banquet, there was probably not much time to spare, for the banquet began at 5 p.m.

Three hundred adults attended the banquet. There was an abundance of good food from the gardens, orchards, farms and herds of the townspeople. The tables were decorated with autumn leaves. A quartet and a double quintet under the direction of Joseph Cosslett provided dinner music. [11]

Through the ceremonies of the day the building became an official state building, dedicated to the light of learning. But through the sacri-

WILLIAM
HOUCHEN

fices that preceded the day, the building had become a symbol of the linking of the community and the institution that would endure through the next 100 years.

When the legislature of 1899 met, Representative John Parry introduced House Bill 55, which called for the reimbursement of the monies borrowed by Cedar City citizens to fund the first year of the school. That part of the bill directed the release of $15,000 already appropriated but withheld until the state received the completed building. It also included a provision to appropriate funds to pay the outstanding note for the heat plant. The bill passed and those obligations were cared for.

There was also hope that an appropriation could be made to reimburse the costs of the building. The Committee scurried about compiling lists of costs and sending letters of suggestions for points of debate to Representative Parry. Their hopes were high as evidenced by their correspondence.

William Houchen, Iron County Assessor, kept a stream of letters flowing to John Parry at the legislature. The originals are endearing, both for their beautiful penmanship, the lack of punctuation and the homely grammar. On January 25, 1899, he wrote:

Hon. John Parry
House of Representatives

Dear Friend,

Yours of January 23 came duly to hand and also your letter addressed to U.T. Jones, M.D Higbee and myself. Uriah and us thought it was alright. We are all anxious somehow or other to hear from you. Well, we have not got the report nowhere ended for the Normal yet and can't say hardly when. I still keep hunting it up. Just got the Jensen bill today, which is over $1376.00 for saw mill account so the lumber account will be high enough as several parties have 70 day labor with teams besides this, and then come all the hauling.

If there should be a committee appointed to visit the school I think we will have most of the account so they could take it back with them. But everybody here now are sick.

Hoping all is well with you and that McCune elected.

I remain very respectfully yours,
W. Houchen

Then, with anxieties showing, he wrote again on January 30:

Hon. John Parry
House of Representatives

Dear Friend,

T.J. Jones was telling me today of having read a piece of your writing in the Deseret News *relative to the Normal School about the way the lumber was got and other inconveniences that we had to go through to get the building ready in time for school.* [12]

The question we thought might be raised that we knew we had to get it ready by a certain time and should of got out the lumber in the fall before. If you will remember there was considerable lumber cut and a great many logs ready to haul to the mill, but on account of so much rain it was impossible to haul them as the wagons soon as loaded with logs or lumber would sink out of sight in that part of the country and it had to be abandoned until frost or snow come, you may have thought of this but we thought you'd have time to read it any way. Also in relation to the bill for the heating plant. Jed sent one to Pres. Kingsbury which was very incomplete as there was a great many items left out. The one you got is the correct one he told me to tell you as you might both present them and the difference would not look well. The building is going to cost from 20 to $25,000 outside of the heating plant. But I am afraid we are not gong to get the accoun[13]...

Finally the totals were assembled and on February 11, 1899, William Houchen sent the following letter to John Parry, again written in his impeccable hand.

Feb. 11, 1899
Hon. John Parry
House of Representatives

Dear Sir,

Enclosed you will find the statement of Cost of the Building of the State Branch Normal School at Cedar City:

Cost of Rock	*$2,300.00*
Brick	*$2,400.00*
Lumber, Lath, Shingles	*$5,950.00*
Lime, Sand, Gravel	*725.00*
Doors, Windows, etc.	*840.00*
Nails, Paint, Screws, Putty, Locks, Painting	*674.00*
Cost of Excavating Cellars	*250.00*
Masons and Carpenters	*$8,900.00*
Real Estate	*$2,500.00*
Blacksmithing, Iron, Etc	*450.00*
Miscellaneous	*150.00*
Total	*$25,139.50*

The following is the Committee's obligations:

Cash borrowed and interest	*$4,359.45*
Due sundry persons for material and sales.	*$4,075.00*
Total	*$8,434.45*

We hope you will be able to get the full amount. Do the very best you can for us. We need it.

Respectfully,

The Committee
per William Houchen

Rep. Parry did do the best he could. But the appropriation was not nearly the full amount. At the end of the following year, December 15, 1900, a long descriptive article appeared in the *Deseret Evening News* which extolled the virtues of the school and the community and provides insight into the outcome of the reimbursement effort.

Altogether the little town of Cedar, with some 1,500 inhabitants, had inside of one year made an actual outlay in money and labor of nearly $40,000, an effort unparalleled in history of the state. For this immense sum the legislature of 1899 made a reimbursing appropriation of $17,000, which, after meeting the cash debts in full, was sufficient to pay the citizens only 56 percent of their due, this loss being borne largely by those who had given their labor. So long as the school exists, it will be a living, speaking monument to their untiring energy, zeal, and devotion to the cause of education, the cause of love, of truth.When a full history of Cedar City is written, no chapter will be of greater interest or importance, nor will any tell more that will reflect more honor and credit on its people, than that which narrates the efforts and toils connected with the establishment of this school. So long as the school exists it will be a living speaking monument to their untiring energy, zeal, and devotion to the cause of education, the cause of love, of truth. [14]

'NORMAL GIRLS,'
1910

Cedar City, in the end, received a great deal of praise, little money. But they had solidified a tradition of cooperative community effort and they had established an intense proprietary affection for their school.

Old Main, as the building was later to become known, was well equipped by the standards of the day. The three-story structure boasted a large chapel for religious programs and assemblies and a library and reading room offering books, magazines, journals and newspapers. The first floor, or basement, held the boiler room and coal bunker, the physical and biological laboratories and the manual training room.

The biological laboratory was furnished with drawered tables specially designed for work in zoology, physiology and botany. It was equipped with compound microscopes, one of the "latest and best microtomes," an incubator for work in embryology, dissecting microscopes and chemical reagents and illustrative specimens. The physical

laboratory equipment was also impressive. It included an air pump, Wimhurst's machine of strong power, telegraph instruments, telephone dipping batteries, sonometer, Leyden jars, levers and pulleys, electric bells, spectroscope, magnets, Geisler tubes, X-ray tubes, Wheatstone bridge, galbanometers, wireless telegraphy apparatus. . . everything necessary for a thorough high school course in physics.

As the second season began, John H. Tipton came to teach physics in the well fitted-out facility. He also taught manual training and found excellent apparatus in that department as well. He had a lathe adapted for both wood and light metal, a forge with an anvil, chisels, saws and planes.

The ground floor housed the principal's office where Mr. Bennion presided when he was not teaching pedagogy and history. Here were also found three large classrooms, a teacher's room and a waiting room. Howard Driggs, serving as secretary and registrar might have shared space in the principal's office and certainly would have occupied the classrooms with classes in English language and literature.

The top floor contained the library, the assembly room and the art room. While the number of books in the library was not excessively large (something over 1,000 volumes), the books were all new and "purchased under intelligent direction." George Decker would have provided said intelligent direction since he was the librarian, as well as the teacher of natural sciences and mathematics. He must

PRINCIPAL
MILTON BENNION,
1899

have had to run from the top floor to the basement in the discharge of his duties. Given his native vitality, he was undoubtedly exhilarated by the exercise.

The assembly room was well used by all the teachers as "Chapel" was held each morning before classes began, each faculty member preparing these devotional programs for a week at a time by rotating turns. Operettas, plays, musicals, assemblies and productions of all kinds were presented there, until the second building provided an auditorium. The assembly room was also fitted-up and used as a gymnasium.

The domain of Miss Spencer would have been almost exclusively the top floor, since she taught music and art, as well as elocution and physical culture.

The student body this second year numbered 118. The faculty was eager to greatly increase the enrollment the following year. The cost of such a fine education was well within the means of most citizens, since there was no tuition charge, and a yearly registration fee of $10 covered any other expenses. The challenge was to publicize the benefits of this new school among the communities of the area.

Young, handsome and impressive of bearing, Principal Milton Bennion made a tour of the southern counties. Legislators and prominent citizens introduced Mr. Bennion to the families who had children eligible to attend BNS. He extolled the virtues of education, pointing out the advantages now available to the young people in the rural areas of the south. Later a small series of "Magic Lantern" slides were created from photographs of the school and the classes. These glass slides were used with a stereoptican apparatus, projecting the images upon a screen. Bennion used the ingenious device in a proselyting effort that included a sort of lyceum circuit entertainment. When the townspeople gathered, the considerable salesmanship of the young faculty member was greatly enhanced by the illustrative slides.

When George Decker became principal he was tireless in his efforts to expedite the growth of the school. An excerpt from a biography written by his son, Ivan, gives some delightful details of his recruitment methods:

Wherever George Decker went, whether on school business or not, he was always on

CHAPEL, 1906

the lookout for chances to make friends for the BNS and to gain new students. Oftentimes he spent money and time which he could ill afford for this end. He organized musical junkets that were made to the various nearby towns of southern Utah to stimulate the interest of young people in going to school at Branch Normal School in Cedar City. Dad and Professor Tollestrup would take a group of us musical students along in two white topped buggies—all travel in those days was via horses, not horsepower—and we would supplement Dad's speeches with musical numbers. Our part on the program would consist of solos, duets, trios, and ensembles of different combinations of instruments. I am not sure that I remember all the kids taken along on the trips but I do remember Lillian Higbee (Macfarlane), piano, Irene Jones (Andrus), clarinet, Hazel Dalley (Granger), flute, Ina Leigh (Gardner), oboe, Cora Jones (Stucki), french horn, Virgil Tollestrup, trombone, Vivian Decker, cornet, and Ivan Decker (me) violin.

Being the youngest of the group, I was flattered that Dad and Mr. Tollestrup considered me worthy of membership in the gang. Sometimes Dad would get another teacher to go along and do some speaking. I remember that the late Dr. M.J. Macfarlane made at least one of the trips when he went south. On the South junkets we gave programs at Kanarraville, New Harmony, Toquerville, Virgin, Hurricane, Leeds, Washington, St. George and Santa Clara. Going the other way we held forth in Parowan, Paragonah,

Circleville, Panguitch, Escalante, Glendale, Orderville, Kanab and Fredonia, Arizona.

I have no idea how influential we were in bringing students to the Branch Normal School; but I do know that all of us kids always had a heck of a time. Since these little journeys were usually made at Dad's expense, he generally persuaded the citizens of the various towns to put us up overnight. Thus we learned about hospitality, the receiving end, that is. Because of the long distance between some of the towns we sometimes had to take along stuff for a noon snack. We stopped one day in the middle of nowhere, sat on a bank near the road and ate Log Cabin Syrup and soda crackers. I was hungry and how good they tasted ! [15]

Whether impelled by the proselyting efforts or not, the students did come. From all the surrounding small towns they came. Families made heroic efforts to enable their children to come to the school. One significant example was the family of Parley Dalley, whose career as a distinguished teacher was spent at the school. Mrs. Dalley had come to this country from Denmark as a convert to the Mormon faith. She had had no opportunity for education at all. As Branch Normal School was about to open in the Ward Hall for the first school season, she determined that her children would have the opportunities that had been denied her. She moved her family from Summit to a small vacant pioneer house, where they lived through the winters, for as

long as her children attended school. [16]

Tillie Macfarlane, eager that her children have the advantage of education, came from St. George and rented the John Perry house on the site that later became the railroad depot. It was large enough to accommodate her own three children, Menzies, Jennie and Emma, as well as numerous other students from St. George, who enjoyed the excellent cooking and the studious atmosphere of the Macfarlane boarding house. [17]

Parents from all of southern Utah were ingenious in finding ways to provide for their children so that they could partake of this newly available schooling. One old photograph, captioned "On the way from Alton to BNS," shows a family traveling by wagon over Cedar Mountain, pots and pans tied to the sides, leading a milk cow.

While the students were eager to come and eager to learn, they did not always demonstrate perfect decorum. From pioneer days there had been the custom in many country towns to allow a certain measure of rowdyism, even tolerating some smoking and some drinking at dancing parties. Now the new faculty was faced with making rules barring such conduct at school socials. [18]

Milton Bennion was the soul of moral rectitude. His educational career was noted for furthering the cause of character education. As first principal of the Branch Normal School, and during the three years of his service, he established a rigid standard of social conduct for the students. The three principals who followed him, J. Reuben Clark, Nathan T. Porter and George W. Decker, continued the pattern he had established, requiring complete abstinence from tobacco, alcohol in any form, profanity and indecent dress. The ruling was not

only imposed upon students and faculty, but the townspeople also had to abide by the rules of the institution if they wanted to attend school functions or use the Normal School facilities. [19]

*T*he "Rules of Conduct" as they were called, did not just pertain to school hours, but had to be observed at all times. If a member of the community smoked, he was barred from admission to any college activity. The rigid imposition of the code upon the townspeople caused bitter resentment in some quarters. Those who had contributed to the construction of the building and then were denied entrance because of their personal habits were understandably irate.

Every catalog or annual from 1897 to 1913 includes a description of the "self governing" structure of the student body. But the most complete description is included in the 1912 issue:

City Government. The student body of the Branch Normal School is self-governing. An organization known as "Branch Normal School City" has been effected, its functions being similar to those of cities of the first class.

Professor Milton Bennion, now of the University of Utah, was the founder of the Self-Governing School System of the Branch Normal School. Through this government the students make their own laws and enforce them. By thus affording a very practical training in civics, the system does much in preparing students for the greater duties imposed upon them by citizenship. The city government has been in operation since it was organized in 1898. It has proved satisfactory beyond the expectations of its founders. The student body has found itself worthy of the trust reposed in it by the instructors and the students themselves are pleased with the condition to such an extent that wherever they go they take steps to procure like privileges. [20]

Specific ordinances prohibited such things as lingering carelessly about while classes are in session (ordinance I) and spitting on the floor (ordinance VIII). [21]

The punishments were not always meted out by student courts, as evidenced by this excerpt from the recorded memories of a young woman student:

One morning in chapel Mr. Decker scorched some of us girls to a cinder. He always went out to the dances, usually held on Friday night. Some of us had been so unwise as to wear lace-yoked blouses without long-handled underwear showing through the lace. His reprimand: "This school is supposed to set an example of fashion, morals, dignity and behavior for the people all around us. Young women who willingly depart from such standards should not upset the regulations of those who will comply, and if they persist in so doing, could be invited to leave." [22]

The strict enforcement of high moral expectations was appreciated by parents and became a decided advantage to the school when in the early 1900s, competition for students became a fierce issue between the LDS Church sponsored academies in Beaver and St. George and the Branch Normal School. No one questioned that standards of behavior at Branch Normal School were equally as stringent as at any of the academies.

The Branch Normal School City organization furnished great training for future civic responsibilities, but it also furnished much of the social activity and interaction of the students. Ernest Hungate Burgess came to Branch Normal School from Pine Valley, Utah, age almost 16. In December, 1899, he wrote in his journal: "Decided on Thanksgiving day to write a journal. It was begun December 2, 1899, while I was attending the Branch Normal School at Cedar. I will write all the important events that happen this winter. My age now 15 years, 11 months."

His treasured document survives, handwritten and extending until May 1904. It is filled with details of student activities, many centered on participation in the "government" of the school.

April 11: A meeting was held at four o'clock today to vote on some laws passed by the city council and to tend to some other business. I came home as soon as the meeting was out and practiced my music...

October 15, 1900: Election week was a busy time for me. I was elected member of the Athletic Executive Committee and also Justice of the Peace for the 2nd year normals. I was appointed with two others to print the ballots on the mimeograph. If we had been successful it would have taken about two hours, but we could not make the machine work very well and soon spoiled all the sensitive paper we had. The result was we had to write 20 ballots apiece with lead pencil...

Nov.10, 1900: We held a mock trial in the justice court of the B.N.S.C. I was the presiding justice. The trial was private, but with two attorneys, witnesses etc, and two instructors there were 10 persons present. The trial lasted about two hours. My decision was that the defendant was guilty. The defendant's attorney was riled, claiming that he had good grounds for a demur which I overruled. No bad results came from it but we all learned very much...

Politics took on reality:

October 13, 1901: Election will be held next week and the campaign is now on. The school thought the class of 1902 were trying to get all the offices and some of the 1903 stirred the rest of the students up against us. They accused us of holding secret primaries and doing worse than we really did. That got us mad and we resolved to get the best of them at any rate. We included about one

fifth of the voters and saw what our chances were. Every brain in the class of 1902 began thinking out plans to out do the other sections and carry the election. Our more mature brains worked it all right in the general convention and we got our men on the ticket. Since they started the opposition we are determined to beat them and by our skillful campaigning that we will pull out all right on election day. The result may be summed up in one word: failure.

March 5, 1901: The election in February was somewhat novel. The girls separated from the boys and so the school was divided on male and female lines. They were far in the majority and could have it their own way. Their mayor, Tillie Gardner, was elected and their recorder, Bess Angel. I ran for attorney general on our side and got elected by a majority of three. One third of my votes were from the other side, so I find it is good to be 'in' with the girls at times. [23]

Each year the faculty increased in number. Each year class offerings and activities expanded, and each year the numbers of students increased. By the school year 1900-1901 the student body had reached an even 200. H. Claude Lewis and O.C. Anderson were added to the faculty, teaching mathematics and music, respectively. The arrival of O. C. Anderson must have been a relief to Annie Spencer, since she could be relieved of that assignment. The catalog also announced a series of public lectures to be given during the winter on scientific, literary and philosophical subjects. Lectures illustrated with stereoptican views were to be frequent. The lectures were intended to extend educational advantages to the community. Maude Eastwood had joined the faculty to teach domestic science, and the circular includes photographs of young women at sewing machines.

There was in the fall of 1900, a most significant occurrence, about which the literature of the school is totally silent, but which sheds a dazzling light upon some realities facing the Branch Normal School that the good citizens of the community had perhaps not yet realized.

From the beginning it was clear that the Cedar City school was a branch of the University of Utah. The classwork offered at the Branch Normal was the same as the first three years of the normal course offered at the University

NATHAN TANNER
PORTER IN HIS OFFICE.

in Salt Lake City. Upon completion of those three years, a student who desired graduation was required to go to Salt Lake City to live, where they could attend the university and receive the fourth year of instruction.

It was a relationship that seemed natural. During the developmental process, while the struggle of the building consumed the people of Cedar City, the relationship had been exceedingly cordial. Everyone who came to teach or administer in the affairs of the branch school had been trained at the University of Utah and were hired by the University of Utah administration. They came to Cedar City with a clear understanding of the mutually beneficial relationship between the University of Utah and the Branch Normal School. There was no expectation that the arrangement would ever change.

Then late in the summer of 1900, after serving as principal for three years, Milton Bennion left Cedar City for New York City to pursue graduate studies. Whether it was a sudden decision and there was not time to change the "Circular" listing, or whether it was an oversight by whomever had responsibility to care for such things, there is no notice of his departure in the catalog of the Branch Normal School. It lists Milton Bennion as serving in his assignment as principal during that year. That was not the case. The Bennions left Cedar City that year with the baby daughter that had been born to them during the three years of their stay.

Young Joshua Reuben Clark Jr. was hired to go to Cedar City and to serve as acting principal of the Branch Normal School in the absence of Mr. Bennion.

J. Reuben Clark had distinguished himself as a student at the University of Utah. He had come to the university from Grantsville, Tooele County, without a high school diploma and entered the preparatory program. With that beginning, earning a degree would ordinarily require six years. Reuben finished in four years, graduating in June of 1898 as valedictorian of his class. While he pursued his studies, he also served as personal secretary to James E. Talmage, who was then president of the university. Upon graduation he served one year as principal of a new high school at Heber City, then taught at the Salt Lake Business College before coming to Cedar City.

As Principal Clark assumed his duties at the Southern Branch, he formed an immediate affection for the young institution he had come to lead. He wrote of the school, "As a place for

securing training of a high school grade, it has few, if any, superiors in the West." Further he said, "For my own part, I was never more happily surprised in a town, a school, and a job than I have been in the present instance. My work has been of the pleasantest nature. I have found the teachers cooperative and think we have as good a body of students so far as earnestness and zeal are concerned as there are in the state. The people have treated me with the utmost courtesy and consideration and are all enthusiasm for the school." [24]

J. REUBEN CLARK

He not only shared the enthusiasm of the local people, but he immediately caught a vision of possibilities for the school that had not seemed to occur to anyone else up until this time. The Cedar City people were so delighted to have a school at all, that they would not have thought, at this point, to suggest that it was an imposition for their young people to have to go to Salt Lake City to finish the four-year course.

J. Reuben Clark had received only an interim appointment. Having come with full knowledge that it was a one-year assignment, he might have gone about his work in an offhand manner. But instead he pursued his duties with amazing vigor and began immediately making creative suggestions for an expanded program and additional facilities.

First, it was immediately obvious to him that very few of the students at Branch Normal School would ever have the opportunity to pursue the fourth year of the normal course. So, with startling audacity, he proposed that the fourth year be added to the curriculum at Cedar City. [25]

Secondly, he proposed the addition of chemistry and mineralogy to the third-year course in place of psychology and the history of education, on the premise that the latter were more reflective and less practical than the former courses. [26]

Thirdly, in the budget proposals he provided

for adjustments in the faculty to include personnel to handle the curriculum recommendations.

Fourthly, he requested an additional building. In doing so he reasoned, "All indications point to an attendance of 250 students during the present year, and every prospect promises a further increase next year. This means either that students will have to be turned away next year, which would violate justice and right, or that additional quarters will have to be provided."

Then he had the wonderful temerity to report that having proposed that the full normal course be given at the school, he had proceeded to have informal talks with the trustees of Cedar City schools, and was ready to recommend a training school for the students to receive practice teaching.

He submitted a budget request for the school years 1901-1902 and 1902-1903 amounting to four times what had been granted before,

including a request for $20,000 to construct a new building and $3,000 for the proposed training school.

One can only imagine the startled faces of President Kingsbury and the Regents when they heard of the bold propositions. They did not hear directly, since Principal Clark went directly to the legislature with his suggestion. The Regents were outraged. [27]

He did not get an appropriation for the new building or the training school. In fact the Board of Regents only recommended to the legislature an appropriation of $16,000. The legislature approved $20,000. In writing to Milton Bennion, Mr. Clark explained:

The getting of the $20,000 from the legislature is something of a tale. In brief this, —The Iron County Representative, McGregor of Parowan by the way, wrote me

J. REUBEN CLARK, JR.
1871-1961

The name of J. Reuben Clark, Jr., on the register of administrators of the Branch Normal School, lends a light brushstroke of class that perhaps no other bit of history could add to the school. In his interim term of one year as acting principal, while Dr. Bennion was on leave of absence, Dr. Clark gave the school and the community a

glimpse of what they could become.

J. Reuben Clark, Jr., born in 1871, is remembered as a true giant of a man, though he was described by Howard Cripps of the *Christian Science Monitor* as a "short and thick-set banker type, whose eyes, prone to twinkle, could [when the occasion required it] sternly dare contradiction."

Cripps was certainly not the only eminent journalist who reported and evaluated the activities of J. Reuben Clark, Jr., during his extraordinarily varied, long and distinguished careers as lawyer, statesman and Apostle of the Church of Jesus Christ of Latter-day Saints. *The New York Times* called one of his many widely- recognized legal papers as a "classic authority."

Primarily a lawyer, he maintained private law practice in Washington D.C, New York City and Salt Lake City until he closed his offices to serve his country full-time. He received a Distinguished Service Medal for his contributions to the Attorney General's office; was the recipient of three service chevrons for service in several capacities during World War I; was solicitor for the Department of State before becoming under-secretary of the department. His timely memorandum to President Herbert Hoover helped to snuff out rebellion

brewing in Mexico in 1929 and led to Hoover's naming him, in 1930, as Ambassador to Mexico. His unfailing fairness and willingness to listen to the other side of the story endeared him to the people of that republic.

Clark's long training, keen mind and winning personality served him well as a representative of the United States. When he received a call from President Heber J. Grant of the LDS Church to become his second counselor, in 1933, he brought all of his remarkable gifts, energy and commitment to that task. However, even after this call, Clark continued to serve the nation, from time to time, in numerous assignments of trust and honor.

There are legends in the LDS Church about J. Reuben Clark's life-long habit of reading "out of the best books" until the wee hours of every morning. He also labored diligently to author books of his own. The University of Utah and Brigham Young University awarded him honorary doctorates.

His devoted wife Luacine Savage Clark and he built a home life together that was as outstanding, and even more fulfilling, than his brilliant professional career. They were the parents of three daughters and a son, all well-known for their own remarkable gifts and versatility.

saying he thought the Branch Normal School had been unfairly treated, and asked me what we wanted. I replied with an itemized statement of needs. Mr. Morris, of Washington County, inquired. I replied ditto. Mr. N. L. Morris of Salt Lake sought light, and got it. Mr. R.K.Thomas officially, as Chairman of the Senate Appropriations Committee wrote, 'What do you want ?' Once more the same matter was sent to the metropolis. Result No. 1, —A joint committee visited the school which we captured. Result No. 2, —We got the appropriation needed. Result No. 3, —I learned I had been guilty of a great impropriety in not referring all the received inquiries to the Board of Regents for answer. Result No. 4, —Not hard to guess. However, we have the money.

In his reply Milton Bennion wrote:

In regard to the inquiries sent to you by the members of the Legislature it appears to me thus: If those members had wanted information from the B. of Regents, they would have sent to them for it. When they sent to you, they wanted it from you. I should have had no hesitation about furnishing it. As to the outcome I should say you won the case.

Mr. Bennion also told Reuben that he was going to teach at the University of Utah the following year instead of continuing with his graduate studies in New York. The next day Reuben received a letter from Dr. Kingsbury informing him that Mr. N. T. Porter had been appointed as the new principal of the Southern Branch of the Normal School. [28]

It was a defining moment. It made clear a reality that would plague the school and the community for generations. There would be little question about who ruled in the relationship between the mother institution and the child.

In his response to the letter from President Kingsbury, Reuben Clark reflects how he felt about the principalship:

As stated by you my engagement was for the present year only. As you may remember, I told Mr. Bennion, yourself too I believe, that it seemed to me whoever the Principal was, he should come here with the intention of remaining more than one year. I am still of that opinion. Realizing the disadvantages of a temporary arrangement, and having

become so attached to the school and interested in its welfare, I believe had the Regents considered it wise to offer me the position for another year, I should have accepted. The school would, I think, have suffered less at my hands during the second than the first year.

The announcement that J. Reuben Clark had been passed over in the selection of the new principal brought the people of Cedar City and the students at the school into action. Petitions were circulated, signed and sent by both groups. Mr. Clark, embarrassed by their action and certainly not desiring to seem to be part of their effort, wrote a detailed letter to Rebecca Little, one of the Regents, in order that at least one of them have the facts. The letter included the following:

...May I ask you to believe that I have not only not solicited this action nor encouraged it, and indeed knew nothing of it until the movement was completed. I should consider participation in any such personal matter entirely improper for a school officer. [29]

The expressed desires of the students and townspeople had no effect. J. Reuben Clark finished his contractual agreement of one year, and on June 8, 1901 returned to Salt Lake City to take up his illustrious destiny. [30] But he left kindled in the hearts of the people of Cedar City and the faculty and students of the Branch Normal

FACULTY, 1901: (SEATED) HOWARD DRIGGS, WILLIAM WARD, ANNIE SPENCER; (STANDING) O.C. ANDERSON, MAUDE EASTMAN, CLAUDE LEWIS, AND GEORGE DECKER.

NATHAN T.
PORTER

School a new concept of their potential.

Clark had written in a letter to his friend Joseph Nelson of Salt Lake City, "The people here are just about disgusted with the management of the Normal by the University autocrats, and justly so I think." [31] That was beginning to be true.

He had written of the school in a laudatory article in the *Deseret News* of December 15, 1900:

As to the future there can be scarcely a doubt. The prospect of the immediate development of the country, together with its consequent rapid settlement, as well as the history of the past, all justify the belief that in numbers, as well as in thoroughness of work, [this school] must soon rank with the very best institutions of the state.

The vision of what they could become had been born.

J. Reuben Clark left Cedar City a hero. He had been open in his affection for the students and had embraced the townspeople who had sacrificed to found the school.

*T*he man selected by those in power in the north to take the helm of the Branch Normal School was Nathan Tanner Porter.

Mr. Porter arrived late in the summer of 1901. He was a graduate of the University of Utah. He was a native of Centerville and had taught school in that community. That he was trusted by the administration of the University of Utah is evidenced by the fact that at the conclusion of three years, he returned to the University of Utah as a full professor and became the first dean of the Law School. In retrospect one feels empathy for the new principal who came into a community that was smarting from the recent rebuff—and on the edge of a crisis because of rampant growth. It is to his credit that the years of his principalship were years of significant progress.

Nathan Porter was faced with an immediate and immense problem. The school was burgeoning beyond its capacity. His predecessor had written of the problem the year before:

The quarters are even now inadequate. Classes have been divided into sections, and the sections crowd the recitation rooms. Students are constantly entering and it is not easy to see how many more can be accommodated. To turn students away is all but criminal, and yet another year promises to bring this condition. All other questions are for the time subordinated and the great problem now placed before the school management for solution is, "How shall we provide for our students of the coming year ?" [32]

Fifty additional students had swelled the ranks since this was written. The student body ready to begin in September, 1901, stood at 250 students. It was apparent that the physical facilities would have to expand to meet the growing enrollment.

When the legislature of 1903 met, the citizens of Southern Utah pressed for an appropriation of $75,000, $25,000 of which was to ensure the construction of another building as large as the Old Main. [33]

The anticipated new building was designed to be harmonious in design with the Old Main, closely resembling it. It was to be called the Science Building. The three-story structure was to contain rooms to house all the laboratories now located in the basement of the Old Main building. There would be a large assem-

FOUNDERS' DAY PARADE, 1909

THE FORGE ROOM, 1903

bly room on the top floor, which would also serve as the center for the music department, and double as a ballroom. The domestic science department would be provided rooms in the basement so that it could be moved from the converted home which had served as its headquarters. Administrative offices were planned for the new Science Building.

The catalog of 1903-1904 shows an artist's rendering of the building; by 1904-5 the building had been completed.

When the building neared completion, the laboratory equipment was ordered, including tables, apparatus and chemicals. Most freight was sent to southern Utah by train, arriving at Lund, then transported by wagon on into Cedar City. The anticipated equipment, accompanied by the man hired to install it, arrived at the station at Lund from Salt Lake City. Unfortunately, no one had arranged for transportation on to the Branch Normal School. The weather was threatening and the man was sitting forlornly on the platform at the isolated station wondering how he could get his railroad car load of fragile materials to his destination when George A. Wood, a young Cedar City man drove his horse drawn wagon loaded with cargo which he intended to load onto an outbound car. He agreed to help the stranded traveler, and together they loaded the science building fittings and materials onto the Wood wagon. It was evening, but because a storm seemed imminent they began the journey, arriving at Iron Springs about 2 o'clock in the morning, where they stopped to rest. At 5 a.m. it began to snow, so they took the horse blankets off their horses, their own bedding and coats and carefully spread them out over the precious instru-

ments and began again their journey through the storm. They arrived at the Science Building in the blizzard, unloaded while snow continued to fall, and rejoiced that their cargo was safe.

The manual training classes which had been housed in the basement of the first building were woefully inadequate and crowded. Principal Porter initiated an ingenious plan to remedy that situation. By using students of the manual training classes as workmen, thus eliminating the cost of hiring workers and also giving students practical experience, he organized the building of a temporary frame structure near the north side of the Main. Into this building they moved the benches, lathes, scroll saws, forges, and other tools for work in wood and metals. This structure, called "The Forge Room," was used to house the department until a more permanent structure was needed. [34]

The new principal accomplished the addition of business courses, as well as German and Latin classes added to the curriculum. He also inaugurated a program of ballroom dancing and drama at the Branch Normal.

In the spring of 1904 Nathan Tanner Porter resigned his post as principal and returned to a professorship at the University of Utah. This time the students were adamant in their eagerness to have input into the choice of a principal.

George Decker was an immensely popular teacher. He had taught for seven years and had earned the devotion of the students for his habit of becoming personally involved in their lives. He was noted for creating part-time work, signing notes or loaning money to students who needed help and taking students home for supper. He was athletic and vigorous, and a

THE SCIENCE BUILDING

superb teacher. And so the students and townspeople who had attempted to influence the selection of a principal three years prior organized themselves for greater impact.

The letter that carried the petition to the regents has not survived the years, but an excerpt of a personal reply from the university secretary is descriptive:

Dear Friend Decker,

The petition expresses in beautiful language the high regard the students have for you. If it concerned me, I believe I would prize the letter more than the petition itself.

I wish to congratulate my friend on his almost certain appointment to a position of honor and trust where he already has the esteem of those over whom he will be called to preside.

Sincerely yours,

R.D. Allen,
Secretary of the University of Utah
and of the Board of Regents

George Decker was appointed principal. He also continued to teach natural science. The faculty now numbered seven teachers, including Miss Spencer and Mr. Driggs who had, with Mr. Decker, been at the school from the beginning. O.C Anderson had come to teach bookkeeping and music, a rather surprising combination, and William T. Ward now taught physics, chemistry, and mincralogy. Maude F. Eastwood taught domestic science and art and Elias Hansen taught history, algebra and commercial law.

The Science Building remained unfinished. The disheveled appearance of the hill had improved only slightly since the completion of the first building.

Principal Decker was eager to improve the appearance of the grounds surrounding the building. He disapproved of the cattle that habitually grazed there. He had already been instrumental in planting some evergreens trees along the path, but had ideas for more sweeping refinements.

Shortly after he became principal, fate brought him into fortuitous relationship with William Flanigan, who became a legend for his work at taming the wilderness of the

NATHAN T. PORTER
1865-1953

Nathan T. Porter was the dynamic young principal of Branch Normal School for three years. A charismatic orator, he also quickly demonstrated his willingness to work hard for the school and the community. He may be

even better remembered at BNS for his encouragement of ambitious dramatic productions and the inauguration of a ballroom dancing program than for the erection of the Science Building and temporary shops for manual training classes.

Nathan Porter was a native of Centerville, Utah, where he began his teaching career in Davis County and later became school superintendent. He had also served a mission for the Church of Jesus Christ of Latter-day Saints in England, before he came to BNS as principal.

Nathan Porter did not limit his attention and efforts to education, however, in southern Utah. He helped organize the Bank of Southern Utah and the Commercial Club, forerunner of the Chamber of Commerce.

After leaving Cedar City, Porter entered law school and was the first dean of the law school at the University of Utah. He later engaged in private law practice in Salt Lake City, associated with Stephen L. Richards, Justice W. Moffat and Herbert Van Dam. It was during this

time that he was appointed a member of the Board of Regents of the University of Utah.

Porter also became prominent in banking circles, serving, at Gov. Simon Bamberger's behest, on the Utah Banking Commission, and acting as chairman of the Utah State Security Commission. He also drew the support of some of the state's leading financiers for development of the Newcastle Reclamation Project, to reclaim desert areas by using dry-land farming methods.

Nathan Porter moved to California in 1921. He founded the National Foods Company there, serving as its president for 10 years and also becoming active in California politics. In 1943 Porter lost the race as a gubernatorial candidate, but was appointed to the Old Age Pension Committee by then-governor Earl Warren.

Nathan T. Porter's wife, Anna Adams Porter, bore eight children, three of whom died in infancy. Two sons, Arthur and James, brilliant young students, died in early manhood. Nathan Porter died at the age of 88 in Inglewood, Calif.

college grounds. The story illuminates the time, the people, and the relationships and is related here in Mr. Flanigan's words:

In the year 1904 I came from Springdale to Cedar City to attend a regional Sunday School Convention. From one of the meetings I walked out to the Branch Normal School campus, then quite far out in the fields, curious to see what there was of interest. I walked about the grounds thinking of the possibilities for beautification.

We men of Dixie were forced to go away from home in those days in order to make a little cash. We took whatever job was available. I was driving stage from Cedar to Lund and for recreation slipping out to the campus to think and study, because the hill so caught and held my interest.

Sometime later I was back home. Passing Father's home my younger sister called to me, "Found any work yet, Will?" "No, not

yet", I replied. "George Decker offered Orin Wood a month's work at the Branch Normal and he isn't going to take it. Why don't you try for it?" she asked.

I caught a freight outfit, took my bedroll and went. I stopped at the old Cedars Hotel. Going out into the street I saw Mr. Proffit surveying the water system lines for putting the Right Hand Canyon water into town for culinary use. He directed me to where George Decker lived. I contacted Mr. Decker and was told to bring my bed and come up to the house, that I would be considered one of the family. Immediately I liked his attitude, his frank and open kindliness. He took me on the job for one month. I knew that I was on probation. After school the next day he sent his oldest son Vivian, down to the hotel with a pack horse to get my things.

I went to work janitoring, tending furnace and doing all the odd jobs in and around the two buildings. Including the

GEORGE W. DECKER
1864-1946

George W. Decker, the first native son of southern Utah to become principal of the Branch Normal School, had been one of the original four faculty at its founding in 1897. The townspeople of Cedar City called him a born teacher; every student in the school signed a petition requesting that he be named principal, when Nathan Porter left the post. The Board of Regents granted their request.

While it was tacitly understood that the popular young educator made personal loans and gifts to poor students who were scrambling for tuition, it was not until after his death that packets of letters of gratitude were found in his personal effects. It could well be that Decker's own desperate struggle to obtain an education prepared him for his life-time encouragement of poor but ambitious students.

The stories of young George's thirst for knowledge are reminiscent of a young Abe Lincoln. This farm boy also read books by the light of a tallow candle or the flickering blaze of a log on the hearth, but the scene took place in the old Presbyterian reading room in Parowan, where he hauled wood by day to pay for the light and heat of his midnight vigils. Upon graduation from the eighth grade in Parowan, George Decker was hired to teach public school in Paragonah.

The young teacher married, and the young couple were parents of a little daughter before they determined together that George must seek higher education. He enrolled at the University of Utah, working as a carpenter on the old Templeton Hotel and the Salt Lake Temple to support his little family. His wife took in washing and worked part-time in a tailoring shop to help George acquire his bachelor's degree.

Upon his graduation, Decker was hired as principal at Payson and then at Parowan, completing summer work at the University of Chicago and at Monterey Bay, Calif., where he conducted a special study on marine life.

George Decker joined the faculty at BNS with this real-life education under his belt. He served as principal until the school became the Branch Agricultural College.

Decker's grown children affectionately teased their father about his unfeigned love for BNS. They told and retold the story about how their mother had painstakingly saved for a for a living room rug only to have to give it up when Principal Decker explained: "I'm sorry! I have to use that money for a new microscope in the biology department." School coffers wouldn't stretch for the crucial purchase.

Upon his retirement the faculty presented him with a leather Morris chair, and the students lovingly gave him a fine gold watch, which he claimed could regulate the sun, moon and stars.

In retirement, George Decker ranched with his two sons in the Parowan Valley, served as superintendent of schools and on the school board, and represented Iron County at the state legislature, but the high point of his life were his years at "his school."

George W.
Decker

bare hill, there were 22 1/2 acres that comprised the campus. There were 19 evergreen trees with the path between and the hitching post. What in the world did they need a hitching post for? For George Decker's saddle horse. He treated his position with dignity and rode to school in style.

My special charge on taking over my new job were three milk cows that seemed to feel that Branch Normal School hill was their special feeding ground. Mr. Decker said, "You try and do something about them. I can't." After several days of trying to fence against the cows I gave up and reasoned, "Well, if we must feed them we will have some of the profit, so I milked the cows and took the milk home. After three or four times the cows came no more. On being questioned and telling him what I did, Mr. Decker bristled, "We will not stand for stealing in this place...but," he added as an afterthought, "I guess it isn't stealing...or is it?" Anyway he smiled so I knew it was all right. [35]

Mr. Decker warmly complimented Flanigan, saying that he had never observed him loafing around town but rather could see that he always made his time count. Flanigan was hired on a yearly basis. He moved his family to Cedar City and began a 33-year mission of beautifying the grounds. He gives some details:

The college land had a field water right, so I began making ditches, planting small plots of grass and always jotting down notes of interest, which have many times been called into use. Creek boulders covered the hill itself. Around the massive ones, I planned spots of

William
Flanigan,
circa 1907

interest. I bought and used powder out of my wages to blast out the blind ones, hundreds of tons of which were laid on the north side to make the circling drive...There was very little expense except the use of a team. I ran my own levels to put the gravity water out where it would cover every spot. I planted trees and shrubs, not from the expensive nurseries, but from our mountains and hills. When water was scarce I sometimes stayed on the job eighteen and twenty hours a day...How I hated a burned spot in the grass. [36]

On the north of the school property was an ugly wash, overgrown with willows. Little by little Will Flanigan cleared the numberless rocks from the land on the hill, borrowing wagons and teams from the men in the town, to haul the rocks he gathered, dump them into the wash, which gradually filled.

The Flanigan era lasted 30 years during which this artist created a beautiful campus from the rocky hillside. Subsequent administrators supported and promoted beautification efforts as the community grew, and the campus became the jewel, set in the center of the thriving town.

Campus improvement included the addition of electrical power to the buildings during the school year of 1908-1909. This replaced the acetylene gas lighting which had been piped from a small brick building behind the main structure. The earliest lighting had been by kerosene lamps.

In 1905 Branch Normal School and Cedar City suffered a significant diminishment as they bade farewell to Miss Annie Spencer after eight years of remarkable contribution.

Many noteworthy romances undoubtedly flourished at BNS, but the one that changed the complexion of the school caught the attention of the students and the populace. Miss Annie Spencer had been joined in 1901 by a charming young assistant. Erastus J. Milne (called Rass or E.J.) of St. George, had gained considerable renown as an athlete in southern Utah as well as at the University of Utah. He came to Branch Normal School as an assistant to Miss Spencer in bookkeeping, typewriting, and in physical education.

Their association ripened over the next four years to friendship, courtship and finally marriage. Each summer between 1901-1905, the two attended classes at Lake Chautauqua, New York, acting as chaperones for Maud Mae Babcock's students who attended summer

E.J. Milne and his Girl's Basketball Team.

classes there during vacation from the U of U. In 1904, Milne graduated from his physical education course and was invited to join the Chautauqua faculty for the 1905 session. Annie Spencer Milne relates the details of her departure from Branch Normal School.

So in June 1905 I said farewell to my teaching career and my friends of Cedar City as our wedding day was to be June 14th. After our graduating exercises were over June 12, we journeyed over rough, rocky Black Ridge behind a span of horses E.J. had hired for the occasion, to Dixieland, St. George where we were married by David Cannon in the St. George Temple. E.J.'s father had painted the interior. His grandfather Jarvis and others of his relatives had helped to build it...Returning to Cedar City the 16th, a drove of cattle of 1,700 head had preceded us, making it a slow, dusty and bumpy ride...we stayed at Cedar City a day or two, then Brother Hyrum Parry drove us in a white topped buggy to Lund, where we boarded the train with all our wedding gifts and belongings. We traveled to Draper, where my father was on hand to greet us. We were happy but broke. I had left my position that paid ninety dollars a month and married a man whom I had every faith in, but who had a job that paid only seventy dollars a month. [37]

Recounting the eight-year tenure of Miss Spencer gives us a clear view of the impact that her activities had upon the community as well as the students. Each year, each faculty member was responsible to present two lectures for the public. Miss Spencer always structured her presentations as recitals, which were enthusiastically hailed by the townspeople. Her attendance at Chautauqua each summer assured that whatever was going on in the eastern schools was quickly included in the curriculum at Branch Normal School.

She had taught music, art, elocution and dramatics as well as typewriting and women's basketball. There is no question that she left an indelible mark upon the students, the community and the school, as she departed.

By 1907 the curriculum was expanding. The offerings fluctuated a bit from year to year depending upon the talents of the faculty that were available. The catalog of 1907 and 1908 reveals a rather cosmopolitan dimension, with German, Spanish, French and Latin being taught by Edwin S. Du Poncet, Ph. D. There were also added that year, business arithmetic, oral expression, music theory, piano, mandolin and guitar, orchestra, band, voice culture, commercial geography and commercial arithmetic. [38]

Two additional buildings were added to the campus. A brick boiler house had been constructed with a $5,000 appropriation from the legislature, and a new shop building was under construction to replace the "homemade" quarters the students had constructed. Electric power replaced the acetylene gas that had lighted the buildings.

The wonderful spirit of the school leaps from between the lines of the 1907-08 catalog descriptions regarding extracurricular activities. Under the heading Chapel Exercises:

ERASTUS J. AND ANNIE
SPENCER MILNE

The
Mandolin
and Guitar
Club

Chapel exercises are held every day, the purpose being to bring students and teachers more closely together, and to instruct along lines of morality. One chapel period each week is given over to the students to carry out programs appropriate for such occasions.

At this period students in literature and science have opportunity to demonstrate that they have power in public speaking and debate.

A choral society was organized for the students. A band and an orchestra were both thriving. There was also advertised in the catalog a mandolin and guitar club, but with a cautious disclaimer:

Mandolin and Guitar. A Mandolin and Guitar club will be organized and instruction to a limited number of students will be given on these instruments; but students are advised to take a better class of instrument. [39]

The relationship between community and the school remained mutually supportive and proprietary. The school not only provided education for young people, but it provided special classes and seminars aimed at the enhancement of practical skills for the adults

of the community. These seminars utilized the expertise of faculty members or visiting authorities on subjects that ranged from nutrition and fashion sewing to electrical installation and the genetics of animal breeding. At one point the school offered to the townspeople a course in elementary law, recalled years later as having benefitted the people in significant ways. [40]

Branch Normal School was the cultural and social sphere around which the town revolved. It boosted the morale of the community; it brought good music and dramatic presentations. And the fiercely loyal townspeople stretched their resources to meet every need that arose. They involved themselves in the recurring dilemmas that faced their school.

Competition for students became an issue. Only a year after the selection of Cedar City as the site for Branch Normal School, the Brigham Young Academy had established a branch in Beaver, 50 miles to the north. It was a good school and drew students from surrounding counties. By 1908, St. George had an academy, also sponsored by the church, which kept their students home. Both these schools offered high school work. The Branch Normal was disadvantaged by the fact that the

Shop Building, 1907

fourth year of their normal course could only be obtained in Salt Lake City. People in the town rallied to the cause. They lowered the rents they charged. They made students from surrounding towns welcome in their homes. They did whatever they could to entice stu-

dents to come to Cedar City, instead of one of the rival schools. Still the survival of Branch Normal School was frequently threatened.

At long last in 1910, the Board of Regents allowed the fourth year to be taught at the Cedar City school. This eliminated the necessity of going to the University of Utah for the additional year of schooling and paved the way for the first class to graduate with four year certificates in the spring of 1911. The granting of the fourth year certificate entitled the student to teach in the common schools for five years without further examination.

Nevertheless, the question arose at every legislative session and among the state's educators generally: Why should Cedar City have a state funded high school, when every other high school was funded by the county or the LDS Church? It was a valid question. And the only way to answer the question was to advance the school to the rank of college.

*T*he University of Utah had made the firm decision that this should not occur. It was their stated intention that Branch Normal School should never advance beyond high school status. The U of U administration and the Board of Regents was convinced that there was not room in the state for three colleges.

It began to appear that the only hope for the school to advance to college level would be to sever its relationship with the University of Utah. There were people who felt that the emphasis of the school should more closely reflect the agrarian society that had fostered it. Those people favored the proposition that now surfaced, that Branch Normal School be transferred to affiliate with the Utah Agricultural College at Logan. Others felt that the cultural advantages that had come from the association with the University would be lost in such a move and that the quality of education would be diminished.

With each succeeding session of the State Legislature it became harder to obtain money to maintain the school. Charges and counter-charges were made. Rep. Wilford Day and State Sen. Henry Lunt could both see that the only hope for the continuance of the school was elevation to a collegiate status. Since it was obvious that the state would not grant monies for the

BRANCH NORMAL SCHOOL FACULTY, 1910. SEATED, L TO R, ALBERT N. TOLLESTRUP (MUSIC), JAMES ROBB (BUSINESS), HAROLD WILKINSON (PHYSICAL EDUCATION), ADA BETZ OR INEZ POWELL (HOME ECONOMICS), J.S. WOODBURY (INDUSTRIAL ARTS), JAMES WESLEY BARTON (SOCIAL SCIENCE). STANDING: MENZIES MACFARLANE (BIOLOGICAL SCIENCE), GEORGE W. DECKER (PRINCIPAL AND HISTORY), PARLEY DALLEY (MATH AND SCIENCE), MABEL NAEGLE (HOME ECONOMICS), ROSWELL BELNAP (LANGUAGES), E.W. MORGAN (ENGLISH).

1909 CLASS

1910 CLASS

SEN. HENRY LUNT

establishment of another state college, the legislators felt that a plan which would achieve this aim and yet bypass direct action by the Legislature must be formulated. The University of Utah could have granted college courses to the Branch Normal School but was determined that the school remain a high school. The two men now looked to the Utah Agricultural College in Logan, where they hoped a simple transfer could achieve their aim. [41]

Both Day and Lunt were ardent supporters of agriculture. Both were active in the sheep industry and farming. They saw in the Logan college the courses they hoped might be taught in the Cedar City school. Both felt that since Iron County was an agricultural region the school should offer courses designed to benefit the farmers. George Decker had initiated a course in agriculture in 1912, with the idea that it would become a more important part of the curriculum, but it did not seem to move quickly enough in that direction.

Apprehension arose among the educators at the school. All were aware of the feelings of their legislators; they feared that the emphasis upon normal courses would diminish. Many of them were content with their relationship with the University of Utah, and favored a known future as a normal school.

On January 1, 1913, the Alumni Association invited Mr. Day and Mr. Lunt to assist in conducting the chapel exercises. The purpose was to acquaint the legislators with the needs of the school. In the assembly Mr. Decker spoke about the policy of the Branch Normal School and its spreading influence, stating that the school had been very conservative in its demands upon the Legislature. As an omen of future action, Sen. Lunt and Rep. Day declared themselves, in short speeches, to be firm friends and supporters of the Branch Normal, and pledged to work for the advancement and avowed needs of the school. They further declared that they would like to see the agri-

culture and domestic science departments strengthened, "...for the needs of our country demand more interest in husbandry, more boys to become producers, while every girl should receive all instructions that the school is giving in domestic art." Thus it was that the legislators publicly announced their conviction that agriculture should be stressed at the Branch Normal School. [42]

Every progressive step of the Cedar City school has been accompanied by political maneuvering and a measure of intrigue, and 1913 was no exception.

Rep. Wilford Day and Sen. Lunt inclined toward the change from University of Utah to the Agricultural College at Logan. The opinions among their constituents were varied. In Cedar City opinions ranged from support of the change to concern that an emphasis upon "hog raising" would negatively affect the status of the school.

Both legislators began inquiries among the members of their respective bodies and received the impression that "industrial education" as a principle had broad acceptance. A vigorous and well organized opposition was mounted by Dr. Joseph Kingsbury, president of the university, Dr. William Stewart, Dr. Joseph F. Merrill and other members of the university faculty. Their legislative representatives also fought the idea.

Midway into the session the two Iron County legislators brought a contingent of their legislative colleagues, accompanied by Dr. Kingsbury, to visit the Branch Normal School. During the days of their visit, a meeting was called by Dr. Kingsbury, which included Sen. Lunt, Principal George Decker, and two representatives who had been appointed by the Chamber of Commerce. Notably absent, not having received an invitation, was Rep. Wilford Day, who really had been the prime mover for the change. At that meeting an agreement was made not to pursue the change during that year.

The legislative group returned to Salt Lake City, arriving on the morning of the last day that legislation could be introduced. Rep. Day hurried to poll his colleagues in the House. He determined that he could garner sufficient support to pass legislation for the change. He contacted A. C. Nelson, state superintendent of public instruction, who told him he thought that the scheme was impossible, but assured him that if it could be done, he felt it would benefit the whole state.

Wilford Day, rushed into town to the office of a Judge Hammond, to obtain help in drafting the bill. "Not even stopping to eat breakfast or dinner, I arrived at the old City and County Building, to introduce the bill at the two o'clock session. I then called Dr. Kingsbury by phone and advised him of what I had done." [43]

The next day President Kingsbury called on Rep. Day. "He tapped me on the shoulder and told me that unless I would withdraw the bill, he would fight me to the bitter end; that he would write to all of the daily papers in Salt Lake; and that he would defeat the measure. I told him that with me it was a matter of principle; that the state demands industrial education and would have it. I told him that if he wanted to fight, all well and good, but that he would find it hard." [44]

No one knows quite what happened overnight in the hallowed halls of the university, but the next day Kingsbury came again, accompanied by Dr. William Stewart, to deliver the message that the fight was off. The minutes of the monthly regents meeting simply state that they will neither support or oppose the move.

Despite that benign declaration, a battle ensued in both houses. Sen. W.S. Hansen carried the bill in the Senate. Sen. Lunt, was not active by reason of his promise to the group who had met with Dr. Kingsbury at Cedar City. University faculty members distributed a letter to all legislators making a bitter attack on the proponents of the measure, calling them "peanut politicians." But notwithstanding the furor of the fight, the bill passed. It now remained for Rep. Day and Sen. Lunt to convince many of the home folks that the change would be for the better.

An article published In the March issue of the student newspaper, entitled: "Do We Want To Change the BNS, to a BAC?" outlines the position of those opposed to the move. Written by a third-year student, Stephen R. Wilkinson of Cedar City, its heated emotional tone is probably indicative of the level of feeling that flowed through the community on both sides of the issue.

In the Day bill it is proposed to change the Branch Normal to a Branch of the Agricultural College. The question is: Is it right for us to do this? And by right we mean that which serves us best. Then will it serve us best to make this change?

First let us consider what we have now. With the exception of the training school we have the complete Normal course. And in connection with this course we have an elementary course in Agriculture. This course has been commenced nicely and is being extended just as rapidly as students are qualified for these extensions.

The instigators of the present bill did not seem to understand that there was no necessity of teaching the advanced subjects in agriculture until some students had prepared themselves for it by first taking the more elementary subjects. The state Agricultural College at Logan has been giving us its heartiest support and encouragement.

The people of Cedar City and surrounding towns are laboring under false impressions,

REP. WILFORD DAY

because they have been told by the instigators of this movement that the present course will be kept here, and the agricultural course will simply be added to it. If the people will read section 2087 of the Compiled Laws of Utah,[45] *they will find this statement is false because it is directly contrary to the laws of the state for such a condition to exist.*

It is advisable for all people concerned to investigate this matter and not make the change blindly at least.

Another expression for which the same people are responsible is: We must make the change or our school would be turned into a county high school, which the county would have to support. The reasons given for this statement are: First, this school is too expensive for the state to support. Second, the surrounding counties are jealous of Iron County for having a Normal School supported by the state when they cannot have a similar institution.

The validity of this statement is also questionable. Let us investigate the first reason. The bill stated that we shall have the same appropriation to support the agricultural school. So the expense problem is going to be entirely done away with by the state giving the same amount of money, but we use it to learn how to feed hogs instead of making public school teachers for the purpose of educating our children.

The second trouble is disposed of in much the same way. The jealousy of the surrounding counties is going to be appeased by the state using the money that they would pay for taxes to feed hogs and cultivate the lands of Iron County instead of using it to produce teachers for the purpose of educating the children of the surrounding as well as those of Iron County.

Then judging from the past we must say that we are jumping out of the frying pan into the fire.

Now let us see what our students are doing for us and the surrounding counties at present. Ninety percent of the graduates of BNS become public school teachers and ninety percent of that ninety percent make a success of that work. And regardless of the number of school teachers produced by our school, we now have to import a great number of school teachers annually. Then when we cut off the supply of teachers we will have to import many more than we do now, and pay the cash which we will have earned by feeding hogs to get someone else

to teach our own children, or else let the youth of our land go uneducated...

Now, as we are informed, this undesired change is sure going to take place. When the fond dreams of the "practical" dairy men and farmers are realized and this country is flowing with milk and buttermilk and grain is blooming 'neath our feet, let us all turn our minds to the happy past and think of the dear old BNS.[46]

The passion of the opposition notwithstanding, the deed was done. The language of the bill changed the parent institution, the name of the school and gave it greatly expanded powers:

The Branch of the State Normal School heretofore established and conducted at Cedar City, in the county of Iron, is hereby constituted a branch of the Agricultural College of Utah, and the state shall maintain the same under the management, control, and direction of the board of trustees of the Agricultural College of Utah, which may offer only such courses of study therein as are permitted by law to be given in the said Agricultural College.[47]

Cedar City people had been edgy through the whole process, fearing that the legislature might decide to eliminate their school. They were now relieved that the school had been preserved. Some were still uneasy about the future, and worried like the impassioned writer Wilkinson, what the change would mean to the school. Some, in loyalty to the University of Utah, still made remarks about "hog feeding," but most citizens must have seen that it was a giant leap forward. There could now be offered any of the courses of study that were given at the Agricultural College, and their school had the potential to become a college!

Dr. John A. Widtsoe, president of the Agricultural College at Logan, lost no time in giving his attention to the new entity under his care. Arriving at Cedar City March 22, 1913. He came to confer with the faculty and students and to acquaint himself with the facilities. He spoke reassuringly to assembled groups and negotiated with individuals.

George W. Decker was much beloved by the students of the school and by the people of the community. He was a vital, exciting teacher. He was a deeply compassionate leader and a champion for the causes of his students. The records are replete with student's grateful declarations of his positive influence upon their lives. As noted earlier, his personal interest in each student took many forms. He paid tuition for those who could not afford it. He fed at his table those who needed sustenance. His was an electric personality. Perhaps he could not always be called "orthodox."

There were some areas of interpersonal stress between Principal Decker and State Rep. Wilford Day. First, they had experienced some disagreement between them over an issue of sheep breeding. Both Day and Decker raised purebred sheep. When Wilford Day brought into the country some cross-breeds to cross with the Rambouillets, which he believed would produce a longer stapled wool, Decker was annoyed and a disagreement grew between them. [48]

Secondly George Decker, in his eagerness that students be given a broad education, could have been considered by some to be too liberal in allowing a science teacher to teach the theory of evolution in his class. The famous John Scopes trial of Tennessee [49] had not yet occurred, but it is clear that the controversy had piqued national camps of opinion. Wilford Day was also a member of the Stake Presidency in the Parowan Stake of the Church of Jesus Christ of Latter-day Saints; he highly disapproved of the subject being allowed at Branch Normal. Some have suggested that this concern was as compelling as any of the other reasons for Day's desiring the change from University of Utah [50]

Thirdly, one could surmise that Decker's attendance at the January meeting with Kingsbury and his consent to the promise of non-support to the move to change to the Agricultural College, may have rankled Representative Day. George Decker did not favor the change. He felt that the relationships with both schools were cordial and beneficial. He also felt that he had already been moving toward the establishment of college level work, as rapidly as was practical.

At any rate, it is clear that by the time John A. Widtsoe left the campus on his initial visit, George Decker knew that he would not be retained as principal of the school. Dr. Widtsoe wrote a letter to Rep. Day and Sen. Henry Lunt immediately upon his return to Logan which, despite its sub-

tlety, confirms that there had been agreement that George Decker would not continue to serve as principal.

An excerpt from Dr. Widtsoe's letter reads:

To find the right man to head the school is not going to be an easy matter. The strongest men will not go and the men of experience in such matters are scarce. We shall do, however, the best we can and I have no fear that we shall succeed... I did not have a chance Monday afternoon to have a final talk with Principal Decker so as to make the situation thoroughly clear. I am writing him today, however, so that there will be no misunderstanding as to the future as far as he is concerned. Mr. Decker showed a splendid spirit during my visit and I can only speak well of the manner in which he handled his part in the situation. [51]

GEORGE W. DECKER

At the end of the school year, 1913, the teaching career of George W. Decker ended. A public meeting was held on campus, where he received a gold watch, a leather rocking chair, and an outpouring of esteem and affection from the students whom he had influenced during the 16 years of his association with Branch Normal School. He then returned to Parowan, where he lived the life of a rancher for a few years, later returning to Cedar City. For the final 40 years of his life, he was frequently visited by former students.

The school had not heard the last from Dr. Kingsbury. He addressed the faculty and student body at graduation exercises that year, using the occasion to inflict a few barbs concerning the change of status of the Branch Normal School. But the wheels had been set in motion and progress rolled forward with increased velocity, as the school prepared to become the new Branch Agricultural College.

PHYSICS LAB, 1905, ABOVE
FACULTY 1929, BELOW: FRONT, LEFT TO RIGHT: GILBERT JANSON, ARTHUR FIFE, J. HOWARD MAUGHAN, ROY L. HALVERSON, PARLEY DALLEY, HAZEN COOLEY. BACK: WILLIAM H. MANNING, LILLIAN WIGHT, IRA N. HAYWARD, ROSE THOMPSON, HAZEL BROCKBANK, ARTHUR J. MORRIS, ESTHER EGGERTSON, MARY BALLANTINE, GEORGE CROFT, ZOE ROBINSON PALMER, GUSTIVE LARSON, RAY LYMAN, HOWARD LINFORD

Graduation—Class of 1906

Old Main and the Creamery

THE 1910 STUDENT BODY

1911 GRADUATION LUNCHEON

HOWARD DRIGSS, AMONG
THE FIRST FACULTY MEMBERS,
HOLDS HIS SON, H. WAYNE
DRIGGS, IN 1906. THE
YOUNGER DRIGGS WOULD GO
ON TO BECOME DIRECTOR OF
THE INSTITUTION.

1907 ARBOR DAY ACTIVITY (BELOW);
HOME ECONOMICS CLUB (BOTTOM)

BAC CLASSROOM GROUP IN LIBRARY

FIRST GRADUATING CLASS FROM JUNIOR COLLEGE DIVISION, 1923 (INCLUDES HIGH SCHOOL GRADUATES)

CHAPTER IV

Branch Agricultural College, 1913-1953

s a matter of fact, in my opinion, the thing that has made this school continue, despite the ups and downs, was that we had dedicated teachers who were more concerned for the service they were giving than they were for their meager salaries."

**Parley P. Dalley, graduate of BNS,
teacher for 50 years at BNS, BAC, CSU and SUSC.**

The contingent of legislators who arrived in Cedar City on Saturday, February 8, 1913, were engaged in spirited discussions about the measure proposed by Rep. Wilford Day that would transfer the Branch Normal School to the Agricultural College. The people of the area were always vocal about anything to do with their school.

There must have developed broad local enthusiasm for the idea, because early on the Wednesday evening following the legislative visit, the Commercial Club of Cedar City met and formed a resolution endorsing the Day bill and exhorting the legislature to pass it. Later on the same night a mass meeting of the citizens of the town congregated to hear the resolution and enthusiastically voted to endorse it. The townspeople of Parowan were meeting at the same time, and they too gave unanimous endorsement of the measure. Uriah Jones, representing the Commercial Club, and E. L. Clark of Parowan were directed by their respective bodies to convey the resolutions to the legislature and give answers to any questions concerning the sentiments of the people of the area.

The *Iron County Record* of February 14, 1913, devoted most of the front page and some inside space to a report of the meetings and to persuasive editorials in support of the move. A bold subheading reads: "Movement has support of the Commercial Clubs of the towns in the south and the endorsement of practically every citizen in Iron County." [1]

Most interesting is a boxed item titled "Special" which read:

A telephone message received by Principal G. W. Decker from Sen. Henry W. Lunt shortly before noon conveys the information that the Board of Regents of the State University have endorsed the Day bill." [2]

"Endorsed" would be too strong a word. The minutes of the Regents' meeting declare that they would neither oppose nor endorse the measure, but the enthusiastic editor used his right to literary license for such a cause.

When, on March 3, the measure passed both legislative houses, it was joyously reported in the *Iron County Record*. "COLLEGE BILL PASSES BOTH HOUSES." An attempt to pass an amendment prohibiting the teaching of courses that would lead to a college degree had been defeated, enabling the school to give any of the prescribed college courses that were taught at the Agricultural College. [3]

There was not perfect accord on the issue in the community, though the newspaper had attempted to make it seem so in its earlier issue. Now the paper was prepared to meet, head-on, the arguments of any dissenters. The type had been set for a lengthy and persuasive article written by Dr. John A. Widtsoe, president of the Agricultural College, and the man who would soon lead the new Branch Agricultural College. The piece was introduced with this short editorial:

The Agricultural College: The arguments respecting the extent and value of such an education as is given in the average agricultural college, that have been heard on the streets and elsewhere since the movement was launched to make the Branch Normal School in this city an auxiliary of the agricultural college, are so widely different that we deem the following extract from the pen of President

JOHN A.
WIDTSOE

John A. Widtsoe of the agricultural college to be deserving of the attention of every citizen of this section of the state.

Dr. Widtsoe's article followed, in which he eloquently defended the value of an education provided by an agricultural college. Some excerpts:

Since the farmer and the physician are both necessary in the world's work, and since there are more than ten farmers for every physician, ten times more emphasis should be placed in the scheme of education on farming than on medicine...Agriculture, domestic science, commerce and engineering, studied scientifically, are equal in educational value to any of the so-called learned professions... A phase of this principle teaches that hand labor should be coupled with head labor for the truly happy life...The Agricultural College of Utah hopes to be the school of the people because it meets the needs of the majority. It frankly admits that it plans to train farmers, housewives, business men and mechanics, but it hopes to train them so that they may feel daily the keen joy which accompanies any pursuit that has been dignified by intelligent mastery.

Two weeks later, when Dr. John A. Widtsoe arrived in Cedar City, he knew that public relations in the community would be as crucial as his role as administrator of the new college.

On Monday evening he spoke at the Tabernacle to the people of the town. Dr. Widtsoe declared that the new agricultural college was never intended to be a Cedar City school, or even an Iron County school, but a southern Utah school. The audience responded with vigorous applause. He then reminded them of their need to improve their agricultural capabilities by chiding them gently with the fact that they were importing butter and other commodities. They might, by increased efficiency of production, as well as in the education of their children, achieve a general enrichment of the people of the area with the advent of the expanded school. He concluded with the question, "Will the people give it proper support?" [4]

Proper support, Dr. Widtsoe made clear, included not only the provision of the added property pledged by the legislators, but also a sprucing up the appearance of the campus and the town. "College towns are invariably clean, attractive, well-improved, and inviting. Their very appearance being an attraction to those from the outside who visit them. While Cedar City is above the average towns in a great many respects, particularly as to liquor and moral conditions, there are other things which should be given attention." He intimated that streets, sidewalks and accommodations for students were on the list of things that needed attention. [5]

Not only had President Widtsoe given the people of Cedar City plenty to consider, but he returned to the Logan campus with many things on his own mind.

The legislative action that opened the way to establishing a college at the Cedar City campus created myriad possibilities. It could become a real college. The enabling legislation provided that anything taught at the Logan campus could be taught at Cedar City. On the other hand he was acutely aware that he would bring the wrath of the state's educators upon him, if he moved either too rapidly or too radically, for they would surely feel threatened if it appeared that the new school would become competition for the financial resources of the state.

*H*e would have also been painfully cognizant that despite his impassioned defense of agricultural education, Cedar City people were watching with intense interest, some half expecting him to constrict the curriculum to "hog feeding." He also knew that it would take time for people living in the neighboring counties to catch the vision of the benefit the school would be to them. They would, in the meantime, offer opposition. And he knew that he must select a person with the right combination of qualities to lead the new school.

In his letter dated March 28, 1913, President Widtsoe wrote to Sen. Lunt and Rep. Day:

It seems to me that the only thing to do is to build cautiously but vigorously an institution that will really be of service. It will be partly the mission of the people themselves to see to it that cooperation and support may be invited from all the southwestern counties. The people of Cedar City, themselves, as the first beneficiaries, must give vigorous support to the School now that it is entering upon its new career. Unless the south can be united in behalf of the School it will be difficult to prevent the question from coming up session after session in the State Legislature. This, of course, you know much better than I do. [6]

President Widtsoe did proceed with vigor. Of immediate concern was whether it would be possible to persuade the best candidate for the principalship to come so far away from civilization. At the April 19 meeting of the Board of Trustees of the Agricultural College, he presented the name of a potential principal, Roy F. Homer, whose qualifications appeared to be well suited to the task. The trustees instructed President Widtsoe to press forward in hiring a new principal and in organizing other faculty and courses for the new school. Roy F. Homer assumed the task at $2,400 a year, a salary only slightly higher than that of his predecessor.

Roy F. Homer came to Cedar City on April 21, 1913 to acquaint himself with the school he had been asked to lead. The student newspaper reports that during his visit he "won the admiration and respect of the patrons, friends and students." It suggests further that: "His close relationship with the Agricultural College and its work will be a big factor in making ours a true daughter of the mother institution...It is needless to say that Mr. Homer will receive the hearty support of the people in this section if he can be prevailed upon to come." [7]

Mr. Homer was, in the end, prevailed upon to come, bringing with him his wife and two children, a daughter, Audrey and a son, Tom. He grasped the reins of the new Branch Agricultural College and prepared to implement the expansion possibilities provided by the transfer. By the time the first student annual, *"The Agricola,"* went to press, his photo was captioned "Our president, commonly and appropriately called Mr. 'Hummer', because he certainly keeps things going." [8]

Principal Homer had to hum. Like the proverbial juggler, he had plates to start and keep spinning while he tossed and caught the balls and brickbats which were the elements of the challenge. The requirements of the transfer to the Agricultural College called for greatly expanded facilities. If the school was to live up to this new mission as an agricultural college, farmland was to be purchased adjoin-

ing the present campus to bring the total property to 40 acres. There would need to be livestock supplied, and an additional experimental farm of eighty acres had to be obtained. The transfer legislation had offered no funds for such things. Principal Homer had to compose a catalog that would list the expanded offerings, and then find teachers to teach them. He even had to find money to pay the Branch Normal School teachers for the last month of the previous school year. Apparently, as soon as the enabling legislation became law, the checks stopped coming from the U. of U. [9]

He had to address these challenges in a manner that would help to win the support of the townspeople and the students and have school ready to open in its expanded form, all in too little time. He had to be a juggler and a magician.

By September 22, 1913, the first day in session as Branch Agricultural College, Mr. Homer was ready. He had distributed 3,000 copies of a letter from Dr. Widtsoe over the whole southern Utah area, giving special attention to alumni, families of former students and church and civic leaders. The letter, deeply reassuring, proclaimed the value of expanded opportunity and promised that nothing formerly treasured would be lost. It assured the people that Mr. Homer was the man of the moment and that every citizen would be well served by the new form of the school. [10]

ROY F. HOMER

Arriving students were greeted with exuberant optimism. Even the new catalog exuded warmth and engendered confidence:

The change to the Branch Agricultural College was made chiefly because of the great need of home builders and homemakers in the marvelous but undeveloped valleys of southern Utah. The "New Education" will give a new and strong impetus to the development of the rich southern counties. Hundreds of young men and women will be taught to believe in the South and will become filled with the glorious spirit of home-making and earth-conquest.

The old school is not dead; it continues under an enlarged mission. This is the only state institution maintained in southern

Utah. It must be made permanent and great...Let's get back of the B.A.C. with a will.

Fears that the change would result in fewer students proved unfounded. Registration numbers were greater than in any previous year. Students came from areas that had never been represented before. Most of the Branch Normal School teachers had been retained and some new people expanded the faculty.

Dr. Widtsoe had earlier written: "The people of Cedar City, themselves, as the first beneficiaries, must give vigorous support to the School that is now entering its new career." Had he been better acquainted with the community, he would have had no concern for their commitment. This was their school and theirs was a firmly established tradition. They would rise to meet whatever need arose.

But the fall term was only months away. Newspaper editorials urged action. Committees were organized yet again. Though they had accomplished much in a short time, September found the townspeople still scrambling to meet help make the magic.

Principal Homer urged them on. He spoke plainly and candidly to the townspeople gathered at the Tabernacle on Sunday, September 7, reminding them that the town did not yet look like a college town. They must transform the streets, sidewalks and houses in order to meet the standard. The Commercial Club designated an Improvement Day designed to make Cedar City a "Spotless Town."

*T*he September 19, 1913 issue of the *Iron County Record* reports some solutions that had been wrought by the citizenry. Headlined, "Generous Citizens Donate Land," the article, which included the photographs of Henry W. Lunt and T.J. Jones, read:

In order to secure the transfer of the Branch Normal School in this city to the Agricultural College, it was necessary for the representatives from our county in the state legislature to pledge to the state a sufficient amount of land, in addition to the school campus, to meet the needs of an agricultural school.

A committee appointed by the Commercial Club secured twenty and a half acres of land with full water right, adjoining the school

TOWNSPEOPLE CLEARING THE LAND, CALLED "GRUB DAY, 1914."

campus, for which the people are asked to pay the sum of $8,775.00, the price to be paid ranging from $350 to $500 per acre. [11]

In addition to the irrigated land, dry land was needed for experimental purposes. The land selected by the committee and Principal Homer, which was chosen because of its location, fertility and other advantages, was valued at $20.00 per acre.

The *Iron County Record* proclaimed:

At the last meeting of the Commercial Club it was announced that Senator Lunt and T.J. Jones would contribute to the College forty of the needed eighty acres of dry land. The forty acres contributed to the College adjoins the forty acres which the committee has purchased for a consideration of $20.00 per acre

The donation by the above named gentlemen represents a gift of $800.00, and the public-spiritedness and generosity of the donors should, and no doubt will, be fully appreciated by the people of Cedar City and that portion of the state directly affected by the school. [12]

People donated livestock. Prize Jersey and Holstein cows came from the herds of the townspeople to form the beginning of a dairy herd. From their own flocks, citizens gave chickens and incubators, resulting in a poultry program.

When spring of 1914 came, they had acquired the land necessary, but it was not ready for planting. There had been no provision made for the cultivation and maintenance of the experimental farm. The county commissioners had agreed to contribute the money to fence the land with a "rabbit-proof" fence. Principal Homer sent out a cry for help. The *Record* reported the result:

BAC EXPERIMENTAL FARM, SPRING 1914.

In response to the "Call to Arms" sent forth by Principal Homer of the BAC to turn out and assist in clearing and plowing the 80 acre experimental farm... about 200 men, half that many women and girls, and perhaps 50 teams responded and Friday and Saturday were busy days on the farm.

Heavy drags, drawn by horses, grubbing hoes and axes in the hands of willing workers, mowed the heavy sage-brush down like magic, and soon the field was a blazing inferno, with the men and boys with the proverbial pitchfork attending the fires and completing the picture. It was a splendid sight, and a most gratifying exhibition of community spirit and the interest that all feel in the welfare of the school.

The 1914 issue of the *Agricola* includes a photograph of carefully tilled seedbeds, ready for the hand of the fledgling farmers. The work of the townspeople and the students had turned raw, brush-covered land into promising plots; before long, barns, feeding sheds and outbuildings began to be erected.

It had taken an amazing cooperative effort. All shared in the exhilaration of accomplishing the expansion, while still preserving the character of the school. There was, however, one great disappointment. The last two years of the normal school training were withdrawn by the State Normal School. The euphoria was undoubtedly marred by a few "sour grapes" feelings for a time.

One discipline unruffled by the transfer was the music department.

This was a town and a school that immersed itself in music. The new school continued to offer a three-year music course. The year they became BAC, the school-produced dramatic offerings were "Sweet Lavender" and "The Perplexed Husband." The band and orchestra continued to thrive under Albert Tollestrup. The band sported a new bass drum proudly emblazoned BAC.

Student publications became more extensive and elaborate. For some years students at BNS had issued a small monthly publication called *The Student*. It had included gossipy news notes, some student literary offerings, athletic details and serious editorial

BAC BAND, 1914

BAC ORCHESTRA, 1914

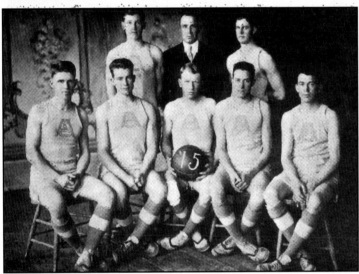

SOUTHERN
REGION
CHAMPIONS,
1914

still shine from the pages, the *Agricola* staff must have believed that no one would ever forget and neglected to list the names of the members of the teams. [14] The coach of both the basketball team and the track team was John S. Christensen. The track team waxed in confidence that they too would become first in the southern region, as a new and improved track was added to the facilities of the campus.

"Girls' Gymnasium," as women's athletics was called, continued to thrive with this avowed goal:

Physical education will directly or indirectly increase the power of sensation, attention, perception, conception, volition. It will regulate and aid in digestion, circulation, respiration, excretion and so on. Through physical education we want to preserve the health of our students. We want to maintain and increase their vitality. We want to prevent them from growing old at 30. Healthy people are happy people. [15]

Intellectual exercise was also encouraged. The first year debate teams won their meets with Murdoch Academy and made a trip north where "honors were showered upon them." They were ranked second in the state. By the year 1915-16, the debate teams were competing with both Dixie Academy and Murdoch on the resolution: "That the Monroe Doctrine should be abandoned." That year the prize debaters were Marion Wooley, Leonard Bowen, Bonner Lambson, and Scott Matheson, whose son who bore his Christian name would one day be the governor of Utah.

The school city, which had been the foremost student organization since the days of Milton Bennion, had to be rechartered and renamed. Now officially granted a city charter under the name Branch Agricultural College City, they continued to function with the same formality that had prevailed through the BNS days. Elections were held each term to select a

compositions such as "Superstitions" and "What Are We To Do With The Negro?" [13] At year's end an expanded edition included photographs of clubs and associations as well as classes and faculty, thereby serving as a sort of year book. *The Student* continued, but when the school became Branch Agricultural College they also added a formal yearbook. Just as the yearbook was named The *Agricola* on the Logan campus, so it was at the Cedar City campus. This is an indicator that the school was, as they had hoped, a true daughter.

The athletic programs for both men and women continued to be an important part of student life. The success of the basketball team spurred the school to considerable confidence as they became the southern region champions. What that means, in terms of who the competitors were, is not quite clear, though the Murdoch Academy of Beaver and the St. George Academy were continual rivals. Unfortunately, though the photographs of the teams

STUDENT
GOVERNMENT,
ABOUT 1914

mayor, recorder, treasurer, councilmen, magistrate and judges. All other officers were appointed, and these included committees for almost all student activities. It was an unique and highly effective system that afforded all students involvement in the affairs of the school city and gave them remarkable training for the civic responsibilities they would encounter in society. [16] Willard Canfield served as mayor of the first term. Ivie Gardner was the second term mayor. Unfortunately, the names of the council members are not included in the yearbook.

*T*he Agricultural Club was organized during the first part of the 1913-14 school year. Its stated purpose was to further the study of scientific agriculture. The members had the benefit of a special library and study room in the Science Building. The Home Economics Club, which had been organized some years earlier, boasted a larger membership, but with that one exception, the Agricultural Club was the largest group.

After the first month, Mr. Homer could write to Dr. Widtsoe the satisfying news that enrollment was 30 students more than the previous year. And that the "Winter Course" would bring many more regular students.

Winter Course was an ingenious arrangement that catered to an agricultural lifestyle and demonstrated clearly the change of emphasis. With the understanding that there were many young men in the southern Utah area who desired education but could not leave the farms at harvest time for the opening of school in September, and that these same young people were needed for spring work at the farms, the school invited them to register for classes during the time they were free during the winter months. They were warmly encouraged to come to Branch Agricultural College for those months. The announcement read in part:

Attention is directed to the announcement of the BAC mid-winter term. This is an announcement which should have an important significance to a large number of young and middle aged men and women of

THE WINTER COURSE

the southern counties of the state—a class of men and women who have the responsibilities of making a livelihood for themselves and perhaps others, and who are unable to attend school during the entire winter, but who can devote twelve weeks of mid-winter between fall and spring work to the improvement of their educational equipment.

After extolling the virtues of education in general, the announcement invites such young people not to neglect or look lightly upon their golden opportunity. There were, in fact, 27 students registered for Winter Course the first year, all young men.

By December the enrollment had neared 300 students. The curriculum now offered five distinct courses that could result in graduation in four years. More than 100 boys were enrolled in agriculture, more than 80 in mechanical arts, more than 120 girls in the domestic sciences and arts.

In December the announcement came that the BAC barn would soon be constructed at the cost of $3,000, and feeding sheds would follow, adding $2,000 more value to the complex.

Veterinary clinics were held each month, attended by students, farmers and stockraisers. The students and farmers learned as they participated in the actual handling of cases.

An intensive session of other courses for farmers and housewives was instituted. "The Farmer's Roundup" included classes on an amazingly wide variety of subjects. Classes were offered in gardening and pasture grasses, fruit growing and dry farming, soil fertility and irrigation skills, the alfalfa weevil and grain judging. There were demonstrations

given in horse handling and dairying, wool marketing and even the much maligned emphasis on hog feeding. The fee was $1.00. The first roundup lasted for two weeks, from February 23 through March 7, 1914, and included entertainments in the evening, dances, banquets and socials. Never did any institution work harder at serving and endearing itself to its constituency. The "Roundup" breathed new life into the town in the dead of winter. Offerings in subsequent years were more modest in terms of length of time.

Pride in the new school grew. In October of 1915 the students and faculty combined efforts to construct a handsome emblem on the hillside above the town. The large white "A" was intended to speak the loyalty and gratitude of the student body. Stated in the dramatic terms of the 1915-1916 *Agricola*: "It is a monument built in view of all the land to bespeak our gratitude to the BAC for splendid opportunities. It was here we learned the beauty of a life of usefulness and how to live it." "A" Day became a yearly outing, upon which the faithful students climbed to the mountain carrying pails of whitewash, to keep the emblem always shining forth. An electrified "A" was placed to emblazon forth from the top of the Main building. It shone with sufficient brightness that games and parties at night were lighted by its glow.

But the school was still a high school. And that chafed the people. The hope, when the change from the University of Utah had occurred, was that very soon Branch Agricultural College would become a college. George W. Decker had already been adding classes of college level, as the students seemed ready for them, but he had been hampered by the firm conviction of Joseph Kingsbury that a college in the south would diminish the state system. So while the content of some classes exceeded average high school level, there could be no college credit given.

Dr. John A. Widtsoe had written to Roy

THE "A," 1915

Homer in the summer of 1913:

We have to deal with a great deal of judgment with the situation at Cedar. Clearly, we cannot now build a college there when we have no high school students with which to fill it. What we must make them understand now is, that what they need is a big, successful high school of a polytechnic kind. The Agricultural College itself had to go through just such a period. Not many years ago it was chiefly a high school with a few score college students in it. [17]

Almost exactly three years later the announcement finally came. The process had evolved under the direction of Principal Homer; and, certainly with the agitation of the people, for though it was called a college, their children still had to leave home to obtain a degree. Not only was there the historic eagerness to enhance the offerings at the BAC, but the county had now begun to clamor for a high school of its own. On July 14, 1916 the *Iron County Record* announced:

BAC TO BE
JUNIOR COLLEGE
Principal R.F. Homer, After Weeks of
Persistent Work, Announces
Success of His Plans
Principal R.F. Homer, who has been in the north on business connected with the BAC for a few weeks, is expected home today or tomorrow. Mr. Homer was seen at Salt Lake the other day by a representative of The Record *and stated that everything was arranged for the introduction of a two years college course into the curriculum of the local school...*

A more formal announcement appeared in the Catalog for the year 1916-1917:

By resolution of the Board of Trustees, passed at a special meeting, July 10, 1916, the Branch Agricultural College of Utah was constituted a regular junior college—This resolution was passed by unanimous vote of the Board on account of their firm belief in the merits and possibilities of the South, their knowledge of its needs, and their desire to extend the service of the institution over which they exercise control. No doubt this advancement of the standards of southern Utah's State School will meet with the hearty approval of all students, patrons, and others

concerned with the up-building of this section.

The first year, college work would begin in all departments. The second year, 1917-18, the sophomore year or second year college work would begin. The high school section would include all four years of work in 1916-17, but thereafter the ninth grade or first year high school work would not be offered by Branch Agricultural College, but would become the responsibility of the Iron County School District.

"However," stated the Catalog, "second, third and fourth year high school courses will be retained in the curriculum until such time as the development of high schools in the various communities and counties of southern Utah makes it desirable to eliminate second year high school work."

A formal notice was sent to surrounding school districts. None of them could send eighth grade graduates for admittance at BAC after the year 1916-1917.

Mr. Homer was so bold as to suggest that he had almost positive assurance that the University of Utah would reinstate two years of the Normal course as given prior to the change from the University of Utah to the Agricultural College. His optimism was born of the fact that the University of Utah was now headed by Dr. John A. Widtsoe, whom, he assured the local folk, is so well acquainted with the needs of the southern counties. [18]

The 1917 *Agricola* invites students to register for an annual fee of $5 and in large letters proclaims the school to be: TUITION FREE.

The dignity of the students is reflected by their dress and deportment. The Ag Club had formed a male quartet, demonstrating again the well-rounded nature of the education obtained at the Branch Agricultural College.

Character education was not neglected. Chapel exercises continued to be held each morning. One lecture remains from Principal

Homer, in which he listed the "don'ts" young men and women of well-ordered lives must observe:

Don't profane; don't smoke or chew tobacco; don't waste time in pool halls; don't match nickels; don't loaf; don't go to excess in buying candy; don't attend too many picture shows or house parties; don't be extravagant; don't joyride; don't read too many novels.

He then added to the list, don't dance improperly, followed by some very plain words of chastisement concerning the behavior he had observed at dances. He did suggest that one of the reasons for improper dancing might be that the offenders didn't know how to dance. He finished with, "There is hope for them when they learn."

Indeed the school seemed to be poised for extraordinary success. The legislature had been generous, appropriating $50,000. That the townspeople were intimately involved with every detail of the progress of their school is evidenced by the account of a "rousing program" held to celebrate the success of Principal Homer at the 1917 Legislature. Amid cheers from students and speeches by prominent citizens, school songs and orchestra pieces, they exulted that the southern boundary line of the state had been extended from Juab County to way below St. George. [19]

All was not well with the world, in general, in 1917, however. World War I was at its height. Men were being drafted. Students were called home to be examined for military service. [20]

Early in 1918, the domestic science department at BAC issued information to the homemakers of the town on ways they could help the war effort. "Share your wheat with the allies," the directive admonished. Then, after counseling housewives about the reduction of consumption of fats, sugars, grains and milk, the directive states:

All the blood, all the heroism, all the money and munitions in the world will not win the war...unless the allies are fed. They will not be fed unless you stand guard each day in your home over your supply of wheat, meat, fats, sugars and milk. Don't think you are so com-

fortably fixed that you can afford to eat what your country needs. Follow directions. [21]

Nonetheless, for a time it appeared that one effect of the war would bring unusual prosperity to the Branch Agricultural College. Announcement was made that the Student Army Corps was to be established at the college. The United States government was to pay the young men who enlisted at the rate of $30 a month. They were to be provided with housing and food, while they continued their studies. As soon as their numbers were drawn by their local draft boards, they were to be issued uniforms. The training was to be done under regularly commissioned army officers based on the campus; as soon as barracks could be constructed, enlistees would be housed there and placed under military discipline.

But the optimism was short lived. Two things altered the plans for the connection with the army. The Armistice was signed, and influenza struck.

People returning to Cedar City from the October Conference of the Church of Jesus Christ of Latter-day Saints and the State Fair, both held in Salt Lake City, began to come down with Spanish Influenza. Newspapers reported that Salt Lake was a "closed city," after the most drastic health order ever issued in the state prohibited all indoor gatherings.

On November 15, Elias M. Corry, Cedar City mayor, issued an official proclamation, co-signed by M. J. Macfarlane, City Health Officer:

INFLUENZA
WHEREAS, it appears that satisfactory progress is not being made in the curtailment and eradication of the Epidemic of INFLUENZA existing in our city, it has been deemed necessary to adopt more stringent measures in dealing with the situation.
NOW THEREFORE, it is hereby ordered:
First. That all persons appearing upon the streets or in any of the public places—Stores, Banks, Hotels, Restaurants, Barber Shops, Etc., (except while actually engaged in eating or in a barber chair) shall be effectually masked with a suitable close-fitting gauze mask of the type approved by the local Board of Health and consisting of not less than four thicknesses of thin cloth, and properly adjusted to strain the breath issuing from the nose and mouth.
Second: Congregating on the streets or in the homes, or visiting by groups at private

ROY F. HOMER
1882-1945

Roy F. Homer firmly grasped the reins of the Branch Normal School of the University of Utah as it made the transition to becoming a Branch of Utah State Agricultual College.

This service covered the grueling years of World War I and the dread influenza epidemic of 1918 and 1919, during which, the school was closed for four months and the home economics department was used as a community hospital. Mr. Homer aided in such operations in every possible way.

The outstanding ability of Mr. Homer as an executive put him in good stead in many community developments. He is remembered by many faculty members for his good judgment, his quiet, efficient manners, his skill in conducting a meeting or caucus and his excellent taste in all public matters. Meetings under his chairmanship were always models of good and exacting leadership.

A fastidious gentleman, he set a good example in dress and manner before the new faculty which was just beginning another phase of life for the college.

Mr. Homer met the practical needs of the school by employing an expert landscape gardener to begin a good campus design for college hill. Much experimental work with pure-bred livestock was begun, as well as development of crops, soils and irrigation projects.

A particular community task was undertaken by public-spirited citizens who, in one day's time, cleared the 80-acre farm on the state highway of a dense growth of sagebrush, preparatory to seeding.

Mr. Homer instituted a program known as the Farmer's Roundup, which was three days of agricultural education for farmers and stockmen, who attended daily lectures and demonstrations. During these Roundups, the Extension Service of the Utah State Agricultural College first brought its influence into this area. Many farmers began to admit to the value of scientific planning of crops and the sanitary handling of milk, and the new era of farming was launched.

He also initiated the Home Economics Club, for many years one of the most influential women's groups in Cedar City.

Roy Homer was a native of Nephi, Utah, and a graduate of the Utah State Agricultural College.

residences, is strictly prohibited. Parents will be held responsible for the observance of this order, by their children of all ages.

Third: All persons having any of the symptoms of Influenza or a cold are required to isolate themselves and report the condition to a Health Officer.

Fourth: Persons nursing or waiting on Influenza patients should isolate themselves from the public.

Fifth: All instructions given in individual cases by the Health Officer or any of his deputies must be complied with. The appointment of a number of deputy health officers is hereby announced.

Failure to observe any of the foregoing stipulations which are effective from and after publication hereof, will constitute a misdemeanor and will be punishable by a fine or imprisonment, or both, at the discretion of the Court.

Given under my hand this 15th day of November, A.D. 1918.

ELIAS M. CORRY,
MAYOR OF CEDAR CITY

M.J. MACFARLAND,
CITY HEALTH OFFICER

The school was, of course, closed. For four months, the duration of the epidemic, no classes were held. It was not the first time disease had closed the school. Branch Normal School had closed for two weeks in the spring of 1901 as a result of a small pox epidemic, but this plague was even more deadly and resulted in a longer recess.

However the campus was not dormant. On the contrary, College Hill continued to be a center of activity. The facilities became the emergency hospital of the community. Quarters in the steam-heated domestic science and domestic art rooms of the Branch Agricultural College were much more comfortable than the icy bedrooms of the average home. The newspaper, dated November 29, 1918, reported the effectiveness of the makeshift infirmary:

A splendid convenience in connection with the existing epidemic of influenza in Cedar City, is the temporary hospital established at the BAC, for the benefit of patients who cannot receive scientific nursing or convenient and favorable accommodations at home. It is in charge of County

Demonstrator Rena B. Maycock and Miss Amy Bowman of the BAC faculty, who have a corps of nurses. It seems to be the history of the patients sent there that they uniformly improve just about as fast as systematic, scientific nursing and care can suggest. The number of patients vary according to the needs of the afflicted, six or seven being as many as have been receiving care at one time. The domestic science and the domestic art rooms of the BAC, steamheated, well ventilated, with a convenient kitchen, are admirably situated for use as a hospital, and if anyone would not improve under the conditions there the chances for them at home would be poor, indeed.

By December the town had become a dull and monotonous place. The young people were straining to break through the restraints. Christmas was coming. But parents were cautioned not to slacken their diligence:

To date the influenza has been six times as deadly for the people of Cedar City as has been the war. Parents who wept when their sons left for battle should remember that their young people at home who are disregarding quarantine rules are taking a far more deadly chance ...if you do not wear a mask properly you may be the direct cause of another's death...It is cowardly as well as dangerous to put your mask up only when you see an officer.

Finally, in February the ban was lifted. After four months the town began to come to life again. Schools reopened, worship meetings were resumed. The afternoon church meetings on Sunday, February 8, were dedicated to President Theodore Roosevelt, whose death a month earlier had passed without public observance in Cedar City because of the quarantine. The announcement of the end of the quarantine included some social opportunities:

The Thorley Theatre will resume its performances and it is hardly necessary to state that the young people will improve the opportunity of having a liberal number of dances and other social gatherings again, after being denied these forms of pleasure for so long a time.
The theatre for the present will be permitted to run on only half capacity and the pool

halls are also permitted to reopen on "table capacity" but no loafers or onlookers are permitted. [22]

The rest of the 1919 school year the school returned to normal. Remarkable development had occurred over the five years since the school had become Branch Agricultural College. The whole school bustled with energy.

The school was proud of the "richness and liberality of the curriculum." The catalog listings testify that the offerings were broad.

It was also liberal in the services they continued to offer. Even though the school had discontinued the first year high school course, they still tried to provide first year high school classes for students who came from counties and districts that had not yet established high schools of their own.

Though the flu epidemic had cancelled the farmer and housewife "Roundup" in 1919, it had been held every year from 1913 until then, and continued afterwards for many years. The 1918 conference list includes men and women from 23 towns. There is little question that the people eagerly embraced the opportunities provided by the Branch Agricultural College to improve their skills and methods. Periodic clinics and workshops in agronomy and animal husbandry were well attended throughout the year. The Home Economics Club included prominent women of the town, while women students focused upon the Girl Welfare Club.

The agricultural and industrial emphasis had flourished, but so had the offerings in the sciences and the arts. Those who had predicted that hog husbandry would supplant the normal school were, no doubt, grateful to be proven wrong.

A teacher training school was established. This crucial element was provided through the cooperative efforts of the State Normal School at the University of Utah, the Utah Agricultural College, the Branch Agricultural College, the State Board of Education and the Iron County School District. Now teaching certificates could be earned by college-level students without their having to go north. It

PRUNING CLASS

was a great boon for southern Utah. A large training-school building was constructed by the Iron County School District.

From photographs in the old catalogs one senses the serious bearing of the student body. Their dress and deportment are indicative of their almost reverential attitude toward the process in which they are involved. That aura was not diminished by the expansion of the "earthier" pursuits when the school became an agricultural college. The students maintained a dignity that seemed to elevate learning, in whatever discipline. A class in pruning is attended by young men dressed in suits, ties and hats, taught by a professor similarly attired.

Prospective girl students were urged to acquire a suitable wardrobe, as suggested by the committee on standardization for school dress. The suggestions:

1. A one piece woolen dress of dark color. 2. A suit (skirt, jacket and wash waist), conservative in color and texture. 3. A one piece dress of wash material such as gingham galatea, linen, pique or percale. 4. Medium or low heel walking shoes and hose of standard quality cotton.

The dress standard is actually more liberal than that of earlier years, when a uniform was to be made of navy blue serge, from Pictorial Review Pattern #6065, Misses Sailor Costume.

NORMAL TRAINING
BUILDING, 1919.

The pattern could be purchased at the Golden Rule Store in Cedar City.

On the subject of discipline the catalog declares:

It is the policy of the administrative officers of the Branch Normal School to give the students all the liberties and privileges they can appreciate. We expect them to assume, in a large measure, the responsibility of maintaining the school's good name. It must be known throughout the state that our student body is made up of young men and women of good morals and industrious habits. Earnestness in study, regularity of attendance, and proper personal conduct are insisted upon at all times. These results are all secured by the BAC City Government...The students govern themselves. The student body government has entire charge of discipline at the school.

Elections twice each year gave many students opportunities to serve in "municipal" positions. The mayor and city council drafted and passed the laws. The police and the courts enforced them. The students accepted the system and were apparently content to abide by it.

The agricultural program progressed each year. The students learned both from instruction and experience. When they needed a hay wagon to harvest their crop, the students constructed a hay wagon.

When a silo was needed to store the crop, the students added a silo alongside the barn, constructed earlier. Theirs was no ivory tower education; the curriculum was designed to prepare students to build the homes and farms of southern Utah.

Everything was accomplished by man power aided by animal power. Six beautiful draft mares became the pride of the agricultural students.

BAC did not intend to be left behind the times. In 1919 the college began the process of building an auto mechanics shop. It would become the fourth building on the hill. Since automobiles were becoming more commonplace, the students were learning to operate and maintain automotive machines. Mr. Homer had purchased a new car himself the year before the *Iron County Record* of May 18, 1918 announced:

Principal Roy F. Homer has a new Buick touring car. The machine was selected from a considerable list of makes, the dealers of which had all been requested to submit their propositions on the sale of the car to the state. The local Buick agents naturally feel jubilant over landing the sale under these circumstances.

The agents felt so jubilant that they took the opportunity to obtain a testimonial from Principal Homer, which they published in the very next issue.

As soon as tractors were introduced to the intermountain region, they were authorized to purchase a tractor. Then Principal Homer went looking for a person to maintain it and to teach these new skills.

The new auto mechanics shop was located south of the gymnasium. It would provide much needed training in the care and repair of the popular cars of the day, i.e. the Model T Ford, the four cylinder Dodge touring car, the

BAC DRAFT MARES

GEORGE
CROFT, 1920

Studebaker 7 passenger, and the Hudson "Super 6."

In order for the students to have something to practice on, townspeople were encouraged to bring their cars and tractors to the new shop for repair or overhaul. That did, understandably, cause some grumbling by the local car dealers. George Croft comments, "When they (car dealers) found we did not unduly interfere with their business they consented to cooperate and sell us repair parts for the cars we repaired in the shop." One wonders if the fledgling mechanics could actually have enhanced the demands upon the local repair businesses. Croft also records that when there existed a family car, students brought it in and worked on it.

Roy F. Homer was persuasive in his proselyting for teachers. George Croft recalls his first encounter with him. "He was a great booster for southern Utah. He talked to me of the many opportunities and the potentialities in what he called the Inland Empire, which was awaiting the advent of a railroad line. [23] He did manage to persuade George that Cedar City and Branch Agricultural College were places of opportunity.

When newly-wedded George and Prudence Croft boarded the train in Ogden Utah, late in August of 1919, they had no idea of the realities of the society they were about to join. They had been regaled with tales of a tropical climate where people lived the easy life, quenched their thirst with Dixie wine and only used water for washing. This enlightenment had been provided by their Logan colleagues, who apparently had little accurate information themselves.

The Crofts came with two suitcases, containing their accumulated worldly wealth. Arriving at Lund, they departed the train into an atmosphere of brilliant sunshine, a southerly breeze, and a vista of wide open sage brush prairie extending eastward to the distant mountains. George's history provides a delightful glimpse of their journey and of Cedar City in 1919:

We all boarded a seven-passenger Buick touring car. [24] The driver. . . was Ben Knell. He had the franchise to haul passengers and mail between Lund and Cedar City. He tied mail bags on the front fenders of his car and

our baggage on two racks built on each side of the car.

The road we travelled consisted of a number of dusty ruts through the sage brush flats. It bore off in a southeasterly direction. We rode merrily along stopping about half way for a drink of water and to fill the car's radiator...We came through the gap in the hills at Iron Springs. I was greatly relieved when I saw that Cedar City was located at the foot of the mountains. I was afraid the town would be somewhere on the flat prairie.

As we came into town I could see three drab looking brick buildings situated on a low, rocky hill. I was told this was the college.

Our conveyance turned south on the main street. On the east corner was an old fashioned wooden building with a porch and balcony along its entire front. Apparently empty, it appeared to have been an old time inn. On the southwest corner was a red stone building with stone steps to the entrance door. A sign indicated that it was the tithing office and store house. [25]

We stopped in front of a large brick building in about the center of the town. It was called the Cedar Mercantile Company. Further north with a vacant lot between, was another large red brick building housing "The Sheep Store."

Across the street from where we stopped we were shown the Cedars Hotel where we could obtain temporary lodging and meals. We crossed the street ankle deep in dust and registered at the hotel. It was managed by a vixen named Perry. You liked her accommodations or else. [26]

The Crofts found a two-room apartment upstairs in the home of Samuel Leigh. George began the teaching career that would last for the next 11 years. His history preserves fascinating details of college and community, and of the physical plant, as it existed then.

At the first faculty meeting I met my fellow teachers. Mr. Roy F. Homer was a rather stout, dignified person, always properly dressed to fit the dignity of his position. . . The physical plant of the college consisted mainly of three brick buildings—the library building to the north, in which was housed the library, the English department and classrooms for typewriting, bookkeeping and stenography. In the basement of that same building was the woodworking shop, the

mechanical drafting room and the advanced woodworking shop. These classes used machinery such as power saws, surface plainer, jointer and a wood lathe. The machines were driven by locally produced single phase electric power and were controlled by exposed knife switches, installed without regard to any safety rules. [27]

The library boasted nearly 5,000 volumes; the catalog declared the intention to spend $1,000 each year to keep the collection current.

The center building, as described by Mr. Croft, contained an assembly hall and the dance floor at the top level, with the music department in two small rooms on the north, surrounding the stairway. The center level also included all the administrative offices as well as the chemistry classroom and laboratory and all of the other science classrooms. The basement of this building housed the agriculture department classrooms and the biology laboratory. It also enclosed a small gas generator which produced the gas used in the chemistry department. The home economics department was also located on the basement level.

The third, and newest, building contained the shops and the gymnasium. The iron work shop and the machine shops both included a good deal of machinery. The shops, the instructor's office and the tool rooms utilized the main floor.

The gymnasium requires some imagination to envision. It occupied the top floor above the shops. A narrow stairway led up from the northeast corner and a steel fire escape descended down the south side from a narrow door in the center of the room. Narrow tiers of seats lined each side wall. During a game the space was so crowded that standing spectators lined the entire boundary of the court. There was a shower and change room, but it consisted of a single shower spray, supplied with hot water from a 300 gallon tank in the forge room. It was heated by a small homemade brick furnace whose fire box was lined with a pipe coil connected to the hot water tank.

The domestic water supply to the town was still unreliable. The water mains were made of redwood, with heavy wire wound spirally around the pipe. Most people kept an emergency supply on hand at all times, but since that was not possible at the magnitude needed at the Branch Agricultural College, the shower room did not always have water. Neither did the gymnasium or the other facilities always have electricity, since the Coal Creek power plant was not to be depended upon.

*T*he industrial education department was distinguished both by genius and by determination. Representative of those noted for their determined effort to gain education were the Robertson brothers, Wells and Von, who came over the mountains from their home in Alton in a team and wagon, bringing household necessities and food supplies from home, leading a milk cow behind their wagon, so that they could be sustained while they learned. Their father came along to drive the wagon home again. Since the road then was little more than a track, and led along the south side of Navajo Lake and into the Deep Creek area, before heading over Cedar Mountain, few would question their fervor for education.

William I. Palmer, who became a noted scientist and years later headed the United States Bureau of Reclamation, first distinguished himself by using the facilities in the industrial department to put together one of the first radios in Cedar City. With the use of earphones, the astonished listener could receive Amy Semple McPherson and her "Four Square Gospel" all the way from Los Angeles.

The agriculture department was flourishing, and each faculty member assumed broad responsibilities. Expansion in the offerings did not mean expansion in numbers of instructors. The 1913-14 catalog lists David Sharp, Jr., B.S, as instructor in animal husbandry and Robert S. Wrigley, B. S., as instructor in agronomy and horticulture. In 1916-17, both still have those responsibilities but Wrigley is also listed as supervisor of farms, and John S. Christensen, their much revered athletic coach, is listed as assistant in agronomy.

The stresses of the job may have caused the rapid turnover in personnel. By the year 1919 William Woolley was serving as instructor in

THREE BUILDINGS, 1919

D.L. SARGENT'S POULTRY CLASS

agronomy and superintendent of farms, with David Sharp still in charge of animal husbandry. But by the next year Sharp had left to become the county agent in Cache County, Stanley Ivins had established himself in a chicken hatching business in American Fork, and the others had also found employment elsewhere. The catalog had no agricultural faculty to list. Principal Homer scrambled to find someone to keep the ambitious agricultural program alive.

Up in Idaho, young David L. Sargent was making his mark in agricultural extension work and had been asked to assume leadership over 4-H work for the state of Idaho. About to accept the prestigious position, he and his wife, Mildred, fretted over the conflict the position would create for him as father of three children, since two-thirds of his time would be spent traveling.

DAVID L. SARGENT. 1920

...Right at the psychological moment, the principal of Branch Agricultural College, Roy F. Homer, called me on the telephone and offered me a position at the college as head of the agricultural department. I was to be head of the department and the only teacher they had.. We concluded that was what we ought to do; so we sent in my resignation as club leader for Idaho, not even having assumed the duties of the office, and came to Cedar City. We arrived here on the 10th of October, 1920... [28]

The Sargents arrived in much the same style as had the Crofts a year earlier.

We crowded into that old car [Ben Knell's hack] and came through ruts and dust, scarcely a green thing in sight and wind blowing and kids a-crying. I began to think, "Well, now, what have I done to myself and my family?" And I thought if I'd ever made a mistake this was it—leaving that beautiful Bear Lake country with water everywhere and that beautiful lake...lots of friends, and come down into this country. [29]

Nevertheless, Mr. Sargent began his duties in earnest. He was listed as instructor of agriculture and superintendent of farms, and he is the only person listed. He taught agronomy, animal

husbandry and horticulture, under which headings were included 21 separate classes. We can only hope that Coach Christensen continued to give able assistance.

The school had long been offering classes in dairying. The administration had been planning to begin a practical dairying operation as part of the curriculum. In the fall of 1921, a Swiss-German dairyman named D.T. Hoffman was hired to proceed with the project. A small manufacturing plant or creamery, set up in the old boiler room at the southeast corner of the Library building, included a churn and a cheese press and a large refrigerator box in the rudimentary equipment.

Milk production from the college herd did not match either their enthusiasm nor their preparations, so David Sargent persuaded the farmers in the Enoch area that they should send their milk to the college instead of each farmer producing and selling a small amount of butter. Soon they found themselves with more milk and butter than they could sell locally. The refrigerator filled up with the surplus of their Desert Gold Butter.

Mr. Sargent approached the principal with the dilemma and a proposed solution:

I told the principal that I just had to get out and sell this butter. So I filled my suitcase with this fine butter, which we had named Desert Gold; and went down into Pioche, Panaca and Las Vegas. I got orders for far more butter than we could produce; so we ran at full speed for three or four years. [30]

It was, perhaps, this kind of extraordinary effort that caused Parley Dalley, a teacher of such remarkable devotion himself, to remark years later, "As a matter of fact, in my opinion, the thing that has made this school continue, despite the ups and downs, was that we had dedicated teachers who were more concerned for the service they were giving than they were for their meager salaries."

r. Hoffman was a wonderful maker of butter. In May of 1922 his BAC creamery butter was awarded first prize in competition with creameries in eight western states with 78 samples submitted. But he was less adept at dealing with the students and moved on to more serene activities in 1923. When he was replaced by Arthur J. Morris, a graduate of the Agricultural College, the creamery continued to expand. Eventually they produced ice cream and cheese, as well as their Desert Gold, and supplied these quality products to the community and the outlying areas.

Classes in poultry production, augmented by coops full of chickens made fresh eggs available to the townspeople for many years.

Though the departments were thriving, smooth sailing was short-lived. Only a few months after D.L. Sargent arrived, Principal Homer, having completed an eventful eight-year administration, abruptly resigned.

The *Iron County Record* of April 1, 1921, reported,

Principal Roy F. Homer announced to the faculty that he will sever his connections with the BAC this spring since this climate does not agree with his health...His successor will be P. Vincent Cardon from Logan...who is now professor of agronomy at the University of Montana. Mr. Homer declares that Mr. Cardon is a very fine and capable young man, and that the institution will be in very good hands.

ormer students remember Mr. Homer fondly. Orien and Jesse Dalley had come to Branch Agricultural College from Summit, Utah. Each of the Dalley brothers remembered Mr. Homer as dignified, quiet, and a fine administrator. Orien, who as a high school student, and in love with Mr. Homer's daughter Audrey, remembers him as a bit stern. [31]

He was editorialized in glowing terms:

Every institution is but the lengthened shadow of some man. The Branch Agricultural College may be taken as the lengthened shadow of Principal R. F. Homer...from a school designed primarily to fit boys and

P.V. CARDON

girls to become teachers, he has changed the institution to a school for practical producing men and women. [32]

It was announced that Mr. Homer would travel, write and generally regain his health and that the Homer family would leave Cedar City at the end of June, 1921.

Farewell parties and receptions honoring the Homers enlivened the community during the month of June. On July 1, Vincent P. Cardon came to assume leadership duties. Mr. Cardon was a son-in-law of Anthony W. Ivins, then chairman of the Board of Trustees. He was a graduate of the Agricultural College, and resigned a professorship of agronomy at Montana State College to come to Branch Agricultural College.

The appointment of Mr. Cardon occasioned also a change in the title of the administrative head of the institution from Principal to Director. "This change," Director Cardon explained, "was made as one of the conditions upon which I accepted the position. The Branch Agricultural College is distinct from any other school in Utah, and therefore should not have an organization identical with that of every district school. The responsibilities of the BAC head are not only greater than those of a high school principal, but they are vastly different. As I understand the duties of my office, I am expected virtually to direct, in this part of the state, through the Branch Agricultural College, the affairs of the present institution, insofar as our equipment and maintenance funds will permit." [33]

But Director Cardon stayed at Branch Agricultural College less than one school year, leaving in the spring of 1922 to accept the position of Director of the Experiment Station at Logan. The school was without a director for two months, giving rise to general uneasiness among the ever-vigilant public.

The appointment of Director P. Vincent Cardon to the post at Logan and his subsequent departure from Branch Agricultural College occurred at the same time as Murdoch Academy was closing at Beaver. J. Howard Maughan, who had served as principal of the Murdock Academy, was appointed to replace Director Cardon. He was well qualified for the position, but he faced serious disadvantages in accepting the Cedar City post. His rocky begin-

J. HOWARD MAUGHAN, 1922

ning reveals much about the proprietary attitude that the citizens of Cedar City maintained regarding the conduct of the day to day affairs of "their school."

There had been, for years, a fierce rivalry between the Murdock Academy and the Cedar City school. It extended into academic competitions as well as athletic contests and had existed from the beginnings of both schools. The faculties and administrators of the two institutions traveled the region during every school recess, vying for students to attend their institutions. The idea of having the former principal of Murdock Academy direct the destiny of the Branch Agricultural College dealt a blow that many people of Cedar City were not sure they could sustain. And the fact that he brought a few of his Murdock faculty members with him, added to the perceived humiliation.

*A*t each successive session of the legislature certain members from the northern counties questioned the advisability of continuing Branch Agricultural College. Most years they were successful in cutting the appropriations to bare bones. In the session just completed a Rep. Peters had actually introduced legislation calling for the closing of Branch Agricultural College. Little wonder that there were raw defensive nerves where the management of their school was concerned. And now the rumor spread that Director Maughan had been placed in the position to prepare for the closing of the school.

As the tales spread and discussion became more lively, the Cedar City Chamber of Commerce decided it was time to intervene in the affair. They appointed a committee of three prominent citizens to look into the matter.

P. VINCENT CARDON
1889-1965

Dr. P. Vincent Cardon came to Cedar City in 1921 as the director of the 24-year-old school. He stayed for only one year, but he left his mark upon the community and student body.

The avowed mission of the beloved school in Cedar City was changing from a teacher education branch of the normal school of the University of Utah in Salt Lake City to performing as the southern Utah arm of the Utah State Agricultural College in Logan.

Cardon was the man for the job. He had already earned a reputation in the field of agronomy on a national level. He was destined to serve the United States in a position of international importance and responsibility as Director General of the Food and Agricultural Organization of the United Nations.

Dr. Cardon came to the Branch Agricultural College in Cedar City, fully trained and extraordinarily experienced as an agriculturist, with the aim of realizing every one of the wonderful possibilities existing in the southern school. He pronounced, upon his appointment, that "BAC should be a real and vital part of the mother institution at Logan and, as far as maintenance funds and equipment will permit, render service of the character that has placed the main institution among the greatest agricultural colleges of the United States. It shall be my aim so to conduct the affairs of the Branch that it will, in every particular, fulfill the purpose for which it was established."

A native of Logan, Utah, P.V. Cardon had graduated from USAC in 1909. His career with the U.S. Department of Agriculture began at that early stage, as he went directly to Nephi to direct the dry land cereal investigation for the National Bureau of Plant Industry. He then accepted an assignment as assistant director of crop acclimatization and adaptation,

traveling throughout the cotton belt of the southern United States to investigate and devise methods of control of cotton pests and work with growers to increase their crop yields.

Dr. Cardon concurrently continued his education, receiving his master's degree from the University of California. He returned to his home state to direct the Utah Experimental Station and serve as editor of the *Utah Farmer.*

P.V. Cardon resigned from a professorship of agronomy at Montana State College to become the director of BAC. He went on from his brief directorship of BAC in Cedar City to establish a solid reputation as one of the most outstanding agricultural experts in the west. Dr. Cardon went to Washington in 1935. His rise there was rapid. He ultimately served as Director of the Graduate School of the United States Department of Agriculture before he initiated, at age 65, the most challenging task of his distinguished career in the above-mentioned position of international eminence.

P. Vincent Cardon had other sides to his personality than the above litany would suggest. As an undergraduate in Logan he had been active in student affairs. He was prominent in athletics and drama, as well as editor of the student newspaper. He married Leah Ivins, and they reared a son and two daughters.

LeGrand Pace, a stockman and banker, U.T. Jones, prominent in church and business, and John Fuller, manager of the local Golden Rule store, began their investigation by inviting faculty members to express their concerns.

By the time the hearing was over, fears were calmed. Most people realized that cooperation among all parties would insure the future of the Branch Agricultural College and that even having been tainted by association with Murdoch Academy, Director Maughan was a man they could admire.

J. Howard Maughan proved to be a pro-active director. He did not leave his fate to the Chamber of Commerce, though he undoubtedly valued their support. He announced a general citizens meeting for the Sunday following his August 4th appointment and invited all the citizens to be present to discuss the work of BAC and plans for the coming year. He wrote reassuring messages through the medium of the newspaper. On August 11, 1922, a bold headline declared,

DIRECTOR MAUGHAN MAKES STATEMENT IN REGARD TO RUMORS ABOUT PERMANENCY OF BAC:

In view of the fact that several rumors with reference to the Branch Agricultural College are receiving rather general circulation in the southern part of the state, it is felt that a definite statement from the institution to the public is imperative at this time...Be assured that the future of Branch Agricultural College was never more promising than at this time...In common with all educational institutions throughout the land—because of a general policy of retrenchment, more support financially could be desired.. However, with economy the appropriation will be adequate. [34]

He further wrote that since the school's service to the state would be measured by the number of people it reached, the pressing challenge was for increased enrollment. He immediately set about to do what he could to bring in more students. On September 1, the paper announced: "BAC Publicity Campaign Now On." Director Maughan organized his own lyceum circuit with musicians, readers and his own persuasive oratory and began to tour the southern Utah towns.

His first meeting was in Minersville on a Sunday afternoon. As a matter of fact, it replaced the sacrament meeting program in the local congregation of The Church of Jesus Christ of Latter-day Saints. The *Record* printed a positive report:

Last Sunday the Director began at Minersville his series of educational meetings. He was accompanied by the LaVoma Quartet, Miss Bernella Gardner, accompanist, Mrs. Leland Betensen, soloist and Mrs. John U. Webster, dramatic reader. Bishop Eyre kindly turned the greater portion of the afternoon meeting over to the visitors and an excellent B.A.C. program was given to an exceptionally large and appreciative audience. [35]

From Minersville he proceeded with his troupe to Beaver, where every seat in the house was filled at the evening meeting. His connections with Beaver County were paying off. The paper reported enthusiastic receptions at every town and outlined Mr.

SHOP, SCIENCE, MAIN BUILDINGS, 1923. NOTE ROAD.

Maughan's itinerary for the following three weeks. He intended to hold two educational meetings a day and cover every town. It was clear that he would win over not only the people of Cedar City, but he would win the hearts of all of southern Utah. He would have his increased enrollment. The naysayers could expect that his tenure would be distinguished by progressive accomplishment.

When the *Iron County Record* announced the September 25 opening of the fall term, the subheading read: "CLOUDS ROLLED AWAY AND EVERYTHING CLEAR FOR A BANNER SCHOOL YEAR. A STRONG FACULTY SECURED."

If the community seems to have been inordinately concerned in the affairs of the school, one must remember that the two were woven together in sometimes complicated ways. The high school was still part of the college. The catalog of 1921-1922 read:

The college furnishes the greater part of the social entertainment of the community. It maintains a lyceum course on which appear the leading lecturers and musical and literary artists of America. Operas, dramas, programs and dances are among the social activities put on, including the athletic sports which mean so much to the life of the community.

On the other hand the college depended upon the community for sustenance, as well. The 1923-24 catalog acknowledges the relationship: "It is confidently expected that all students coming to BAC for the coming school year will find comfortable and agreeable quarters. The housekeepers are generous and kind and spare no pains in making the home life of the students, for whose living conditions they take responsibility, home-like, congenial, and pleasant." Board and room was available for $20 to $35 a month.

The Home Economics Club was begun by prominent local women whose purposes included the raising and maintaining of a fund to give financial assistance to any student "...who would be compelled to leave school for the want of money."

One of the good causes of the Home Economics Club was the root of a treasured tradition, cherished for the next two and a half decades. These wonderful women, ever vigilant to find worthy contributions in their cause, purchased a large cast iron bell, which they intended as a gift for the high school. As the high school building had a flat roof, which could not accommodate the bell, the resourceful ladies offered the bell to the Branch Agricultural College, with the suggestion that it be placed in the cupola atop the main building, called by this time, the Library Building. The fact that the imposing gift weighed 1,800 pounds presented a daunting challenge.

The students in the mechanic arts department, with their inventive teacher, Mr. Croft, solved the dilemma. Flexing their collective

J. HOWARD MAUGHAN
1893-1976

The BAC faculty under the direction of J. Howard Maughan was outstanding. A great lover of the out-of-doors, he established a number of wholesome and fun-loving events which became traditional to faculty activities, including an annual Spring Breakfast at commencement time, and the annual venison dinner.

His great interest in relating Boy Scout activities to the college helped spearhead the movement in southern Utah. He was chosen to be second president of Zion National Park Boy Scout Council following William R. Palmer...In his 30 years' service to scouting, Mr. Maughan received many honors, including the coveted Silver Beaver Award.

Born in western Idaho in 1893, the son of Harrison Davenport and Elizabeth Freestone Maughan, he received his education at Oneida Stake Academy in Preston, Idaho, his bachelor's and master's degrees from the Utah State Agricultural College and further advanced study at the University of Wisconsin. He was a member of the United States Air Corps during World War I.

Maughan began his teaching career at the Murdock Academy in Beaver. Following his principalship there, he came to Branch Agricultural College as director. Under his leadership, the BAC began to emerge as southern Utah's school. Enrollment began to expand into numerous southern Utah counties, and real proselyting was established as part of the school's program. College work began to lead out over high school courses. A year after his arrival, the first diplomas were presented to those who graduated from the college division. The track and football field was constructed through an expansive program under the leadership of M.J. Urie. The gymnasium building on the north end of the knoll was built.

After leaving BAC Mr. Maughan became senior agricultural economist for the United States Department of Agriculture, a position he retained for 17 years. He left that position in 1951, when his call came to head the New England States Mission of the LDS Church. Always an active and devout member of his church, he had served in many capacities.

His ability as a forceful and forthright speaker placed him in good stead for positions of trust. He was a member of the Utah Academy of Science, Western Farm Economics Association and was listed in American Men of Science.

J. Howard Maughan married Hattie Bagley in 1921. They were the parents of three daughters and two sons.

SUU • A Heritage History • 93

muscle power they employed the department hoist and some steel cable and managed to fit the bell into the small tower. They also fashioned a mechanism whereby it could be rung. The bell rope extended from the operating crank, terminating in a loop just below the ceiling. A tall pole with a hook facilitated the ringing of the bell, which occurred every morning at 8 o'clock, reminding the townspeople and students of the hour and of the school. The bell also rang to announce every athletic contest, at home or away, in which the Branch Agricultural School was victorious. And every time the bell rang for 25 years, it reminded the townspeople of their connection with this school they had worked so hard to build and still marshalled their energies to sustain. [36]

On a Sunday morning in December, 1948, fire destroyed the roof of the building. The bell crashed to the basement and was ruined.

In the spring of 1923 the first class graduated from the Junior College division. Junior College work now became the greater emphasis, phasing down, as planned, the high school offerings to three upper years in 1923-24 and two upper grades in 1924-25.

J. Howard Maughan was indeed a man of great vitality. He loved the outdoors and began immediately to organize vigorous activities for the students. He instituted an annual pilgrimage to Zion National Park during the first year of his administration. He fostered a hiking club. And he pressed for improvement of the athletic facilities.

However, there was no slackening in the academic requirements imposed upon the students. The Forum Club was organized as a scholastic honor society which pressed for scholarly attainment. Some "special rulings" declared that stringent attention to behavior would continue to be the rule:

1. There is a special rule requiring that all students must attend regular chapel exercises. Any student who absents himself from chapel without reasonable excuse shall be liable to five percent deduction from his final grades. The committee on chapel attendance

shall act upon all excuses and make all deductions.

2. The following ruling is in effect: Ten percent will be deducted from the final grade of students who leave school before the regular closing of school preceding holidays, or who fail to return promptly upon its re-opening following the holidays, or who absent themselves on days not designated by the faculty as school holidays, or who are leaders in a "no school today" movement, or

A 1920s MILLINERY CLASS

who are absent during a more or less general movement to attend events held in town. The enforcement of this ruling is under the jurisdiction of the Attendance and Scholarship committee.

3. All students of the college will be required to be in the library between the hours of nine and three-twenty except when in classes or during the noon hour. Violators of this rule will be subject to the same rule applying to chapel absences.

There were more strictures, all equally exacting of the student. Nevertheless, Mr. Maughan hastened to organize groups that would enhance the social atmosphere. He initiated the application of a charter to the first greek letter sororities. Phi Alpha Beta became the first, followed a year later by the Vivenda Club, the forerunner to Xi Lambda Tau.

KING
HENDRICKS,
1924.

The city government that had governed the school since 1897, was altered to become a commissioner form of city government. Instead of a mayor and councilmen, the officers were now commissioners, given responsibility over finance, publicity, publications, athletics, dramatics and debating, and records. The winds of change stirred ever so slightly. Student police, magistrates and attorneys still wielded power.

It was appropriate to have a debate commission as the debating societies were a major part of student life. A council of six faculty members assisted the debaters. Each of the six meets merited a page in the annual yearbook. The debaters were most often successful, even though they aspired to meet universities in Nevada, California and Arizona.

King Hendricks, director of dramatics, produced six plays during the year of 1924. He required that aspiring actors and actresses demonstrate unusually good scholarship, before being allowed to try out for a part.

But the music department was not to be eclipsed "Never before," the *Agricola* exults, "in the history of BAC has there been such activity in the music department as this year...The band, built up of beginners, has become one of the finest college bands in Utah. A symphony orchestra, little dreamed of, is an actuality...The vocal department has also been active, presenting *The Musical Cocktail*, a variety show of Broadway themes, *Messiah* on New Year's Morn, and *The Fire Prince*, besides numerous concerts."

WILLIAM
MANNING,
1924

The *Agricola* then extolled the music faculty, W.S. Berryessa, who conducted the orchestra and the band, Ernest Oborn, piano instructor, and Ralph Hansen, instructor in violin.

Then, especially, the publication lauds the "untiring efforts, the spirit of service and the cheerful disposition of the new head of their music department, recently arrived to make his home in Cedar City, William H. Manning. Cedar City was about to discover what the students already knew — that a town and a school need have no limiting restrictions when it came to music.

The Public Service Bureau had been formed to furnish musical programs for various organizations, with the stated purpose of bringing BAC into the community life of the people of southern Utah. A chautauqua company had been organized with three groups of entertainers to tour towns considered to have less cultural advantage .

Basketball, track and field and baseball carried full teams and had successful seasons. Stock judging teams were as prestigious as athletic teams.

In addition to all these traditional activities, Branch Agricultural College became, at the behest of J. Howard Maughan, the headquarters for scouting in southern Utah. Men from the faculty staff became the scout officials. The college organized classes to train leaders, and a troop was organized among the students. They functioned as an exemplary unit, complete with "good turns." They cleaned the cemetery and chopped wood for widows.

The Ag Club remained the largest men's organization. But the BAC National Guardsmen were prestigious, perhaps because they appeared so resplendent in their uniforms.

On March 11, 1925 the school celebrated the first Founders' Day. Howard Maughan decreed that the founders of the school should be honored thereafter, during March of every year. Anyone who had once believed that Director Maughan might not dedicate his energy and vitality to his new community and the school, quietly changed his mind.

In 1926, the Branch Agricultural College City government, dearly maintained since 1897 and the days of Milton Bennion, was abandoned. The Branch Agricultural College adopted a more traditional format of student government. They now elected a student body president, vice president and secretary. They also had class representatives and managers of activities. Interestingly, they still had a full police force and a commissioner of discipline.

In 1927 the music department presented four grand operas, *Il Trovatore, Carmen, Bohemian Girl* and *La Traviata.* All the activities continued to thrive, from stock judging to debate, from baseball to scouting. The yearbook contains a special Sheep Section to boast the quality of their champion ewes and lambs. But the big news was that there was to be a new gymnasium.

The 1927 legislature appropriated $30,000 for the building of a new gymnasium. Local enthusiasm knew no bounds. The old shop-gymnasium building was notorious for its inadequacy. Not only was the plan poorly conceived, with the shop facilities downstairs and the gymnasium on the second floor, but there was insufficient seating capacity for the devoted townspeople and students who wanted to cheer their teams to victory. Often as many as 500 cheering fans crowded the periphery of the floor, making it almost impossible for the teams to play the game. Inadequate fire escapes created very real hazard.

The $30,000 was half enough to construct the building. The appropriation carried with it the implicit requirement that the local citizens must raise an equal amount to match the legislature's appropriation. The people began immediately to search for sources to provide the money. The alumni association pledged $6,000. The community borrowed $25,000 from the State Bank of Southern Utah and the Bank of Hurricane, local people placing their names on the loan, with the faith that the loan could, in fact, be paid off as all others historically had been. Fund-raising activities focused upon paying the interest on the loan.

The student association of 1927-28 agreed to eliminate debating trips in order to contribute their $500 share. The students decided to forgo having a yearbook that year. Each student promised to contribute 50 cents. The faculty sacrificed funds saved for parties, emergency loans, and any other source they could find, to make their contribution of $1,000.

The local newspaper ran an update on the progress of the gymnasium fundraising in every week's issue. The arrival of the architectural firm of Cannon and Fetzer in Cedar City was big news. The excavation was news. The contractors caught the spirit, and the work moved forward with vitality. The cornerstone ceremony was a celebration such as the town had not held since 1898.

On March 16, 1928, they danced at the first college prom in the new gymnasium, on a ballroom floor twice as large as the old one. Everyone who could walk turned out to dance.

The facility was wonderful. It would now hold all the fans at basketball games. And with their newly prestigious basketball court, it seemed appropriate that football and track facilities should be upgraded as well. Director Maughan took advantage of the momentum authorizing the project to begin immediately. The willingness of the townspeople to donate labor and again back loans justified indebtedness amounting to $25,000. They leveled the playing field, finished a new track and constructed bleachers along one side. By autumn the stadium was ready for the football season. Once again the citizenry's leap of faith had resulted in a blessed reality for BAC The next year the 1929 legislature appropriated money to redeem the outstanding notes and interest.

During the summer of 1928, as soon as the new gymnasium was complete, the old gym was converted to become the first women's dormitory. Thirty girls could now be housed above the mechanical shop, on the top floor where once the rafters rang with the rowdiness of enthusiastic players and supporters. Hazel Brockbank, a professor of education and Lillian Wight, professor of home economics, supervised the girls.

Despite the heroic efforts to rise to special occasions, the school was still running in the red. The precarious economic condition of the country and the penury of the legislature had kept the school in a position of gradually increasing debt.

In the autumn that year, 1928, a young man came, sent from the Logan campus to serve as financial officer of the Branch Agricultural College. Hazen Cooley arrived in Cedar City ready to take up the task of

TUG-O-WAR, 1926

HAZEN
COOLEY,
1928.

eliminating the deficit. Up to this point the financial accounting had been a part-time duty of an assigned faculty member. This began a career of service to the college and the community that spanned the next 46 years.

Hazen Cooley's meticulously kept files provide much insight into the affairs of Branch Agricultural College. He was frequently faced with the necessity to write to farm families whose children had not had quite enough money to pay tuition in full. "Could they send the six dollars still owing on Johnnie's tuition?" He wrote to tell a struggling father that, sorry as he was, he could not refund even a few dollars from the tuition paid by his son who had to leave school before the end of a term, "...for money reasons." [37]

The fees of the high school students continued to be a vital resource. College enrollment continued to be uncertain. Iron County School District had contracted to pay the college $105 for each enrolled high school student. The district was rarely able to pay the full amount. Some years they paid $70 per student, some years $85. But they provided a source of cash and enrollment that helped the college survive during a period when they might have failed. The Iron County School Board had as their ultimate objective the withdrawal of their students from the college and the establishment of an autonomous Iron County High School. Mr. Cooley's history records:

Director Maughan and I discussed this at great length and concluded that a college with 100 students would be in a most difficult situation. . . We asked for a meeting with the school board and discussed with them the situation that would ensue. I told them that at this time the College would be severely injured by withdrawing the students. Dr. M.J. Macfarlane was then president of the school board. He told us that it was not the desire of the board to do anything that would harm the college. The board subsequently voted to postpone any action in the withdrawal of high school students, and they also voted to increase the contract $1000 for the year, even though the enrollment was expected to decrease.

We did not know that the depression years were ahead. Prosperity was just around the corner, we were told. With the deepening of the depression, Gov. Blood asked each institution to cut their appropriation by 20 percent. Iron County School district increased their contract another $1,000 just to help out, though their enrollment had diminished.

Then the bottom dropped out of the economy. The 1933 legislature seriously considered dropping the entire appropriation to BAC. In fact, they did just that. The bill was written so that the BAC appropriation was included in that for Utah State Agricultural College. Walter K. Granger then fought for an amendment, which passed, to the effect that Utah State must appropriate at least $25,000 each year of the biennium to the Cedar City branch. And that is exactly what was allotted to BAC, which was $30,000 less than the school had been getting.

The Iron County School Board came to the rescue again and raised the amount they paid each of the following six years, as Utah State kept the appropriation awarded to Cedar City at an impossible $25,000.

Thus for 10 years the Iron County School Board postponed their desire to develop a Cedar City High School as a separate entity, while Branch Agricultural College was in financial distress.[38] Except for this help, patience, and cooperation, there may not have been a college in Cedar City after 1933.

In the spring of 1929, Director Maughan was granted sabbatical leave to attend the University of Wisconsin at Madison. It is clear that Director Maughan intended to return to Cedar City after his year at Wisconsin. Henry Oberhansley is listed as acting director in both the 1929-30 catalog and again in 1930-31. However, at the end of Howard Maughan's schooling at University of Wisconsin, he returned for a time to his ranch at Lava Hot Springs, Idaho, working with his brothers to build up the ranch. Later, he accepted a position with the United States Department of Agriculture to become Senior Agricultural Economist, stationed in Logan. He remained in that position for 17 years.

During the years while he was on leave from Branch Agricultural School, he continued to correspond with Mr. Cooley, making sure that any unfinished details were completed with impeccable integrity.

Henry Oberhansley came as acting director in 1929, intending to stay a year; he stayed 15.

He came at a time when there was continued strong community support for the school, but heavy financial duress. The great depression was just over the horizon, and many people were struggling sufficiently that sending their students to college was a luxury they could not afford.

The campus included the main building, now called the Library building; the Science building; the Mechanical Arts building, now housing the girls dorm on the top floor; the auto shop; a small boiler house and the newly constructed gymnasium. A graveled road encircled the three center buildings and crossed north of the auto shop, then continued around the rock garden between Old Main and the gymnasium, down the hill and onto Center Street. The football field had been graded, but not yet planted with grass. West of the football field stretched the barns, the sheds and the farm house.

*M*r. Oberhansley came to Branch Agricultural College from the Logan school, where he had served for 11 years. Three of those years he had served as assistant leader of the 4-H clubs in the extension division. Eight years had been spent in the education department as a professor and as head of the department. He brought with him his wife, Salome Barney, and two young sons, Billy and Victor.

He was faced with keeping strict economies in the operation of the school. In accordance with this need, and perhaps as a result of his natural administrative style, he imposed stringent requirements upon the faculty.

The faculty was a closely-knit group. Under Howard Maughan there had been an easy congeniality encompassing them. Faculty members enjoyed having their summers free, so that most were able to pick up extra work to supplement their incomes. A lively social atmosphere existed, and the cultural life of the college provided plenty of pleasurable entertainment.

Mr. Oberhansley was forced to find ways to cut costs in every area. He announced that he would require all faculty members to remain on duty throughout the summer season, outlining specific assignments they were expected to perform. Some of them chafed a bit under this ruling. George Croft, who had plans for summer work with the Utah Parks Company, was assigned to help on the farm and do repair work on the school buildings

during the summer months. The requirement altered the course of his career, for the Utah Parks Company, upon learning that he would not be available for summer work, offered him a full time position, which he accepted. His resignation was a significant loss to BAC.

Nevertheless, the director's pattern had been established. In some cases the assignments were incongruent with the personalities of the individuals. Grant Redford taught English, but was mandated to repair the ceiling in the gymnasium during the summer months. On one occasion the director called by the gymnasium to check up on the work and found that Mr. Redford had gone home to help his wife bottle peaches. Mr. Oberhansley used the incident as a symbol of "goofing off" and mentioned it in faculty meetings, to the humiliation of the errant Mr. Redford.

Henry Oberhansley did not spare himself. He took personal responsibility to mow all the lawns of the campus. Ben Cooley, who replaced Mr. Croft as teacher of mechanical arts and building trades, made all campus repairs. When LaVeve Petty Whetten came in 1939, to teach business and dance, she also worked in the Registrar's Office, and in free moments redecorated her small office. She remembers doing the painting herself, the color: Bastow green.

Due to the harsh economic conditions, Director Oberhansley also strived to make the most of all his resources. Faculty members were encouraged, when they had to leave the campus between the hours of 8 a.m. and 5 p.m., to leave a note on Mr. Oberhansley's desk, telling him where they had gone, why they had gone, and when they would return. Members of the faculty were required to attend every student dance. The director checked, and if faculty members were missing, it was important to have a good excuse. Eddie Peterson had set Friday, 11th of February as his wedding day, but found that the director would not give him permission to be gone on Friday. Students, hearing of his dilemma, came to his aid. They suggested he quietly go ahead with his trip to Logan for his wedding and promised to see that nothing would happen that would call attention to his absence. [39]

Getting more work from fewer people did not make up for the devastation of the 1933

HENRY OBERHANSLEY

legislature. Those who were fortunate enough to have positions, had to take significant salary cuts of 20 to 25 percent. In 1931-32 Hazen Cooley's salary was $2,600 a year. He took a sabbatical leave the next year and returned in 1933 to a yearly salary of $1,900. All salaries were cut at the same proportion. [40]

Funding from the legislature in 1928-29 had totalled $55,075.27. In 1933-34 the appropriation fell to $27,870.91, but enrollment had jumped from 113 in 1928-29 to 255 in 1933. Mr. Oberhansley faced times of genuine crisis.

On the morning of May 8, 1931, fire began to smolder in the building which housed the mechanical arts shop and the girls' dormitory. Someone sounded the alarm. The fire department arrived and expeditiously hooked up the hoses, only to discover that water had not yet been turned into the hydrants on campus since the winter. By the time the firemen had connected with the hydrants on College avenue and had strung hoses across the street and up the hill, the fire was out of control. It was impossible to save the structure. The girls had time to carry out their treasures, and help arrived to save some of the furnishings. Except for a few small tools, the valuable machinery in the shop downstairs was lost. [41] For the remainder of the year, the girls who had been living in the building moved to the women's physical education area of the new gymnasium.

Speculation circulated that one of the girls had left an "electric flat iron charged," but the cause of the blaze was never definitely determined. The newspaper reported that 1,500 people watched the blaze and that charred

HENRY E. OBERHANSLEY
1885-1945

Henry E. Oberhansley served as director for 15 years. The span of his leadership was brought to a sudden close by his untimely death in April of 1945. Dr. Oberhansley's era included the greatest single change in the growth of the school to that point: the complete separation of the high school division from the College. Many BAC supporters looked upon the move with great trepidation, but were grateful to acknowledge later, that the decision had paid sustantive dividends to the college and to Cedar City.

Conscientious and untiring in his devotion to his work, Director Oberhansley began a serious effort to strengthen the bond between BAC and its mother institution, Utah State Agricultural College. Through his cooperative strivings the Vocational Education program of BAC was advanced in practical ways, courses in the curriculum of the southern school being brought into parallel with those at USAC. Mr. Oberhansley also initiated the third college year in agriculture and furthered the landscaping program of the campus. His marked ability as a trusted financeer added stability to the financial position of the school.

This director is perhaps best remembered for his great concern for the professional stewardship of faculty members—that they were diligent in the classroom, careful in personal assignments and fully accountable for the nurturing of their students. Immaculate of appearance himself, he required good grooming of those with whom he worked. His many kindnesses to students who had to work to finance their schooling were known only to a few close friends. His utter devotion to his young son, Billy, who died during his term as director, was widely and warmly noted in the community.

Director and Mrs. Oberhansley established many cultural programs on the campus, including the Ladies Faculty Club, with its annual Spring Luncheon, and the reception for graduates.

Born in Payson, Utah, in April of 1885, Oberhansley assumed his first teaching assignments in Payson and Provo schools, before serving as principal of Parowan High School from 1916 to 1918. The following year he joined the faculty of USAC, where he was assigned briefly as assistant director of Boys' and Girls' Clubs in the Extension Division, but soon became a professor in the department of education. He closed his eight year stint there as head of that department, leaving in 1930 to complete his master's degree at the University of California.

As a citizen of Cedar City, Henry Oberhansley was prominent in numerous civic groups, serving as president of the Rotary Club, director of the Chamber of Commerce and on the central committee of the coordinating council, and chairman of the Iron County Red Cross. In business circles the director was president of Cedar City Home Building Society and director of the Cedar City Finance Company. He participated in the Utah's Citizens' Commission on National Defense and in post-war planning affairs on a statewide level.

Henry E. and Salome Barney Oberhansley were the parents of two sons.

shingles were carried by the wind and found as far as three blocks from the campus.

Fortunately, the building was fully insured. By July 8 a contract had been awarded to Hyrum Kunz, a local contractor, to construct a new mechanical arts building, south of the auto shop. A few days after school began, September 8, 1931, the new building was ready for occupancy.

Whether the new shop facility inspired more innovative ways to teach building arts, or whether C. B. Cooley had already decided upon his creative course, it is not clear. But he began a method of teaching building skills that involved the actual construction of a home, from planning to completion. He started with an ambitious project. In 1932, Mr. Cooley and the young men in his classes began to build a residence for the directors of the school. Called the Directors Cottage, the finished product was a lovely, two-story, Cape Cod-style home, nestled among the pines on the campus, just east of the three main buildings. Mr. Oberhansley gladly moved his family into the new home at the beginning of the 1933 school year.

Young building-trades students went away from the year's experience feeling capable from their house building adventure. Many of them became the contractors and builders who constructed the next generation of southern Utah homes.

From that beginning, the building-trades classes, under C.B. Cooley's direction, constructed a house each year. The college conducted auctions of the completed houses, which one by one became the homes of prominent and respected townspeople. After World War II, when surplus buildings became available, the building and trades students became a valuable resource. They organized into teams which helped to bring war surplus buildings onto the campus and remodel them to fit the needs of the college.

Faculty members were regularly granted sabbatical leave to pursue advanced studies. There was even a fund, called the Faculty Loan Fund, available to help struggling faculty members to realize their goals of higher degrees. Correspondence of the time reveals

DIRECTOR'S COTTAGE, 1933

that the stresses of economic struggles were very real in the lives of teachers, trying to become more proficient in their disciplines. Hazen Cooley received letter after letter, requesting that he "hold" a loan payment check, until later in the month, or until months later. Everywhere are evidences that financial stress was a fact of their lives.

Through all the years of the '30s the college struggled. The great depression gripped the nation and the school. With the continued cooperation of the school district, high school students swelled the numbers to a respectable size. Without them there would have been an impossibly small student body.

The school and the town were sustained in their spirits by the extraordinary quality of cultural bright spots that flowed from the college. However grim the times, there were operas and plays, there were dance programs and art exhibits, there were evenings of chamber music and grand orchestra and band concerts.

Roy Halversen had arrived in 1927, to join William Manning in the music department. Though he left again in 1929, to spend a romantic year in Berlin with his newly-wedded bride, Maude Macfarlane, he returned in 1930 to form the magic team of Manning and Halversen. Their prolific production of musical events is astonishing. A gladly receptive community found their lives graced with joyful activity in the midst of economic deprivation.

The yearbook of 1932 declares:

It was said three years ago when the music department presented five standard grand operas in one week, that the department had

C.B. COOLEY, 1940.

MARY
BASTOW,
1928

reached its peak of achievement. But those who had such thoughts have ample cause to think again. This has been one of the most fruitful years we have ever enjoyed. The Violin Choir of 15 violins has graced us with the classics. The orchestra has surpassed anything it has ever done. The band is bigger and better than ever. The greatest achievements have been the wonderful evenings of chamber music presented by the String Quartet and the Sunday afternoons with the Instrumental Trio. The Chorus and the Male Quartet, the Glee Clubs and the Mixed Quartets have delighted audiences at home and abroad in surrounding towns and have been a credit to their teachers and their school.

Mary L. Bastow had come in 1929, immediately becoming the community authority on all that was beautiful and in good taste, as well as the driving force behind brightening up the drabness she found on College Hill. In the years that followed, Mary L. had her finger in everything. People who built new homes would not have thought of choosing colors for their rooms without consultation with Miss Bastow. People designing a garden waited until she could help with the decision on where to plant the row of lilacs. She told A.J. Morris, director of the dairy, that he ought never to wear green; it made his complexion sallow. A young woman with an inferiority complex about her flaming red hair was used every day in class as an example of beautiful coloring, until by her own admission, she believed she was beautiful. Mary L. Bastow added color to the community in a myriad of wonderful ways. [41]

ROY
HALVERSEN,
1928

*I*n 1936 a disquieting blow fell upon the school. The State Department of Education increased the minimum requirement for teacher certification to a bachelor's degree. The prized teacher training program was taken from Branch Agricultural College. Once again the final year of training for teachers had to be taken at Logan. In that same year the Board of Trustees did authorize that the third year in agriculture could be completed at BAC.

Despite the hurdles a new hope for imminent success was kindling. Little by little appropriation of funds from the legislature edged back upward, until by 1939-1940 it had almost reached the point it had been 10 years before. Through intensive proselyting efforts and outreach programs, student enrollment had also begun to increase. In 1939-40, college enrollment stood at 300. The administration judged that at last the Branch Agricultural College could soon survive without the sacrifice of the Iron County Schools. That year the 10th grade was taken from the College.

It was the beginning of a time of great vitality. They added the women's residence hall which had been sorely needed. Zoe Palmer, serving as dean of women, worked untiringly to make the dorm a reality. Girls moved into the new facility in September, 1939, eight years after fire had destroyed the first dormitory. C.B. Cooley's building trades classes focused efforts upon a men's residence complex, adding a few units each year.

Greek letter organizations multiplied. Two sororities and three fraternities were active and engaged in service and social affairs.

Young Edwin L Peterson, dean of men, supervised the Greeks. He also coached the high school in football, basketball and track. At

ZOE PALMER, 1939

EDWIN L. PETERSON

LAVEVE PETTY, 1939

WOMEN'S DORMITORY, 1939

the same time he taught three high school classes and three college classes. Double and triple duty was an accepted pattern for every faculty member.

College athletics was thriving. LaVeve Petty established a popular women's intramural program which involved almost every girl. Men's intramurals were as fiercely competitive as the teams that fought for victory against neighboring schools. "Tuff" Linford led the intramural sports, as well as league basketball and football.

The constant round of concerts, operas, plays and dance programs kept pace with athletics and made life vibrant and alive for the community and the college.

In 1940-41 the 11th grade high school class left BAC to become the junior class of Cedar City High School. The College, though ever so slightly wobbly, seemed at last ready to move forward without the sustaining hand of the Iron County Schools. The academic programs were strong. The agriculture and normal programs were both sustaining. Extracurricular and athletic programs were thriving and the community centered on them with pride. The school looked forward to a whole new era of prosperity.

Two months later, on December 7, 1941, the Japanese Air Force attacked Pearl Harbor. The United States was at war. The draft was initiated and young men left for military service. BAC enrollment dropped to 85 students, of which only 11 were men. This new crisis again engendered the entirely reasonable fear that the college might not survive after all.

Walter K. Granger was member of Congress, serving in the United States House of Representatives. He again proved to be the right man at the right place at the right time.

At the outbreak of the war, the Army Air

Corps needed more training facilities for the large increases in recruits. Rep. Granger was a member of the Congressional Military Committee. He suggested to the Air Corps that they investigate the Branch Agricultural College for the establishment of an Air Corps College Training Detachment. Without such a recommendation, such a small place as Cedar City would not have come to their attention.

Rep. Granger then alerted the people of the area to the things the Air Corps would need in such a facility. The people hastened to prepare. When an investigating team from the Air Corps visited Cedar City there was a well prepared presentation awaiting them. The impressive El Escalante Hotel was available for housing, supplemented by other facilities of the Utah Parks Company. The Iron County Hospital was alert and ready to offer health care. The Cedar City Airport was nearby, sufficient for their needs, and the changeable weather promised to give young pilots varied experience. Most impressive was the amazing fact that the Board of Trustees had authorized for the college a unit of pilot training in February, 1940, almost two years before. The college was ready with a superb faculty, eager to provide the needed educational facilities.

FOOTBALL, 1940

U.S. REP.
WALTER K.
GRANGER

The committee investigated facilities from California to Montana. Their report was that they had found nothing to compare with what awaited them in Cedar City.

As a result of Rep. Granger's quick thinking and the unified effort of the community, the 316th Army Air Corps Training Detachment was established at Cedar City at the Branch Agricultural College. The permanent party personnel arrived in Cedar City, in February, 1943 to prepare. On March 5, 1943 the first 300 pre-flight aviation students arrived in Cedar City. The students took a stiff five-month military indoctrination academic course. During the academic portion of their course they studied mathematics, physics, history, geography, English, medical aid and civil aeronautics and regulations. During the last month the students were given ten hours of flying in the cockpit of a 75 H.P. aircraft. After the pre-flight training in Cedar City, the students were transferred to bases in California, where they were classified as navigators, bombardiers, or pursuit pilots.

When the program closed June 30, 1944, 2,276 cadets had been trained at BAC. General M.F. Scanlon of the Army Air Corps Western Flying Command wrote Director Oberhansley:

CADETS,
EL
ESCALANTE

It has been a most satisfying experience to me, personally, to witness the outstanding service you have rendered our Air Arm. I desire that you and your faculty claim your just share of credit for the present success of our combat air forces. [43]

The faculty and administration rallied to the call. Because the regular enrollment was so diminished, most of the faculty were shifted to the air crew training program and became the training force for the cadets. Roy Halversen, whose string programs suffered by the departure of so many students, became director of academics for the cadet training. The teachers and administrators threw themselves into the accelerated program with zeal, teaching long hours, and adjusting the content of their classes to meet the needs of the cadets.

The student body adjusted well. Their yearbook of 1943 states: The war has taken over BAC and the B.A.C. has taken over the war." Actually the adjustment of the student body was unavoidable. The men of BAC had gone away to serve in other branches of the military and the girls did all they could to make the cadets feel welcome in this place, which one former cadet reported seemed to them a one horse town. [44]

The cadets constituted a disciplined presence. Classes began at 7 a.m. They marched from their billeting at The El Escalante Hotel and the Utah Parks Company's east garage, singing as they marched in formation, in the early morning darkness.

Their presence in the town was a constant reminder that the nation was at war, and the townspeople responded with patriotic zeal, doing all they could to help the cadets to feel welcome. The military men entered in to the social life provided for them and provided some of their own.

The people of Cedar City established a unit of the U.S.O., staffed by volunteers who gathered in the cadets whenever possible. They organized frequent open air dances which gave ample opportunity for local girls to meet the airmen, now far from their homes. Marriages naturally resulted, and from those marriages came prominent Cedar City families of the next generation. Robert Avedisian, a cadet far from home and family, remembered that the Utah Parks Company loaned him tables, lamps and a bed, to furnish the small apartment to which he brought his bride, Lazon Woolsey, a Cedar City girl he had met at a dance. It was a kindness repeated many times in many forms. [45]

United States Savings Bond rallies united the talents of the town and the capacities of the cadets in presenting spirited programs, the object of which was to add money to the effort. The cadre of cadets included some tal-

ented musicians, who wrote and performed original songs that lamented their loneliness for home and friends and extolled the virtues of the town that had adopted them.

> *When it's lights out in Cedar City,*
> *I'm thinking of you, Sweetheart,*
> *When the cares of the day,*
> *Seem miles and miles away,*
> *And there's only you in my heart.*
> *When night falls in Cedar City,*
> *And the mountains fade from view,*
> *I hope and pray the day has been a happy*
> *one for you* [46]

The Air Corps program was a financial wind-fall for Branch Agricultural College. The salaries of the faculty who taught the cadets, were paid by the federal government, leaving that portion of the state appropriation to be used for other purposes.

And it came at a wonderful time. Extensive mountain grazing property located in the Cedar Canyon-Cedar Mountain area had just been made available to the College by Kumen Jones, who had accumulated the land over many years. The college again borrowed money—this time to obtain the property which would augment their experimental range and grazing program. By the end of the cadet training program, enough had been saved of the state appropriation to pay off the notes covering the purchase of the Mountain Ranch and the Valley Farm. Gov. Herbert Maw gave special permission for the use of what seemed to them a miraculous surplus.

By June 30, 1944, the cadets were gone. They had impacted the lives of the people of the town. But most important, they had impacted the school. Once again the school had survived a crisis and was saved.

The *Agricola* of 1945 is a very thin book. The sophomore class numbered 29. Of that number five were men. The freshman class consisted of 53 students. There were 10 freshmen men. Somehow, with 15 men in the whole school, they managed to field a basketball team. Since most of them had never played before, they were none too proficient. But that didn't matter much, since the war made competition between schools impossible. The Home Economics Club was active; the Ag Club no longer existed. Girls' intramurals continued. The students held dinners. No dances. The "stiff-upper-lip" was evident, but college life at Branch Agricultural College carried on.

Then Director Oberhansley died. On Thursday, April 11, 1945, Henry Oberhansley left his office, not feeling well. He rested at home during the day, intending to see his physician the next morning. But the next day the college and the community awakened to the distressing news that Mr. Oberhansley had died quietly in his sleep, during the night. The cause of his death was listed as a heart attack.

Surely the 15 years of his service had been some of the most dramatic and stressful. He had weathered storms of many varieties. He held tight the reins while he steered the school through the threat of extinction that arose time after time. He had seen her through the great depression, a major war, a devastating fire, and extensive campus construction. The roller coaster ride of his years as administrator must certainly have taken a toll. There had also been personal sorrows to endure. A child, Billy, suffered a chronic illness and died while his father served as director. Victor, the only other child of the Oberhansleys, was serving in the Pacific war zone at the time that Henry Oberhansley died. Mrs. Oberhansley left Cedar City and many friends, after 15 years, stunned by the sudden change in the course of her life.

His unexpected death was a shock to the town and the college. Parley P. Dalley was asked to assume responsibilities of interim director, and he agreed to serve until a new director could be appointed.

Parley Pratt Dalley was a wonderful choice. He had come to teach at Branch Normal School in 1909, and had attended as a student some years before that. By 1945, when he accepted the assignment as acting director, he had been a faculty member for 37 years. After his student days at Branch Normal School, Dalley had gone away to gain a degree at the University of Utah and returned to teach science. Most of those years he had served as head of the science department. No other person associated with the school had had such a long and illustrious history connected with the college.

Commencement was less than a month away. Plans for a full week of cultural events, teas and receptions had been formulated, but were still tentative. It was all familiar to him, since he had participated in many graduations, but now he had to finish his teaching and become the director at the same time. He rose to the occasion and life moved on for a sobered, but resolute college community.

They went ahead with the annual "A Day," during which the students and faculty "housecleaned" the whole campus including all the buildings. Then, because the student body was so small that year, all students were invited to go along on the annual Zion Canyon two-day trek. It was a tradition usually reserved for sophomores, but the war years had diminished their numbers so greatly that the sophomores needed the freshman class to make it a party.

The students took their annual exchange program to Dixie College, then took the long way home and presented it to the Hurricane High School student body. The sophomore class observed their annual "sluff day", and failed to show up for classes. A feeling of normalcy returned.

At the end of the graduation exercises on Friday, May 18, 1945, school closed. Students from out of town returned home. And the townspeople waited while the Board of Trustees met.

They waited and speculated. Several local names were on the list of possible new leaders for the school. Ianthus Wright had just become superintendent of Iron County Schools and people thought he might be interested. Burns Finlinson,

dean of students, a popular teacher and head of the social science department, was mentioned. Some conjectured that Gustive O. Larson, director of the LDS Institute, might be chosen.

It had been announced that President Franklin S. Harris, newly appointed president of the Utah State Agricultural College at Logan, had recommended H. Wayne Driggs, associate professor of English at Brigham Young University. Some of the trustees expressed astonishment at the suggestion. "Why would you present an English professor to be head of an agricultural college?" President Harris replied, "The man's field of study is not the important factor. You don't need an agriculturalist; what you need is an administrator. This young man has administrative abilities."[47] On Friday, when the trustees emerged from their meeting, the decision was announced. H. Wayne Driggs would become the director of Branch Agricultural College.

Dr. H. Wayne Driggs had lived in Cedar City before. As a very young child he had resided in Cedar City with his parents, while his father, Howard R. Driggs, taught at Branch Normal School. A graduate of the University of Utah, he received his doctorate from New York University. After teaching at New York University, he headed the English Department at Hofstra College at Hempstead, Long Island. He had worked at Brigham Young University under Dr. Franklin Harris, who recognized his superb qualifications for the assignment.

He was the most highly educated of the men who had come, to this point, to lead the school—the first who had already earned a doctorate. And of some significance is the fact that he was the first, since J. Reuben Clark, who had come without an already established link to the mother institution.

Dr. Driggs was committed to a summer professorship at the University of Wyoming which did not end until August. His arrival to take up his duties was delayed until he had fulfilled that obligation and preparations for the fall term fell upon acting director Dalley, who continued to function well.

PARLEY P. DALLEY, 1945

When he arrived in August, the conditions awaiting Director Driggs were vastly different than those faced by his predecessor, Henry Oberhansley. The war was ending; young men and women who had interrupted their education to fight the war were beginning to return. The government had established funding for educating these young warriors under the G.I. Bill of Rights. For the first time, proselyting efforts were not a primary concern. There would be a burgeoning enrollment.

The newspaper carried the customary advertisement, a plea for people to open their homes to make room for the returning students, just as it had every year since the beginnings. But this year there was a greater urgency.

When H. Wayne and Elizabeth Swenson Driggs arrived in Cedar City, with their four young sons, they had a home waiting. The Director's Cottage was a pleasant place and fitted their family. But immediately Dr. Driggs was faced with the concern that he had more students arriving from out of town than had ever before come to the college, and his facilities for housing them were woefully inadequate.

The men's dormitory, down the hill from the main buildings, had been constructed little by little in an ever-evolving process. Building trades students under the direction of C.B. Cooley, had completed sufficient units to

DR. HOWARD
WAYNE DRIGGS

house approximately 48 men and a supervising family, but returning veterans would soon arrive, some of them bringing their families. The housing shortage was a critical stumbling block.

The enlargement of the women's dormitory had been planned for some time, but war priorities had postponed it. Now Dr. Driggs has-

tened to find a way of financing the project. As early as September 1945, he had announced his intention to expand the building, and had begun contacting banks and bankers. The loan would be self-liquidating, but time was a crucial element. So he went to his home town bank in Mt. Pleasant to borrow part of the money. In November, C.B. Cooley was in Salt Lake City working out final plans.

MEN'S
DORM,
1945

Student housing was not the only crucial issue. Expanded space for common areas, faculty housing and married student housing were needed as quickly as possible. Though the need was real, the problem of insufficient funding was an ever-present reality.

One advantage Director Driggs found as he began his work was that his faculty was accustomed to extraordinary effort and were totally committed to doing things not specified in their employment contracts. [48] The tradition of struggle made it natural to them to be involved in every aspect of the school. They expected to paint their own offices and sew the draperies for them. They expected to help in planting shrubbery and flowers to beautify the place. They expected to spend their summers traveling to persuade students to attend BAC. They expected to participate in whatever project or effort would further the cause. Now, in early 1946, they were about to embark on an amazing series of projects that would change the face of the campus and enable the beginning of an era of expansion.

In the desert north and west of Delta, at a lonely place called Topaz, was a sad little compound of hastily built structures–grim reminders of the tragic outgrowths of war.

*I*n June, 1942, six months after the beginning of the war with Japan, the United States government had begun the construction of a Japanese internment camp. Consisting of hundreds of sterile buildings, the site included blocks of housing, mess halls, offices and schools. To this western desert place were brought thousands of people of Japanese descent, the children of whom were citizens of the United States. It was a shameful action, borne of war-time hysteria and prejudice. But the camp was active and functioned as a place of internment until 1945 when the war ended.

As the unfortunate folks were released to rebuild their lives, the buildings became available and quickly obtainable for those institutions who acted with dispatch.

The administration and faculty of Branch Agricultural College were on their toes.

They made trips to Topaz to assess the available resources and to bargain for them. Once the arrangements were made, they teamed up to help move the buildings to the campus and to reconstruct them.

Dr. McRay Cloward, who was manager of housing at the time, remembers:

Faculty and staff cleaned and painted buildings and assisted in transporting war-surplus materials, furniture and even buildings from military bases and from Topaz, the Japanese Relocation Center near Delta, Utah.

I made a number of trips to Topaz with Vic Davis, Eugene Hardy, Reid Cox, Hazen Cooley and Ed Matheson. Cooley, secretary and treasurer of the college, worked many hours overtime on his regular job but still found time to go on some of those trips... Victor (Vic) Davis always went along as the truck driver and chief mechanic for the "Old Mack" truck, which was never entirely free of mechanical breakdowns.

On one particular trip, the truck sputtered a couple of times and then quit entirely near the town of Fillmore. This happened to be one of the most important trips because the carpets and furniture from one large dormitory had been assigned to the college for pick-up. When "Old Mack" was running again a week later, we were almost too late. Much to our disappointment, others had been there ahead of us and had taken many of the choice items...We did bring back a truck load of greatly needed furniture, mattresses, a few small carpets and a variety of miscellaneous items. [49]

One notable acquisition became the "Chicken Coops," more properly known as staff housing. The undignified designation flowed from their unimaginative design. These remnants of Topaz were eight small apartments moved onto the southeast corner of the campus, and provided homes for an ever-changing procession of young faculty and staff families for many years. The residents poured concrete sidewalks, planted the lawns and shrubbery and paid $28 a month rental fee.

In July, 1946, The *Iron County Record* announced the purchase of 50 war-surplus trailer houses from St. Johns military base near Tooele, Utah. The contract for moving them to Cedar City and setting them up, called for the completion of the trailer village before the end of August. Plumbing and sewer construction was to be accomplished by the college. That was not overly complicated, since two central buildings contained all laundry, bath, and shower facilities. The trailers of "Trailer Town" had no running water. They were heated by open-fire oil stoves, fueled by 55-gallon oil drums placed at the end of each box-like structure. Safety was apparently not a serious concern. It has been noted that residents were identifiable to their classmates, by the odor of the fuel oil that attended them. The trailers were equipped with ice boxes, large

STAFF HOUSES, OR 'CHICKEN COOPS'

TRAILER TOWN, 1946

enough to accommodate a 25-pound block of ice, and a small amount of food, and a tiny two burner hot-plate type stove for cooking. [50] Trailer Town became home for 50 student families or groups of four single students.

Men's dormitory facilities were expanded by moving in from Topaz a three-wing barracks type building called Dorm B, which housed nearly a hundred men students and two supervisory faculty families. The presence of the faculty families was simply another extracurricular responsibility, accepted by the teachers as a logical part of their commitment. It also gave them a place to live in a town that was severely limited in housing possibilities.

The flood of new students taxed the resources of space and personnel. The return of some young teachers as they were released from military assignments, helped create the balance. Coach Nelson "Ty" Tydings returned from naval air service to assist in physical education and competitive athletics, and Edwin L. Peterson came back from army and air corps assignments in the Panama Canal Zone, Texas and Arizona. Peterson returned to the social science department and to head public relations for the school. Young Twain Tippetts, released from the U.S. Navy, came as a new faculty member to teach drama and speech. A few months later popular teacher William "Pa" Manning, returned from Logan, where he had been transferred when enrollment fell so abysmally, at the beginning of the war.

*I*t was, indeed, the largest enrollment in the history of the school. In December 1946 Elva Oldroyd, registrar, announced that enrollment had passed the 400 mark. The hoped for enrollment for 1947 was 500 students. This was to be the Jubilee Year. Fifty years since the establishment of the Branch Normal School was a significant anniversary

and it was planned to be a great celebration.

There was private celebration in the hearts of the women students who had endured the bleak social life of the war years. The ratio of men to women students reversed and now stood at 325 men to 115 women. Even with the number of men students who were married, prospects were more positive for single young women.

Extra-curricular activities began to thrive again. With the added numbers of students there was need for expansion of organizations that fostered sociability. Sororities and fraternities that had floundered and failed during the war years were now reorganized. These included the Xi Lambda Tau, Chi Theta Iota, Phi Sigma Xi, and Sigma Kappa Rho. New ones were initiated: Iota Iota, Gamma Psi Upsilon, Tau Epsilon and Zeta Nu. Competitive assemblies and intramural sports were a vital part of campus life.

Service organizations, Intercollegiate Knights and Spurs, were established. There were county clubs, i.e. the Millard Club, the Garfield Club, gathering together students from their respective home areas. The Ag Club flourished again, as did the Home Economics Club. Myriad new organizations bespoke the vitality of a growing school.

The official symbol was changed from "Aggies," and the teams began to be called "Broncos." It was, perhaps, the first evidence of a stirring of desire for independence from the mother school.

The growing student body gave rise to great need for a student center. Once again the solution came from Topaz. An office building was dismantled, hauled home and reassembled to become a cafeteria, a book store, student body offices and a large recreation space. Called "The Commons," it housed the staffs of the yearbook and the newspaper and brought relief from some of the inevitable overcrowding of the main classroom buildings. The construction effort was modest and quiet, managed "in house" and overseen by Reid Cox, whose responsibilities were titled "director of repairs." C.B. Cooley used his corps of students as well as other young people who wanted work.

Vitality surged through the community as well as the school. And in keeping with long-established tradition, businesses and towns-

XI LAMBDA TAU ASSEMBLY, 1950. BACK: BONNIE STEPHENSON, VIRGINIA THORLEY, ZOE PORTER. IN TUB: CAROLYN YOUNG.

people did everything they could to connect with the school in helpful ways. The "new" gymnasium was becoming highly inadequate, both as a ballroom and as a basketball court. The elegant Hotel El Escalante, newly re-opened after the war, became the site of many of the social activities of the school. Formal balls and sorority teas were almost always held at the more prestigious site.

The year 1947 was especially significant for the state of Utah. It marked 100 years from the coming of the first settlers to establish a society west of the Rocky Mountains. And it was the 50th anniversary of the founding of Branch Normal School. Cedar City people celebrated their great events and they called this year the Golden Jubilee.

May was targeted for the week-long observance, which included a three-night run of the Puccini opera, *La Boheme*, commence-

ment activities and an original Golden Jubilee pageant, "College Cavalcade."

The pageant was a memorable conclusion. The re-enactment of the founding and progress of the school moved through five separate episodes. It was an effective production, authored by Fae Decker Dix and Dr. Wayne Driggs. It flowed with beautiful original poetry recited by J. H. Plummer as lyric narrator, Emron Jensen as the epic narrator and a full contingent of choral readers. The site of the presentation was the football field with the audience seated on bleachers along the sides of the stadium. Faculty and staff spared no effort to make it a fitting commemoration. [51] Changing so many scenes presented a challenge, which was met in an ingenious manner. Young Twain Tippetts had seen a production in which water sprayed upwards in a magical silver curtain, shielding the audience from the bustle of on-stage arrangements. As the production

HOTEL EL ESCALANTE, 1946

director he determined to engineer the effect for the pageant. It took the cooperation of the city fire department, with a truck that could pump water at high pressure through long lengths of pipes of decreasing diameter, thus creating an even height with the silvery streams.

Day after day the firemen came to practice their part, until it worked perfectly. And the final presentation did proceed perfectly except for one small moment that went awry. Someone accidentally nudged a length of pipe, turning the spray toward the audience seated on the bleachers, and causing a brief interruption in the flow of the production. Those unfortunate folks, seated in the best seats of the first few rows, were thoroughly dampened by the force of the cold water. The production paused while they dried off the best they could, recovered their dignity and

STUDENT CENTER, CIRCA TOPAZ.
WOMEN'S DORM IN BACKGROUND.

MISS UTAH, 1947   MISS IRON COUNTY, 1947

the show could go on.

Each of the five episodes portrayed an era of the history of the institution and paid tribute to the pioneers who had settled the state and those who founded the school:[52]

> *Long have the quivering winds of Time*
> *Borne mute eloquence of your story,*
> *Long have the shimmering sands of Ox-*
> *trekked prairies*
> *Hummed the vibrant murmur of your*
> *blood-wracked trail.*
> *Yours the faith of saints,*
> *And faith in your children's children —*
> *And we are they!*
> *How came you by this great abiding love*
> *Of future generations?*

The pageant concluded with a grand procession led by royalty, for the school could boast two queens, June Decker as Miss Iron County and Donna Southwick as Miss Utah.

Following were graduates in caps and gowns and faculty in academic robes, displaying the colors of their disciplines: maize for agriculture; golden yellow for science; light blue for education; orange for engineering; white for arts and letters, history, english and languages; pink for music; russett for forestry; light brown for commerce; sage green for physical education; copper for home economics and vocational education.

As the procession finished, the chorus swelled softly into "Lift Thine Eyes," the lights faded and the voice of the lyric narrator spoke the final prayer:

> *Lend us thy hand in blessing, God,*
> *Keep our hearts humble,*
> *For through thy grace we know much*
> *good,*
> *Commit our ways and all our trust to thee,*
> *Lord—teach us how to share the good we*
> *know,*

> *And live with gratitude forever in our*
> *hearts,*
> *Lifting our eyes bravely to the conquest!*
> *Amen.*

It was good timing for the people to receive a reminder of their debt of deep gratitude. There loomed immediately ahead another difficult demand.

Nothing could disguise the fact that the gymnasium, which the town had so nobly supported during its construction only a few years before, was hopelessly obsolete. It could hold neither the expanding student body, nor the enthusiastic local fans. There were 500 narrow bleacher seats. 250 were allotted for students and there was always a scramble for those. The 200 season tickets that were available to the townspeople were allotted by priority drawings.

Again, two advantages meshed to create the solution. The people of the town marshalled forces. The Chamber of Commerce organized a Fieldhouse Committee and began gathering contributions for the project, pledging themselves to accomplish the excavation phase of the process. And, glittering in the sunshine of the desert, the Topaz High School gymnasium stood abandoned. Its iron girder skeleton and full basketball court with hardwood floors waited, for some creative souls, not fearful of the enormous task of dismantling, removal and reconstruction. The committee obtained the building, the federal government aided in the actual dismantling and transporting of the parts to Cedar City.

The state allotted $30,000 of the estimated $60,000. The Southern Utah Livestock Association, realizing that the building could also furnish needed livestock show space, were quick to join the effort. The city and the school district joined in.

Fred Markham, an architect from Provo, was engaged to find ways that the building could be re-designed to facilitate everything from livestock shows to concerts and athletic events. It would seat 3,000 people. It would be the largest building in southern Utah.

By December, 1947, the Topaz salvage had been transported to Cedar City. Civic groups were raising funds, and the project was attended by an air of excited commitment. On April 8, 1948, 1,500 people gathered for the groundbreaking. Gov. Herbert Maw, piloting his own plane, had come to town to turn the first spade of earth. Groundbreak-

WAR
MEMORIAL
FIELDHOUSE,
1948

ing for the new heating plant was slated for the same day.

The governor was high in his praise for the school and the community, saying:

No school has received less from the state for building purposes than has the BAC, yet the school has continued to grow because the people of the community have provided needed buildings through their own efforts.[53]

It was well-earned acknowledgement, and as if to confirm the truth of the governor's statement, Dr. Driggs presented him with a check for $17,000 from funds appropriated from the Southern Utah Livestock Association and from the Iron County School District, to be used in the completion of the new fieldhouse.

Gov. Maw responded by pledging his support to the continued growth of the Branch Agricultural College, a declaration gladly received, since the fieldhouse was not the only expansion effort in the minds of the people on the campus and in the town.

There was still the cumbersome requirement placed upon students at Branch Agricultural College, of going north to finish school. The awarding of a bachelors degree, and the fourth year of training was still withheld. There was really only one explanation. The student body of the Logan school was augmented significantly by transferring students, exactly as had been the case with the University of Utah and the Branch Normal School.

The students and the community, indeed the whole southern Utah area, chafed under the imposition. Dr. Driggs had proposed the expansion, indeed had plead with the legislature for the expansion. The Cedar City Chamber of Commerce had requested that the governor intervene. In August of 1947, Gov. Herbert Maw had come to Cedar City, and in a speech before the Chamber of Commerce had stated that he was heartily in favor of the proposition:

The need for this expansion is apparent. The local school is in a position to provide the service, and the young people of the southern part of the state should be given the same privileges of continuing their studies as are the young people of the more thickly populated northern sections. Certainly if Utah is to have another four year institution, southern Utah is the place for it.[54]

It was really a decision of the Board of Trustees of the Utah State Agricultural College. The legislation changing the college to BAC and to the governance of the USAC, was amazingly broad. It enabled the teaching of any courses taught at Logan. There was, however, the matter of the proprietary interests. A four-year program at Cedar City would rob the northern campus of transfer students from all the junior colleges in the southern part of the state, as well as the natural transfers from BAC.

An active committee, headed by Warren Bulloch, then president of the Cedar City Chamber of Commerce, was hard at work. They contacted school superintendents of surrounding counties, who most keenly felt the need for teachers trained and ready to serve in their schools. The superintendents responded with written pleas for the action. They enlisted the help of anyone whom they felt could lend support.

By the time the presentation was ready it was a bulky 26-page document containing letters and signatures from every organization in the southern part of the state. Everyone from members of school boards and city councils to virtually every civic club, to the ladies auxiliary of the Veterans of Foreign Wars had made a statement regarding the need for the four-year degree in education to be granted at BAC.

*P*ressure on the Board of Trustees mounted. In January, 1948, 15 counties of southern and eastern Utah, through the Associated Civic Clubs, adopted a resolution calling for expansion of the academic program at Branch Agricultural College, to include the granting of degrees in elementary education. Present at the conference was Secretary of State Heber Bennion, who also served on the Board of Trustees of the Utah State Agricultural College. He promised to "study" the proposition when it came before the board.

When a Logan newspaper reported Gov. Maw's address to a USAC men's faculty dinner club, in which he seemed to have equivocated slightly on the matter of the expansion at BAC, someone from Cedar City picked up on it and pounced on him. The governor quickly wrote Dr. J. S. Prestwich, member of the Board of Trustees, reaffirming his support for the expansion. [55]

The Logan Chamber of Commerce formed a committee to study BAC expansion. Their visit to Cedar City was reported in the *Iron County Record* of February 26, 1948:

Adrian Hatch, George Preston and Guy Cardon, representatives of the Logan Chamber of Commerce, spent Monday in Cedar City studying the need and feasibility of proposed expansion at Branch Agricultural College. After a thorough investigation the gentlemen concluded that in their opinion the expansion program would strengthen the Utah State Agricultural College at Logan, rather than weaken it. They stated that they are of the opinion that the need for expansion is apparent, that the state college administration should do more to make the Cedar City school an integral part of the state college, and that the state should spend more money for new buildings and the repair of old ones on the BAC campus.

The Logan Chamber of Commerce gave the crowning endorsement. As surprising as their involvement seems, shortly after their visit on April 15th, 1948, the Board of Trustees of the Utah State Agricultural College authorized the expansion of training to award bachelor's degrees in elementary education and a full three-year course in agriculture. Teacher training would be carried out in conjunction with Cedar City elementary schools.

Director Driggs had been untiring in his quest for expansion. Warren Bulloch, as president of the Chamber of Commerce, had given unfailing leadership, as had J.S. Prestwich, as a member of the Board of Trustees. The whole education community of southern Utah rejoiced. It had been a long journey from Branch Normal School days to the achievement of this milestone. Dr. Driggs was jubilant. The community and the area realized that a substantive step had been made in the effort to provide equal educational opportunities to young people of the entire state.

The catalog for the fall quarter of 1948 included more than 100 new courses, with 90 hours of upper division credit courses included in the curriculum. Dr. Reese P. Maughan was appointed chair of the newly-expanded education department, coming directly from Arizona State College at Tempe. Interestingly, Dr. Maughan had formerly been in charge of the school system at the Topaz relocation center, where he had organized the curriculum, hired the teachers and supervised the operation of the schools. He must have felt right at home among BAC's "new" buildings.

One hundred forty-two students received diplomas at the commencement exercises in May, 1948–more than twice as many as in any previous year. The fall registration, continuing the trend, was again the largest number of enrolled students. And now they were prepared. Housing was more plentiful, if not lavish.

The Commons Building had just been completed, landscaped and decorated. It encompassed student union facilities, including a soda fountain called "The Hitching Post," offices for the yearbook and newspaper staffs and student body offices.

STUDENT BODY OFFICERS AT THEIR NEW OFFICES

*T*ranscending all other developments was the fact that registering students could look forward to the completion of a degree without transferring to a larger school.

Work on the fieldhouse progressed, with local contractor, Leo Palmer, supervising the work. No contractor had actually bid on the construction of the building, and Mr. Palmer had accepted the job under "force account." It was hoped that the facility would be ready for the fall livestock show and for the winter sporting events.

The new girls' dormitory was complete and Blanche Houchen became the matron. Mrs. Fern Kimball managed the now completed cafeteria. It promised to be a wonderful year. And for almost the whole fall quarter, the course of events ran smoothly.

Then, on a wintry Sunday morning, December 12, 1948, as Jack Walters and his father Roy, were returning with the newspapers Jack was to deliver to the homes on his route, they were startled to see smoke pouring from a ventilator on the top of Old Main. They rushed to the home of Eldro Rigby, manager of the college farm, who lived less than a block away, to sound the alarm. By the time they reached the Rigby home, flames were visible on the roof. Mr. Rigby called the fire department and then called Edward Matheson, school custodian, who was first to reach the blaze. Mr. Matheson threw off all electrical switches to the building, but the fire was already blazing through the dry attic, where it had begun.

Students, alerted, rushed to the scene, formed a human brigade up the steel fire escape and began to retrieve all that was possible of the precious books and artifacts, collected over the 50-year history of Old Main. For a time they worked in an orderly fashion, passing books carefully from one to the other. As the flames began leaping through the library itself, students snatched armloads of books and dropped them from the top floor to the ground below. Only moments before the burning roof fell, the students left the building, to watch helplessly as the remaining treasures were consumed by the inferno.

It was tragic that this building, so beloved and cherished, should

burn just a few weeks beyond the 50th anniversary of its dedication. The most dramatic moment occurred as the cupola containing the bell was consumed. With a plaintive clang, almost like a cry, the bell crashed ringing from floor to floor, falling finally to the ground. Perhaps the most sadly poignant was the sight of aging professor Parley Dalley, at the corner of the building, pouring water toward the flames with a garden hose. In approximately three hours, the blaze was under control. Only the outer walls remained of the upper floor. Several old men, who 50 years before had been young men filled with dedicated determination, now stood sadly by. These were men of the lumbering expedition and the building crews of 1898. They watched tearfully. Rob Will Bulloch, whose home was only a few hundred yards from the campus, spoke:

It was the older men then, who could see what could be done, and they filled us with enthusiasm so that we did what was needed. Now it is our turn to enthuse the young ones to get this building rebuilt. [56]

As the depth of the tragedy sank into the cumulative consciousness of the community

DECEMBER 12, 1948, COURTESY OF YORK JONES. NOTEBOOKS AND TYPEWRITERS IN FOREGROUND.

and the College, some things were immediately clear. The art department, as well as the library, had been demolished. The wonderful collection of materials, books, paintings, slides, that Professor Mary Bastow had spent her lifetime assembling, were all lost. Her personal loss was greater than any individual. Nevertheless, her resolve was exemplary as she met with administrators and faculty members on Monday morning. The question in all their minds: How best to get on with the business of education, even with the debilitating events of the previous day.

Only about 20 percent of the library collection had survived the fire. And those few books were in unorganized disarray. They were carried to the cafeteria and placed in a semblance of order, but it was a pitiful resource. Fortunately the business department on the lower floors had been protected by the falling books and the machines and equipment from that department were salvaged.

By Monday afternoon regularly scheduled classes were in session. While cramped into inadequate spaces, none of the classes were forced to move off-campus. The business department moved to the small gymnasium. Students and faculty, without hesitation, entered into a spirit of cooperative effort. Virtually no class time was lost.

On Wednesday, Dr. Franklin S. Harris, president of USAC, arrived in Cedar City to survey the loss and help to determine the best way to proceed. Some people thought rebuilding was impractical.

But Dr. Driggs was dedicated to the concept of restoring the historic and much-loved building. Within a week he had made a formal request for an interim appropriation to rebuild Old Main. Though the state had insured it for only $30,000, Wayne Driggs was firm in his determination to restore it without delay.

And the sentiment of the town was firm. Hazen Cooley describes the response:

The fire again brought the town and college into cooperative effort. Feeling that any delay in repairing the building was unthinkable, men of the community and some members of the college Board of Trustees met with two members of the state Board of Examiners to request a deficit appropriation. These men sat stolidly in the meeting and would not take "no" for an answer.

There had been a change of administration and Gov. Maw had only a few days left in his term. He was out of the state and the other members of the Board of Examiners were reluctant to act without his being present. But they finally agreed to present the matter favorably to the governor when he returned, which would be a day or two before the first of the year. This they did and after hearing the situation the governor agreed to a deficit appropriation of $150,000 so that the repair could begin immediately. This left the insurance to refurnish the building and replace whatever books could be obtained. The action gained six months to a year's time in getting back into the building. [57]

DECEMBER 12, 1948

Robert Gardner, Cedar City architect, rushed to prepare plans for the remodeling of the building. An immediate determination was made that the remodeled building would contain classrooms and offices for faculty who taught there, restrooms and utility areas. It was agreed that a new building would have to be provided for housing a library.

Two lower floors of the building were spared. Replastering of all the walls and refinishing of all floors would be required. The top floor would have to be completely rebuilt. The old timbers hauled through the icy winter many years before would be replaced with steel trusses, and the roof would be covered with asbestos shingles.

Students and faculty regrouped and moved life forward again. Band and orchestra concerts were presented as scheduled. The music department presented *La Traviata* starring Emma Lou Warren and Wallace Adams. The student body presented a varsity show, and the campus was flooded with hundreds of high school students at the 16th annual Vocational Day.

Heartening humanitarian responses to the misfortune of the fire came flooding in. Sympathy poured forth from all over the state. The Utah Conference on Higher Education appointed Dr. Blaine Winters to manage a drive for books from teachers throughout Utah, and contributed volumes began come in. Utah artists, and some from the intermountain area, donated paintings to replace those that had been lost. Service organizations at Utah State Agricultural College instituted a drive to help replace the destroyed books, and friends and patrons in Cedar City began an active effort. The National Guard Armory became the gathering place, where people could deliver their contributions and where the materials could be sorted and catalogued. Clubs organized fund raising activities to benefit the library collection.

*T*hat spring the Board of Trustees approved the first summer session to be held at Branch Agricultural College and printed 500 catalogs describing 40 courses that would be offered this first summer session. Dr. Maughan was named to head the first summer school.

Early in May the actual rebuilding work began on Old Main. The Ballard-Flandro Construction Company of Salt Lake City, were already on campus engaged in the construction of the heat plant. They were low bidders on the reconstruction and quickly had a demolition crew at work, tearing down the top floor to the window level. They promised to rush the work to meet a completion deadline for the beginning of school in September. There was a dramatic moment when the original low bid was considerably higher than the available money. For a time the restoration of the beloved structure was threatened. Judicious whittling pared the bid from $166,778.01 to $141,778.01 and the work moved forward.

No amount of optimism or work could restore the beloved old cast iron bell. A fund drive was launched by students, alumni and townspeople to place a carillon in the cupola of Old Main. The electronic carillon could approximate the sound of the swinging bell, and could broadcast Christmas carols across the wintry campus. By December it was installed and little by little people transferred their affections and forgot the original bell.

The struggle to complete the fieldhouse was an ongoing saga. The community established a process for the sale of bonds so that they could make contracts on remaining phases of construction. The Chamber of Commerce committee on education assembled 75 workers, each of whom were committed to contact five people in and around Cedar City to sell the fieldhouse bonds to them. Bonds were sold in $25, $100 and $500 denominations. The bonds would be paid from a ten cent seat tax levied on each ticket for every event. Cliff Ewing was chairman of the bond sales effort. [58] It was another example of the meshing of town and school, in harmony with long-held tradition.

In the spring of 1949, Director Driggs made the official announcement that an ROTC unit would be established on the Branch Agricultural College campus. It would provide the first two years of a four- year training for commissioned officers in the United States Air Force. Students who enrolled in ROTC would be automatically exempt from the draft.

Enlistment was brisk. ROTC soon became a significant force on the campus.

Perhaps no one knew exactly what a challenging task faced the regular Air Force officers as they came to make cadets from farm kids. But the farm kids were enthusiastic and the presence of the ROTC added an air of military grandeur, in a rather unsophisticated time.

"PA" MANNING DEMONSTRATES TO WALLACE ADAMS HOW TO WOO JANICE MERRYWEATHER.

When the fieldhouse finally became a reality, it was appropriately called the War Memorial Fieldhouse, in memory of all former students who were killed or had died while serving in the armed forces. As the day arrived for the building to be dedicated, the ROTC was called upon to add dignity to the event. A

MAJ. O.W. HARRIS AND DR. H.WAYNE DRIGGS

delightful memory of Lawana Nelson Warner from that occasion, demonstrates just how challenged the staid Col.Oliver Harris must have been by his assignment.

An event which was supposed to be grand turned out to have some unexpected humor. The new field house was dedicated early in the basketball season of 1950. The governor of Utah was an invited celebrity. The faculty and student body made preparation to put on their best show. The halftime activity was to be maneuvers by the ROTC drill team. Sergeant Hill had spent hours with the boys and they were ready. Unfortunately, Sergeant Hill celebrated that evening by becoming too drunk to lead the commands — so, hurriedly, Donald Staheli, a student officer filled in. Acquiring the rifles was part of the mounting stress for the team because Sergeant Hill, in his condition, had difficulty locating the key to the room where the rifles were stored.

Moments before they were to march before the noisy spectators the boys found their *assigned positions in their formation and they followed Donald Staheli's first command, "Forward March". On, "To the rear March," the back right corner cadet did not hear the command and kept on marching straight. When he found his mistake he turned around and hurriedly found his position with the group again. The crowd found the maneuver humorous which raised the noise level. "Double to the rear march" was hard to hear and as a result cadets found themselves facing their counterparts, marching in the wrong direction. From there it got worse. One of the cadet's hats went flying when it was knocked ajar by a miscued rifle. Don Knight was quick to reach down while marching in formation and picked up the hat. Everything the boys did now only added to the humor. The crowd was delighted. The drill team was mortified. There were spectators who requested a return performance, promising to pay double the price for admission. It never happened. The experience was far too painful to repeat. It never would have been as funny the second time anyway.* [59]

Despite the comic aspects of the occasion, the ceremony did retain some dignity. Held in conjunction with a Friday night basketball game, in December 1950, a bronze plaque was unveiled, which read: "To the men of BAC who gave their lives in the service of the American way of life, this building is dedicated by humble and grateful people. May our tradition of competition and fair play displayed here stand as proof that their sacrifice was not in vain."

Dignitaries abounded, a dedicatory prayer was offered by Oscar Hulet, local educator, and a capacity crowd watched as the Broncos narrowly defeated the San Bernardino State College Indians, 68-67.

William H. Manning retired that year. A young Blaine Johnson came to lead the vocal department, but his call to active duty in the National Guard interrupted his plan. "Pa" Manning agreed to return for four weeks, until something could be organized. Loa Johnson, Virginia Larson, wife of LDS Institute Director Gustive Larson, and Reed Berrett, a local business man, divided the duties, until the end of the Korean War, when Dr. Johnson was released.

But the music department had some good news too. Commencement exercises in

ROTC, 1952

the spring provided the setting for the announcement of a gift by the Frank J. Thorley family. The Thorleys presented the college with their stately home located just across the street from the campus. It was for the use of the music department and would now be known as the Thorley Music Hall. It was the first time an entire building had been given to the school and could not have been more appropriate.

The music department had been crowded into a tiny space in the science building. Having a music building gave students studios for practice and eliminated their necessity of finding access to a nearby church, a tree shaded glen, or a crowded dormitory closet. It provided rooms for private lessons and even performances of vocal or chamber music recitals.

Commencement, 1950, was an historic occasion. Twenty graduates received the first Bachelor of Science degrees ever awarded at the school. Along with their degrees, the graduates all received teaching certificates in elementary education. Though the degrees were awarded by Utah State Agricultural College, all of the course work had been completed on the campus at Cedar City. All of the teacher training had been accomplished in conjunction with Iron County schools. A source of certified teachers that could be tapped by rural school districts, at last, poured forth from the institution at Cedar City.

THORLEY HALL, 1950

*T*he exhilaration of graduation activities had barely subsided when shockingly somber news clouded the campus and the community. Director Driggs was discovered to be suffering from acute leukemia. It was a death sentence. No method for slowing the progress of the disease was known in 1951. Dr. J. S. Prestwich diagnosed the malady. Doctors at the University of Utah Medical Center confirmed that his was the most virulent strain of the disease. He returned home to Cedar City to be with his family as long as possible. He died within three weeks, July 20, 1951. He was 49.

H. Wayne Driggs was a participant. He was involved with the students. He took small roles in their dramatic productions and went on the road with them. He knew the first name of each student. He was seated front row, center court, 50-yard line, at athletic competitions and responded with emotion to the success or lack of success being experienced by the teams. He joined the local service clubs and taught Sunday School to his neighborhood at church.

The Driggs children included four young boys, the eldest 16, and one baby girl, born 18 months before. The children roamed the college hill. For the students, interacting with the Driggs children had become as much a part of college life as interacting with each other. Dr. and Mrs. Driggs hosted special parties and teas always at the "cottage," so students were as emotionally tied to the family of their director, as they were to the warm congeniality of their relationship with him. This sudden departure was anguishing for the shocked students, and though most students had returned home for the summer, word spread quickly to them wherever they were.

It had been six years of great vitality for the school. Enrollment had doubled, the four year program had begun, housing facilities had been tripled, the fieldhouse built, the mountain ranch expanded, the ROTC initiated and the summer school started. Student activities had been infused with excitement and kindled with vigor.

Sadness permeated the community as his much-loved widow departed with her children, to return to her family home in Pleasant Grove. Returning students would feel the loss of all of them, when they came back in September.

On Saturday, July 28, following the funeral services, the Board of Trustees of the Utah State Agricultural College met in Logan, Utah, to choose a new director. They were decisive in their choice. Dr. Daryl Chase, then serving as dean of students and director of public relations for USAC, was named to fill the position.

Dr. Chase brought with him a rich educational background. A graduate of the University of Utah, he had earned his doctorate from the University of Chicago in 1934. By the time of his appointment to lead Branch Agricultural College, he had been an educator for more than 20 years, and had served as dean of students for five of those.

Dr. Louis Madsen had replaced Dr. Franklin S. Harris as president of USAC and BAC, the previous October. He came now with Dr. Chase, arriving in Cedar City on the next Tuesday to assess the needs and to turn the responsibility to Dr. Chase.

Within weeks, the Chase family arrived. Daryl Chase and his wife, Alice Kofford Chase, and their nine year old son, Peter, were welcomed by a community sensitive to the dif-

ficulty of their situation. Not only had they been abruptly uprooted, but they came to a school and a town still stunned by the departure of a remarkable leader.

Dr. Chase had immediate challenges. School was to begin in a little over a month. Catalogs were being prepared, but needed to be mailed. Additions to curriculum were in the planning stage. While the old library building had been restored, what was left of the library collection still had no adequate home.

That September, J. Harry Plummer, registrar, announced a 20 percent increase in freshman registrations. The ROTC moved into the old gymnasium, and courses were expanded to include a third year. Fourteen new courses were included in the catalog, many in upper division work. A new college hymn was composed, with music

HOWARD WAYNE DRIGGS
1902-1951

H. Wayne Driggs was the director of Branch Agricultural College for six years during the exciting era of the school beginning with the close of World War II. Enrollment had plummeted during the war years, but the return of the young G.I.s heralded a dynamic period of growth for the school. Dr. Driggs was credited with the establishment of an ROTC unit, the long-anticipated expansion of the education department to a four-year program, inauguration of the summer school and the ambitious undertaking

of planning, funding and construction of new and future buildings.

Driggs' building projects included the erection of a new fieldhouse and plans and appropriations for an auditorium, library and men's dormitory. Director Driggs acquired abandoned buildings at Topaz for transport and reconstruction at BAC, for needed campus buildings, including a trailer village to solve the critical housing shortage; all at tremendous savings to the school.

Dr. Driggs was the director who stood gripped with horror as he witnessed beloved Old Main go up in flames. He was the director who stood firmly behind the decision to preserve the outer shell of the historic building, gutting the interior to make way for an immediate renovation.

Careful consideration of options in the solving of all types of challenges, as well as building projects, was a hallmark of Dr. Driggs personal administrative style. Speakers at his funeral after his untimely death at age 49 of acute leukemia, noted that he was a teacher and director who always did painstaking "homework" before making any presentation to the Board of Trustees, state legislature, faculty or townspeople of Cedar City.

Friends and distinguished educators extolled his friendly humanitarianism and winning personality. They praised his remarkable vision, his unselfish

habit of giving credit where it was due, his open-door policy as a director and inimitable good cheer. His wife often said that he had a "bit of grease paint in his blood," as he not only loved attending theatrical productions but enjoyed playing small roles in campus productions. He was also an enthusiastic sports fan and consummate booster of BAC athletic events.

A tall, handsome figure at well over six feet, Wayne Driggs impressed people with his keen intellect and earnest dedication to his chosen field of education as a professor of English.

His father, Howard R. Driggs, was one of the earliest teachers of the school during the BNS period. The family had moved to New York state when his father took a position at New York University. Years later, after he received his Ph.D., son Wayne joined his father on the English education department at NYU; both were master teachers.

Widely acknowledged for literary talent, Dr. Driggs authored the famous Book of Mormon pageant, *America's Witness for Christ*, produced annually at Palmyra, New York, as well as many contributions to educational, professional and church journals.

Dr. Driggs lost his first wife, Mamie Rowland Driggs, and their infant daughter in childbirth. He and Elizabeth Swenson, his accomplished second wife, were the parents of five children.

DR. DARYL
CHASE, 1952

by Marian Decker and words by Professor Richard Rowley. The spirit of the place was still dynamic.

Then a momentous thing happened! For the first time in nearly 50 years the state of Utah appropriated money from the building fund to construct a new building on the campus of Branch Agricultural College. In response to a quiet lobbying effort that had been proceeding for some time, initiated by Dr. Driggs and community leaders, the state building board announced the allocation of $400,000 for a new building. It would house the displaced library collection. It would replace the old auditorium, still nestled on the top floor of the 50-year old science building. This was news!

The history of every building on the campus up to this time had included striving and struggle. It was a history replete with public-spirited townspeople signing notes, creative adaptation of second-hand buildings hauled from afar and reconstructed; innovations; making do. But never since the science building of 1904, had there simply been an appropriation. Now the state would fund a new building.

Mayor L.V. Broadbent issued a statement:

We are very pleased that the state has realized the value of the Branch Agricultural College enough to make a direct appropriation for a new building. Naturally, we are very pleased.

It was tantamount to being legitimized at last.

Then people began to give book collections to BAC, in honor of Dr. Wayne Driggs. It began at first as a proposal to the Utah Conference on Higher Education, where the members voted to establish a memorial collection. Dr. Driggs had been chairman of the conference at the time of his death. Dr. Blaine Winters was appointed to head the campaign. Whole collections of books began to pour in from private donors. Other colleges began to respond, and members of their faculties sent treasured

volumes. Books came from former colleagues of Dr. Driggs in New York. Books came from churches and former students. Thousands of books had been contributed before the flow ebbed. It was a great boost to the meager resources of the library. It was a fitting tribute to a departed leader.

Housing the collections was a nightmare. Books were placed in several places on campus, from the basement of the restored Old Main, to the gymnasium and even to the agriculture building. Wherever there were shelves, there were books. It was the ultimate insecurity for the library staff, while they waited for the new building to begin.

By November, 1952 the location and final plans were announced. The building, the largest on the campus, would be a combination library and auditorium. It was to be located northeast of Old Main. It would be designed in "conservative modern" style by M.E. Harris, architect, of Salt Lake City. The auditorium section would seat 935 people. There was to be an orchestra pit with a lift, a spacious and well-equipped stage, modern in every aspect; the library would hold all the books and more. By the end of the year the plans were final, and it was anticipated that work would soon begin.

Dr. and Mrs. Chase hosted students and townspeople at an afternoon reception at the newly-redecorated director's cottage. It was clear that a mutual affection had developed.

The year 1952 brought the announcement of emeritus status for Parley P. Dalley after 43 years of teaching. His students established a scholarship in his name. He taught for an additional 10 years.

*T*he promise of a new auditorium where the performing arts could thrive still seemed distant, and creative minds could not postpone their dreams. For a long time Professor Richard Rowley had pondered the possibility of a

THE LIBRARY/AUDITORIUM

student varsity show, written, directed and acted by the students. In 1952, as adviser to the *Agricola* and to the *Bacian* newspaper, he saw the show he'd envisioned as a possible solution for the ever-underfunded publications.

The group of students he approached with the idea were activists. They grasped his idea and began to brainstorm together. Through the Christmas holidays they worked at birthing a production. When they finished they had written a classic musical comedy plot. "Country boy meets city girl and love blooms" carried the main theme, while charming sub-plots involving the town miser and three old maids, and a nice widow with two charming children added warmth and comedy.

The young playwrights made a fortunate connection with Miriam K. Stallings, a Salt Lake City song-writer and composer who provided them with 13 original songs to enhance their invention, and they were on their way.

Ever-supportive faculty added expertise. Roy Halversen trained and conducted the orchestra, while Wallace Adams taught the original songs to young singers and conducted the chorus.

The result was a rollicking, if ever so slightly amateurish, production. They had mounted their show in the decrepit old auditorium, another of the hundreds of presentations of all kinds that had enriched the community from the stage of the building constructed in 1904. There would not be many more productions staged there, but it had served long and well.

DARYL CHASE
1901-1984

Dr. Daryl Chase was appointed as director of Branch Agricultural College in 1951, following the death of H. Wayne Driggs. Under his administration, the school officially had its name changed to the College of Southern Utah. Dr. Chase also was effective in procuring increases in legislative appropriations, making possible faculty raises and new construction. He was a man who could get things done.

In December of 1954 Chase left College of Southern Utah to become president of Utah State Agricultural College. Chase, president of USU for 14 years, until 1968, was credited with doubling its enrollment. This unprecedented growth demanded funding for 13 new buildings, including what became The Chase Fine Arts Center. He encouraged the exchange of foreign students and established technical aid programs in Iran, Bolivia and Brazil.

The growth of CSU and USU, during his administrations was not physical alone, though the increase in enrollment and the new facilities on both campuses were a testament to his vision. His insistence on quality programs and excellence of faculties were his best legacy. His ambition to see USAC become a university in every sense of the word was ratified by the change in status and name to Utah State University in 1957. Despite this change, he made sure that the university retained its reputation as one of the great producers of experts in agriculture, forestry and conservation.

As an educator during his entire professional career, which included service as a teacher or administrator at LDS Church institutes in four states, he influenced many young people for the better. A man who understood the needs and aspirations of young people, Dr. Chase was not just a remote administrator, but befriended many students. The advice he often gave them is still perceptive and pertinent:

"While acquiring broad knowledge of nature and of man and a mastery of some phase of art or science, do not neglect to cultivate your spiritual nature also."

Even in retirement as administrator, Chase did not slacken his efforts. His vitality and wisdom were deeply engaged in his work as director of the Man and His Bread Museum, also established through his inspiration, and he returned to active teaching as a professor of history.

Daryl Chase's life was characterized by the dedication of all of his ability, energy and vision to the highest standard of achievement. He had his roots deep in the soil, having been reared on a farm in Nephi. To that background he added scholarship in religion and history and enjoyment of the creative arts. He had a delightful sense of humor that allowed him to smile at man's inconsistencies, yet he had great faith in the people. He taught that "war is not inevitable, that a just and lasting peace is attainable."

Scholar and author, master teacher, dean and director, administrator and builder—for high achievement in service to mankind, he received an honorary Doctor of Humanities award from CSU at the 72nd annual commencent in 1969.

Dr. Chase died at the age of 83. A USU faculty member described Chase as a man who believed in elegance. "He always looked like a president. His death was the end of an era."

There is no record whether or not the production added to the meager resources of the yearbook, but the student varsity show had been born.

That summer Branch Agricultural College met the federal government. A new men's dormitory was sorely needed. The enrollment consistently included twice as many men as women, but the housing facilities for men were still limited to the old Topaz building, Dorm B, and the original 12-unit dorm. Funds were available through the Federal Housing and Home Finance Agency in Washington D.C. and formal application had been made. The agency sent a person to investigate, who visited Cedar City and returned without contacting anyone. Then he issued a report which stated that Cedar City was too small a town to qualify for a loan.

Hazen Cooley was dispatched to Washington D.C. to plead the cause. Rep. Walter K. Granger helped by arranging an appointment with the loan administration personnel. Hazen was persuasive. Did they realize that BAC was the only four-year college within 200 miles? Did they understand that 80 percent of the students came from out of town and needed housing? Finally he persuaded the agency people that they should grant the loan. [60]

In July of 1952 the federal loan of $250,000 for the dormitory was announced. The addition of this money brought the total available for construction on the campus that year to $700,000. The total also included $50,000 for the remodeling of Thorley Hall and various repairs. The new dormitory, called Oak Hall, would house men students. The original boys' dorm became available to married students with their families. Boys' Dorm B and Trailer Town were to be hauled away.

Whether or not the government loan agents were impelled to generosity by awareness of the plight of Trailer Town is hard to say. But the college administration was eager to quietly dispose of it. It was important to make way for a parking lot for the War Memorial Fieldhouse, but it was even more important to realize that perhaps luck was running out. That spring, a woman firing the furnace in one of the laundry areas, had forgotten to open the water valve on the hot water tank. With a deafening explosion, the steam pressure blew up the furnace and the tank and sent metal shrapnel flying in all directions. Fortunately no one was inside the building on that early morning. But it was time to bid trailer town a fond farewell. [61]

Some projects were simpler than going to Washington for money. In the autumn of 1952, Dr. Chase appointed a committee of faculty members to suggest ways to repair or renovate the old cabin on the Mountain Ranch property. It had served the Jones family for generations before the college bought the place, and had sheltered students and faculty from the worst of the elements since that time. It was in a dilapidated condition. The committee recommended that it be torn down and another built in its stead. There followed a legendary cooperative effort of the faculty and staff that strained the talents of the most able handymen among them, and enlarged the capacities of those not so naturally inclined.

From the felling of the timber and the

OAK
HALL

peeling of the logs to the final chinking to make it tight, the work was done by committed faculty and staff. When they had finished, they had built, completely by their labors, a lovely little cabin that would be used for generations hence. [62]

When the renovated Thorley Music Hall was opened to the public on February 8, 1953, it contained tangible evidence of the characteristic community support. Two new pianos had been given by the Lions Club and the Rotary Club. Furnishings, paintings recording equipment and a record collection had all been contributed by businesses and individuals. And the neighbors on the street had joined together to put new curb and gutter along the front of the house.

It was a reciprocal friendship. The college was equally vigilant in watching for needs in the community. Not only was the school the provider of rich cultural resources for the whole area, but it was also the source of practical assistance. One week a tractor maintenance course began; another week a course followed, "Making Home Work Enjoyable," which included a demonstration on ironing. In February, 1952 the BAC agriculture department announced:

Faced with a need for a reserve of persons trained in sheep-shearing techniques, a committee of Iron County stockmen headed by Douglas Clark is making tentative plans for a sheep shearing school to be given at Branch Agricultural College this week. The school will train young men acquainted with sheep-raising practices through having been brought up around sheep or through caring for farm flocks and who expect to go into the sheep business. Instructions will be on the machine-type shearing.

Other offerings included a short law course focused upon water rights. When someone at the college perceived a need in the community, they hastened to help. It was a mutually beneficial alliance.

The call for bids on the library/auditorium building resulted in a heavy dose of reality. The wondrous features that had seemed too good to be true, actually were too costly to fit the appropriated funds after architects fees and other costs were deducted. The architects pared down the features. The 1953 Legislature appropriated an additional

$200,000. The call for bids went out again. Finally, in May, the contract was awarded to Jensen Brothers Construction Company of Salt Lake City. Dignitaries gathered and ground was broken. The cost of the building was to be $486,440.

It was a momentous spring. President David O. McKay, president of the Church of Jesus Christ of Latter-day Saints, came to address the graduates at the commencement exercises, held for the first time in the War Memorial Fieldhouse.

That year, 1953, retirement was announced for two revered faculty members: David L. Sargent, who had headed two departments and been on the faculty for 35 years and Mary L. Bastow, who had been head of the art department for 24 years. It was the end of an era.

MOUNTAIN CABIN RANCH, 1955

It was also the beginning of a new one. With little fanfare, the Board of Trustees announced the changing of the name of Branch Agricultural College. The Trustees reported that the new name had been selected because it more clearly designated the service that the college rendered to the people of that part of the state. After 40 years of being BAC, the school was to be called College of Southern Utah.

1915 'AGRICOLA' STAFF

A D.L. SARGENT BIOLOGY CLASS OF THE '20S

THE NEW GYMNASIUM, 1928

WAR MEMORIAL FIELDHOUSE UNDER CONSTRUCTION

AN ADVERTISEMENT IN THE 1948 'AGRICOLA' YEARBOOK URGED STUDENTS TO 'MEET THE GANG AT THORNTON DRUG.'

THE TRADES AND INDUSTRIES CLASS CONSTRUCTING THE MEN'S DORMITORY, LATE 1940'S

DINNER-DANCE IN THE BASEMENT OF THE EL ESCALANTE HOTEL, 1947

THE BAC BAND HEADS DOWN MAIN STREET IN A 1950 PARADE.

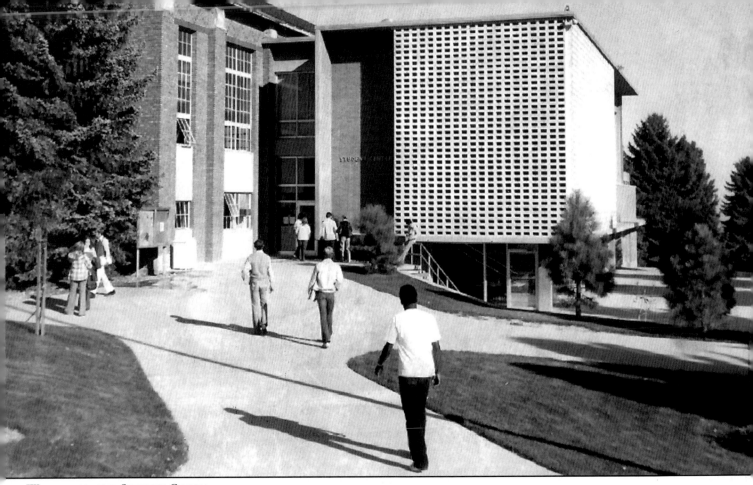

WALKWAY TO THE STUDENT CENTER

A CLASS ON THE UPPER QUAD

CHAPTER V

College of Southern Utah, 1953-1969

"*That old school has had one hard scratch, and if it hadn't been for those many people who worked for small wages, and those who gave freely of their time and talents and money, it wouldn't be there today.*"

William Flanigan

Director Chase was a fine administrator. He perceived the college as an ever-expanding influence upon the growth and development of southern Utah. He could see that it had become more than a community college. It was a regional educational center. There were many who had been troubled for a long time by the fact that the institution had always simply been called by the name of the school that governed it. The college needed a more valid name and people began to press for it.

When the Board of Trustees met at Cedar City on May 23, 1953, Dr. Daryl Chase, then director of the college, and Edwin L. Peterson, representing students, faculty and civic groups, presented a formal petition requesting that the name of the college be changed to one more in harmony with its history and mission. [1]

The signatures on the petition expressed the interest of a broad range of individuals and organizations supportive of the change. It was signed by the BNS-BAC Alumni Association, the student officers, the faculty association, Cedar City Chamber of Commerce, Southern Utah Livestock Show board, Business and Professional Women of Cedar City, Cedar City Lions Club and the Cedar City Junior Chamber of Commerce. When the board received the petition, Chairman Thorpe B. Issacson asked that copies be mailed to any absent board members and any whose terms were to begin on July 1 of that year. They then deferred action until the next meeting.

At the board meeting on June 27, 1953, the trustees approved the measure calling for the name change, with only one dissenting vote. In making the announcement, they stated that the new name more clearly designated the service that the college rendered to the people of that part of the state.

Adjustment to the change took some time. For more than 40 years the school had been Branch Agricultural College. It was second nature for the town, the college, the alumni and others associated with it. But most people sensed an intangible increase in prestige with the new name. The change of the name did not signify any change in status. In fact, the full and official name was: College of Southern Utah, Branch of the Utah State Agricultural College. Everyone agreed that so long a title was cumbersome, so for general identification the designation was to be College of Southern Utah or simply CSU. There was quiet pleasure in no longer being called a branch, especially since Snow College had become a branch of USAC at about the same time, being called Snow Branch Agricultural College.

The process of changing printed materials and signs began immediately. The students changed the name of their newspaper from *Bacian* to *Cantus South Utahn*. Cantus was defined as meaning "The Principal Voice." Admittedly, it was a stretch, but they managed to get their new initials in the title.

The townspeople anxiously watched for signs of progress on the new auditorium/library building. It was a slow beginning. Excavation work was begun in July, then soil testing delayed the work. By the end of summer, the structure began to be visible. Student excitement and citizen enthusiasm rose with the walls.

The advent of the new auditorium would

expand the possibilities for cultural events for the community and the college. The only performance facility on the campus was still the very inadequate auditorium on the top floor of the old science building. For more than 50 years the auditorium had been the site of operas, plays, musical performances and all assemblies. The fact that it was considered to be haunted by a deceased music student, who played "Deep Purple" in the dark of the night, added drama and intrigue, but sound and lighting technology were primitive, and the entire music library was stored on the front row of auditorium seating since there were no shelves or file cabinets. A lot of people eagerly anticipated the completion of the building.

*I*n August 1953, a little more than a year after the loan had been approved, final plans for the new 200-man dormitory were approved. L. Robert Gardner, Cedar City architect, prepared the plans and called for bids. The goal was to have the facility ready to house students for the 1954 school year. Though the building was designed in the most economical style possible, bids were higher than anticipated and frustrating delays occurred. Work finally began November 5.

Not only would the dormitory provide housing for men students, but it would facilitate the solution of the problem of parking for events held at the new fieldhouse. Trailer Town and Dorm B could not be moved until it was completed.

An upheaval in the administration of Utah State Agricultural College required the selection of a new president, and rumors circulated that Dr. Daryl Chase would be chosen. Dr. Chase was among those interviewed for the position. But when the selection was made, Henry Aldous Dixon became the president of USAC, and Chase remained at the Cedar City school.

Summer school offerings expanded under the direction of Twain Tippetts. Southern Utah students, young and adult, took advantage of the opportunity and especially large numbers of teachers came to renew certificates or pursue expanded qualification. Evening school, under the direction of Ben Cooley, drew townspeople and students who worked in the day, attending school at night.

Proselyting for students was always necessary. It was an effort that had hardly changed since the beginning of BNS. All faculty members gave up some of their summer days to scour surrounding counties for prospective

students. Once contacts were made, they telephoned and wrote letters to keep in touch. They were motivated not only by a chauvinistic affection for the school; their very jobs were on the line.

Eddie Peterson recalls knocking at the front door of a family in the small Utah town of Marysvale. Receiving no response, but sensing that someone was inside, he proceeded in the direction of the back door, hoping to rouse them there. He walked around to the back, just in time to intercept the lady of the house with a coffee pot in her hand. He introduced himself as a representative of the college in Cedar City, and the woman invited him in. With a sigh of relief she exclaimed, "Thank goodness. I thought you were the ward teachers."

Dr. Peterson also remembers driving with Director Chase to all the area county fairs, a rich resource for prospective freshmen in agriculture. When Dr. Chase displayed impressive familiarity with livestock and farming methods in his conversations with the young farmers and their families, Peterson could not hide his astonishment. "You thought I was a city slicker, didn't you?" Chase chided. "Well, I grew up on a dry-farm just outside Levan." [2]

Chase stories abound in the memories of his faculty. One anecdote concerns his encounter with Gov. J. Bracken Lee as he went to lobby for increased funding. Gov. Lee wanted a list of faculty and staff, which Director Chase provided forthwith. The governor's purpose was to figure for himself the teacher-to-student ratio, and determine just how efficiently funds were being used at CSU. Upon receiving the list he divided it by the number of students, and then informed Dr. Chase that the ratio was too low and he could not support additional funding. Whereupon Dr. Chase pointed

out that a number of the staff personnel on the list were actually herders of the college sheep flock. "I'm still counting them as part of your staff resource," replied the governor. "Then," remonstrated the director, "we will have to count the sheep as students." [3]

Notwithstanding his "hands-on" style of administration, the tenure of Dr. Chase at College of Southern Utah was destined to be brief. In November 1954, Henry Aldous Dixon was elected to the United States House of Representatives and Dr. Daryl Chase was appointed president of Utah State Agricultural College.

*T*he appointment was announced on a Friday in mid-November. The Chase family left almost immediately to assume their duties in Logan. Dr. Dixon planned to leave shortly for Washington and would have limited time to orient Dr. Chase. Hazen Cooley, executive secretary, was appointed to serve as acting director at College of Southern Utah. There was no crisis involved in that, since Mr. Cooley had been intimately involved in all details of the school since 1929. Cooley was legendary for his inimitable grasp of every aspect in the operation of the school, as well as his careful attention to every particular.

But the townspeople were again thrown into anxiety. In September the school had announced the largest enrollment ever to register in a fall quarter. The legislature was only a month away and experience had shown that the institution needed strong representation when the battle over the apportionment of funds began. It was always a big-boys versus small-kids contest. Now, with no permanent director and the president consumed with his own stresses, the defense of the interests of the school became an understandable concern among townspeople and faculty. [4]

Charles R. Hunter, chairman of the CSU committee of the Board of Trustees, held his cards close to his chest. There were, he said, many people interested, and he would not divulge the names of any.

Never mind his reticence, there was plenty of conjecture to keep the matter alive as the preferred subject of conversation. Everyone speculated and "inside" information flowed. Theron Ashcroft made a public statement that he was not interested. D.C. Schmutz did the same. Eddie Peterson and Reese Maughan each admitted interest. C.B. Cooley was mentioned, as was J.H. Plummer, dean of students.

Ianthus Wright, superintendent of Iron County Schools, was again mentioned.

The December 2 paper announced that Charles R. Hunter had left for meetings at which would be interviewed 22 men who were under consideration. It also reported that J.H. Plummer had declared that he had no interest in the appointment, which was to be announced on the following Friday.

On December 9, the headline read: "Board Takes No Action On CSU Director." And there was another reminder of the dire difficulty of a school with no one to fight for its funding in the approaching legislature. One bit of information filtered from the frequently-meeting trustees. They would not consider a director who had no doctorate degree.

The December 16 *Iron County Record* brought the news that the field was narrowing and that the board would meet again on that day to give the matter further consideration. Experience had taught the paper's publisher that promises of specifics were hazardous. There appeared only a cautious hope that the decision might be made soon.

December 23, two days before Christmas, the headline was downright discouraging: "AC Board of Trustees Fails To Name New Director for Local Institution."

The College of Southern Utah committee of the board, composed of five members with Charles R. Hunter of Cedar City as chairman, was not prepared to make any recommendations at the meeting, and since only three members of the committee were in attendance, no effort was made to take committee action on the day of the meeting. Mr. Hunter stated that 14 men were under consideration for the appointment, some of them active candidates for the position and the others available if the appointment was offered them. The next meeting of the

HAZEN
COOLEY

CHARLES
R. HUNTER

THE BRAITHWAITE FAMILY: ROYDEN AND ALICE WITH BOBBY AND
ELAINE AS KARL AND DOUG FLANK THEM.

trustees was to be held January 3. [5]

Mr. Hunter had assured his constituents that they need not worry about the January 10 opening of the legislature. Gov. J. Bracken Lee and Dr. Daryl Chase were to be depended upon to watch over the interests of CSU.

The Board of Trustees did not name a director at its January 8 meeting. The trustees did, however, announce that they were searching for a replacement for Edwin L. Peterson. The election of Henry Aldous Dixon to Congress had unsettled CSU more deeply than at first perceived, and Eddie Peterson left to go to Washington as Mr. Dixon's administrative assistant.

Finally, the announcement came. Dr. Royden C. Braithwaite, a native of Manti, Utah, and dean of the college of family living at Brigham Young University, was named to head College of Southern Utah. He was well educated, holding a master's degree from Stanford, and a doctorate in education from Cornell University. His experience was varied.

Trustee Hunter must have been relieved to introduce the new director to the students, faculty and townspeople. As he flanked Dr. Chase and made the announcement he assured the students and the public that Dr. Braithwaite had been invited to apply and was unanimously accepted by the board.

DR.
ROYDEN C.
BRAITHWAITE

Dr. Braithwaite came quickly to assume the stewardship. He brought with him to Cedar City his wife, Alice Todd, and three boys: Doug, age 15, Karl, age 12, and Bobby, age 4. First daughter Elaine was born soon after.

The arrival of the new director and his family coincided with the completion of the new library/auditorium building. The town was invited to a reception to introduce them both. It was a well attended event.

The reception for the new director, on April 3,

was only the first of the festivities. The completion of the auditorium was an event momentous enough to rival the completion of the first building on the campus in 1898. And the people were not unmindful of the connection as they celebrated through the springtime.

Roy Halversen had been chairman of the building committee; now he was appointed to chair the committee to plan and execute the dedication week.

*T*he festivities would also celebrate the completion of the new men's dormitory. The dedication program would encompass both buildings. Hazen Cooley had chaired the building committee for the dormitory and now served on the dedication committee.

The long-awaited first performance in the new auditorium was the second of the flurry of events. Blaine Johnson and Roy Halversen had readied Sigmund Romberg's *The New Moon*. It was to star Virginia Rose, John Davis and Larry Jones, and would make make full use of the expanded capability the auditorium provided. There was to be a full orchestra, beautiful scenery, fencing, dancing and rowdy fights. [6]

The whole town awaited eagerly. This was a town steeped in the tradition of grand opera, light opera, and drama of every kind. But this was the first time that a facility had been provided that could do justice to the work and the talent expended. The new stage was graced by a remarkable orchestra lift, one of the few in Utah. The opera played for three nights, and every seat was filled at every performance.

man of the committee to prepare the brochure. She had spent the years since the fire, struggling to hold together the meager remains of the library collection, all the while working and planning for this dreamed-of facility. Her own sense of relief is interwoven in the words of gratitude expressed by the poem she placed inside the front page of the dedication booklet. The poem had originally been written for the program of the 50th anniversary celebration in 1947, but it seemed also to speak Lael's feelings of this day.

Tribute to the Founders

For these are they who blazed the weary trailways,
With faith in what the future proferred men,
Who, dauntless, surged beyond the realm of doubting,

Then, with only time to get the scenery removed, Richard Rowley was ready with two classic Greek plays. These were the first dramatic performances in the new auditorium. *Oedipus the King* and *Antigone* played on two consecutive nights, and again the house was filled by an enthusiastic audience of townspeople and students.

Young Richard Rowley must have been inspired by the new facility. Later that year he produced three more plays: *Arsenic and Old Lace*, the classical Greek play *Prometheus Bound*, as well as an old time comedy, *Desperate Desmond's Dastardly Deed*.

The dedication ceremonies were to be the centerpiece of the commencement week activities. Committees made up of faculty and administrators had worked untiringly through the whole planning-construction process, and now they worked to prepare an event befitting the magnitude of the occasion.

RICHARD ROWLEY

A deep awareness of history ran through the consciousness of the people and the content of the festivities. Their sense of triumph at the end of what had been a long struggle brought them to identify with the struggles of the founders.

Eulalia B. Jones, librarian, was chair-

Believing still, though barriers crowded hope,
Whose vision from the mists of golden purpose
Brought light for generations yet unborn—
No trembling force from Nature's opposi tion
Dared thwart the chartered course they laid themselves.
Strong hearts, swift courage, and the love of work,
The willingness to serve a mighty cause—
Though splendors of their fighting days have ended,
Our gratitude shall live each day renewed.

Fae Decker Dix

'NEW MOON' OPERA

The poem, no doubt, had double meaning. Three directors and large committees had worked to bring the dream to reality. Many people sensed the connection between the generations.

The dedication ceremony was held in the evening on May 18, 1955. Of course the seats were filled. Gov. J. Bracken Lee came to speak. Thorpe B. Issacson, chairman of the Board of Trustees, spoke, as did Dr. Daryl Chase. There were prayers and music. The chorus and the orchestra performed numbers from Handel's *Messiah*, accompanied on a new nine-foot Steinway grand piano. It was a time of joyful celebration.

The new Men's Dormitory was dedicated at the same time and in the same ceremony. It engendered significant enthusiasm, for it too had been a long time coming. Hazen Cooley, who had been so instrumental in accomplishing the loan from the federal government and had chaired the planning committee, now happily saw its completion and the beginning of its use.

That year, Ward Robb graduated as valedictorian of the upper division graduates. With the achievement of his degree he could receive the official title of registrar. He had been serving in that office since 1947, while he took classes toward a degree. Finally, his role became recognized. His career with the college extended over more than 39 years.

One of the first visible changes made by Director Braithwaite was the name of the student newspaper. Perhaps he didn't really know the meaning of the word "Cantus" either. Soon after his arrival, a contest was announced and students invited to submit potential names. The name *Thunderbird* was selected. March 27, 1956, was the first issue bearing the new name. A further change came later in the fall when the name of the yearbook was changed to *Pictograph* to replace the long-standing *Agricola*. The new name was intended to connote "culture" rather than "agriculture." The sense of mission broadened. It was also the beginning of an American Indian motif for the campus.

In 1956, seven faculty members were on leave: Twain Tippetts had been away since the summer of 1954. McRay Cloward, Gwyn Clark, Lanice Moore, Conrad Hatch, Blaine

LAEL JONES

WARD ROBB, 1956

Johnson and Max Robinson were also on leave. Robinson was loaned to Pakistan to assist that nation with problems in range management. Gwyn Clark was in Tokyo, serving at the university as an aide in their teacher training program. The influence of CSU was beginning to broaden beyond the borders of southern Utah.

William H. Manning came back to the college to fill the vacancy caused by Blaine Johnson's leave. That year he teamed again with Roy Halversen, and they produced *Il Trovatore*, the same opera he had introduced to Cedar City 30 years before. He promised that the double-cast production would surpass anything he had ever produced. [7] He must also have reveled in the new possibilities provided by the auditorium.

With the state-funded construction of the auditorium building, the gates began to swing open. In 1957 a new trades and industries building was completed. In 1958, a federal loan was approved to enable the creation of a student center from the old gymnasium. In 1959 plans were approved and funds appropriated for a new science center.

The trades and industries building vastly expanded the possibilities for industrial education, which had been a major thrust at the college from its beginning. For Professor Ben Cooley, Eugene Hardy and Victor Davis, it was a wondrous fulfillment of a dream and a struggle. They had built the department of vocational and industrial education in cramped, inadequate nooks and crannies. They had pleaded and planned for the building for more than 12 years. Their striving for the funds was only part of their effort. They traveled southern California studying facilities. They visited industries to find what kind of training would prepare young people for the most needed jobs.

Ben Cooley, in the process of finishing his 10th project house, would now remodel and use the old facility that had housed all three for the woodworking and carpentry division. The space for Vic Davis' automotive mechanics area was tripled. Eugene Hardy, now had up-to-date facilities for teaching welding, machines and paint. Both Hardy and Davis were graduates of the program at BAC. They had experienced the whole evolution of the program. The building was finished at the time of the 60th anniversary of the founding of the school. No one celebrated with greater fervor than these three men. They used their summer vacations to move their equipment down the hill to the new facility. Since they had no forklifts, they used a sled pulled by a horse. As one of the features of Homecoming Week, the public was invited to admire the realization of their dream.

Early in 1957, a statewide conference for elementary educators and administrators was held at the College of Southern Utah. The conference received high praise from the participants, who numbered two-hundred more than had been expected. But the significant outcome of the conference was the praise for the teacher training program at CSU that seemed the universal response of the educators. It boded well for the future.

It was a time of vitality and change with seven new people joining the faculty. Ada Carpenter and Marie Krueger came to the home and family living department. Eugene Woolf was signed to teach English and humani-

HARL JUDD

ties. Max Weaver replaced Gaell Lindstrom as professor of art. Harl Judd, looking just over 19, came as an engineering instructor.

Joseph Fillerup, sporting a brand new doctorate, came to head the department of education and supervise summer school, replacing Dr. Reese Maughan. George Barrus became the full-time public relations person, taught journalism and supervised the newly named *Thunderbird.*

There was expansion in Logan too. That year the state granted university status to

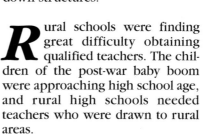

EUGENE WOOLF

Utah State Agricultural College. The name of the institution became Utah State University, much to the chagrin of the University of Utah, which had enjoyed the distinction of being the only public university in the state. Now CSU was again a branch of a university.

At the end of 1957, Dr. Braithwaite and Hazen Cooley, accompanied by Dee Broadbent, USU business manager, headed for San Francisco to confer with the Federal Housing and Home Finance Agency. They wanted a loan to remodel the old gymnasium into a student center, to replace the old Topaz office building, still valiantly serving. They needed $250,000. If they received preliminary approval there, the request would go to Washington to the Community Facilities Administration for final approval. In February the telegram arrived, bringing the good news. Gardner and Rasmussen, architects, were already at work on the plans. It would be the end of the hand-me-down structures.

Rural schools were finding great difficulty obtaining qualified teachers. The children of the post-war baby boom were approaching high school age, and rural high schools needed teachers who were drawn to rural areas.

For a long time it hadn't made any sense that CSU could grant degrees in elementary education, but to certify in secondary education, a student was forced to attend one of the state universities. The 1913 enabling-legislation for the college had explicitly vested in the Board of Trustees of Utah State University the power to establish at the Cedar City school any courses taught at the Logan campus. Requests to expand the educational offerings at CSU to include degrees in secondary education had fallen on deaf ears.

In November 1958, the college received a visitation from the Northwest Accreditation Commission, whose purpose was to evaluate

C.B. COOLEY

EUGENE HARDY

VICTOR DAVIS

institutions of higher education in the five western states and Alaska. The commission members stayed on the campus for the better part of a week, and in December they issued their report:

The association praised CSU for providing a very satisfactory educational program for students in southern Utah. They also praised the community of Cedar City for the excellent moral and financial support given to the college. The report commended the faculty members for the keen interest they show in helping students "find themselves" and

achieve success in educational programs best suited to their needs...

The report is long and effusive in praising the work offered at the College. The education department was singled out for special recognition:

Praise is particularly directed to the efforts in the field of elementary education and the close cooperation with Iron County Public Schools. The College of Southern Utah is a thriving, stable institution which is pro-

ROYDEN C. BRAITHWAITE
1912-1991

Royden C. Braithwaite became, in 1955, the director of the College of Southern Utah, which had recently changed its name from Branch Agricultural College to CSU. Because the school had been a branch of other institutions for its entire history to that date, its senor official had held the title "director." When CSU gained its independence in 1965, on the 10th anniversary of his tenure, Braithwaite technically became its first president.

When Royden Braithwaite, new to Cedar City, accepted the directorship of CSU, he said that he was so impressed to learn of the faith, dedication and farsightedness of the settlers of the town that he really wanted to be a

part of their school. In honoring Braithwaite on the occasion of the naming of the Royden C. Braithwaite Liberal Arts Center, a precedent at the college, speakers proclaimed that Braithwaite's relationship with the school was "a love affair from the beginning."

The campus was a beautiful place to him. He walked the grounds with joy, alone or with students or visitors, saturating himself with the sensations of the seasons or refreshed by a clean, new vigor after a rain. From the beginning, he worked from his vision of what the campus could become; the campus itself almost doubled in acreage and holdings during his tenure. Of the 28 structures on the campus in 1991, at the time of his death, there were few that he had not built or renovated. Each addition—building, waterfall or outdoor classroom—represented part of his vision for the body of the college. He knew the inner operations as well as the stone and mortar. He knew the faculty and staff, which grew during his administration from 50 to 235. He knew the students individually, though the enrollment more than quadrupled during his era. These were people, not numbers to him. He inspired his peers and the students, helping them to become "whole people."

Royden Braithwaite served the institution longer than any other chief administrator, for 23 years. Other leaders, in an accepted process of personal and professional growth, had used the college as a stepping stone. Despite periods of ill health, formidable difficulties and inevitable criticism, and lacking quick gratification of his

goals, Braithwaite gave a quarter of a century of his life in striving for the success of the school. When the school became SUU, Braithwaite's replacement, Gerald Sherratt said, "If we are about to explore a new world as a university, it is because he brought us to the edge of that new world."

Royden Braithwaite had prepared himself well before he came to CSU at age 43. A native of Ephraim, he had graduated from Snow College, where he was studentbody president. He had served an LDS mission to Texas and Louisiana before returning to school in Utah, graduating from BYU, where he was an honor student, summer school student body president and senior class president. It was at BYU that he met his wife, the former Alice Todd, who graduated the year they were married in 1938.

In addition to teaching seminary in Heber City, Braithwaite was director of the LDS Institutes of Religion at Dixie College and Weber State College. He served as chaplain in the U.S. Army in Italy during World War II.

After the war, Braithwaite taught in the LDS Institute at Utah State University before returning to school at Cornell University to earn his doctorate in human development in 1950. He served on the faculty at Cornell as a professor until he returned to Utah to be coordinator of student activities at BYU, where he was also co-dean in establishing the College of Family Living.

Royden and Alice Braithwaite reared three sons and one daughter, all of whom earned advanced degrees and went on to emulate their father and mother in service to their communities.

viding the people of southern Utah a fine institution of higher education. It is constantly striving for increasing facilities and services to meet expanding needs. The College and the community are working harmoniously to make this institution, its program and its facilities one to be proud of.

The Commission noted the areas of needed improvement: increased budget for operating needs, science facilities, a gymnasium for physical education instruction and more library services. They recommended that the program be expanded to offer four-year degrees in secondary education. [8]

It was praise gladly received by the college and the town. Indeed, the college and the community were working harmoniously together. The Chamber of Commerce had already appointed a committee to work for the expansion. In January, the committee had met with Dr. Daryl Chase. They received assurance from him that their request would be an agenda item at the next board meeting.

*T*he accreditation report and the recommendation for expansion gave courage to the committee. They could approach the issue with greater confidence. They marshalled the people of the whole area to relay their supportive sentiments to the Board of Trustees before the next meeting.

The *Iron County Record* of February 12, 1959, reported:

Civic groups and interested citizens, spearheaded by a committee of the Cedar City Chamber of Commerce, this week flooded the office of the president of Utah State University at Logan, with telegrams and letters, issuing a cry for an expansion program at the College of Southern Utah that would offer training for secondary teachers in a four-year degree program.

Dixie Leavitt, chairman of the chamber committee, and his group have been working for several months gathering material and working with President Daryl Chase of USU and members of the Board of Trustees, governing board for USU and CSU...The flood of letters and telegrams this week denotes the extreme interest of citizens in this area in the growth and development of the college and also gives credit to the committee for its fine work in preparing the "case" for the expansion program on the campus.

*T*he make-up of the committee was impressive. Except for the 29-year-old chairman, the membership of the committee included some of the town's most venerable citizens: Warren Bulloch, Dr. John Beal, Rep. Kumen Gardner, Sen. Charles R. Hunter, Jim Urie, Loren Whetten, Lehi M. Jones, Elwood Corry, Dr. L.V. Broadbent, Dr. J.S. Prestwich, Kumen Jones, Jim Heywood, Wilson Lunt, Ianthus Wright, Mayor Arnold Anderson and D.W. Corry, president of the Chamber of Commerce, who served as liaison to the chamber board.

The "flood" of communication had some effect. Before the paper had gone to press an inserted box flashed this news:

Word was received late Wednesday that the committee on the expansion of the college has been invited to meet the entire Board of Trustees Saturday morning, February 14 at the regular meeting of the group. A delegation is being formed to accept the invitation. [9]

The delegation journeyed to Logan, where they were reported to have received a courteous welcome. The Board of Trustees appointed a special committee to make a thorough study of the proposal.

They believed they were on their way. They were, in fact, at the beginning of a long and arduous journey.

When the Board of Trustees met in March, it received the report of the special study committee which included R.J. Potter of East Garland, Henry Hurran of Logan, David W. Evans of Salt Lake City, Ralph Blackham of Moroni, Mrs. Eve Ashton of Vernal, and Alma Sonne of Logan. Two USU officials, L.M. Neuberger and John C. Carlisle, were part of the group. Dr. Royden Braithwaite was assigned to provide them information.

The study committee reported that they had met, received the formal request and had heard a "thoughtful and sincere defense of the request from Dixie Leavitt and D.W. Corry." They had discussed the petition and decided that, while there were strong arguments in favor, there were the matters of finance, quality, coordination, accreditation and related matters. The committee concluded that it needed time to study the situation sufficiently to make valid and just considerations.

Leavitt and Corry returned home to strategize with their fellow workers. Nothing had ever happened easily or quickly in the

TOM
CHALLIS

progress of the school. This was not likely to break that pattern. They issued an invitation to the members of the special committee and to President Chase to visit Cedar City. They asked that they be given information outlining whatever would be needed to accomplish approval of the expansion. It was a project they intended to see through to completion.

In April, the requirement was announced that CSU would need to undergo an additional accreditation investigation in May. The Board of Trustees would consider the measure when that report was received.

The full Board of Trustees was to meet in Cedar City on May 29th, following the commencement exercises. The expansion committee asked to meet with the board following their meeting.

*T*hat fall of 1959, eight new faculty members and a new head librarian greeted a record number of students. Arthur Tom Challis came with a newly earned M.S. in library science. It was a career move that became permanent. Paul Warby and Paul Vorkink were hired to teach auto mechanics and English. Kent Myers, a graduate of the BAC, began his teaching career in the English department. Dr. Morris Shirts came that autumn to join the education department. But there was sadness too. Ben Cooley died suddenly, having given thirty years of his life to students of the building trades. That was also the year that a dramatic young man named Fred Adams came to replace Richard Rowley, who had gone away to Stanford University to complete his doctorate. He came with curly dark hair and a dashing mustache. His resume listed a master's degree from BYU, acting honors and attachment to theatre. It was never to diminish.

The students were oblivious to the politics that pervaded the consciousness of faculty and administrators. For students at CSU in the '50s, it was a time of vitality and creative possibilities. Much of what enlarged the sphere of their education was generated by the students themselves. They focused on assembly programs they wrote, directed and produced. They organized entertainments and expanded their own horizons. The story of the first marching group is illustrative: told by a 23-year-old bride, Barbara Grimshaw Dykstra, sharing dorm supervisor duties with her young husband, pregnant with her first child and open to new adventure: [10]

In the fall of 1958 a group of girls, in and out of the dorm, approached me to be their adviser for a precision marching drill team. It was sort of an "in" thing which had been going around and had a lot of appeal for girls who wanted something to do outside the campus curriculum. Whether or not they had approached the women's physical education staff I never knew. I had never done anything of this nature before, but why not?

We managed to get Director Braithwaite to approve our attempt, made arrangements to use the Women's Gym at 6:30 a.m. Mondays through Fridays, took several deep breaths and went to work.

I borrowed my sister's portable record player, bought an album of marching and fight songs of the collegiate and military worlds and spent my nights lying awake composing choreography in my mind. Fortunately, after a few weeks the girls had more bright ideas than I did and we began to

ELAINE SOUTHWICK, FRED ADAMS, HARRY PLUMMER, 1959

make real progress.

About this time I began waking up sick, so along with the record player, record and other necessities I carried soda crackers and munched them between calling cadences, turns and other instructions. This meant things got garbled some with my whistle-blowing signals suffering the most. The result was that I was still nauseated and unreliable at best. Fortunately, the girls found it more amusing than debilitating so that after dissolving into spasms of hoots and giggles, the lines would re-form and we would be back on task.

We called ourselves the Broncettes and when the basketball team went on the road, so did we. The girls were talented, dedicated and quick to learn. White majorette boots and kicky uniforms finished the look. These girls were a class act...In the spring of 1959, we prepared and presented a review in the fieldhouse. It was an evening of exultation and reward for the sacrifice and hard work of those early morning hours. It was also a notice of planned continuance and stability. Even though the school offered only a two-year program for most students, somehow the Broncettes would go on.

The Broncettes found new sponsors and have endured over the years, with name changes evolving with the names of the teams. The Broncettes became the Thunderettes, then, in the '80s, the Waukeenyan Dance Drill Team. It is a tribute to those young women of the academic year 1958-59 that their dream of fun and promoting school spirit should live on in the centennial year.

*I*n January 1960, the Utah State University Board of Trustees met in Cedar City again. This time the Chamber of Commerce expansion committee was

THE BRONCETTES

forceful in getting their attention. The board meeting was to be held on Saturday, January 9. The committee successfully petitioned for meetings on the Thursday evening and Friday at noon preceding the meeting of the board. Ever faithful, Morgan Rollo reported those meetings in the *Iron County Record:*

Thursday evening and Friday noon, Daryl Chase, president of USU, Milton Merrill, vice president and trustee R.J. Potter met in session with 26 members of the Cedar City Chamber of Commerce committee appointed to promote the expansion program at CSU. This committee is headed by Dixie Leavitt and he presided over the two sessions. Meeting with the group was Dr. R.W. Farnsworth, trustee from Cedar City. At the conclusion of the meetings President Chase indicated that he expected the expansion into the four-year program in secondary education to move forward and hinted that the promoters may be "pleasantly surprised" within the next two or three months.

But the report from the Saturday meeting of the trustees did not even hint of pleasant surprises. They simply suggested that the matter should continue to be studied. And that if and when the expansion should occur, it should be adequately financed. [11]

Nineteen-sixty was the year that the school would lose the revered and respected presence of David L. Sargent to retirement. While he taught as emeritus for a time, his final retirement was to become that year a reality. Dr. Wesley Larsen tells of his hiring to replace David L. Sargent:

It was spring of 1960 and I had just completed my doctorate and 12 years of teaching at Carbon College. Following an interview, President Chase said to me, "Go down to Cedar City and tell them that I have hired you to begin teaching next fall." That was typical of Daryl Chase. No one ever doubted for a minute that he was "the boss." My teaching assignment was to replace the recently retired Dave Sargent to instruct in comparative anatomy, vertebrate embryology, physiology, entomology, zoology and genetics. I have no illusion as to why I was hired. The College had just been reviewed by the Northwest Accreditation Association and found lacking in faculty Ph.D.s. So that year Drs. Richard Thompson, Wesley Larsen and returning Conrad Hatch filled that gap. We were the only Ph.D.s other than Director Braithwaite. [12]

Dr. Larsen describes the atmosphere of warm camaraderie:

In 1960 the College had about 600 students with classes held for the most part in the Science-Administration and Old Main buildings. It was a rare day when one didn't meet all the other faculty members and students, whether in the halls or at mail call in the wooden student center. Almost every afternoon the faculty would gravitate to the home economics department for Ada Carpenter to dip out home made ice cream. Treasurer Hazen Cooley's brain was the campus computer and let me tell you it was better than any computer yet invented. Bessie Dover alone managed the service desk and telephone switchboard. Ward Robb was "Mr. Efficient." He could do anything with office machines.

The spring of 1960 was a hectic time at the College of Southern Utah. Director Braithwaite became ill. Hazen Cooley again stepped up to become acting director, during the period of Dr. Braithwaite's recuperation. Construction of three major buildings had been approved and was poised to begin.

It was an important milestone in the history of the school. Nearly $1 million in new buildings would soon be under construction. A new women's residence hall would cost nearly $285,000, a new student center at just over $300,000 and a wonderful new science building was to be built at an estimated cost of $900,000.

The dorm and the student center were financed by federal loans that would be repaid by rental and fees. The Science Building would be built with an appropriation of state money.

In May of 1960, ground was broken at the Valley Farm property, six miles west of Cedar City, for a new dairy barn. Professor V.R. Magleby was to supervise the operation of the new facility. The training in agriculture, though no longer the leading area of focus for the school, was still an important part of the education offered by College of Southern Utah.

By the end of July, the bid for the construction of the new science center had been awarded to Weyher Construction of Salt Lake City. Ground breaking ceremonies were conducted on August 1, and the most elaborate and costly building on the campus was under way. The science center promised to be one of the most modern in the West. It was to have a total floor space of 50,000 square feet and

would double the classroom space on the campus. The building was designed by Gardner and Rasmussen of Cedar City.

As men with shovels gathered to ceremonially break ground for the science center, some were painfully aware of the Director's Cottage nearby. The ground upon which the new facility would be built was occupied by the home of the director. The home that had been part of the warm traditions of the college would have to be removed. A closed-bid auction was conducted to sell the house. The Braithwaites were high bidders. They moved the house to a lot on South 700 West, expanded it, and it quickly resumed its role as home for a family, a place from which emanated hospitality for students and guests of the college.

V.R. MAGLEBY, 1960

By September 1960, Blackburn and Gower construction company of Cedar City was ready to begin work on the student center. The women's dormitory was not far behind. Then both were dedicated in March 1962.

That fall quarter, Parley Dalley began his 52nd year as a faculty member at the school. In an interview with the *Thunderbird* he revealed, "I didn't intend to be a teacher. But jobs in chemical engineering were scarce at that time. A position was available at my old school, BNS, so I took it. I've been here ever since."

The effort toward expansion continued. It was a frustrating process. The trustees deferred to the newly-organized Coordinating Council on Higher Education. The Coordinating Council on Higher Education suggested more accreditation examinations. So the National Council for Accreditation of Teacher Education (N-CATE) came to investigate. It was an arduous and lengthy process.

Happily, when N-CATE had completed their examination, they announced that they had given full accreditation to College of Southern Utah. It seemed the last hurdle must surely have been successfully scaled. When President Daryl Chase spoke at commence-

ment exercises in early June 1961, the news-paper reported:

Dr. Daryl Chase, president of Utah State University, announced at College of Southern Utah commencement exercises Thursday night, that the Board of Trustees had approved the establishment of four-years training in secondary education and a full liberal arts college at College of Southern Utah. He did not elaborate on the announcement at the exercises other than to say that this would be done "as soon as feasible."

College of Southern Utah officials and supporters were elated with the announcement that the long sought program had been approved, but remained mystified when nothing more definite was announced either by the president or the board before the group left Cedar City Friday to attend graduation exercises at Snow College, and apparently nothing has been announced since...

The Cedar City Chamber of Commerce committee, elated over the board action, met with the Board of Trustees briefly Friday morning to seek information on plans for the program and to assure the board of full community support in the new undertaking. In reply to a direct question as to when the program would be put into effect, and what the plans would be, Dr. Chase stated that he could not answer the question until after the meeting because the procedure would be determined at the board meeting in session. However the question was not brought

before the board and no discussion of it whatsoever took place.

Following the meeting President Chase stated to the press that the program had been approved and that the board would "move toward establishment of secondary education and a full liberal arts college at College of Southern Utah." He gave no indication, however, as to when this would be accomplished, or what steps were being taken to put the program into effect, other than to state that the question would undoubtedly be placed before the Coordinating Council on Higher Education before the trustees took further action. [13]

The Coordinating Council on Higher Education had been organized in 1959 by legislative decree, for the purpose of coordinating the requests that came before the legislature. The body had the power of recommendation to the legislature.

It often seemed to the expansion committee and the college administrators that the Coordinating Council had become a convenient delaying detour, to which the Board of Trustees could send requests when they did not want to grant them or to deal with them. While that perception may have been formed by their impatience to move the school forward, the fact remains that the request was ping-ponged back and forth between the trustees and the coordinating council, each invoking some requirement. When that requirement had been met, it was always necessary to receive authorization of one or the other of the two governing bodies, and so it went—on and on.

While progress seemed elusive to those striving for expansion of the college role, progress on the campus was visible and consistent. It was a time of vitality and change.

Elaine Southwick was named dean of women. Her responsibilities included all women student activities and women's housing supervision. She was to direct the inter-sorority council and the Associated Women Students organization. Harry Plummer was dean of academics. The tradition of multiple tasks was still alive. Harry Plummer also taught languages and other classes. Elaine Southwick taught English and special night school charm classes for career women.

On November 7, 1961, the "million dollar lady," as the new Science Center was called, was ready for dedication. Under the chairman-

DEAN
HARRY
PLUMMER

ELAINE SOUTHWICK

their new facility, he had taught in less adequate facilities for many years. It was a dream come true for him.

It was a joyous time. The building doubled the classroom space on the campus. At $900,000, it was the most costly building built in Cedar City up to that time. Constructed on five levels, it housed 12 laboratories, nine lecture rooms, nine classrooms and 18 offices. And it was beautiful. The entrance was decorated by an elaborate mosaic, created from over 65,000 pieces of tile, by professor Max Weaver.

The United States Air Force Band ushered in the week with a concert on Tuesday. The Utah Symphony presented a concert on Friday. The people of the town lined up to tour the building, then trooped en masse to the football game with the Weber Wildcats pitted against CSU's Thunderbirds.

At the dedication ceremony Dr. Willard Libby, winner of the 1960 Nobel Prize in Chemistry, was the highlighted speaker. Gov. George Dewey Clyde spoke, as did Alma

ship of Professor Theron Ashcroft, an elaborate week of dedication events was planned. Professor Ashcroft not only chaired the festivities, he probably felt most festive. While the whole science faculty were delighted with

FACULTY AND STAFF, 1961. PHOTO COURTESY OF ADA CARPENTER. FRONT ROW: LAEL JONES, LAVEVE WHETTEN, AUDREY DUNCAN, ROYDEN BRAITHWAITE, REED FARNSWORTH, WESLEY LARSEN, REP. CHARLES R. HUNTER, HAZEN COOLEY, ADA CARPENTER, MARY KAY CROFT, SHIRLEY STOUT, MABEL DALLEY, PARLEY DALLEY. SECOND ROW: LAWRENCE COOPER, INEZ COOPER, JOE FILLERUP, MEL ROPER, EUGENE HARDY, RICHARD ROWLEY, ROY HALVERSEN, GEORGE BARRUS, CAROL DRAPER, GWYN CLARK, MARY MCMULLLIN, WILDE, ELAINE SOUTHWICK, MCRAY CLOWARD, TOM CHALLIS, RICHARD THOMPSON, A.W. STEPHENSON, PAUL VORKINK. BACK ROW: VAN BUSHNELL, GORDON SLACK, MORRIS SHIRTS, GLENN WAHLQUIST, CONRAD HATCH, BRUCE HOWARD, CLEO PETTY, HARRY PLUMMER, WESLEY LARSON, ELDRO RIGBY, D.C. SCHMUTZ, RICHARD GILLES, THOMAS LEEK, GERALD HANSEN, KIM JONES, V.R. MAGLEBY, JIM WATSON, DOUGLAS JACKSON, JOE ROBERTS, GEORGE LEBARON, KENT MYERS, FRED ADAMS.

THERON
ASHCROFT

Sonne, chairman of the Board of Trustees. Dr. Reed Farnsworth, member of the board, gave the dedicatory prayer.

In December that year, the athletic department moved into competitive athletics with four-year schools. Beginning with the 1962-63 season, CSU would no longer compete with junior colleges.

Everywhere were evidences of progress, and each was an incremental step in strengthening the petition for expansion. The quest was still a consuming passion.

In February 1962, the trustees finally made a public expression of approval of the request. The *Iron County Record* reported:

A big step forward in the campaign to expand the four year program at the College of Southern Utah was taken Saturday, when the Board of Trustees of Utah State University, of which CSU is a branch, unanimously approved the expansion of the program.

Four years of training in elementary education has been provided at the southern Utah school for some time, and it has been proposed for some time that this program be expanded to include at least a bachelor degree level in secondary education. The vote of the Board of Trustees Saturday not only seems to assure this expansion in the near future, but also leaves the way open to expand the local state institution to a full

liberal arts college, offering degrees in a number of fields. [14]

A full liberal arts college was the ultimate aim. The secondary education degree was needed, and was considered a step in the direction of liberal arts. CSU wanted to be able, eventually, to offer degrees in various disciplines. This recognition by the Board of Trustees was significant progress. From that time on, the expansion proponents began to publicly speak of their desire to expand beyond the secondary education request and to openly mention their goal for the full liberal arts designation. The report went on:

The next step in the process will be the consideration of the proposal by the State Coordinating Council of Higher Education. This body is charged with the legal and moral responsibility to investigate and examine proposals for new programs in higher education, and to make budget recommendations to the Governor and the Legislature.

It is clearly understood that the Board of Trustees has the legal authority to establish any program, new or expanded, at the College of Southern Utah which is offered at the parent institution. However, the Coordinating Council of Higher Education must consider the overall effect on higher education in the state of such proposals, as well as the cost of such expansions.

The Board of Trustees has made an official request of the Coordinating Council to examine the request of College of Southern Utah and to advise the Board of Trustees at the earliest possible date of its opinion regarding the feasibility and desirability of such a degree program. Should the Coordinating Council of Higher Education be favorable to the establishment of the program, it is recommended that the Board of Trustees authorize the President and the Director to establish such a program immediately, providing funds from any source are available. It is hoped that the first year of the program can be initiated in the fall of 1962.

Should the opinion of the Coordinating Council be unfavorable, the Board of Trustees could, it is understood, exercise its legal prerogative and make its decision. Funds with which to operate the expanded program would come from Legislative appropriation. It has been pointed out that the secondary education program in selected *areas leading to a degree can be established at the College of Southern Utah for a modest additional expenditure; $26,810 the first year; $61,162 the following year and each succeeding year thereafter.* [15]

It was clear: The legislature had the final power in the issue. Even after authorization was obtained, legislative action would be needed to get the necessary funding.

Though hope still burned brightly, there were times when the embers were fanned more by determination than by encouragement. In March 1962, the Coordinating Council for Higher Education offered the first report subsequent to the official request for an opinion.

In the initial report considerable attention was given to the question of whether or not the expansion should be limited to secondary education or whether CSU should be developed to a full four year college...The economic, cultural, political, and educational implications of a move toward the secondary degree program were discussed.

The council appointed a joint-special committee, consisting of members of the Utah State Board of Trustees and members of the Coordinating Council on Higher Education. The purpose of the special committee was to conduct further study. It was chaired by Alma Sonne.

That year, "Satchmo" came to town. On March 22, 1962, Louis Armstrong and his All-Stars presented a two-hour jazz concert to help the school celebrate the completion of the new Student Center and the new women's residence halls, called Manzanita Courts.

Again, there were grand dedication festivities. Dr. Wesley P. Lloyd, dean of the graduate school at Brigham Young University, was the guest speaker for the dedication ceremonies. Dixie Leavitt gave the dedicatory prayer. Dr. Reed Farnsworth, trustee, presided.

LOUIS ARMSTRONG

In the last week of May, the special committee made its report:

The direction which the College of Southern Utah in Cedar City will take in the future toward growth and expansion was outlined Wednesday in a "policy statement" adopted by a special committee of the Utah State University Board of Trustees and the Utah Coordinating Council on Higher Education.

*At a conjoint meeting held in the Hotel Utah, both groups unanimously concurred that **when conditions warrant** (emphasis added) expansion of CSU towards a general four-year college, growth should lead to a liberal arts college with teacher educational programs rather than merely a teachers college.*

"As a special Board of Trustees committee on the recommendation expansion of College of Southern Utah, we have made a careful examination of studies and reports on the subject," Alma Sonne, chairman and spokesman for the committee, stated. "It is our recommendation, and we shall so recommend to the board, that the requested secondary education program not be granted at this time."

However, Mr. Sonne continued that when a larger undergraduate enrollment base is established and economic resources are available, the College of Southern Utah should expand its upper division to create a general four-year liberal arts college with teacher education programs.

"In the interval, gradual steps should be taken by the Board of Trustees through the University administration to increase the number of faculty and to broaden the curriculum of CSU as rapidly as availability of funds and other factors justify," the chairman concluded. [16]

It was not what the Chamber of Commerce committee or the faculty and staff at the college had hoped to hear. While it sounded reasonable, even promising, it also sounded distressingly familiar. Their experience over the preceding five years of effort made them wary.

There had been forming in the minds of some of the committee members, and especially in the mind of the chairman, Dixie Leavitt, a conviction that the accomplishment of their goal was eventually going to

THE ADAMS MEMORIAL THEATRE:
FRED ADAMS' VISION.

happen through the Utah State Legislature, if it were to happen at all.

WhRep. Kumen Gardner ran successfully for Mayor of Cedar City in November 1961, thereby leaving the crucial Iron County legislative seat open, Leavitt resolved that he would be vigilant in persuading someone to run who had a keen interest in the expansion effort, and who could be effective.

One day in the spring of 1962, a visitor to Leavitt's office commented, casually, that this was the last day for candidates to file for election to statewide offices. It had slipped his mind. He was jarred to the realization that the hope for legislative action in the process of expansion at the College hung upon having a representative there from Iron County. It was his stewardship.

He spent the rest of the day making contacts with potential candidates. After two dozen fruitless phone calls, he realized that it was 4 p.m., and that Parowan, the county seat, was 20 miles away. After several unsuccessful attempts to reach his unsuspecting wife, he made the decision. Hastily leaving his office, he drove rapidly to Parowan and filed for the Utah House of Representatives on the Republican ticket. It was probably the least pre-meditated beginning to a political career in history. As Dixie Leavitt walked out of the court house at 4:45 that day, an old friend, Lorin C. Miles, walked in to file on the Democratic ticket. Leavitt had entered politics. His driving purpose was to move the College of Southern Utah forward. It was a quest that would span almost three decades of his life. [17]

That summer, the first Utah Shakespearean Festival announced that participating students would attend CSU Summer School classes to prepare them for the event, which would run July 1 through July 14. Fred Adams would teach courses in advanced acting, literature of the English Renaissance and Shakespeare. The *Iron County Record* reported on the fledgling venture:

Construction is progressing on the five and one-half ton outdoor setting which is an exact replica of the original productions of Shakespeare's plays. Gary McIntyre, Cedar City, is in charge of sets and scenery.

Work is nearing completion for the costumes of 'Hamlet.' Costumes for 'Merchant of Venice' and 'Taming of the Shrew' have been finished...Mrs. Lee Thompson and Gaylynn Sherratt are supervising costumes [18]*...The plays will be presented nightly in rotation so that visitors may see all three in three nights.* [19]

RICHARD
THOMPSON

The CSU Museum of Natural History opened that fall. Under the direction of Dr. Richard Thompson, it included collections from the zoology, botany, geology and anthropology departments. It was housed in the old student center, recently vacated. Another creative use of the Topaz mementos.

Students registering for fall quarter of 1962 numbered 931. The stretch toward a 1,000 student school was almost, but not quite, realized.

The three primary needs outlined in the first accreditation report were slowly being filled. 1. The science center was now a reality. 2. The library was increasing. The Library Development Foundation, established in July 1962, under the chairmanship of Cedar City businessman Elloyd Marchant, was striving to augment the collection. They solicited contributions from individuals and organizations of the

ADA CARPENTER

community and raised funds for the project. And thirdly, plans were now prepared for a physical education teaching facility.

Trustee Reed W. Farnworth announced that the building board, the governor and the trustees had all sanctioned the physical education building project. He even believed that it would pass the legislature. Senator Charles R. Hunter had introduced a bill calling for a half-cent sales tax increase, earmarked for buildings. First-time legislator Dixie Leavitt, working the measure through the House of Representatives, was learning valuable lessons on what it takes to get an intensely desired measure though that body.

By end of the semi-annual legislative session in 1963, CSU had received appropriations for doubling the campus heating plant and, more wonderfully, the $900,000 to build the physical education building.

The low bidder for the job was Alder-Childs of Salt Lake City. Ground was broken on September 13, 1963, and the much needed facility was under way. Gardner and Rasmussen had designed the building to include handball courts, dance studios, a large gymnasium, classrooms and a swimming pool. It would be the town's first indoor swimming facility.

In the spring of 1964, approval came from the Board of Trustees to begin teaching third year courses in a number of classes. The news article read:

It is now official. The College of Southern Utah will offer third year work in a wide range of fields beginning with the fall quarter of 1963. This announcement was made Tuesday, April 30, by Dr. Richard Thompson, administrative assistant for curriculum development, speaking for Dr. Royden C. Braithwaite, CSU director. Liberal arts junior year work will be offered in American studies, art, business administration, English (literature), English (communications), history, zoology, and speech. These junior year programs will lead to the B.A. or B.S. degrees.

The article continued with credits given and expressions of hope that it was a transition into becoming a full liberal arts institution.

That autumn, Walter Charles Johnson of Middlesboro, Kentucky, became the 1,000th student to register for fall quarter. It was the first time a single quarter registration had exceeded 1,000 and was the first quarter that

junior work had been given in fields other than elementary education.

Ada Carpenter was appointed dean of women. Craig Jones joined the department of business and social sciences. And Dr. Morris Shirts was made chairman of the division of education as Dr. Joseph Fillerup left to teach in Kenya, West Africa.

More dormitory space to accommodate the growing student numbers was under way in January 1964, and the construction of the physical education building progressed on schedule.

The Alumni Association initiated a petition campaign in its own drive to influence the four-year liberal arts effort. Under the direction of Van Bushnell and Naomi Platt, alumni in every town in southern Utah were enlisted to circulate petitions asking for the increased status of the college. The petitions addressed Dr. Royden Braithwaite and were sent into southern Nevada and northern Arizona communities. The documents declared that the undersigned person deeply desired a full liberal arts college in southern Utah and urged quick and positive action.

Minutes of the May 16, 1964, meeting of the Board of Trustees record:

A meeting of the Academic Affairs Committee was held last week to consider the establishment of a four-year liberal arts college at the College of Southern Utah. As a result of this meeting, and the one held this morning, the Committee unanimously recommended to the Board of Trustees that approval be given to the following plan of action:

(1) That the administration of both the University and the College be instructed to prepare sound cost estimates for the establishment of a four-year liberal arts college at the College of Southern Utah. The Coordinating Council of Higher Education should be invited to participate in making this cost estimate through its staff. The cost estimates should be prepared and approved by the Board of Trustees prior to September 1, 1964.

(2) Following the study aforementioned the administration be instructed to prepare a legislative bill which, if passed, will authorize a four-year liberal arts college at the College of Southern Utah. Budget requests to the Coordinating Council and the Legislature will include a request for funds

to establish the program with the beginning of the 1965-66 school year. [20]

Dr. Braithwaite issued an exultant statement:

The action of the Board of Trustees on May 16, 1964, authorized the administration at College of Southern Utah and the president of Utah State University to prepare an educational program with cost estimates, in order to realize our dream of a full fledged four-year liberal arts college. Of course this would be a major step forward in the fulfillment of the destiny of the College. . . This means that we are not only authorized but instructed to prepare an educational program of high excellence with a statement of financial costs of such a program. As a consequence of this action the administrative officers and faculty may proceed with unsurpassed unity in this professional challenge. It also means that the students, their parents, citizens of our southern region of the state, may share in the genuine joy of working toward obtaining the money necessary to implement the full-fledged liberal arts program. A very realistic, promising program for action is being organized. We plan to keep all citizens informed of the work that needs to be accomplished. [21]

*T*he study committee estimated the cost of adding the fourth year at CSU at $156,651. The Board of Trustees, at their October meeting, authorized a line item for that sum to be added to the CSU budget. The administration of the university was assigned to prepare legislation to effect the advancement to four-year liberal arts status. [22]

Ward Robb, registrar, announced on October 1, 1964 that the enrollment at College of Southern Utah had reached an all-time high. It was an 18 percent increase over the previous year, with 1,186 students enrolled fall quarter. Extra sections were added in many classes. Somehow, it seemed that something wonderful was about to happen.

That year, Sen. Charles R. Hunter decided not to run for another term in the Utah State Senate. Rep. Dixie Leavitt filed for his seat and became the senator from Iron County. J. Harold Mitchell of Parowan became the representative from Iron County to the Utah House of Representatives. The two legislators anticipated that the college expansion legislation would be a pleasurable task afforded them early in the 1965 legislative session.

ROYDEN
BRAITHWAITE

At the beginning of 1965, Director and Mrs. Braithwaite were honored for 10 years' service to the College of Southern Utah. Little did they guess what kind of year was just ahead.

As the legislative session progressed, no documents came from the administration at Logan. Sen. Dixie Leavitt, for whom this quest had been a seven-year mission, was impatient. He reminded the USU administrators of his imminent need to receive the proposed legislation they had been assigned to prepare so that he could introduce it in the senate. Still nothing came. Repeated urging brought no results. Some excerpts from his history reveal the dynamics of those days:

We were still fighting for four-year status for the college...the process of higher education in the state was a cumbersome and clumsy process. I was becoming acutely aware of this as I tried to get action on our quest. There was a coordinating council on higher education and each institution had its Board of Trustees. The lines of authority were cloudy. There was much room for buck-passing and not a lot of clarity as to who had the authority to do what.

The Board of Trustees maintained that they didn't have authority to grant what we wanted and suggested that it needed to be done by legislative action. It really was just another stumbling block placed in our path, but they did agree to help me draft the legislation so it would be done properly. Daryl Chase had been given the assignment to prepare that proposed legislation. At that time we didn't have attorneys at our disposal to prepare our bills and had to get them done the best we could.

We were well into the session and Dr. Chase hadn't come through with anything. I was constantly in touch with him and finally he came in with just a paragraph statement. It was highly inadequate to present as a bill. I was so upset at what he had brought me that I decided to take matters into my own hands. I went to a

lawyer, my brother-in-law John F. Piercey, and told him that I needed help to draft the legislation. I was so annoyed at the lack of cooperation and the constant flow of obstacles, that I decided that we should not only fight for our original quest for four-year status, but that we should go for independence from USU, and establish ourselves as an independent four-year liberal arts institution.

To the surprise of everyone and the annoyance of many, we drafted two bills. The first, Senate Bill 97 granted College of Southern Utah four-year liberal arts status and the right to confer baccalaureate degrees. The second, Senate Bill 209, was an audacious and undiscussed move. It made CSU independent from USU, and gave her an independent Board of Trustees.

Rep. Harold Mitchell, Dr. Royden Braithwaite, Senator Dixie Leavitt watch as Governor Rampton signs SB 209.

Little question it was a move of breathtaking audacity. There had been no previous discussion of independence. Leavitt was not only a freshman senator, but his party was in the minority. Nevertheless, he introduced the bills into the senate and went to work to line up support–checking off legislators, one by one, as he enlisted them.

Senate bill 97 passed both houses with no dissenting votes. College of Southern Utah would become a four-year liberal arts college. The class work for the degree could all be completed at the Cedar City campus, although the degree would be granted by the authority of the Board of Trustees of Utah State University.

As the legislative session drew down to the last few days, Senate Bill 209, the measure to make CSU independent of USU, languished low on the calendar. It was not moving to the top of the board to come out onto the floor. Sen. Leavitt approached a powerful rural colleague for help.

Thorpe Waddingham was the senator from Millard County. He was also the majority leader in the Utah State Senate. Waddingham had formed an affection for the intrepid young senator from Iron County and held a genuine fondness for the school which educated many of his own constituents. He agreed to help. Sen. Waddingham made a motion to move S.B.209 to the top of the calendar, under suspension of rules. Opposition came mostly from Cache County legislators,

but the motion carried.

The measure came out for debate and passed the senate by a vote of 25 to 0. It was sent immediately to the House of Representatives, where it passed by unanimous voice vote. Rep. Mitchell had done his work well. [23]

Leavitt wrote:

There was a great deal of excitement and apprehension in me as I worked to get it through. It was a daring expansion of my original intent, and I felt almost as though I were doing something questionable. But I felt strongly that if the college were ever going to move ahead, we had to have our own board and become an independent institution...it was an audacious attitude, but I felt that I was right. The pressure was intense. But the wonderful thing is that even with the opposition, we were successful and the bill passed.

The members of the 50-Year Club, at a luncheon meeting in Cedar City, hardly noticed when Parley Dalley was called from the room. He was absent from the gathering for a few minutes, then he returned with a spring in his step that belied his 85 years. He stepped to the podium and announced, "I have just spoken to Senator Leavitt on the telephone. The vote has been taken in the legislature and the measure passed unanimously, making this school an independent four-year liberal arts college." [24]

Morgan Rollo exulted in a headline that proclaimed:

UTAH STATE LEGISLATURE APPROVES INDEPENDENT GOVERNING BOARD FOR CSU.

> *Gov. Calvin L. Rampton is expected to sign into law within the next few days a bill that will divest the College of Southern Utah from the controls of the Utah State University Board of Trustees and establish an independent governing board.*
>
> *In a surprise move in the Utah State Senate last week, a bill was introduced by Sen. Dixie Leavitt of Iron County and Sen. Thorpe Waddingham of Delta to create the independent board...The passage of both CSU bills without opposition in the legislative body of the state indicates wholehearted support of the continued growth of College of Southern Utah.* [25]

By May, Gov. Rampton had appointed 12 men and women to serve on the first governing board of College of Southern Utah. Six were named for two-year terms: Mrs. Lula Issacson, Lorin Wheelwright, Marion D. Hanks, all of Salt Lake City, Mrs. Doyle Sampson, St. George, Dr. Reed Farnsworth, Cedar City, and R.J. Potter of Tremonton, Utah. Six members were named to four-year terms. They were: Lowell Sherratt, Kumen Gardner and Warren Bulloch of Cedar City, Edmund Flynn, Salt Lake City, Eugene Overfelt, Gunnison, and John T. Vernieu, Richfield. According to law, the Secretary of State, then Clyde Miller, was an automatic member of the board, as was the president of the Alumni Association, who was then Gail Miles.

Swearing in ceremonies for the new board were held on July 8, 1965, at the Family Living Center in the science building. The first action was the election of Warren H. Bulloch as chairman of the board, with Dr.

Reed Farnsworth as vice chairman. The executive committee named included Kumen S. Gardner, Mrs. Doyle Sampson and Eugene Overfelt. Then. by unanimous action, Dr. Royden C. Braithwaite was named President of the College of Southern Utah.

It was the beginning of a new epoch. No one was more keenly aware of that than was a young senator, who wrote:

> *I remember the thoughts that went through my mind after it was over. I had worked hard and I was feeling a sense of pride in the accomplishment. When the first Board of Trustees was named, I remember that I almost wanted to go meet with them and tell them first-hand what a battle it had been and give them my own charge of responsibility to make it work. I remembered the old Founders' Day stories, the Old Sorrel story, the stories of Will Flanigan planting the trees. I was aware that the things that had just happened would eventually take a place in the chronology of the development of this college. I knew the significance of the change I had wrought.* [26]

*F*or the first time in the 68-year history of the school, there would be a governing board whose sole concern was the well-being and progress of this institution. For the first time the needs and aims, the goals and aspirations of the college would not be filtered through the eyes of a mother institution. For the first time they could craft their own mission statement and form their own strategy for its fulfillment. No longer would the administrators go, like errant stepchildren, hats in hand, to plead for a share of state dollars, hoping that their "superiors" would not consider those requests counter to their own. They would, rather, stand now on an equal basis with their peers. Now they would compete for students and funding on the basis of the excellence of their programs and the educational atmosphere they could provide. It was, indeed, a whole new beginning.

The 1965 legislature appropriated almost $2 million for new buildings. Included in the funding would be the construction of the new library for $750,000, a new fine arts center (music building) at

SUU's PHYSICAL EDUCATION BUILDING, WHICH WAS DEDICATED ON OCTOBER 29, 1965.

A.W. STEPHENSON

$500,000 and a new greenhouse at a cost of $17,500. The monies were to cover some maintenance and remodeling projects. There was also money included to fund the four-year program that would evolve over the next two years.

Change encompassed the campus. The football stadium would need to be moved to make room for the new music building. L. Robert Gardner began plans for the new library. John Rowley was authorized to plan the new greenhouse. Plans moved forward for remodeling the administration building.

The new trustees were inundated with needed projects. A beehive of activity ensued. The basement of the science building was remodeled to store costumes, so that the space in the old agricultural building could be released to the health and counseling service. They authorized professor Melvin Roper to engage his building trades class in remodeling the food services area of the Student Center. Classrooms and offices were remodeled and redecorated.

When school opened for fall quarter 1965, the enrollment neared 1,600 students. Some 800 were entering freshmen. There was indeed new vitality.

That October ground was broken for the new music center; and on October 29th, the CSU Physical Education Building was dedicated by Elder Marion D. Hanks, member of the Board of Trustees.

At year's end, the trustees were laying plans for long-range development of the campus that could, in their words, eventually provide for 3,500 to 4,000 students. [27] At the time it seemed a far-away dream.

As the school settled into the new era, administrative restructuring began. Eugene Woolf became an administrative assistant to the president.

GEORGIA BETH SMITH

Gordon Slack, who had been at the college since 1959, was named assistant treasurer. Dr. Conrad Hatch was named administrative assistant for academic affairs. Dr. Richard Thompson became chairman of the Division of Social Science, which had formerly been combined with the Division of Business, headed by A.W. Stephenson, who remained as chairman of that division. Dr. Harl Judd was approved as chairman of Engineering and Physical Science, which had previously been shared by Dr. Hatch and Theron Ashcroft.

Lee Morrell and Robert Jones came to join Dr. Judd's department as assistant professors. It was a homecoming for young Dr. Jones. He had grown up on the campus carrying boxes of books for his mother, Lael Jones, whose task it had been to re-catalogue the books rescued unceremoniously from the 1948 library fire and stacked in nooks and crannies all over the campus until space was built to house them.

The drive to obtain books for the library moved, of necessity, to a state-wide effort as President Royden Braithwaite appealed to the people of the state to aid in the overwhelming task of raising $490,000 to purchase the needed library books. Trustee Warren Bulloch declared, with a small measure of chagrin, that it was the first time in three quarters of a century that the citizens of the community had been forced to look beyond the boundaries of the town for assistance. But since the college had reached far beyond the community borders in service, it was now necessary to appeal for help. Edwin Flynn of Salt Lake City agreed to head the committee.

Georgia Beth Smith became dean of women, replacing Barbara Adams. Lyman Smart was hired as director of development.

At their last meeting of 1966, the Board of Trustees sent to the upcoming legislature appropriation requests totaling $5 million. The College of Southern Utah had quickly joined the ranks of the "big-time." Unfortunately, the Coordinating Council on Higher Education recommended only slightly over half that amount, and administrators and trustees scrambled to justify their request.

A welcome boost in fortunes came in February 1967, in a federal grant for $373,923, making possible the construction of a new library. It would be constructed just north of the almost completed music building. The total cost was estimated at $1,123,923.00, but the grant gave encouragement to begin the planning.

The United States Steel Company vacated their Cedar City office and gifted its 8,204 square foot building to CSU.

That year, 1967, saw a reorganization of academic disciplines. Dr. Conrad Hatch was named vice president for academic affairs. Under his charge, the disciplines were divided into five schools and deans were appointed for the first time.

Prior to this time division heads had been designated chairmen. Five new deans included Professor A.W. Stephenson, dean of the School of Business and Technology, Dr. McRay Cloward, dean of the School of Continuing Education and Public Service, Dr. Morris Shirts, dean of the School of Education, Dr. Wesley P. Larsen, dean of the School of Science, and Dr. Eugene T. Woolf, dean of the School of Arts and Letters.

The late '60s and early '70s were a time of unrest and conflicting values among young people. The discord was reflected on college campuses all over the nation. President Braithwaite quietly prepared. In his wallet he carried telephone numbers for all police officers in southern Utah, which he knew would bring immediate help. But he also intensified attention to his students, mingling daily to feel the pulse of his campus. The few incidents which did occur were handled quietly.

Commencement week of 1967 included groundbreaking ceremonies for the new library building, and the graduation exercises featured Esther Peterson, assistant secretary of labor for the United States of America. She was also honored as a former faculty member.

That July, the Board of Trustees was reorganized and Kumen Gardner became the chairman. He replaced Warren Bulloch, who became a member of the Coordinating Council on Higher Education. The system of recommendations for funding was still capricious and complicated. Representation on the council was important to the college.

Each week the local newspaper reported progress made on the drive for books and funds for the library. Gifts continued to roll in. Some books given were appropriate for a college library and some were not useful. But the library staff received them all graciously and gratefully. The interest and involvement of people of the area and all over the state warmed their hearts,

DR. EUGENE WOOLF

DR. CONRAD HATCH

DR. MORRIS SHIRTS

DR. MCRAY CLOWARD

DR. WESLEY LARSEN

WARREN BULLOCH, KUMEN GARDNER AND GOV. CALVIN RAMPTON

even when the books did not. Money was the greatest need, and it trickled in.

Meanwhile, the library building progressed on schedule. Early in 1968, plans to add a wing to Manzanita Women's Residence Hall were announced by the Board of Trustees. They intended that it should be ready for fall quarter, 1969. Funds for that addition were granted by the Office of Housing and Urban Affairs. The trustees also announced construction plans for the first wing of a married

student housing project, to begin immediately.

Tom Leek designed the school seal, which was adopted by the trustees. The seal was composed of two columns and the arching words: "Learning Lives Forever." It included the founding date, the site of the college and the name of the school at the base. It was not

destined to last long. Another name change stirred in the wind.

Dr. McRay Cloward announced that 115 courses would be taught at summer school. There would be 60 faculty members. Expansion was evident in every area.

The Board of Trustees announced construction plans for a new administration building, a new heating plant, seating at the new football stadium and an all weather track. Funds for the new administration building were awarded from the U.S. Office of Education and announced by Sen. Wallace F. Bennett. The stadium, at a cost of $102,000, was pushed with intensity by Blackburn and Gower Construction Company. It was ready for the first football game, slated for September 28, 1968. The stadium seating was to be funded by a student fee of $2 per student, per quarter.

The secondary education program, so long in coming, received full accreditation from the Utah State Department of Education. It was a well-deserved validation.

Higher education in the state of Utah had become a hodge-podge of management systems. Five autonomous boards governing institutions of higher education, each establishing goals for their institutions, often overlapping in the development of costly programs while each battled for the same tax dollars, had created a situation in which the largest and the fittest had much the advantage. It also allowed duplication of programs, with no responsibility for the delineation of roles and missions of the differing schools

The funding fracas was especially fierce in the case of the small schools. Snow College and College of Eastern Utah budget requests both still filtered through the boards of the large universities and the coordinating council. Dixie College, Utah Technical College and Utah Valley Trade Technical College were all under the auspices of the Utah State Board of Public Instruction. They competed for funds with elementary schools and high schools of the state.

Even with the release of the College of Southern Utah from the budget scrutiny of Utah State University Board of Trustees, the college budget request still had to pass before the Coordinating Council of Higher Education before it got to the legislative committee. Sen. Dixie Leavitt, who was responsible to gain funding for both Dixie College and College of Southern Utah, found himself working in an impossible milieu. He recorded his observations:

Once I understood the appropriations process, it was clear to me that all the smaller schools were at a great disadvantage in having their requests filtered by the larger schools. Self interest meant that any request that might have run counter to the needs of the larger university had no chance of being granted, because it had little chance of being presented. The whole force for CSU was Royden Braithwaite and Hazen Cooley. Before they came to the legislative committee, they had already been before the Board of Trustees of Utah State University and the Coordinating Council on Higher Education. By the time they got to the legislature, they had been so browbeaten they hardly had the courage or the confidence to speak their own need. The universities would be attended by their boards, their alumni, their deans and their presidents. Their hearings would have the appearance of a small congress. The log-rolling effected by such an impressive entourage left little for the pickings of the poor relatives down south. [28]

It was clear that a more efficient and more equitable system was needed before the playing field could even approach being level. In the 1967 legislature, Senator Leavitt had called for a comprehensive study of the whole system. The study was authorized by the legislature that year. The Coordinating Council on Higher Education commissioned a study of their own. Two concurrent studies began immediately following the close of the session.

Both studies led to the conclusion that a single overarching board should govern all higher education in the state. That prompted the Higher Education Act of 1969 or Senate Bill 10, which called for a system of higher education governed by a single governing board.

Under the provision of the law, each institution would then have an institutional advisory council. But stewardship over the overall system of higher education would rest in the Board of Regents. Large institutions generally opposed the measure. Smaller schools championed it. The bill was authored by Sen. Dixie Leavitt, Senate District 29, who led the debate in the legislature. Notwithstand-

ing some opposition, final passage was unanimous. The state of Utah now had a system of higher education. Schools were no longer branches of other schools. Every school now took its place with all other institutions under a governing board charged with the legal authority and obligation to consider each school created equal.

There were other changes pending. For some time, the name College of Southern Utah had not really described the mission nor the functional breadth of the school. The initials caused confusion with Colorado State University. It was now an autonomous state college and many believed the name should reflect that status. In January, committees were appointed with the purpose of selecting an appropriate name. Chamber of Commerce committees were invited to participate. Campus organizations and individuals were urged to submit suggestions on three-by-five cards, including arguments why that suggestion appealed. These were to be submitted to Kenneth Benson, director of student affairs. Prizes were offered and suggestions flowed in.

The Board of Trustees encouraged the selection of a new name and set forth some criteria: 1. Inclusion of the word "state" in the title. 2. The initials should be short, snappy and easy to pronounce. 3. The name should set the institution apart from others. 4. The name should be connotative of the area. Deadline was January 23, 1969.

Suggestions ranged widely. Some samples: Kolob State College, Rainbow Canyon State College, Brian Head College, Mountain State College, State College of Southern Utah, Bonneville State College, Beehive State College, Great Basin State College, Basin Rim State College, Southern Utah State College, Utah Western State College, and Robert Kennedy State College, in memory of the recently slain U.S. senator from New York.

At the February meeting of the Board of Trustees, the name was selected. Southern Utah State College, SUSC, it would be. Legislation was drafted and sent to the legislature, where it was introduced and passed. The new name would become effective July 1, 1969.

But for the current year, College of Southern Utah had a lot going on.

The Northwest Accreditation Association awarded CSU a five-year accreditation. A

information at a time, the heralded new wonder was placed in a special room in the library. Beginning computer classes were announced. The announcement made no mention of the extraordinary events attending the acquisition of the computer. Those details emerge from the personal history of Dr. Judd:

The college had received a handed-down IBM 407, used primarily in the Registrar's Office. It had to be programmed by using panels that could be wired to do the tasks. Ward Robb and Barbara Nelson became very efficient at this. It was slow and had no memory other than the panels. USU had an IBM 1620. It had 4K of memory. They were getting a new computer and were willing to give it to CSU for a small price. Computers were not built to be moved around and it had to be prepared for shipping by IBM personnel so that damage during shipping would not occur. We somehow convinced our administration that we should get this computer. USU was anxious to get rid of it. In fact, they had moved it out of their computer center into the hall in the basement of their Old Main building, and sent word that if we wanted it we had to get it soon. It was big and heavy. CSU did not have enough money to pay to have it shipped by regular moving company.

Bob Jones and I decided that the only way was to find a truck of some kind, drive up to Logan and get it. CSU did not have many vehicles to choose from. There was an old army truck that was used by the grounds department. It was not roadworthy for such a long trip. We found that the Valley Farm had a cattle truck that could make it. The cattle truck had racks on and it had been well used for its designed purpose. We took with us a roll of plastic and some ropes. It was also necessary, in order to keep the warrant valid, that we have insurance. We somehow found $200 to purchase the insurance.

With excitement and anticipation, off we went. The weather was nice in Cedar City but as we went north it became more and more stormy. We arrived late and stayed at the Baugh Motel. We arose early and discovered that it had rained during the night. We drove the truck to the east door of Old Main and were ready to load. With help from USU personnel and the IBM

WARD ROBB, BARBARA NELSON, YVONNE
THOMPSON AND THE 407

signal compliment, since at that time most schools received shorter periods of time.

Dr. Harl Judd, assistant dean of the School of Science, invited the public to view the new computer equipment. About the size of a piano and capable of storing 40,000 bits of

DR. BRAITHWAITE HELPS MOVE BOOKS.

service engineer, we somehow got the computer loaded. The more we moved around in the truck the more sloshy the "stuff" on the bed of the truck became. There were three pieces of equipment and a hundred or more cardboard boxes of cards that held the programs and applications. There were also boxes of documentation.

We finished loading up and took off for Cedar City. We did quite well until we got almost to Provo and it started to rain. We pulled off the freeway at the Center Street exit and found a Texaco service station. We asked them if we could pull our truck in so that we could pull the plastic over our equipment and boxes. On home we went. When we finally got it home and unloaded, we plugged in the computer and it worked! [29]

Dedication of the new library was announced, but later was postponed. Some equipment had not arrived in time for the May 2 date. But the library was sufficiently prepared to move books onto the shelves.

Volunteers formed themselves into a human conveyor belt to move 45,000 books from the old library to the new. Beginning at 8 a.m., the students, faculty and townspeople pushed through the entire day. Each book was placed in its proper place in the library as it reached the new building. Campus organizations competed against each other to supply manpower for the activity. When the day was over, Dan Jones, student body president, announced the successful transfer of all the books, and declared the Student Education Association winner of the contest, having turned out a total of 76 workers.

The delay in the construction of the library had something to do with the science department. Well

HUMAN CONVEYOR BELT MOVES BOOKS.

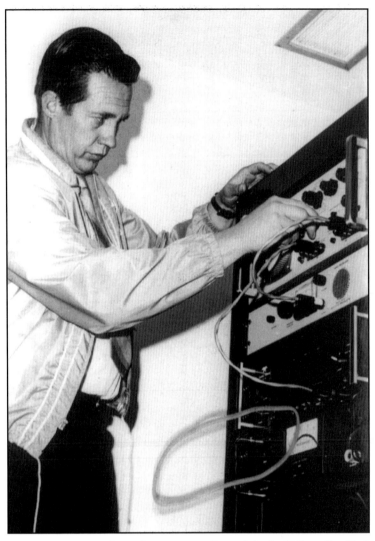

DR. HARL
JUDD AND THE
SEISMOGRAPH,
1969

Special effort was made to keep the piers free of the building because the instruments were sensitive. There was a strip around each pier that had no floor.

There were four rooms. Two of the rooms had two piers each. In one room the piers were used to hold the equipment that sensed the earthquakes. The other room with piers was used to hold the equipment that recorded the earthquakes. The third room held the time-keeping instruments and served as an office and a storage area. The fourth room was a darkroom. The records were made on photographic paper and these had to be changed and developed every day. The developed records were mailed to the U of U weekly. This became very demanding.

"Demanding" is an understatement. Every day, the records had to be developed and the paper changed. A visual display machine in the science building became a regular attraction for students and faculty, who dropped by often to see if there had been a quake. The families of Dr. Lee Morrell, Dr. Robert Jones and Dr. Judd wove the keeping of the seismograph into the fabric of their lives. Their older children learned to service the system when their fathers were busy. And there was information available beyond the natural seismic activity:

It was interesting to discover that the Saturday night dances were recorded on the record. It was easy to determine the length of each of the musical renditions, the length of the pauses between selections, and with a little bit of knowledge of music, the actual musical number could be determined. This was possible because some of the numbers were "foot stompers" and some were "quiet." This difference showed up on the records. The Saturday night dances were supposed to end at midnight. The seismograph record could be used to verify whether or not they actually stopped at that time. [30]

When new technology rendered the station obsolete, the Judds, Morrells and Jones openly rejoiced.

*C*ommencement exercises that spring bestowed honorary doctorates upon Dr. Daryl Chase, former director of the college, and Juanita Brooks, prominent southern Utah historian.

It was the last formal occasion for the school called College of Southern Utah. A new era was about to begin.

into the construction of the building, Dr. Harl Judd was contacted by personnel of the seismograph station at the University of Utah, who had established a network of stations to monitor the earthquake activity in the state. Cedar City had no station close enough to provide adequate coverage and Dr. Kenneth Cook, director of the project, wondered if CSU would be willing to have a station on campus, which they would also be responsible to maintain. The science department was always willing and the timing was good, for the station could be built at ground level in the library building in process. A change order ensued.

The station would require several small rooms and some special piers to hold the instruments and equipment. These piers were constructed of unenforced concrete and were about 5 feet by 10 feet by 12 feet high. Each pier required about 30 cubic yards of concrete and extended nine to 10 feet into the ground.

Oak Hall

Archery class, 1954

SINGING WITH 'PA' MANNING

A CSU chemistry class

1956 cheerleaders included Jackie Winterrose, Maxine Haws and Sherma Ann Huntington

Air Force ROTC women

Doris Okerlund and Pat Urie were 'Sponsors,' supporting ROTC units in 1958.

THE 'BUNNY HOP' STARTS MOVING AT A SADIE HAWKINS DANCE.

PING PONG HELPED RELIEVE STRESS AMONG CSU STUDENTS.

PARLEY DALLEY & 'PA' MANNING, JUNE 3, 1965

CHAPTER VI

Southern Utah State College, 1969-1990

" *A* campus is more than just buildings. The
thing that overrides the buildings and pulls
them together is the organization of the
outside spaces; the outside rooms, the vistas,
and the surprises around the corner."

President Royden C. Braithwaite, 1976

*A*t eight o'clock on the morning of July 1, 1969, a new SUSC flag was ceremoniously hoisted up the flagpole at the Cedar City campus. The new SUSC banner joined the flags of the United States of America and of the great state of Utah. It was the official opening of a day of celebration and the official beginning of Southern Utah State College.

The day included speeches and a reception, carillon concerts and intramural contests. President Braithwaite lauded the students for providing the major impetus for the name change.

The new flag had been created by the staff of the Utah Shakespearean Festival. Constructed by Mary Judd and presented by Fred Adams, it featured the SUSC emblem on a white background, bordered in turquoise and coral.

Dr. Harl Judd brought his scout group, Troop 347, to conduct the flag ceremony, and Brent Boyter played "Post to The Colors" on his trumpet as the flags were raised. A large birthday cake, baked by Garth Jones, was served as guests concluded tours of the campus.

By October the new library was completed, fitted out and ready to be formally dedicated. A week of celebration was planned to coincide with Homecoming Week. The theme of the week was "Tabernacle of Knowledge on Temple Hill." It referred to pre-college days when campus hill had been dedicated for construction of a temple of the Church of Jesus Christ of Latter-day Saints. Arthur Tom Challis chaired the committee for arrangements and conducted the dedication program, at which G. Homer Durham, newly appointed Commissioner of Higher Education, gave a dedicatory address. Elder Bernard Brockbank, assistant to the Council of the Twelve of the LDS church, pronounced the dedicatory prayer.

The activities of the week were widely varied, including a concert featuring Cynthia Williams Dunaway and the String Ensemble and a lecture by Dr. John Seymour. Then, in case the proceedings were too somber, they included the traditional mud football game called the Mud Bowl, featuring the Greek

GOV. CALVIN RAMPTON SIGNS BILL CHANGING THE NAME OF THE INSTITUTION TO
SUSC. OBSERVING ARE PRES. ROYDEN BRAITHWAITE, TRUSTEE KUMEN GARDNER
AND STUDENT BODY OFFICERS.

HOMECOMING
QUEEN JACKLYN
SMITH IN THE
TRADITIONAL
MUD BOWL
CONTEST.

than in any of the written accounts detailing the two structures.

*T*he once-simple campus was becoming so complex that visitors needed a directory map. Both college and community resources were used to erect a large marker on the northeast corner of the campus which identified buildings and points of interest and announced coming events.

On March 16, 1970, Roy Halversen died. For 43 years he had been at the core of the cultural life of the community and the college. There fell upon the town a cloak of sadness—a tangible diminishment of life in Cedar City had occurred. The traditions he had fostered would continue, and the mention of his name would engender warm, affectionate feelings for generations to come. He was posthumously awarded an honorary doctorate at commencement that year.

sorority women and the requisite participation of the Homecoming Queen. A Glen Yarborough concert topped off the evening.

Early in 1970, the Utah Historical Society selected Old Main and the Old Administration Building for listing as historical sites. The honor was of significant interest to Mabel and Parley Dalley. Both of them had attended school in Old Main, when it was the only building on the campus. Both had watched the construction of the second building. Parley had taught in both buildings for more than 50 years. They were present at the ceremonies, more of the history alive in their memories

Later in the spring of 1970, the Board of Trustees announced a major organizational restructuring: Conrad Hatch, formerly director of academics, was now called vice president of academics; Paul Southwick, formerly director of financial affairs, became vice president of financial affairs; Eugene Holman became dean of students instead of director of student personnel services; Gordon Slack became the business manager and Jim Robinson became director of public relations. No new hirings were needed to effect the changes. It was touted as a move to streamline operations, since all of the people involved were already aboard.

PARLEY AND MABEL DALLEY, CIRCA 1900

PARLEY AND MABEL DALLEY, 1970

By 1970, THE CAMPUS HAD GROWN LARGE ENOUGH
THAT A MAP WAS NEEDED TO AID VISITORS.

SUU · A Heritage History · 163

Almost as soon as Southern Utah State College became an independent four-year school, its influence began to be felt throughout the schools of Utah and southern Nevada.

· A large percentage of high school athletic coaches in the state of Utah and surrounding areas were graduates of SUSC.

· The National Science Foundation awarded funds enabling SUSC to provide in-service workshops for elementary science teachers. The project, under the direction of George LeBaron and Dr. Lee Morrell, included a three-week summer course for 35 teachers selected from southern Utah and Nevada. The science teachers returned for 10 follow-up sessions throughout the year; the schools of the area benefitted from the ripple effect.

· A new center for diagnostic services and therapy for handicapped children received students from surrounding school districts. Arlene Smart directed the program, and Cedar City citizens contributed materials and resources. Antone and Fern Hunter carpeted and draped rooms in the north wing of Hawthorne Hall in bright tones of red and yellow. Speech therapy, swimming lessons, social therapy, and development in motor and comprehension skills were offered to severely handicapped children, many for the first time.

· The campus became a popular venue for conferences and special workshops. Participants came to take part in conferences dealing with areas such as agriculture, education, business, community development, religion, law enforcement, health, home economics and philanthropy.

· KCDR-FM radio station bloomed on campus. Included in the student personnel were Gerald Howes and Fred Esplin, both of whom became radio personalities.

· The traditional "Snow Week" was expanded to become the "Winter Classic" in conjunction with the brand-new Brian Head ski resort. Activities were held both on the campus and at the resort.

Commencement exercises honored T.H.

Bell, United States Commissioner of Education, as well as Roy Halversen.

Just as the College had appealed to the community every autumn for 73 years, so again that fall of 1970 Rex Michie, housing coordinator, announced: "We are desperately short on married student housing." He urged the people of the community to find space in basements, attics and any other spot that was not being used. Just as they had for 73 years, the people of the town responded.

Though hard times had eased slightly, there was never enough money to buy all the equipment needed by the college's academic programs. The faculty was no less inventive and adaptable than earlier groups had been; they were still willing to go beyond contractual requirements. For example, Professors Blair Maxfield and Lawrence Cooper needed a rock-cutting machine to prepare specimens for microscopic examination. They were short on departmental funds, but long on dedication. Working Saturdays, evenings and through the summer of 1970, they invented a machine that could slice rocks to 3,000ths of a millimeter, so that the mineral composition could be analyzed under petrographic microscopes. As the machine quickly excited the admiration of geologists at other institutions, the two might have profited greatly from their joint genius, but they kept their attention focused upon teaching and made only tentative motions toward marketing their invention. Years later, others re-invented and marketed the same machine and made fortunes.

ROY HALVERSEN

JIM ROBINSON AND BESSIE DOVER

The Faculty and Staff Associations produced the Mary Chase comedy *Harvey* to a three-night sell-out crowd, donating the proceeds to the scholarship fund. Dr. Paul Vorkink directed the effort and played the role of Elwood Dowd.

In January 1971, Boyd Adams announced that he would leave his position as head basketball coach to pursue doctoral studies. He had served during the crucial years as the department moved from competition with two-year schools through the transition to four-year school competition and the entrance into the Rocky Mountain Athletic Conference.

When graduation time arrived, Elder Bernard Brockbank gave the baccalaureate address and alumnus Ellis L. Armstrong, commissioner of the United States Bureau of Reclamation, addressed the graduates and received an honorary doctorate.

Dr. Harl Judd stepped up as new dean of the School of Science, succeeding Dr. Wesley P. Larsen, who became administrator of research and the college grants officer.

In July, the Chamber of Commerce requested a report on progress at the college and received a glowing account from Dr. Braithwaite. Enrollment had surpassed other years, the faculty was considered to be the best ever, and six separate building or improvement projects were under way on the campus.

Private donors were making possible the construction of the Utah Shakespearean Festival Tiring House. Funding had been approved for the new administration building at $680,000. Two new parking lots were under way, estimated at $20,000. Phase A of the married student housing was begun and would cost $280,000. An entirely new campus lighting system had been undertaken, the cost of which would total $175,000. The peripheral road system was being improved at a cost of $10,000.

Dr. Royden Braithwaite and Merrill Kunz, controller of buildings and grounds, reported that the old married-student housing, called Ponderosa, would be demolished to create the parking lot for the new administration building. The museum would be enlarged, sidewalks re-routed, lawns and flowers replaced. All in all, it was a time of general improvement; spirits were high.

But the administration faced tough sledding on progress with their new building. The August bid opening revealed that the design was much more costly than available funds. After making some modifications, a second call for bids was issued. A December opening found the low bid $77,000 higher than the $683,000 available. Finally, in February 1972, at a special session of the legislature, an additional appropriation was obtained and hopes for the building brightened. On February 10, groundbreaking was held and the new administration building was begun.

Another significant building took its place in the affairs of the campus. On February 13, under the direction of institute director Joseph Felix, dedication ceremonies were conducted for the new L.D.S. Institute Building. Elder LeGrande Richards of the Church's Council of the Twelve Apostles offered the dedication address and the dedicatory prayer. It was an eventful week on Center Street in Cedar City.

Recruitment for enrollment involved almost everyone on campus. At the March 1973 meeting of the Board of Trustees, Frain Pearson, chairman of the SUSC Recruitment Committee, reported the progress and noted that much of the high school recruitment was channeled through the LDS seminaries—not so different from the days when Howard Maughan toured southern towns speaking in sacrament meetings about the virtues of BAC. It was still a gentle time; no one sued or made a fuss that the school was focusing on LDS students.

Pearson also reported that 681 recruitment packets had been distributed among the high schools and

THE NEW INSTITUTE BUILDING

junior colleges of Utah, Arizona and Nevada, and that 91 LDS mission presidents had received SUSC recruitment packets. As each school in the college was responsible for making its own effort, faculty members were encouraged to contact students personally and by letter. Then someone had the bright idea to stage a contest. Competitive students rose to the challenge, picking up 703 packets. Recruitment materials were placed at Brian Head Resort and in all the motels in Cedar City.

Professor Robert Jones reported that SUSC scientists had delivered 55 lectures throughout Utah and surrounding states in keeping with their recruitment.

The athletic department faculty were naturally involved in a constant recruitment effort. But the focus was never just upon winning teams. They looked for worthy students, gave all the financial help they could and often reaped extraordinary fruits. One illustrative account is told by Dr. Bruce Osborne:

I was on a recruiting trip in Southern Nevada. I went out to Boulder City to visit with Bob Lunt. Bob is an alumnus of the school and a good coach. I asked him, "Who are your outstanding players that I ought to offer a scholarship?" Without thinking he replied, "I have a kid that is such a quality young man that you ought to offer him some help." As an afterthought he added, "He's not really much of an athlete, but he's a superb person." Bob told me that the kid worked as a shoe-shine boy at a local barber shop and gave me directions to find the place. I went to the shop and told the barbers that I was looking for a boy named Harry Reid; that I had a $60 scholarship I wanted to offer him to come to College of Southern Utah. The men explained that young Harry Reid would be there at work in two hours and asked that I come back. I later learned that as soon as I left their shop they closed their doors and began to canvas the other businesses in the area. They had gone door to door gathering contributions to add to my $60. When I returned they gave me $500, so when I met Harry Reid, I had $560.00 to offer him for a football scholarship. That was more money than we had to offer any player. He accepted the scholarship. I brought the money home and gave it to Hazen Cooley and it paid for his two years at the college.

Harry Reid graduated from CSU in two years, went on to graduate from USU, and later from law school. He became a renowned

United States Senator. Bob was right. He really didn't make much of a football player, but what a great heart; what a great young man ! [1]

That spring, Eulalia B. Jones retired from the library after 10 years at the school. She had come to BAC just after the library fire had destroyed most of the collection. Students had dumped armloads of books from second-story windows, and hers was the task of making sense from boxes of salvaged books stashed in every conceivable spot. In 1950, she had become head librarian, overseeing the move to the auditorium/library building, and had assumed the responsibility for receiving and cataloging the enriching contributions that had come from all over the United States. [2]

Also that spring of 1972, Dr. Harold Hiskey was appointed as the new dean of the School of Business, Technology and Aerospace Studies. Dr. Kent Myers was named dean of the School of Education. Sterling Church became the new dean of students, taking up his duties again after an assignment at Brigham Young University. Betty Ann Kingsford became his assistant dean, then dean of women.

The commencement of 1972 was a fine affair. Honorary doctorates were awarded to three distinguished citizens. Lucy Beth Rampton, first lady of the state of Utah and daughter of P.V. Cardon, who had served during 1921-22 as director of Branch Agricultural College, was

PROMINENT ALUMNUS
UNITED STATES SEN. HARRY REID

honored. Obert C. Tanner, a benevolent supporter of the college, was also lauded. He and his wife, Grace Adams Tanner, an alumnus of the College, were the major donors to the Adams Memorial Theatre, just nearing completion.

Morgan Rollo was awarded an honorary doctorate posthumously, having died in March of that year ,1972. Cited for his dedication as a journalist and his service to his community, he had been a second generation owner and publisher of the *Iron County Record* and had to his credit a long and impressive list of projects and committees that served his town. [3]

Elder Marion D. Hanks of the LDS Church delivered the baccalaureate address.

*I*t was announced that summer that Wayne Mifflin had been chosen as director of the Upward Bound project. The goal of Upward Bound was to identify and help culturally and financially disadvantaged students to pursue post-high school educations.

The Utah Shakespearean Festival celebrated its 10th anniversary in the new theatre and presented *The Tempest, King Henry IV, Part I,* and *The Taming of the Shrew*. It was becoming a more sophisticated enterprise, still largely staffed by the department.

Events commemorating the 75th anniversary

of the founding dotted the calendar through 1973. The drama department prepared historical plays to emphasize the historic nature of the year's activities: *The Little Foxes* early in the year, and *1776* in the winter quarter. The Ladies Faculty Association organized its monthly meetings around historical themes. The art department created a gallery of photographs of personalities connected to the history. A year-long tree planting project culminated in the planting of the 75th tree.

*T*he 1973 yearbook, *SUSC Tavi*, featured a special section of historic photographs and a careful listing of the names of the men who had been instrumental in the construction of the first buildings and those who had managed the political achievements. Because the listings and the photographs, painstakingly assembled by Inez Cooper, caught the interest of the people of the community, the yearbooks were offered for sale to the public through the Alumni Office.

It was fitting that SUSC should host a forensic tournament that year. Debate competition had always been a prominent part of extracurricular activity at the school, and Professor Steve Van Dyke touted this jubilee year tournament as the largest high school forensic tournament in history of the state.

Soaring to heights of which the founders had never dreamed, Dr. Robert Moss of the School of Education and Boyd Redington, head of the photo service at SUSC, organized a Sky Divers' Club and sent parachuted divers free-falling from the sky on Saturdays throughout the year. The Sky Divers' Club was an outgrowth of an aerotechnology program offered under the School of Continuing Education and Public Service, and would qualify the student for a private pilot license. Courses could be completed in one quarter at a cost of $718.

Wives of married students loved the boon of free baby sitting services during school athletic and social events. Students were able to obtain the free service simply by calling the office of Betty Kingsford, who had come up with the idea.

It was a good year to initiate a new fundraising plan, and the annual Telethon was born under the direction of the SUSC Development Office, headed by Dennis Agle. That year, students made more than 1,100 calls, resulting in 389 pledges totaling $3,734 contributed to the scholarship fund.

The Founders' Day celebration included two assembly programs. The first, themed "Our

Glorious Past," was narrated by Lanell Lunt and Otto Fife, flanked by popular alumni musicians Christine Winterrose, Naida Gardner, Gladys Isom, Janice Olsen and Mary MacDonald. Gov. Calvin L. Rampton came to speak at the Thursday afternoon program, and the SUSC band closed with a patriotic salute.

Bulldozers moved onto the campus in early May to begin the "mall project," which was designed to transform the area between the student center and the music building. Benches, overhanging arbors, kiosks and walkways would be interspersed among shrubbery and flowers. Waterfalls cascading down from the student center level to the site of the new administration building were to form the basis for hillside landscaping. It was pure "Braithwaite," a reflection of the president's desire for the campus to be a place of extraordinary beauty. The work proceeded at a frenzied pace in order to be complete for Commencement, scheduled for June 1. President Braithwaite kept an encouraging watch on the progress, walking across the site several times a day.

When Commencement Week dawned, a decision had been made to hold the exercises on the campus quadrangle. The construction of the administration building had rendered the parking lot by the War Memorial Fieldhouse unusable. Spring rains had made the greens of the campus unusually beautiful, and so the first of the traditional outdoor graduation ceremonies were held on the lawns east of the school's two oldest buildings

If any of the founders were watching from an exalted sphere, they would have been astonished at the changes 75 years had wrought. Where one building had once stood on a rocky hillside, 44 buildings dotted a campus of 102 landscaped acres.

Paul H. Dunn of the LDS Church delivered the baccalaureate address at services which had quickly moved indoors to the Auditorium to escape the sudden rain. Sen. Dixie L. Leavitt delivered the address to the graduates the next morning under threatening skies, with graduates and friends seated on rows of chairs on the grassy quad where cows had grazed contentedly a generation before.

That summer, the

THE MALL

beautification efforts on the campus were enhanced by the SUSC School of Sciences project. The faculty of that school planted three bristlecone pine trees in commemoration of the 75th anniversary. Southern Utah State College had chosen the Bristlecone Pine, a tree of the southern Rocky Mountains whose prime characteristic is an extraordinarily tenacious hold upon life under every adverse condition, as its symbol.

The Utah State Board of Higher Education approved a nursing program to train licensed practical nurses and registered nurses. Offered in cooperation with Weber State College, it was called the LPN/RN Program. A critical shortage of nurses in the southern Utah area was the impetus for initiation of the courses. Students from Dixie College could take general education and nursing support classes at Dixie College, then transfer to SUSC to complete the nursing courses and the major portion of their clinical experience. At that time, the Iron County Hospital was the only accredited hospital in the area.

As the summer of 1973 ended, the long-awaited move to the new Administration Building began. It had been on the drawing board for nearly 10 years. A stormy financial path had further delayed completion, but now it was finished. The registrar, the cashier, the financial affairs office, the controller's office, the dean of students, student personnel offices, the vice presidents and the president all moved in to adequate and attractive new offices. For them, it was the best part of the jubilee celebration.

In the spring of

THE TELETHON SAW GREAT SUCCESS.

1974, ground was broken for a new trades and industries building at 800 West and Center Streets. The old building, which had seemed so wonderful a few short years before, had become hopelessly inadequate as the programs multiplied. Ross Hilton, chairman of the SUSC Industrial Arts and Technology Division, reported that the division included more than 20 vocationally oriented programs, which would be housed in this new building designed by Jack Rowley. A low bid of $1,024,000 was received from Carter Brothers Construction, who were awarded the job. Work progressed rapidly through the year. Spring break of 1975 allowed time for moving into the completed facility. Courses were moved from all over the campus into the 24,000 square foot building.

From the beginning of the Air Force Reserve Officers Training Corps in 1949 until the mid 1960s when the college became a four-year school, an active two-year program had been maintained. When the college assumed four-year status the ROTC program was dropped. Then, in 1971, a four-year ROTC program was

TRADES
AND
INDUSTRIES
BUILDING

reinstituted and had become a valued training program.

Word came early that year that 12 programs across the nation were to be phased out. The program at SUSC would be one of those because the number of cadets enrolled was too small to justify continuation.

A higher percentage of the student body was enrolled at SUSC than at other universities, as high as 3.5 percent participating, but since the total enrollment was under 1,900 students, the SUSC program did not meet Air Force guidelines. The Institutional Council accepted the decision "with regret."

As always, the aim of serving the community and the students drove the evening and the summer programs; summer forum presentations included lectures on topics of interest for

both students and the public. Faculty members gave lectures in their areas of expertise or their areas of interest. David Conine lectured on "Energy Alternatives for the Home," Fred Adams presented "Shakespeare Production," and Dr. Morris Shirts gave a lecture entitled "Those Stupid Studebakers." All the visual aids belonged to him. He owned nine Studebakers at the time, "five going, three getting ready and one for parts." [4]

The old Administration Building, originally constructed in 1903-04, when it was called the Science Building, was placed on the Utah Heritage List. The structure originally housed science laboratories and classrooms, the home economics department, administrative offices, an auditorium and ballroom, and some student offices. At commencement time, one particular office was called the "weeping room," where graduating students bade farewell to classmates and friends.

All the principals and directors of the college from 1904 on had their offices in the building until in the middle 1960s the building was condemned and vacated. For a decade, it stood empty, awaiting the allocation of funds to repair it. Because of the building's grand historic value, restoration was favored. The building was named to the Utah Heritage List and plans were drawn and the Board of Trustees approved the project at $92,000.

When construction began in 1974, only the outer walls of the building were preserved, while the interior was gutted and completely restructured. The old brick exterior was cleaned and restored as nearly as possible to its original state.

Adaptive preservation was completed in the structure in 1975 with Boyd A. Blackner as the architect and Carter Enterprises as the general contractor. Renamed the Old Administration Building, the building housed the School of Continuing Education and Public Service, offices of the School of Arts and Letters, a weaving room, classroom and conference space, and temporarily, the School of Business. In addition, the College established an art gallery on the building's first level, which was named in honor of President Royden C. Braithwaite.

The Braithwaite Fine Arts Gallery became home of the College's growing permanent art collection. It was designed to administer a vigorous exhibition program of traveling faculty and student art exhibits for the cultural edification of the campus and the community. In the years to come, it would host prominent artists for lectures, art demonstrations and related cultural activities. It would also provide students the opportunity to examine and participate in the procedures of a gallery program.

Almost simultaneously, construction began to convert the basement level of the 1970 science building for use of the expanded nursing program of the home economics department. The building's basement level had previously consisted of empty unusable space. The remodeling produced classrooms, offices and training rooms with hospital beds and equipment, allowing the program goal of two-year registered nurses training to move forward in its new facility.

DR. GWYN CLARK

DR. KENT MYERS

In 1975, the Institutional Council announced the creation of a new department of business, formed by consolidating the departments of accounting, business administration and business education into one department. The new department of business was to be chaired by Dr. Robert Moore.

The departments formerly called elementary education and secondary education became, through consolidation, the new department of education to be headed by Kent Myers.

James Miller was named dean of the School of Education, replacing Dr. Gwyn Clark, who had recently retired. Dr. Clark, who had been a stalwart in teacher education, had taught for 24 years. She continued with emeritus status to supervise student teaching at SUSC.

Dr. Gwyn Clark spoke that spring, 1975, at the baccalaureate exercises, sharing honors with Sen. Wallace Bennett, who spoke at the commencement program. The moment gave grateful students an opportunity to laud their much beloved teacher. Gwyn Clark had been the spark that lit the flame of teacher education at SUU. [5] She had made it her mission, from 1950 to 1974, to transmit her passion for teaching to her students. The Fulbright scholar inspired prospective teachers on three continents, but her focus had been her southern Utah charges.

A poignant presentation occurred in the summer of 1975 when Ramona Chamberlain, gifts and exchange librarian, received from Geneve Plummer, widow of J. Harry Plummer, his complete library of books, periodicals and recordings. The materials were written in Russian, Latin, French, German and Spanish. The collection of 367 books, 425 periodicals and various recordings rendered a substantial boost to the foreign language section of the library. J. Harry Plummer, at the time of his death on July 12, 1972, had been serving as chairman of the language department and professor of Spanish. He had taught and held administrative positions for 26 years.

Professor Plummer had been largely self-educated in languages. His acumen in French, Latin and Spanish had been gained over the years, working late at night, poring over the books and listening to the recordings that his widow now gifted to the library. He was the father of the language department, simply learning to teach whatever subject was needed at a particular time.

*B*undled in topcoats in late autumn, college and area dignitaries participated in groundbreaking ceremonies for a new Life Science Building on the corner of 300 West and 200 South. It would house soil labs, a greenhouse and office space. The new structure would expand educational possibilities in life sciences beyond wildest dreams of earlier faculty. It would be built at a cost of $365,000 and would be ready for fall quarter 1976.

A welcome gift from an "anonymous donor" opened the way for the fulfillment of yet another dream. From the time of his arrival as a member of the faculty in 1966, Dr. M. Robert Jones had longed to establish an observatory. Southern Utah is an especially advantageous place for observing the heavens, because of the clarity of the atmosphere. Faculty members of the School of Science had done the best they

AL TAIT AND A STUDENT CONSIDER BANANAS GROWN IN THE NEW LIFE SCIENCE GREENHOUSE.

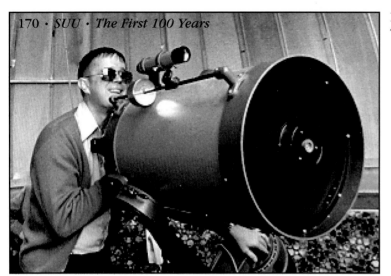

Dr. M. Robert Jones exults in the Observatory, 1980.

could to establish an observatory on the roof of the science building, using available equipment in the department.

In a characteristic manner, Dr. Harl Judd, dean of the School of Science, laboring along with his two young sons, constructed a redwood deck on the roof of the science building. Crafted with piers for mounting the two eight-inch Newtonian reflector telescopes and a three-inch refractor, this structure on the roof became the SUSC Observatory.

Dr. Jones, head of the department of physical sciences, enthusiastically advertised:

Arrangements for special astronomy lectures and observing sessions can be made by contacting the SUSC department of physical science. We gear the lectures to the age and interests of the group.

Dr. Jones noted that the observatory was open to the public, weather permitting, from 9:30 to 11:30 p.m. Daylight Savings Time. [6] The department was flooded with requests from cub scout and boy scout groups, 4-H classes as well as astronomy buffs who wanted to view the heavens.

One observer had an especially clear view of the inadequacy of the facility young Dr. Jones was trying to establish. Eulalia B. Jones, retired from long service as librarian at SUSC and mother of Robert Jones, made a gift of a powerful new telescope, with the provision that the name of the donor would be kept secret.

Late in November, in plenty of time for Christmas, the gift arrived. It was a 14-inch Schmidt Cassagrain telescope which doubled the resolution and tripled the light-gathering powers that had been available in the smaller equipment. Another pier was installed on the redwood deck on the roof. The four telescopes had to be carried in and out with each use. The

new instrument made it possible to see fine-grained objects and to take photographs and spectrograms. People could really see the stars.

Then another gift opened another door. Arthur Armbrust, a developer from Wheaton, Illinois, purchased a quarter section of land in the hills west of Cedar City. A magnanimous man, wishing to contribute to the community well-being, he offered five acres to Southern Utah State College to be used for a worthy project. Professors Jones and Judd knew exactly the project. But the college had no funds for the undertaking.

In October 1976, Dr. Jones sent a formal proposal to the College Development Board, chaired at that time by Dennis Agle, asking them to raise the projected $23,000. Mr. Clayton Frehner, who was chairman of the Development Board, had been instrumental in the Armbrust gift. The board agreed to take on the project and Mr. Frehner accepted the chairmanship of the observatory committee.

The project was embraced with the same spirit that always attended worthy projects at the school. People agreed to donate their skills and materials. Raymond Gardner, architect, contributed his time and talent to making the design. Professor Lyman Munford pledged his building trade students to construct the building and went to work getting donations from the materials suppliers in the town. On October 10, 1977, ground was broken. On September 26, 1980, the observatory was dedicated and named for Professor Theron M. Ashcroft, who had shared the dream and the wonder with countless students over a teaching career that lasted 34 years of the school's history.

Athletic programs were never completely overshadowed by academics. The school also needed new playing fields. The administration developed an extensive complex during 1976 that encompassed the area between 800 West and 1150 West and comprised of two softball fields, a regulation baseball field, complete with dugouts, and a regulation football practice field, all adjoining Thunderbird Stadium. The ingenious aspect of these new fields was a sprinkling system that used water from the Cedar City sewage treatment plant. At the completion of this new project, two-thirds of the campus was under a system that could be sprinkled with used water. It was recycling ahead of its time.

Clayton Frehner

The aging Old Main building, constructed in the winter of 1898, was greatly in need of renovation too, although it had been extensively remodeled following the 1948 fire. In 1977, the building was similarly gutted and an entirely new interior was constructed inside the familiar exterior. The 17,016 square feet of floor space was completely reapportioned with all new partitions in the all new floor plan.Some of the pioneer flavor of the building was preserved in rock arches in the first level of the building.

When the work was completed in late 1977, the building now housed the School of Education, the English department and some other offices of the School of Arts and Letters. Modern classroom-laboratories on the top floor added a new dimension to the purpose for which the building was first erected, the training of teachers.

Actually, the 1977 renovation was the Old Main building's fourth incarnation. Originally built in 1898, it had been remodeled once before the disastrous fire of 1948 and the resulting third remodeling that followed. But through all its various remodeling, the original outer walls were preserved and the appearance of building remained the same, adding a sense of continuity to the campus.

*I*n November 1977, Dr. Royden Braithwaite announced that he would retire after 23 years as head of the college. The account of the announcement was accompanied by accolades describing the significant accomplishments of those 23 years. When the Braithwaites had come to the campus in 1955, enrollment numbered 427 students. At the time of his retirement, the enrollment was just over 1,900 students. He had begun his term under the Board of Trustees and the administration of Utah State University for 10 years, and then had shepherded the transition to an independent four-year liberal arts college, serving longer than any other president, nearly a third of the 81-year history. He had seen the student body quadruple, and the structures on the campus double in number. Every area of the expanded and beautified campus bore his imprint.

The announcement came near the day of his 65th birthday. The Trustees announced that a search committee had been appointed to find his successor.

There was no "lame duck" respite for the retiring president; he had many things to finish up. Five major additions to the campus were under construction. The Life Science Building was

midway to completion, Old Main and the old science building were both undergoing extensive remodeling, the industrial education building and the administration building were in the finishing stages.

Dr. Braithwaite had been deeply involved in helping to prepare an application for the authority to grant the master's of education degree at SUSC. The petition was before the Board of Regents and required his vigilance until the end of his term. Announcement came in September that a master's program in cooperation with USU would be granted. While it was not a triumph, it was a beginning. James Miller, dean of the School of Education, called it a step toward "proving the point" that SUSC was moving rapidly toward readiness to grant the higher degree independent of a university. Dr. Braithwaite would enjoy watching the achievement of the goal after his retirement.

The honorable Scott M. Matheson, governor of the state of Utah, and Elder Nathan Eldon Tanner, of the first presidency of the Church of Jesus Christ of Latter-day Saints, both came to participate in the late April festivities honoring the outgoing president. Appreciation Day was a celebration filled with activities: in the morning, a groundbreaking ceremony for a new solar-heated business building; in the afternoon, the dedication ceremonies for the

INEZ
COOPER

five newly-completed buildings; and in the evening, a gala banquet honoring President and Mrs. Braithwaite. President Tanner was the featured speaker at the banquet. He praised the influence and spiritual uplift that emanated from Royden Braithwaite which would, he said, continue to be felt for years to come.

Inez Cooper, SUSC archivist, enumerated Braithwaite's accomplishments in terms of development, declaring, "In his 23 years the College has grown to include five Schools, offering 20 majors with 36 minors, with seven composite majors, 10 special majors for elementary education, eight professional programs and 12 vocational education programs." [7]

Students and staff members remembered his proclivity for establishing treasured traditions. He began the campus tree-lighting ceremony and always personally turned on the lights of the big pine tree, where students, faculty and staff and their children gathered to initiate the season. He always arranged a Santa Claus, music, games and fun. He found a place in the canyon east of Cedar City which he named Thunderbird Gardens, and introduced it as a spot of solitude and reflection. He formed the framework for the symbolic connection of the Bristlecone Pine to the school he loved.

He created a weekly President's Assembly, held every Thursday in the Auditorium. Faculty and staff members performed, and all the students were invited. Most of the assemblies were serious offerings, but the one most memorable was hilarious. That program included Ada Carpenter dressed as a cave woman in a beautiful soft calf-skin costume. ROTC Major Bowes flew across the stage on a wire "vine," flinging Ada across his shoulders as he flew. Dr. Gwyn Clark read "I'm A Little Teapot," Blaine Johnson sang "Mac the Knife" while Roy Halversen played the jazzy number on his violin. [8]

A portrait of Dr. Braithwaite, painted by Alvin Gittins, was unveiled and presented at the retirement dinner. The students dedicated

the yearbook *Tavi* to their retiring leader.

A fitting farewell came with commencement in June. Dr. Braithwaite was invited to deliver the baccalaureate address.

He accepted an assignment to teach psychology and education courses, relishing the prospect of being on the "front line again."

In May, the Board of Regents named Dr. Orville Carnahan as the 12th president of Southern Utah State College, effective July 1, 1978. At the time of the appointment, Dr. Carnahan was serving as associate commissioner for higher education for the Utah System of Higher Education. The search committee had screened more than 100 applicants, submitting five names to the regents.

Dr. Carnahan was a native of Malta, Idaho, whose credentials were impressive. He had served as president of Highline College in Midway, Washington, as president of Yakima Valley College in Yakima, Washington, and as chancellor of Eastern Iowa Community College in Davenport, Iowa. He came to Cedar City with his wife, Colleen (Arrott) and their family of four children.

President Carnahan began immediately to acquaint himself with his task. By early in January 1979, he was ready to announce major organizational changes: The School of Continuing Education and Public Service was to be eliminated, the programs administered under that school now becoming the responsibility of the Dean of Academic Affairs. A new position of vice president for academic affairs was created, that person to assist in administering the programs transferred to the new office. McRay Cloward returned to full-time teaching duties. In line with established policy of rotating duties of the deanships, Dr. Hal Campbell became dean of the School of Arts and Letters, relieving Dr. Eugene Woolf for broader teaching responsibilities.

Inauguration festivities brought Gov. Scott M. Matheson, Dr. T.H. Bell, commissioner of Higher Education, and a host of other political and educational leaders to the campus on a crisp April day. They had come to participate in the formal installation of the new president of Southern Utah State College. An academic procession began at the music building and proceeded across the campus to the SUSC Auditorium, where President Carnahan received his charge of responsibility from Kumen Gardner, chair of the Institutional Council, Donald Holbrook, chair of the Board of Regents, and Dr. T.H. Bell.

DR. HAL CAMPBELL

Dr. Bell emphasized the need for courageous and morally righteous leaders. He suggested, "...we lack leaders who have the courage and character to tell us what we don't want to hear even if is right and good and in our long-range best interest. We desperately need leaders with strong convictions, who will choose the right, even if it means defeat at the polls or criticism in the ranks of the constituency. We need leaders who can speak in a straight and forthright manner those universal truths that tell us to stop spending today, for we are leaving our children a heritage of staggering debt." Commissioner Bell declared the incoming president to be such a man, predicting that the College would grow and prosper under his leadership in the coming years.

In his response, President Orville D. Carnahan emphasized his commitment to vocational education and liberal arts education in side by side availability. "Whatever the future holds, SUSC has a tradition of community support and commitment to tradition imbedded into the college...We will keep that spirit alive and make this unique and distinct school the college we have the potential to become. We must gauge our efforts and our successes by a yardstick of excellence, educational excellence, and intellectual excellence. A major thrust for our college should be quality of instruction, provided by master teachers. We must provide a climate of freedom, freedom of inquiry, not freedom to evade or avoid professional and social responsibilities; a climate of freedom, not of license. We need to provide an atmosphere conducive to learning, inside and outside the classroom..." [9]

As he concluded his response, President Carnahan stated, "The President for this college must be an idealist but with both feet firmly embedded in reality."

He was right.

Even before his inauguration President Carnahan had faced extenuating challenges. A pending tax revolt had caused Gov. Matheson to call for a $15 million budget cut. Of that amount, $6 million was apportioned to higher education. This was money that had already been apportioned by the legislature and had been already included in the budgets of the schools—not a pleasant prospect for a new president.

Dr. Carnahan opposed the attempt to make up some of the deficit by levying a steep tuition hike to out-of-state students, realizing that the schools nearest Utah borders would be most adversely affected. SUSC would sustain a more serious loss than neighboring Dixie College, because the tuition increases were greater for four-year schools.

*T*he Institutional Council supported President Carnahan. The action was, they agreed, at cross-purposes with the Regents' recent charge to increase enrollment at SUSC to 2,500 students. Despite their protest, the tuition hike was implemented.

It was not just the political climate that brought challenge. The students could, on occasion, foment some stress. *The Thunderbird* published an "Other Side of The Campus Issue," which celebrated the ease of obtaining illegal drugs, the proliferation of liquor and other unsavory activities in the dorms.[10] While investigations proved that the problems were much overstated by the enthusiastic editor, the new president must have reeled a bit.

Good things helped to balance the scale:

· An accreditation team visiting SUSC gave a resounding vote of confidence to all 12 vocational programs and full accreditation.

· The cooperative master's of education program took classes off campus to 91 students in St. George, Kanab and Richfield.

· The Board of Regents recommended the completion of the third floor space in the administration building, which would add 5,000 square feet of new space.

· The SUSC forensics team, under the direction of M.L. Smith, brought home sweeping victories from debate meets around the western United States and then hosted the first national forensics tournament at SUSC—a resounding success.

· The Utah Shakespearean Festival competed a successful 18th season. Three plays, *The Merry Wives of Windsor, King Lear* and *All's Well That Ends Well*, ran July 18th through August 18th. They had managed to clear the debt of the Adams Memorial Theatre, and festival planners gratefully turned their attention to

DR. ORVILLE CARNAHAN

FRANK J.
PETTY

KUMEN GARDNER

landscaping the grounds.

•Computer cataloging was introduced at the Library; the Library went on line with the Ohio College Library Center (OCLC). It was a beginning that seemed miraculous at the time.

•The SUSC Women's Resource Center began to open broad vistas for women students. Their successful fall workshop, "Networks," attracted wide participation.

•The program established as The Indian Education Center became the Multi-Cultural Center, adding an instructor in the Navajo language, a remedial specialist and a Paiute research specialist.

After more than 14 years service on either the Board of Trustees or the Institutional Council, 12 of these years as chairman, Kumen Gardner retired from the council. He had seen the school through daunting challenges, some defeats and some triumphs, serving untiringly and effectively. At commencement exercises on May 29, Mr. Gardner was awarded an honorary doctorate degree.

Frank J. Petty, Cedar City postmaster, was elected to replace the retiring Mr. Gardner. James Hoyle, Cedar City businessman, became the vice chairman.

Bringing to a close 28 years in athletics at SUSC, Cleo Petty announced his upcoming retirement. He agreed to stay one more year on emeritus status. He had served 28 years as baseball coach, 10 years as basketball coach, 12 years as athletic director and 16 years as chairman of the athletic department.

Petty was the rare combination of athlete and musician; many people would rather hear him play the piano than watch his basketball team. He was noted for remembering each individual player and that player's athletic peculiarities.

The November 28, 1978, dedication ceremonies, attended by enthusiastic townspeople

and students, marked the official dedication of the Music Building. The event was held in the 250-seat recital hall to be named for Frank A. Thorley, whose family had earlier generously given their home on 200 South Street to house the department. The prayer of dedication was offered by Kumen S. Gardner. David W. Evans of Evans Advertising in Salt Lake City was the featured speaker in a mostly musical program.

The budget cuts were real and they were difficult to deal with. December of 1979 brought a memo from President Carnahan to the faculty and staff with the news that the campus would be shut down from December 21 through January 1 in an attempt to save an estimated $11,000.[11]

No one was happy that January of 1980, with the mandated four percent cut in the budget, and President Carnahan struggled with the resulting pain to his faculty and staff. He assured them that there was also good news. He hoped—was in fact confident—that a salary adjustment for SUSC faculty and staff was in the offing. It continually chafed that salaries at SUSC were lower than at other state institutions.[12]

However, an anticipated 12 percent salary increase dwindled to eight percent, and President Carnahan informed the community that he feared that dire consequences would result from the cuts being required by the Legislature. The behavioral science major was dropped; others were being reviewed.

These stresses took their toll. President Carnahan suffered a mild heart attack shortly after the completion of the legislative session,

COACH CLEO PETTY, 1979

THE MUSIC
BUILDING

which required that he rest six weeks away from the university.

But these trials proved again the traditional resilience of the school. The customary community response came in the form of the Southern Utah State College Foundation. Organized to help maintain and extend the facilities and services of the college, the foundation named William I. Palmer, son of an early BNS student, William R. Palmer, as first president. Anne Ashcroft Judd was an effective vice president. Their stated goals were ambitious, including the establishment of a new student center and of a western and southern Utah history collection.

A donation from Dr. John Seymour assisted in the establishment of the Palmer Room, which would house the history collection in the Special Collections area of the library. Achieving the badly-needed student center was destined to take a little longer.

Young scientists flooded the campus for the eighth annual Southern Utah Regional Science and Engineering Fair. Fair director, Steven Heath, invited the public to attend and view remarkable exhibits prepared by more than 200 junior high and high school students from the southern Utah region.[13]

The music department produced Bizet's *Carmen* for the third time in the 30-year career of Dr. Blaine Johnson. The production was a fitting finish to his three decades at the college, providing an appropriate setting for the announcement that he would retire. Johnson's years had spanned the eras of BAC, CSU and SUSC. Beginning in 1951, when BAC

was still a two-year college, Dr. Johnson and Roy Halversen produced the great operas of the world. Keeping alive the tradition established by William Manning and Halversen, the new team produced the major musical works for orchestra, chorus and soloists. They dared to produce Verdi's and Mozart's difficult requiems. Every year from 1951 through 1979, he had conducted Handel's *Messiah*. He had enriched the lives of literally countless students and had expanded the cultural horizons of the whole region. In 1974, he founded the Manning-Halversen Oratorio Society, generously passing the conducting privilege to others, to provide stimulation and growth opportunities for many who would not otherwise have had such a resource. As with the departures of William Manning and Roy Halversen, the people of the town and the school felt a deep awareness of diminishment at Dr. Johnson's retirement.[14]

The SUSC marching band needed spiffy uniforms, but the road to raising the funds was long and fraught with other, more pressing, needs. Driving home from a meeting in Salt Lake City in December of 1977, Dr. Eugene Woolf heard a tantalizing item on the radio, date-lined Washington D.C. The new White House ceremonial uniforms, designed during the Nixon administration and considered too European for American tastes, were being put into mothballs. When Dr. Woolf fired off a letter to the White House information officer, the reply was discouraging. It was not possible to sell or give away official inventory. Woolf was undaunted. He contacted Sen. Jake Garn, who contacted the General Service Administration, who asked for some justification for such a presumptuous request. Dr. Woolf applied his persuasive pen to a letter. After a painful period of waiting, he was informed that the uniforms had been turned over to the Secret Service, but that his letter would be forwarded.

DR. BLAINE JOHNSON

DR. PHILLIP C. CARTER

PAULINE H.
NELSON

Six months later, in May of 1980, word came that 80 of the handsome black, white and gold uniforms, which had been worn only once by the White House guards, were being sent to Southern Utah State College. The music department rejoiced. There was the problem of $400 for the freight bill and another significant sum for cleaning. When those items had been paid for, the department had $65 remaining in their budget for the year.

The White House uniforms presented some difficulties. To belong to the White House Ceremonial Guard, the guardsman had to be at least six feet tall and in excellent physical condition. Since the majority of SUSC's band members were less than six feet and some were a bit heavy for the uniforms, extensive tailoring was necessary and not always successful. Television reporters invariably trained their cameras upon the most ill-fitting uniforms, and one national television program, themed to the "Whatever Happened to...," devoted an entire segment of the program to the unhappy history of the uniforms at the White House.

Among other problems, the buttons of the uniforms had been removed since they had been engraved with the presidential seal. Despite the difficulties, the handed-down uniforms served the marching band for the next six seasons.

Southern Utah State College announced a new policy of placing increased emphasis on what they called outreach or off-campus programs. Pauline Hafen Nelson became the assistant vice president for academic affairs, assuming responsibility for federal programs, community services, conferences and workshops, evening school, summer school and off-campus programs. The beginning thrusts of the outreach programs were in elementary and secondary education, allowing persons in outlying communities to complete degrees through classes offered weekly in

their towns. Cedar City residents who worked during the day were offered sequential courses taught entirely in the evenings and on weekends. Dr. Phillip C. Carter, chairman of the SUSC department of teacher education, was responsible for the educational offerings.

Typical of students who attained degrees from the outreach effort was the first graduate from Garfield County. Mrs. Marilyn Bulkley was one of 15 outreach graduates in the 1981 class. A mother of four, she had lacked 30 credits toward graduation when she married and settled in Panguitch.

*T*he library collection of western history received significant enrichments in June of 1980, when the family of the late Gustive O. Larson gifted his impressive collection of books, pamphlets and other publications to SUSC. Mr. Larson had been the first director of the LDS Institute on the BAC campus, serving there for 20 years before accepting an appointment as professor of history and religion at Brigham Young University. Tom Challis, librarian, gladly received the collection.

These were times of heated oratory and strong political opinions on the campus. The debate over the proposed MX missile base in the western desert of southern Utah brought fiery opponents to SUSC, stirring up the students, who added their voices with vitriolic condemnatory letters to the editor of the school newspaper. Community members had looked to the base as a possible answer to economic woes. The College sponsored a four-part lecture series on "Growth and the Quality of Life in Utah." It was designed to temper the tempest.

The ever-present budget cutting also drew feverish criticism from the students and

C. DAVID NYMAN, STUDENT WAYNE
GOULDING AND EUGENE T. WOOLF
ADMIRE THE NIXONIAN HANDIWORK.

faculty. President Carnahan appealed to his faculty and staff for cool heads and gentle hearts and for specific suggestions of ways costs could be cut, each looking at his own area:

Please do not use this as an excuse to vent displeasure at those other places on campus with which you are dissatisfied. If you make references outside of your own area, please do so only on the basis of some objective documentation to substantiate your recommendation.

I know we can survive this crisis and I also know that we can do so only by a team effort. Nowhere else in southern Utah is there a pool of talent and expertise and knowledge like that which is housed at SUSC. I think this is a real challenge to our ability in exercising that talent, ability and knowledge. May I have your responses as quickly as possible? I

will accept anonymous responses, but prefer that you identify yourselves, and any suggestion you make will be given serious consideration.[15]

One suggestion stands out on the record. When commencement time neared, the faculty announced, with the approval of the administration, that they would not wear the traditional caps and gowns at the ceremony. They intended the gesture to speak a silent but striking protest over the extremity of the funding crunch. Faculty members would donate the $13 fee that would have been spent for graduation regalia to buy books for the library. The students' protest of the decision was not silent. Seniors screamed that the moment for which they had long striven would become a drab event.

Shortly after school ended in June of 1981, the announcement that Dr. Orville D. Carnahan

ORVILLE D. CARNAHAN
1929-

Orville D. Carnahan was born on Christmas Day, 1929. He spent his formative years in Idaho, graduating from Raft River High School in Malta in 1948. His decision to attend Utah State University reveals what was already a well-cultivated interest in education and the natural growth processes of the earth. After earning his first degree in vocational agriculture, he returned to his home state to earn master of education and doctor of education degrees

at the University of Idaho. He served in the U.S. military, spending 15 months of his two-year span in the Far East. That experience only served to further inspire his dedication to education and he returned to the United States to begin what would be a highly varied and influential career as a teacher and administrator. Beginning as a vocational teacher in the Jordan School District, Dr. Carnahan later served as a teacher and principal in the Valley School District of Eden, Idaho. He also spent three years as an instructor, director and supervisor of student teachers at the University of Idaho Training School.

In his efforts as an administrator in higher education, Dr. Carnahan earned a reputation as a champion of learning in all its particulars. He first served as vice president of Yakima Valley College in Yakima, Wash., later becoming its dean of applied science. He next became chancellor of the Eastern Iowa Community College District in Davenport, Iowa. He then returned to the Pacific Northwest, where he served for five years as president of Highline College in Midway, Wash.

Such extensive and varied service to collegiate institutions facing a wide spectrum of challenges and opportunities made Dr. Carnahan the most logical choice to fill the next post he would assume—that of associate commissioner of higher education for the

Utah System of Higher Education.

In June, 1978, Dr. Carnahan welcomed a request to focus his energies and commitment on a single one of the state's institutions of higher learning and became the 12th president of Southern Utah State College. His efforts over the next three years would become instrumental in preparing the school for the explosive development and change to come.

Among his accomplishments during his tenure at SUSC were the construction of the Ashcroft Observatory, the securing of funding through the Grace and Obert Tanner Foundation for the building of the fountain at the entrance of the auditorium, and the strengthening and expansion of the institution's academic programs.

As his stay at SUSC came to an end, his fierce commitment to the people of his adopted state of Utah found him contributing in many ways to the well-being and vitality of the higher education system. He served as president of the Salt Lake Community College and later became a member of the House of Representatives, where he proved a staunch and effective defender of education.

A dedicated father and family man, Dr. Carnahan and his wife Colleen Arrott reared four children, who have gone on to significant service in the tradition of their parents.

had been appointed to head Salt Lake Community College startled the community and the college. The appointment was effective immediately. President Carnahan resigned; the Carnahans left Cedar City by July 1 to assume their new assignment. There was not even time for farewell fanfare.

*T*he Board of Trustees appointed Dr. Harl Judd, dean of the School of Science, to serve as acting president. It was a natural choice. Dr. Judd was chairman of the Deans' Council. He had recently been appointed acting academic vice president. Now, suddenly, he was Southern Utah State College acting president.

The Deans' Council, which included the academic vice president and the four deans from the four schools on campus, directly administered the academic programs. Dr. Judd now found himself juggling three of those positions. He was dean, acting academic vice president and acting president.

The Board of Regents appointed a selection committee, but there was no time for waiting. Summer school was in session; the Utah Shakespearean Festival was in the midst of its 20th season; plans and preparation for the upcoming fall quarter placed heavy demands upon the acting administration.

HARL JUDD
AS ACTING
PRESIDENT,
1981

Help came in August with the arrival of Dr. Terry D. Alger, who had been associate director for academic affairs for the Utah System of

Higher Education. As the new vice president for academic affairs at SUSC, he shored up the team.

Two assistant vice presidents, Dr. Phil Carter and Pauline Nelson, reported to Dr. Alger. Paul R. Southwick, who had been at SUSC since 1967, was financial vice president, and Dr. Sterling R. Church, beginning his 10th year at the school, was dean of students. The Deans' Council was in place. The team pulled together and the college moved forward with no waiting. They worked while they watched for the selection committee to produce a president.

Acting President Judd continued to work with Dixie College President Alton Wade and USU President Stanford Cazier to find a way to lower out-of-state fees for students from border communities. He proposed expansion of the trades and industries building and establishment of a new behavioral and social science building. He missed the contact with his students and longed to return to his classroom, but he forged ahead with administrative tasks.

The busy season included a report from the salaries committee, chaired by Professor Bob Moore, with the discouraging news that the average garbage collector in Orem City earned $2,000 a year more than the average professor at SUSC.

• Communication department chairman Frain Pearson announced that $130,000 had been granted to SUSC's television and radio instructional broadcasting facility. The department could add a new FM transmitter, two new mini-television cameras and a new control board and editing equipment for the campus television station. The federally-funded grant

would also make possible an experimental telecommunications network, using SUSC as the southern base, linking the college with University of Utah's Channel 7 to provide educational programming to the entire state.

· Dean Harold Hiskey announced that there were 467 students majoring in business in fall quarter of 1981. The business school was commencing a finance major and classes in entrepreneurship, credit management and business policy were to be added that quarter.

· Friends of the Gallery, a committee of townspeople headed by Dr. Rodney Brown, kicked off a drive to raise funds for the Braithwaite Art Gallery on campus.

· The forensics squad reported success at all levels of competition. M.L. Smith evaluated the SUSC team to be among the top 20 in the nation.

· Homecoming Week featured the induction of the Class of 1931 into the 50 Year Club. Alumni Association executive secretary Peg Thorley pled for "lost" alumni to respond with their new addresses.

Dr. Judd was wearing the mantle well. The school moved forward.

*I*n mid-summer an announcement from the Utah State Office of Higher Education listed 13 members of a search committee appointed to select the 13th president of Southern Utah State College. It was a representative group. Four regents, three institutional council members, two faculty members, one from the staff association, the chair of the alumni council, a student and a community member.

Regent Jay Dee Harris of Tremonton, Utah was chairman. The committee membership included Mary D. Lunt, Wayne Owens, Holly Sloan, Frank J. Petty, James Hoyle, Dale Zabriskie, Richard A. Dotson, Dr. Harold Hiskey, Bessie Dover, Lorraine Warren, Shelley Benson and Dixie Leavitt. Don R. Carpenter was appointed by the Board of Regents to act as executive secretary to the group.

The committee met on August 12, 1981, in Cedar City, announcing that it would organize a nationwide search and setting October 19, 1981, as the closing date for applications and nominations.

If the volume of response was an indicator, Southern Utah State College had become a visible entity. Applications poured in and committee members examined each of them. By the closing date they had received 126 applications. The committee interviewed and deliber-

ated over a period of five months. Finally, they sent five finalists to the Board of Regents for a decision.

While the regents interviewed and deliberated, the community conjectured and in some cases lobbied. All of this was concurrent with an especially busy time in Cedar City. Planning for anticipated growth and striving to maintain the integrity of the downtown area, Cedar City had established a redevelopment agency. Committees were working to bring into reality a convention center/ special events center that could accommodate athletic events and large gatherings. Since cooperative effort among the county, the community and the college was always a paramount priority, the town hoped this new president would have vision. Their hopes were realized.

In December, the decision was reached. On December 15, 1981, Mr. Kem Gardner, chairman of the Utah State Board of Regents, and Mr. Frank J. Petty, chairman of the Institutional Council, announced that Dr. Gerald R. Sherratt, vice president for university relations at Utah State University, had been selected as the 13th president of Southern Utah State College.

Dr. Sherratt was a home-town boy who had become, through significant achievement, well prepared to return home with honor. A graduate of Branch Agricultural College, he held bachelors and masters degrees in educational administration from Utah State University and a Ph.D. degree in the administration of higher education from Michigan State University. Cedar City people remembered him as the energetic yell leader from the very early '50s. Since that time, he had been assistant to three presidents of Utah State University. He had served as director of development, director of alumni relations, and as vice president for university relations, as well as heading USU's ambitious fundraising programs, which had obtained nearly $10 million for the construction of buildings and other campus facilities.

Sherratt's Cedar City roots ran deep. A descendant of Cedar City's earliest settlers, his grandfather and several uncles were among the group of men who made up the logging party of 1898, organized to obtain lumber to construct the school's first building.

JERRY SHERRATT, BAC, 1951

GOV. SCOTT MATHESON, LT. GOV.
DAVID S. MONSON, PRESIDENT
SHERRATT, JOHN BERNHARD AT
INAUGURAL CEREMONIES.

The town and the college received the news gladly.

The new president had a penchant for communicating his aims and enlisting the populace. In his first published interview with the student newspaper, he assessed some problems and solutions:

One of the main problems is that we can't get the state to give us enough money. If the state will give us the same amount of money as other schools we will soar ahead...We have the highest quality teaching you can find. But how can we expect to keep the teachers at the salaries we pay? We need more money to be able to increase their salaries and attract an even greater number of superb teachers. [16]

He decried the inadequacies of the Student Center, and declared his intention to move expeditiously toward something more suitable. Then he finished:

Southern Utah is an uncommonly fine school. We have quality teaching, a beautiful campus, and a good learning atmosphere. The only trouble is people don't know we exist. I intend to let them know we are here and what a fine school we really are. [17]

Full realization of just how financially stressed a school could be came quickly to President Sherratt. He took on the federal government, protesting budget cuts in student financial help. He urged the congressional delegation to oppose cuts in financial aid to students. It was a familiar story: new president, great initiative and vitality, not enough money. Sherratt was determined to write a happy ending.

The school and the community were soon given an indication of the flair that would grace this new administration. Activities began on Friday, May 20, with a reception at the president's home. Displays and demonstrations depicting the activities of each academic area were presented in each department. People strolled the campus and enjoyed small concerts through the afternoon at the Adams Memorial Theatre. The Inauguration Gala that evening was an event to remember, with a line-up of Hollywood entertainers.

Broadway actor Russ Tamblyn, who had been among the stars in Sherratt's favorite film, *Seven Brides for Seven Brothers*, was a delightful master of ceremonies. Billie Loukas, soprano from the Utah Opera Company, captivated the audience with popular ballads. Hit singer Jimmie Rogers pleased the crowd with "Honeycomb," "Kisses Sweeter Than Wine" and "Waltzing Matilda." Comedian Warren Burton added hilarity with such exotic musical instruments as the Tartini Balloon and the Renaissance Nose Flute.

The featured moments came with the premier performance of the Burch Mann American Folk Ballet.

Next morning, the ceremonial rites commenced with an academic procession from the Thorley Recital Hall to the Auditorium. A capacity house awaited. Dignitaries presented salutations. They included: Lorraine Warren, president of the alumni; ASSUSC president Donald Hulet; assistant director of student activities, Dave Taylor; Richard Dotson, president of the Faculty Senate, and Gov. Scott M. Matheson.

The investiture was performed by Kem Gardner, chairman of the Utah State Board of Regents. The inaugural address was delivered by Dr. John Bernhard, president of Western Michigan University. The response by President Gerald R. Sherratt warmed the hearts of faculty, students and townspeople who had gathered to confirm their heartfelt welcome

He began by honoring the presidents who had preceded him. A descendant of each

DR. GERALD R. SHERRATT AND MISS BURCH MANN ON INAUGURATION EVENING, 1982.

DR. SHERRATT DELIVERING INAUGURAL REMARKS

deceased president had been invited and was honored. Presidents living and present were lauded. Then President Sherratt praised his own former teacher, Mrs. Zoe Palmer, as an exemplary educator and suggested, "I think it is appropriate that at a ceremony which celebrates the processes of education we point with pride to a teacher who represents what education is all about, and how in the hands of a master teacher, lives can be changed."

Paying homage and honor to others was a pattern that was to become a trademark of his administration.

Dr. Sherratt enumerated significant changes that had occurred in society and in the school. He finished with these words:

There are seasons, in human affairs, of inward and outward revolution, when new depths seem to be broken up in the soul, when new events are unfolded in multitudes, and a new and undefined good is thirsted for. There are periods when the principles of experience need to be modified, when hope and trust and instinct claim a share with prudence in the guidance of affairs, when, in truth, to dare is the highest wisdom.

If there is one thing I have sensed about this institution and about those who have tied their destiny to the College it is a conviction that SUSC has arrived at a point in its history when to dare is, indeed, the highest wisdom.

So let this institution dare to dedicate itself to the highest ideals of advanced scholarship, to become a prime example of the academic rigor and intellectual capacity for which every college strives--but not all attain. Let SUSC be a campus whose love for the intellectual life is reflected in all it does.

And let this institution dare to devote itself to the highest ideals of humane development, to become a place noted not only for excellence of its programs for imparting knowledge, but also for those that develop imagination and judgment and inspire commitment. Let SUSC be a campus whose interests are directed to what is significant, worthwhile and noble.

The ceremony and solemnity of this event is not meant to celebrate the new president, but rather to serve as a signal of both the continuity and change that are endemic to institutions of higher learning.

No college or university in America can equal the unique and dramatic heritage of SUSC. As the English clergyman Joseph Parker once said: "Our yesterdays follow us; they con-

stitute our life, and they give character and force and meaning to our present deeds."

The character and force and meaning of Southern Utah State College does indeed reflect its yesterdays. The College exists today as the sum of all that has gone before:
• of its students, who infused the institution with their vitality and zest for life;
• of its faculties, who bestowed their dedication and zeal for teaching;
• of its administrators and staff, who endowed it with their dreams come true.

Let us hope that the coming years are as significant and meaningful as the eighty-five years that have gone before and that the spiritual and creative presence of the institution's yesterdays will continue to enrich and ennoble its tomorrows.

The inauguration festivities finished with a flourish, as the premier performance of Burch Mann's American Folk Ballet played to rousing ovations. The local newspaper art critic wrote: " If you were present and it didn't make you want to get up and dance, you were either dead or drunk." "This town will renew my spirit," said a tearful Burch Mann in response to the enthusiastic audience approval.

The Carnahans came to the campus in 1979 to find that there was no official residence to receive them. The Braithwaites had purchased the Director's Cottage and moved it to make room for the science building in 1960. Since that time the Braithwaites had resided in their own home, located almost adjacent to the campus. Orville and Colleen Carnahan were not able to find a home in the neighborhood,

THE
PRESIDENT'S
RESIDENCE

and rented a house some distance from the campus, then quickly found the distance inconvenient.

The college owned a comfortable home directly across 200 South Street from the campus, purchased earlier from Mr. and Mrs. Stanley Bradshaw. For 17 years it had been the Family Home Living Center, where countless young women had learned, on site, the arts of gracious living. Now the program was changed to a non-resident program and moved to the science building. The home became the official residence of the president. The Carnahans resided in the home for the final year that he led the college. It was then ready to receive President Gerald R. Sherratt, and was to remain his residence from 1983 until his retirement in 1997. He brought to the home his elegant flair; he furnished it to his taste, and made it a center of gracious hospitality, where innumerable guests were warmed at his hearth.

In case the people of the town had believed that the inauguration had been a one-time panache, they needn't have worried. Following closely on the heels of the gala events of the inauguration week, came "Miss Kitty" of the popular television series *Gunsmoke*, Amanda Blake, now retired from her movie and television roles, had become a civic activist, prominent in laudable causes. She still carried the mystique of fame from her movie and television days. Ms. Blake delivered the baccalaureate address.

Spencer F. Eccles, chief executive of First Security Bank, addressed the graduates of the second largest graduating class in the history of the school. Three hundred five graduates received diplomas that day.

Commencement time, 1982,

brought announcement of some arrivals and some departures. One of the significant arrivals was Dr. Michael D. Richards, as assistant to the president of Southern Utah State College. Dr. Richards had been a trusted colleague of President Sherratt at USU, where he had served as director of alumni relations. Prior to his position at USU, he was a member of the faculty at the United States Air Force Academy. His Ph.D. degree in administration of higher education was from the University of Denver. He came to Cedar City, bringing his wife and young family. His career at SUSC was to parallel that of the new president. Cedar City became the permanent home of the Richards family.

At commencement time came the announcement that the Burch Mann American Folk Ballet would make Cedar City its permanent base, and that the dance program at SUSC would expand to include the uniquely appealing and accessible ballet style created by Miss Mann. The goal of the American Folk Ballet was to create dances that would speak to the soul of the people. It was a fortunate addition. Miss Mann's decision to relocate from Pasadena, Calif., where her dance company was located and where she had conducted a dance school for several decades, to Cedar City, Utah, came as a result of a long-standing friendship with Dr. Gerald R. Sherratt. He perceived this a helpful facet of his effort to make the school visible and develop a dance program in the performing arts. Mann had been courted by Utah State University, and her decision to come to SUSC was a matter of considerable disappointment in Logan.

Dr. Wesley P. Larsen, professor of biology, announced that he would retire at the end of the 1981-82 year after a distinguished career that included 23 years at SUSC. Colleagues and students greeted the news with dismay.

Dr. Larsen was noted for the excitement he brought to his teaching. Each day he came to class with an article of interest, a new specimen, a new idea. His innovative teaching methods were acclaimed. He was a former dean of the School of Science, had been awarded numerous honors and was revered by students who had made significant marks in scientific fields, many of whom credited their successes to the

MICHAEL D. RICHARDS

WES LARSEN

KEN BENSON

superb instruction and encouragement received under the tutelage of their friend and mentor, Dr. Wesley Larsen.

A warm mixture of sadness, tenderness, admiration and gratitude attended the announcement that R. Kenneth Benson would retire after 14 years as director of student activities.

Benson was the man on campus who had worked most closely with the students. His job description had included the coordination of student activities, training and advising of student body officers, supervision of dormitories and coordination of the Student Center. An actual description of his influence must extend to include the offering of encouragement to the discouraged, nourishment and healing of bruised student psyches, inspiration to the faltering and help to the helpless and the needy.

A student during the College of Southern Utah era, Benson had lettered in track and field, football and wrestling. His massive six-foot-four inch frame, coupled with remarkable ability, had drawn draft offers from professional football clubs. But the Bensons returned in 1969 to southern Utah where he spent his career promoting the progress of students at Southern Utah State College. Noted for his skill in outdoor living arts, and for his sincere and gentle spirit, he bade farewell to his task amidst accolades and well-wishes from colleagues and students alike.

"Like the giant trees that grace our campus, this giant of a man has weathered the storm and has come through standing tall," said Dean Sterling Church in a farewell tribute.

*T*he dream that had dwindled downtown, when the hope of a special events center seemed beyond their financial reach, breathed with new life when a proposal came from the college. The *Iron County Record* of March 11, 1982, reported:

Cedar City and Southern Utah State College may yet get a special events center. Such a center was the main topic of discussion Monday morning at the meeting of the Cedar City Redevelopment Advisory Committee. The committee gave approval to new SUSC president, Gerald R. Sherratt to look into the possibilities of the college building such a needed facility.

The committee some time ago had arrived at a consensus that such a center was economically unfeasible over the next several years, but Sherratt told of the college's need for such a facility and his desire for a much-modified version of the original plan. The committee passed a resolution approving his efforts at exploring further with the Utah State Building Board and the Utah State Board of Regents.

The modification of the original plan was that the center would be built on the campus of the college, rather than downtown, and that it would contain only an arena, and not a concert hall and convention center, as had been originally hoped. The college had a good site available. This project would be another dream requiring a concerted joint-effort to benefit both the community and the college,

KEN BENSON COUNSELING

in perfect harmony with long established tradition.

On March 14, the *Color Country Spectrum* reported that the building had been proposed by Dr. Sherratt at a meeting of the Institutional Council. The estimated cost of $3 million was undoubtedly much too modest, but it eased the idea into motion. Enthusiastic support mounted quickly. By July 29, the editor of the *Iron County Record* urged:

The Southern Utah State College Special Events Center campaign is now on, and we at the Record *would encourage everyone in Iron County to throw their support behind such a worthy project.*

A special events center or convention center has been discussed for some time now by a number of organizations in Iron County, most recently by the Cedar City Redevelopment Advisory Committee, which could see such a center as a major impetus to development and growth of the city, as well as the county. At the same time a number of groups at the college have wanted such a center to improve the quality of athletic events, as well as make it possible to attract larger concerts and programs of many types to SUSC and Cedar City.

Now the groups have joined together to accomplish this goal, and they are expanding on the original committee of 250 people who have committed themselves to the effort; and they are asking for the support of everybody. We think that support deserving. . . Heading the committee are leaders of SUSC and Cedar City. Co-chairman Royden C. Braithwaite, former president of the college, has brought the SUSC Foundation into the effort. Co-Chairman Dixie Leavitt, chairman of the Redevelopment Advisory Committee, has swung the support of the redevelopment agency. There is a broad base of support... It is a good cause. It is good for the entire

county. Again we urge your support. [20]

Gerald R. Sherratt had demonstrated his capacity for consensus building. The practice he'd gained in fundraising at USU was now benefitting his home town. A truly massive organizational effort ensued. Committees of fund-raising volunteers swelled to 26 sub-committees, with 52 co-chairmen and 10 administrative assistants. The core of support amounted to almost 350 people, who all went around with blue "Whom Do You Know?" cards and red and white contribution/pledge cards in their pockets. They made voluminous lists and solicited everyone on them. The scene was reminiscent of the founding days of BNS, when "the beggars" went door to door conscribing whatever the household could give.

The goal was $1.1 million in donations. The committee also intended to bond against student fees, and though it was a very tight money year for the state, they planned to go with a request to the legislature.

As fundraising events proliferated, people turned out to spend their money for the cause. The Lions Club sponsored a steak fry; the Elks Club held a demolition derby; the Rotarians pledged two years of the club's weekly fines, which totaled $5,000; women's clubs made and sold quilts. Auctions, home shows, garage sales and fashion shows all added to the growing fund. A contribution of $1,750 came from the Associated Students' "Hospital of Horrors," a spook alley located in the old Iron County Hospital building.

A pre-sale of seat options elicited a spirited response, probably from fans who had long craned their necks from uncomfortable seats in the old field house. Three hundred seats sold almost instantaneously, raising $125,000, according to Jack Bishop, SUSC development director.

Newspapers around the state gave a boost to the effort. The *Deseret News* published a long editorial:

IN OUR OPINION,
If there's a more inadequate, outdated, or seedy college auditorium in the country than the one at Southern Utah State College, its existence is certainly a well-kept secret. Known locally as "The Barn," the Cedar City field house has been there since 1946 when it was moved from the old Japanese relocation center at Topaz. The chairback seats in the gymnasium were built in the 1890's. The

ORIGINAL PHYSICAL CONCEPT OF THE
SPECIAL EVENTS CENTER.

FROM TOP: RICHARD ROWLEY, WARD ROBB, ANTON LAMBERT

bleacher seats are uncomfortable and unsafe. About the only polite way to describe the men's dressing room and shower is as extremely primitive; there are no such facilities for women. The building has no insulation, and cracks in the cinder block facade let cold air seep inside.

The acoustics are so bad that lectures held in the field house have been virtually unintelligible. Concerts staged there have been inaudible. The lighting system is inadequate too.

Because the field house seats only 1,400, SUSC has no place to assemble its entire student body of 2,400. The campus auditorium seats only 1,000. No wonder that visiting performing groups, such as the Utah Symphony have declined to appear at SUSC. Earlier visits by Ballet West have been discontinued. No wonder too, that SUSC wants to tear down the field house and replace it with a new $4.3 million Special Events Center...

The earnest editor then called for the legislature to approve the state bonding program and to see that SUSC received the funding needed to make their building a reality, while acknowledging that there were plenty of crucial projects on the state list:

But few, if any, of those other projects reflect as much involvement at the grassroots and willingness to sacrifice as there is in Cedar City. Let's rid Utah of the dubious distinction that comes with having possibly the worst college gymnasium in the country. [21]

The editorial piece extolled the effort that Cedar City people had made in raising $1.2 million to that point, with thousands more to come from gifts and further events. It was a nice assist. It made the effort visible statewide.

The drive was touted as the most successful fund-raising campaign in the history of the state. Gifts came in amazing forms: A large office building and five acres of land in the Fiddler's Canyon subdivision; a $15,000 building lot and a home appraised at $60,000; a corporate gift of $45,000. An anonymous donor gave $50,000; a former local school teacher withdrew her life savings of $1,500 and gave it to the project. More than half of the faculty and staff at SUSC signed up for payroll deductions to make their contribution and Cedar City's public school teachers donated $25,000.

While they worked and the little pots of money filled, the realistic projected costs swelled too. The project was clearly in the hands of the legislature.

Fall quarter of 1982 saw a startling increase in enrollment. Recruitment had been, from the first, a necessary effort. From early days of faculty members visiting in the living rooms of rural high school seniors, the effort had become a more sophisticated process—colored brochures were mailed to graduating seniors and college representatives visited the schools with professionally prepared presentations. Whatever magic was working, the 14 percent enrollment increase was startling. Enrollment stood at 2,378, the highest number in the school's 85-year history.

*A*fter 35 years at SUSC, Professor Richard Rowley announced his retirement. He had linked his destiny with the school as a young teacher when the institution was a small two-year college. A member of the faculty since 1947, he was chairman of the communication department when it was organized in 1968 and when the communication major was authorized in 1972.

Ward Robb would retire at the end of the 1983 school year after 37 years as a staff member. He had served successively as assistant college secretary-treasurer, cashier, registrar, secretary to the institutional council, chief admissions officer and veteran's coordinator under five presidents and two acting presidents. Robb had been honored as outstanding staff member at the 1980 commencement.

Anton H. Lambert was granted early retirement as an assistant professor in the SUSC

KEM GARDNER

School of Business and Technology, department of industrial education. He had taught all aspects of police science since 1963.

On March 1, 1983, Sen. Ivan Matheson brought Sen. Kay Cornaby, senate majority leader, for an official visit to SUSC and a public hearing to help in the consideration of the funding request for the special events center. Four hundred people crowded into the hearing to express their support of the building. The legislators toured the War Memorial Fieldhouse, including the nether-region shower rooms, so eloquently maligned in the *Deseret News* editorial and also saw for themselves the difficult dilemma of cramped classroom space. The people of the town and the college were at the edge of their collective chairs as the vote on funding of the building requests was slated for the following week. [22]

Former state senator Dixie Leavitt, co-chairman of the fund raising effort, used the privilege accorded former legislators to buttonhole representatives and senators at their desks to urge their support for a bond containing funding for the Special Events Center, and Sen. Ivan Matheson taped posters to the marble walls of the Capitol building. Finally, on March 10, 1983, with 20 minutes remaining in the 45th Legislative session, an acceptable compromise was achieved between the Senate and the House of Representatives. The funding measure authorizing $43 million in construction for Utah's colleges and universities squeaked by the senate with two votes to spare and cleared the house by a margin of 46-22.

For SUSC, it meant that the state would fund $2.5 million for the Special Events Center, $3.2 million for the general classroom building and $1.5 million to convert the heat plant to a coal-burning facility, a $100,000 renovation for the science building and some money to repair building settlement problems.

Mike Richards, assistant to the president, was delighted:

Of course we're delighted about the building projects. In many ways it will mark a new era for the college and for southern Utah. We'll now finalize selection of architects for these projects and get them under way. [23]

It did seem like a lot of money.

March 11, 1983, the day following the close of the 1983 legislature, was Founders' Day at SUSC. President Sherratt called it the "best of times" for SUSC, as he exulted over the success of the petition for funding for the three building projects. Sen. Ivan Matheson and Rep. Haze Hunter were named "honorary alumni" for their help in making the appropriation a reality. The two had worked hard at winning the support of their colleagues, and the president expressed gratitude for their work.

But not everyone was happy. Kem Gardner, chairman of the Utah State Board of Regents, invited to Cedar City as the featured speaker at the Founders' Day program, was grim-faced. He took the opportunity to decry the penury of the legislature and called it the "worst of times" for higher education in the state. A small increase in funding for higher education caused the chairman to fear for the future. No money had been appropriated for salary increases; he feared enrollment "lids" were ahead.

Nevertheless, he failed to dampen the celebration at Founders' Day. Spirits were high at one institution—Southern Utah State College.

On Tuesday, April 19, 1983, Dr. Gerald R. Sherratt and Dr. Michael D. Richards traveled to Logan armed with an exciting and, as it turned out, brilliant new idea to present to the Utah State Board of Regents. As they had worked to plan for the new special events center and the general classroom building, there evolved the idea to combine the two buildings using the concourse that encircled the arena of the special events center as the hallway of the general classroom facility. Classrooms would be built on the outside perimeter of the concourse. It had become clear that the plan was workable and would save a considerable amount of money.

*T*heir presentation was convincing. Before they left Logan, the regents had given approval to the "co-location" of the two facilities.

The architectural firm of Fowler, Ferguson, Kingston and Ruben (FFKR) of Salt Lake City was engaged to plan the new dual-concept building. College officials and the state building board planned to break ground in

ROSS HILTON

November. President Sherratt reported the advantages of the unique plan:

The unique concept of combining the Special Events Center and the classroom building has saved about $800,000. Working out details of the plan has taken time, but the new facility will fulfill many needs of the college and be a lasting asset to the community...The center, the largest public building ever to be built in southern Utah, will be located on 800 West Street between Center and 200 South streets. It will house, in addition to the arena and dressing room areas, television and radio studios, various art studios for sculpture, ceramics, graphics, painting, and print making; two classrooms holding 100 students each and three smaller classrooms; a statistical laboratory, a video perception laboratory, and several psychology laboratories.

The area will seat 5,000 spectators, all in chairback seats and will be the focal point for a wide variety of community and cultural activities. Once envisioned as a domed building, the Special Events Center will have a more cost-effective conventional roof, with the cost-savings directed toward enhancing the rest of the building. Skylights will encircle the arena's edge. Beyond the arena concourse will be the variety of academic space. [24]

*T*he task of raising funds for the special events center still loomed large. Coach Jack Bishop realized that he could no longer be effective as both head football coach and part-time director of development. He chose, reluctantly, to become the full-time director of development.

Two more retirements were announced in the spring. Dr. Morris A. Shirts and Dr. Ross C. Hilton both announced their retirement at the end of the school year. Dr. Hilton had been at the school since 1969 as a chairman of the department of industrial arts and technology and then as assistant dean in the School of Business and Technology. Dr. Shirts joined the faculty in 1959, serving as dean of the School of Education, and had been instrumental in bringing that school to new heights.

A retirement dinner honoring five retirees feted Shirts, Hilton, Anton Lambert, Richard Rowley and Ward Robb. It was the end of an era. Among the five men their service totalled 128 years. In terms of contributions the sum was immeasurable. A dinner honoring all who had retired from the institution became an annual affair, representing Dr. Sherratt's flair

and fondness for commemorations as well as the honoring of those who gave so much of their lives to the furtherance of the College and its students.

At the same time, rumor had it that the president didn't like the school colors of Columbia blue and white with orange trim, and had plans to change them. The editor of *The Thunderbird* challenged such audacity. The president protested his innocence. While admitting that the colors weren't much to his liking, he declared himself neutral on the issue of the change. [25]

Since those who designed publications for the college recruiting felt that the printed materials should reflect a robust, expanding image for the institution, they elected to use a vibrant red instead of the more passive Columbia blue and white with orange trim. The materials were well received but they didn't match the school colors.

MORRIS
SHIRTS

At the end of spring quarter 1983 wide controversy surrounded the issue. It was shaky to stand on the issue of tradition, for it was hardly long-standing. Branch Normal School had adopted red and white as the school colors. When the school became BAC in 1913, they had changed their colors to azure blue and white, in order to match those of Utah State Agricultural College. When Utah State changed to navy and white, BAC followed suit. When BAC achieved independent status in 1965, the colors were changed to turquoise and coral. Not until 1980 were the colors changed to Columbia blue and white with orange trim.

The debate continued. Some loved the colors. Some didn't like them at all. Almost everyone had a strong opinion, but there was a substantive reason, beside personal preference, for the change. Uniforms were hard to find in those colors. Special orders were necessary and costly. In the summer, Mark Wade, ASSUSC president, wrote a letter to President Sherratt suggesting that the color change might be a good idea. It was all Sherratt needed. He appointed a committee with representatives from the administration, the faculty, student government and the Institutional Council to study the issue.

BRENT
SORENSEN

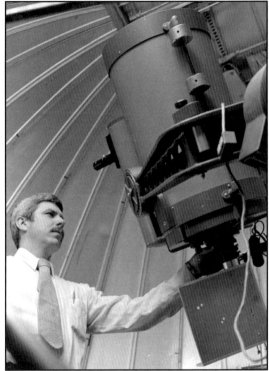

In early September, the committee recommended to the Institutional Council that they institute the sixth change of color in the 86-year history of the school. The choice was to adopt scarlet and white as the school colors with royal blue as the accent color. The proposal received an unanimous vote, with one abstention. It was done.

In the next issue of *The Thunderbird*–the first of the new school year–an editorial complained that it was a pity and a little high-handed that the change had come while most of the student body was away for the summer.

Had the founders of the school been able to watch the furor over the school colors, they might not have been surprised but they would have been astonished at the magnitude of help available to students. Jack Cannon, director of SUSC financial aid programs, announced that four kinds of financial assistance would be available to students. Work-study, grants, loans and scholarships would provide in excess of $2 million for the upcoming school year. Cannon reported that most students were eager to work to earn the assistance.

Three "aid" centers, established to help students succeed, flourished on the campus. The Learning Center helped with reading skills, study skills for exams, writing skills and textbook uses. Testing for learning styles and helpful analysis was provided. Free tutoring was available in a quiet, relaxed study environment. Preparation for graduate school entrance exams was available.

The Health Center offered free medical services. The center prescribed medications for simple ailments and arranged doctor's appointments for serious problems. To receive the service, a student need only carry seven credit hours.

The Multi-Cultural Center offered support and help of many kinds to students from all cultures. It was especially geared to help minority students become an integral part of SUSC.

In the fall of 1983, Professor Brent Sorensen came to be the director of the Ashcroft Observatory and assistant professor in astronomy and physics. Professor Robert Jones transferred to teach computer science, after filling a primary role in the establishment of the observatory.

*A*s the days of 1983 dwindled, there was much to reflect upon with satisfaction:

• A survey completed by Rex Michie, college placement officer, revealed that SUSC graduates were more successful in obtaining jobs than their counterparts from other schools around the nation.

• For the first time, private giving to the college in one year had exceeded the $1 million mark. Many of these gifts were specified as scholarship funds. Endowments and the contributions to the new special events center brought the total well beyond the million mark, far more than in any other year.

• The newly-inaugurated Convocation series, bringing an array of prominent speakers, attracted record audiences of students and townspeople. John Ehrlichman, John Dean, Martin Luther King III, and actor/activist Mike Farrell of *M*A*S*H* fame, were among the con-

CONVOCATION SPEAKER MIKE FARRELL

troversial and impressive speakers who came in a single year.

• SUSC students were winning state and national honors in record numbers, and faculty members garnered impressive awards in a variety of national and state honors, not all of which were education awards. Dean of the School of Education, Dr. James Miller, was named Brigadier General of the Utah National Guard.

• Construction was completed on the third floor addition of the administration building, bringing some relief to crowded office sharers.

• A high acceptance rate of SUSC students by professional schools was recorded, including three of four applicants to veterinary school, five of five applicants to dental school and all four applicants to medical school.

• A new fire alarm system was installed across the campus at a cost of $65,000. It became immediately notorious as an unnecessarily sensitive system, since dust from a floor being swept or steam from cooking carrots set the alarm shrieking through Manzanita residence halls. Exhaust from a car passing in the middle of the night often wakened the neighborhood. After months of racing to shut off the offending noise, one frustrated student, alone in the halls over Thanksgiving holiday, disconnected the wires to the system with his pocketknife. The campus police said there would be no penalty.

It was a most eventful year.

Good news came early in 1984, when the evaluation of the Northwest Association of Schools and Colleges was released. The October study brought high praise from the accrediting group. The committee was highly impressed with the faculty, praising the commitment of the teachers, who carried an excessively heavy teaching load. They gave accolades to all four schools, singling out the education department, English, fine arts, communication, business and teacher education programs for special praise. It was a surprise to no one that the committee reported a concern that the library and the general financial base needed strengthening.

The reaccreditation was happy news, though fully expected. What the College hoped for, without such assurance, was that the legislature would look as kindly upon them as had the accrediting association. The budget presentations before the legislature were carefully prepared to articulate the need. They were not disappointed. SUSC joyfully received a 12 percent hike in the budget, which provided for a 13 percent raise for faculty, a 10 percent increase for staff, much needed computer equipment and significant funding for library improvement.

A contest calling for suggestions of names for the new special events center/classroom building resulted in the selection of "The Centrum." Groundbreaking ceremonies for the eagerly-anticipated structure was scheduled for Founders' Day, March 10, 1984.

On that day, more than 500 people gathered at the construction site. President G. Homer Durham, Council of the Seventy, Church of Jesus Christ of Latter-day Saints, offered the prayer. Speakers included Kem Gardner, chairman of the state Board of Regents; President Gerald R. Sherratt; Rep. Haze Hunter; Sen. Ivan Matheson and Ray Kingston, principal designer of the Centrum.

"This building represents the largest public contribution per capita of any building in the state's history," declared Gardner. "It represents a high water mark of physical and moral development of this area. Since the building of Old Main in 1897, no public enterprise in the state has met with more enthusiasm and involvement."

President Sherratt noted, "The community contributions have exceeded the $2 million mark. That averages out to $160 for every man, woman and child in Cedar City. Like Old Main, this is no ordinary structure, being brought together with sacrifice, love of education, and faith in the future of southern Utah."

Twenty-plus state and local leaders lined up, shovels at the ready. They responded to the command called out by President Sherratt, "Put your shovels in. Now dig it up !"

And so the ground for the $8 million structure was broken.

That night, at the Founders' Day banquet, J. Reuben Clark was inducted into the College's Hall of Honor. It was a fitting gesture, for he had had from its beginning the vision of the potential of the school. And he had loved it.

When Dean Hal Campbell resigned to devote more time to teaching, Professor Rodney Decker was appointed dean of the School of Arts and Letters. Professor Wayne Hinton replaced Professor Decker as chair of the department of behavioral and social sciences.

The construction industry was booming in the five-county area of Beaver, Iron, Washington, Kane and Garfield counties in 1984. A shortage of trained construction workers posed a challenge and an opportunity for SUSC. The building trades department, headed by Lyman Munford, had continued the tradition begun by Ben Cooley of practical

laborers they needed.

SUSC had found a modern version of the tradition of meeting the needs of her community, established long ago when sheep raising and milk production were compelling community requirements.

While the building and trades students were making news, the method of disseminating it was changing. The publications council had voted in 1982 to dispense with a yearbook and to use the funding to expand the student newspaper, renamed *The T-Bird Times.* The staff found it tough going and by the end of the year the effort was led by a new adviser, Larry Baker, who was charged with producing a regularly published newspaper. New typesetting equipment and advertising support from local merchants enabled an eight- to 12-page paper to be issued each Thursday. Again the name became *The Thunderbird,* and it reported campus news, including meetings and issues. An opinion page was a popular and well-used feature. In June, the first issues of a summer paper ever at the institution, *The Summerbird,* appeared.

In the 1983-84 school year, the paper came out each Monday and totaled 33 editions. That year, the newspaper won more awards than any other paper at the annual Rocky Mountain Collegiate Press Association convention,

training for students, but the scope had been limited to the project houses they could build and market. Now contractors of the area were desperate for qualified help. In the words of Van Bushnell, assistant to the provost for vocational education, "Because we are an area vocational school, the college needs to meet the needs of industry, and this time it means meeting them just as soon as we possibly can."

Industrial education department chair Don L. Blanchard announced the formation of an ingenious cooperative program whereby the college could concurrently prepare students for specific employment opportunities while serving the needs of community industry. The program participated substantively in the construction of a Federal Aviation facility at the Cedar City airport, The Centrum, a United States Post Office in Parowan and significant building at Brian Head Resort.

The department linked with Job Service, the Five County Association of Governments, and contractors engaged in the building to form the innovative program, mutually beneficial to all partners. Called the Consolidated Building Construction Program, the joint effort provided a half-day of classroom instruction and a half-day on the job experience. At the end of one year, the students received certification in the trades, and contractors found the

RODNEY DECKER

WAYNE HINTON

including the President's Award as the best journalistic operation in the 16 states encompassed by the organization. *The Thunderbird* continued to distinguish itself year after year, garnering far more awards than any other paper in the region, including those from much larger universities.

Some 10 years later, in September of 1994, the institution saw the first appearance of the *University Journal,* which was the brainchild of President Sherratt and was a totally revamped campus newspaper, published Mondays, Wednesdays and Fridays, generally with 20-page editions. The paper now contained campus and local news as well as state, national and world news, sports and photos from Associated Press, and was one of only a handful of campus papers in the country to utilize the full range of AP services.

The *University Journal,* which used professional staff leading and teaching the students, acted as an adjunct to the general education program of the institution and contained educational writings and commentary from faculty members. It also provided real-world journalistic experience for students, as editor Larry Baker utilized students as photographers, editors and writers. Two associate editors, selected each quarter for internship credit, worked 40 hour weeks and emerged as experienced newspaper people, prepared for journalistic careers.

As the building trades and journalists were on a roll, the program of accountancy was also running smoothly, as usual, when the Utah State Legislature abruptly threw a wrench into the works. In 1981, the Public Accountants Licensing Act had been passed by the Utah Legislature. The act made it mandatory by 1986 that, before Utah applicants could sit for the national CPA exam, they must have not fewer than 30 semester hours of additional post-baccalaureate study (the equivalent of a master's degree).

The legislators had been told that such a law would upgrade the profession of public accounting by raising the entrance requirements. Opponents argued that the act was merely a means of limiting the number of those who could sit for CPA exams, thus insuring that there would be fewer certified public accountants to dilute the monetary fee the CPAs could charge.

Southern Utah accountants were generally opposed to the act, as was the Utah State Board of Regents. For SUSC and Weber State,

the implementation of the act meant that accounting graduates of the two schools would have to get an additional year of education at one of the three universities (Brigham Young University, University of Utah, and Utah State University) which offered master's degrees in accountancy before sitting for the CPA exam, and officials at the two schools worried that accounting students would elect to bypass both schools.

Accounting was one of SUSC's largest academic areas and the implementation of the act could bring a sharp reduction in enrollment in the College of Business.

Unable to get the act repealed, SUSC and Weber asked the Utah State Board of Regents for authority to grant a master's degree in accountancy. It would be the first graduate degree for both schools. The request was met with instantaneous opposition by the two established public universities, who fought vigorously to restrict the two schools to undergraduate degrees. A period of intense lobbying of Regents began, SUSC and Weber pitted against the University of Utah and Utah State University. The showdown came in July, 1984 when the Board of Regents met in Cedar City for a midsummer meeting.

In the end, the approval of master's of accountancy programs at both SUSC and Weber State passed by a wide margin, perhaps one of the most important votes in SUSC's history since the college could now offer a master's degree, with the possibility of more to come in the future.

At SUSC, the business department worked to prepare the master's programs they had petitioned to offer while they battled for authorization. Professor Roger Hillyard assumed the chairmanship of the department and the administrative duties as Professor Gary Giles resigned as chairman to begin work on the advanced degree curriculum.

By fall quarter of 1985, the SUSC business department had built a cur-

GARY N.
GILES

riculum with the necessary classes to fill the higher requirement. And the students came. The vitality of the department was restored. In June, 1985 the Northwest Accreditation Agency accredited the master's of accountancy at SUSC.

As with all the stories of adversity in the history of the school, once weathered, a stronger, more vital entity emerged.

The 1984-85 legislative appropriation request was as dramatic as that of the previous year when the special events center funding was the thrust of the effort. This year brought very practical needs to the fore. First on the college's capital facilities request was funding to purchase the last remaining home on the east side of 800 West Street, as well as a block of homes east of 800 West where the college hoped to construct a parking lot to accommodate patrons of Centrum events and provide additional student parking for the school's ever-increasing student body.

Priority number two was for a pot of money to repair settling buildings and other general repairs such as the upgrading of wiring throughout the campus and an air conditioning system for the science building. Another priority was funding to demolish relics of the Topaz era—the old War Memorial Fieldhouse and the building which had served, since it was hauled in from Topaz, as a student center, library, bookstore, office building, classroom building and finally as a museum.

Not much glamour, but necessities nonetheless.

A respectable college band could only be

content with second-hand regalia for a limited time. New uniforms were ordered that included beautiful bearskin hats befitting a genuine pipers' band. Unfortunately, some people questioned, conservatively, whether authentic bearskin hats were not too extravagant for a small school in the western wilds. People joined in on both sides of the discussion until it seemed that it would become a genuine controversy. President Sherratt, whom one suspects had his heart set on the elegant trappings, found a solution. He paid for them personally. The hats arrived from England and, costly or not, they were sensational. A genuine departure from the previous SUSC band uniforms, handed-down from White House pageantry, the hats were handsome. They evoked visions of a British ceremonial band, and paired with bagpipes, the band added a dignified touch to formal occasions. Band director Dennis Bacon assured critics and supporters alike: "This college was not destined to follow others, but to create a path of its own. When people hear us play and see us perform, they'll be glad to say, 'Hey that's our band'!"

People caught the spirit of the pipes. They loved the sound and the illusions of grandeur. There are those who believe that the spirits of the Scottish founders attend all official affairs.

In a departure from general policy, SUSC officials announced that they would rename the Business Building. The designation The Dixie Leavitt Business Building would be an acknowledgement of Leavitt's involvement

THE SCARLET
AND BLACK

with the affairs of the college from 1947 until 1984, and gratitude for the skillful political acumen that saved funding for the building when it had seemed to be lost. In response to the attendant commendations, Leavitt said, "I am not sure the honor is appropriate, but I must confess I like the idea that future generations will know how much I loved this school."[26]

As the school year ended, two faculty members, Inez Cooper and Vic J. Davis, ended their careers with Southern Utah State College.

Joining the SUSC faculty in 1956, Mrs. Cooper had worked in public relations for three years, prior to becoming SUSC special collections librarian and historian in 1962. Mrs. Cooper's contribution was especially valuable because until that time many of the primary historical materials were being lost to libraries in California and northern Utah. Her interest was manifested in her writing as well as in her diligence in preservation.

Vic Davis joined the faculty in 1941. His 43-year teaching career spanned the administration of six directors and presidents. He helped to pioneer programs in industrial education and saw departments through evolutionary changes and improvements. His beyond-the-call of duty service included driving the college bus to transport students to all varieties of extracurricular activities for more than a quarter of a century.

The Cedar City Lions Club roared onto the scene in the spring of 1985 when SUSC officials announced that the prominent service club would provide the leadership for the phased expansion of Thunderbird Stadium. The first phase of the expansion was to be the addition of 1,500 concrete seats on the east side of the stadium playing field. The seating would run from end zone to end zone and was to be 10 rows high. The project would bring the total seating capacity to 4,500.

The Lions Club planned to solicit volunteer labor and some contributions of materials. Volunteers came from all the civic clubs of Cedar City, as well as students. Some people

DIXIE LEAVITT AT THE DEDICATION OF
THE BUSINESS BUILDING WHICH
WOULD BEAR HIS NAME.

VIC J. DAVIS

donated money to hire replacements for their labor when they could not work themselves. Planning began in the spring, and the project was completed in time for fall football.

Soil settlement, which had caused damage to buildings all over the campus, signaled to Spindler Construction Company, general contractors on the Centrum, that soil testing would be prudent. The tests revealed the presence of the shifting soil prevalent in the Cedar City area. To remedy the problem, it was necessary for the contractors to install 200 caissons beneath the structure, some of which were drilled to a depth of 70 feet. The extraordinary nature of the process put the project behind schedule almost from the beginning. The progress of the building became the center of interest. People passed by frequently to watch the headway of the much-anticipated facility. It became the regular route of President Gerald Sherratt, who was joined by fascinated townspeople day after day, as they watched walls emerge above the cavernous opening.

The Centrum officially opened on November 22, 1985. There was much work still to be done, but the McDonald Tip-Off Tournament was scheduled, with the first game on that Friday night. The gala event began with fireworks outside the building at 6 p.m. Then, with 5,100 people watching, the largest indoor crowd ever assembled in southern Utah, Sen. Ivan Matheson walked onto the floor, took the oversized pair of scissors offered him by Michael Richards, and cut the red ribbon stretched across the arena floor. Dignitaries representing state, county and city government entities, representatives from the design and contracting firms and subcontractors, as well as college officials and students all were appropriately honored and thanked.

Cheerleaders shouted, "Come on Big Red, let's go!" The crowd cheered as the Thunderbirds recovered the tip-off, carried the ball down the court and made the first basket, going on to win the tourney. An exhilarated crowd that night had the sense that the win signaled great times ahead; surely the place would be magic.

A small flap with the fire marshal arose after the beginning basketball games of the season. The fire marshal ordered that the venue of the remaining games be returned to the War Memorial Fieldhouse because of the unfinished state of the building. The concern was that the fire alarm system in the Centrum was not yet operative. Of course the fieldhouse had never had a fire alarm system. The arena in the Centrum actually had a fully operating sprinkling system and 12 operating extinguisher stations. The fieldhouse had never had either. The Centrum had 17 exits, the fieldhouse only five. After some further discussion, the state fire marshal agreed that the remaining games could be returned to the not-quite completed Centrum. When the Centrum was completed, the state fire marshal ordered that the field house be closed permanently.

The administration faced the end of 1985

PRESIDENT SHERRATT VISITED THE CONSTRUCTION SITE OF THE CENTRUM ALMOST DAILY.

with the assurance of two conflicting factors. Enrollment was rising and the state legislature had asked for a 2 percent budget cut. It was not a happy prospect. The regents had approved significant increases for SUSC, in view of programs changes and continued salary inequities. Equipment needs at SUSC were backlogged at $2.7 million. As it was not a new difficulty, the school faced the year with customary stoicism.

True to his early aim of bringing his school to the consciousness of the people of the state, President Gerald Sherratt conceived an ingenious plan: "Bring them here as families." Plans were formulated at the end of the summer of 1985. It was vintage Jerry Sherratt. It was also an idea gaining popularity throughout the nation. Thirty-three states already had summer games.

Cedar City and SUSC would co-host the first Utah Summer Games in the summer of 1986. Vaughn McDonald, assistant to the president for college advancement, was made the chair of the initial games.

Jack Bishop, chairman of the games committee, announced the three stated goals of the committee:

· To promote a good, wholesome amateur athletic competition in Utah.

· To promote SUSC's athletic image and the image of the College in general.

· To promote economic development.

A minimum of 12 sports were required to gain sanction of the United States Olympic Committee. The committee expected 1,500 athletes the first year. They expected that the figure would rise to 5,000 within the following three years. Ceremonies opened the games with fireworks and fanfare on July 1, and elaborate final formalities closed them three days later.

The dream came true, like most dreams that emanate from the hill in the center of town, because the community embraced it. The Utah Summer Games became legendary, not only because of the efforts and the talent of the athletes, but because they constituted another example of volunteerism, true to the tradition of the town. From the first year hundreds of people worked to make it a success. The hundreds became time-keepers and punch-pourers, hosts and registrars, sandwich makers and expert encouragers. And the citizens of the state became much more aware of Southern Utah State College and her town.

Joyous news came early in 1986. The dream of the long-needed, long hoped-for, long striven-for student center could be realized. For years a percentage of the student fees had been earmarked to build the new facility. No funds were available from the state of Utah, but as interest rates fell, it became possible for Southern Utah State College to obtain a student revenue bond to finance the $2.2 million project.

Vice President for Student Services Dr. Sterling R. Church, made the announcement as he issued an invitation to townspeople, students and faculty to be present at the groundbreaking activities on March 10, 1986.

The new center was planned to house the bookstore, the food-services area, offices for student leaders and pleasant gathering areas. It would feature an atrium, designed to become the living room of the campus, said the delighted Dr. Church.

The Founders' Day groundbreaking ceremony was well attended by students and friends of the college. Invited guests included all student body presidents since 1950. Any lingering nostalgia that the War Memorial Fieldhouse would be shortly removed to make room for the new structure diffused in the excitement.

SUSC debaters took their 17th first place sweepstakes for the year at a national tournament at Weber State College. The debate team had consistently won national honors in all events over a period of years. In 1986, they were the proud possessors of 350 trophies and were headed for still more contests. From the 1898 founding of BNS, debate had consistently been an important extra-curricular activity. It simply expanded from the days of early teams' laborious travel to St. George and Beaver for competition, to these seasons of skimming the skies of the nation to meets all over the land. One wonders if modern teams felt a connection to those of the past

The men, women and children living in Cedar City in 1897-98 had not thought of themselves as heroic. But those who received their legacy honored them with a statue of heroic proportions placed near the Centrum. The Old Sorrel Monument, a magnificent piece by sculptor Jerry Anderson, depicted dramatic details of the struggle of men and animals to bring the lumber into the town in the winter of 1898. It symbolized the effort of all the people, whatever part they had played in the accomplishment.

Funding for the monument came from private donors, many of whom were descendants of the original founding families. As an appropriate memorial to monumental achievement, it was, perhaps, intended to signify a double meaning--remembrance of the pioneering people in the miraculous creation of the first building, and a memorial to the superb effort of many who had worked to make the Centrum, this

VAUGHN McDONALD

STERLING R. CHURCH

OLD SORREL MONUMENT
DEDICATION, MAY 9, 1986
YORK JONES PHOTO

newest miracle, happen.

Finishing touches on the Centrum were finally complete. The grand building was ready to be formally received and formally dedicated. The committee was polishing details of two separate and significant dedications- of the fabulous building itself, and the magnificent Founders' Monument that stood along side.

The famed Mormon Tabernacle Choir came to sing. Governor Norman H. Bangerter was to speak. Hugh Pinnock of the First Quorum of the Seventy of the LDS Church would offer the prayer. Even a famous movie and stage actress, Celeste Holm, who served on the National Endowment of the Arts, came to add sparkle to the already dazzling occasion and to emphasize that the building was to be a center for the arts as well as athletics. It was a grand affair.

The dedication of the monument was held at three in the afternoon. Somber folks remembered their forefathers. A time capsule, carefully prepared by Diana Graff and filled with items representative of the 1980s, was placed inside the base. It included music tapes and newspapers, a program of the Centrum dedication, a copy of the book *Dr. Mac, The Man, His Land* by L.W. Macfarlane.

At eight o'clock that evening, with 5,000 people who had come to claim chair-back seats half an hour before, the choir began to sing. The Mormon Tabernacle Choir presented a full concert of 12 selections. The glorious presentation included excerpts from *Elijah, Glory to the Lamb, Deep River, An American Tribute, Come, Come Ye Saints* and a rousing finale of *The Battle Hymn of the Republic.*

Celeste Holm gave the dedicatory address, recounting the drama of the founding of the school. She praised the industry and creativity of founding pioneers, both past and present. President Sherratt also addressed the crowd, as did Gov. Norman Bangerter; Michael O. Leavitt, chairman of the Institutional Council; Elder Hugh Pinnock and Cedar City Mayor Robert Linford.

As the people filed home after the inspiring event, every person was aware that a new day had dawned in southern Utah.

At the end of the school year 1986, Conrad and Elva Oldroyd Hatch retired from teaching at SUSC. Theirs was no ordinary story. Their lives were intertwined with the school in remarkable ways. Both had come to Branch Agricultural College from small Utah towns; Con from Koosharem, Elva from Venice, both graduating from Richfield High School. Con came to BAC as a student in 1940, and served as student body president before he graduated with an associate degree in 1942. Elva came later to complete her associate degree. Both then transferred to northern universities to complete further schooling, Con earning bachelor's and master's degrees in physics and chemistry from Brigham Young University, Elva a bachelor of science at Utah State Agricultural College. Both returned to the campus of BAC. Elva came in 1945 as secretary to Director Wayne Driggs, BAC registrar and teacher of English and speech. Con came in 1948 as a teacher of physics and chemistry. The two quickly became the object of campus matchmakers, notably Roy Halversen, Theron Ashcroft and "Pa" Manning. The trio did good work, for Hatch and Oldroyd were married in February 1949.

The Hatch family established their home in Cedar City, leaving only for a three-year period while Con completed his doctoral studies, but except for that brief absence, the campus was as much their home as their home. Dale, Elaine, Lynn, Larry, Paul, Anne and Linda; all seven of their seven children graduated from SUSC.

Dr. Hatch had served as professor, department chair, dean and academic vice president. Now, at his retirement, he quietly arranged one last contribution. He would, he said, like to teach one more year.

This time he would accept no salary, but rather would contribute his year's salary to fund two endowments. One would furnish a scholarship in the physical science department, and one in his wife's name in communication.

"I don't think I'll ever have a lot of money to donate," he said, "but I thought I could donate my time."

The giving of what one could, in expression of love for the institution, is the long-established tradition of the school. It is a grand tradition.

That summer of 1986, the Utah Shakespearean Festival celebrated its silver anniversary, and the Utah Summer Games opened its first season with pomp and pageantry.

Early in the 1986-87 school year word came down from the governor to the regents, to the Institutional Council, to the administration that the financial outlook for the upcoming year was not bright. A $48 million revenue shortfall was projected. All institutions of higher education were being asked by Gov. Norman Bangerter to slice a 6 percent reduction out of their projected budgets. It would be painful.

The SUSC administration announced a tuition hike, acknowledging, however, that the added revenue would not alter the necessity to cut back. Every program on campus would have to be reviewed and analyzed for reduction or elimination. There would even be cuts in personnel.

The major reductions in programs and staff resulting from the governor's mandate were announced on Friday, October 10, 1986.

The process had been thorough and laborious. The academic programs that would be eliminated were: bachelor of social work, agriculture emphasis in biology, health education emphasis in physical education, minor in health education, one- and two-year certificates in the metals program, and philosophy. Departments would be consolidated.

Every office in every department was affected. The president withdrew the schools' memberships in any professional associations that required the paying of dues. Counseling services were cut. Health services now would carry a cost to the student. Custodial services and building maintenance costs were cut. The engineers turned down valves in the heating and cooling plants to save energy cost.

Students who had completed much of the work in the eliminated majors and minors paraded in front of the buildings with hand-made signs that read: "Please don't take our dreams away" and "Don't jerk social work."

ELVA OLDROYD AND CONRAD HATCH, 1949; THE HATCHES, 1996.

People really suffered the losses. Those nearing retirement were offered the option of early retirement. Some staff people simply had to search for new jobs. The employment of several tenured faculty members was terminated, resulting in a law suit which took six years to resolve. A jury finally agreed with the school's position that the cuts were appropriate and lawful.

President Sherratt, sensitive to the wounds in people and programs, pointed out, "There is no fat or loose change we can call on to make the cuts that are requested of us."

Students in social work quietly carried placards in their protest effort. But agriculture students, angry about the loss of the biology emphasis in agriculture, circled the campus in a parade of tractors, horses and farm trucks. The students were joined by a few area farmers and ranchers, enlisted to make the protest more impressive. They honked loudly, letting frustrations grow into a rowdy demonstration. Administrators were sorry, but unable to acquiesce to their demands. Instead, they appointed a study committee made up of prominent local ranchers and agriculture specialists from the western United States to study the future of the agricultural program, which had once

MARK
BARTON

been, long ago, the very back-bone of the school.

There was no other way. The Institutional Council, in their February 1987 meeting, voted unanimously to increase student activity fees from $234 to $264 a year. The ASSUSC reluctantly ratified the move. SUSC fees were not exorbitant when compared with other institutions of higher learning in the state, but $30 meant something to students, and the hike was felt as a twinge of discomfort caused by the economic distress of the state. Twenty-five percent of the student fees still were dedicated to the Student Center under construction.

At the same time funding was being curtailed, enrollment was burgeoning. That fall Mark Barton, announced that the number of full-time and special students had almost reached the 3,000 mark for the first time. He analyzed the reasons for the increase:

• More transfer students from larger universities who desire more personalized education;

• Greater exposure through the 7,000 people who visited the Summer Games;

• The great variety of visitors who came for the Shakespearean Festival;

• "Project Image," a new advertising program initiated by Institutional Council Chair Michael O. Leavitt. Funded by the Cedar City Corporation, Iron County Commission, and a significant donation from Utah Power, Project Image focused upon the academic achievement of SUSC students. The campaign advertisements appeared on television and radio stations, and on billboards throughout the state. The campaign had a major impact upon the public image of SUSC and helped set the stage for the name-change campaign that was to come a few years later. [27]

Enrollment had doubled in 10 years. Summer school had more than doubled just in the last summer, and the future appeared bright as college officials targeted an enrollment of 4,000 in the next three years. Of course, more students to educate with less money sharpened the sting of the budget cuts.

The demolition of the War Memorial Fieldhouse revealed a treasure. There were, when the worn out shell had been cleared away, some large trusses of significant value. All the better to retrieve a dream shelved by lack of funding. There had long been a hope to construct a pavilion at the south end of the stadium which would provide drama to the pageantry of activities staged there. The trea-

sured trusses, valued at $250,000, were carefully dismantled and stored away to be used in the new project. Private funds were enlisted to do the truss work. And when later the completed structure bore the names of Jay Dee and Alice Christopherson Harris, dear friends of President Sherratt, it became clear that they had gifted the funds to facilitate the dream.

Provost Terry Alger announced the return, after a two-decade absence from the Cedar City campus, of ROTC to Southern Utah State College. Late in 1986, Dr. Alger, along with Dr. James Miller, dean of the School of Education and also commanding general of the National Guard 1st Corps, and admissions director Mark Barton had met with ROTC officials at Brigham Young University to consider the feasibility of an ROTC unit on the campus of SUSC as a satellite program of BYU. Leadership training and other advantages would come to the school with the program. The arrangement required only that there be 10 or more students enrolled. SUSC administrators were assured that triple that number would be interested. Scholarships were available to qualifying students.

Arrangements proceeded, and the program opened on the SUSC campus fall quarter of 1987. ROTC was to remain on the campus until the end of the 1991 year, when it was phased out.

During the 1987 legislature, tax protesters had demonstrated in the rotunda of the State Capitol against tax increases, and students had lobbied loudly in favor of tax increases. When the dust settled, the legislature had adopted a $152 million tax increase, the largest in the history of the state. No one was completely happy, but SUSC fared as well as they could have hoped, and they were grateful to have been allotted $11.4 million, though they had asked for $12.3 million. They could now fix the cracks in the buildings. The library would be able to stay open for regular hours. There would even be some merit pay increases.

The State Board of Regents announced a permanent 10 percent tuition increase.

The USA's 50-starred flag and the USSR's solid red sickle and hammer flew side by side in the Centrum on Wednesday, April 29, 1987. The occasion was an historic USA/USSR Goodwill Tour. The town turned out to warmly welcome the Russian athletes for "Western Days." An enthusiastic group gathered at the airport to welcome the gymnasts; a cheering crowd lined Main Street for a two-hour long parade; and the dazzled capacity audience at the Centrum continued to express the town's genuine warmth and new-found affection for the young Russians, who were experiencing America and the American West for the first time.

The Russians received the best round-up of Americana that Cedar City could offer. They returned the compliment through their spokesman:

When people heard they always ask me,' Where is Cedar City?' Now I know what to tell them. Here, we found real America. I have meet people who are handsome. They are courageous. They are friends. I am very impressed.

It had been a week to remember for people on both sides of the world.

Library Awareness Week was launched early in May by ASSUSC President Monica Moe. The effort was timed to coincide with the spring meeting of the Board of Regents. It was to be a peaceful and dignified demonstration, but it was to be a statement: the old library was inadequate; drives to obtain more and more books were futile without a new facility to house them. *The Thunderbird* for the week dedicated eight full pages to making the point.

PLANT OPERATIONS HEAD GORDON SLACK

THE QUARTER-OF-A-MILLION DOLLAR TRUSSES OF WAR MEMORIAL FIELDHOUSE

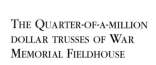

Randall Christensen, librarian, articulated his frustration with trying to serve the students with inadequate resources. Diana Graff, library director, looking ahead a few years, voiced her worry about the impossibility of serving the 4,000 to 5,000 students projected by the year 2000, in the current cramped library. [28]

Moe and senior student Jay Lane took copies of the special issue of *The Thunderbird* to reinforce a strong appeal to the Institutional Council. The regents responded with the promise of a site visit in July and a forthcoming decision on whether or not they would carry the appeal through the process to the Legislature. By the July meeting of the Board of Regents, the Institutional Council was on board. The request for the new library was the top priority item in their $38 million request for facilities at Southern Utah State College.

Gordon Slack, director of the physical plant at SUSC, announced the purchase of the final home on 200 South and 800 West Streets. To make way for a new parking lot, across the street west from the Centrum, 14 houses would be moved or demolished. All had been purchased by Southern Utah State College, an expenditure of more than $900,000. Now the owners had a deadline of June 1 to vacate them. Three hundred cars would occupy the space where a neighborhood of families had lived out their lives. When students leaving for the summer returned in the fall, the face of the place would have been altered forever. The returning students would find six new tennis courts, a nearly completed Student Center, an automated mechanized sprinkler system that could save them from being drenched during daytime classes and, though they may not notice, many of the old damage-spots from soil settlement would have been repaired.

SUSC students reporting to register for the fall quarter of 1987 sensed a new burst of activity along with the new look.

• In addition to President Gerald Sherratt's traditional welcome reception for new and returning students, the new ROTC unit whirled cadets and prospective cadets around town in a helicopter for a bird's-eye view of the town and surrounding mountains. It called attention to the opportunity for ROTC scholarships available to those would sign up for four-year stints.

• Arriving students heard the reassuring sound of construction at the new Student Center nearing completion.

• A new performing arts theatre, funded by an Economic Development grant to Cedar City, was well on the way to its debut.

• Cable television and telephone hook-ups had been added to remodeled campus housing over the summer.

It promised to be a busy year.

Hundreds of fans and family members cheered as Boyd Adams became the 18th person inducted into the SUSC Athletic Hall of Fame. He was described as a lifetime fixture in the department, having participated as a player and as a coach of several sports. He had seen the department through

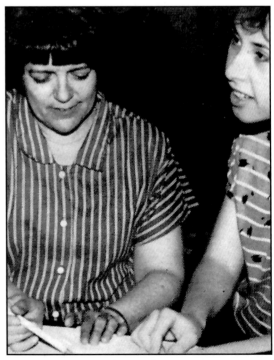

LIBRARY DIRECTOR DIANA GRAFF WORKED HARD TO MAINTAIN HER FACILITY DESPITE A LACK OF ADEQUATE FUNDING IN 1986.

the transition from a two-year to a four-year program and then on to a Division I program. He had been named NAIA District Women's Basketball Coach of the Year in acknowledgement of his instrumentality in laying the groundwork to bring women's athletics to the next level of competition.

At the close of the 1988 general session of the state legislature, SUSC had fared amazingly well. The $12 million appropriated for SUSC's budget was actually a few percentage points ahead of the increase allotted the other senior institutions in the state. Of course, there were some down sides to the outcome.

The legislators authorized a study of all

BOYD ADAMS IS INDUCTED INTO THE SUU ATHLETIC HALL OF FAME IN 1987.

library needs in the state, including the SUSC Library, which meant that more time would elapse before the new library could become a reality.

The funds to remodel the old student center were not granted. Even with these disappointments, the scene was not as grim as it had seemed other years.

*A*fter weeks of extended construction deadlines, the new Student Center opened for business. The new center seemed like wonderland compared to the former facility, and students reveled in the luxury.

Bookstore, food service and post office employees raced to complete the move and settled in to serve, while students poured in to explore, exclaim and relax.

The closure of the old student center meant there was no longer a campus ballroom, but dances

NEWLY ARRIVED ROTC UNITS PROVIDED FREE HELICOPTER RIDES TO STUDENTS IN THE FALL OF 1987.

could be held in the Physical Education Building.

On the day before the 91st commencement, the Student Center was dedicated in style. The reception honoring the past student body officers presented a chance to show off the new offices to old officers who had served in much less commodious quarters. It was also a good time to honor many who had conserved student body fees so that the building could become a reality.

Everyone was invited to see the new home of the student body. Guests passing through the new building paused with appropriate sentiment before a plaque commemorating the War Memorial Fieldhouse, the long-time home of the Thunderbirds, which had stood on the spot. They marveled at the magnitude of a mural created by art department faculty member Anton Rasmussen, which covered the walls of the Kolob Canyons living room in the center of the building depicting the natural wonders of the Zion Canyon country.

People filed through the spacious Bookstore. They admired the food service areas, including a snack bar called The Country Store, they became acquainted with the Thunderbird Circle dining room, designed to feel "uninstitutional" and welcoming. Student hosts, excited by their elegant new home, were glad to show it off.

*I*n the afternoon, at a dedication program, Elder Marion D. Hanks, Church of Jesus Christ of Latter-day Saints, offered the prayer to dedicate the new student center.

After 25 years as teacher and later as head of the home economics department, Ella Van Groningen retired. She had been the resident adviser of the Family Living Center for 17

WORK ON THE NEW STUDENT CENTER MOVED ALONG IN 1986 AND 1987 (ABOVE). DEAN OF CONTINUING EDUCATION PHIL CARTER AWAITED FUNDS TO RENOVATE THE OLD STUDENT CENTER INTO A FACILITY FOR LIFELONG LEARNING (RIGHT).

THE NEW STUDENT CENTER WAS A GREAT HOME TO ALL ON CAMPUS.

years. "Miss Van" had instructed, expanded, and refined an ongoing series of girls, who left her presence as young women of substance.

Dr. Eugene Woolf, professor of English and philosophy, formerly dean of Arts and Letters, retired after 35 years of teaching. He had established the O.C. Tanner Distinguished Lecture Series and would continue to administer that program as well as become a principal figure in Centennial events some eight years later, but he concluded a distinguished career as a beloved classroom teacher.

The threat of another round of proposed tax cut initiatives on the ballot at election time in 1988 brought President Sherratt to his soapbox. Tax cuts mandated by three proposed initiatives would pare $300 million from the coffers of the state. SUSC administrators estimated at least $3 million would be cut from their budget if the roll-backs were to become law; this at a time when enrollment was at a new all-time high. Reported enrollment for fall quarter stood at 3,436 full-time students.

The effort to persuade the voters to reject the tax revolt was ultimately successful, but the first quarter was tense. A housing shortage added to the stress, and college officials appealed once again to the community for help in housing the influx of students.

Efforts at recruitment had been effective and successful. Ironically, now they feared they would have to turn students away for lack of classes.

The College Cabin, created by the hands of devoted faculty and staff nearly 35 years previously and the site of countless warm and wonderful events, had over the years diminished to a run-down state. The wooded site along Highway 14 was a wondrous spot. The potential for improving the small structure into a much more usable resource began to germinate in the minds of forward-looking faculty. Why not create a mountain conference center where many more people could enjoy the magic of the mountain? Volunteer committees were appointed; plans were formulated. Work began under the direction of special instructor Jerry

'Miss Van' retired in 1987 after 25 years at the institution.

Lawrence and under the auspices of a series of Summer School workshops entitled "Cabin Construction" and "Cabin Renovations." The project had long been the dream of Dr. Phillip Carter, and now, as assistant provost, he was in a position to promote its fulfillment. The ambitious project proceeded until the tiny, deteriorating cabin was magically transformed into a facility that could be used for conferences, workshops and the enjoyment of faculty and staff families. By the end of the summer of 1988 the project had begun to transform the property. Vaughn McDonald, assistant to the president for development, extolled the virtues of the new, expanded resource for summer courses, retreats and seminars. Naturally he also appealed for donations.

A tender part of the project included the restoration of a tiny sheep-camp cabin tucked away in the corner of the property. It was ramshackle, but filled with nostalgic memories for those who could look backward to an earlier day. They could not tear it down, so Richard Dotson found time on summer days to make it tight and secure again so that passersby in winter or summer could find shelter, just as shepherds had done generations before.

History was repeating itself in very positive ways. Once again faculty, staff and friends of the college had stepped forward, hand in hand, to dedicate time and money, materials and effort, to enhance a treasured tradition.

The state required that all colleges plan for future growth. The startling rate of growth experienced at SUSC suggested that expansion was the watchword. At the end of 1988, the required master plan detailed renovation or expansion of almost every building on the campus.

A top priority was the renovation of the old student center. Constructed in 1927 as a gymnasium, it now sat still and useless, though filled with potential. Second was the needed expansion of the science building. The $9 million library had already been presented as a priority item to the Regents and the Utah State

Eugene Woolf retired after 35 years of teaching.

Building Board. Expansion of the stadium and the new Student Center were on the drawing board as well. Other plans were afoot to double the size of the Dixie Leavitt Business Building, make additions to the Physical Education and Industrial Education buildings and acquire land to expand the Utah Shakespearean Festival. The expansion plans were targeted to make the campus facilities adequate to accommodate 5,000 students, which at that time looked to be a long way into the future. [29]

Sometimes one crucial need collided with other needs equally pressing. When the needed library was finally funded, Oak Hall, the only campus facility for married student housing, would have to be demolished, as it stood on the site designated for the library.

For 30 years Oak Hall, with its tiny rooms and cramped spaces, had housed young student families. It had the capacity to house 50 families, 40 percent of whom were usually single-parent units, and over the years it had housed hundreds of them. Though occasionally residents called it by less than affectionate appelations, [30] they also suggested some advantages—apartments were so small one didn't need much furniture; laundry facilities and television hook-ups were free; and the units could be put "in storage" through the summer for only half rent.

The legislature kept the people of the state

President Sherratt rejoiced over the defeat of the tax rollback on the evening of November 1, 1988.

THE
COLLEGE
CABIN

on tenterhooks through the 1989 session. No one could be sure the $52 million bonding bill would pass until just a few moments before midnight. When the smoke cleared, SUSC had been granted $3.7 million to renovate the old Student Center into an Academic Service Center, enabling SUSC to host large conferences and workshops and to improve the acoustics and decor of the Great Hall. Planning funds were appropriated for the new library, and with them came the assurance of a construction appropriation the following session.

*I*n another important way it was a good session for the college. Faculty salaries, though not at the requested level, were brought more nearly into line with peer higher education institutions in the state and nation. The session marked the beginning of a good year.

After decades of service, two distinguished faculty members announced their retirement in the spring of 1989.

As McRay Cloward had joined the College faculty in 1947, his association with the school spanned more than 42 years. Early in his career he had been housing manager, manager of the bookstore and coordinator of student aid. Later he had become dean of Continuing Education and Public Service and numerous other projects related to group dynamics and community development. His involvement with campus projects had included acquisition and disposition of the Topaz buildings, the college cabin, and countless other additions to the

school. He had been a campus favorite with students and staff. The place would not ever seem the same.

Likewise, after 29 years as professor of chemistry and a noted researcher, Dr. Joseph L. Comp retired. SUSC's highly successful water testing laboratory had come into being under Professor Comp's direction in 1976; he served as its director from its inception through 1988. Services of the certified water lab include complete water analysis on everything from culinary water and irrigation water to sewage treatment plants.

The water lab was established for the two historic dual reasons–to provide practical laboratory experience for SUSC students and to provide a much needed service for this part of the state.

Drama had always played a primary role in the grand tradition of Cedar City and Southern Utah State College. With the dedication June 23, 1989, of the magnificent Randall L. Jones Memorial Theatre, "grand" took on new meaning.

The Randall L. Jones Memorial Theatre was born of a cooperative project of the community of Cedar City, Southern Utah State College, and The Utah Shakespearean Festival. In response to a study entitled "Economic Development Through Expansion of the Performing Arts in Southern Utah," the three entities jointly sought and received grants from the Utah State Department of Community and Economic Development and the United States Department of Health and Human Services.

While numerous other donors contributed to equip and embellish the lovely place, a generous donation from the family of Randall L. Jones determined that the theatre would be designated by his name. Jones was a Cedar City native who became an architect and returned to Cedar City to practice his profession, designing the El Escalante Hotel and many other homes in Cedar City. His love of his home country was his impetus for promoting the beauties of southern Utah. He was considered one of the founding fathers of the tourist industry in southern Utah.

The dedication was a sparkling affair with music and tributes, the unveiling of the Randall L. Jones portrait in the foyer of the theatre, refreshments under the trees surrounding the beautiful building, and people from all over the state celebrating a future of expanded possibilities in a city that had always embraced elevating dramatic arts.

That evening, 767 excited patrons encircled

the stage in plum-colored velvet seats to enjoy a superb performance of Tennessee Williams' *The Glass Menagerie.* It was a grand beginning.

Also part of the opening was the debut of a play, commissioned by the Festival to open the new theatre, entitled *Nothing Like the Sun,* dealing with Ben Jonson's writing of the epitaph for his friend William Shakespeare. It was meant to be a one-man vehicle for Festival favorite Patrick Page and directed by R. Scott Phillips of the USF. The playwright was Doug Christensen who, as an SUU student several years earlier, had served as the editor of both the student newspaper and the student literary magazine. After attending graduate school at Temple University, he returned to southern Utah to write this, his third play. However, he died, two weeks short of his 31st birthday and before the play's completion. The decision was made to carry on with the project, with Page and Christensen's longtime friend and newspaper adviser Larry Baker to speculate on how the late playwright might have proceeded and to complete the writing process. Despite continuous alterations made up until, literally, the last minute, the play was a success and has been performed many times since, with royalties going toward an SUU journalism scholarship in Christensen's name.

*T*he summer school added to its usual breadth some new and exciting programs. The Governor's Honors Academy began, introducing some of the state's most remarkable young scholars to the campus in a two-week long seminar of special honors academic programs. A summer youth equestrian camp brought youngsters to the campus.

One especially clever course brought students to the cabin to learn the art of cabin-construction finishing. The students gained experience while they put the finishing touches on the newly rebuilt cabin, which became the site for watercoloring workshops and ceramics classes. In addition to special programs. the usual full core of academic courses continued to be offered.

As fall quarter of 1989 arrived, the school suddenly struggled with an unexpected challenge. Registration brought the largest increase the school had ever experienced. An increase of 22 percent translated into 3,612 students, a greater increase than any school in the state. The image campaign had worked almost too well. But the good news was that the campaign

was attracting scholars. The GPA of scholarships applicants was 3.87.

DOUG
CHRISTENSEN

Out-of-state students poured in, 100 more than the previous year. D. Mark Barton, director of admissions and records, rejoiced over the success and wondered where they would house them all.

The idea had been germinating at SUSC that perhaps the time was right to move for a change of designation from a college to a university. Education officials were aware that Weber State College intended to petition the legislature for that change at their school. Research had shown that the title "university" on a diploma made a graduate more marketable in a competitive job arena. Even though there was no difference in the graduation or course work requirement, there existed, nonetheless, an illusive prestige to the appellation "university." The other side of that coin was that prejudice attended a degree that read "college." Were Weber State College to "advance" to the rank of university while SUSC remained a "college," even though the courses the two required for graduation remained exactly the same, there would occur a tangible disadvantage to SUSC.

The administration decided to seize the moment and join the movement. At first, Weber State College resisted being joined in the effort by their southern cousins. But very shortly the political realities became clear. [31]

Only legislative action could ultimately accomplish the change, but the recommendation of the Board of Regents would be an important factor influencing the legislature. Neither school had the legislative votes nor the regent votes to do it alone. And they would need both to accomplish their goal.

On October 19, 1989, when the Board of Regents met on the campus of College of Eastern Utah at Price, Utah, the Institutional Council of SUSC and Institutional Council of Weber State College made startling proposals.

In a petition addressed to Wm. Rolfe Kerr, State Commissioner of Higher Education, and the State Board of Regents, the SUSC Institutional Council requested a change in designation from Southern Utah State College to Southern Utah State University.

Following the presentation of the Weber contingent, and in a committee of the whole, K. L.

RANDALL LUNT JONES PORTRAIT (TOP) AND AN
INTERIOR VIEW OF THE RANDALL LUNT JONES
MEMORIAL THEATRE.

McIff, chairman of the SUSC Institutional
Council, presented the request and spoke to the
issue. The petition stressed that university
status should not be based upon an institution's
size in enrollment, but rather the critical factor
should be the institution's proscribed mission
and role. He described the mission and role of
SUSC, as defined by the Utah System of Higher
Education: "to provide baccalaureate degrees in
the liberal arts tradition in the arts, humanities
and sciences, and the professional areas of business, education and technology. Additionally,
SUSC provides students with master's programs
in education and business." Mr. McIff called the
attention of the regents to the fact that this
mission concurs precisely with that of other
schools across the nation known by the name
of university. The Regents were aware that a
strong national trend toward re-naming colleges
as universities existed throughout the states.

Regent Michael O. Leavitt moved that a study
of the matter become an important dimension
of the strategic planning then under way. He
emphasized that the conduct of the study
should focus only upon a change of names and
make clear that no change of mission would be
considered for either institution. The motion,
seconded by Regent Clifford LeFevre, was
unanimously adopted.[32]

Commissioner Kerr directed that both
schools prepare formal institutional proposals
containing specific data and justification for
their requests. The battle had begun to gain the
support of the Board of Regents.

Administrators of Southern Utah State
College hurried home to prepare to make their
case.

It was an idea not gladly received by all other
institutions in the system. Objections began to
flow to the office of the Commissioner.
Opposing parties argued that the title "university" should be reserved for research institutions. They protested that both colleges were
too small to be called universities. They reasoned that the change would further drain the
already strained financial resources of the state.
They declared that "academic drift" would
result, since no matter what the petitioning
schools declared at the moment of request,
their heads would soon be turned by the newly
prestigious titles and they would soon request
expanded roles. They railed eloquently against
the proposal.

Commissioner Kerr and his staff solicited
expressions of opinion on the issue from higher
education officials in Utah and other states, in a
quest for comparative data to aid in the analysis
of the issue. Eager to maintain civility in his
ranks, he urged that cool heads should prevail
in an emotional issue that admittedly had great
potential for divisiveness. A dignified understatement.

The battle lines had been drawn long before

the formal proposals, with their persuasive arguments, had been heard and considered. *The Salt Lake Tribune*, always closely aligned with the position of the University of Utah, hopped onto the issue in a lead editorial in its October 30 issue:

Utahns Beware: There's More To A University Than A Title

Utah's four-year colleges dropped a bombshell on the Board of Regents the other day: They want to be universities. This proposal must not be taken lightly.

After eloquently disdaining the audacity of the thought, the editor persuasively enumerated why the change should not occur, then continued:

It would be naive for the regents and other state officials to expect a name change to be only that. More likely the new designation would push the camel's nose further into the tent, precipitating a wider array of graduate programs at SUSC and WSC. If Utahns want, can afford and can fill two more public universities, fine, but everyone should approach the issue with eyes wide open.

Everyone in the administration of Southern Utah State College had their eyes wide open to the fact that the opposition was powerful, armed and ready.

The Board of Regents met at Snow College on November 17 with myriad issues to consider, but the "renaming" of the two colleges was on everybody's mind. Commissioner Kerr made a formal recommendation that: "...the regents avoid taking a position on this important issue until institutional proposals are submitted, institutional and comparative data are available, and both institutional and systemwide ramifications of the requested name changes can be fully examined." [33]

Regent Ian Cumming, statesmanlike, confident and correct, commented, "...this item has plenty of opportunity to be divisive—between the Legislature and the Regents, between Institutional Councils and the Regents, between the presidents of the institutions themselves; therefore we all have to forebear as best we can and do what is proposed in the Commissioner's recommendation." He then offered a motion to approve the recommendation. Regent LeFevre seconded and the Board voted unanimously in favor.

Cumming, who was chair of the subcommittee assigned to study the measure, then moved to adopt another resolution, which Regent Leavitt seconded and the Board unanimously affirmed:

The Commissioner and his staff are directed to review the requests from Weber State College and Southern Utah State College to be renamed universities, and to prepare a report for discussion in the December Board of Regents meeting.

In completing this assignment, the Commissioner is directed to analyze the issues in context with the existing Board of Regents Master Plan and the strategic plan that is in progress. He is also directed to consider the challenges and long-term best interests of the system, not just the two institutions in question. Finally, the presidents and staffs of all institutions are directed to avoid engaging in any activities that would further emotionalize this issue and do damage to the Utah System of Higher Education. The Utah Legislature empowered the Board of Regents to undertake the management of the Utah System of Higher Education. The issue of name changes for two of our institutions may have significant systemwide implications. We ask that our institutional councils, presidents and legislators allow us to complete our work in a careful and rational manner. [34]

Not everyone remembered the part about not engaging in activities that might further emotionalize the issue.

The Ogden *Standard-Examiner* took on presidents and provosts of the universities that bordered Weber State College on either side. The presidents and provosts fired back.

Nor did newspapers at the state's southern end lack for incendiary content. The Institutional Council of Dixie College formally opposed the change, saying, "...such a change would cause serious dislocation that will benefit some citizens and not others." [35]

Dixie College president Dr. Douglas Alder released his letter to the Regents giving a dignified but spirited defense of his firm opposition.[36]

Never mind the regents' resolution. Emotions were enflamed by faculty senates, student body officers and interested citizens, which included almost everyone.

At SUSC they were feverishly preparing a presentation for the crucial December meeting of the Board of Regents. The Commissioner had outlined the rules: Each school would be allowed 15 minutes to make their presentation. The staff of the Board of Regents would then present to the Regents the considerable volume of data they had gathered, followed by 30 minutes of open discussion. [37]

The formal proposals prepared by SUSC and WSC were mailed to the Regents from the office of the USOHE on December 8, a week before the upcoming meeting, along with a charge from Commissioner Kerr, to study the proposals with care.

In keeping with the intent of the Commissioner and the staff to help the Regents come to a position on the requests in a careful and rational manner, they had conducted a thorough and deliberate study. In that process, they had accumulated letters from presidents past and present; statements from executive officers from other state higher education systems; heads of several national higher education associations and organizations; missives from students, alumni and virtually every Tom, Dick or Harry who had an opinion on the issue, who could also write. The voluminous mass of material would be distilled into a manageable form by the long-suffering staff, headed by Don A. Carpenter, associate commissioner for academic affairs. Their extract would be handcarried and delivered to the Regents at the December 15 meeting.[38] They'd have plenty of material to work from.

*T*he presentation prepared by President Sherratt and his able crew would be succinct, persuasive and visual, the compelling points to be illustrated with a series of slides. A printed *pièce de résistance* would be placed in the hands of each regent: The team had created a small, dignified, but tastefully presented brochure entitled: "Why Southern Utah State College Deserves to be Called a University." At a glance the regents, and later the legislators, would be able to see why that was true. A black and white photo of Old Main graced the booklet cover, as did a discreet line crediting the Alumni Association with its publishing. Should anyone be so crass as to criticize the cost of the booklet, the bases were covered; no college funds had been used.

When the Regents met on December 15, 1989, they gathered on the neutral ground of their Triad Center offices. There were no absentees. A capacity crowd of large contingents from every constituency was present for the opening committee-of-the-whole.

The Regents disposed, with dispatch, of three agenda items that engendered cursory interest.

The "nomenclature issue" was next on the agenda.

Though he had little need to explain to those present, Commissioner Kerr declared that in the comprehensive review conducted by the USOHE staff, the information gathered so far had clearly indicated that there were two sides to the issue.

Commissioner Kerr first introduced President Steven Nadauld of Weber State College, who discussed five issues underlying Weber State College's proposal:
· National Patterns of Nomenclature in Higher Education,
· Institutional Mission,
· Resource and Program Implications,
· Implications for the Utah System of Higher Education; and the
· Role of Teaching. [39]

President Gerald Sherratt was next introduced. He presented the case for the "university" label, using the prepared slides. Then he distributed the leaflet. The small persuasive piece elicited an immediate and heated response. Committee chairman Cumming, who had appealed so eloquently for cool heads to prevail, was visibly irate. It was not just that the leaflet was classy. It was not just concern for cost. It was a masterpiece of convincing brevity. At a glance it stated the case for, and dispelled the prevailing reasons against, the nomenclature change. Mr. Cumming was not pleased with its potential impact.

The minutes record, benignly, that a lively discussion ensued, with most of the Regents and several Presidents expressing their views on the name change issues.

At their January meeting, the Board of Regents would decide whether or not to support the legislation already prepared to effect the change.

An inveterate champion of the institution would draft that legislation.

Dixie Leavitt had surprised himself when he agreed in 1987 to run again for the seat in the Utah State Senate he had vacated in 1976. He had anticipated that, after having served for 14 years, most of the crucial and exciting issues would have been resolved. That had certainly not proven to be the case. The potential of this last giant step forward for his alma mater fired his excitement for the task. Before the 1990 legislative session opened, Senator Leavitt had prepared legislation to facilitate the leap.

Early in the session, Leavitt introduced Senate Bill 119, calling for a change in the name of Southern Utah State College to

Southern Utah State University.[40] Previously, he had approached Sen. Haven Barlow, sponsor of a bill to change the name of Weber State College, suggesting that the two bills be joined into one. Weber officials were wary of SUSC's efforts, worried that joining might scuttle their endeavor. Sen. Barlow declined. Sen. Leavitt went to work to enlist support among his fellow senators. When the bill was introduced it bore his name as the prime sponsor, but signing on with him as co-sponsors were 18 of the 29 senators. A majority in the senate requires only 15 votes. Sen. Leavitt was chairman of the public education committee, and while he was not overconfident, he felt quite certain that he could shepherd his measure successfully through. Barlow was expending the same kind of diligence. Both senators watched the proceedings in the Board of Regents with interest. The Regents were equally aware of what was happening in the senate. Everyone sensed that the issue would pass the senate, with or without the recommendation of the Regents. Their support was, however, much more crucial in the more unwieldy setting of the House of Representatives. Many more votes there would be influenced by the way the Regents voted on the matter. [41]

When the Regents met on January 26, 1990, at Salt Lake Community College, anxiety hung palpably on the air. A vote would be taken at this meeting to decide whether or not the Regents would lend support to the name-change legislation or oppose it. Again, the drama played to a full house.

Most of the regents were fully aware of the sentiments of the others; all knew that the vote would be extremely close. Thirteen voting regents were present. Elder Robert Hales was absent. Evelyn B. Lee, recently appointed to fill the vacancy created by the resignation of Don Holbrook, was present but, not having been confirmed by the Utah State Senate, was ineligible to vote. This was considered fortunate by the proponents, for she was widely believed to oppose the name change. Her nay vote would have created a tie, thereby requiring the tie-breaking vote of Chairman Douglas Foxley. No one was quite sure where he stood.

Commissioner Kerr presented his recommendation regarding proposals from Weber State College and Southern Utah State College to be renamed "universities." He said it has

been his desire to elevate the consideration of these proposals from a political campaign to an analysis of the central issues. On the one hand was the desire for the name changes; on the other was the necessity for preservation of already scarce state resources and prevention of the dilution of the roles of other institutions in the Utah System of Higher Education. The Commissioner said a large stack of letters received in his office attested to the fact that it was not an easy, black and white issue. He read two letters illustrating the extreme positions.

Commissioner Kerr referred to Tab M in the Regents agenda, which listed three options for Board consideration:

Option #1
The Regents could deny the WSC and SUSC requests, concluding that university status is not in keeping with their current institutional missions and that the risk of academic drift would be greatly increased notwithstanding institutional assurances to the contrary. This obviously would be a "win" for some and a "loss" for others.

Option #2
The Regents could approve the requests, concluding that university designation is in keeping with national trends for institutions of similar size and scope serving similar roles and that the requests reflect changes in name only and not changes in mission. Again, some would "win" and some would "lose."

Option #3
The Regents could reasonably conclude that neither Option #1 nor Option #2 resolves this issue, but that they both leave damaging scars and a divided system of higher education. Instead, the Regents could pursue the following course: (1) Agree that by September 1990, the Board will reaffirm and refine as necessary the structure to clearly identify three types of categories of institutions in Utah higher education and (2) In establishing this structure, the Regents will adopt appropriate and reasonable criteria that will define and describe the functions and missions of teaching or comprehensive universities, as distinct from the categories of community colleges and of graduate/research universities. [42]

Commissioner Kerr recommended Option

#3. He stated that he was not opposed to the name changes, with the condition that the structure and criteria as proposed in Option #3 be put in place.

Regent Ian Cumming quickly moved to approve the Commissioner's proposal. Regent Fred Stringham seconded the motion. Delay was more palatable than acceptance.

At this point, Regent Leavitt offered a motion for a brief recess, which Regent Jack Goddard seconded. The meeting recessed at 10:30 a.m. to 10:35 a.m., when Chairman Foxley recognized Regent Leavitt to make a substitute motion. [43]

What young Regent Leavitt actually asked in his motion to recess was that the Regents be allowed to "saunter," a term not in ordinary usage in Board of Regents practice. He did more than saunter. There were 13 votes present that day. He knew the minds of all, except one. Only one, Regent Karen Haight Huntsman, was not openly committed to either side. Though Leavitt had discussed the proposition with her, she had remained undecided. Huntsman had southern Utah roots. She was also personally associated with the University of Utah in significant ways. She had reason for allegiance in both camps. Leavitt went quickly to her side. "It looks to me that it pretty much comes down to you," Leavitt said. Huntsman was thoughtful. Then she replied, "I'm with you." [44]

The "post-sauntering" portion of the meeting is recorded in the minutes:

Regent Leavitt said that in spirit he was in total agreement with the Commissioner's recommendation; however, his proposed substitute would provide for the Board to take a position on the name changes. He said it is crucial to continue to have three categories of institutions. The substitute motion, offered by Regent Leavitt and seconded by Regent Clifford LeFevre, follows:

Whereas, "Comprehensive or Teaching University" has become a widely accepted classification describing non-doctoral granting institutions with some graduate education through the master's degree; and Whereas, both Weber State College and Southern Utah State College fit within this classification; and

Whereas, the Board of Regents holds the need to maintain three distinct categories of institutions as a center objective to the master plan; and Whereas, the Board of Regents has the statutory responsibility for "system development of the role or roles of each institution within the system of higher education;" and

Whereas, the Board of Regents desires to adopt appropriate and reasonable criteria that will define and describe the functions and missions of teaching or comprehensive universities, that are distinct from the categories of community colleges and of graduate/research universities;

Be it hereby resolved that:

1. The Board of Regents requests that the Utah State Legislature and Governor Norman H. Bangerter enact legislation that will, effective January 1, 1991, change the name of Weber State College to Weber State University and Southern Utah State College to Southern Utah State University.

2. By September 30, 1990, the Board will reaffirm and refine as necessary the descriptions and roles of its institutions to clearly identify three types or categories in Utah higher education. In establishing this structure, the Regents will adopt appropriate and reasonable criteria that will define and describe the functions and missions of teaching or comprehensive universities, as distinct from the categories of community colleges and of graduate /research universities. [45]

In the discussion that followed, several Regents and Presidents spoke both for and against the substitute motion. These included Regents Stringham, Goddard, Cumming, LeFevre, Rogers, and President Stanford Cazier of Utah State University. Presidents Sherratt

REGENT MICHAEL O. LEAVITT

and Nadauld offered assurances.

The roll-call vote was called:

Charles W. Bullen	Nay
Aileen M. Clyde	Nay
Ian M. Cumming	Nay
John B. Goddard	Yea
Karen H. Huntsman	Yea
Stephanie K. Jessen	Yea
Michael O. Leavitt	Yea
Clifford S. LeFevre	Yea
Paul S. Rogers	Yea
Steven E. Snow	Nay
Fred H. Stringham	Nay
Jay B. Taggart	Yea
Dale O. Zabriskie	Nay

Everyone was counting for himself. At Zabriskie's "Nay," there was a long and pregnant silence. After the long moment, Chairman Foxley, jarred every so slightly from his customary composure, declared, "I guess it passes."

Then Regent Zabriskie, recovering his aplomb, suggested that the Regents move forward, setting aside divisiveness, and demonstrate that spirit by making the vote unanimously affirmative. Zabriskie moved to make the vote unanimous. Regent Taggart seconded his motion. The motion received 12 yeas. Regent Ian Cumming voted nay.

It now remained for the Regents to inform the legislature of their decision. Their annual meeting with the Senate Committee on Higher Education was already scheduled. They carried the copy of the approved motion with them as they met with the legislators of the committee.

Chairman of the Senate Committee on Higher Education was Senator Fred Finlinson, noted for his fervent support of the University of Utah. The committee received the report of the Regents. Senator Finlinson seemed unimpressed. "Well, he drawled, "seven to six—what kind of vote is that?"

Regent Leavitt was quick to reply. "It is, Mr. Chairman, in a democracy, a majority. It is the same as though the vote had been 13 to zero." [46]

Senate Bill 119 moved forward in the process of becoming law. Sen. Leavitt had altered his measure to make the effective date January 1, 1991, to conform with the Regents' motion, but another question had been raised. He had begun receiving telephone calls and letters protesting the proposed name: Southern Utah State University.

PRESIDENT SHERRATT WAS TENSE AS THE REGENTS VOTED ON UNIVERSITY STATUS FOR THE COLLEGE.

The Thunderbird of January 29, 1990 had blared the headline: Regents OK 'SUSU.' Perhaps it was the impact of seeing the abbreviation in print, but many had begun to have second thoughts about whether or not they liked being called SUSU. They were forthright. "SUSU (soo soo) is a pig call," one wrote. Others could foresee the name being an instrument of derision in heated athletic contests. "It confuses us with USU," said another. Sen. Leavitt called the administration for a clear signal. They would confer and get back to him.

While he waited for consensus from the College, time was getting short. He wanted to get the measure onto the floor for debate. Finally, he made the decision himself. Senate Bill 119 read: AN ACT RELATING TO HIGHER EDUCATION; CHANGING THE NAME OF SOUTHERN UTAH STATE COLLEGE TO SOUTHERN UTAH UNIVERSITY. Section five read: This act takes effect on January 1, 1991.

The number of signatures on the bill indicated that the measure would pass; still there was opposition. Speaking in opposition to the motion were Sen. Black, Sen. Carling and Sen. Cornaby, all of Salt Lake City, Sen. Lyle Hillyard of Logan, and Sen. LeRay McAllister of Utah County. After a 20-minute discussion, the measure was voted favorably and moved onto the second reading calendar. The following day' Senate Bill 119 was voted favorably out of the Senate and referred to the House of Representatives.

When Rep. Haze Hunter had polled his colleagues in the House of Representatives, he found that most were in favor of the measure. When Rep. Martin Stephens of Ogden introduced a house version of the Weber State name-change bill with signatures of 54 house members into the House Education Committee, he amended SUSC into that bill. That action confirmed to Rep. Hunter that

the support was steady. "Like a good poker hand, I knew what I had and decided not to press because the bill had the support." [47]

The Senate name-change bills were scheduled by the Speaker for "time certain," debated 15-20 minutes each, then called for the vote. Both bills passed the Utah House of Representatives by two-thirds majority. [48]

An enthusiastic group of students, faculty and staff sat in the House gallery, barely able to contain their excitement. Their school was about to be named a university. The group had struggled through a snowstorm to be there for the moment.

Perhaps they could be forgiven if their cheers did disrupt the tranquility of the august body calling for a few extra strokes of the Speaker's gavel.

At 11:15 on February 14, 1990, Valentine's Day, Governor Norman H. Bangerter signed the legislation into law. Bells rang across the campus in Cedar City to celebrate the moment.

Months would pass while SUSC prepared to become SUU. A few days' euphoria and celebration preceded the settling down to work:

At halftime of the SUSC-Florida International basketball game, Sen. Dixie Leavitt and Rep. Haze Hunter presented the pen the governor had used to sign Senate Bill 119 to President Gerald Sherratt. The two legislators received two of the first scarlet sweat shirts with Southern Utah University emblazoned across the front.

For the first time in history, a legislative appropriation of $5.6 million for a new college building seemed almost eclipsed in the con-

sciousness of the school. The university status issue had relegated the funding for a new Science Center to second billing. Dr. Harl Judd and the sciences faculty turned their attention to planning the project, which would turn out much differently than originally planned.

Honors came as students continued to excel. Peter Tagg, a senior majoring in public relations, earned the sweepstakes award at the national forensics tournament at the University of Alabama. It was the first time, even with the hundreds of trophies and awards earned by forensics teams, that a

SEN. DIXIE LEAVITT PRESENTS TO PRES. GERALD R. SHERRATT THE PEN USED BY GOV. BANGERTER TO SIGN SENATE BILL 119 INTO LAW.

student from SUSC had earned this coveted first.

The Institutional Council proclaimed that students graduating in 1990 could choose to have a diploma issued from SUSC, or wait a few months to receive one issued from Southern Utah University.

The Council selected a design, from among several created by Larry Baker, director of publications, that would become a new seal for Southern Utah University. The attractive new emblem, engraved with the date of the founding, would be ready to signify the new entity on January 1, 1991.

The fledgling university was poised to take flight at the official moment.

PETER TAGG

'SOUNDS UNLIMITED' PERFORMS IN A TRAVEL BUREAU PROGRAM IN 1979.

'THE GRASSROOTS' PROVIDE DANCE MUSIC IN 1969.

THE THUNDERETTES, 1975

REGISTRATION, FALL 1978

UNDERBIRD STADIUM, 1970S

THE SUSC FINE
ARTS GUILD,
1972

THE LIBRARY, 1997

CHAPTER VII

Southern Utah University, 1991-1997

"*As we embark on our new status as a university, let us remember our past. Our goals should not be safe, or conformist, or common. Ours should be uncommon goals as befit our uncommon heritage. I firmly believe that nothing we can foresee, or sense, or conceive is beyond SUU's capacity to do.*"

President Gerald R. Sherratt

Bells rang and fireworks lighted the sky; people swayed and stomped to a trio of dance bands in disparate corners of the campus. University status called for a more than ordinary celebration, and the University Gala of December 31, 1990, was designed as a commemoration commensurate with the occasion.

The law changing the name of Southern Utah State College to Southern Utah University had provided for the change of designation to occur exactly at midnight, as the new year began. This new year, symbolic of the new university era, was ushered in at Cedar City in a style never dreamt of.

FRED ADAMS WAS AMONG THE MANY WHO ENTERTAINED AT THE UNIVERSITY GALA.

The Daily Spectrum ran a special commemorative issue tracing the long and winding road to university status—recounting the dark days of wartime when enrollment fell to 67 students, when there were not sufficient men students to maintain a fraternity and not enough students or money to muster a band. The tone of the exultant paper suggested that hard times would never come again; the people celebrated as though they really believed it.

The events of celebration were spread over a 48-hour period and began with the unveiling of the new sign proclaiming the name Southern Utah University. Meticulous effort had virtually cleared away all old designations and created new signs and new emblems so that when the transition moment came, there would be no residue of lesser days.

Beginning early on New Year's Eve with the "Grand Buffet," a table laden with "culinary delights," hundreds of people dined as they enjoyed the nostalgic "big band" music of the Seegmiller Band, then proceeded to the Centrum for the Command Performance.

Music from country to grand opera, interspersed with humorous presentations and folk dancing, entertained the large and exuberant crowd of celebrants. The array of talent was grand and diverse, and the appreciative audience responded with joyous reception. As the entertainment ended, 5,000 people rose to sing *Auld Lang Syne,* signaling the passing of the year and the passing of old times at the school they loved.

The dazzling display of fireworks at the stadium welcomed in the new and people went home exhilarated by the pleasant prospects of a promising future.

After the ball was over the realities surfaced. There was still a serious need for expanded facilities. For almost 10 years the college had battled to have its need for a new library acknowledged by the Board of Regents and the legislature, but the building was still very low on the State Building Board priority list. New university status had absolutely no effect upon that. The library stayed low on the list, but students organized a fund-raising drive, and administrators strategized another approach.

The inadequate amount of both single student and married student housing was viewed as the crucial question that threatened the growth potential of the new university. As, historically, they had always done, the college administrators appealed to the community to awaken to the impact that the problem posed for the town and the school.

The science building–the Million Dollar Lady of the '60s–was grossly outdated and, though it housed 45 percent of the classes taught on the campus, there were heating and cooling deficiencies, problems with soil settlement, mechanical facilities totally inadequate for many of the laboratories, and it did not meet basic earthquake design requirements. Plans had been formulated and some funds allocated to remodel the building to remedy these faults.

State regulators required a panel of engineers and architects to review the initial plans to ascertain feasibility of cost and procedure. This group determined that a complete gutting of the building would be necessary to bring the structure up to specifications and that the cost would be just about equal to constructing a new building.

Added to the cost factor was the dilemma of where to teach the classes and labs during the lengthy construction process. The question campus administrators had to face was whether to remodel the existing science building or to opt for a separate new building which would require the process of lobbying for funds to begin all over again.

Dr. Harl Judd records the small drama of decision as school officials and science faculty members met at the state capitol:

The decision had to be made before the

meeting concluded. I remember four of us going into a corner, Mike Richards, Al Tait, Dale Brinkerhoff and myself trying to make the best decision possible. Where would a new building be placed? What would the people back home think of us allowing our existing building to be torn down? We discussed this and deep down we felt that the new building was the way to go...we gambled and won. It was the right decision. [1]

The decision was followed by their determination to plan the best possible facility. The faculty and administrators of the College of Science wanted the new building to enable them to provide an education in the sciences for the students at Southern Utah University that would be equal to any school in the nation. The realization of the dream has been evident as students have contributed excellence in scientific pursuits, all over the world.

While student enrollment in winter traditionally dropped from fall quarter numbers, this first university year saw an increase of 16 percent over previous winter quarters. Class size increased, and the faculty, determined to protect the traditional advantage of smaller class size and greater personal interaction between student and teacher, committed themselves to heavier loads and longer hours. A survey made by the Board of Regents proved that the commitment of the teachers were wholehearted and real. The survey showed that Southern Utah University faculty worked an average of 56 hours a week, 10 hours more than the national average and the highest in the state of Utah. [2] It also revealed that the salaries were considerably lower at

DAVE LEE, 'THE PIG POET.'

Southern Utah University than at comparable schools in the state and the nation—not exactly an enticement to draw aspiring young professors to establish careers at SUU. The fact remained that the professors already dedicated to the school were providing superior educational experience, and the steady enrollment increases indicated that the word was out.

One dedicated professor, who had consistently added luster to the institution, was named to a prestigious list of Utah's 12 best writers. Dr. William David Lee, well-published poet and favorite teacher, now was designated as among the most accomplished from a listing of 300 writers through Utah's history. Lee was a transplanted Utahn, with roots so embedded in red soil that he seemed not able to accept the enticing offers that came again and again as a result of his considerable prominence in the literary world. His love of the area and loyalty to the school kept him, so that he continued to be a benefit to countless students.

He enjoyed the unique position of a poet whose work was beloved in his time. He wrote of rural life, in an era when it had become a style of living desirable to a larger audience. He wrote with humor, wit and sensitivity, so that his seven published books, and his numerous appearances in magazines and anthologies were eagerly sought and warmly accepted. His readings were memorable performances, and the nation was his stage. Honors mounted, including the 1995 Utah Governor's Award and the coveted Western State Book Award for *My Town*, Professor of the Year designated by the students, the institution's Educator of the Year Award in 1990, and selection as Utah's first poet laureate in 1997. Still the southern Utah earth clung to his boots, and he centered at Southern Utah University.

Perhaps it was coincidental that along with university status came an expanded diversity of concerns and issues. The times were tumultuous. War had erupted in the Persian Gulf and students, again called up for active duty, were leaving school to respond. Women's issues, already

at the fore of national media attention, took a tangible form in the literature of the new university. Cultural diversity, long a reality on the campus, was more frequently examined. The presence of Native American students had been a decades-long association; now Russian students and instructors piqued the interest and added another cultural connection. Consciousness of the need for environmental preservation was manifest in fiery speeches and earnest attempts at recycling. Less benign were the recurring references to AIDs and seminars stressing responsible sex. Workshops and discussions articulated the issues concerning Utah's abortion laws and vigilant editorializing warned of increased incidence of substance abuse—a far cry from chapel exercises of former days.

The long and colorful history of the 1927

gymnasium took an interesting new turn. The structure, the result of intense community and college joint-effort, had already lived its quota of lives. First the site of men's athletic activities and strongly-supported sports events, it became, in the face of small wartime enrollment, the home of the Air Corps cadet program, returning to postwar duty as the athletic center when public athletic events were staged again. When the War Memorial Fieldhouse was completed, the old gym was devoted to a women's facility. It had always doubled as the campus ballroom. From there it became the student center; now plans were complete for another "recycle." The building was to be remodeled into an academic service center, housing Continuing Education and the Life Span Learning Center, which would greatly enhance the ability of the university to draw

PHI ALPHA BETA SORORITY MEMBERS SUPPORTED THE PERSIAN GULF WAR EFFORT BY WRITING LETTERS TO U.S. TROOPS IN SAUDI ARABIA.

conferences, workshops and seminars to the campus.

The initial plans proved too grand. The bid came in at $900,000 more than the $3.7 million appropriated by the legislature and serious redrawing of blueprints halted the forward motion while the project was pared down.

Added stress was caused when the legislature adjourned without passing a building bond, deferring the decision until an April special session. Finally, with funds allocated and plans down-scaled to meet available money, work began to move forward by autumn of 1991.

On the 94th anniversary of the founding of the school that he had served for 23 years, former president Royden Braithwaite died. Flags on the campus flew at half-staff. People who had worked under him and students who had learned from him spoke their admiration in hushed tones. Famous for inspiring his faculty to strive for dedication, devotion, decision, development and destiny, now they remembered him fondly. "He was a father figure, a genuinely decent human being--he graced the earth," said a saddened David Lee, " but his greatest attribute was the way he made everyone feel important, no matter who they were. He was incredibly fair and even-handed; he was my hero, my role model."

During the years of Dr. Braithwaite's leadership

HAROLD H. HISKEY

he had shepherded the school through crucial changes of role and designation, had seen 13 buildings from planning to completion and had made beautifying the campus a major focus. The respectful nostalgia that hovered over the hill and the community was borne of deep and genuine affection.

After 19 years as dean of the College of Business, Dr. Harold H. Hiskey announced that he would accept the invitation to assume the newly-created position of vice president of regional services. It was an exciting new opportunity for the respected administrator. He would have the charge to form partnerships with communities in the region to solve specific problems and advance the economic and social development of southern Utah. Dr. Gerald R. Sherratt announced the purpose of the new position:

Dr. Hiskey's role will be to work actively toward blending regional issues and concerns with the institution's strengths and potential. The creation of the new position is part of the development of SUU as an interactive university.

Higher education is being propelled into the 21st century on a wave of cultural and economic and societal transformation. What is needed today are new models of excellence. Southern Utah University, caught in these dynamic changes, must seek out new ways of confronting the challenges. He will be responsible for developing a deliberately articulated strategy of interaction with the communities of southern Utah.

By October of 1993, the Utah Center For Rural Life had been established and a state-wide summit on rural issues held. An advisory council of rural leaders helped to focus the direction of the activities of the Center. The yearly summit became an established pattern and gained in prominence and influence with each succeeding year.

The Center for Rural Life prepared and presented reports to the Utah State Legislature on the state of rural life in Utah and provided a newsletter for exchange of ideas among rural residents. The training of economic development practitioners, focusing upon enhancing economic well-being in rural areas, resulted in new and innovative programs for development.

Seminars and workshops were organized to

acquaint rural people with the Utah Education Network (EDNET), and to enlarge their ability to utilize technology, thereby reducing their isolation

The university was trying to continue doing what the school had always done, namely to meet the needs of the people and the communities of the school's constituency. Since society had become more complicated and demands were broadening, the school would employ the genius of Dr. Hiskey, a talented educator familiar with rural Utah from the days of his childhood, to assure that the services offered by the University would still meet the real needs, as the school had done since the days of Farmers' Roundups and Homemakers Conferences.

When SUSC hosted the USA-USSR Gymnastic Friendship tour in 1987 and again in 1989, a remarkable connection was established between Southern Utah State College and the republic of Russia. There resulted a friendly and mutually-nurturing relationship. In the spring of 1991, Boris Notkin, a popular Russian television commentator and educator, visited SUU to deliver a speech for the Tanner Lecture Series. Notkin was warmly welcomed to the campus and a friendship developed between President Sherratt and Boris Notkin. During the course of his visit, Notkin requested that the university accept the son of Moscow mayor, Gavriil Popov, as a student. As arrangements for young Khariton Popov's enrollment were progressing, an invitation came to Dr. Sherratt to visit Russia as a consultant to Mayor Popov, who was working to learn about and apply the experience of American universities in the development of a similar institution of higher education in Moscow.

*P*resident Sherratt accepted the invitation, which resulted in an extraordinary week-long adventure for him and an ongoing, mutually beneficial relationship

with educational and governmental leaders in Russia and other former republics of the former USSR. Assigned a car and a driver, Dr. Sherratt experienced a whirlwind schedule. He was docketed every day and every evening to participate in different aspects of Russian national life.

He consulted on the establishment of the American-type university in Moscow and he discussed American government with the framer of the new Russian constitution.

In the course of the visit he dined with Mikhail Bouniaev, dean of mathematics at Moscow State Pedagogy University, and his wife Alla Paroaiatnikova, a teacher of American literature at Moscow State University. That meeting resulted in the ultimate emigration of these two Russian educators and their taking up new careers as members of the faculty at Southern Utah University and becoming permanent residents of Cedar City.

Mayor Gavriil K. Popov came to visit the SUU campus and his student-son in October of 1992, received an honorary doctorate, and extended an invitation for an ongoing educational exchange.

In harmony with that goal, Dean Robert Salmon and Professor Tim Lewis visited at the International University in Moscow, bearing large numbers of books on business, economics and accounting as a gift for their library. Tim Lewis became the first visiting professor from SUU to teach at IU Moscow, followed by David Rees, Andrew Madsen, Denise Woodbury, Joe Merrill and Steve Evans.

Through these connections, Yuri Shenkovich, a prominent physician in Russia and producer of a highly popular television program, "Travel Club," came to SUU to film a documentary on the university, which was

MOSCOW
MAYOR
GAVRIIL POPOV
AND PRESIDENT
SHERRATT

ALLA PAROAIATNIKOVA AND MIKHAIL BOUNIAEV

shown repeatedly on television in the Russian republics. Russian students who come to SUU have usually heard of the school from this television program. Exchanges of students and faculty have brought rich experiences on both sides of the world. The ripple effect of friendship has been wide and deep.

Students arriving for the first fall quarter at SUU may have thought they were entering a war zone. A giant hole where the library parking lot had been was becoming the foundation for the new science building; the replacement parking lot at 500 West and 200 South would not be ready until late in October. Another gaping hole startled people who were looking for the Multicultural Center at its previous site on 200 South, which was also becoming a parking lot. The MCC moved, along with Student Support Services, to the north end of South Hall. Work was progressing on the Academic Service Center, which was not expected to be completed until late in 1992. Two soccer-sized practice fields were under construction west of the Centrum. Physical Plant was in the process of being moved to 200 South 1200 West, where a new motorpool and grounds building was under construction. There were few spots untouched by progress in process.

Nevertheless, student numbers soared as registration of freshmen students greatly expanded. Total enrollment broke all records at 4,292, some 500 more than the previous fall.

Administrators, determined that the school's famously low student-to-teacher ratio should not elevate with the enrollment, added more sections of popular classes and announced that the one-to-twenty ratio of the previous year, would be maintained.

Seven new faculty members and one new dean helped to accommodate the numbers. Robert O. Salmon became the dean of SUU's College of Business, Technology and Communication. The university was not so successful in absorbing the numbers into student housing. The problem was discernible and real in apartments built to house six, but where seven students were crunched. The university appealed to citi-

ROBERT O. SALMON

zens of the town to build housing, since the construction projects on campus were at optimum level with no resources to apply to student housing. Yet again the townspeople responded. Developers began to build. Ordinary citizens, with innate affection and concern, became developers of sorts and began to provide private housing for future student growth.

Significant government cuts in work-study funds lessened work opportunities for needy students. A hike in the minimum wage scale, at the same time, also diminished the funds available for campus jobs. Rex Michie, financial aid officer, appealed to businesses in town to hire students whenever possible.

Great news came from the Board of Regents at the end of the year. In their yearly funding recommendations the regents included a $10.4 million request for the much-needed library at SUU, $12.9 million for Phase II of the Student Center and money to fund the burgeoning growth of Southern Utah University.

As Southern Utah University reached its first anniversary, tallies showed that the percentage of enrollment growth had surpassed all other schools in the state. The academic reputation of the school was increasingly a factor in the growth; the American College Testing scores of entering students had elevated significantly.

A new fiber optic network was completed, which gave students the advantage of greater speed and the ability to receive and send both audio and video data. The technological revolution was manifest at SUU.

"SUU is the fastest growing four-year institution in Utah," said D. Mark Barton at the beginning of fall quarter 1992. Available scholarship funds were based on 10 percent of the collected revenues, and the increase in students meant more money for new scholarships. Surveys reflected that personal attention from faculty and staff was the number one reason students chose to attend Southern Utah University.

For more than 90 years the school at Cedar City had practiced an open admissions policy. Early students of Branch Normal School who were not prepared for college work, had even been offered a class called "The Preparatory Course" to make up for a lack in their scholastic opportunity. But in 1990 a surge of student enrollments at Utah campuses had prompted the Board of

Regents to adopt more selective admissions policies at the four state universities. In 1991 studies began on the best method for indexing admissions, and in February 1992, the Regents approved a system for SUU that was implemented in the fall of 1992. As a result of admissions indexing, it was estimated that 10 percent of students applying were not admitted, but student success and retention increased. [3]

*M*ore stringent admission standards simply made it more difficult for students to gain admission. The policy was implemented by university officials with some regret, for the school had long received young people with inadequate preparation, who had nevertheless quickly responded to the opportunity and the unique personal attention of dedicated faculty. However, the funding restraints created the necessity for careful screening, and the success rate of the students who were admitted increased.

While admissions were tightened, and aspiring students were turned away, SUU maintained the tradition of providing every possible help. The amazing service of the Home Economics Club of early days had provided funds for students stressed with financial concerns, but even they would have been astonished at the array of services provided for students at the new university. The school offered subsidized child care during finals; there was a food bank for times when the term "starving students" became literal. Shuttle service to and from St. George brought students from the neighboring town and back again for $3 a day. The "ride board" was a year-round service listing people who were traveling throughout the country. Students could share expenses and get a ride to almost any location in the U.S.A. A fitness center, a wellness center, a job-placement center, career fairs, counseling, even free assistance in filing income tax returns was offered. Almost any need that could beset a student could be addressed through the assortment of services.

Early in 1996, Daphne Dalley was employed as a "learning success specialist." She

DAPHNE DALLEY

worked with faculty and staff to assist them in finding ways to help students succeed. A workshop, "Keeping A User-Friendly Campus," used modern jargon, but the spirit of giving students a boost had been around for a very long time.

In July of 1992 Southern Utah University announced that the new academic service center would be named in honor of veteran state legislator R. Haze Hunter, who had successfully shepherded the funding for the remodeled building through the legislature. The facility would be known as the R. Haze Hunter Conference Center.

Designed to house a variety of academic services, the building would provide a permanent home for the fast-growing division of continuing education and public service, which had been fitted into nooks in different parts of the campus, again and again outgrowing constricted quarters.

In September of 1992 the renovated building once again became a focus of activities

AT THE DEDICATION OF THE R. HAZE HUNTER CONFERENCE CENTER, R. HAZE HUNTER ACKNOWLEDGES THE UNVEILING OF HIS PORTRAIT.

on the campus. Now much more impressive than in its former incarnations, the halls of the building, which once rang with the shouts of exuberant basketball fans and saw dreamy prom goers sway under twisted crepe-papered ceilings, became the scene of the most elegant university occasions.

The Steve Gilbert Great Hall, superbly designed and furbished through funding provided by Steve and Cyndi Woodbury Gilbert, became one of Utah's most elegant meeting places, serving as a theatre, dining room, and concert hall. Mrs. Gilbert was a graduate of SUU, had served in student body offices as a

student, later as president of the Alumni Association and a member of the Board of Trustees. The contribution to the Great Hall was one of many instances of their support of the University.

The Great Hall became a gallery, as original oil portraits of people prominent in the history of the school were unveiled one by one. Beautifully designed academic banners representing the scholastic disciplines, hung from the beams of the towering ceiling, adding the final flair to the splendid room.

An arrangement of three stained-glass panels, depicting scenes from the university history; proclaimed the motto: "Learning Lives Forever." In light and translucent color, the windows became the focal point of the magnificent space. The beautiful panels were designed by Peter Cook, a student in the performing arts. The design was executed by Frank Adams, local artist in the stained-glass medium. [4]

A series of nicely-appointed meeting rooms, some named for prominent supporters of the school, gave the university a new capacity that had been lacking through the whole of its history.

*T*he culmination of five years' earnest labor came to fruition when on January 4, 1993, students attended classes in the new Science Center for the first time. [5]

The $5.6 million building now stood completed, a stalwart 70,000 square foot structure with the capability of providing wonderful laboratories and superb equipment. The College of Science faculty had designed the building. Each member of the faculty now felt that SUU could offer high quality education in the field of science, unsurpassed anywhere else in the country.

Dr. Paul Burgoyne, head of the department of biology, was exultant.

"This building will not only provide a lot more space, but more up-to-date technology," he boasted. "We will have state-of the-art electronics and consoles housing computers, VCR's and ceiling-mounted television projectors in at least five rooms."

Dr. Michael Richards added his approval: "With the new electron microscope, we will have more comparable technology, which has worked its way into the curriculum of physics, mathematics and chemistry, and we will be able to support the latest in electronic media systems that are now a part of teaching in general, across the campus."

The Center acquired physics equipment through a National Science Foundation grant of $32,000, SUU's first in more than 20 years. Prof. Desmond Penny explained his delight in receiving the grant, "We will use these funds to foster a change in our approach to teaching in the labs...we will institute workshop physics into our teaching, which becomes an exciting exploration of physical laws for students," he said. "SUU will be at the forefront of revolutionizing the way physics is taught throughout the country."

Remembering the level of the laboratories joyfully established in the "new" science building of 1904, the term "revolutionizing" did not seem an overstatement.

A general renovation of the "old" science building into what would be known as the General Classroom building, to be finished by fall of 1994, would complete the evolution of the revolution.

PAUL BURGOYNE

When the legislative session ended in early March 1993, there was rejoicing in the halls of SUU. Rarely in the nearly 100-year history had the legislative session inspired euphoria, but this year the appropriation would increase SUU's operating budget by 16 percent. The unprecedented boost would finance a 6 percent increase in faculty compensation, fund the unexpected enrollment growth, and maintain the new Science Center. It would also fund "urgent student support services," such as extended library hours and increased staff in the Student Development Center. Perhaps most exciting

DEMOLITION OF OAK HALL

THE PLANS FOR THE NEW LIBRARY SHOWED A BEAUTIFUL AND FUNCTIONAL BUILDING.

state-of-the-art facility became a reality.

Technology and media would gain a new home with the completion of the new building, because 40,000 square feet of space in the existing library would be made available to house computer labs and offices.

Groundbreaking ceremonies for the new library in November of 1993 were festive and impressive. Hans Chamberlain, chairman of the Board of Trustees conducted the gathering, which included short speeches by Louis Ulrich, architect and designer of the impressive structure; library director, Diana Graff and President Gerald R. Sherratt. The library would be the second largest building ever built on the campus, second only to the Centrum, also designed by Ulrich. With the ceremonial earth-turning, the project was officially on its way.

The expansion in facilities and services came in the nick of time. An astonishing head count of 5,026 students registering for fall quarter of 1994 broke all previous enrollment records. SUU had become the fastest-growing university in the state system. Every class category except sophomores increased in numbers. Registration of out of state students increased by 44 percent.

It had become more difficult to hold the cherished student-teacher ratio, but adding classes, larger teaching loads and added faculty numbers kept the ratio stable.

was the approval of a bond for SUU's new library. Construction was slated to begin in the summer.

Rejoicing and regrets collided in June 1993. Forty-eight families sadly searched for new homes as bull-dozers poised to demolish the 38-year old Oak Hall complex to make room for the promised new library. Built in 1955 and originally intended for single students, the complex had sheltered married student families in the tiny apartments for more than two decades. Some militant folks protested the "heartlessness" of administrators in the face of the perpetual housing shortage, but the fact remained that Oak Hall, sadly worn and decrepit, stood on the spot where would rise the multi-million dollar library, long needed and long awaited.

Somehow the residents located new places to live, and the excavation began. The old landmark toppled, along with the ancient cottonwood trees that had bordered the walk and shaded passersby for generations. But the new library promised to be worth all the sacrifices. Even the protracted nightmare of the torn-up campus would be forgotten when the

When the 1995 legislature ended its session, it had given SUU an appropriation of $24,585,800, an increase of 8.79 percent above the previous year, the highest percentage increase among the universities and the second highest in the

GROUNDBREAKING FOR THE NEW LIBRARY

Utah System of Higher Education. All signs pointed to a growing acceptance of SUU as a valued institution.

In 1982 the campus had four computer terminals and four communications lines connecting then SUSC to Weber State. At the time, Weber provided primary computer services for both SUSC and WSC until an amicable separation occurred in 1984. For the next three years, the institution implemented a "package" software system for administrative computing and installed embryonic computer labs in business and science. In 1987-88 a six strand, fiber-optic network was installed to connect the major academic buildings on campus with data service. Administrative computing was supported with a DEC VAX 780 cluster, and computer labs were operating in four colleges. Academic and administrative user groups were organized to insure that computing systems met the needs of the University in an economical manner. In 1988 approximately 1,000 student accounts were established on the VAX cluster.

By 1996, technology on campus had ballooned to nearly 1,500 computers, five electronic classrooms, an EDNET hub (the statewide educational television system) to serve six counties of southwestern Utah, 24 local area networks, and more than 6,000 accounts for computer use. Every freshman entering SUU received an account for e-mail and Internet assignments; students had global access to information. The new library was fully equipped with computers and other equipment to search global knowledge-bases. The once basic fiber backbone had been superseded by a 48-strand fiber optic network, meeting the latest international standards for Asynchronous Transfer Mode technology. Sixty percent of this network upgrade had been funded and completed. Voice, video, and data communication would be provided simultaneously with the new backbone.

With the University's level of technology, distance learning and student support services assumed larger dimensions and broader service

STEVE ADAMS

areas. Courses had been offered over the EDNET system since the mid-80s. In 1995-96 six SUU courses were offered on the system; nine were scheduled for 1996-97. For the first time, Art 101 was designed for and offered on the World Wide Web, reaching students on three continents. Five courses were planned for 1996-97.

The next steps in information technology would include capabilities to apply for admission, register for classes, and obtain campus information via the Internet. [6]

Long time technology professor, Stephen R. Adams, died on October 18, 1995 of pancreatic cancer, only a few weeks after his illness was diagnosed. For 25 years he had been a much-loved teacher of technical education, woodworking and facilities management. He had been honored as Utah's Outstanding Technical Educator in 1994 and had received both the Distinguished Educator and the Outstanding Educator of SUU awards. Other faculty members had enrolled in his classes, eager to learn both his craft and his teaching methods. All extolled his superb capacity for nurturing relationships with his students and for his patient, calm manner. His impact upon countless students over the years was the embodiment of the university motto, "Learning Lives Forever."

In response to student demand for baccalaureate programs in St. George, the Regents had established a University Center to deliver courses and programs apart from Dixie College. For several years the Center had been operated by Dixie College, and offerings were "brokered" between Weber State, Utah State and SUU. This arrangement became unwieldy, and turf battles broke out among institutions. To make the Center more viable, SUU proposed being the sole, accountable manager. Staff and budget of the Center were transferred to SUU's jurisdiction, and SUU became the primary sponsor of bachelor's degrees at the Center. It became possible to take a degree in business, education or criminal justice from SUU, without leaving St. George. Under SUU's direction, enrollment at the center increased rapidly. [7]

Higher education state-wide verged upon a quandary over whether or not to change from a quarter system to a semester system. Over the preceding 20 years nearly 1,400 United States colleges had switched from quarter calendars until more than 80 percent of colleges and universities in the nation operated on a semester system. Persuasive arguments for the change cited the advantage of longer terms which allowed students to explore subject matter in greater depth, and fewer breaks between terms, as well as better utilization of campus facilities.

The one-time conversion costs would be real, but potential savings would result. Textbooks, primarily designed for semester courses, could be better utilized, resulting in savings. Students would be positively affected by being given a chance for earlier entry into the job market.

A lively debate included the perspective of teachers who would be required to alter the outlines of their courses. Their effort would, however, have the effect of updating the curricula and would demonstrate willingness to reform, to change and to improve.

The debate closed in January 1996, when the Board of Regents voted to convert eight of the state's nine public colleges and universities to a semester calendar. (Utah Valley State College in Orem already followed a semester calendar.) The Regents authorized Dr. Cecelia Foxley, Commissioner of Higher Education, to seek $500,000 to fund planning for the change.

Committees formed to create guidelines, and faculty and administrators began using every spare moment to prepare for the future. Indeed there would be updating, there would be reform, there would be concerted effort to improve. The Utah State System of Higher Education would operate on a semester system. The change would occur by fall of 1998.

Southern Utah University had long sought to affiliate its intercollegiate athletic program with the Big Sky Conference and had been encouraged by several Big Sky presidents to seek membership, particularly Eugene M. Hughes, president of Northern Arizona University, who had told other Big Sky presidents that Northern Arizona would consider withdrawing from the Big Sky if SUU were not admitted. But SUU's bid was opposed by the presidents of Montana University and Weber State University, and there were not enough votes in favor of SUU's entrance to reach the required two-thirds majority. The departure of Northern Arizona's president, Eugene Hughes, for the presidency of Wichita State University in Kansas was another blow to SUU's Big Sky aspirations.

In 1995, when the Big Sky elected to add four more universities, SUU was again excluded, the new president of Northern Arizona University, Dr. Clara M. Lovett, joining with Montana University to oppose SUU's entrance. President Sherratt then approached Gov. Michael O. Leavitt for assistance in contacting the two institutions in SUU's behalf. Governor Leavitt sent letters of support for SUU to all the Big Sky schools, stressing his belief that Weber State and SUU belonged in the same conference. Arrangements were made to bring President Lovett to SUU for a

GEORGE FENSTERMACHER, DIRECTOR OF THE SUU ST. GEORGE CENTER.

campus visit, and Governor Leavitt and President Sherratt flew to Flagstaff for a meeting with the Northern Arizona president. That trip, plus Dr. Lovett's summer visit, resolved her resistance to SUU's bid and she became one of SUU's strongest backers.

By the spring of 1996, SUU was told by Weber State University's new president, Paul Thompson, that the necessary two-thirds vote for SUU admittance was finally attainable and that at the annual conference meeting in May, the motion would be made to admit SUU into the Big Sky. It was a matter of some disappointment to SUU, then, when the school learned that the president of the University of Montana threatened to have his school leave the conference if the Big Sky voted for further expansion. Given Montana's ultimatum, SUU's supporters backed away.

A few brief weeks after the Big Sky's meeting in May, SUU was contacted by the commissioner of another conference, the Mid-Continent Conference with headquarters in Naperville, Illinois, with a preliminary inquiry as to whether SUU would be interested in affiliating with the Mid-

Continent, a prestigious conference which sponsored all sports except football. SUU was elated with the news and conveyed back to the Mid-Continent that it was indeed interested in joining.

The advantages of affiliation with the Mid-Continent were obvious and in many respects a decided advantage over the Big Sky. As a Mid-Continent school SUU would receive media coverage in such major cities as Chicago, Indianapolis, Kansas City, Cleveland and Pittsburgh. For the first time SUU would be in a conference with an automatic berth in the NCAA basketball tournaments. And, surprisingly since the Mid-Continent member schools are in Illinois, Indiana, Ohio, Missouri, and Oklahoma, there would even be some travel money savings, airfare out of Las Vegas to the large cities of the mid-west being substantially less than by commuter airlines into places like Missoula and Bozeman in Montana.

With SUU's enthusiasm, the Mid-Continent was ready to move. A site visit was arranged,

SUU receiving the committee's spirited recommendation. On August 14, at news conferences held in both Salt Lake City and Cedar City, SUU announced it would join the Mid-Continent Conference effective fall quarter 1997. Given that SUU had courted the Big Sky for ten years, only to be spurned at each occasion, the school's entrance into the Mid-Continent, a conference with many advantages over the Big Sky, was remarkably swift. The University couldn't believe its good fortune.

Observers might easily be so occupied with assimilating all the visible and tangible changes occurring over the first six years after the school became Southern Utah University, that they might miss the significant and simultaneous academic evolution. Each program advancement was accompanied by the traditional dramatic struggle; each required dedicated people with vision and passion to prepare, propose

GERALD R. SHERRATT
1931-

Gerald R. Sherratt was the first graduate of SUU (he received his associate degree in 1951) to return as the school's president. Born in 1931 and reared in Los Angeles, California, of descendants of pioneer Cedar City families (he is a descendent of five of SUU's founding families) his parents moved back to Cedar City in 1943 and Sherratt

attended junior high school and high school in Cedar City, graduating from Cedar City High School as "boy of the year" in 1949.

While attending BAC, he was cheerleader and president of his fraternity. He received BS and MS degrees from Utah State University (where he was twice named "class personality") and a Ph.D in administration of higher education from Michigan State University. He served in the U.S. Air Force and then joined the student services staff of Utah State University, followed by three years as editor and assistant executive secretary of Sigma Nu Fraternity in Virginia (he was the fraternity's international president in 1976-78). Returning home to Utah in 1961 as staff associate at the University of Utah, the next year he began a 20-year stint at USU, where he moved from director of high school relations to assistant to the president, to vice president for university relations. He also directed USU's office of alumni relations, development and summer school. He founded USU's Festival of the American West and a pageant he wrote, *The West: America's Odyssey*, was presented at USU every summer for 25 years.

In November 1981, he was appointed

president of SUU, then named Southern Utah State College, and took office on January 1, 1982. His 15 1/2 years as president was the second longest tenure of the 13 men who served as principal, director, or president during SUU's first century. It was also the period of the school's greatest growth, enrollment increasing from 1,800 in January 1982, to more than 5,600 in the fall of 1996. During his administration, 16 new buildings were constructed, extensively remodeled or acquired; the Utah Summer Games was launched; the school earned university status and added its first two graduate programs; the athletic program was elevated to NCAA Division I status; and new admission standards were adopted. In addition to these quantitative, tangible improvements, the image of the university flourished under his leadership, until it became known, internationally, as a superb and unique institution of higher learning.

Sherratt also served on the Board of Trustees of the 2002 Winter Olympic Games in Salt Lake City, was a member and chairman of the board of the Salt Lake Branch of the Federal Reserve Bank of San Francisco, and president of the Utah Higher Education Foundation.

and produce a program. Each success brought benefits to students and communities.

The Utah State Board of Regents, at its March 1990 meeting, approved SUU's request for a baccalaureate degree program in special education to address the state's well-documented need for teachers in this area. With approval of the new major, teacher education students at SUU were now able to obtain double majors in special education and elementary or secondary education.

In 1993, SUU was granted approval to offer a baccalaureate degree in criminal justice, a major in biology teaching, and a minor in geography. Both the biology major and geography minor received the approval of the Regents with little opposition from the other universities in the state. But the request for a criminal justice degree at SUU generated considerable discussion.

Weber State University had been granted an exclusive state-wide role in providing baccalaureate-level offerings in criminal justice and SUU's request for approval of a criminal justice degree would end that exclusive Weber State role. University officials were able to show, however, that the current SUU program in criminal justice, conducted at the associate in science level since 1972, had sufficient enrollment that would warrant expanding to a full baccalaureate level. The University was able to also solicit wide-spread support for its proposal from throughout southern Utah and from area law enforcement agencies. The request was approved by the Regents on November 5, 1993. Within three years enrollments in criminal justice doubled, verifying SUU's claims that the new degree was indeed needed in southern Utah.

In 1994 the Regents approved that a certificate in international relations be offered by SUU. University officials were convinced that adding an international dimension to the school's offerings was essential if its students were to compete in business, education, cultural and other areas where international borders were rapidly disappearing. As a result of being able to offer the certificate, the University has moved to establish institutional relationships with universities in Russia and Mexico, with other countries on the horizon.

BURCH MANN

In 1995, the University sought approval for an independent master of education program. For 18 years SUU had offered a cooperative master of education program with Utah State University, but the University believed it was now able to offer the degree independent of USU since SUU faculty were teaching all of the program's courses in the fall, winter, and spring quarters and half of those in summer quarter. The request was opposed by both the University of Utah and Utah State University, principally because the two schools did not want SUU involved with graduate programs. As so often before, SUU sought the support of area school districts and at the May meeting of the Board of Regents held in Cedar City several superintendents spoke in SUU's behalf. The result was the unanimous vote of the Regents in favor of SUU's request. With another master's program, in addition to accountancy, SUU was elevated to a Masters II University status by the Carnegie classification system. By the fall of 1996, SUU had more than 500 students enrolled in its graduate programs.

In December of 1995, the Regents approved an associate in science degree in paralegal, responding to a request from area lawyers for graduates with paralegal training. As with SUU's request for a master of education program, the paralegal program was approved by the Regents over the objections of other Utah schools, primarily Utah Valley State College which saw SUU's request as a threat to their own paralegal program.

In June 1996, the Regents approved a bachelors degree program in dance at SUU. For nearly a half century SUU had offered dance classes through the department of physical education. In the middle years of the century, for example, LaVeve Whetten had earned an enviable reputation as a dance teacher, one of her students, Joan Jones Woodbury, going on to form the Ririe-

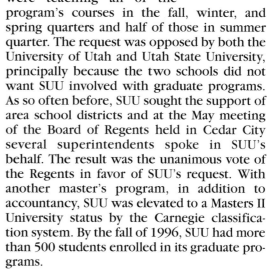

LONGTIME FACULTY MEMBER QUENTON BOWLER, IN HIS FINAL YEAR OF SERVICE BEFORE RETIREMENT, SHEPHERDED SUU THROUGH ITS TRANSFORMATION INTO AN INDEPENDENT MASTER'S GRANTING PROGRAM IN EDUCATION.

Woodbury professional dance company.

In 1982, however, noted choreographer Burch Mann had moved her professional dance company to Cedar City and established a dance program in the department of theatre arts, using her daughter, San Christopher, and lead dancers of her company as instructors. By the early 1990s, the University merged its two dance programs, the one in physical education and Mann's program in theatre arts, as a single dance program to be housed in the department of theatre arts and dance. The enrollment growth of the dance program, which doubled following the merger, culminated at the June 1996 meeting of the Board of Regents when SUU's request for a dance major was approved, again over the objection of the University of Utah but with strong support from southern Utah community colleges. The approval of the dance major came only several weeks before the death of Burch Mann and was a matter of delight to the ailing choreographer, when she heard the welcome news. By the fall of 1996, enrollments in dance courses were second in size to music in the performing arts.

*I*t was clear that the new title of university, acquired in 1990 with such system-wide hesitancy in higher education, was paying extra dividends for Southern Utah University. Directly correlated with the title change was a broadened diversity in the faculty, as recruitment of new faculty became more national in scope and as the institution began providing its undergraduate students with heightened opportunities in scholarly activities.

Donations to the school from foundations and individuals also increased rapidly. In a three-year period, from 1993 to 1996, the amount of private giving to SUU eclipsed the entire previous 96 years combined.

In significant ways the community was becoming defined by the remarkable activities centered at the University. The 1989 completion of the Randall Jones Theatre had allowed the Utah Shakespearean Festival to literally double in size and scope. By 1991, when the festival celebrated its 30th

anniversary season, it had expanded to a 10-week season. Six plays revolved through the week, with matinees bringing the weekly total to 20 presentations. Playgoers were entertained through the days with workshops and tours and festival goers could feast, Elizabethan style, each evening before curtain time.

By 1993 nearly 300 designers, technicians and actors made up the team who opened six plays in six nights, with no major hitches. Reviewers joyously extolled the quality of the productions, from the merriment of the Greenshow to the rich variety of shows now offered in addition to the traditional Shakespearean plays. And people began to order tickets long in advance.

The Festival had become one of the most famous Shakespearean festivals in the country. It had become an institution at an institution, and the town, which had fostered and supported both, now gladly accepted the designation of itself as The Festival City.

From its modest beginning as a three-day sports event, the Utah Summer Games had developed by 1996, its 11th annual event, into Utah's premier amateur sports festival. Modeled after the Olympic Games, the Utah Summer Games held annual qualifying competitions in five regions. The Utah Summer Games opening ceremonies had become an extravaganza attended by more than 10,000 spectators caught up in the spirited entertainment fare, the induction into the Utah Summer Games Hall of Fame of renowned athletes and coaches, and wondrous fireworks displays, each succeeding year surpassing the previous one.

Open to all ages and skill levels, the Utah Summer Games attracted competitors in sports ranging from the martial arts and horseshoe pitching to cycling and equestrian. Large fields of competitors were always drawn to basketball, swimming, track and field and soccer. It had grown from 748 athletes in 1986 to nearly 7,000 in 1996 with an anticipated 8,000 for the games scheduled for 1997.

Hundreds of community volunteers welcomed the participants, working at a variety of posts, these people from all the neighbor-

THE UTAH SUMMER GAMES UNIFIED THE STATE IN CEDAR CITY.

NELLIE PUCELL UNTHANK MONUMENT

hoods of the town added the dimension that made the Utah Summer Games unique among the nation's events: people serving for the joy of serving.

*H*urrying toward the century mark, Southern Utah University was engaged in extraordinary expansion in preparation for the celebration of a lifetime. The beloved school would celebrate its centennial throughout the 1997 academic year, commemorating one hundred years since the founding of Branch Normal School. Faculty, staff and students anticipated the approaching celebration. Tangible improvements appeared on every corner of the campus and loyal supporters marshalled creative means to call attention to the observance.

University supporters, in the long-standing tradition, combined resources to present a remarkable centennial gift: The Centurium Monument. Placed just south of the Centrum, the circular structure contained bronze statues representing 12 of the best-known thinkers of the western world. It was intended to celebrate the accomplishments, knowledge and unselfish contributions that flow to humankind from educated, thoughtful people. It would become a place for reflection and inspiration, and would symbolize the lasting purposes for which universities are founded. A circle of bricks, engraved with the names of contributors to scholarships and

endowments, bespoke the tacit understanding that effective accomplishments of the centuries have always required the linking of the world of academia with the commerce of the citizenry.

Statuary on the campus of Southern Utah University was becoming a trademark, emulating the universities in Europe and the eastern United States. Beginning with the Old Sorrel Monument, a relationship had formed between sculptor Jerry Anderson and the University. In August of 1991 the Nellie Unthank monument, a lovely tribute to pioneer courage, had been placed atop campus hill by the Sons of the Utah Pioneers. Anderson would now create, one by one, the statues to be placed in the Centurium. The collection would prove to be of unique magnitude and one more significant distinction of a remarkable institution.

A little further west, the stadium was evolving into a splendid place. In March 1995 specialists from the Utah Division of Risk Management had declared the existing seating condemned. The aging structures did not meet safety or fire codes and the administration was faced with finding the means to bring it to standard.

President Gerald R. Sherratt envisioned an extraordinary improvement. "The Coliseum will not be the nation's largest," he said, "but when it is completed it will be among the most beautiful stadiums in all of American higher education and perhaps the finest track and field arena in the American west."

The price tag for realizing the dream was $2.1 million, and private gifts would have to make up $1.6 million of that amount. The pressing project would have to rely upon support from alumni and friends. A vigorous campaign was mounted with Clayton Frehner as chairman and Rich Wilson as co-chair. The effort received a boost with two significant gifts: one from an anonymous family for $500,000 and a grant of $500,000 from the George S. and Dolores Doré Eccles Foundation. The Coliseum would be named for the Eccles in honor of their pivotal contribution.

Work on the Jay Dee Harris and Alice C. Harris Center moved nearer to completion and the beauty of the structure epitomized the transformation of the campus over the years, in stark contrast to the old photograph of the football team on the quadrangle in front of the first buildings, spectators sharing the space with grazing cows.

LIBRARY
READING
ROOM

Just before the dawning of the centennial year the beautiful new library was dedicated. The spectacular structure would house some of the most up-to-date services of any library in the state. The dedication celebrated the 99th anniversary of the founding of the school.

It was a dazzling day, filled with commemorative activities. Participants brimmed with excited anticipation for the first views of the new library. And the reality was as wonderful as they could have hoped. The building was startling with its uniquely designed, enormous windows, almost any spot in the building offering spectacular views of the campus and the surrounding mountains. Light filled the building and Diana Graff, the excited director of the library, exulted, "You can see to Delta!"

Dr. Graff had headed the long and careful planning of the library, which had been implemented through $10.4 million in state funding and significant private contributions. It would double the library space on the campus, provide 1,200 student study stations and bring technological/electronic teaching/ learning resources to state-of-the-art level.

No dignitary declined the invitation to attend the dedication ceremony which featured David McCullough, Pulitzer Prize winning author and renowned scholar, as the guest speaker. Utah Gov. Michael O. Leavitt, an alumnus of the institution; Cecelia Foxley, commissioner of higher education; David Jordan, chair of the SUU Board of Trustees; Dr. Gerald R. Sherratt, SUU president; a delighted Diana Graff and Tosh Brinkerhoff, SUU student body president, each added exuberant expressions.

Representatives of the architects from the firm of Fowler, Ferguson, Kingston and Ruben of Salt Lake City were present to receive accolades for their design, as were members of the construction firm of Carter Enterprises of Cedar City, justly proud of their work.

That afternoon history was repeated in a ceremonial book brigade, which moved volumes from the 1969 "old library" down the hill to the shelves of this wondrous new facility. The same hand-to-hand process had involved students and faculty 27 years earlier, as they had moved the books from the auditorium/library to the now outmoded building, awaiting revamping into the Electronic Learning Center, a facility for computer laboratories and electronic learning. This time there were thousands more volumes, but the same emotional investment, the same gratitude for the progress of their school and the same excitement to begin using it.

Elegance in design and furnishings beckoned students to the Special Collections area on the garden level. Rooms that memorialized historian William R. Palmer, choreographer Burch Mann and her daughter San Christopher, and philanthropists Grace and O. C. Tanner and Dr. John Seymour had been created for quiet study or contemplation. Study carrels, reading rooms and instructional media were all now available at a level never before possible.

The students responded eagerly. The planning, the worry, the work were now all richly justified.

A visual tribute proclaimed the excitement of the up-coming landmark centennial celebration to the people of Utah in parades of the 1996 summer season. A parade float depicting the Centurium, the symbol of the Centennial celebration, was designed and constructed by Joyce and Richard Messer and appeared in the parades of significant celebrations. First appearing in Salt Lake City at the Days of '47 parade, the entry won the Mayor's Award. The Washington County Fair Parade and the Iron County Fair Parade followed, with the float receiving the top awards. Finally, featured in the SUU Homecoming Parade, the float declared exuberant anticipation of the gala events of celebration.

Immediately south of the Jay Dee and Alice Harris Center at 1150 West and 200 South, the Southern Utah University Staff Association planted the Centennial Parterre, a garden of 21 partitioned flower beds, each uniquely beautiful, each plant identified in a prepared guide. By August, 1996 the garden was in perfect bloom, another example of an extraordinary contribution by caring people.

When Dr. Gerald R. Sherratt first arrived back in town in 1982, he had found some disheartened friends about to reluctantly relinquish a dream. The dream, which had sometimes burned as brightly as a hope, was that they could somehow build in their town a trio of wonders in one: a special events center, a concert hall and a convention center. Committees had been organized and plans formulated, but financial realities had dimmed their prospects.

History records that hope rekindled, fueled largely by the enthusiasm and leadership of Gerald R. Sherratt, and that two of the three desired components were accomplished with the linking together of college and community in the building of the Centrum. Special events, sporting events, concerts and extravaganzas were staged there. The community gladly agreed that two out of three wasn't bad. The dream of a convention center would have to wait.

In 1986, the long needed center for student

JOYCE MESSER

activities was constructed on the site of the old War Memorial Fieldhouse. It was considered, in the minds of most, a welcome but independent building. But in the ever-creative consciousness of President Gerald Sherratt, it was "Phase II." His vision extended to Phase III, which would be a much larger facility that would eventually connect the new student center to the Centrum. It would be an amazing complex, unique among college campuses, and certainly one more shining example of cooperation among community, college and private citizens. And it would, if the dream could be realized, fulfill the long-hoped-for aim: a place to host large gatherings and conventions in southern Utah.

H opes were high, vision was vigorous, but the realities of funding still seemed unattainable. Then, in the spring of 1993, there came a quiet, anonymous gift of $2.5 million dollars. The gift

THE ROTUNDA OF THE SHARWAN SMITH CENTER

came from a family whose children had loved their own expanding experiences at Southern Utah University.

Because student fees would contribute to the financing, the students were invited to participate in the planning phase. Student fees would fund a major part of the ballroom, the fitness center, the game room, a small auditorium, a post office and some meeting rooms.

The state would appropriate $5,036,000, which would be used exclusively for the student services complex. Services, dispersed all around the campus, would be brought together in one convenient arrangement. Health and counseling services, financial aid, admissions and records, and student support services would all move from scattered temporary quarters to this new and permanent location.

The convention center dream would come true with funding from the Iron County Commission. The state legislature had authorized an optional restaurant tax, which had been implemented in Iron County. The monies accumulated enabled the county to make a contribution of $1,250,000 toward a meeting complex, incorporated into the building, which when not in use for conventions, would be available for student and university use. It was an innovative and creative linking of community and institution, which would be eagerly imitated in other localities.

The generous private gift of $2.5 million from a family, who insisted upon remaining anonymous, would furnish the building's rotunda, other special areas, as well as new furniture and equipment needed in the building. It would make possible movie theatres, lounge areas and a food court. The days of the Topaz-building Student Center seemed very far away.

In the fall of 1988 there had come to the campus, as an entering freshman student, a most remarkable young woman. The third of three siblings to come to the school, she followed her sisters, Glenna and Stacie. Tall and beautiful, filled with music and the joy of life, she was immediately beloved by her teachers and her peers. Naturally chosen to lead her fellows, she possessed an uncanny ability to engender both respect and admiration. The words of William Shakespeare seemed to describe this child: "'Tis human

fortune's happiest height to be a spirit, melodious, lucid, poised and whole. Second in order of felicity is to walk with such a soul."

A former queen of the "Days of '47" celebration in Salt Lake City, an accomplished scholar and a popular student body officer, she set aside her studies and her leadership post to become a missionary for her church in far-away Argentina. Returning to graduate from Southern Utah University, she garnered honors as her proud family looked on.

Not so long after these joyous, exuberant days, an unspeakable tragedy occurred. The lovely young woman was gone untimely from her adoring sphere, taken from life in a jarring automobile accident. Anguish permeated the very atmosphere at the university. A shining, exemplary light had faded from view.

Sharwan's grieving friends and fellow student leaders offered an idea that comforted them. Could the promised new

SCULPTOR JERRY ANDERSON

current and future students is being named after such an ideal role model. [8]

On Founders' Day, March 11, 1997, 100 years, almost to the hour, from Gov. Heber M. Wells' signing of the authorization for the founding of a Branch Normal School in southern Utah, a large congregation of thankful and solemn people assembled in the ballroom to dedicate the Sharwan Smith Center, a facility that could not have been imagined a century before.

In the center of the magnificent rotunda stood a seven-foot statue of Sharwan Smith. Sculptor Jerry Anderson had crafted a marvelous representation of vibrant young womanhood. Using films, photographs and treasured perceptions of those who had loved her most, the artist had captured the essence of Sharwan's joyous vitality with exquisite skill. Looking up, one felt warmed by her smile and the wave of her hand. The statue stood in the center of the rotunda, where all student activities would now revolve. It was intended to inspire an understanding of the link between joy and superb performance.

The Founders' Day commemoration was memorable, with a century to celebrate and the wondrous new building to stand as a symbol of all the dreams and strivings of 100 years. The dedication program had been planned to include the sentiments of each of the entities and personalities responsible for the fruition of the dream. The emotions of the day were akin to those of the founders on March 11, 1897, a century past, when word arrived that they would have their school.

Sterling W. Church, vice president for student services, welcomed the assembled group, introducing David Jordan, chair of the Southern Utah University Board of Trustees. Trustee Jordan closed his remarks with a quotation from John S. Woodbury, one of the founders of the school, "Our children have all studied, graduated and grown to manhood and womanhood in the shadow of the school. What would this town have been without the school?" Jordan added, "What

student center bear the name Sharwan Smith? It would be appropriate, they felt, that this place where students would come together to mingle and befriend each other be named in honor of their friend whose inclusive, welcoming nature had warmed their lives. They approached Sharwan's parents, Hyrum and Gail Smith, who hesitated. It was a decision, the Smiths believed, that should be made by University administrators.

On Thursday, May 2, 1996 President Gerald R. Sherratt made an announcement:

The new Southern Utah University Student Center-Centrum Complex will be named the Sharwan Smith Center, after an outstanding student leader on our campus. Sharwan Smith was an exceptionally gifted young woman, with an extraordinary personality. SUU longs to exemplify the same traits of character and ability that made Sharwan such a remarkable young woman. I cannot conceive of a more appropriate name for this wonderful new center.

Other leaders echoed the president's sentiment. Sterling R. Church, vice president for student services, expressed his accord:

Sharwan typified the ideal student in so many ways. Her wholesome, open, active and positive nature deserves emulation. We think it very appropriate that a facility which will impact the lives of so many

Sharwan Smith

would this school have been without the town?"

Roy P. Urie, Iron County commissioner, expressed satisfaction in the linking of the county with the University in the new facility and remembered his own fortunate connection to the institution. He spoke of John Urie, his founding ancestor, his happy years as a student at BAC, the education of his children, and suggested that his family had "generated generations of students," continuing with his grandchildren, currently enrolled at SUU.

The superb acoustics of the new building were demonstrated as the SUU concert choir sang brilliantly, John Rutter's "For the Beauty of the Earth" and "All Ye That Hath Breath Praise Ye the Lord." by Rene Clausen. Valerie Ekins Olson, SUUSA president, challenged students and townspeople present to "rise to the occasion and build upon the superb foundation laid by founders of every generation."

With great tenderness, Gail Smith described her daughter, Sharwan. Smiling through tears she expressed the hope of their family that the monument and the building would inspire generosity and inclusiveness, a quest for knowledge, and joy in the human experience—the ideals that guided Sharwan's life. Hyrum Smith echoed her expressions, adding his own warm remembrances, and left the audience recommitted to a quest for excellence.

President Gerald R. Sherratt, whose vision had kindled the miracle now coming to fruition, remembered the BAC student commons of the '50s, with its modest cafeteria, as a wonderful place, because students had gathered and learned there. He celebrated the startling difference between that wooden structure and this amazing new facility, which will also be wonderful for the same reasons. From memory he quoted President Theodore Roosevelt:

...It is not the critic who counts, or the man who points out where the strong man stumbled, or where the doer of deeds could have done them better. The credit belongs to the man (or the woman) who is actually in the arena, whose face is marred with dust, and sweat and blood, who strives valiantly, who errs and comes short again and again, who spends oneself in a worthy cause, who knows in the end, the triumph of high achievement, or if he fails, at least by daring greatly his

place will never be with those timid souls who know neither victory nor defeat.

"The founders," President Sherratt said, "were not timid souls. Because they spent themselves in a worthy cause, today we know the triumph of high achievement." He likened the Smith family to the founders—"courageous, in daring greatly to give themselves to worthy causes and in spending themselves in the cause of a better life for all those who call this region home."

Sharwan's three sisters, Stacie, Glenna and Rebecca, performed with poignant courage, two songs—"The Shawl," and "Flowers and Bones." The girls carried on without the fourth member of their Smith Four quartet, their now memorialized sister, Sharwan. Scenes from Sharwan's exuberant life flowed onto a large screen in a video presentation produced by Troy Church, accompanied by her clear and sensitive singing.

Marion D. Hanks, a member of the first Board of Trustees of the University, Emeritus General Authority of the Church of Jesus Christ of Latter-day Saints and dear friend of the Smith family, paraphrased the 45th Psalm to describe Sharwan: "She is anointed with the oil of gladness above her fellows. Her name shall be remembered in all generations." He then pronounced the dedicatory

prayer upon the grand new edifice.

As 1997 neared, ringing in the year for the 100th anniversary of the founding of Southern Utah University, there stirred a sense of destiny fulfilled. The man who had guided the course of the school for the last 15 of the 100 years had been ignited by a rare fire, to build the capacity and expand the influence of the institution. Was there a connection that hailed back 100 years?

The ancestral line of President Gerald R. Sherratt includes five of the families most intimately connected with the struggle to establish Branch Normal School. Directly descended from the Bladens, the Bullochs, the Heybornes, the Rosenbergs and the Sherratts, the 13th president's birthright was the same passion that had driven the founders.

The Bladen family boasted Thomas and Cornelius, both driving forces in the construction of Old Main. Thomas was a member of the five-man committee which supervised the building; Cornelius was the fiery leader of the lumber expedition. Husky, 38-year-old James Bulloch Sherratt was responsible to keep the road open for the wagons and sleighs going to and from the logging site; Rosenbergs and Heybornes were prominent in the expedition and the construction. The founders' passion and pride, passed down in family tradition, had kindled Sherratt's obsession.

During his administration the school had grown in size, in prominence and in academic standing, more than at any other period of the 100-year history. The achievements during that period were widely attributed to the extraordinary personal gifts of Gerald R. Sherratt, but the fervor that caused him to apply his gifts to the cause so intensely espoused by his forefathers, was inherent.

A pensive Sherratt acknowledged that there had been myriad moments when he had felt the influence of the founders in propelling forward the affairs of the school. Just as the beginnings had required the enormous effort of the founding folk coupled with the overreaching help of divine power, the day-to-day progression over this era of such remarkable development had been inspired by the dedication and devotion of those who had given birth to the school. And it would surprise no one that the last great occasion of the 15 Sherratt years, the celebration to mark the centennial anniversary, would be an event unsurpassed in the history of any university.

*T*he celebration would be funded by the generosity of nearly 400 people who had affiliated with the Centennial Society, formed especially to ensure that SUU's unique founding, and the sacrifices it entailed, were properly acknowledged and extolled. The Society's chair was Eldon Schmutz, long-time Cedar City resident and friend of the University.

In anticipation of Southern Utah University's centennial anniversary, the institution launched a fund raising campaign with a goal of raising $17.5 million before the end of 1998. As part of the centennial campaign an internal campaign was organized among faculty and staff. Chaired by Dr. Eugene Woolf and Professor James Bowns, assisted by division chairmen, succeeded in raising nearly $150,000 from the staff and faculty. The fund would grow through payroll deductions and would be used for scholarships and endowments, educational support in the form of computers and scientific equipment, library enhancement and faculty enrichment.

Fervor for the upcoming celebration had borne fruit throughout the fall of 1996. The Centennial Parterre had provided a rich focal point. A Centennial faculty symposium in September 1996, added academic emphasis to the celebration as it welcomed Pulitzer prize-winner Jane Smiley; Carol O'Connor and Clyde Milner, co-editors of the *Oxford History of the American West*; Katherine Coles, poet and author, and Thomas C. Henderson, chair of the computer science department at

MARLO MADSEN, GRANDDAUGHTER OF LONGTIME FACULTY MEMBER ADA CARPENTER. PLAYED 'CARMEN' TO ROUSING APPLAUSE.

University of Utah. The visiting authors and scholars participated in lectures and panels attended by invited faculty from all Utah colleges and universities.

The academic emphasis continued through the first four months of 1997 with a series of faculty lectures by invited scholars from the western United States, each guest remaining three days to interact with students and faculty.

Music resounded with extraordinary brilliance as concerts and recitals also filled the early calendar. The Warsaw Philharmonic Orchestra dazzled concert-goers in January with the first concert of the centennial year, sponsored jointly by Cedar City Music Arts and the SUU Centennial Committee. The Founders' Day concert of the Utah Symphony Orchestra with mezzo-soprano Frederica Von Stade on March 11, thrilled affectionate supporters.

In February, the committee took the celebration to far-flung alumni, gathering them in at Centennial Galas at Kingsbury Hall in Salt Lake City and Cashman Field in Las Vegas, Nevada. Talented SUU student groups, including a dance ensemble, Opus, the SUU Choir, Ballroom Dance Team, Acclamation, theatre ensembles and other dancers provided entertainment.

Presentation of Bizet's opera, *Carmen*, which had become almost a tradition through the years, was now produced by the music department as a Centennial offering, under the direction of Carol Ann Modesitt. Opera lovers flocked to the performances to enjoy the colorful presentation, touched by the added dimension of nostalgia.

At the 1997 legislature, the last session at which President Sherratt would make appropriation requests for Southern Utah University, one last, especially satisfying triumph occurred. The physical education building that had seemed adequate in 1964, had suffered from the characteristic soil-settlement difficulties, and it was simply too small. Beginning in 1992 the university had petitioned, planned and plead for a new facility. Several years' disappointment and the burgeoning need made success even more sweet. The request to the legislature was presented by Dr. Gerald R. Sherratt and Dr. Michael D. Richards at the first budget hearings. In the final appropriation $1.1 million was granted to SUU for the planning phase of a new physical education building. The architect would be engaged and begin planning the projected 90,000 square foot facility. It was to include a swimming pool 50 meters long and 25 meters across, a large playing floor with a running track around the perimeter, classrooms and laboratories. Eventually the building would cost almost $22 million, but with the investment in planning the commitment was assured.

The April performance of the world-renowned Guarneri String Quartet brought an outpouring of delight. Called by *New Yorker* Magazine "the preeminent string quartet in the world," the Guarneri made this centennial year visit through the generosity of Orien Dalley, celebrated alumnus of Branch Normal School and, in his younger years, a member of the faculty of BAC. Mr. Dalley's dreams for developing musical opportunity in his native southern Utah had never dimmed, but had been manifested in gifts of music and instruments to the school. Now the presence of the Guarneri, with Orien Dalley's son John as a principal, came as a significant centennial gift.

Reminiscent of the pageantry of the *College Cavalcade*, produced in 1947 on the occasion of the golden anniversary of the university, the production entitled *Centennial! The Show* pulled out all the stops. One hundred years of progress had provided the place, (The Centrum), the technology and the talent to create an extravaganza that would usher in the new century and that would be remembered until the beginning of a new millennium. The event, produced by Mitzi McKay, dramatized in song and dance the succeeding periods of SUU history. Large crowds enjoyed the stunning performances, which included the American Folk Ballet and other SUU performing groups and ended with indoor fireworks.

The theatre arts and dance department had readied the musical *South Pacific* for a seven-night run at the Randall Theatre. Under the direction of professor Richard Bugg, the favorite show was a major Centennial event, playing to a full house each night.

The culminating crescendo came with the events of May 1 and May 2, 1997. On May Day afternoon the Jay Dee and Alice Harris Center was dedicated. The magnificent stadium crown had evolved through a process that bespoke the creative genius of the retiring president Gerald R. Sherratt. His imagination had been kindled by the removal of the steel girders from the War Memorial Fieldhouse, and the completed central pavilion fulfilled all expectations, filling the need of the growing gymnastics program and becoming the campus ballroom. As the need for offices and administrative spaces for the university athletic programs had become more critical, the benevolence of Sherratt's old friends, Jay Dee and Alice Harris helped to expand the facility, designed in the classical Greek style, until it became a triplet of buildings, completing the dream that the stadium would rank among the most beautiful in all of American higher education.

The dedication ceremony that Thursday afternoon paid tribute to the Harrises for their generosity, symbolic of a century of contributions, great and small, that had flowed from the people who loved and blessed the university.

*T*hat evening the Centennial Gala and Ball, sponsored by the SUU Student Association, enlivened campus and community as students and townspeople danced together in the new ballroom at the Sharwan Smith Center. Entertainment included country music star Collin Raye and a trio that carried on the Centennial theme, three singers from an earlier era: The Golden Boys, with '50s pop idols Frankie Avalon, Bobby Rydell and Fabian.

At 9:00 on Friday morning in an open air pavilion located directly south of the Centrum, the Centurium, a gift to the university exemplifying "The Life of the Mind," was dedicated. Created to celebrate the spirit of the university, as exemplified in people whose lives demonstrate a passion for intellectual freedom, the exaltation of reason, the spirit of discovery and the fire of genius, the 12 statues represent persons in history who embodied these virtues.

After the dedication, luncheons were served at the student center for students and friends, while the Centennial Society gathered for lunch at the Great Hall, greeted by former President of the United States, George H. Bush. At the conclusion of the luncheons, participants in the grand academic processional assembled.

The ceremonial procession of 1,200 people included distinguished guests—Boards of Regents and Trustees; the Centennial Society members; 100 students from each of the classes of 1997, 1998, 1999, and 2000; alumni or representatives from each graduating class of the hundred years; faculty, students and emeriti from every era. The procession moved solemnly from the upper campus behind a bagpipe band to the Centrum filled to over-flowing with people who treasured the University as their heritage. The Centennial Convocation was about to begin.

Honored guests filed from the procession to the podium, including the Honorable Michael Okerlund Leavitt, Governor of Utah, President Gordon B. Hinckley of the Church of Jesus Christ of Latter-day Saints and British Consul General Merrick Baker-Bates, all of whom gave tributes to the founders of the University. A glittering slate of speakers graced the occasion: Dr. Michael DeBakey, world-renowned cardiovascular surgeon; astronaut David Scott; Evgeny Sidorov, Russian Minister of Culture, former U.S. Surgeon General C. Everett Koop and George Bush, former president of the United States.

The music of the Mormon Tabernacle Choir added glory to the day.

And somewhere, in another sphere...

...there were the Adamses, the Ashdowns, the Arthurs, the Armstrongs and Ahlstroms; the Bauers, the Bensons, the Besses, the Bladens, the Browns, the Bullochs, the Bryants, the Burbecks, the Bergstroms; the Chatterleys, the Corrys, the Corletts, the Cosslets, the Carrigans, the Condies, the Chaffins and the Clarks, the Connells and the Coverts...

...there were the Dalleys, the Dixes, the Dovers, the Duttons, the Deckers, the Driggs, and the Daughertys; the Elikers, the Fifes and the Fretwells; the Gowers and the Goulds; the Haights, the Hansens, the Harrises, the Heybornes, the Higbees, the Houchens, the Hunters, the Humphries, the Hallmans and the Hollands; the Jensens, Heber and John, who operated the lumber mill; the Jones, the Jacobsens, and the Krumans; the Leighs, the Lunts and the Lamberts; the Macfarlanes, the Mackelprangs, the Mathesons, the Muries, the McConnells, the Middletons and the Nelsons...

...there were the Palmers, the Parrys, the Perrys, the Pendletons, the Perkins, the Poynors, the Pryors, and the Pucells. There were the Rollos, who made the brick, and the Roots, the Roches, and the Rosenbergs; the Sandines, the Sawyers, the Sherratts, the Schoppmans, the Spencers; the Taits, the Tailors, the Taylors, the Thorleys, and the Tuckers. There were the Unthanks and the Uries; the Walkers, the Websters, the Wilkinsons, the Williamses and the Woods...

...all of whom had been present at the laying of the cornerstone of Old Main—watched rejoicing. [9]

Afterword

On occasion, past and present converge in the affairs of men and of institutions. On March 21, 1997, a group gathered to hear the announcement of the selection of a new president of Southern Utah University. The new president would lead Southern Utah University into its second century, the announcement coming just 10 days beyond the centennial of the school's founding. A sense of history hung palpably in the air.

Kenneth G. Anderton, chair of the Utah State Board of Regents, made the announcement. Dr. Steven D. Bennion was named president of Southern Utah University, to succeed Dr. Gerald R. Sherratt, retiring as president

STEVEN D. BENNION

after nearly 16 years of extraordinary service.

Dr. Steven D. Bennion is the grandson of Milton Bennion, hired in March, 1897, as first principal of Branch Normal School. This reminder of the institution's roots gave added impact to the moment.

The selection process had been long and careful. Dr. Bennion was selected from a pool of 109 nominees and applicants for the position. A search committee comprised of university representatives, trustees, regents and community leaders chose and interviewed 10 semi-finalists, recommending four finalists to the State Board of Regents. The Regents made the final appointment.

Dr. Bennion brings to the task extensive experience in higher education, having served as president of Snow College and of Ricks College, serving at each post for seven years. He had earlier been Associate Commissioner for Planning for the Utah System of Higher Education.

Dr. Bennion earned his Ph.D. in educational administration with a minor in organizational behavior at the University of Wisconsin; his masters degree in public administration at Cornell University and his bachelors degree at the University of Utah, where he graduated Cum Laude.

Dr. Bennion is married to Marjorie Hopkins. They are the parents of five children and have five grandchildren.

Dr. Steven D. Bennion's appointment was an historic and symbolic capstone to the first 100 years of SUU's history. Milton Bennion had taken up the task as principal of Branch Normal School as the school took its first faltering steps. A young bachelor, he married Cora Lindsay after his first year at Branch Normal School. He had been at the beginning of his education and his career.

Dr. Steven D. Bennion takes the reins of a flourishing university, at the dawn of its second century, moving forward with momentum, secure in direction. Thirty years older than when Milton Bennion took the institution's helm, Dr. Bennion brings the professional experience and maturity required for the task in 1997. He may nonetheless sense, as did Gerald Sherratt before him, that heroes from an earlier era are cheering him on.

PART 2

The Developing Disciplines

CHAPTER VIII

Teacher Education - The heart of BNS-SUU

It's hard on us to help you out of the nest, knowing that the cold world is the only place we have to send you off to.

Bessie Dover

The settlement of Cedar City and other southern Utah towns and villages led to immediate establishment of schools. In Cedar City the first formal school was organized in the Old Fort in 1853 in the home of Joseph Chatterley, with Matthew Carruthers as the first teacher. Matthew Carruthers was well prepared to teach, having been university-educated in Scotland. He was also a leader in the Iron Mission and supervisor in the Iron Works. After a short time, John Chatterley replaced Carruthers as the teacher. A building was erected in the northeast corner of the fort, which became the school and public meeting hall. When the fort was abandoned, a school building was constructed on a new city site. The Social Hall was built just south of this building; both were used as schools.[1]

Teachers who followed Carruthers and Chatterley in these schools were Martin Slack, John V. Adams, J. M. Macfarlane, Paddy O'Brien, Robert Heyborne, Lewis Fisher, John Duncan, William Leigh and John Edwards.

Several informal schools were also organized in homes of the early residents of Cedar City. The teachers in these home schools included Jane Spikins, Jane Parry Mackelprang, Annie Wood Romney, Lewis Fisher, Keturah Macfarland and Mary Ann Lunt.

There was no mandatory attendance in these early schools, the school year being governed by the need for the children to help with work at home and in the fields. However, the demand for schooling continued to grow. The Social Hall was the main school building for 25 years. In 1881 the people determined that the time had

come to formalize the system and erect a new building. Construction was begun that year at 100 East Center Street, site of the present Rock Church, and classes commenced in the new school on January 15, 1883. Matthew Dalley was one of the first young men of Cedar City to have attended school elsewhere. Dalley came home to teach at this school. His first contract called for a salary of $60 per month—1/3 cash, 2/3 produce. Monies to support the school probably came from a combination of gifts, tuition and city funds.

In 1890 public schools became a reality by territorial law. Each city was made a sub-district with power to elect a board of directors and hire a superintendent. By 1896, and statehood, the Social Hall school had outgrown its six classrooms.

The need for trained teachers in these Cedar

HOWARD R. DRIGGS PREPARES STUDENTS FOR THEIR TEACHING CAREER.

City schools and in the other towns and villages of Iron, Millard, Washington, Beaver, Kane, Piute and Garfield counties was burgeoning. High schools and academies were being established. The remarkable growth of public schools was the natural result of the high priority given to education by the pioneer families; there was always a need for qualified teachers. This demand led to the establishment of the southern Branch of the State Normal School of the University of Utah, known as the Branch Normal School (BNS).

The training of teachers for the public (common) schools of Utah was the purpose of the Southern Branch of the State Normal School. From page 11 of the 1988-89 BNS catalog:

"The Branch Normal School will this year offer two courses of study. 1. The first three years of regular four years leading to normal certificate. 2. A preparatory course for students 18 years of age who are not prepared to do work of the normal course."

Dr. Milton Bennion, first principal of BNS , re-articulated this primary purpose—to establish a state-supported institution to train elementary school teachers for the public schools, especially the schools of southern Utah—in a retrospective statement in "College Cavalcade," a historical pageant published in 1947:

The BAC first bore the name "Southern Branch of the State Normal School" because its primary purpose was to prepare teachers for service in elementary schools. At that time the requirement for teacher certification was a good secondary education supplemented by professional training in the art of teaching.

The curriculum at the BNS for those students seeking a "normal" education was almost identical to the curriculum at the mother institution, The State Normal School at the University of Utah. Admission to the normal course in the period from 1897 to 1909 was proof of completion of the eighth grade. In the beginning the normal course was basically a three-year high school course, then a fourth year combination of high school subjects and special subjects in teacher education.

The teacher education courses were: history of education, pedagogy, educational psychology, school accounting and training (student teaching). The State Normal School also offered a four-year kindergarten course, which was not added to the BNS Course offering until 1910. Even though the teacher education courses were listed in the BNS Catalog, these courses

were, for the most part, only offered at the State Normal School. BNS students were required to attend these classes at the normal school in Salt Lake City to complete the course of study and receive a normal diploma, or teaching certificate.

The first state legislature gave the University of Utah and the State Normal School unusual powers governing the training of teachers. The Laws of Utah of 1896, page 275, reads:

The University of Utah shall be the highest branch of a public system of education of this state, and as far as practicable, its courses and methods of instruction shall be arranged to supplement and continue the instruction in other branches of the public system, and with a view to afford and complete a thorough education to students of both sexes in arts, science and literature and such professional branches as may be included in its courses of instruction.

The principal of the State Normal School was given authority to issue teacher's certificates and diplomas which, when endorsed by the chairman of the State Board of Education, had "the force of corresponding certificates issued by the State Board..." This practice continued until 1934, when the State Board of Education became the sole agency to issue public school certificates. Thus, the State Normal School, as a department of the University of Utah, was given preeminence in the new state of Utah in the training of teachers. A law in 1896 provided one of the greatest supports ever given students entering the teaching field, the Normal Scholarships. The 1896 law stated:

The Normal School shall be continued as a Department of University for students of both sexes, and its courses of instruction may extend for a period of four years or until graduation, and its courses shall include practice teaching and instruction in pedagogy. One hundred free Normal Scholarships may be maintained in the Normal School, the holder shall be exempt from all registration or entrance fees. Fifty appointments to such scholarships may be made annually: Each appointment to be for a period to two years provided: that students may be reappointed to scholarships. Appointments to normal scholarships shall be made by the superintendent of public instruction, on nomination by the county board of examiners, or city boards of education when such places are not under the supervision of superintendents of schools. It shall be the duty of the Superintendent of Public Instruction on or before the last day of May of each year to apportion scholarships on the basis of total school population.

Students who received these scholarships were required to declare in writing that they intended to become teachers, and that if they left the program without becoming teachers they would repay the scholarship monies they had received. BNS could apply and receive a share of those granted for the State Normal School.

BNS was the embryo of a university, yet like all things newly-created its life was dependent on the support of its "mother" institution. That support was given as long as the local political and educational leaders of the fledgling school were satisfied to remain a branch of the University of Utah, unable to offer college-level courses at the Cedar City campus. Remarkable educators were appointed, and they attracted students to the new school. The faculty, along with determined southern Utah political leaders, assured the BNS a bright beginning and continued growth over the next 17 years. It also brought an increased level of educational opportunity to a whole region.

*I*n 1900 the first class of the Southern Branch of the State Normal School had completed the course work necessary for graduation. Ten students are shown as members of that class in the Alumni Booklet published in 1940, but only six students completed the normal course in the three years.[2] The other four were slowed by their necessity to complete the preparatory course.

The six who completed the normal course were granted scholarships to proceed to the University of Utah to complete the fourth year. They had promised, as required, that they would upon completion of their schooling teach at least three years. A brief review of these students and their teaching careers gives a view of the educational impact of the Branch Normal School upon the whole region. It was an impact that was realized in a remarkably short time and clearly validates the vision of the founders. These six first graduates, shown in the accompanying photograph, included:

Emma Gardner (Abbott), one of 13 children of Royal Joseph and Chloe Louisa Snow Gardner of Pine Valley, Washington County. She completed her elementary education at Pine Valley and Central schools, then came to Branch

First Graduates, Branch Normal School,1900. L to R: Emma Gardner, Joseph Wilkinson, Alice Redd, Ella Berry, Julius Sylvester Dalley, Amelia Dalley.

Normal for her secondary training. Emma fulfilled her scholarship "contract," teaching 23 years at Mesquite, Nevada. Emma married David Arthur Abbot of Mesquite. She became the principal of the school and served in numerous civic capacities.

Joseph T. Wilkinson Jr., born in Leeds, Utah, the fourth of five children of Joseph T. Wilkinson and Elizabeth Emily Wells. The family moved to Cedar City, where they worked together publishing the *Iron County Record*. Joseph, called "Josie," married Annie Jarvis Webb. He taught at schools in Hurricane, Rockville, Springdale and Moccasin and Cane Beds, Arizona. His normal schooling framed a teaching career that extended over many years.

Alice Redd (Rich), the 13th child of Lemuel Hardison Redd and Keziah Jane Butler of New Harmony. After her graduation she taught for a year at Pioche, Nevada, then went to Paris, Idaho, to teach at the Fielding Academy. She married a fellow teacher, Abel Sargent Rich. They settled in Brigham City, Utah, and three of their six children became teachers.

Ella Berry (Leigh), the seventh of eight children of William Shanks Berry and Rebecca Rocena Beck. The Berry family settled early in Kanarraville. Ella attended the Parowan Stake Academy and entered with the first class. After her graduation from the University of Utah she taught just three years in the Iron County School District before marrying Harry Leigh, a budding young Cedar City businessman. The business prospered, as did their family of nine children.

Julius Sylvester Dalley, born to James and
Johanna Bolette Bertleson Dalley in Summit,
Utah. He was an apt student and allowed to
attend school through the fifth reader, and to
continue in that grade when no higher education was available. At the opening of the
Parowan Stake Academy he entered there and
then became a member of the first BNS class.
After his U of U graduation, he began teaching
in the basement of the Parowan Tabernacle. He
taught at Summit and Monticello, Utah and
Moccasin, Arizona, finishing a long teaching
career in Kanab, Utah. He was a strong civic
leader, involved in education for his entire life.

Amelia Dalley (Green), a half-sister to Julius
Dalley. She was born to James and Petrine
Bertleson Dalley. She and her twin sister,
Minnie, were the ninth and 10th children of
this family of 14. She married George Bernard
Green. Her teaching career began in Summit in
a one-room school that included grades one
though eight. One of her pupils was her broth-
er Parley, who finished the eighth grade with
Amelia as his teacher.

This group of six friends went together to Salt
Lake City for their obligatory year at the
University of Utah. Petrine Bertlesen Dalley,
leaving three-year-old Parley in the care of relatives, went along as their chaperone and house-
mother. They rented a small house and all lived
together, while they completed their graduation
and certification requirements.

As Utah began the transition from a territorial government to statehood, education for all of its citizens became a major
political and economic agenda. In rural communities intelligent and dedicated, but non-cer-
tified, local citizens had been paid in kind.
Professionally trained teachers who held a normal certificate insisted on cash payment, if they
were to move to the hinterlands of the state.
When BNS opened the doors of the Ward Hall
that September of 1897, it was the beginning of
an era that would change the thrust of public
education in southern Utah and eventually
southern and eastern Nevada and northern
Arizona forever.

Even though the curriculum was at the high
school level, the program resulted in an
increase of educated citizens in the rural counties. In reviewing the records of graduates from
1900 to 1913 it was not possible to determine
which students followed the normal course
(college) and those who had completed a high
school (secondary) course of study. It is estimated that 70 to 90 percent of the graduates
each year were graduates of the normal course.

Some of those who did not complete the normal course were hired as teachers by town and
county schools. The State Board of Education
had established a system of licensing teachers
which allowed students who had the equivalent
of a high school education to "sit" for licensing
examinations. College professors and town and
county administrators were named as examiners. Students who met the academic requirements and passed these exams were awarded
teaching certificates. Some of the BNS students
who completed the normal course at BNS but
were not able to afford the additional year at the
University of Utah became teachers through
this system. That BNS graduated 307 students in
the years 1900-1913, the number fluctuating
from year to year, was remarkable for a new
school with a very small faculty.

The slow but consistent growth and maturity
of BNS was not without serious challenge. The
people of Beaver, Parowan and St. George, who
had been earnest contenders for the establishment of the branch college, began immediately
to find ways to provide secondary education in
their towns. The establishment of LDS academies, with ties to Brigham Young Academy in
Provo, marked the beginnings of a public system of secondary education. High schools were
soon to be established in southern Utah counties. As chronicled in this history, other towns
continued to smart from what they perceived as
the unfair advantage of BNS/BAC, which was
supported by state funds, while their local
boards of education had to scramble for funding.

Graduates of BNS in the first 17 years were,
for the most part, students who completed the
normal course and either went away to Salt
Lake to complete graduation requirements or sat for
teacher certification examinations. The need by

the citizens of southern Utah to have these col-lege-level education courses taught at BNS was rebuffed by the faculty and administration at the University of Utah. Political action by south-ern Utah legislators became intense as they pressed for the need for Branch Normal School to become a college.

When the Utah Legislature acted in 1913 to change Southern Branch of the State Normal School to Branch Agricultural College (official name: The Branch of the Agricultural College of Utah), it was a moment of great significance for teacher educa-tion at BNS-BAC. The mother college, USAC, was facing the same problems as BNS in getting legislative approval to establish teacher educa-tion programs, and it was not until 1921 that the legislature was to give that approval to USAC. Even though the northern school did not have a teacher education program in 1913, the law giving birth to the Branch at Cedar City was the opening of the door for future professional training of teachers at BAC.

It is evident that BAC took some action on its own in 1917, four years later. The administra-tion hired faculty to teach education and psy-chology courses, probably college-level courses. By that time similar classes were being offered at USAC, but a footnote in the catalog indicated that these classes were given under the direc-tion of Brigham Young College, which was later to become Logan High School.

The normal training curriculum was again added to the BAC catalog in 1918-19. The con-nection with the state normal school was reestablished; the principal of the state school became responsible for recording credits earned at BAC and was the issuer of teaching certificates. Faculty for teacher training were authorized by a joint process involving the Normal School, faculty at BAC and the Iron County School District. This led to a strength-ening of the relationship between these part-ners that become very important in the build-ing of teacher education in southern Utah in the years to follow.

By 1925 the college had three academic divi-sions: the junior college division, the normal division and the high school division. In that same year the State Board of Education became responsible for certification of teachers.

The decade of 1926 to 1935 was a period of transition. A few markers are helpful in retrospect. In 1928-29 the word "Normal" was dropped from the course head-

ings, but "normal graduate" was still used. The catalog now showed a department of education and psychology.

The appointment of Henry Oberhansley as director of BAC in the fall of 1929 was a plus for teacher education. Professor Oberhansley, who had been an assistant professor of education and pedagogy at USAC in 1921, had been one of the team which had planned and directed the first teacher education programs there. His spe-cial interest in teacher education gave assur-ance that he would shepherd the program at BAC as the curriculum grew. Oberhansley was to remain the teacher education leader at BAC until 1944.

The first day of the year of 1936 new state teacher certification requirements were approved, and the term "Normal" did not appear in the 1936-37 catalog in reference to earning educational credits. The department of education and psychology still offered the course work in teacher education, but now stu-dent teaching was not listed and the certifica-tion requirements which had been printed in previous catalogs were not shown. The State Board of Education had won the battle with the State Normal School in becoming the sole teacher certification agency of Utah.

The new state certification requirements demanded a third year of training for the ele-mentary certificate with the fourth year and the bachelor's degree to be required in the near future.

On February 14th of 1936 the BAC Committee of the Board of Trustees approved seeking a third year of work in education at the Cedar City campus. Director Oberhansley sent a written request to President E.G. Peterson at USAC to add the upper-division program to the BAC curriculum. He followed up with a list of the courses, which were the same as those offered at USAC.

Mr. Skidmore, the state superintendent of public instruction, resisted the move on the grounds that Dixie, Snow and Weber Junior Colleges would soon want to do the same thing. A hot political controversy fomented about who really governed BAC, and the issue of whether BAC was, in fact, destined to be a "junior" col-lege. Trustee M.J. Macfarlane rose to defend the cause of BAC and urged the granting of the third year.[3]

Out of this turmoil ensued the formal growth process toward a four-year elementary educa-tion degree program.

In 1937-38, in an administrative reorganiza-tion of BAC, education became one of 11 acad-

MARY
MCMILLAN
EGGERT,
SUPERVISOR
OF TEACHER
TRAINING,
1949

emic disciplines in the Division of Liberal Arts. The following year the Division of Education was organized. Teacher education courses offered 35 hours of credit, enough credit for the equivalent of a three-year college program with the fourth year to be completed at USAC or some other four-year college. The departments of art, music and physical education became part of the Division of Education. A special course was taught by each of these three departments which enriched the elementary education course of study. William Manning taught a music methods course, Mary Bastow taught a methods course in art and H.B. Linford taught a similar class for health education.

In 1940 Burns Finlinson was hired to teach education and psychology courses, which had been previously taught by Director Oberhansley. Of the 64 BAC graduates that year, 20 of them were education graduates, one indication of the continuing prominent place of teacher education at BAC. Professor Finlinson did not return after a leave in 1941-42. Betty T. Berry and Donald K. Nelson were hired in 1943, Berry to teach education and Nelson to teach library science, which were offered by the Division of Education.

H. Wayne Driggs became the director of BAC in 1945, serving concurrently as chairman of the Division of Education. Professor Driggs continued the uphill struggle for expansion which had commenced under Professor Oberhansley.

*T*he Golden Jubilee year, 1947-1948, celebrated 50 years of BNS/BAC. A significant element in the larger event was the celebration of 50 years of educational leadership and teacher training.

In May of 1947 Dr. H. Wayne Driggs announced the formation of a teacher education advisory council, following up on the decision of the USAC Board of Trustees to expand the elementary education program so that all requirements for the bachelor's degree in education could be completed at BAC.

The following is an excerpt, quoting Dr. Driggs from *The Bacian* in May of 1947:

School superintendents of southern Utah districts have

DR. REESE P.
MAUGHAN

formed an advisory council to assist the college in setting up the practical program in training elementary teachers... The addition to the training facilities in southern Utah means that students will be able to get their bachelor's degree in elementary education without having to leave the region..(and) able to qualify for state certification to teach in the elementary schools of the state... With the authorization of the USAC Board of Trustees for the addition of third year work in other departments, any elementary student will be able to fill his junior year with subjects related to education and devote the entire fourth year to practice teaching and studies in the major field... The expansion program has come as a result of the efforts of the people of southern Utah who saw the need for the new offering at the college.

The appointment of the advisory council, along with the hiring of a department chairman to head the expansion, was the capstone of the first 50 years of teacher education at BNS-BAC.

Two-year degrees could now be granted by BAC and a four-year program was in place, though that degree would be given by USAC. The stage was now set for ushering in, during the next 50 years, the development of an independent four-year college and then a university, whose teacher education program would open the way for the offering of other majors and minors.

The announcement of the bachelor's degree program in elementary education in the BAC catalog for 1948-49 made waves, with a ripple effect. It was a boon, of course, for students currently enrolled at BAC, but it also caused other students from southern Utah and Nevada who had enrolled in programs at BYU and the U of U to transfer to BAC.

The requirements for a B.S. Degree in elementary education were published in the 1948-49 catalog. There were 14 specific requirements. The final two requirements are interesting:

13. The candidates must be of good moral character and must have discharged all college fees.

14. Attendance in person at the Commencement and Baccalaureate exercises...is mandatory, unless excused in writing for very urgent reasons...

In September of 1948 Dr. Reese P. Maughan became the chair of the Division of Education

and chair, as well, of the department of education within the division. Dr. Maughan assumed responsibility for establishment of the curriculum, a major share of the teaching load and the task of recruiting students within BAC and other colleges to enter the new program. More than 30 students began their professional career in that program during 1948-49. Maughan's appointment to the faculty was reported in the *Bacian* of Tuesday, September 7, 1948:

Dr. Reese P. Maughan, of Arizona State Teacher's College at Tempe, Ariz., has been named professor of education and Chairman of the Department of Education here at BAC to direct the first year's expansion of the teacher's training program at the college...

The new program...will be done in cooperation with Iron County school system. Dr. Maughan comes highly recommended as an organizer, having served as director of child welfare and guidance of the San Luis Obispo school system. During the war years he did a splendid job of organizing the school system of the Topaz Relocation Center, where he had complete charge of the organization of the curriculum, the hiring of teachers and the direct responsibility for the operation of the school system at Topaz.

The newly expanded teacher training program will mean that for the first time students of southern Utah will have an opportunity to obtain a bachelor's degree in a school located in southern Utah.

The response to the program was so immediate that summer school was added in 1949. Students were not only attracted to summer school to take major courses in elementary education, but students in the arts and sciences could now take upper division courses in their academic disciplines which were part of the requirements for their minors; these courses had been added to support the elementary education major. Graduate students in education also came to summer school to earn credits to renew their State Teaching Certificates. Summer school was an immediate success.

*T*he second 50 years was off to an explosive start. The first graduating class was scheduled for 1950, and new admissions insured that 20 to 30 graduates would be completing the bachelors degree work during the first five years.

The class of 1950 had two things in common with the class of 1900. The students of 1900 and

of 1950 were trained to become teachers. Both classes were "firsts." The class of 1900 constituted the first graduates in teacher training ; the class of 1950 were the first of thousands who would earn their bachelor's degrees in education at BAC. They both led the way.

Twenty men and women graduated with bachelors degrees awarded by Utah State Agricultural College but earned at the Branch at Cedar City. Those who received those first historic diplomas included: Maxine Berry Adams, Wallace Adams, Chester Benson, Morris Buhanan, Hallie Thorley Duckworth, Ila Gurr Sherratt Corry, Victor Frei, Hilda Foy Gardner, Rayone Brown Grenawalt, Arlo John Hafen, Ida Jolley, Miriam Hunter Luke, Andrew J. Mitchell, Vana Oldroyd Nelson, Claud L. Robinson, Helen Stones, Robert L. Stratton, June Decker Thorley, Barbara Williams and Agnes Wilson.

Many of the students attended commencement exercises on both campuses.[4]

These first 20 graduates were the vanguard of the modern era of teacher education at

GRADUATION DAY, 1950: MORRIS BUHANAN, ILA GURR SHERRATT, MIRIAM LUKE AND MAXINE ADAMS.

50 YEARS OF GRADUATES: ALICE R. RICH, AMELIA D. GREEN, AND JULIUS DALLEY, CLASS OF 1900, WITH MRS. VANA NELSON, CLASS OF 1950.

JOSEPH
FILLERUP

GWYN
CLARK

BAC/SUU. During the next 15 years (1950-1965) 570 men and women graduated from the elementary education program. This 15 years of growth and development allowed for the refinement and strengthening of the course work in the elementary education major and the development of academic minors in each of the other departments of the college. This would, in turn, lay the ground work for the academic majors needed for the prospective secondary education program.

Daryl Chase was named director of BAC in 1952. He was to serve only for three years and then returned to USAC to become the president of the college.

In 1953 the name of the college was changed to College of Southern Utah, Branch of Utah State Agricultural College. In 1954 Royden Braithwaite was appointed director of CSU, and he followed the precedent of previous directors by holding an academic professorship in the Division of Education.

In the fall of 1957 Joseph Fillerup replaced Reese Maughan as chairman of the Division of Education. The mother institution, Utah State Agricultural College, changed its name to Utah State University.

In response to the need for kindergarten teachers, the department offered new classes in child development, which were added to the Division of Home and Family Living. The steady growth of enrollment in the elementary education major resulted in a concurrent enrollment in the other divisions of CSU which provided required course work for the minors of elementary education majors. All of these majors earned at least 44 quarter hours of credit in the other divisions of the college. This additional academic preparation beyond the major in elementary education added some upper division credit to departments and divisions of the college which were soon to have academic major programs of their own.

The public school superinten-

dents in the area and the faculty of the Division of Education began a needs assessment for secondary teachers which continued from 1959 to 1964. In 1961, when the Division of Physical Education, Health and Athletics was created, P.E. and health courses were removed from catalog offerings of the Division of Education.

Morris Shirts, who had been hired as a faculty member in the Division of Education in 1959, became acting division chair in 1962 while Joseph Fillerup was on leave. Dr. Fillerup extended his stay in Africa; Dr. Shirts became division chairman in 1964. At this juncture three departments were formed in the division: departments of elementary education, secondary education and psychology. That same year the third-year courses for majors in secondary education were added to the teacher education curriculum. The other academic divisions at CSU submitted plans for academic majors for secondary education students. The intention was that secondary students would complete their fourth year and receive their degree at USU.

*T*eacher education was again at the forefront of major change in the history of BNS/SUU. Legislative leaders from Southern Utah boldly laid the next major milestone in the path of progress, in 1965, by presenting and shepherding the passage into law at the Utah Legislature a bill which made CSU an independent four-year state college.

The year of 1965 also marked a milestone in teacher education per se. The department established the fourth year of the secondary program course work, and minors for secondary education majors were added in all the academic disciplines. The course work for a minor in child development was also added; students could now earn Early Childhood Education Certificates at CSU. Certification course work for elementary and secondary school librarians was also added.

No more was there a need to affiliate as a branch of other universities at the undergraduate level, but the completion of graduate degrees in elementary and secondary education was another thing. CSU was destined for a new relationship with USU.

In 1966 the Division of Behavioral and Social Sciences resulted in the removal of psychology programs from the Division of Education. In 1968 a major administrative reorganization occurred at CSU. Academic schools replaced the divisions of the former structure. Morris Shirts became dean of The School of Education,

PAUL VORKINK

*M*y time at SUSC was a highlight of my life. Upon arriving on campus in 1970 I experienced feelings that I had never felt before. I hungered for the things that SUSC would offer me. When Susan Memmott, Judy Brown and Susan Hafen and I moved into a house together we instantly felt accepted, even loved, by not only the college personnel but also by the townspeople of Cedar City.

I was average in every way - grades, abilities, understanding and experience - but the people in town treated me as if I were important to them. I believe we really were important to them. So many people and their families invited us into their homes for meals and visits. Professor Phil Carter, Ken Benson, Gary Giles, Robert Moss, Fred Adams, Eugene Holman, Bessie Dover and others shared their families, homes and food with us. They became best friends, surrogate parents, helping us socially, emotionally, nutritionally and spiritually, as well as academically.

There were snowy days when Ken Benson picked us up in his big four-wheel drive truck; otherwise we would not have made it to classes. Dr. Gwyn Clark often called me at home to make sure that I'd be on time or remind me of things I needed to do. One day when we could only afford rice and noodles at Lin's AG Market, the owner, Ray Orton, noted the sparse contents of our bag and slipped in a freshly-roasted chicken, free of charge. We would have been mal-nourished if it were not for the times we took our guitars and sang, as Sue, Lou and Sher, for Rotary, Kiwanis and Lions' club banquets, and were rewarded by delicious meals.

At graduation, I had already accepted a teaching position, but I really did not want to leave SUSC. Dr. Kent Myers, sensing my ambivalence, invited me into his office for a chat. He told me to just go out there and become the best Sheryn Daugherty that I could possibly become. I think it was Bessie Dover who also tried to help me out of the nest, by saying "It's hard on us, too, knowing that the cold world is the only place we have to sent you off to."

Where else in the world could anyone find a school and community that are so determined to do all they can to help the individual!

Sheryn Daugherty

which welcomed back physical education into the school. Three departments—elementary education, secondary education and physical education were organized within the school with Gwyn Clark, Paul Vorkink and Cleo Petty as department chairs, respectively.

Library personnel who taught the library science and media courses also held academic rank in the School of Education, the school librarian certification program being renamed the Basic Media Endorsement. Dr. Shirts organized a college-wide Secondary Advisory Committee. Faculty members from departments which had majors and/or minors that had been approved as programs meeting State of Utah certification requirements were appointed to the committee, which would key the development of academic programs to meet the needs of students seeking to become professional educators.

A new girder in building university status for the Cedar City school was raised when the name of the college became Southern Utah State College the following year in 1969. The change to SUSC identified the institution as an independent four-year college.

Teacher education programs continued to be the most productive programs on campus in

terms of the number of graduates and the number of graduates licensed as professionals. It was now clear that course work beyond the bachelor's degree for re-certification of teachers should be a priority. Public and private school teachers throughout southern Utah, southern Nevada and northern Arizona needed such a program.

When the faculty of the School of Education began to formulate plans for a master of education program, they met with intense resistance from the University of Utah and Utah State University. In 1970 some fifth-year courses were added to the teacher education curriculum to assist these teachers. The fifth-year courses were ranked above undergraduate credit, but were not truly graduate courses because no authority had been give to SUSC to offer graduate work.

The demand for a master's program was shown to be real by the completion of a needs assessment in which teachers and administrators in the public schools were polled. Dean Shirts and his faculty prepared the first planning documents for presentation to the Board of Regents concerning credit beyond the bachelors degree. The deans of education from the colleges and universities in the Utah system of

DR. MORRIS
SHIRTS AND
STUDENTS

higher education met often in 1971 and 1972 as the Teacher Education Ad Hoc Committee.

The matter of graduate programs came to a head on January 14, 1972, when the following recommendation was presented:

Dr. Oral Ballam, dean at USU, moved that this committee (Ad Hoc) recommend a five year moratorium at the established four-year institutions on the development of formal master's degree programs in teacher education, but that at the end of that time, the decision be reviewed.

The motion was seconded by Jerry Anderson, dean at University of Utah, and passed with Dean Shirts protesting with the only "no" vote.

The Board of Regents failed to accept the recommendation, and someone suggested a proposal to explore the possibility of a cooperative master's program between SUSC and one of the state universities.

The state universities at Salt Lake City and Logan applied pressure on Utah legislators and higher education officials to limit the graduate programs to their schools. However, the salaries of professional educators in the public schools was becoming directly tied to the number of graduate credit hours and the advanced degrees held by teachers and administrators, so the need for the master's program at SUSC did not go away.

The School of Education now had large numbers of graduates with a fairly small number of

DR. JAMES
MILLER

faculty, so experimentation in administrative organization was on-going. In 1970 the three departments were replaced by two divisions: Education Division, with Robert Moss as chairman, and Physical Education Division, with Bruce Osborne as chairman.

In 1972 the School of Education was reorganized with Kent Myers as dean; the divisions were designated as departments with Gywn Clark, chair of elementary and Paul Vorkink, chair of secondary. President Braithwaite and Dr. Myers presented a formal proposal for a master's of education program to the Commissioner of Higher Education, but the proposal was rejected. Dr. Homer Durham, the commissioner, indicated that "the University of Utah had masters programs in place which could easily accommodate the needs of all public school personnel."

The School of Education began planning for a cooperative master's program with either USU or the U of U. A political plus for this approach was the fact that Weber State College had also been pushing for a master's program in teacher education and had a tentative working agreement with USU. However, it would be another six years before a cooperative program between SUSC and USU would be approved by the Board of Regents. It was a lesson in history. Southern Utah State College would need the political power which came from associations with the northern Utah universities, as had BNS, to get its first graduate program.

In 1974 a teacher certification program for training teachers of children with learning disabilities was added to the SUSC teacher education curriculum. The courses for a minor in health education were added to the offerings of the newly-formed department of physical education and health.

Also in 1974 the teacher education programs in the state of Utah came under fire from the Commissioner of Higher Education's Office and the Utah Board of Regents. A quota on the numbers of graduates in teacher education was imposed on each state institution. It had a brief leveling effect on the number of graduates from state colleges and universities, but inasmuch as the program producing the greatest numbers of teacher education graduates in Utah was a private university, Brigham Young University, the quota system was short lived.

In the academic year of 1974-75 James Miller replaced Kent Myers as dean of the School of Education. A minor in reading education was approved by the regents, and additional courses in teaching reading were added to the curriculum. The reading minor had incorporated within it the course work needed for the new certification program at SUSC for teacher education students who were to become teachers of children with learning disabilities.

At the beginning of the 1975-76 academic year Dean Miller organized the school with one department in teacher education and one in physical education. This structure was still in place in 1997. Kent Myers was named department chair in teacher education. A resource teacher education minor was added, which was to be the forerunner of a minor and then a major in Special Education. In 1978, Dr. Phillip Carter was named chair of teacher education. On September 1, 1979, the SUSC Reading Center and Clinic were established in the department of teacher education with Kent Myers as the director.

In 1979 the SUSC-USU Cooperative Master's of Education program was approved by the Board of Regents. James Miller became the SUSC director of the master's program, along with his duties as dean of the School of Education.

In 1980 a program for the preparation of middle school teachers was approved by the State Board of Education. Special outreach programs were held in the school districts throughout southern Utah by teacher education faculty to train teachers who needed course work to qualify for this certificate.

Also in 1980, the first annual SUSC Reading Conference was held on campus. It attracted teachers from Utah, Arizona and Nevada in goodly numbers and has remained a strong summer quarter event. Nationally renowned reading specialists and authors of children's literature come to campus for the event. State and local authors and educators also present workshops and seminars during the conference.

Summer school became summer quarter for the programs in teacher education. The demand for all required courses for elementary and secondary education majors had increased to the point where it had become necessary to provide a complete offering of course work all four quarters of the year.

In 1982 Mark Webster was named chairman of teacher education, and the curriculum was adjusted using Teacher Education Competency Guidelines. The next four years were years of curriculum consolidation. An increase in the number of outreach programs was made, with teacher education programs being offered each quarter in centers at Richfield and St. George. This created a dramatic increase in the number

of teacher education students; the professors in the department now had 60 to 90 students to advise each quarter.

Quenton Bowler was named chair of the department of teacher education in 1986. Graduate classes were offered off-campus in communities where the enrollment was sufficient. "Taking the program to the people" became a significant part of teacher education training. Faculty and staff were called upon to provide courses in increasing numbers at off-campus teaching stations. The cooperative master's program became stronger as a result.

DR. DONALD BARNES

In 1988 the course of study for the resource education minor was revised and renamed the special education minor. Enrollment in this program continued to grow. Also in 1988 the department of teacher education created an academic advisor office, and Gayle Garrett was hired, full-time, to advise the hundreds of education students. Faculty members could now deal with problems associated with the courses they taught, while Mrs. Garrett handled admission and academic scheduling advisement.

MARK WEBSTER

*I*n the politically explosive year of 1991 SUSC finally became a university; the name changed to Southern Utah University. That year the major in special education was approved, under the leadership of Dr. Donald Barnes.

Throughout the final five years of the first 100 years, the professional teacher education program in elementary education continued to produce the greatest number of graduates of any program at the University.

In 1994, upon the retirement of James Miller, Dr. Quenton Bowler served as acting dean of the School of Education while university administrators made a nation-wide search for a new dean. Kevin Robinson was appointed chair of the department of teacher education.

During the 1994-95 academic year, the cooperative masters program with USU was rescinded, and an independent master of education degree program was approved for SUU. The Board of Regents minutes of May 5, 1995 state:

DR. PHILLIP CARTER

Southern Utah University: Convert the Existing Cooperative Master of Education Degree with Utah State University to an Independent Master of Education Degree Administered by Southern Utah University. Southern Utah University officials requested authorization to convert to an independent Master of Education Degree. Concentrations in the program would include Language Arts, Science, and Social Studies within Secondary Education and Elementary Education...

A revised recommendation read:

It is the recommendation of the Commissioner that the Regents review Southern Utah University's proposal to separate the Master's of Education degree program from the joint program with Utah State University, raise additional questions and issues that need to be addressed, and, if satisfied, approve this proposal during the May Board meeting. It is further recommended that SUU Center at Dixie College be the only off-campus location approved by the Regents for the delivery of the independent M.Ed Program. Any future proposals for delivery of the program to additional off-campus sites will be presented to the Regents for consideration...

Regent Rogers asked about the number of participants in the cooperative M. Ed. Program. The response was an average of 100 historically, with an excess of 20 graduates each year.

The motion was unanimously adopted.

FRED
LUNENBURG

Teacher education at BNS-SUU had been connected to the University of Utah for its first 17 years and to Utah State University from 1913 until 1965, when the undergraduate program became independent. The graduate program had a USU connection for fourteen years, but now all teacher education programs were directed by the administration and faculty at Southern Utah University.

The dream of the pioneers, of a university independent of all others was now a reality.

In 1995 Fredrick Carl Lunenburg, a native of New York City, was hired as the dean of the College of Education, Southern Utah University. Prior to his becoming dean, he was professor of administration and higher education at the University of Louisville. He had previously taught English in high schools and served as a principal and superintendent of schools.

The growth of BAC to SUU has been possible because academic and support programs have been continually studied and improved. An enormous amount of time and effort has been spent by the faculty and staff in making sure that teacher education programs were accredited.

Four state and national groups have studied the programs over these 50 years and their recommendations have helped to improve the curriculum, the administration of the programs, and the services to students. The four groups are: NACTE (The National Association of College of Teacher Education), NASDTEC (National Association of State Directors of Teacher Education and Certification), The Northwest Association of Schools and Colleges and the Utah State Office of Education. The programs are fully reviewed every 10 years with a more concise review at five years. All programs are fully accredited at this date.

Innovations in the training of teachers were a continuous part of the second 50 years of teacher education at BNS-SUU. Cooperation with local school districts in Utah, Arizona, Nevada and California are elements of those innovations, as were special field experiences in thousands of classrooms. The continuous growth of the elementary education program and the addition of certification programs in secondary education, middle school education, early childhood education, media (library), and special education greatly expanded the need for classrooms where field experiences and student teaching could be completed.

*I*n 1950, teacher education was the only bachelor's degree program on-campus, and the need for originating and maintaining contact with public and private schools, who would be hiring the BAC teacher education graduates, was met by the teacher education staff and faculty. Placement files were created for each graduate; superintendents from Utah and Nevada came to BAC to interview candidates for professional employment. From the beginning a very high percentage of all graduates were placed in teaching positions. When SUSC became a four-year independent college, campus-wide placement services were added, student placement files being maintained at the Campus Placement Office.

In November, 1964, the Education Division staff helped organize some team teaching programs in the public schools and decided that they should practice what they preached. Dr.

Paul Vorkink and Dr. Morris Shirts teamed for a class entitled the "The American School System." "Introduction to Education" was taught by Dr. Paul Vorkink and Dr. Kent Myers. A third class was added in the second year of the experiment. Professor Vern Kupfer and Dr. McRay Cloward taught "Psychological Foundations for Teachers." It was a "fused" class which combined educational psychology and child growth and development. The results of the team teaching over a four-year period were generally positive and were reported in the *Educational Forum* in May, 1968.

A block of education courses was organized for majors, so that all courses could be taken in one quarter. This opened the way for a student to meet the required field experiences, spending one to three weeks of that quarter in an elementary or secondary classroom as an assistant to the teacher.

The block experience, which has prospered since its beginning, has made it possible for students to have in-the-field work at schools in Arizona, California, Nevada and Utah and to interact with a diverse faculty and student body in a variety of school settings. It continues to be a hallmark of the teacher education program as SUU begins its the second 100 years.

Using other professional fields as a model, the School of Education also organized internship programs with school districts in southern Utah. The Elementary Education Intern Program was initiated in 1968 by Dr. Robert Moss, continued informally until 1976 when it was formally approved, and ended when interns reported that mentoring was not often available when needed. The internship was the final year of the student teacher education program.

During the fifteen years from 1950 to 1965 almost all student teaching was completed in the Iron County School District. During the 1970's the growth of the program and the need for students to have experiences with children from minority populations caused the teacher education faculty to seek other localities as well as Iron County for field experiences.

An accreditation team advised that... "An in-depth experience (one or two weeks) should be provided elementary education majors in working with culturally and ethnically different (Chicano, Indian, Black, poor White) children." Dr. Gwyn Clark contacted Richard V. McMullin, principal of the Bureau of Indian Affairs Schools in Kayenta, Arizona, and made an agreement to have a limited numbers of elementary majors complete an early fall block of student teaching

in the Kayenta Schools. Inasmuch as there was no money in the budget for this experiment, Mr. McMullin agreed to house up to 12 student teachers in the BIA dormitories and allow students to eat in the BIA cafeteria. Students were assessed a fee of $100 to help defray the cost of supervision and travel. Nine students were selected from those who applied and successfully completed the five- week experience in the fall of 1973. This early fall experience was to become a regular option in student teaching and continues to this day.

DR. ROBERT MOSS

A short-lived experiment was conducted with the National Park Service. As the number of students in elementary and secondary education continued to grow, more and more students needed to be able to student teach during the summer quarter. Very few schools were available. The National Park Service had opened an environmental school at Bryce Canyon for the children of employees and park visitors.

During the spring of 1971 Dr. Morris Shirts worked with Jim Shaack, Chief Park Naturalist at Bryce Canyon, working out a pilot program for student teachers there. The program was discontinued in the late 70's for two reasons: excess costs and the experience did not prepare teachers for professional work in the public schools. However, the program was a harbinger of things to come. As the number of students in Utah public schools was growing rapidly in the 70's and 80's, year-round schools were opened in Provo, Jordan and Washington school districts. Summer quarter student teaching in these schools is now a common practice.

DEAN KENT MYERS

In 1974-75 the State Building Board seemed ready to approve the construction of a new building at SUSC. Dr. Morris Shirts had completed a planning guide for a new education building, and it appeared that the request for funding for that new building would be approved. The School of Business had also submitted plans and a request for a new building. In consultation with President Royden Braithwaite, Dean Kent Myers and Dr. Shirts, the previous dean, the teacher education faculty was asked to consider, instead of a new facility, the possibility of having Old Main remodeled for the School of Education. The

THE REMODELED OLD MAIN, HOME OF TEACHER EDUCATION

decision was made to have Old Main remain the home of teacher education.

In July of 1975 the planning guide for remodeling Old Main was submitted to the State Building Board and approved later that year. In addition to offices, classrooms and public areas, the new Old Main was to house a reading center and laboratory and a TV studio with an observation area. During 1976-1978 faculty and staff were shifted to other buildings, and Old Main was remodeled. When the original stone walls were uncovered during remodeling, the beauty of the stone and arches were so striking that plans were changed to leave the walls on the first floor exposed. This touch added to the historical "feel" of the grand old building. The department had come full circle.

At this writing teacher education remains in this historic building along with the reading center, but the TV studio has been converted to a computer lab, with TV taping completed in other campus facilities and in the Old Main classrooms using portable equipment.

The choice of old over new allowed the business building to be built a bit earlier, but put a space limitation on teacher education, which at the end of the 100 years is a reality. Additional offices and labs for teacher education will be located in the remodeled library building.

*E*ven prior to the remodeling of Old Main, the faculty had begun video taping teacher education students in micro-teaching situations on campus, and even some student teaching in the public schools, although the equipment was bulky. Morris Shirts, who had trained in audio-visual education, was able to put a television package together which allowed some portability and a quality picture. This innovation was a reality-check for both teacher education students and

faculty, who participated in evaluations, using a standard form. The feedback of performance from the faculty member was important, but the student's personal feedback of his performance was even more instructive. Many students really saw themselves as a teacher for the first time using these taped experiences. The camera told it as it was.

The TV studio was used for the micro-teaching and for faculty members to develop model lessons which were video taped and used as exemplars with their students. It was also the intent of the faculty to have outstanding teachers from nearby school districts bring their students into the classroom-studio and teach a lesson, while SUSC students observed. However, problems with logistics made the idea impractical. As the size of portable equipment became smaller and the quality of the picture better, the video taping was done in classrooms on campus and in the districts.

In 1994 the studio was remodeled to become a computer lab. The computer and the video recorder have proven to be important tools in teaching and in evaluation of student performance in the SUU teacher education program.

In February of 1951 the Branch Agricultural College Education Association (BACEA) was chartered. This organization, patterned somewhat after the Utah Education Association, had many social as well as professional functions. While student education organizations were already functioning at other colleges and universities, this was a "first" for BAC. The chartering was reported in the *Bacian* as follows:

A new club, organized for students majoring in education, has been formed on the Branch Agricultural College campus. The new organization has been formed to foster better student-teacher relations, promote educational ideals on the campus, bring prospective teachers in contact with educators in the area and encourage outstanding high school graduates to enter the field. Members of the new organization signed their charter at a banquet this week. Ianthus Wright, superintendent, Iron County schools, was the guest speaker at the charter banquet.

The student education association has been an active force in college and university throughout the past fifty years. The student leaders have received leadership and professional training which they could have obtained in no other way.

The enrollment in the programs of teacher

education at SUU over the last 50 years has been the most extensive of all the programs at the university. A total of 6,135 students have graduated and been recommended for professional certification in elementary and secondary education at Southern Utah University since 1950. Of these, 5,789 received bachelor's degrees and 346 received master's degrees. An additional 150 to 200 students who completed a degree at another college or university have completed their professional training in teacher education at SUU and have been recommended for certification.

Follow-up studies of these graduates have given the faculty helpful data for a continuous strengthening of training. The studies indicate that most of those trained in teacher education at BNS-SUU remained in the profession. Specific data on the number of graduates who went on to become school administrators (principals and superintendents) is not available, but the number is considerable. Many have also become teacher educators and administrators in colleges and universities throughout the nation.[5]

*F*or 50 years the strength and power of the teacher education program at Southern Utah University has been the dedication and caring of faculty and staff members.[6]

In 1966 Dr. Morris Shirts created the annual Pestalozzi Award to recognize the outstanding elementary and secondary graduate. Representative of all those who served with valor are four who received the special Pestalozzi award, given under very special circumstances, to educational leaders who had made significant contributions to teacher education at SUU.

While it is impossible to honor all the effective and caring faculty leaders in teacher education from BNS to SUU, it seems appropriate to include in this brief outline an abbreviated personal sketch of teacher education faculty members who received the special Pestalozzi awards.

• Dr. Morris Shirts, who received a special Pestalozzi award in 1972, was one of those who "made it happen" at SUSC. He was the first dean of the School of Education when SUSC became an independent four-year state college. His 25 years of service as a teacher and administrator helped create the reality which SUU enjoys as a pre-eminent teacher education program. He joined the staff of Southern Utah State College as an associate professor in 1959, was appointed chair of the Division of Education in 1962, and when the college was organized into

DR.
MORRIS
SHIRTS

schools in 1967, he was appointed dean of the School of Education and professor of education.

Dr. Shirts' distinguished career included two years as an advising professor to the National Teachers' College in Iran. In 1959 upon completion of the assignment in Iran, Morris Shirts came to SUSC, where he added substantively to the education program on many levels.

Dr. Shirts published many articles in professional educational magazines, as well as a book on Little League Baseball. He devoted many years to the welfare of boys, including as coach and as a scoutmaster. For two consecutive years his Boy Scout Troop 347 was recognized as one of the top 50 troops in the LDS Church. He organized Boy Scout hiking trails in southern Utah and spearheaded the establishment of a Boy Scout summer camp in Parowan Canyon. He was also active in the identification and preservation of historic sites in the area. He died early in 1997.

• Dr. Gwyn R. Clark, Special Pestalozzi Award recipient in 1974, was the spark that lit the flame of teacher education at BAC-CSU-SUSC. She taught at the university for 24 years—from 1950 through 1974. Dr. Clark taught her students to work hard, have a passion for teaching and always have a genuine concern for each student. She was instrumental in helping to build SUU's reputation for excellence in teacher education.

After 1950 Dr. Clark served as an assistant, associate and full professor in the department of elementary education. While at SUSC she served both as coordinator and chairman of elementary education.

In 1955-56 she served as a Fulbright teacher of English at the Tokyo University of Education and its attached schools. From 1964-66, and also during the summers of 1967-68, she served as associate professor of education and supervisor of the laboratory school at Haile Sellassie I University in Addis Ababa, Ethiopia, where, under the auspices of USAID, she helped to establish a school of education.

Dr. Clark published articles in *The Utah Educational Review, Elementary English, Peabody Journal of Education, Educational Leadership* and *Haile Sellassie Journal of Education.*

While at SUSC she held such offices as advisor to AWS and SEA, vice president and president of the faculty senate and editor of the faculty senate handbook. She had also served as chairman of a Title III project to develop a competency-based teacher education progam. In addition to the Pestalozzi Special Award, Dr. Clark also received, in 1974, the Outstanding Teacher Award, presented by the Southern Utah Chapter of Phi Delta Kappa.

After her retirement in 1974 Dr. Clark served on the Iron County School Board for 10 years. She was honored by the Business and Professional Women as one of the three outstanding women of Utah in 1988. SUU granted her an honorary doctor of humanities degree in 1992.

· Dr. Kent E. Myers, who was awarded the Special Pestalozzi Award in 1990, is the author of *SUU History, Teacher Education,* from which this outline history of the department of Education has been distilled. Dr. Myers is an emeritus professor of education at the time of this publication.

Dr. Myers was a teacher's teacher. His students' most common comment has been, "He teaches the way he wants us to teach, and he cares about us... When his comment on a student teaching evaluation read, 'I see a teacher,' you knew you had arrived." For Kent Myers, being called a "teacher" was the highest of all accolades.

Myers completed his master's degree in 1959 at BYU and accepted a position as an instructor in the English department of the College of Southern Utah that fall. He was awarded his doctoral degree from the University of Utah in

1964. The following year he was hired by the department of teacher education at the newly independent state college, Southern Utah State College.

While at SUU Dr. Myers was department head in teacher education, twice, and dean of the School of Education. He was the first director of the SUU Reading Center and organized the annual Reading Conference. He was named Professor of the Year at SUSC in 1969 and Distinguished Educator at SUSC in 1981 and 1988. He was named as Educator of the Year in 1987 by Phi Delta Kappa. He was also listed in *Who's Who in American Education*. He has also authored several professional and literary works.

During his tenure at SUU Dr. Myers also served as visiting faculty at BYU-Hawaii, was an honor faculty member at Arizona State University and a fellow at the University of British Columbia. Dr. Myers retired as professor of teacher education in 1990 and served one year as vice president of the Pacific Rim Institute of Culture and Language at Irvine, California.

· Cleo M. Petty, who received the Special Pestalozzi Award in 1979, began teaching at Branch Agricultural College in 1951.. He served as athletic director, department chair, HPER, and head coach of basketball and baseball. His first year at BAC saw the "Broncos" finish in sixth place at the NJCAA tournament in Hutchinson, Kansas. His baseball team finished in third place a few years later at the NJCAA tournament in Grand Junction, Colo. He received his M.S. degree from Utah State University during 1958-59. After returning to BAC (later changed to CSU) conference championships were won in both basketball and baseball.

Statistics reveal that after coaching and teaching for a period of 28 years at BAC, CSU, and SUSC, more than 425 athletes have been members of either his basketball or baseball teams. During recent years his baseball teams have won three RMAC championships, one NAIA District title, and finished in second place several other times. His wife, Jane, and all four children have graduated from the institution at Cedar City. He has devoted many years to youth baseball and organized the first Little League team in Cedar City during 1951.

Over the generations, scores of devoted faculty members inspired and trained literally thousands of teachers, whose influence extended into tens of thousands of lives—the fulfillment of the dream of the founders.

EARLY BNS GRADUATE EMMA GARDNER, BACK RIGHT, NEXT TO PRINCIPAL RALPH HUNTSMAN AND HER FELLOW TEACHERS AT MESQUITE ELEMENTARY.

CHAPTER IX

Physical Education and Athletics

We will run, we will score, 'til the thunder roars.

The small frontier college of the late 1890s provided limited opportunity for sports competition. Such was Cedar City's isolation then in a rugged, almost forgotten corner of the American west. In spite of this factor, the school mounted basketball, track and baseball teams to give its students a chance to participate, and competitions were scheduled with other schools and with towns and all-star teams, although the athletes had no chance to compete for titles or awards. For a quarter of a century, the school's teams competed wherever an opponent could be found.[1]

During the years from 1897 to 1923, the absence of nearby competitors limited the potential success of the institution's athletic program. Nevertheless, the reputation of the school's teams were enhanced by the quality of the seven coaches who served during this period: K.K. Steffensen, Harold H. Wilkinson,

BNS BASEBALL 1904, ERASTUS MILNE, COACH

Forrest Fletcher, Ernest Milne, Ernest Nohr, John C. Christensen, and John A. Young, who also served as the school's first true athletic director. The coaches were able to establish a strong loyalty to the institution through their hard work and emphasis on good sportsmanship.

BNS was essentially a high school, and athletic competition was with similar institutions. When the school made the transition to BAC in 1913, the college was still primarily a secondary school, and its basketball and track teams competed with other Utah high schools. In 1916, and again in 1918, SUU basketball teams won the Utah high school state championships. The school also won the state title in track and field in 1916. That period is known as the first "golden era" for sports at the college.

For SUU's first 44 years, the school included a

BNS TRACK TEAM, 1904, ERASTUS MILNE, COACH

BNS
WOMEN'S
HURDLES,
1903

high school division, and for the first 26 years college-level competition was limited to other two-year colleges in southern Utah, augmented with some high school teams. Sports competition was essentially confined to basketball, baseball and track, although an unsuccessful attempt was made to establish football at BAC in 1914, but the sport could not be maintained beyond the initial year. Women's athletics, though called "physical culture," included track and basketball.

In 1923 a new era began for SUU athletics. The emergence of other institutions in the mountain- states with similar athletic programs enabled the establishment of a new league and for the first time the school's athletes had the opportunity to compete for trophies and league titles. The athletic conference was organized with six other Utah and Idaho colleges. The conference's southern division consisted of BAC, Dixie College and Snow College; the northern division included Brigham Young College (Logan), Westminster College, Weber College

HAROLD
WILKINSON'S
WOMEN'S
BASKETBALL,
BNS, 1912

and Ricks College.

In the years that SUU competed in the Intermountain Collegiate Athletic Conference (ICAC) and its predecessor associations, a span of four decades, a distinguished cadre of coaches gave added luster to the institution's athletic fortunes. Among the standouts were John Young, Howard "Tuff" Linford, Hyrum Hunsaker, Nelson Tydings, Lee Liston, Murray Maughan, Ray Lindquist, Dave Gates, Cleo Petty, Bruce Osborne and Boyd Adams.

The decade that began in 1940 was destined to challenge SUU's athletic program as never before. The advent of World War II virtually depleted the male members of the student body and football was abandoned in 1943 for the war's duration. The same year, the school's basketball team again took top conference honors, but the following year a lack of players, due to the war, necessitated the canceling of basketball also.

With the end of World War II, enrollment at the college increased substantially and a full athletic program was reinstated. Competition resumed and the school's affiliation with the ICAC was renewed.

In 1965 the college received full baccalaureate status and stopped competing with junior college teams. For a time SUU participated as an independent school. In 1967 the school aligned its athletic program with the Rocky Mountain Athletic Conference, a venerable athletic alliance that traced its history back to 1909 and had included, at various times in its history, the University of Colorado, Colorado State University, Utah State University, Montana State University, the University of Wyoming, the University of Utah, Brigham Young University and Idaho State University. The RMAC was affiliated with the National Association of Intercollegiate Athletics (NAIA).

As for the front office, four men held the position of athletic director during the decade. The list included Petty (for the first two years), Bruce Osborne (1962-65), Boyd Adams (1965-67) and Osborne once again, this time for a

E. LEE LISTON

HYRUM
HUNSAKER

JOHN YOUNG
AND HIS
BASKETBALL
TEAM IN
THE FIRST
GYMNASIUM,
CIRCA 1920s

period of 12 consecutive years.

In 1967, at a meeting of presidents of 15 institutions, including Southern Utah University, the RMAC was reorganized into two divisions—mountains and plains—with SUU positioned in the mountains division. The conference separated into two independent conferences in 1972, with SUU in the division that retained the Rocky Mountain Athletic Conference name and consisted of institutions in Utah, Colorado and New Mexico.

Southern Utah University was a highly respected member of the RMAC for 19 years, during which time it accumulated an enviable record in the sports sponsored by the conference: football, basketball, baseball, women's basketball and women's volleyball.

In 1986 SUU withdrew from the RMAC to become an independent NCAA program at the Division II level, affiliating its football program with the Western Football Conference. The remaining sports conducted their programs as independents. The Western Football Conference had been formed in 1982, and the members of the conference, in addition to SUU, were California State University, Northridge; Santa Clara University; California State University, Sacramento; California Polytechnic State University, San Luis Obispo; Portland State University; and California Lutheran University.

In the fall of 1987, SUU elevated all of its athletic programs, except football, to the NCAA Division I level, competing as an independent. In doing so, it adopted an athletic format known as the "Santa Clara model," patterned after Santa Clara University, which conducted all its sports at Division I with the exception of football which, for cost containment considerations, was kept at a Division II level.

In the early 1990s, however, the NCAA adopted rules requiring that all sports be conducted at the same division level on a campus, eliminating the opportunity for SUU to conduct football at the Division II level. The new rules forced schools to either drop football, as Santa Clara did, or elevate the sport to Division I-AA status, as SUU, Northridge, Sacramento, and Cal Poly did.

On April 14, 1993, Southern Utah University, together with three other charter institutions, California Polytechnic State University at San Luis Obispo; California State University, Northridge; and California State University,

Sacramento, formed a new all-sports athletic conference named the American West Conference. The union of the four universities gave the conference a unique blend of both rural and urban institutions. All four universities were committed to continuing football, though at a cost-containment level which restricted the number of coaches and scholarships the football program could have. It was the hope of the charter institutions that other universities, which were also interested in restricting the costs of football, would later affiliate.

The American West Conference was to last but three years, as the three California institutions passed campus referendums increasing student fees for athletics. With more funds avail-

TRACK, 1916. L TO R, REAR: GELES CARROLL, FERNARD ESPLIN, DEVENHAM MORRIS, JOSEPH ARMSTRONG, ADAM SEEGMILLER, RALPH SANFORD, COACH JOHN CHRISTENSEN. MIDDLE: LEONARD BOWEN, LOREN SHURTZ, CLAIR GARDNER, CLYDE BUNKER, JUNIOR MCCONNELL, ALDRICH THORLEY. FRONT: - WHITAKER, ALTON NIELSON, ROSS GARDNER, WELLS WILLIAMS, SCOTT MATHESON, WILL JONES.

GYMNASIUM, 1927 (NOW THE HUNTER CONFERENCE CENTER)

able for their athletic programs, the schools abandoned their cost containment policies. Subsequently, Cal Poly was offered membership in the Big West Conference and took it. Both Northridge and Sacramento affiliated with the Big Sky Conference, leaving SUU without a conference. After a year as an independent, SUU accepted affiliation in the Mid-Continent Conference, effective the fall of 1997.

Facilities for physical culture and athletics were severely restricted during the BNS era. The school's athletic field was initially located west of Old Main, but its oval track was extremely steep and deemed totally unsuitable. In 1907 the athletic field was moved to a better site east of the existing school buildings, and the new grounds were laid out and planned after the stadium at the St. Louis Exposition.

The Utah Legislature, in 1907, appropriated $10,000 for a shop/gymnasium. The two-story building, which resembled the older two campus buildings but was considerably smaller, was erected in the summer of 1908. The lower floor was devoted to shops, while the upper floor was used as a gymnasium and later as a girl's dormitory. The gymnasium floor was small, with seats only on the sides, since there was limited space between the end lines and the walls. It was to be the home of the BNS/BAC athletic program for the next 19 years.

NYLES HUMPHRIES, 1927 GYMNASIUM

In 1927 the Utah Legislature appropriated $30,000 for the construction of a new gymnasium to be located north of the Old Main building. An architect was selected and plans for the new building were put out for construction bids. When the bids were opened, the lowest was $59,770, nearly twice the state appropriation. The Board of Trustees authorized proceeding with construction provided the State Board of Examiners would appropriate funds sufficient to cover the deficit. The Examiners agreed to allocate $6,000, on the condition that the college alumni association would match the sum. A loan was then underwritten by a number of Southern Utah citizens for another $25,000. The completed building cost $60,720. The construction of the gymnasium couldn't have come at a better time for in the winter of 1930 the old shop/gymnasium was destroyed by fire.

Prior to 1937, the college had but one coach for both the high school division and the college division. Often the college level athletes would be designated to coach the high school teams. In 1937 Edwin L. Peterson was hired as the first high school coach, Howard "Tuff" Linford retaining the college-level teams.

During the administration of J. Howard Maughan, improvements were made to the track and football field. In 1929 the field was repositioned to run north and south instead of the previous east and west orientation. It was leveled with a team of horses and scrapers, bleachers were built on the east slope, and concrete walls were constructed around the track. Grass was planted on the football field and shrubs were added to the slope.

Major improvements of the physical facilities during the 1940's added much to the school's athletic programs. With the help of the American Legion and the local power company, lights were added to the stadium in 1946. Attendance at night games showed a marked increase.

AERIAL VIEW OF THE WAR MEMORIAL FIELDHOUSE, CIRCA 1950'S

The BAC pep club, in 1937, sparked new enthusiasm when it presented the Dixie Junior College team captain with a wooden axe, as part of a stunt, after the BAC team had defeated Dixie in an athletic contest. The skit sparked such enthusiasm that the student body presidents of the two schools collaborated on an idea - that the competetive energy which the presentation of the axe had generated could be perpetuated. The long-standing tradition of exchanging an axe was thus born in the spirit of cooperation between fierce competitors.

Charles Merkley, a Dixie College instructor, crafted a fitting replica of an authentic battle axe with the names of the two schools emblazoned on the two sides of the ornate axe head, from which shimmered the school colors of each school in braided and tasseled silk.

The axe, prominently displayed at each Dixie and BAC game, was ceremoniously carried off by the victorious team and guarded until that team was next vanquished by its arch rival. At the end of the school year the school which had tallied the most wins took possession for the summer months.

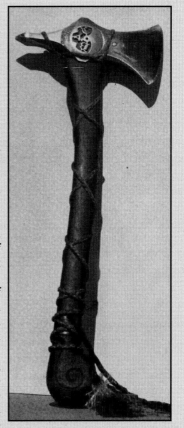

The axe became an emotional focus. Once, in February of 1941, the Dixie team somehow failed to retrieve it, though they'd won the game. Pretty Ravenna Leigh, BAC's only girl cadet, and her co-pilot, Quinn Jones, flew the axe to Dixie and presented it to Jack Rencher, Dixie College student body president

When the traditional rivalry was discontinued at the beginning of fall quarter of 1963, as BAC left the junior college ranks to compete against four-year schools, the question arose of what to do with the axe. The BAC Executive Council decided that BAC should present the axe to Dixie. Not so fast! BAC's Letterman's Club spearheaded a wildly-supported drive to override the council's decision by offering other alternatives: the axe could be cut in half; the school with the best win-loss record should keep the trophy or an exact duplicate be made, so that each school could have the prize. When the last alternative was agreed upon, Rice Machine Company in Cedar City presented a beautiful copy for inspection, which was accepted by student body presidents Derrill Larkin of Dixie and Richard Henrie of BAC. The two flipped a coin for the original; both carried home a treasured axe.

Director Royden Braithwaite of BAC and Acting Dixie President, Lorraine Woodbury, indicated their satisfaction, Mr. Woodbury concluding, "This should certainly be most conducive to the future good feelings between these two fine institutions."

The inadequacy of the college gymnasium had been apparent for more than a decade and community and college leaders began planning for a new field house. The Utah Legislature appropriated $30,000 toward the building, the Cedar City Livestock Association, Iron County School District and Iron County contributing another $17,000.

Ground breaking ceremonies were held on April 7, 1948, with Gov. Herbert B. Maw driving a bulldozer to break the ground. Unfortunately the project experienced several delays. There was a lack of bidders for the concrete work, and when bids were finally received and opened, the amount was higher than the available funds. The project was set back again when the second bids exceeded revenues. An appeal to the State Building Commission to let construction begin, while fund-raising efforts were still underway, was approved; work on the building began. To reduce costs, materials from the Japanese Relocation Center in Topaz were obtained, but due to insufficient funds, construction slowed. Completion of the building was assured in May, 1949, when the USAC Board of Trustees approved a plan for the selling of bonds to finance construction costs. The college imposed a student field house building fee of $6.00 per year and also directed that the gate receipts at the field house be used to retire the bonds. On February 24, 1950, the first basketball game was played in the field house. It was officially dedicated on December 8, 1950, as the War Memorial Field House.

In 1965 the department moved into a new $3 million physical education building with a large gymnasium, natatorium, two handball courts, a dance studio, classrooms and offices. Constructed with funds provided by the Utah Legislature, the completed building gave the physical education program a decided shot in the arm. The department had never before had access to a swimming pool, and the lack of one had always been a detriment to the program. The gymnasium was actually three gymnasiums in one and allowed the department to schedule a variety of activities at the same time.

What was not anticipated, however, was the collapsible nature of the soils upon which the facility was built. Three years after the building opened, cracks began to appear in the swimming pool area, and water began leaking out of the pool. In 1977 an attempt was made to pour grout under the pool to prevent further leaks but the building was to be vexed by similar problems related to soil conditions for the next two decades.

In 1968 the school moved its stadium to a

ARCHITECT'S
RENDERING
FOR NEW STA-
DIUM, TO BE
COMPLETED IN
THE SUMMER
OF 1997.

new site west of the campus. The relocated stadium had seating for people, together with rest rooms and an oval track. Remodeling in 1987 added offices, as well as dressing and training rooms. The total cost of the original construction and the remodeling was $246,510.

The opening of the 5,300-seat Centrum in 1985 provided a giant leap for SUU's athletic program and represented the reward of an amazing community fund-raising effort launched in 1983 with the formation of a committee of more than 300 volunteers. A total of $2.1 million was generated in less than nine months. Translated to a per capita figure, the campaign yielded about $150 for every man, woman and child in Iron County.

Impressed by the success of the fund raising effort, the Utah Legislature appropriated $5.7 million for a facility that would uniquely combine an arena with classrooms and other academic areas. Construction began in March of 1984, and after some delays caused by the conditions of the soil upon which the building was to rest, the facility was complete. SUU hosted its first basketball game on November 22, 1985. With the completion of the Centrum, SUU moved into a new athletic age.

In the twelve years since the opening of the Centrum, there have been other improvements in SUU's athletic facilities. The college stadium, renamed the Coliseum of Southern Utah, was renovated in phases. Under the leadership of the Cedar City Lions Club, concrete seats on the east side of the stadium were built, much of the labor being provided by the Lions Club and other community volunteers. A south colonnade with fountains and staging platforms, new rest rooms and ticket concession and storage facilities were later added. A major renovation of the west stands in 1997, funded by $1.5 million in private gifts and a $600,000 revenue bond backed by student fees, provided five new chair-back seating sections, open-air corporate boxes, a new press box and a series of skyboxes.

At the south end of the stadium, the Jay Dee and Alice C. Harris Center was constructed, also in phases, through private gifts and student fees. The center's distinctive architecture, with its pair of obelisks and Grecian elements, anchored the Coliseum and gave it a unique appearance. The building's center gymnasium contained facilities for the SUU gymnastics team. The west wing included dressing rooms; offices for the gymnastics, track, softball, and the baseball coaches; and, on the second floor, an athletic department suite for the athletic director and his staff, the academic counselor and the sports information offices. South of the Harris Center the University constructed a four-court outdoor tennis complex.

A mong the men's sports SUU has sponsored over the years are football, basketball, golf, baseball, track and field, and wrestling, but clearly the two dominant sports have been basketball and football.

Athletic competition at the college level began during the 1920s. Small enrollments at the college and the lack of facilities limited the number of competitive athletic events in which the school could participate. The two major sports were basketball and track.

The small college gymnasium was inadequate in all respects. Not only was it adverse to good training, but it was not large enough to hold the crowds who wanted to come to watch the basketball games. But the hardships did not hinder the enthusiasm of the athletes, who earned a reputation for being clean and sportsmanlike players.

Serving as coaches in the period prior to World War II were Jack Christensen (1914-26) John A. Young (1927-28) H. B. "Tuff" Linford (1928-36) Hy Hunsaker (1935-36) and Linford again (1936-40.)

The 1924 basketball team had a 13 and 1 record. The SUU basketball team won the conference championship in 1928, 1929, 1930, 1931, and 1934. In 1929 the college won the Utah-Idaho Junior College Tournament.

The school's success in basketball in the late '30s and early '40s was not as great. Because of World War II, league play was suspended in 1943, in favor of a single tournament, which SUU won by defeating Dixie College in championship play. No team was fielded in 1944 but basketball returned in 1945 with Lee Liston and Ty Tydings as coaches. Ray Lindquist replaced Tydings in 1947 and served for five years. He was succeeded in 1952 by Cleo Petty.

In 1946 the BAC Broncos earned a spot in the Western States Basketball Tournament, composed of the top 16 teams in California, Oregon, Washington, Arizona, Idaho, Wyoming, Colorado, New Mexico and Oklahoma, and captured fourth place honors. In 1947 and 1948, the Broncos were again selected to attend the Western States Basketball Tournament, placing eighth in 1947.

In the 1950s, Southern Utah University entered its second "golden era." In 1952 the SUU basketball team, under coach Cleo Petty, qualified for the region tournament in Ogden,

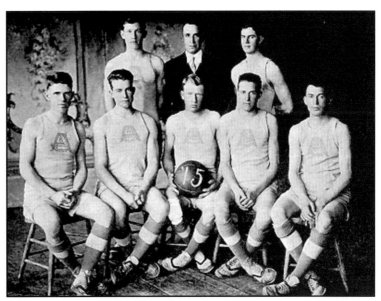

Utah. In the three-day tournament, the Broncos defeated Northern Montana, Boise College and Weber State. This championship qualified them for the National Tournament held in Hutchinson, Kansas.

Steve Lunt records this account of the SUU basketball team at the national tournament:

To get to the national tourney, money had to be raised as there was nothing left in the budget. Raffles, auctions of donated articles, and bake sales were held to raise the money. Two automobile companies donated the use of automobiles. Finally mustering enough money, the team left and drove most of the way in a snowstorm. On the opening day of the tournament, SUU defeated Graceland College 81-60, and also defeated Grays Harbor College 76-69 in the second round, to make SUU the dark horse and Cinderella team of the tourney. In the semi-final game, SUU lost a real heartbreaker 70-68 to Hibbing College. SUU played for third and sixth place honors on the last day, and lost to Hannibal College in an overtime 63-61, giving SUU sixth place in the nation. Don Marshall, from Minersville, was named to the Jr. College All-American team. Final records showed 23 victories and ten defeats. Named to the All-Conference teams were Boyd Adams, Don Marshall, Bob Hortin and

COACH JACK CHRISTENSEN'S BASKETBALL TEAM, 1915

STEVE LUNT

Neil Christiansen. Named as player of the year was Don Marshall.

Among the outstanding players of the decade of the 50's were Max Bond, Dent Sorensen, Don Tuft, Boyd Adams, John Wood, Keith Cooley, Bob Davis, Jerry Frame, Jim Spencer and Paul Rasmussen. Boyd Adams replaced Cleo Petty as coach of the men's basketball team in 1959 while Petty took a sabbatical. In the school's final three years as a junior college, the top players were Ray Greenberg, Larry Dehlin, and George Rekoutis.

The year 1963 marked a milestone for SUU's basketball team which began competition with four-year colleges and universities. Boyd Adams served as head coach from 1963 to 1971, followed by Stan Jack (1971-80), Tom McCracken (1980-83), Bob Schermerhorn (1983-87), Neil Roberts (1987-92) and Bill Evans (1992 to present.)

In 1967 SUU affiliated its athletic program with the Rocky Mountain Athletic Conference. In basketball, SUU won the RMAC conference championship in 1978 and again in 1983, and was runner-up on seven other occasions. Among the leading players of the period were Larry Moore, Dave Pinamonti, Skip Mead, Al Winfield, Scott Gilmore, Hal Hamblin, Kohn Smith (who was to later serve as head coach at Utah State University), Steve Laing, Robert Dunn Lee, Kerry Rupp, Marc Wilson, Butch Douglas, Dave Knudsen, Dean O'Driscoll, Karl Anderson, Shawn Daniels, Derrick Johnson, Russell Otis and Michael Alexander.

The year 1988-89 was SUU's first as a Division I institution. Neil Roberts, an outstanding athlete at Cedar High School and basketball player at BYU, had replaced Bob Schermerhorn the previous year as coach of the SUU men's basketball team, and posted a 16-11 win-loss record. Roberts' first year at the Division I level produced a 10-18 record, but the next year the T-Birds won 16 to 12 losses. Roberts stepped down as head coach mid-way through the 1991-92 year, but the team went on to win 20 games to but 8 losses. Roberts' legacy to SUU was the knowledge that the school could be competitive at the Division I level in basketball.

Replacing Roberts as basketball coach was Bill Evans, who took SUU into the newly-formed American West Conference. During the AWC's three years of competition, SUU was conference champion twice and runner-up once.

Among the top players of the Division I era were Reggie Ingram, Jon Gaines, Keith Berard, Andy Ward, Richard Barton, Dana Achtzehn, Davor Marcelic, Peter Johnson, Jerry Naulls and Ted Thomas.

Howard B. Linford, known to everyone as "Tuff," came to SUU in 1928 and inaugurated the college's football program that fall. He coached at SUU from 1928 to 1940, except for a sabbatical year in 1935-36. The first season consisted of three games, with the "Branch Aggies" winning two and losing one. By 1930 there were five games on the schedule.

Football grew rapidly in popularity in the 1930's, capped by an undefeated league championship in 1931. SUU's 1934 team won four games and lost but one, Westminster College and Snow College being the only two schools to appear on the schedule.

Hyrum Hunsaker served as coach during Linford's sabbatical and had a split season of two wins and two losses. Linford returned in 1936, and in 1938 the team won the runner-up spot in league standings. The 1940 team posted the best marks of the era with seven wins, two losses, and a tie. Linford resigned as coach and was replaced by Nelson "Ty" Tydings.

World War II interrupted the football program for two years (1943 and 1944.) Football resumed in 1945 with Tydings and Lee Liston as coaches. In 1946, Murray Maughan took

BOYD ADAMS

HOWARD B. "TUFF" LINFORD

MURRAY MAUGHAN

ROY
LINDQUIST

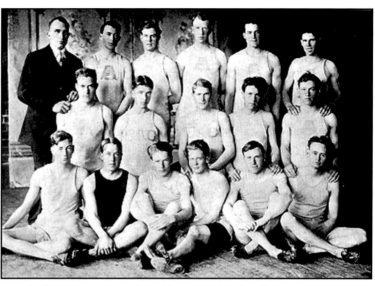

over as head coach. Maughan added the nation's number one ranked team, Compton College of Compton, Calif., to the schedule, and on game day it began to snow and continued to snow the entire game. Compton won the contest, 26-18, but it was the closest game Compton had for several years.

Maughan resigned as coach in 1950 and was replaced by Dave Gates, who in turn was replaced by Bruce Osborne in 1954. Osborne's initial coaching year was one of the most successful in SUU's history to that date, posting a six win and one loss record.

In 1956, Dee Smith, a guard on the football team, was selected to the National Junior College All-American Football Second Team. Other standouts of the period were Lewis Edwards, Kent Myers, Don Keeney, Jim Porter, Ron Hauser, Clifford Craig, Eric Gardner, Jim Marshall, and Ron Mayne.

The 1961 football season was the first since football began at SUU that a team failed to win at least one game, but the school rebounded the next year to a third place league finish. The annual game with Dixie College that year was notable because of an accident involving the team bus in a rain storm just south of Cedar City. In order to get the team to St. George, cars traveling south were stopped to transport the players and their equipment to the game, whose unusual score ended six to two for SUU. Ron Mayne earned junior college All-America honors, a first ever for football at SUU. After graduating from college, Mayne pursued a career in professional wrestling under the name "Mad Dog Mayne." His career was cut short when he was killed in an automobile accident.

In 1963 SUU's football program ended junior college competition as the four-year college era began. Serving as football coaches have been Osborne to 1964, followed by Bill Reeske (1965-66), Tom Kingsford (1967-77), Jack Bishop (1978-82 and 1986-95), Don Conrad (1983-86), Rich Ellerson (1996) and C. Ray Gregory (1997). In the 19 years SUU participated in the RMAC, the team placed in the top three in football in the conference nine times and was twice runner-up to the conference championship.

Among the outstanding football players in the '60s and '70s were Rick Traasdahl, who was named to All-American NAIA honors in 1965,

and whose jersey, number 60, was retired at the time; Doug Wolter, Pat Rippee, John Pensis, Bob Schexnayder, Doug Berry, Bill Jones, Don Conrad, Jeff Keel, Stan Jones, Gil Roderiquez, Dave Castro and Lane Martino. Lenny Walterscheid was drafted by the Chicago Bears of the National Football League, where he became the defensive captain and the Bears' kickoff return specialist.

In the seven years SUU participated in the American West Conference, the Thunderbirds earned second place honors three times (1989, 1991, and 1992) and third place once (1990.)

JACK
CHRISTENSEN'S
BAC TRACK
TEAM

DIXIE LEAVITT, BAC FOOTBALL, CIRCA 1949

BRUCE
OSBORNE

BILL
REESKE

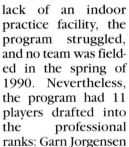

JACK
BISHOP

The conference's coveted Pat Malley Award was won three times by SUU athletes: Everett Kelepolo in 1989 and Steve McDowell in 1990 and Jared Hunsaker in 1993. The 1991 season was SUU's best, the team winning seven games to three losses and one tie.

Outstanding SUU football players in AWC play were Brent Bailey, Ken Smith, Chad Richard, Richard Bailey, Thane Marshall, Kelvin Minefee, Herkey Marksen, Randy Bostic, Steve McDowell, Rich Carter, Brad Mathews, Zed Robinson, James Armendariz, Ryan Monier, Mike Key, Darren DeGracie, Curtis Lindsey and Kevin Cuthbertson.

From 1993 through 1995–three years–SUU's football team played in the American West Conference as an NCAA Division I-AA program. Jack Bishop's team in 1993 tied for the conference championship. Rick Robins, Kevin Cuthbertson, Anthony Brown, Jeff Galyean, Craig Van Woerkom, Benji Hoskins, Jared Hunsaker and Daniel Harris were among those receiving media accolades.

At the end of the 1995 season, Jack Bishop elected to concentrate on his athletic director responsibilities, turning over the head football coaching position to Rich Ellerson, who posted four wins to seven losses in his single year at the helm of the independent football program.

Baseball was added to the athletic program during the 1940s; however, participation was limited. For example, in 1947 SUU was ICAC champion, but only three games were played and but four in 1948. In 1949 a baseball league was organized involving SUU, Weber, Snow, and Carbon colleges. Under the direction of Coach Cleo Petty, the 1963 SUU baseball team won the ICAC title, the District Seven championship, and finished third in the NAIA tournament. Steve Calhoon and Gordon Loveless were named to the NAIA All-American team.

From 1964 through 1989, SUU's baseball team had but four winning seasons (1964, 1965, 1966 and 1986) although it took top conference honors in 1952, and the conference and region championships in 1963. Plagued by budget restraints and the

lack of an indoor practice facility, the program struggled, and no team was fielded in the spring of 1990. Nevertheless, the program had 11 players drafted into the professional ranks: Garn Jorgensen to the Oakland Athletics (1980), Tony Pappas to the San Francisco Giants (1980), Dave Lenderman to the Chicago Cubs (1983), Darren Garrick and Darrell Pruitt to the Chicago White Sox (1984), Todd Moriarty (1984) and Rick Lundahl (1986) to the San Francisco Giants, Mike Ryser to the Oakland Athletics (1987), Brian Whittaker to the Cincinnati Reds (1987), Bill Robertson to the Milwaukee Brewers (1988), and Dave Mineer to the Colorado Rockies (1993). As free agents, Jed Murray went with the Seattle Mariners (1980) and Thane Woodard, Floyd Armstrong, and Blaine Reber to the Salt Lake Trappers (1989.

Baseball coaches, in the four-year era, have been Cleo Petty (1963-79), Stan Jack (1979-80), Hack Mitchell and Don Conrad (1980-81), Larry Wilson (1981-84), Bill Groves (1984-89), Gordon Dotson (1990-91), Steve Rollo (1991-92), Tom O'Gorman (1992-93), and Jeff Scholzen from 1993 to the present.

Brent Orchard, golf professional at the Cedar Ridge Golf Course, was instrumental in getting golf started at SUU. He served as coach of the golf team from 1967 to 1977, followed by Gale Parcell (1977-78), Tom Kingsford (1978-91), and John Evans (1991-).

The 1984 golf team won the RMAC championship and came within four strokes of the NAIA District Seven title. Among the outstanding student athletes in golf have been O'Neil Brerton, Neil Jenkins, Bob Roberts, Jeff Carr, Kim Thompson, Tom Higbee, John McArthur, Kevin Averett, Dean Cooper, Stuart Adams, Brett Wilkinson, Todd Mills, Ken Thornock, Jason Mitchell, Jason Reynolds, Cameron Cowan, Corey Monsen and Tom Johnson.

The University sponsored a wrestling program for 20 years from 1960 to 1980, when the sport was discontinued permanently. Among the stalwarts

CLEO PETTY

TOM
KINGSFORD

DAVID
GATES

on the wrestling team were Keith Seals, Ladd Holman, Lafe Parrish, Craig Rollo, Phil Howa, Robert Sanders, Eusebio Sams, Joe Taylor, Ron Parker, Neil Callister, Dave Hatch, Paul Logue and Ken McKnight. The teams were coached by Bruce Osborne, Bill Reeske and Joe Lopour.

Information on the early years of track and field is incomplete but the sport has been a part of SUU from almost the beginning. It is known that Vertis Wood entered the BYU Invitational Track and Field Meet in 1927 and placed fourth among competitors. Track and field was hampered by bad weather and a lack of student interest in the 1930s but had significant growth in the 1940s, except for the war years when the sport was discontinued.

In the late 1940s and early 1950s SUU produced a series of powerhouse teams led by Dan Lindsey, Bunny Fullmer, Boyd Rollins, Bob Nowers, Bob Peterson, Dahl Gleave, Gareth Spencer, Darwin Woodbury, Dixie Leavitt and Murray Edwards, among others. Six consecutive conference championships were posted from 1946 through 1951.

Among those serving as coaches in track and field and in cross county (which was added in 1975) were Nelson Tyding, Lee Liston, David Gates, Bruce Osborne, Steve Lunt, Boyd Adams, Ben Davidson, Joe Lopour, Paul Maggio and Eric Houle.

Outstanding track and cross country athletes in the period from 1950 to 1997 have been L. Dee Shakespear, Ben Davidson, Robert Shirts, Will James, Travis Anderson, Dave Houle, Eric Houle, Tim Pilling, David Dix and Travis Anderson.

Women's athletics began at SUU in 1968 with the hiring of Kathryn Berg as a physical education instructor and coach. Prior to 1968, participation in sports by women was limited to sports days with other Utah colleges. These teams were coached first by long-time physical education and dance teacher LaVeve Whetten, then successively by Kathy Major and Kaye Hart.

From 1968 to 1970 the school sent teams to meets staged by the Wasatch Area Athletic and Recreation Federation for College Women (WARFCW.) The Federation, organized to further athletic interests and activities for women

SUSC
CHEER-
LEADERS

in northern Utah, allowed regional colleges to enter two teams in its Friday and Saturday competitions. It was not uncommon in basketball to play five games in a day and a half, and players jokingly insisted they were really participating in marathon and endurance tests.

The WARFCW disbanded in 1970, and the college affiliated with the Association of Intercollegiate Athletics for Women's (AIAW) Intermountain Division, which included colleges and universities in Utah, Idaho, Wyoming, and Colorado. Membership in the AIAW meant increased opportunities, with the advent of regional competition and established sports seasons with specific numbers of scheduled games, and season-ending championships. Opportunities for national competition were also available through divisional and regional play.

Many of the women who participated in athletics during the early years played in at least

WOMEN'S
BASKETBALL,
1915

ATHLETIC
ASSEMBLY,
LAVEVE
WHETTEN,
KATHRYN
BERG, AND
JOE LOPOUR,
1972

two sports and often three. They traveled, played and practiced under conditions that were not the best. Practice times for women's athletics were scheduled outside the traditional academic day so that classes, intramurals and men's athletic practice times would not be inconvenienced.

From 1968 to 1973, women athletes wore a standard uniform of a white shirt and shorts, provided by the athletes themselves. In 1970 Coach Berg made fabric turquoise numbers which she sewed to the uniforms. In 1973, the college purchased its first set of uniforms for women athletes.

The women's programs competed in the

WOMEN'S BASKETBALL,
1971

KATHRYN
BERG

AIAW's Intermountain Division from 1970 to 1976, and from 1977 to 1979 they were in the AIAW's Rocky Mountain Division. The women's program participated in the Rocky Mountain Athletic Conference from 1979 to 1985. During those seven years, SUU had the conference's premier program. The school's teams had an opportunity to compete at the NAIA national level in all of the sports the college sponsored.

From 1988 through 1993, SUU's women's teams competed at the NCAA Division I level. As independents, home contests were difficult to schedule, but away games included contests with many of the nation's top women's teams.

The women's program competed in the American West Conference, for the three years that the conference was in existence, in basketball, track and cross-country and tennis. The University won the basketball championship two years, and the cross-country team placed second at the 1995-96 meet.

During the 1996-97 school year all SUU teams competed as independents awaiting affiliation in 1997-98 with the Mid-Continent Conference.

Serving as gymnastics coaches have been Kathryn Berg (1968-71), LaDawn Allen (1976-77), Kathryn Berg again (1977-88), Brent Hardcastle (1988-91), and Scott Bauman (1991 to present). Competing at the NAIA level from 1977 to 1988, the program suffered from a lack of funding and inadequate facilities. Everyday the equipment had to be set up by the athletes and coaches themselves, which reduced the amount of time available for practice. Through the years 1989 to 1991, the gymnastics program experienced considerable change. The school moved from college to university level and the program made the transfer from NAIA level to the top level of the NCAA. Money and resources improved, and a modern practice facility was constructed.

In the gymnastics program's first year at the NCAA Division I level, SUU achieved the nation's largest jump in scores, an advance of almost 13 points. The following year the program made another three-point jump and qualified the first athlete at the NCAA Division 1 level in post-season competition. The 1990-91 season put the Lady Thunderbirds on the national map. The team broke the elusive 190 mark on several occasions during the year and registered wins against such top 20 teams as Utah State, Boise State, and University of

Denver. The 1995 season saw the women gymnasts shatter all campus records. The team would surpass the old record of 192 set in 1993 numerous times and narrowly missed the regional team championships. In 1996 the SUU team scored a high of 194.2 against the University of Utah, which put SUU gymnastics in the upper echelon of the sport and gained national rankings as high as 13th.

Serving as softball coaches at SUU have been Kathryn Berg (1968-72), Christine Cooper (1972-73), Sandra Bryant (1974-75), Joe Hillock (1975-76, Joy Peterson (1976-79), Val Peterson (1979-80), Bruce Osborne (1981-82), Karma Zeeman (1982-83) and Joy Peterson again (1984-97).

While competing in the RMAC, the Lady Thunderbird softball team went to three NAIA national tournaments, and pitcher Christine Razmic was named to the NAIA All-American team in 1984. Coach Joy Peterson earned District 7 Coach of the Year honors five times. Softball was elevated to NCAA Division I status in 1988 and in 1990 the team affiliated with the Western Athletic Conference, one of the two best softball conferences in the nation. In 1990-91 the team was recognized as being the number two academic team in the nation, and in 1992-93 the team placed among the top 10 softball academic teams in the NCAA.

Kathryn Berg was the first head coach for women's basketball (1968-72 and 1973-74). She was followed by Christine Cooper (1972-73), Sandy Bryant (1974-75), Joe Hillock (1975-76), Joy Peterson (1976-82), Boyd Adams (1982-88), Clay Anderson (1988-90), Gordon Kerbs (1990-91), Larry Shurtliff (1991-96), and Joe Hillock again (1996 to the present).

The 1974-75 and 1975-76 teams qualified to advance to regional and national AIAW competition. The 1975-76 team was selected for the first small college national tournament and was led by Cheryl Eyraud and Laura Bailey. In 1976-77 Coach Peterson's team placed first in the RMAC and third in the region with an 18-4 record. The SUU women's team had six winning seasons in the 1980s, capped by a 18-8 record in 1987-88. Boyd Adams' team captured the RMAC championship, the bi-district tournament and went to the NAIA nationals in Kansas City, Missouri. During one of the best seasons for women's basketball in SUU's history, the players were saddened at mid-season by the illness of Coach Boyd Adams, who died of cancer the following summer. Competing in the American West Conference in 1994-96, under the direction of Coach Larry Shurtliff, the team

GYMNASTICS TEAM, 1987-88

won two championships and completed a perfect conference win-loss record both years.

Southern Utah University's volleyball program began in 1968 and was discontinued 21 years later. Kathryn Berg served as its first coach (1968-75), followed by Joy Peterson (1976-87), and Alema Teó (1988). In the RMAC, the volleyball team won seven consecutive championships (1978 to 1984), and participated in two national NAIA tournaments. Volleyball coach Joy Peterson was named RMAC coach of the year seven times. Lori McCurdy was named to the NAIA All-American team in 1981. In 1985-86, after nine years as a volleyball power in the NAIA's District 7, the SUU team had its first losing season in ten years. In 1988, the sport was discontinued as part of a campus-wide funding reduction ordered by the Utah Legislature.

Kathryn Berg was also the first coach for women's track and cross-country teams. For the sport's first eleven years (1968-79) Berg was coach, succeeded by Ben Davidson (1979-86), Joe Lopour (1986-90), Paul Maggio (1990-92), and Eric Houle (1992 to present.) In 1970, at the Intermountain AIAW Track Meet at Idaho State University, SUU placed second behind BYU. Geneva Harris took first in the shot put, Patti Pead took javelin honors and Irene Harris set a new intermountain discus record with a throw of 114 feet. In 1979 two outstanding athletes, Mary Diamani and Michele Hebberd brought home national championships, Diamani in the 1500 meter race and Hebberd in the high jump. Other national competitors were

WOMEN'S
SWIM
TEAM

Jolene Fisher in the marathon and Jill Reynolds and Lisa Bounhius in the javelin. In 1995 the SUU women's team placed second in the American West Conference cross-country championships.

Women's swimming was a varsity sport at SUU from 1968 to 1973. Kathryn Berg was swimming coach from 1968 to 1971 and again from 1972 to 1973. Steve Tomlinson coached the team for a year in 1971-72. The team competed against swim teams in Utah and Idaho, but the sport was discontinued because the college found it difficult to field a full and competitive team.

Women's tennis was added in 1993 to meet NCAA requirements that the school have seven sports for women at the Division I level. Coach Lenny Lee has coached a team that has had an improving record each of the four years the sport has been sponsored by the school. In his initial year as coach, the team consisted of students enrolled at SUU who had an interest in playing tennis. Recruiting players to the team began in the sport's second year.

CHEERLEADERS,
1969

The lyrics to SUU's popular fight song are relatively new, but the tune (composed by the legendary music professor William "Pa" Manning in the late 1920s) has spanned four of the University's five name changes and symbolizes both the continuity and change of the institution itself–as well as it's physical education and athletic programs.[2]

We will cheer for the red and white.
Of our fighting SUU
Hear our battle cry,
Echo through the sky,
As our team goes blazing through.
They will fight, fight, fight,
When they hear us shout,
As we sing our victory song,
We will run, we will score,
'Til the thunder roars,
And the T-Birds win once more.

From 1923 to 1965–43 years–the school competed in sports as a junior college. During the more than four decades, the college developed a number of rivalries but none so intense as with Dixie College in St. George, Utah. Because of the close proximity of the two schools, it was only natural that athletic competition played a major part of student activities. Sometimes the rivalry caused students to extend their extra-curricular activities in trying to out-do the others in various pranks which would upset the other student body. Over the years there were many incidents that kept the competitive spirit between the two schools alive.

One year students from BAC attempted to paint the Dixie "D" on the hill above St. George in the colors of BAC and were caught and reprimanded. In retaliation, members of the Dixie student body marked a large "D" by sprinkling salt on top of the snow on the football field. This was not discovered until the next spring when a 35-foot "D" appeared on the field in the grass where the turf had been killed by the salt.

Another well-known incident occurred when three or four former Cedar High School students and athletes at the college took the Dixie Rebel flag from the balcony of the Dixie field house after a ball game. Immediately after the game, Dixie officials noticed the flag missing. SUU students had been observed in the vicinity of the flag. A call to the Utah Highway Patrol in Cedar City caused them to set up a roadblock just south of town. The SUU students were stopped and asked to get out of the car while the patrol officer searched it. They failed to find the flag, because it had been folded carefully and placed under the back of a coat being worn by Ken McKnight. A few days before Dixie College was to play SUU in basketball in Cedar City, the flag was observed being used as a saddle blanket on a horse that Gary Anderson was riding around campus. Word went out by President Braithwaite, Cleo Petty and Bruce Osborne that the flag was to be returned to Dixie College immediately. At the halftime of the Dixie-SUU basketball game the flag was presented to the Dixie student body by lowering it from the ceiling of the field house where it had been secreted by those who had stolen it and had been unobserved by anyone from either college. When the Dixie student body saw their flag being lowered from high in the girders of the War Memorial Field House, a near riot broke out. It required more than 15 minutes to clear the floor, quiet the students and continue the game.

Attendance at the Dixie-BAC basketball games was always at capacity, and those who wanted to attend often came to the games an hour or more before starting time. The games were broadcast over KSUB radio, but the gym was so crowded that the announcers were placed in the corner of the building over the heat vents.

Edwin L. Peterson, together with Arthur Higbee, did the play-by-play announcing for KSUB. When the BAC-Dixie games were held in St.George, several broadcasts were plagued by pulled power lines, forcing the station off the air for some time. Peterson noted that the pulled lines often came when BAC was ahead.

On one occasion, the game was very close, Dixie being ahead by one point. A BAC player was fouled,and the referees gave him two shots, which, had he made them, would have given BAC a one point victory. The Dixie College gym had a track which ran around the top of the gym at the height of the scoreboard. The track was filled with spectators and a Dixie fan leaned over the scoreboard waving a cowboy hat over the hoop. The BAC athlete asked the referee to stop the spectator from waving his hat over the hoop, but the referee refused. BAC attempted the foul shot—but, distracted by the waving hat, missed—prompting Peterson to remark on the air, "Well, the crowd won that one." Angered by Peterson's statement, the president of Dixie College banned KSUB from future broadcasting in the Dixie gym.

KSUB was not a powerful station, and at night other stronger stations would essentially push KSUB off the air, frustrating listeners in nearby counties who wanted to hear the games. On nights of game broadcasts, several carloads of BAC supporters would park their cars on top of the hill south of the Zion Canyon junction on U.S. Highway 89, where the radio reception was better. Some of the BAC players were from Kanab and since the KSUB signal often did not reach Kanab, the fans drove to the site where they could hear the game.

With the end of World War II, the school took on a new look. Out was the old nickname "Branch Aggies." In was the new "Broncos," complete to a half-sized replica of a horse that was pulled around the gymnasium floor. To the tune of "Ragtime Cowboy Joe," the student body would sing:

O how they swing into line,
As the score begins to climb
When the Broncs (stomp, stomp)
When the Broncs begin to stomp,
Got a team, What a team.
As the hills give back the rattle
When the Broncs go into battle
When the Broncs (stomp, stomp)
When the Broncs begin to stomp,
And the Aggie folks will grin,
As those rompin' stompin' victory trompin'
Bunch of Broncs begin a stompin'
Up the score goes.
Who can stop the Broncos?
BAC will win !

The colors of the school have changed several times during the century. For SUU's first 15 years the school shared the red and white colors of the University of Utah, its mother school. From 1913 to 1961, the school colors were those of Utah State University: navy blue and white. In 1961 coral and turquoise were selected as the school colors. The difficulty locating manufacturers who could produce uniforms in coral and turquoise colors eventually led to the substitution of orange for the coral and a royal blue for the turquoise. In 1983, however, the school elected to discard the orange and blue completely and returned to the school's original red and white colors. Scarlet was selected as the shade of red, and royal blue was approved for an accent color to be used in the trim of uniforms.

When SUU ceased being a junior college and became a four-year institution, a new athletic rivalry began with Westminster College in Salt Lake City. The two schools both competed in the Rocky Mountain Athletic Conference, and

> *S*outhern Utah University was, for me, a wonderful community of learning, a place that awakened my mind and my soul. The surroundings were breathtaking, the pine trees an oasis for me after coming from a life in the desert. The faculty and staff were extraordinary, professionally, of course, but personally, as well. Their caring, one-on-one attention to students created an atmosphere of personal nurturing that made SUU a home away from home. One of my fondest memories is of the night University President Royden C. Braithwaite bought me a hamburger.
>
> SUU is the place where I learned that education is important. While this may seem pretty obvious, you must remember that I was a kid from Searchlight, Nevada, who had no exposure to formal schooling beyond my two-room schoolhouse. The adventure of going off to college was one thing; the realization of the importance of education came later.
>
> I had come to SUU as a student athlete, academics playing a definitely secondary role in my mind. However, I got hurt on the playing field, and the injuries forced an outlook reversal. It was not immediately evident that the calamity would be the proverbial blessing in disguise, but for the first time in my life I began to get good grades. A new kind of exhilaration followed from flexing my brain muscle, to rise to the challenge of becoming an academic man. As I found myself actually enjoying the rigor of this new kind of discipline, I began to get a glimmering of the importance of a good education.
>
> The classroom doors of SUU opened up a whole new paradigm for me, full of exciting possibilities. I am grateful to all those individuals at SUU who encouraged me in that time of tremendous personal growth.
>
> United States Sen. Harry Reid, Nevada

because the axe had engendered so much enthusiasm as a part of the SUU versus Dixie athletic rivalry, and since SUU and Westminster were both in-state institutions and both RMAC members, there was an opportunity to contest for athletic supremacy between the two schools. With this in mind a "saber" was designed as the trophy to indicate the winner of the SUU vs Westminster football and basketball games. At the conclusion of a game the two student body presidents would meet in center-court or mid-field to exchange the possesion of the saber, if posession was to change. The school would display the saber on its campus until the next game. This continued until Westminster dropped the intercollegiate athletic program in 1978-79.

From the end of World War II to the spring of 1961, SUU athletic teams answered to the nickname of Broncos. In 1961 the Bronco name was dropped in favor of Thunderbirds, the designation that has identified SUU teams in the 36 years that have since passed. The Thunderbird was a mythological bird of very large size which featured prominently in the lore of some North American Indian tribes and was the source of thunder, lightening and rain.

*T*raveling throughout the mountain west and beyond was sometimes an adventure for the school's athletes and their coaches. Coach Jack Young, who served the college for seven years from 1923 to 1930, recalled many occasions when athletes and coaches

were required to pay part of their meals and lodging on team trips. Travel was usually made in the coach's car and in donated vehicles from various Cedar City businesses. On some occasions, the athletes stayed in the homes of the athletes they were playing against, or in dormitories or on gymnasium floors. A basketball trip to northern Utah to play Westminister College, Weber State College, or the freshman team at BYU could require several days; such were the questionable road conditions in winter time.

Coach Boyd Adams and one of his basketball teams had their station wagon catch fire on Wolf Creek Pass in Colorado. Adams and his athletes were able to cut the ties on the luggage rack atop the vehicle and save the uniforms and personal items of the players, but the station wagon was a total loss.

Coach Kathryn Berg, traveling to Ricks College in Idaho with a van load of women athletes, hit black ice on a turn near Kanosh, Utah, and the vehicle rolled. Much of the luggage on the top of the van was destroyed, but the 10 or

CAR WRECK, ATHLETICS TRAVEL, 1969

12 women in the van sustained only minor injuries. The van was, however, totaled, with its ceiling mashed down to the top of the seats. After that, Berg was not quick to volunteer to drive athletic teams on their away trips.

On occasion, it was the coaches and administrators who were plagued by mishaps when traveling on behalf of the school's sports programs. Once Coach Cleo Petty, who had been in Kansas City, Kan., for a national convention, was returning home by train. A severe snow storm forced the train to be snowbound in Garden City, Kan., and the passengers were taken off the train and housed and fed in the local gymnasium. Petty was an outstanding pianist and some of the other coaches from Utah and Wyoming persuaded him to play the piano for the stranded travelers. With Cleo playing the piano, the passengers spent the evening singing and dancing, all of which was duly reported, with pictures, in *Time* magazine.

Kathryn Berg was among several campus officials who returned home from the 1997 NCAA convention aboard a plane bound from Atlanta to Salt Lake City. Preparing to land in Salt Lake City, the pilot attempted to lower the landing gears, only to discover the gears would not lock into place. Reporting the plane's condition to the passengers, the pilot informed them he would severely rock the plane from side to side to force the gears to engage but alerted the passengers a free-fall could result. The maneuver was not successful, and a bypass over the airport tower was needed for the tower to assess whether the gears were down, though it was not known if they had actually locked into place. Consequently, the passengers were put through the emergency landing procedures and informed they would land in four minutes. If the gears held, the trip would be safe. If not, a crash landing was assured. The gears did hold, and the crash was averted, but one passenger had a heart attack in the landing process.

Given the amount of traveling required of the school's teams and their coaches over the years, but especially in the RMAC era, in which the majority of travel was by car, bus, or van over mountain passes, often in winter time, it is fortunate that no serious injuries or major accidents occurred.

*A*thletics is, of course, a human endeavor, and SUU's century of sports competition is laced with stories that speak of its human dimension. There are, for example, many instances of administrators, faculty, staff and townspeople assisting students in their

*S*outhern Utah State College will always hold a special place in my heart, as that is where I made several life-long friends - both students and faculty members. Because it was a small school, it offered me the opportunity to excel on the football field and to mature in other important ways. I attribute much of my later success on the national athletic scene to the encouragement and instruction of people who cared about me during my four years there. The faculty of the school and the people of Cedar City really supported the students of the college. It was a great atmosphere in which to learn about myself and life, as well as to acquire the basic skills I needed to compete in professional football and in the business world.

—Leonard Walterscheid, still listed several times in the SUU record book, was the only graduate to go on to compete in the National Football League, playing for the Chicago Bears.

endeavors to gain an education and compete in sports.

In 1954, football coach Bruce Osborne recruited a young man from Provo, Utah, to come to SUU to join Osborne's team. A few days prior to the beginning of football practice sessions, the young man informed Coach Osborne that his summer's earnings were not sufficient to pay his college expenses, and he would be unable to come to BAC after all. Osborne encouraged him to come anyway, informing the potential student that he would find a way to help him financially. The business department provided a $60 tuition scholarship, and a Cedar City businessman, Nelson Marsden of Marsden's Men's Shop, agreed to interview the athlete for a part-time job. The young man

BNS BASEBALL TEAM

LaVeve
Whetten

showed up for the interview in old clothing, but they were neatly pressed. Marsden later said he hired the athlete when he noticed the highly polished, old, worn shoes he was wearing. The athlete worked at Marsden's for three or four years, married, and after graduation, went on to a very successful career in business in California, where for many years he sent back contributions to the college scholarship fund.

The physical culture classes presented during the BNS period for both men and women were primarily gymnastics in the winter months and outdoor sports in the fall and spring. Posture was stressed in the women's classes. Women were also permitted to participate in tennis, basketball and golf, and free gymnastics modeled after the German, French and Swedish styles. Females wore a divided skirt, loose waist and shoes. The male uniform consisted of dark trousers with a modified tee-shirt, and tennis shoes.

Prior to 1965, coursework in physical culture—later renamed physical education—consisted primarily of activity courses in which all students were required to participate. Students could complete the physical education requirements for an associate degree by taking six credits in various sports classes or in dance.

In February of 1965, the Utah State University Board of Trustees and Utah Coordinating Council gave approval to SUU to grant baccalaureate degrees in 18 areas, including physical education. The school was now prepared to begin turning out physical education majors. The curriculum was expanding and deepening.

In the 32 years that have since passed, the department of physical education has earned a distinguished reputation, and its graduates pepper coaching and teaching ranks throughout the intermountain west and beyond. Twenty-two men and women have held professional rank in the department in the intervening years. Of those, ten served for more than 20 years each.

LaVeve Whetten came to the school in 1939 and retired 35 years later in 1974, with several periods in which she took time off to raise a family. In addition to her teaching assignment, she served for a period as dean of women, advised sororities, the Women's Athletic Association, the Broncettes and the Thunderettes. When Whetten arrived to take her teaching assignment in 1939, the position also required her to teach three or four classes in secretarial science, coach the women's sports and supervise the women's intramural program. She was a woman of many talents and abilities.

Cleo Petty, who had played varsity basketball for Utah State University for four years (two of which he served as team captain), joined the BAC faculty in 1951 and served as head basketball and baseball coach, athletic director, and head of the physical education department. In his first years as basketball coach, his teams won the region championship and placed sixth in the national tournament. He retired in 1979.

Boyd Adams played basketball and baseball at SUU and lettered in the two sports at USU. He served as head basketball coach at SUU for a year in 1958, spent a year as an assistant coach at the University of Nevada, Las Vegas, and rejoined the SUU faculty in the fall of 1962 as teacher and head basketball coach. He coached the school's basketball team from 1962 to 1971 and the women's basketball team from 1982 to 1988. His death in 1988 ended a colorful and distinguished career as an athlete, coach and teacher.

Bruce H. Osborne attended USU, where he participated in football and track, served a stint in the U. S. Marines, then enrolled at BYU where he twice earned all-conference honors in football. He coached at Delta and Provo high schools before joining the SUU faculty in 1954 as a teacher and coach of football, wrestling, and track. In addition to his coaching responsibilities, he served as chair of the physical education department from 1967 to 1979. Few in the history of intercollegiate athletics and in the department of physical education can match the dedication and leadership of his SUU career.

Steve Lunt attended Cedar High School and CSU. He was appointed to the SUU faculty in 1965 and served as assistant football coach (1965-71), assistant basketball coach (1965-79), assistant baseball coach (1965-66), head track and cross-country coach (1972-79), and as head athletic trainer (1965-71.) Lunt served as athletic director from 1979 to 1987 and as chair of the physical education department (1979 to the present). He also served as assistant to the president for special projects where he created campus opportunities in which upwards of 80 high schools participated in sporting events at SUU in a single year. In 1994 he was selected to receive the Circle of Fame Award from the Utah High School Activities Association for outstanding contributions to Utah high school activities, the only college or university faculty member to receive the honor to date.

Kathryn Berg joined the SUU faculty in 1968, and in the University's centennial year she is the school's senior female professor. Berg, who also serves as associate athletic director, has coached women's teams in gymnastics (1968-71, 1977-78), volleyball (1968-75), basketball (1968-72, 1973-74), softball, (1968-72, 1973-74), swimming (1968-71), and track and field (1968-79). In addition, she directed the women's intramurals program, was assistant chair of the physical education department and assistant athletic director. She also directed a series of synchronized swimming water shows.

Tom Kingsford was appointed to the department faculty in 1967. He coached the SUU football team (1967-78), and was golf coach (1978-1991). At the retirement of Cleo Petty, he assumed leadership of the school's intramural program. Kingsford retired from SUU in 1991.

Joseph H. Lopour was appointed to the faculty in 1971. He served as assistant football coach (1971-81) and as head coach of the SUU wrestling team (1971-79). He also coached both men's and women's track and field teams (1986-90).

Benjamin Davidson arrived at SUU in 1979 and served as trainer for the athletic department (1979-1993.) He also coached women's and men's track (1979-90.)

Joy Peterson was appointed to the faculty in 1976. She coached the women's volleyball team (1976-87), women's basketball team (1976-82), and women's softball team (1976-79, 1983 to the present).

Others who have served with professional rank in the department of physical education include Bill Reeske, Kathy Major, Kaye Hart, Sandra Bryant, Don Conrad, Bill Groves, Brent Hardcastle, Steve Kazor, Stan Jack, Gordon Kerbs, Terri Lauterbach-Cotts, Tom McCracken, Bob Schermerhorn, Nancy Stringham, Craig Morrison, and Jean Reeves.

In 1986 an article written by *Deseret News* sportswriter Dan Pattison focused on the large number of high school coaches who received their undergraduate degrees at SUU and commented on their successes on the high school sporting scene. In the article he described the department as "The Coaching Factory." The title has often since been used as a moniker for the department.

In 1988-89, to bring campus recognition to the success of SUU alumni in the coaching ranks, Dr. Lunt instituted a night to honor SUU alumni whose teams had competed for a state high school championship during the year.

Honored at the half-time of a basketball game, the number of winning coaches each year stretched side by side from one border of the arena floor to the other. In the 1995-96 school year, for example, SUU graduates coached 19 state championship teams in Utah, five state championships in Nevada, and one each in Arizona and New Mexico.

Several alumni in the coaching ranks have earned national honors. Herb Stinson of New Mexico's Aztec High School was named as the nation's high school wrestling coach of the year in 1965, and Russell Otis of Dominguez High School in southern California had his basketball team ranked at number one in the nation in 1996. David Houle of Mountain View High School has several times earned national championships for his women's track and cross-country teams.

SUU's ORIGINAL OLYMPIC CHAMPION, S. FOREST FLETCHER OF CHICAGO. HE COACHED ATHLETICS AT BNS FROM 1912-13 AND COMPETED IN THE 1912 OLYMPICS, SETTING FOUR WORLD RECORDS.

THE READING
ROOM OF THE
NEW LIBRARY,
DEDICATED IN
1996.

BNS
LIBRARY,
1908

CHAPTER X

The Library

ooks had to be stored wherever there was a bit of space. There was a tiny room under the stage...where boxes could be stashed. They called it 'Peter's Prayer Room' because one had to enter in a kneeling position.

W hen school opened in the fall of 1898[1], George W. Decker, librarian of the year-old Branch Normal School, occupied an office on the third floor over the "most spacious, well-stocked library that southern Utah had ever seen."[2] So declared the first circular of the Branch Normal School. The "spacious and well-stocked library" may well have been the only library in southern Utah. The circular also stated:

Several hundred dollars have been appropriated for apparatus and books, which will be immediately purchased and be ready for use in the opening of this school year.

The record shows that the amount spent to purchase books and apparatus, which probably included tables, chairs and other furnishings as well as books, totaled about $800. So the dog-eared and well-worn books loaned by townspeople and teachers were necessary and welcome. Some books, bearing the insignia of Branch Normal School and the nameplates of early citizens and teachers, still grace the shelves of the Special Collections rooms nearly a century after this first library opened.

The Old Ward Hall, which had sheltered the school the first year, had no organized library. Books in frontier Utah were hard to find. Each faculty family had a few treasured volumes, and the four faculty members unselfishly used their own books to teach and to loan to their students. When the first building was completed in 1898, it was called the Library Building and some books were on the shelves. It was the home of the library for 50 years.

In the early history of most colleges and universities, the principal, director or president was often the librarian in addition to his administrative role. This was the pattern of the first librarians in the 19th century and earlier. These were well-read individuals of knowledge and wisdom, well equipped for selecting the best and needed books and magazines for the library. Principal Milton Bennion served the first year as librarian of the non-existent library, but the assignment fell to George W. Decker in 1898, and he continued in that post until his retirement in 1913.

Mr. Decker also taught mathematics and natural science. Assistant librarian was Annie E.

BRANCH
NORMAL
SCHOOL,
LIBRARY ON
THIRD
FLOOR

READING ROOM OF BRANCH NORMAL SCHOOL

Spencer, who was also a teacher of art, music, elocution and physical culture. So, while the library was the object of considerable pride, library administration was in addition to teaching assignments. The task of the librarian was not taxing, since the program and materials were simple. Some tables with eight chairs, a few pull-out maps and a single world globe would have been the complete furnishing. With so few books on the shelves it was necessary to insure that students did not keep books too long. There was one desk near the exit, with a stamp pad and a pencil.

The collection at BNS was extolled in the first school circular:

The Library is furnished with collections of standard works in literature, history, pedagogy and science, besides miscellaneous books and public documents. Some of the best American magazines and journals and the latest newspaper of the state are also provided. All students have free access to those from 9:00 a.m. to 5:00 p.m. on school days and at such other times as sufficient subjects of students may desire to use the Library.

DONALD K. NELSON, 1945

At the time the Branch Normal School changed to Branch Agricultural College George Decker retired and vacated his post as both principal and librarian. It is amazing that he had maintained both tasks through all these years. For the year 1914-15, Almeda Perry served as librarian. Roy F. Homer, then principal of the Branch Agricultural College, said,

The Library consists of nearly 4,000 volumes of standard works in literature, history and science and other departments of knowl-

edge, besides a large number of the best magazines and papers of the nation. Additions to the Library are made constantly.[3]

Caroline Keturrah Parry was made the librarian for the year 1915-1916. A daughter of Representative John Parry of BNS founding fame, Miss Parry was credited with cataloging the library collection of 4,000 books into the Dewey Decimal classification system, which was used until 1977. Miss Parry was second in a long list of women who served as librarians.

College catalogs continued to advertise the growing collection. In the 1918 catalog is found:

The Library consists of nearly 5,000 volumes of standard works—of literature history, science, plus magazines and papers. During that year upwards of $1,000 was expended, and it was the policy of the institution to expend that amount each year. New furniture was added to the equipment of the reading room making it one of the most attractive quarters in the school.[4]

The new furnishings and the cataloging system must have made life more pleasant for Annie E. Pettigrew, who came in 1918 and remained until 1924. She was replaced by Clara Farnsworth, who stayed with the task for three years, leaving in 1927. From 1927 until 1935, a gap occurs in the record, and no librarian is recorded. Knowing that these were years of austerity at the school, it could well be that teachers assisted with the library.

Marie Tinsley came in 1935 and served until 1939; she was replaced in 1939 by Vera Chadwick. In 1941 young Donald K. Nelson came to assume the duties of librarian. He served eight years, until 1949.

The third-floor library experienced uninterrupted serenity for slightly more than 50 years. Then, on December 10, 1948 an early morning fire erupted in the dried roof timbers. The ensuing damage caused years of displacement for the library collection.

The cataloging system had been completely destroyed. Don K. Nelson hired Eulalia B. (Lael) Jones, who had extensive experience in library practices at the University of Utah, to begin the task of re-cataloging the library. Jean Whitney was hired to assist her.

Only 20 percent of the library holdings was saved, and most of the rescued books and materials were dumped unceremoniously from the third-story window after a hand-to-hand brigade proved too dangerous and too slow. The art collection of Mary L. Bastow and most of her art supplies were lost. Treasured volumes that could not be replaced were burned or damaged beyond recovery, and there was no appropriate space to house the scrambled remains. The librarians began to search for a place to store what was left of the library collection.

It quickly became apparent that there was no area that would contain the library as it had been. Boxes of books would have to be stored wherever there was a bit of space. There was a tiny room under the stage in the girls' gym where boxes could be stashed. They called it "Peter's Prayer Room" because one had to enter in a kneeling position and couldn't stand upright inside. Boxes were also stored in the equipment rooms in the basement of the gym.

When the fire-damaged building was cleaned enough to be re-occupied three classrooms on the south side of the bottom floor became the library. The circulation desk and the stacks with the most necessary books were moved into these three rooms. Other books were stored in boxes all over campus.

During this confusion, Donald K. Nelson accepted the position of librarian at Brigham Young University. Nelson departed, leaving Lael Jones as librarian, confronted with putting back together the library system, receiving books from the book drive that had been instituted by sympathetic supporters and beginning to plan for a new facility.

*I*n the aftermath of the fire, Director Driggs had begun talking about a beautiful new library building for BAC which would rise from the ashes of the old as the fabulous Phoenix bird of Egypt rose again, in the freshness of youth, from its funeral pyre. Two years later Driggs was successful in obtaining an initial appropriation of $400,000 for the building of a new auditorium/library.

Dr. Driggs died before the dream became a reality. At the time of his death, he had been serving as president of the Utah Conference on Higher Education. At its annual meeting held in Cedar City a month after his death, his successor, Dr. Daryl Chase, proposed that every educator in the state contribute a book to the college library as a fitting memorial to Director Driggs. Under the chairmanship of N. Blaine Winters, this committee of educators added more than 8,000 books to the collection. Each had a gift plate in it naming the donor. Each book that arrived had to be catalogued and space found to store it while plans for the new

LIBRARY
FIRE,
1948

library moved slowly forward.[5] Finally, on March 28, 1955 the completed library/auditorium was officially turned over to the school.

After six years of juggling the volumes of books that came as gifts and managing in the cramped quarters in the basement of Old Main, Lael Jones faced the challenge of moving to the new building. Students, faculty and volunteers were recruited to carry the books from the stacks in Old Main and from various storage places to the new facility. This building served two purposes, with the library comprising two levels on the west end of the building and the auditorium occupying the east side. This was the first time a building had been built entirely with state money on the Cedar City campus.

With the imminent move to the new library, work on building a viable collection began in earnest. The Northwest Accreditation Association had pointed out many deficiencies in the area of the library collections over the past visits. The book budget for 1958-1959 was only $2,000; however, the following year the budget was increased to $5,000. The College of Southern Utah was spending $7.00 per student for library books.

Lael Jones served as the sole library staff for ten years, from 1949 to 1959. She relied on student-help, but ran the library with exceptional devotion and professionalism. The American Library Association had recommended two full-time professional librarians and a full-time secretarial assistant, plus student assistants for a library the size of CSU's.

EULALIA
BROWN
JONES,
LIBRARIAN
1949-1959

ARTHUR TOM
CHALLIS,
1959

CAROLINE
KETURRAH
PARRY
WOOLEY,
1960's

Dr. Royden Braithwaite, then college president, became keenly aware of the extraordinary demands placed on Jones and hired Arthur T. Challis as a new librarian. With the appointment of Tom Challis, Lael became head of technical services and cataloging; Challis became the library director in charge of administration, reference, circulation and selection. Over the next ten years more full- and part-time librarians were hired. In 1967 several new people were added to the library staff: Ramona Chamberlain as circulation librarian, Elma Hardy as serials librarian and Sharon Leigh and LaRue Higbee as part-time assistants to Lael Jones.

President Braithwaite established a Special Collections area in the library in 1960 to collect and preserve regional history and rare and expensive books and artifacts. The following year Inez Cooper was appointed Special Collections librarian. Although this area contained only a single desk and two small file cabinets, it was important in providing a place to collect, catalog and preserve local history. One of the first additions was a collection of BAC textbooks which had belonged to Principal George Decker and which Tom Challis rescued when it was learned that some boys were throwing books out the attic window of an abandoned building.

The first major collection donated to the college to be housed in Special Collections came from Dr. John Lawrence Seymour, who became acquainted with the library through a chance meeting with Ruth Challis, a hostess at Utah Shakespearean Festival. Dr. Seymour was looking for a home for his music, books, artifacts and antique furniture, and the college was building a new library that would have suitable space for such materials. The collection was appraised and accepted, and a room in the new (1968)

library was designated the Seymour Room. Eventually, Dr. Seymour made his home in Cedar City establishing the Seymour Room as his working headquarters. He became a valuable library resource, sharing his music, literature and collected treasures from all over the world with students and townspeople.

Accreditation was necessary to the progress of the college and the inadequacy of the library music, literature and collected treasures from all over the world with students and townspeople.

Accreditation was necessary for the progress of the college, and the inadequacy of the library seemed a significant stumbling block. However diligently the library personnel worked at building library services and programs, the library still did not have the facilities or materials to satisfy the accreditation requirements. In July of 1946 the Board of Trustees authorized the administration to request funds from the Utah legislature for a new library. The legislative battle for funding ran in tandem with the fight for four-year liberal arts status and independence from Utah State Agricultural College. It was a triumph when the $750,000 appropriation for planning the library was achieved. On March 29, 1965 the planning committee was announced. The committee included Brent Palmer, Craig Jones, Eugene Woolf, Inez Cooper, Hazen Cooley, Gordon Slack, Richard A. Thompson and A. Thomas Challis, chair. In October architect Robert L. Gardner was appointed to design the five-story building. The trustees accepted the preliminary design and the realization of another dream seemed near.

In autumn of 1966, Gov. Calvin Rampton announced his support for the new building,

LIBRARY GROUND BREAKING, LEFT TO RIGHT - FRONT: TOM CHALLIS, DR. OLIVER PETERSON, MRS. ESTHER PETERSON, PRESIDENT ROYDEN BRAITHWAITE, EUGENE WOOLF. BACK ROW: CRAIG JONES, HAZEN COOLEY, MRS. L. SWEET, RUSSELL DAVIS, GLEN SWENSON, MAYOR LOREN WHETTEN.

promising that it would not be among the buildings he intended to cut from his 1977 budget, but cautioning that there would not be funds to stock its shelves.[6]

A new book drive commenced. This time a member of the Board of Trustees, Edmund Flynn of Salt Lake, agreed to head the drive. Public-spirited individuals and businesses rose to the challenge, as they had always done in the past. The drive was given a beginning boost with a gift of $1,500 from California Pacific Utilities Company, and the momentum accelerated.

The 1977 Legislature appropriated the remaining construction funding for the library and on commencement day, June 3, 1967, ground-breaking ceremonies were held on the site.

As the shiney shovels finished their symbolic duty, Blackburn and Gower construction company machinery began their work of excavating the basement of the new library.

The $1,130,500 library building progressed remarkably well and was completed in 21 months. There were some difficulties associated with the construction, especially unfortunate for the elevator company. In digging the elevator shaft they hit large dolomite limestone boulders. Small charges of dynamite were necessary to crack the stones, then picks and shovels broke them into pieces that could be loaded into trucks. More than 100 days labor were used in sinking one 90-foot shaft. By the time the task was complete the Montgomery Elevator Company regretted having been awarded the contract.

Despite the trial of the dolomite boulders, the work moved rapidly. Though the dedication was not held until November, 1969, the building was substantially complete, so permission was granted to move the collection into the new facility on March 18, 1969.

Ramona Chamberlain, circulation librarian, organized the move. A human chain involving more than 350 people from every constituency in the College and community came to help - housewives, professors, students, janitors, administrators and businessmen formed a human conveyor belt. Everyone wanted to be a part of this historic event.

From eight o'clock in the morning the volunteers worked through the day to push the project along. The line began next to the stacks in the old building and ended at the stacks in the new library. Library staff members filled in gaps in the line and worked on both ends to try to keep the books in order. For the first time in the

history of the school, there was a library housed in a building whose primary purpose was to be a library.

When the building was dedicated on November 14, 1969, the week-long celebration leading up to the grand occasion included the formal opening of the Seymour Room on Wednesday, November 12, and an evening musical recital at the Thorley Music Hall on Thursday night. Friday's festivities began with tours of the beautiful new building, a luncheon and the dedication program in the Auditorium. The one-hour program included remarks by G. Homer Durham and dedicatory remarks and a prayer by Elder Bernard Brockbank.

During the course of his address Dr. Durham suggested that friends and supporters of the library make contributions to the collection and that they be given library cards in return.

LIBRARY UNDER CONSTRUCTION, 1968

MOVING THE BOOKS, MARCH 18, 1969

LIBRARY STAFF, CIRCA 1970s:
LEFT TO RIGHT, FRONT ROW: HELEN KETCHEM, LA RUE HIGBEE, CLARA WAHLQUIST, DAVE JENSEN, TOM CHALLIS, SECOND ROW, LEFT TO RIGHT: INEZ COOPER, MARJAN WAZEKA, ELMA HARDY, SHARON LEIGH, RAMONA CHAMBERLAIN, LAEL JONES.

Immediately after the ceremony, two long-time boosters of the college rushed forward to be the first to contribute. Professor Emeritus and Mrs. Parley Dalley purchased the first two cards, followed closely by Lanell and Lucy Lunt, who received cards three and four.

There were surprises in store when the library was finished in 1969. The builders had inadvertently sealed some bats in the upper part of the building. In the evenings they crawled out of the vents and swooped across the lobby and through the chandeliers until they were finally exterminated.

The new library required additional employees and changes in library assignments. LaRue Higbee became the full-time reference librarian, Helen Ketchem the reserve room librarian, and Clara Wahlquist was hired as library secretary.

President Braithwaite announced the appointment of David Jensen as assistant library director and coordinator of instructional media services in 1969. Space for the instructional media center had been provided on the second level of the new building. Jensen's responsibilities included: developing an instructional media resource center, supervising the new curriculum library, overseeing two television studios and managing the campus printing center and copy machines.

Librarians had taught several library classes [e.g. cataloging, library orientation, etc.] over the years to prepare students planning for work in school libraries. The existing education curriculum expanded under Jensen's direction to include a state endorsement and minor in instructional media. While these courses changed over the years, they always included library administration, selection, cataloging, utilization, media production, library orientation, photography and other offerings.

When Lael Jones retired in 1972, she had been a participant in a dramatic evolution in library service. She had served as the sole librarian for 10 years, during which time she had directed the saving and rehabilitation of the rescued collection and had received thousands of volumes as gifts, finding a place for them all. She had worked in three buildings, actively counseling in the design process of two of them. For more than 20 years she had cataloged and classified all the materials in the library. She had trained student-workers in the art of cataloging, including her meticulous method of hand-lettering the call numbers on the spine of books. As this grand lady finished her work, she could look back with pride upon many thousands of students she had guided and quietly taught. Her fellow staff members, who gathered for a photograph shortly before her retirement, revered and respected her.

With the retirement of Lael Jones, Sharon Leigh moved up to work as head of cataloging and Randall Christensen was hired to assist her. The following year Diana Graff was hired part-time to assist in acquisitions and later, when Elma Hardy retired, Diana assumed the full-time responsibilities for both serials and acquisitions. The media center also added a new employee. Sue Dutton was hired as media center secretary and eventually became assistant coordinator.

During this time the library started Dialog computer reference searches utilizing a nation-wide on-line database, and cataloging was great-

LEFT TO RIGHT, FRONT ROW: ADA S. PALMER, WILLIAM I. PALMER. BACK ROW: RODNEY I. PALMER, A. THOMAS CHALLIS, INEZ COOPER AND RICHARD I. PALMER

ly improved by joining OCLC, a national automated cataloging system. Already the library was experiencing the first inklings of a coming radical shift in librarianship and information technology occasioned by the computer revolution.

The growing size and complexity of the library collection necessitated a change in the classification system used to organize the books. The Dewey Decimal Classification was replaced by the more sophisticated Library of Congress Classification, a system much better suited to a college library. This meant not only changing the procedures then in use, but every book in the existng collection had to be recataloged under the new system. The retrospective conversion of the collection was not entirely finished until 1993.

On June 1, 1978 the library announced that the family of William R. Palmer, noted southern Utah historian, had gifted the entire collection of their father's manuscripts and books to the college. The collection of 33 boxes would be housed in a special room prepared to preserve and display the collection. It would be called the Palmer Western History Room. Included were diaries, letters, journals, copied public records and original manuscripts collected by Mr. Palmer during his 82-year lifetime. The family also donated much of the furniture and artifacts from the Palmer home to the collection. This gift represented 18 years of discussion between the library and the Palmer family. The valuable collection had been actively sought by many other university and historical agencies, both in and out of state. The Palmer Collection paved the way for others to consider the University as a repository for their family papers.

Inez Cooper had taken great joy in the beautiful Seymour Room and was pleased and excited by the addition of the Palmer Room to Special Collections. With the Palmer family's donation, Cooper began the cataloging and painstaking preservation of 33 boxes of treasured materials. It sometimes seemed that the materials that had taken a lifetime to assemble would take a lifetime to process.[7]

In 1980 Tom Challis, who had served as library director for 20 years, became serials librarian, and Diana Graff was hired as the new director. One of her first jobs as director was to supervise the completion of the Palmer Room so it could be dedicated during Homecoming of 1980.

Though the Palmer Room was dedicated on November 7, 1980, the catalog to the Palmer Collection was not completed until almost four years later. The catalog provided name and subject indexes to the entire collection—papers, letters, photographs, maps and memorabilia.

The Palmer Collection was only the first of four major additions to the SUSC Library Special Collections during the 1980s. It was only shortly after completing the enormous Palmer Collection project that another impressive and valuable collection was added to Special Collections. In 1984 a fine collection of Shakespeare materials was purchased from Howard and Mabel Smith of Las Vegas, Nevada, using special gift funds. The collection included many rare and valuable editions of Shakespeare's works including: the second printing of the first edition in Nicholas Row's edition of Shakespeare; Sir Thomas Hammer's 1744 edition "for a gentleman by a gentleman;" and six of eight volumes of the first collected works of Shakespeare published in America.

John L. Seymour, the library's resident scholar and a long time benefactor of SUSC died on February 1, 1986. Dr. Seymour had a special affection for southern Utah, SUSC and the SUSC Library. He had previously donated a large collection of books and artifacts to the library and upon his death he left a sizable endowment to provide for the cataloging, care and maintenance of his materials and for the general support of the library.

A third important collection was added to Special Collections in 1987 when Homer and Belle Jones presented the library with a collection of southern Utah photos and negatives representing 30 years of photos from the Zion Photo Shop which was owned by the Jones'.

Before the decade closed Special Collections received a fourth donation. Dr. Orien Dalley presented to the library a valuable collection of books, scores and records to enhance the library's music resources.

The 1980s also saw the creation of Southern Utah State College Press, formed to publish materials relating to southern Utah, Utah histo-

Dr. John L. Seymour in the Seymour Library Room

> *As a music major I had to fulfill a language requirement. I took the Humanities 100 class from Dr. Harrison, which gave me some German, French and Spanish, but I wanted to study Italian also, as I was exploring the idea of going into opera management. The same name kept coming up - Dr. John Seymour. I put on my best student suit, got my best student books on Italian and opera and knocked on the door of the Seymour Room at the library.*
>
> *The most glorious music I had ever heard was coming from the room, which I soon found to hold a horse hair couch, original art and lots of other beautiful things. A little man with gray hair on a balding head and the kindest blue eyes in the world came to the door. Here was Dr. John Seymour! I told him that I had done the language study required for a student with ambitions in arts administration, but I wanted to study Italian at Yale that summer and I had no way to prepare. Could he advise me?*
>
> *He said, "My young lady, studying Italian is no easy task. Are you prepared to take it seriously?" When I assured him that I was very serious, he invited me to sit on his horse hair couch, turned down the music on the phonograph and produced an Italian book. I was beginning my Italian studies with Dr. John Seymour.*
>
> *We sat in his office three times a week for about eight weeks. He was patient and wonderful. I learned more than how to conjugate verbs and pronounce phrases in Italian. I learned about the context of the phrases and about the culture and the mentality of the Italian people. I can still see the tears on his face and feel the tears on mine as we listened to Italian operas. He would go off into places that the special world of opera opened up - Egypt, Bavaria, Russia - and I would go with him. One day as we were listening to Joan D' Arc I suddenly realized that I had traveled to the heart and mind and life of Dr. Seymour, and it was the most wonderful place of all.*
>
> *I hold special memories of the man who gave me the greatest education of all of my years. He taught me how to carry the essence of beauty and pain and the challenge of loss and renewal in all of its bitter-sweet forms. He gave me a dream world that became a reality.*
>
> Rebecca Patterson, 1986 SUU applied music graduate.

ry and SUSC. Books published by SUSC Press include:

Mayors of Cedar City by York and Evelyn Jones.

Three Score and Ten in Retrospect by John S. Boyden and Orpha Sweeton Boyden.

Reflections by Elva Matheson.

Sojourn in Israel. by Inez Cooper

As more students began to enroll and more faculty were hired, it became obvious that library services had to grow as well. In 1980 the Learning Center opened on the first floor of the library, funded in part through a Title IIIA grant. The Learning Center provided classes in remedial reading, writing and peer tutoring services for many disciplines across campus. The provided services proved so valuable that the Learning Center continued under college funding after the three-year grant period ended.

In the 1984-85 school year, the 15th anniversary of the completion of the library building, library personnel began the early stages of planning for a new building to meet the needs of the growing campus community and to more adequately support the increasing technological demands of operating a quality college library. It was a shock to some "old timers" who still

considered the current building as the "new library."

The Statewide Academic Library Study was completed in September of 1988 and presented to the 1989 Utah State Legislature. The proposal recommended a new building of 60,000 gross square feet that "can be added to when the need arises."

Plans, studies and needs assessments notwithstanding, the library had real growing pains to deal with in the present. In the meantime the library added more stacks, tables and chairs in 1988 to try to keep up with the study needs of the growing student population.

The year 1990 marked a major change in library operations and heralded a new era in library and information services. The library began operating an automated library system purchased from Dynix, a fledgling Utah company, which would later prosper into one of the moving forces in library automation worldwide. This new computerized system tied together many library tasks and services through one integrated system. The main benefit to faculty and students was the OPAC (Online Public Access Catalog), the computerized index which replaced the cumbersome card catalog. The purchase and switch-over to this automated system was only the first step in an on-going race to make use of new technologies in providing quality information services to the SUSC community. Under the direction of Randall Christensen, the library made this first bold step into the world of computer-based library resources which continued to expand exponentially until the present time.

In 1991 the college was granted university status, and the SUU Library was born. Library personnel took it all in stride because the only constant in the library was change. The rapid growth of computer technologies, especially networking and the internet, continued to push the library into new arenas. Randy Christensen was appointed as library system administrator, and in 1993 he was relieved of his reference position to work full time as system administrator with the help of several part-time students and SUU academic computing. In the early 1990s on-line and computer-based information retrieval revolutionized libraries and library services and the university library provided a high standard of quality research resources throughout this very turbulent time.

In 1992-1993 the Utah legislature appropriated the funds for construction of a new library at SUU and planning began in earnest. The valuable contributions of the library staff and faculty and the tireless efforts of Dean Graff were a major factor in the ultimate success of this huge undertaking. The new building was designed by the Salt Lake firm FFKR, and the bid for construction was awarded on December 15, 1993 for an estimated total cost of $10.4 million.

Through the generosity of Burch Mann, a long time SUSC/SUU supporter, a beautiful new home for Special Collections was added to the design of the new library. The Christopher/ Mann Room became the heart of Special Collections and a show piece for the new library. Opening off the Christopher/Mann Room, the Seymour and Palmer Rooms were recreated in the new library along with a new Grace A. Tanner Room funded by the Obert C. Tanner Foundation.

As construction of the new library commenced, additional responsibilities were added to the growing list of services provided by the library. A faculty development office was funded by the faculty senate, and its administration fell under the stewardship of the library director. The Center for Faculty Development began operation in 1992, and through the succeeding years provided an increasing number of services to the faculty including: an annual Regional Fall Faculty Development Conference;

LIBRARY STAFF, 1997

in-house faculty development grants; the Laptop Computer Technology Initiative; the Instructional Design, Evaluation and Assessment Lab (IDEA Lab) and the Sandwiches and Scholarship brown bag discussion group. In 1993 the Center grew to include the Academic Grants Office created to assist and advise faculty in finding funding sources and preparing grant applications.

In 1994 the library director accepted the responsibility for guiding SUU's participation in the expanding EDNET system. The technical operations were already being administered by the library's media center director, Sue (Dutton) Stratton and the curricular and teaching responsibilities for SUU's courses offered over the system were added to the burgeoning responsibilities of the Center for Faculty Excellence. With teaching faculty culled from the campus best, the SUU courses on EDNET became some of the finest offered over the entire state-wide system.

On March 8, 1996, the new library was dedicated in ceremonies marking the 99th anniversary of the founding of the university. The program included a welcome by David Jordan, chair, Board of Trustees; remarks by Gerald O. Sherratt, president, Southern Utah University;

LIBRARY FACULTY, 1997

Tosh Brinkerhoff, student body president, SUU; Cecelia Foxley, commissioner of Higher Education and Michael O. Leavitt, governor, State of Utah. The keynote speaker, introduced by Dean Rodney D. Decker, was David McCullough, a distinguished historian and author.

Diana Graff, dean of library services, accepted the building on behalf of the University. The dedication was part of the Founders' Day program that included the dedication of The Centurium, the Southern Utah Honors Program and the Founders' Day banquet.

In the afternoon of that day a traditional "book brigade" was held where students, faculty and community members passed the first 1,000 books by hand from the old building to the new. This was the beginning of six very long days. For the bulk of the move, the book brigade was retired in favor of rolling carts designed specifically for the move. Library faculty and staff, assisted by 20 students, moved the entire library collection, some 200,000 volumes, in less than a week. In addition to moving the books and serials, much of the furniture had to be assembled and put in place.

On March 20, 1996, the first day of spring quarter at 7:00 a.m., a ribbon-cutting ceremony was held, and the first students came to study in the new building. All the books were on the shelves, and 98 percent of the furniture was positioned in its permanent place. The dream was finally a reality.

The school's fourth library was designed from the ground up to take advantage of the many new technologies supporting research at the college level. Not only was the building wired with the latest in networking servers and connections, it was planned with the future in mind with spare conduits and outlets on every floor awaiting whatever new technologies might be coming.

Due to the expanding work force and many varied services provided in the library, Vik Brown was made associate library director in the fall of 1996 to aid Dean Graff in administering the growing work load.

That same school year Sharon Leigh, then serving as the serials librarian, retired after more than 30 years of library service. During her tenure she had worked in all areas of the library including cataloging, acquisitions, serials and reference. She participated in the planning of two new buildings and was witness to the enormous changes wrought by computer technology, telecommunications and the internet. Since the founding of the first library room in Old Main in 1898, no library employee had served longer at her post than Leigh.

Throughout its 100-year history the library has provided quality service to the school's students, faculty and staff, as well as the southern Utah community at large in support of curricular, professional and life-long learning needs. Libraries are asked to serve not only as guardians of the past but also as harbingers of the future. The solid foundation established over the last 100 years, briefly chronicled here, bodes a bright future for SUU and southern Utah. Libraries and librarians have a vital role to play in the Information Age—organizing and channeling data for use by their communities. The library faculty and staff of today (1997) and the future are dedicated to harnessing information-power to benefit and enlighten faculty, students and the southern Utah community.

THE 1969 LIBRARY

CHAPTER XI

Art in the barren desert

he pupils must feel that every time they hang a picture, change the furniture in a room, choose a coat or hat or tie, an artistic decision is made.

Branch Normal School was a school of the early frontier yet, amazing as it may seem, the curriculum of the first year, and most years following, included a course in art. True, the offering was small, and 100 years later at SUU, a full-fledged university, it is still a small department, but it enjoys a remarkable reputation as one of the finest small-school art programs in the country.[1]

Although they numbered only four in 1897, the faculty of the BNS was noteworthy. Those four teachers taught 118 students in two categories: 55 preparatory students, and 62 second-year normal students, with two listed as regular students. Miss Annie Spencer, noted for her versatility and refinement, was the art teacher. A description of the outline for art students was listed under the heading of "Normal Drawing." The program was ambitious:

The aim of this course is to prepare students to illustrate all subjects studied, and to acquire thereby a knowledge of the elementary principles of art. To this end chalk-modeling; freehand drawing from objects, models, and casts; water coloring of design and objects and outdoor sketching are employed. The expense of materials need not exceed $1.50 for one year. Required of first, second, and third year students: two recitations per week during the first, second and third years. Drawing primarily is sought to cultivate the aesthetic instinct and develop the owners of observation..... sketching, with colored crayon, water color, pencil, and pen and inks.

MISS SPENCER'S "NORMAL DRAWING", 1898

From her arrival in 1897 until she left Cedar City in 1905, the art department was Annie Spencer's domain, along with reading and physical culture. After Miss Spencer's departure a Miss Miller is listed as head of the art department in 1905 and 1906. The requirements and class descriptions did not change.

In 1906 and 1907, according to the catalog, a Miss Donahue became the teacher of art. Added to the art course was a class in "clay modeling, provided to develop the students' power of observation." We are reminded that the primary goal of an education at Branch Normal School was to train teachers. Anyone expecting to teach was required to complete a class in "black-board work of rapid sketching."

When a Miss Christensen came as the art teacher in 1908 and 1909, the basic philosophy was the same, but the requirement became a bit more stringent:

The student is given credit according to the amount of work done. Studies made of still life objects and easy subjects for the student are selected. Course I consists of work in charcoal sketching; course II consists of water color work and canvas. An apt student should be able to complete a few studies in each course. Two years special work should prepare a student as an art teacher in the public schools of the State." Course III consists of oil on board.[2]

BRANCH NORMAL SCHOOL FACULTY ABOUT 1910. REAR LEFT TO RIGHT: MENZIES MACFARLANE, GEORGE W. DECKER, PARLEY DALLEY, MABLE NAEGLE, MR. STEPHENSON, MR. BELNAP, E.W. MORGAN, FRONT LEFT TO RIGHT: TOLLESTRUP, JAMES ROBB, HAROLD WILKINSON, INEZ POWELL, J.S. WOODBURY, JAMES BARTON

Enid M. Severy was hired for the years of 1909 and 1910 but canceled her contract before school began. She was replaced by Mabel Naegle (later to become Mrs. Parley Dalley), who taught art and physical training for girls. To teach general high school courses the student was required to enroll in free-hand drawing for four periods in the first year of study.

The art department expanded in 1910 and 1911 with the hiring of Mr. John A. Alder.

Adah F. Betz took over the job of art instructor in 1911 and 1912, which was the first time an instructor was hired with a background solely in the field of art. Her resume included:

Education: Chicago Art Institute 1904, Campana Art School, water color; instruction in water color with J. W. Forkner, 1905; china

work with Amy McPherson, Jennie Stewart; Oil painting with Franz Bischoff, 1909; Instructor in Keith O'Brien Art studio; conducted private studio in Salt Lake City, 1906, 1907, 1908; and in charge of Keith O'Brien Art department, 1910.

Listed in the catalogue that academic school year under "Four-Year Normal Course" was 'drawing', with four recitations as previously listed, but in the elective category, a course "special art," which was graded on the merit of work, was also taught.

The institution expanded its focus in 1913 and 1914 with an addition of "Commercial Art." This included commercial arithmetic, geography, spelling, commercial law, stenography, typewriting, penmanship, music, drawing and art. Again, only first and third year art was listed under "Courses of Study": Art I: Drawing; Art II: Design; Art III: Watercolor and oil - with special courses provided when required.

During the years of 1916 and 1917 the art course encompassed the principles of art and the forms of expression from "true experience and proportion." Harmonization of color combinations was studied to "cultivate the students' taste for the beautiful." Line and mass were emphasized and also the history of art and free-hand lettering. Interestingly, the course correlated with domestic art and domestic science for girls who wished to learn design of clothing.

An interesting article from the *Iron County Record* of Friday, October 17, 1919, was headlined: "Art Courses at BAC Are Practical."

The art department of the BAC is alive and giving art that is useful. It is endeavoring to make the art courses efficient in the sense that the time of the pupil shall not be wasted; that he shall be taught mastery of himself as well as of his materials. The public school art is getting farther away from the 'easel painters' studio, and teaching art that will influence the students' daily life through all time, not something he will have to unlearn or forget. We believe in teaching art for use. This is our creed. The pupils must feel that every time they hang a picture, change the furniture in a room, choose a coat or hat or tie, an artistic decision is made. They must feel that art is a real and vital thing, and that a sense of beauty is as necessary to the good citizen as a sense of morality........In this course he learns two things. One is to know and appreciate the value of practical aesthetics in any business he may undertake, whether it is the proper spac-

ing of a typewritten legal form, the display of goods on a counter, or in a window, or development of art in advertising and industries. The other thing is that they learn the enormous solace of art in pictures, etc., and museums become to them a place of delight.

This article is reflective of common attitudes toward art education nationwide at this time: art should be practiced and should be used to develop appreciation in the beholder.

In 1919 *The Student,* the school newspaper, published this article by Mary Urie:

To most of us, art has meant only painting and statuary, is something beyond our power to create or to own, not a practical subject that could be applied in every day life. In our school this is not the case. It is the aim of the art department to adapt the courses to every day life. We must all wear clothes. It is the purpose of the costume design course to cultivate taste and give an insight into the principles of good line, color and harmony in dress. All fabrics, all costumes are designed well or ill, and the girl who knows unerringly how to select lines and colors best suited to herself has at all times an advantage over her less fortunate sister, who has not a knowledge of good design. . . . a girl does not necessarily have to be an artist to accomplish this. In the pottery and terra cotta class modeling and various treatments of pottery are taught. In the course in interior decoration, artistic, harmonious color, good design and the arrangement of draperies, rugs, and ornaments are considered. Batik and lacquer, inexpensive crafts, but very effective in home decoration, are studied.

Functional art was in vogue, and the instructors at BNS were in tune with the times.

When Margaret Whiting was listed as instructor in art in 1921 and 1922, the art course was under the heading "Vocational or Applied Art." From a quote in this catalog:

The College is now prepared to offer courses in all forms of applied art, a kind of art that is needed in the rural sections of the country. Home decoration, pottery and china design, dress decoration and design and all kinds of advertising art, such as sign painting and magazine advertising. The work done at the BAC in vocational art is unexcelled by any other school in the State of Utah.

There was no art teacher nor any art classes

listed for the years of 1922 and 1923, but from 1923 through 1925 the catalogue listed art under "Normal Arts for the Teacher" and was placed under auspices of the education department. The course dealt with art from the point of view of the teacher and suggested that " the class offers practical correlation of art with the child's life."

FRED BRAITHWAITE'S 1921 ART CLASS

*A*fter a gap of several years, when the teaching of art was focused upon teacher training, the school established a department again and demonstrated the commitment by hiring Mary Lovina Bastow to teach art and English. Miss Bastow was a graduate of Brigham Young College Normal Course in 1908 with a B.S. from Utah State Agricultural College in 1914-1915 . She had taught at USAC in 1916.

If the administration had had a tenuous commitment to offering an education in art, that changed quickly with the arrival of Mary L. Bastow. Hers was a presence that enlarged the commitment of the community and the college. Over the years of her career, she would expand the devotion to art, both of the citizens of the town and the school. She was a force for action, leading out in instruction and the securing of representative works in collections of the college.

For the next two decades, Mary L. Bastow *was* the art department. The first years of her employment could not have been very satisfactory because the country was in the throes of the worst depression in history. Materials, wages, and students were at a premium. However, the courses she taught were varied

MARY L.
BASTOW

and encompassed an astonishing breadth. She brought beauty into the lives of her students at a time when there was little beauty anywhere else. She taught design, color appreciation, freehand drawing and art appreciation, advance design and color courses, (given in 1930-1931); costume design, and interior decoration, applied art, divided into the following categories: basketry, textile decoration and stitchery, china decoration, decoration of furniture , i.e., lampshades, trays, etc. and public school art methods. In 1939 an additional course appeared in the curriculum, namely "Professional Design." To quote the catalogue description:

This will give the students interested in design and color much opportunity to express themselves creatively in color and design. Various problems that have application to everyday life may be selected, such as decorative landscape design, design for textiles, wallpaper or stage design, etc. Elementary color and design, or equivalent is a prerequisite.

In 1937 and 1938, the art courses taught were under the Division of "Liberal Arts" for the first time. In 1938, Miss Bastow taught 'Housing Problems,' which covered house design, garden design, house planning, building construction, heating, lighting, plumbing, etc. Included under this category were training in how to select the type of house and how to supervise the construction and equipment of the home.

MARY MACDONALD, LUCILLE BROADBENT, PRUDENCE CROFT, MAX WEAVER AND CARMEN JONES ENJOY EXHIBIT.

Drawing for the elementary grades was also included that year. In 1939 a "Division of Art" was finally designated, with E. A. Jacobsen, USAC, dean, and Mary L. Bastow, chair.

The art department was located on the top floor of Old Main and occupied the north side of the building. (The Library was located across the hall on the south side.) Miss Bastow climbed three flights of stairs many times a day for 24 years.

Students remember the incredible variety of classes that she taught and the stringent requirements she placed upon them:

I remember taking Miss Bastow's class in cross-stitch, and needle-point one year. Later, I took interior design, home-planning and construction. It was a requirement that we compile a scrapbook, complete with house plans drawn to scale, done in color, and with the landscaping and over-all design of the house. The classes she taught in interior design were always filled.[3]

Hazen Cooley remembers,

It was almost a daily occurrence for someone to stop Mary as she walked, to ask for help in re-decorating their home or how to landscape their lot. Not only did she advise contractors on colors for painting the walls, but she actually mixed five gallon cans of paint herself, and when it went on the walls, it was beautiful.

In 1940 Eugene Jorgensen, a Cedar City Junior High School faculty member, conceived the idea of sponsoring an annual art exhibit as one method of stimulating interest in art. He enlisted the enthusiastic support of "Mary L" and a newly-organized women's fine arts guild. Together they planned and executed the first exhibit, at which one hundred and twelve paintings were shown, featuring artists from many sections of the United States. An encouraging response greeted the exhibition, but it became evident that wider community support could make the project more successful.[4]

The Iron County School system actively supported the project through the leadership of Superintendent Ianthus Wright, himself a staunch supporter of the arts, who wrote:

Should you visit the schools and homes of a little community in southern Utah, you may be interested and perhaps a little surprised to find excellent original works of art adorning hundreds of walls. You may also be interested to hear a local business man, farmer, teacher or housewife discussing outstanding contemporary artists and their works. These are experiences that one may have by visiting Cedar City, Utah.[5]

At this fortuitous time a community coordinating council was being organized to sponsor and coordinate various civic activities. Attending members of the council had already been appointed to study community beautification, the town calendar, music arts and health. The junior high school asked the coordinating council to appoint a fine arts committee, whose specific responsibility was to perpetuate the annual exhibit. The committee was organized and set for themselves the following objectives:

> *To establish an annual Art Exhibit in Cedar City.*
> *To foster art as a cultural influence.*
> *To exhibit all forms of contemporary painting.*
> *To cultivate an understanding and appreciation of art by encouraging the purchase of good painting for homes as well as for public buildings and offices.*
> *To work toward securing a permanent art collection and a gallery in which the collection could be housed and the annual exhibit could be hung.*

The cooperative effort of multiple organizations made the art exhibit possible. Iron County, Cedar City Corporation, Cedar City Chamber of Commerce, Iron County School District, as well as the Branch Agricultural College were all involved in sustaining the exhibit. But significant contributions were required of various departments at the college. Elegant Sunday afternoon programs, prepared and presented under the direction of the music department or occasionally the dance department became a much-cherished tradition as part of the art exhibit. Distinguished visiting artists lectured, under arrangements made by the art department, and always the art department personnel were intimately involved in the details of the show. Carpentry work, necessary in the presentation of paintings as well as the un-crating and re-crating of the works, involved faculty and staff from the college industrial arts department. Faculty members were represented on all the commit-

tees that kept the enterprise alive.

Housing of the exhibit presented a challenge. It moved from one public building to another, from one elementary school to another, each year or two in a new location. Schools loved having the exhibit hang in their halls, and students of all ages delighted to see the paintings. In 1953, when the college gymnasium was the venue, it was necessary for the committee to wait until the final strains of music from the spring formal prom had faded away, then work feverishly through the night to get the paintings hung in time for the Sunday afternoon opening of the exhibit.

The final home for the Cedar City Annual Art Exhibit was the Braithwaite Fine Arts Gallery, in 1974, where it continues as a much-anticipated event each spring.

The December morning fire that destroyed the BAC library collection, took perhaps a deeper toll upon the art collection, lovingly assembled by Professor Mary Bastow. The loss is detailed in the following article published by the *Iron County Record*, December 16, 1948:

GAELL
LINDSTROM

> *Mary L. Bastow, head of the art department of the Branch Agricultural College, suffered severe loss in a fire that extensively damaged the college library building Sunday morning. Miss Bastow had collected the Interior Decoration Library, one of the west's most valuable and extensive, and the entire supply of materials and information was destroyed. The department also lost valuable original paintings including two paintings by Maynard Dixon, and one by Eve VanEyk. A number of etchings, lithographs, and wood cuts were on display at an exhibit at the El Escalante Hotel and escaped destruction. Tapestries, wall hangings, needlepoint, furniture, china, pottery, and many other interior decoration materials were lost and cannot be replaced. Miss Bastow suffers a great personal loss in equipment valued at $3,000 in addition to her work. A painting which she had finished preparing for final work Saturday was lost in the blaze. Mural drawings and other art work, the product of many years, were burned.*

The retirement of Mary L. Bastow from full

PROFESSOR
MAX
WEAVER
AND SHERRIE
HILL

THOMAS
LEEK, 1963

MARY MACFARLANE
MACDONALD, 1963

time teaching came after 24 years as head of the art department. Professor Gaell Lindstrom, who had been teaching in the Cedar City Schools, began that summer to teach a college summer school class and was hired to fill the position as art department head. The emphasis of the department changed under Mr. Lindstrom's direction. Mr. Lindstrom, a renowned watercolorist, brought a greater emphasis in that medium. He added watercolor, design I & II, photography, ceramics, and lettering.

Lindstrom was instrumental in starting the ceramics program. He found space for the ceramics studio in the old men's dorms which were, at one time, barracks brought in from the desert. He was a potter, water colorist of the first degree and photographer par excellence. He was truly a "renaissance man" and his enthusiasm generated a new excitement, not only for the serious student, but for townspeople as well.

Professor Max Weaver took the reins of the art department with the departure of Mr. Lindstrom in 1957. Lindstrom had accepted a full professor's appointment at Utah State Agricultural College.

Professor Weaver came to Cedar City from Provo, Utah, where he had taught in the Provo school district. A native of Logan, Utah, Professor Weaver had studied with many notable artists. At CSU, one of his contributions was a ceramic mosaic-mural which was placed in the foyer of the newly-built science

building on campus. The mosaic ceramic pieces were made by students, and Professor Weaver supervised the design and placement of the pieces. He contributed greatly to the arts in Cedar City and taught night classes both in ceramics and painting.

He was named head of the department in 1961. Much of his art work reflects his connection to the red-rock country of southern Utah.

When Professor Weaver left for a teaching position at BYU in 1961 an exhaustive search of applicants from many parts of the United States resulted in the hiring of Professor Thomas A. Leek. A native of Salt Lake City, Professor Leek was well-qualified to teach the following classes: design, drawing and painting, printmaking, art history, and art education. His credentials were impressive: B.F.A., Art Institute of Chicago and M.A., BYU, Provo, Utah. Other graduate study was done at the University of Chicago, University of California at Los Angeles, and the University of Iowa in Iowa City, Iowa.

Professor Leek began to build the department with the addition of faculty. That his students respected him and benefitted from him is illustrated by an excerpt from a letter written by a former student:

Now Tom Leek was not the kind of professor whose courses you took if you were faint-hearted, cowardly, lazy, uncommitted or unconfident—all or most of which I was. He was demanding and rigorous, critical, difficult to please, intimidating, and smart, and initially seemed humorless. He would often begin courses in a new quarter by announcing that if anybody was taking this course for elective or general education credit, "there must be an easier way," thereby allowing the process of natural selection (which I had just learned about in Professor Wes Larsen's biology class) to reduce the class size. Nevertheless, I found myself intrigued and challenged by Leek's amazing skills, diversity and knowledge and if I worked really hard (usually putting in about twice as much time or more than most of the other students) who all seemed to have much more talent than I, there would be an occasional pat on the head from T. Leek, and at times he would do something with his face that I found out later was a kind of smile. It was subtle and I wondered if it hurt him very much to do that.[6]

Recognizing the limitations inherent in studying the great works of art in a small rural community, T. Leek took students and interested members of the community on numerous trips to Los Angeles and San Francisco. He was a knowledgeable guide.

Mary M. MacDonald, a Cedar City native, was appointed to teach ceramics, three-dimensional design, senior art portfolio and art appreciation. She was educated at BAC, Mills College in Oakland, Calif., and USAC In Logan, Utah. Her duties included color and design consultant to the College, and she also worked with the architects on various buildings on campus.

Mrs. MacDonald taught until 1965, when she moved to Lander, Wyo., and taught classes at Central Wyoming Community College. Mrs. MacDonald returned to the college in 1976 and taught continuing education classes and team-taught with Carol Abraham.

Appointed to teach ceramics, sculpture, design, and art appreciation in 1966, Robert L. Gerring taught in the department until 1976.

Glen Dale Anderson was appointed as the third member of the art department faculty in 1967 and taught art education, art appreciation, drawing and painting. Anderson had earned a Master of Fine Arts from Utah State University. He taught in the department until 1983. In 1974 Mr. Anderson received the Utah Art Education Association's Art Educator of the Year award. As assistant professor of art at SUSC, he exhibited in western states art shows and worked on in-service programs demonstrating various art media throughout the area He served as assistant professor until 1983, when he transferred to the education department at the college.

He was noted for his humorous and entertaining approach to teaching and an inimitable manner of involving students.

*I*n the quest for a fine arts gallery on the campus, Professor Tom Leek was a moving force and when the Old Administration building was renovated as a classroom building, he seized the moment and was instrumental in obtaining space in the basement for the gallery. Professor Leek proudly described the new facility:

The new Fine Arts Gallery opened in January 1976—another dimension to the arts at Southern Utah State College. The Gallery is named in honor of Dr. Royden C. Braithwaite, president of the college and an ardent supporter of the arts. Consisting of 2,000 square feet and equipped with excellent lighting, display and security systems, the Braithwaite Fine Arts Gallery is located in the lower level of the Old Administration

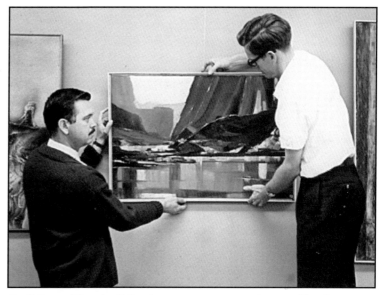

TOM LEEK AND
ROBERT
GERRING

Building. The building's recent renovation involved an "adaptive preservation" program, which included a sensitive, thorough and economical restoration of the second-oldest building on campus.

"The Braithwaite Gallery, the only secured, non-commercial gallery south of Springville, Utah, is a cultural resource center for the visual arts in a broad rural area. A high standard of excellence is maintained in the gallery. In addition to the care and exhibition of the college's permanent collection (a substantial collection now includes paintings, graphics, ceramics, sculptures and weaving with a total value approaching $500,000), important traveling exhibitions are scheduled year-round. Faculty and student exhibitions are held and the well-established Cedar City National Competitive Exhibition is presented annually. Illustrated lectures, art demonstrations, art film series, music concerts and related special events are presented regularly.[7]

GLEN DALE
ANDERSON,
1978

It was an appropriate tribute when the gallery was named for Dr. Royden Braithwaite, for he had been an ardent supporter of the work of the department and the arts in general. When Braithwaite spoke of the gallery, he revealed something of his own philosophy and spirit.

There are moments in our lives, there are moments in a day, when we seem to see beyond the usual. Such are the moments of our greatest wisdom, if one could but recall his vision by some sort of sign. It was in this hope that the arts were invented—signposts toward greater knowledge.

The Art Spirit, as communicated in the philosophy of Robert Henri, permeates the spirit and educational philosophy of Southern Utah State College—the quest for knowledge, human fulfillment and the betterment of mankind includes the experience of beauty revealed in the creations of the environment of the world in which we live.

ARLENE V.
BRAITHWAITE

The arts of man flourish at Southern Utah State College. The campus is more than its buildings: it is the stately groves of trees, the lawns and shrubbery, the sidewalks and malls, the playing fields and outdoor classrooms; it is the residential and dining areas, the laboratories and recital halls, the offices, the classrooms, and hallways; it is the outdoor sculpture and water-falls; and, most especially, it is the Library and the Fine Arts Gallery and the substantive, priceless permanent art collection. It is the inner world of the experience of each student, each faculty member, each citizen who becomes involved in the designed processes of education which constitute the genius and uniqueness of Southern Utah State College.[8]

Professor Leek was promoted to full professor in 1978-79. He resigned his position in 1985 to pursue his painting in California and Salt Lake City.

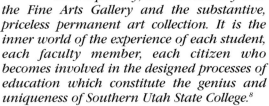

As funding needs mounted and appropriation realities became more clear, Friends of the Gallery was organized to offer volunteer service and fund-raising efforts. In yet another demonstration of the linking of town and school in worthwhile causes, they became so supportive and performed with such amazing effectiveness that, by the second year of operation, the administration considered reducing the basic budget and eliminating one full-time gallery person. Dr. Rodney Brown led the Friends of the Gallery from 1977-1984, Mary MacDonald was president through the years 1984-1986; Dr. C.J. Thinnes was elected to serve 1986-89 and Ann Marie Gardner provided leadership from 1989 through 1994.

The budget cut did not materialize, but the gallery has continued to depend upon mentors and friends. The Braithwaite Fine Arts Gallery is funded in part by a joint grant from the Utah Arts Council and the National Endowment for the Arts, Washington D.C., as well as Friends of the Gallery and other private contributors.

In 1975-76, Carol Jean Abraham was hired to teach ceramics, sculpture, mixed media, and art appreciation. She was a gifted artist and developed a Thixatrophic porcelain body which was "revolutionary" in the ceramic arts and was featured in many national publications.

The art department at this time was housed in the old Industrial Education building (or shop building) on the south end of the campus. There was a ceramics studio, dark-room for photography, painting and design space, and later a graphics studio when the building arts vacated the south end of the building. This also opened up a space for extended ceramics and sculpture. The old chemistry building, just north and adjacent to the art building, was converted into a painting studio. This was the art department home until the Centrum was completed in 1986, with classrooms, studios, and offices in addition to the space for athletics and performances.

Richard R. Adams was appointed to teach ceramics, sculpture, and other related subjects in 1977. His background was impressive: California State University at Long Beach, M..S.; Utah State University, B.S.; and Indiana State University, M.F.A. He brought an excellence to the department with his unique talent. His fragile, beautiful porcelain, encased in a sphere of plastic containers was exquisite. His wife, June, complemented him artistically in every way. She also had an M.F.A. from Indiana State University and was appointed as Professor Leek's assistant curator at the gallery. She later became curator when Professor Leek left the college in 1986. June was energetic and organized. There were many fine arts tours to art centers while she was employed, and she strengthened the organization "Friends of the Gallery" with innovative projects and ideas. The Adams' left the institution to accept positions at Indiana State University in 1988. Richard had planned the ceramics studio and sculpture studios to be built in the Centrum.

Arlene V. Braithwaite was appointed to the department in 1978. She received her A.P.A., B.F.A., and M.Ed., Art Emphasis from the University of Utah, Salt Lake City, Utah. Arlene has taught 13 different classes during her stay at S.U.U. She has served as head and is in charge of the art education composite major. She has initiated on-site visits to secondary schools and in classroom teaching experiences to prepare art education students for their student teaching. Her art work is primarily pastel paintings of the local landscape and figures. She has had her work exhibited in state and regional shows. She has served as Art Guild adviser and chaperoned student trips to Los Angeles, San Francisco, New Mexico, and Arizona. As head, she linked with the communication department in the establishment of a graphics computer lab and initiated summer art education workshops.

Mrs. Braithwaite was instrumental in planning the art studios in the Centrum. The move, in 1985, provided the first adequate home for the art department. She served as head of the department from 1989-1991 and 1995 to the time of this writing (1997).

Appointed as associate professor of art in 1984, Mark Talbert is a nationally recognized ceramicist. He taught at SUU through 1996. During his stay he served as department head and built a strong ceramics program. He was known for his large-scale and elegantly formed ceramic vessels.

Mr. Talbert received his B.A. degree from Fairfield State in West Virginia and his M.F.A. from Utah State University. "Art, he explained, is not a talent you are born with but it is a way of thinking. The trick to art is not making one good pot, but training yourself to think creatively, so that you will have life-long success." Talbert left SUU to pursue an arts administrative post at Tamarack, W. Va.

Assistant professor of art, 1983-1985, Nina Marshall was a painting and print-making instructor whose work dealt with objects and figures of personal significance to make insightful and emotional communication. She often worked multimedia, coloring a serigraph with pastel or combining drawing and painting in one image.

Assistant professor of art, 1985-86, Linda Lutz taught painting and drawing. Her media was primarily oil pastel and oil paint. Linda used the southern Utah landscape as a source for many of her abstractions. She was a caring teacher to whom students responded with enthusiasm.

Anton Rasmussen was an associate professor of art from 1986 to 1989; he received both his B.A. and his M.F.A. from the University of Utah. Rasmussen came to SUU after serving as the director of the Bountiful Arts Center. He is known for his large scale, panoramic paintings of southern Utah, including a series of murals for the Salt Lake City International Airport. His work ranges from idealized landscapes to abstract explorations of paint. He served as

department head during his stay at SUU. He was a robust, friendly person, and was very well-liked and admired by his students and colleagues.

As associate professor of art in 1986 to 1988, Mark Bangerter previously taught at Boise State College. He received his B.F.S. and his M.F.A. from the University of Utah. He taught painting and printmaking. Mark was an accomplished portrait painter and did numerous portrait commissions for the president of the University during his stay at SUU.

Hong Yu Ji served as assistant professor of art from 1986 to 1988. He came from State University of New York at New Paltz, where he was awarded a master's degree in painting and printmaking. He earned a bachelor's degree from the Central Academy of Fine Arts in Beijing, China. Primarily a figure painter, Yu Ji had his work purchased by the Pennsylvania Art Academy and has received numerous awards while in the state from the Springville Museum and Dixie College Invitational. He was a demanding instructor and, for the serious art student, an unlimited resource, placing many of his graduates in painting programs across the nation. He initiated evening figure drawing sessions for the students who wanted to work beyond class time.

MARK
BANGERTER

Martha MacLeish served as assistant professor of art from 1991 to 1992. She received her B.A. from the University of Massachusetts and M.F.A. in painting from Yale University. Her multimedia, large scale, non-objective paintings challenged viewers to rethink their assumptions about art.

Eric Brown, instructor from 1994 to present (1997), teaches art history, art appreciation and drawing. He received a B.A. from SUSC in 1974 and M.F.A. from Drake University. He is a talented figure painter who also uses his art background with his cabinet-making skills to craft furniture that are works of art. He is considered the department's scholar, and he is sought by students for his thoughtful opinions.

Perry Stewart, associate professor of art from 1990 to present (1997), earned his B.A. and M.F.A. in illustration from Utah State University. Mr. Stewart established the illustration composite major at SUU. He is actively involved in professional illustration and is a master teacher. The work of his students has been recognized nationally at the New York Society of Illustrators Student Competition. Stewart is currently working with the communication department to develop a graphic design major, which will train students in computer graphics.

Del Parson, an associate professor at SUU from 1994 to 1995, received both his B.A. and M.F.A. from BYU. Del is a well-known portrait painter and illustrator for the LDS Church. He has proven to be an excellent resource for students of painting, especially those interested in the figure. Mr, Parson is currently teaching painting at Dixie College. He has painted many of the portraits that hang in the Great Hall.

Brian Hoover, assistant professor of art, received his B.F.A. from Kutztown University and M.F.A. from State University of New York at Buffalo, New York, in printmaking and painting. Mr. Hoover's painting is enigmatic, using figures and symbols that suggest a narrative but one that would vary with the viewer. He primarily teaches painting, printmaking and drawing. Hoover is an excellent teacher, but due to his youthful appearance, he has been mistaken for a student. He has been instrumental in establishing a new printmaking studio in the former drawing studio on upper campus.

Susan D. Harris arrived at SUU in 1996. She received her B.A. from the University of Illinois and M.F.A. from Utah State University. Susan is an active professional ceramicist who is very involved in National Council on Education for the Ceramic Arts (NCECA), and has served as their exhibition's chair for the past five years. Her ceramic vessels appropriate forms and surface designs from other cultures and times and are combined with her own personal references to create intriguingly complex pieces. She teaches ceramics, sculpture and three-dimensional design.

*T*he department philosophy aims toward broadening cultural backgrounds of all students and, at the same time, toward offering a solid foundation for the serious art students, major or minor.[9] Objectives include assisting students to obtain a liberal arts education; helping prepare students for teaching careers in elementary and secondary schools; preparing students for professional careers in industry and studio practice; qualifying students for advanced study and providing cultural enrichment.

The art department is growing. There are at this writing more than 90 art majors. Offerings in art include ceramics and sculpture, art education, painting and illustration. The department's physical facilities are located in the Centrum and include spacious ceramic, painting, drawing and sculpture studios. A new computer lab will open in 1997 to provide art students with current technology for art production.

The art department has set up a new computer graphics lab in cooperation with the communication department. This state-of-the-art computer lab allows students to do illustration, graphic design and fine art on computers.

The faculty is committed to maintaining the "one-to-one" education that art majors have always received. This is probably the main reason that the department consistently graduates such a large percentage of its majors.

The department's students and faculty are receiving recognition nationally and regionally. Illustration students John Snell and Mike Malm were recognized in New York City, in 1995, by the New York Society of Illustrators. Their work was selected from thousands of entries to hang in the society's prestigious Annual Student Show.

Brian Hoover, assistant professor of painting was honored at the Springville Annual Spring Salon with the Award of Merit for his painting, "The Harbinger." He was also featured in the University's publication, *Sanctuary,* with several pages of full-color reproductions of his work.

Arlene Braithwaite was elected president-elect of the Utah Art Education Association, the statewide professional organization for art educators.

Art graduates are currently being placed directly in the professions of illustration and teaching or go on to graduate school. Phil Hermansen, the designer for the Shakespeare Festival; Wayne Kimball, professor of printmaking at Brigham Young University; and Karen Gilg, nationally recognized printmaker and sculptor, are SUU graduates.

In 1996 the department welcomed Susan Harris to teach ceramics and sculpture. Susan's work was included in the September 1996 issue of *Ceramics Monthly,* the professional journal for ceramicists nationwide. Her work is featured in one-woman and group-juried national exhibitions around the country.

*T*he list of accomplished artists, teachers, illustrators and printmakers that have emerged from Southern Utah University, in its various stages, is long and illustrious.[10] Mary MacDonald included those lists in her *History of the Art Department.* In this brief outline one testimonial must represent all.

Between the lines of a warm and humorous letter written by a renowned and successful artist, W. Wayne Kimball, once a quavering student, one senses the proof of the pudding.

Kimball graduated from College of Southern Utah in 1968. His resume reveals a litany of accomplishments and honors, degrees and certifications since he graduated from CSU. Presently (1997), he is Professor of lithography and drawing at Brigham Young University. His work has been shown in nearly 300 exhibitions, represented in scores of private and public collections, and reproduced in more than fifty publications. He is listed in art-world publications that do not even hint that he was not a child prodigy. But by his own expression:

...my motivation for getting into art in the first place was so that I could look at the pictures and not have to deal with written stuff.

When I came to College of Southern Utah, I was actually a mathematics major (worked with Parley Dalley -- holy smoke! and Kim - "heres, the deal, see" -- Jones) with ambitions of being a really cool quantitative guy who was also athletic. The athletic fantasies that I had didn't hold up very well for long. I was bound to get kicked out of sports anyway because I had such a lousy attitude - quit football, didn't make basketball, and hated to run. Besides, a person can encounter serious hurt doing athletic things.

The art business was all an accident. I remember very clearly how it happened. One day just as our freshman year (1961-62) was getting under way, my roommates, Bruce Christensen and Steve Steffensen and I bumbled into the art building to taunt Steve's and my cousin, Margaret Mabey, who was taking the ceramics class. The activity looked really fun and very slippery (and quasi-athletic--had to use those kick wheels). . . so we figured that this was the class for us, and we all three enrolled for ceramics the next two quarters. I took ceramics for four quarters before Mary MacDonald persuaded me to take some of the foundation art courses. (She had clearly seen enough of me by then). So to satisfy her I enrolled in a lettering class from Tom Leek. . . At any rate, that proved to be a decisive period of time for my career. While at home with my parents one weekend, the subject of what I would major in naturally arose. I think we spent time discussing every major in the catalog (except art because that always brought with it the embarrassing implication of what would I do for a living?), and finally my dad

commented that since I had gotten such a "kick" out of my art classes, why didn't I major in that? What a question. That came from a man who was a banker--and anybody knows that no self-respecting banker would ever allow his kid to major in art. And here he was, actually suggesting it. And that was the moment when my decision was made and I never looked back (until I got to graduate school.) Of course, Professors MacDonald and Leek had carefully crafted everything for that moment. From there, I elected to take art education as a composite major (thinking there might be some job potential in public education) because I was in no position to select a single medium-based studio major such as painting or sculpture, having had by that time practically no exposure to any of those disciplines. (The studio aspect of the art education major at that time required a fairly extensive and balanced series of courses in all the studio disciplines).

Graduate school was, in fact, an extremely difficult endeavor for me. As I look back, I have no idea how I survived it, but with the superlative undergraduate education that I had received, it helped set the stage for an unbelievably exciting and rewarding career. I see myself as living proof that an aimless attitude can lead to something.

The essence of the department lies in the tradition of the school. Again and again young people come to discover their potential and to receive the inspiration and instruction to achieve it. That was the vision of the founders.

THE
BRAITHWAITE
BUILDING,
1996

BNS FACULTY,
1912, SEE PAGE 303
FOR IDENTIFICATION

'THE STUDENT' STAFF,
1916

CHAPTER XII

Language, Literature & Humanities

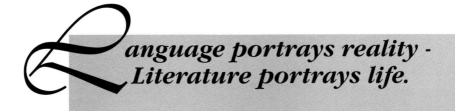

*anguage portrays reality -
Literature portrays life.*

When the first tiny circular of the Southern Branch of the State Normal School appeared in 1897, it gave as "Requirements for Admission" in reading and spelling the following:[1]

The applicant should be able to recognize and define all the parts of speech and tell their respective varieties; to decline nouns and pronouns and understand their properties; to compare adjectives and adverbs; to explain regular and irregular, transitive and intransitive verbs; to analyze participial, infinitive and prepositional phrases; and to explain and analyze easy sentences, simple, compound and complex.

The students's knowledge of the use of capital letters and punctuation marks and his ability to compose good sentences will be tested by a short article to be written at the time of examination.

He must be prepared to read clearly and intelligently any selection in the Franklin Fifth Reader.

He must be able to spell the words found in the Modern Spelling Book (the book in use in Utah).

At the back of the book was an announcement to give hope to those not yet prepared to enter the Normal School:

As there are in the more remote settlements many young men and women who have not had the advantages of a complete common school education, it is designed to offer for students over 18 years of age special instruction in the subjects required for entrance.

Admission to this preparatory course was by examination or by giving evidence of ability to do the work required. Classes were offered in grammar, reading, writing and spelling. Howard R. Driggs, secretary and registrar, was to teach language and literature and Annie E. Spencer, assistant librarian, was to teach elocution. Mr. Driggs would also teach penmanship. Three courses in English and two in reading were offered.

In 1899-1900 Annie Spencer began teaching Reading, which she continued through 1905. In 1901-02 oral expression was offered, described as follows:

HOWARD DRIGGS' ENGLISH CLASS, 1902

ANNIE SPENCER
AS ROMEO AND
BLANCHE
THOMAS AS
JULIET

*Training in thought-getting, and the power
of adequate expression, voice building, pronunciation, articulation, the criteria of vocal
expression - quality, force, time, pitch - and
underlying principles of reading. Special
attention paid to expressive reading and
developing a standard of criticism.*

Howard Driggs was away on leave in 1901
and the catalog lists Blanche Thomas as English
assistant, with Annie Spencer for reading. This
must have been a most dramatic year, as the
SUU photo archives attest. Annie Spencer
played Romeo to Blanche Thomas as Juliet.
Thomas also played Ophelia, with Spencer as
her Hamlet. Lantern slides were made of the balcony scene and a scene from *Hamlet* for use in
proselyting for the Branch Normal School in
nearby communities.

In 1903-04 the preparatory course became
the sub-preparatory course with the same classes offered. Instruction in foreign languages
began in 1903, with German being taught by
Willard Jones, continued the next year by
Charles R. Mabey who, in 1904-05, also taught
English grammar. Reading and interpretation of
literature were taught that year by John T.
Marshman.

In 1906-07 English classes were taught by F.Y.
Fox and George W. Decker, the principal of the
Southern Branch. Edwin S. Du Poncet, Ph.D.
expanded the foreign language offerings to
include German, French, Spanish, and Latin.
German included both an elementary course
and German 2, devoted mostly to prose and
drama. Spanish was recommended for "those

young people who may wish to fit themselves
for the consular service as clerks," adding, "For
those who wish to become teachers in our
Spanish possessions such a course will be very
valuable." Latin was offered for those "having
aspirations for medicine or other scientific
work."

Besides continuing with all the languages
through the next year and teaching English, Dr.
Du Poncet was the drama director. Nevada
Watson Driggs remembered that when she was
a student at BNS he directed several plays. *"Miss
Walker, the singing instructor and I were in*
She Stoops to Conquer," she said. *"He directed
other plays, but I can't remember any except*
Trilby, *which I was not in."* (From an undated
letter to Inez Cooper.) English classes were
taught by Edward A. Morgan, Menzies
Macfarlane, and Mr. Decker and reading by a
Miss Donahue.

In 1908-09 English, literary interpretation,
rhetoric and oral expression were taught by
Morgan, Macfarlane and Decker; German was
taught by T. Willard Jones and Latin and Greek
by Herbert Hussong.

In 1909-10 Roswell C. Belnap began teaching
German; he also taught English along with
Morgan. Hussong continued with Latin.

[Enid M. Severy is listed in the catalog to
teach oral expression, but a penciled note
signed by Parley Dalley says she did not teach,
that she cancelled her contract before school
began and was replaced by Mabel Naegle.]

In February of 1910, a monthly school publication, *The Student,* was begun. The first editor-
in-chief was A. Nevada Watson (later Nevada
Watson Driggs), who had taught school the year
before so that she could finish at B.N.S. She was
only 17 at the time.

"The Student, as its name signifies," according to an announcement in the magazine, "represents the students, and is controlled entirely
by a staff of students. It is a school magazine the

ANNIE SPENCER AS HAMLET AND BLANCHE
THOMAS AS OPHELIA.

purpose of which is to give experience in managing and editing papers and to encourage literary efforts."

Under the heading "THEMES FROM ENGLISH CLASSES OF BRANCH NORMAL," the March 1910 issue of *The Student* included "Dreams" by Richard Tweedie and "Uncle David" by A. Nevada Watson.

The Student also gave faculty members a place for publication. In the April 1910 issue there appeared an article by Roswell Belnap, "The Spirit of Our Secondary Schools." Myrtle Decker's "Mark Twain's Philosophy" was featured in March 1911.

News of the language and literature classes included the information that English A had just finished reading *Ivanhoe* and was again studying technical grammar; English B students were reading *Silas Marner;* English C, studying Milton, was "deep in his masque *Comus.*" The German class, having had the exam on *Gluck Auf,* was studying those "STRONG" verbs, and that the "members of the class can certainly bear witness to the fact that these verbs are strong and much opposed to being conquered"

In 1910-11 English and oral expression were taught by Myrtle Decker, English and reading by John A. Alder, and English and interpretation of literature by Roswell C. Belnap, who also taught German. Clifford Ashley [or Ashby - the name is spelled both ways in various publications] and a Miss Palmer were added to the English faculty the next year. The faculty photo of June 1912 in *The Student* includes also, as teachers of English, Dr. M.L. James and Kate Palmer Macfarlane, most probably the Miss Palmer of the year before, and Robert S. Gardner, who taught German that year, as well as shop and mathematics.

In the final year of BNS, Myrtle Decker taught English and Elocution, Jean Brown taught English and Public Address, R.S. Gardner taught German and Clifford Ashley taught French.

The 1897-98 circular announced that the policy of the instructors of the school would be to "encourage and assist in establishing student organizations which tend to promote a broader culture." Among these were to be literary and debating societies. By 1902-03 the students of the Normal had a debating club, "conducted exclusively by men," and a literary and domestic art society, "exclusively for women."

The committee for literary and debating societies in 1911-12 was comprised of Mr. Ashley and Miss Decker. On March 2, 1912 the

THE FIRST EDITORIAL STAFF OF *THE STUDENT* - BNS 1910. LEFT TO RIGHT - BACK ROW: LILLIAN HIGBEE, DOLPH ANDRES, NEVADA WATSON, RICHARD TWEEDIE, GLADYS MCCONNELL. FRONT ROW: IVAN DECKER, ARTHUR FIFE, RASS MCFARLANE, LEON WINDSOR, LINDA SLACK

Students' Literary Society held a reading at which Myrtle Decker and Elsa Anderson read two pieces. There were also two musical numbers by Mr. Ashley and the trio: Misses Winnie Corry, Ina Neilson and Vira Perkins. Another reading was held on March 16, 1912.

Gordon Matheson sang and Mrs. K. P. Macfarlane read an original essay. In April the Students' Literary Society held two more programs. One was a talk by Amasa Clark and the

BNS FACULTY, 1912: TOP ROW (LEFT TO RIGHT): R.L. WRIGLEY, AGRICULTURE, ANIMAL HUSBANDRY; JAMES ROBB, BUSINESS; HAROLD WILKINSON, PHYSICAL EDUCATION, PHYSIOLOGY; R.S. GARDNER, SHOPS, GERMAN, MATHEMATICS; J.W.BARTON, HISTORY, EDUCATION; CLIFFORD ASHLEY, BIOLOGY, FRENCH; A.N. TOLLESTRUP, MUSIC. BOTTOM ROW (LEFT TO RIGHT): PARLEY DALLEY, PHYSICS, CHEMISTRY, MATHEMATICS; MYRTLE DECKER, ENGLISH, GIRLS' PHYSICAL CULTURE; K.P. MACFARLANE, ENGLISH; JENNIE LEIGH, DOMESTIC SCIENCE; ADAH BETZ, DOMESTIC ART; DR. M.L. JAMES, ENGLISH, MATHEMATICS; PRINCIPAL G.W. DECKER.

FORENSIC
LEAGUE,
1903

other a reading by Irene Mackelprang.

In 1912-13, four literature and language-related groups were defined in the catalog, including one for alumni:

Students' Literary Society. All students are invited to become members of the Students' Literary Society. This organization aims at the promotion of general culture in literature, and at developing power in public speaking, parliamentary procedure, and different forms of public entertainment.

Wranglers' Club. Any boy interested in debating may become an active member of this organization on recommendation of some member of the association. Its purpose is to give special opportunity for a study of argumentation and for practice in debate. Besides regular debating, current events and other interesting topics are discussed.

Le Cercle. This organization comprises all the girls and women teachers of the school. Some sessions are devoted to literary programs, others to social features. The purpose of the association is intellectual and social betterment.

MYRTLE
DECKER
JANSEN,
1917

The Litsic. An organization of alumni. It was organized in the fall of 1909 with Menzies Macfarlane president. It gives the opportunity to the alumni residing in the vicinity of the school for meeting and discussing literary and scientific topics from the standpoint of the graduate and mature minds.

In 1913, with the change to the BAC, came a downsizing of the English faculty, with only Myrtle Decker and Jean Brown listed, to teach composition and literature, drama, oral expres-

sion, and debating. Though German and Latin were offered in the 1913-14 catalog, no teacher was indicated for either one. Dramatics and debating, etc. were to be managed by student organizations, with assistance from faculty committees. The student was to be given "all the encouragement that the new administration could lend."

By 1916-17, Myrtle Decker had become Myrtle Decker Jansen and was the only instructor listed for English. The classics for study in her composition class ranged from the *Iliad* of Homer to Burrough's *Birds and Bees*, with sixteen books to be read outside of classwork. German and Latin were still listed, but no instructor indicated. But a German club was mentioned for those "who read and speak Deutsche."

Lottie H. Kunz and Eunice Jacobson were the English faculty for 1918-19, with classes such as advanced rhetoric, Tennyson and lyric poetry and A Study of the Modern Novel added to the basics. French was listed, but still no instructor.

The Student, published monthly, gave students an "opportunity to try their ability at writing." In 1919-20 that opportunity was no longer optional. The catalog announced:

All students registered in the English department will be required to contribute to student publications. ... Each student will be asked to do some newspaper reporting as a part of his English work. Students will be expected to engage in chapel talks and college and intercollege contests.

A new class was offered:

SOCIAL STUDIES IN MODERN LITERATURE: This course is a general reading course designed for fathers and mothers or college

STAFF OF *THE STUDENT*, 1916

students. It is an attempt to understand current social conditions. Both drama and novel are studied. Four hours credit each term.

In 1921-22 English students were required to make contributions to *The Student* and to take part in the tryouts for debating and public speaking contests. Lottie Kunz was now Lottie Esplin and the next year she was joined by Marian Gudmundson who taught English and French. King Hendricks joined the English faculty in 1923, and Ruby Woodard was an English assistant.

The March 14, 1923 issue of *The Student* reported the following, under the heading DOINGS OF THE FRENCH CLASS (published without accents):

Une vingtaine de Francais regale la faculte et l'etudiants dans la chapelle exercises a dix heure et demi A. M. Lundi, Mars onzieme. Nous sommes un vrai regal de nous allie voisions. Nous sommes refraichi sans delassements.

Lottie K. Esplin became the first head of the English department in 1924, assisted by Gudmundsen and Hendricks: Hendricks also taught Latin. In 1926, Hendricks became head of the department of English, a position he held until 1935.

When Aileen Dixon, head of the dramatics department left in December, 1926 to be married, her classes were taken over by Zoe Robinson, Mr. Janson and Mr. Hendricks. *The Goose Hangs High,* the play she was directing, went on as planned with Hendricks directing. He also taught French that year.

In 1926 a German class was organized under William H. Manning for students interested in learning conversational German. The announcement said that it would be given twice a week in the evening at a time most convenient for those desiring to take it. Musical students especially were expected to be interested in the course. Manning taught German intermittently until 1950, as well as music.

The Student sponsored a Christmas story contest in 1927, the prize to be "probably a gold pencil or pen." [No record could be found of the winning story or writer, or the actual prize.]

Ira N. Hayward and Esther Eggertsen joined the faculty in 1927, Roy L. Halverson in 1928. That year private training in interpretative reading was offered for the first time, open to a limited number of high school and college students who had sufficient coursework or practical

experience to justify private work.

In 1929 Allen Cannon joined the faculty to teach English and French, and Mary Lovina Bastow taught English as well as art. Story telling and children's literature was taught by a Miss West. Elementary Latin was offered in 1932, and private instruction in interpretation was available for ten dollars per credit hour. Among new instructors in the 1930s were Marie Tinsley, English and Charles B. Drake, French and German, 1935; Grant Redford, English, 1936; Mary Coughlin and Ray B. West, Jr., English, modern languages and speech, 1936; Clara Woodhouse, English, 1938.

LOTTIE K. ESPLIN, 1925

Ray B. West, Jr. became the first chair of the division of English, Speech, and Languages in 1939, followed the next year by Grant Redford. On March 25, 1941, *The Bacian,* the college newspaper, announced: "*The Rocky Mountain Review*, the only literary quarterly published in the intermountain area, and edited by Grant Redford and Ray B. West, Jr., of the BAC faculty, has just issued its winter number." *The Review* was published for some years at BAC.

New faculty during the 1940s were Frances Elva Knott and Gwendolyn Hansen, English, 1942; Ione S. Bennion, Harry Plummer, and Donald K. Nelson, English, 1943; Betty T. Berry and J.G. Van Zandt, English and modern languages, 1943.

N.A. Pedersen, became the dean of the Division of English, Modern Languages and Speech in 1943, with Grant H. Redford continuing as chair. Preston R. Gledhill became chair in 1944; in 1945 Carlton Culmsee became dean. H. Wayne Driggs, Twain Tippets and Harry Plummer all joined the English faculty in 1946, and Richard M. Rowley and Elva Oldroyd the next year. Modern languages were taught by Manning, Plummer, and Alene H. Grover. The German Club was still active. *The Bacian*, Nov. 11, 1947 reported:

KING HENDRICKS, 1927

The German Club held another 'get together' [Nov. 3 at the home of Mr. and Mrs. George Wood] :

...In the course of the evening, our hostess, Mrs. Wood, served hot doughnuts and cider. At this time a ban was put on speaking English. Naturally there were several violations and the regular fine of one cent

GRANT REDFORD, 1939

RAY B.
WEST,
1939

per English word was assessed.

And in February, another activity of the German Club:

Each student with his pet German words will stand up before the class and tell his favorite story in German. The extreme interest and desire for many of the students to learn German has almost forced them into a condition of servility towards their book. (Bacian, Feb.3, 1948)

The May 19, 1948 issue of the *Bacian* announced a new literary magazine that would contain short stories, essays, poetry and feature articles written by students in Rowley's creative writing and advanced composition classes and Tippett's English composition classes.

There was also an article about a book being compiled by the English 12 expository writing class to be called *Southern Utah, Its Resources and Possibilities,* with each member of the class writing a chapter.

TWAIN
TIPPETTS,
1948

Twain Tippetts became chair of the Division of English, Modern Language, and Speech in 1948. A literary magazine was published during the spring quarter of 1949, containing the best student writing in short story, essay, poetry and feature article done by students in English classes at the college. Members of the creative writing course assembled and edited the magazine, advised by Mr. Rowley.

Gwyn Clark joined the faculty in 1950, and a new class was offered: Learning to Like Literature.

On Nov. 15, 1950 the fifth annual poetry recital was held, with 36 students taking part— the theme: Poetry Around the World. There was a special memorial group of poems to Edna St. Vincent Millay, who had died just a short time before. Some original poetry was also presented. Professor Tippets remarked that interest in poetry had grown in the city and the schools, with one of the largest classes enrolled that year, a class containing the highest percentage of male students. A poetry recital was presented by the group in Panguitch and in some other communities in the area.

For the dedication of the new fieldhouse, Tippetts and the students of his radio class took charge of the assembly. The class arranged a script that told the story of the building from the beginning. Kent Myers acted as narrator and, with the help of the radio class, the story of the Bronco Barn was presented. (*The Student,* Dec. 12, 1950)

In spring quarter of 1952, a new "reading accelerator" was used to help increase reading speed of students. According to Professor Tippetts, some students had made spectacular gains in both speed and comprehension, some as much as 100 percent increase.

In the last year of BAC, 1952-53, Culmsee was still dean of the division, Tippetts was still chair, and Plummer, Clark and Rowley completed the faculty.

The English and languages faculty was basically the same in 1953-54 as BAC became CSU. Carlton Culmsee was dean of the Division of English, Modern Language, Speech, and Journalism, with Twain Tippetts, chair, J. H. Plummer and Gwyn Clark, instructors. (Rowley was on leave.) There were some interestingly titled new courses:

*Humanities I. Reading to Stimulate
   Abundant Living
English A. Drill in Essentials of English
Communications 1. Read Well
Communications 2. Speak Well
Communications 3. Write Well*

By 1958 Eugene Woolf and Elaine Southwick were among the English and languages faculty, which was now part of the division of Language Arts and Humanities. Introduction to humanities was offered for the first time.

Paul Vorkink joined the English faculty in 1959, as did Fred Adams and Kent Myers.

The March 7, 1959 issue of the *Deseret News* announced a contest for CSU students. They were invited to submit papers based on research and personal interviews concerning the history of CSU. The contest was sponsored by David L. Sargent, emeritus professor, Dr.

Braithwaite and Harry Plummer. Unfortunately, no contest entries seem to have survived.

The Division of Humanities, English and Fine Arts, which encompassed languages and literature in 1961, was

GWYN CLARK,
1958

divided the next year into the Division of English and Language Arts and the Division of Humanities, Fine Arts, and Languages. Culmsee was the dean of both divisions. Rowley was chair of the first and J. H. Plummer, chair of the second.

Four majors were offered in English and language arts: the standard English major, the English teaching major, the writing and mass communications major, and the American studies major. New classes offered were reading improvement, speed reading, great books and ideas and teaching English and speech.

Under the direction of Professor Paul Vorkink, a reading development lab was set up, as described in the *Iron County Record,* Oct. 19, 1961:

The reading improvement program is composed of a remedial section for students having reading difficulties and an elective section for students who desire to increase their reading speed and comprehension....The class instructors use some equipment such as the Rateometer which covers any printed page at a regulated rate of speed forcing the student to keep ahead. A special control reader flashes words, sentences or complete articles onto a screen at adjusted speeds....The program was begun in 1959 at CSU under the direction of the English department staff.

Problems of philosophy was offered as part of the humanities program. In modern languages, French, German and Spanish all had two-year programs, plus readings, and there was a Spanish readings and conversation class.

Richard M. Rowley attended the English Annual Creative Problem-Solving Institute in 1962, after which he set up a summer institute called Creative Problem Solving and taught classes and workshops on that subject and also creative thinking at CSU and in the surrounding communities.

Rowley had earlier been active in starting the Theatre Matinee program held in the Bootstrap Theatre in Old Main. Each Wednesday students would present plays varying from *Prometheus Bound* to *Othello* to Ibsen's *A Doll's House* and Susan Glaspell's *Trifles* to *Cyrano de Bergerac.* Rowley's dramatic interests carried him off campus to Zion to film sequences for *Singaway,* a musical drama he wrote and produced.

CSU students in a class taught by *Deseret News* writer Lavor Chaffin in July 1962 toured southern Utah, collecting information for arti-

cles. They visited Silver Reef, a mining ghost town in Washington County, Old Iron Town, west of Cedar City, and a number of other interesting places.

In July of 1962, a *Deseret News* headline announced:

CSU ZEROES IN ON FAULTY ENGLISH

The article that followed, written by Jim Robinson (*Deseret News* correspondent), explained the new program:

ELAINE SOUTHWICK, 1956

Professor Richard M. Rowley, Chairman of the Division of English and Language Arts, is in charge of the unique program, which stresses English in all classes at the college. Initiated a year ago, the program is a means of attacking the problem of student deficiencies in basic English fundamentals. A copy of the basic English handbook used in the freshman English course was distributed to each faculty member, with an explanation of its use. Professor Rowley says this is to give instructors a background into what is expected of college students in English and also to provide a review of basic English rules for teachers. CSU teachers are encouraged to grade all papers that students submit on the basis of English rules, as well as ideas and subject matter. This grading method calls for a double grade, one on the basis of ideas and the other an English grade. Thus a grade of A/D would tell the student that his ideas are very good, but his English is pretty bad. Other improvements: making research paper style guides available to teachers and special English review sessions at faculty meetings.

RICHARD M. ROWLEY, 1955

PAUL VORKINK WITH STUDENTS, 1964

J.H.
PLUMMER

Red Slip Used: Mr. Rowley says a teacher should not be expected to read a paper that is obviously not on a college level. This is when the red slip is used. A square yellow sticker tells a student that the paper he submitted has good ideas, but is lacking in some phase of English— clarity of expression, punctuation, organization, etc. The sticker was purposely shaped like a highway caution sign because it indicates that a student should use caution and more care in his English habits.

New faculty in 1962 were Gwen Sandburg and Heber G. Woolsey. CSU students of Spanish studied spring quarter of 1963 in Mexico, attending Mexico City College. Harry Plummer, chair of the CSU Division of Humanities, Fine Arts, and Language accompanied the students.

By 1964 Bonnie LoJean Boden (later Hobbs), Geneve Plummer and James A. Work were part of the faculty; an honors course in basic communication had begun, and Spanish students could again spend spring quarter in Mexico City, a program that continued for several years.

In 1965, when CSU became a four-year liberal arts college, a student could qualify for the bachelors degree in any of four areas in English: the English literature major, the English communication major, the teaching major in English (for secondary teachers) and the composite major in language arts (for secondary teachers). There was also a composite major in speech-English-theatre arts, an English minor and a minor in languages—German, Spanish or French. In 1966 the Major in German was added. New courses were teaching English in the secondary school, foundations of linguistics and methods and materials for the teaching of languages.

The foreign language offerings were greatly expanded with three-year programs, followed by literature classes in French, German and Spanish. German classes also included phonet-

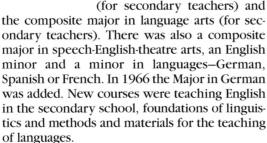

LYNN
BROADBENT

ics and pronunciation, cultural history of Germany, history of the German language, applied linguistics and a senior seminar. Kenneth W. Childs was a new faculty member that year.

Robert A. Christmas joined CSU faculty as assistant professor of English with a teaching emphasis on creative writing in 1968. English and languages were now part of the School of Arts and Letters with Eugene T. Woolf as dean and also chair of the English department. Other new English faculty were Bruce Jorgensen, Elva Hatch, Iris Corry and Marilyn Hawley.

Harry Plummer was chair of the department of languages, which included Lynn Broadbent, E. Leon Chidester and Herbert Ludwig. A Spanish major had been added, and *Don Quixote* was taught in two parts, in alternate years. Latin American Culture and Latin American literature were added to the curriculum.

When CSU became SUSC the organization of the School of Arts and Letters remained the same, with Eugene Woolf as dean; Robert Christmas, chair of English; J. H. Plummer, chair of languages. Rowley, Childs, Jorgensen, Corry, Elva O. Hatch, Geneve Plummer and Marilyn Hawley completed the English faculty; Broadbent, Chidester, Ludwig and Bruce L. Knowlton, the language faculty.

Joining the faculty in the 1970s were Robert T. Wazeka and William David Lee, English (1971); Michael Cohen and Gretchen Robertson (later Jones), English; Terry M. Blodgett, German; James Mills, French and Dick

LEON CHIDESTER

Carlson, Spanish (1974); S.S. Moorty, English (1976); James Harrison, German (1977); Sage L. Platt, English (1979).

David Lee became head of the department of English in 1974, followed by Michael Cohen in 1982 and S.S. Moorty in 1986. Leon Chidester was chair of the department of languages from 1974 until 1982, followed by Terry Blodgett.

Class offerings were greatly expanded, offering more specialized English and American literature classes and adding a class called foreign literature in translation. New language classes were offered, such as introduction to descriptive linguistics, phonetics and diction, and history of languages. English as a second language classes were begun in 1978; Introduction to foreign language study, in 1980.

New faculty in the 1980s were James M. Aton, Lana Johnson, S. S. Moorty, Sarah Ann Solberg and Carolyn Young, English (1982); Bruce Lee, English (1984); Marilyn Robinson, English (1986).

On July 1, 1987, the English and language departments were combined to form the language and literature department, with Dave Lee as head. Humanities classes were included in this department. Joining the faculty that fall was Robert Fronk, French (1987).

In 1988-90, still under the School of Arts and Letters, the department of language and literature comprised the following:

David Lee, head of the department.

S. S. Moorty, director of composition.

James Harrison, director of humanities.

Other faculty included: Michael P. Cohen, James M. Aton, Terry M. Blodgett, E. Leon Chidester, James Mills, Sarah A. Solberg, Dick L. Carlson, Christina Brown, Jane Roberts, Marilyn Robinson and Robert Fronk.

New classes, such as American Nature

Writing, Medieval World View, Shakespeare and the Renaissance, and Wilderness and the American Mind, expressed the interests and expertise of the faculty. A French major was added in 1989, and a French club was organized, with Mills and Fronk as advisers. At Christmas time the club learned French Christmas songs and went caroling. They sold pizzas as a way to help raise funds toward the French tour planned for the summer of 1990.

TERRY BLODGETT

New faculty were Julie Simon, English composition and John H. Olson, a one-year replacement for English faculty on leave. Danielle Beazer (later Dubrasky) joined the English faculty in 1990.

When SUSC became Southern Utah University in 1991, there was a growing demand for lower division English classes, so Douglas Bonzo, Jan Harrison and Larry Baker began teaching English and Paul Rea came in the fall of 1991 to be director of writing.

Other new faculty during the last years of the first century of the school were Thomas Porter (Spanish), Elise Leahy (French and Spanish), Jeanette Bagley, Maria Smith, Jane Roberts, Stephanie Chidester, Vi-Ann Prestwich, Robert Behunin, Shauna Eddy, Bill Ransom, Eric Morrow, Scott Richey, Glen Bessonette, and Rhonda Miller, all to take part in teaching English. And Alla Paroaiatnikova, of the business department, began teaching classes in Russian.

JAMES HARRISON

The department, the University and the community were saddened by the death, in January of 1995, of Jan Harrison, who had taught in both the English and music departments.

In the mid-1990s, sophomore composition (English 202) was replaced by humanities-based writing courses with such subjects The Eastern World View, taught by S.S. Moorty; Writing from Environment, taught by Michael Cohen; Shakespeare and Renaissance, taught by Rob Behunin; and Youth Culture, taught by Larry Baker.

Under the direction of Julie Simon, English 101 classes were standardized, with requirements focusing on expressive, explanatory, and

RICHARD CARLSON

JAMES MILLS

JAMES M. ATON

S.S. MOORTY

analytical forms of writing. Essay contests were planned, with winning papers to be collected and used as a textbook for future students. Under Simon's direction, a writing lab was set up in the Braithwaite building, continued by Shauna Eddy and now supervised by Glen Bessonette, assisted by student tutors, to help students with class assignments, compositions and computer programs. The lab, now named Plato's Cave, open to any student or faculty member, quickly became a popular and productive place on campus.

In 1997, three foreign languages: Spanish, German, and French offer both a major and minor, and there is hope that a minor may be offered in Russian. Latin, Hebrew, Greek and Japanese are taught occasionally, and Italian is being offered for the first time this year.

Humanities includes basic liberal arts courses as well as classes in philosophy and creative writing. New humanities courses include the west and wilderness; philosophy of values: truth, goodness, and beauty; philosophy of language: introduction to logic; philosophy of values: justice, freedom and equality; and the European enlightenment and its reflexes.

Majors and minors are offered in English with three options: literature, secondary education, and creative writing, and the catalog lists 45 different classes in English. Two literary journals are published by the department, *Tailwind* and *The Paunsagunt Review*. The Literary Guild sponsors poetry readings, featuring poets such as William Kloefkorn, Katherine Coles, Leslie Norris and, of course, Dave Lee and Bill Ransom. Writing workshops are held each summer at the SUU Mountain Center, under the direction of Dave Lee, taught by nationally known poets and writers. A summer study-trip, called San Juan River Canyons: People, Stories and Environment, conducted by Jim Aton, gives students a chance to observe, think and write on the river. Shakespeare classes are taught each summer to complement the Utah Shakespearean Festival, and study tours of France are offered every three years.

*T*he history of the language and literature department is, after all, the story of the teachers who brought their interests and experience, their expertise and enthusiasm into the classrooms, where they taught grammar and composition, literature and humanities, linguistics and foreign languages and a myriad other things during the hundred years from BNS to SUU.

From 1897 to 1997 more than 140 people were involved in this effort. Some stayed only a short time, leaving behind only scant information, like a Miss West who taught storytelling and children's literature in 1929-30 and Dr. M.L. James, instructor of English in 1911-12, who left behind only her picture with the faculty of that year and a brief mention in *The Student*.

Some began in English and then changed to other departments, like Gwyn Clark and Kent Myers who moved to education and Fred Adams who taught English as well as drama in his early years at the college. Some took time from their major assignments, like William Manning who taught German as well as music and sponsored a German club for many years. There were those like Harry Plummer, Richard Rowley, and Eugene Woolf, however, who devoted their entire professional lives to teaching in the department.

And there are those who are taking the teaching of language and literature into the second century of SUU—both the professors who teach advanced classes and those often un-named teachers who help students learn to organize their thoughts, judiciously use Spellcheck and avoid comma splices, and those who help their students to take those first faltering steps toward learning to communicate in another language. All these teachers make 1997 not an ending, but another beginning.

MICHAEL COHEN

CHAPTER XIII

Music hath charms

The philosophy has always been to produce the greatest works of music and to provide opportunities for students and community members to combine efforts in our productions.

There was great music in Cedar City before the Branch Normal School was established. The first settlers leavened their spiritual dedication with significant music, including works by Bach, Beethoven and Mozart. This love of great music, mingled with deep spiritual values, was heightened by a thirst for education, lightened by the spirit of play and by genuine enjoyment of one another, all underpinned by an unabashed love of the desert mountains with their gnarled old juniper trees.[1]

Expansive imaginations took the musical experience of the college and community far beyond what might have been considered possible. They produced world-class music—Verdi's massive "Requiem," the cantatas of J.S. Bach, and the masses of Mozart, compositions requiring a sophistication in taste and demand in musicianship expected only in the very large universities.

The department faculty always adhered to the philosophy succinctly stated by Roy Halversen in the 1932 yearbook:

The philosophy of the music department has been, and still is, to produce the greatest works of music and to provide opportunities for students and community members to combine efforts in such productions.

These questions arose many times: Do these activities contribute pragmatically to a prospective teacher? Do they develop in him or her the classroom skills needed to succeed as a music teacher? There was always agreement on this one principle: that having fledgling teach-

ers aspire to perform great music would stretch their minds, broaden their horizons and probe their deepest feelings, thereby expanding their comprehension and skills.

Even in the old fort the people had a ward choir and a band, both of which grew in numbers and expertise when the people moved to the present site of the town. J. M. Macfarlane, composer of the beloved Latter-day Saint hymns "Dearest Children, God is Near You" and "Far, Far Away on Judea's Plains," was the first choir leader. Remembered as a genial, talented leader, Macfarlane served in Cedar until the late 1860s when Brigham Young called him to St. George.

John Chatterley took over the choir baton until Gomer Coslett and Joseph Coslett assumed stewardship of the choir. Coslett, another gifted composer, is known to present members of the LDS Church for his hymn, "We'll Sing All Hail to Jesus Name." He led the struggling pioneers in singing until his death in the '70s.

James Haslam was another thoroughly-educated musician, who had been a military band leader in Switzerland before he sacrificed, as had others, comfort and culture to help make a new home in the southern wilderness of Deseret. Haslam organized the band of the old fort, which disbanded when the settlers moved to the new site. John Chatterley manifest his versatility by directing a new band, organized in 1880. Cedar's first settlers loved celebrations, dances and programs, and they loved their band. The musicians had celebrations of their own, including an annual banquet for the members and their partners, followed by a dance to which the whole community was invited.

The founders of the Branch Normal School valued music as an integral element in the curriculum of their college. When the doors of Cedar City's Ward Hall opened for the historic beginning of advanced education in the little town, Annie Spencer joined Principal Milton Bennion, George W. Decker and Howard R. Driggs in greeting the eager young students. Annie must have been a one-of-a-kind woman. She was a delightfully confident member of the extraordinarily fine, if small, faculty; her teaching load included elocution, physical education, drawing and music. She had studied organ under the noted Professor Evan Stephens, who had recommended her for the position.

Each day in the new school began with spiritual preparation. Annie was not only a champion of the tradition of the morning devotional, she provided the accompaniment on the pump organ for robust congregational singing of such favorites as "Sweet Hour of Prayer" and "I Need Thee Every Hour." When the student body of the fledgling school moved into Old Main on Temple Knoll, the hour of music, prayer and a thought for the day had become a rich tradition.

Three years after the founding, in the school year of 1899-90, the school gladly welcomed to the faculty the noted musician O.C. Anderson, who was hired to form a music department at BNS. A graduate of Brigham Young Academy, Anderson was well equipped for the challenge. He had been chosen, at age 13, by John Haslam as the youngest member of the Mt. Pleasant band and had later shown promise as a pianist, studying at BY Academy under a master of the great tabernacle organ on Temple Square in Salt Lake City. After graduating from the academy, Anderson taught music in Mt. Pleasant before taking the assignment at BNS.

O.C. ANDERSON, 1902

Mr. Anderson requisitioned the school's first upright piano, which was still in use 50 years later, and established classes in piano and organ and a course in the fundamentals of music.

When Nathan T. Porter became principal in 1902, he acknowledged O.C. Anderson's possession of a wide range of talents by asking him to teach a new course of study in business. In those days every professor had multiple assignments.

By then Anderson had organized a band, which provided a rallying spirit for the students and for the community. The roster of this first band rings with prominent Cedar City names: George Lunt, Robert A. Thorley, John N. Webster, T. Willard Jones, Warren and Wesley Taylor, Clarence Jones, James Cottam, George Taylor, Willard Nielson, Sadie Jones, Willard and Randall Lunt and Paul Poyner. These all became noted citizens of Iron and Washington counties.

Mr. Anderson aspired to the development of a more balanced musical curriculum, to include choral work. One of the members of the first ladies chorus of 11 voices was Annie Spencer, along with Emily Jones, Miss Porter, Mattie Booth, Agnes Coslett, Mamie Taylor, Ann Jones Gardner, Lucy Jeppson and Miss McMullin and Miss Jones.

Just as Annie Spencer possessed the ability to teach music and act as accompanist in addition to her greater expertise in the field of communications, then called elocution, O. C. Anderson must have been an accomplished public speaker. When President Kingsbury of the University of Utah begged to be excused as principal speaker at the commencement exercises of 1904, it was O. C. Anderson who was invited to fill in on this important occasion. This was to be his swan song, as he left BNS shortly thereafter to teach at the Dallas, Texas Conservatory of Music. Anderson articulated the importance of his experience in Cedar City by saying in his commencement address that he had "learned to appreciate more keenly than ever before, the true meaning of life."

Dr. Blaine Johnson, in his complete and detailed history of the department of music, has assessed Anderson's impact:

Mr. Anderson's contribution was the establishment of honest musical instruction based on correct and accurate principles as exemplified in the great masters. His heroic efforts

MISS ANNIE SPENCER, 1898

established a core of musical studies that would last throughout the college's history.

O. C. Anderson also acknowledged the powerful influence, in the development of the fledgling music department, of Joseph Coslett and other pioneer musicians, who were not formally connected to BNS but were forerunners in the tradition of cooperation between the community and its school.

When George Decker became principal of the Branch Normal School in 1904, he appointed Albert Tollestrup as head of the BNS music department. Tollestrup was a large man of great humor who "had a way with people" but was an exacting instructor. He had acquired considerable experience before he came to Cedar City, including having been sent by Karl G. Maeser, principal of Brigham Young Academy, to go to Morgan and there build up an academy. His expectation that music studies would be a cardinal academic discipline at BNS was illustrated by his successfully promoting the purchase of the Chickering concert grand piano, which is still, in 1997, in the University's music department, having been rebuilt and refurbished. The school had no band instruments when Tollestrup came to BNS he managed to secure instruments and added uniforms in 1905. He also transcribed all the music for the early productions, because the students weren't advanced enough to read the music as published.

In 1906 Miss Emily Larsen was added to the music staff for one year.

In a study entitled *A Historical Study of Musical Development in Cedar City, Utah from 1851 to 1931,* Cynthia Williams Dunaway outlines the driving forces behind the establishment of a great tradition of music in the Southern Utah University. In her analysis of the impact of Albert Tollestrup she describes with thoroughness the multi-faceted talent, the personality, the training and the devotion to his art and to the community of this man who replaced O.C. Anderson.

She writes:

He endeavored to help {students} become acquainted with the best orchestral and concert band music of the time...He pioneered efforts to combine campus and community forces, thus introducing this medium of culture to the people of Cedar City.

Tollestrup's students performed frequently for the community. One remarkable recital was

AUSTIN DALLEY, TOLLESTRUP, BETH HAMBLIN, MARTHA LANGFORD, EARLY 1900S.

by Lillian Higbee Macfarlane in which she treated the town to selections by Beethoven, Chopin and Mozart.

Mr. Tollestrup's single greatest contribution may have been his introduction to the curriculum of oratorio and opera. Beginning with Alfred Gaul's *Ruth* in 1908, oratorio became a mainstay and centerpiece of every year's offering, except for the brief interruption of all academic programs occasioned by World War II.

After producing a succession of popular operettas, in spite of BNS's inadequate technical facilities, Tollestrup masterminded a serious attempt at opera with Andran's *Olivette*, which included Scott Matheson, father of a future governor of Utah, in the cast. Caroline Parry, the art instructor of that year, painted a large picture of a ship for the final scene, which was appreciated as having added immeasurably to the effectiveness of the opera.

Handel's *Saul* starred Chauncey Macfarlane

LILLIAN HIGBEE MACFARLANE RECITAL

MR.
TOLLESTRUP
AND
ORCHESTRA,
BNS, EARLY
1900s

ORIEN
DALLEY

and included Lehi M. Jones, Belle Perry, S. J. Foster, Jennie Corry, Katie Dalley, E.M. Corry and Mattie Hunter.

The Mascot, for which admission was 50, 35, or 25 cents, was the springboard opportunity for Elora Urie, Pearle Urie, Gordon Matheson, Parley Dalley, Robert Gardner, E. M. Corry, Walter Lunt and Tedd Fawcett.

Maritania a more ambitious show, helped to season the talents of some of the above listed cast: Elora Urie, Parley Dalley, Gardner and Lunt. Isabell Jackson and Ellen Nelson supported Urie in the lead role.

Albert Tollestrup was a hands-on director, according to Dunaway:

He shows the pages how to court the maids, the soldiers how to drill - rewriting the orchestra score, planning the sets and is trying to make dancers out of the lords and ladies.

For decades oratorio and opera were the glittering jewels of a tradition of college-community activities. After 85 years, these elements are still part of the guiding principal of the university.

Two years before Albert Tollestrup left BAC, in 1917, to return to private teaching, William "Bill" Knudson appeared on the scene. A native of Provo, he had studied at The Boston Conservatory of Music. Having been instructed "to build up the vocal department," he organized the first ladies chorus and chose Bernella Gardner as his accompanist.[2]

Knudson continued the tradition of producing operettas, such as *Little Almond Eyes* and DeKoven's *Robin Hood.* His innovation was to introduce a new organizational format by invit-

ing various instructors in the school to assume responsibility for some phase of the production: John Moser, an art instructor, supervised set design and construction; Parley Dalley and Miss Knowles took dancing as a project; Miss Skidmore was responsible for costumes. These caring faculty members received praise in the *Iron County Record* for their efforts.

Students earned three hours of credit upon completion of three years of participation in opera and operetta. This practice by Principal George W. Decker established a firm academic basis for the more generous accreditation for participation in musical theatre that continues to the present.

After Mr. Tollestrup left the faculty, Kenneth Roylance carried on teaching violin and H. LeRoy Frisby instructed in piano and voice. Frisby organized a male quartet. H. Peyton Johnson instructed violin and directed the band and orchestra. The following year Frisby was replaced by Marion Nichols. The opera of that year was *Bos'n's Bride..* The Craftmen Glee Club was organized. James West came to teach but stayed only one year. Norman McCarty came in 1921 and taught three years. He wrote school songs, stirring the students to sing in assemblies, or chapel, as it was still called.

The people of Cedar City loved the rich tradition of great music at their school, had flocked to the college operettas and operas and looked forward with enthusiasm to participating in the annual oratorios. A desire for more enrichment in their own lives led to the formation of an offshoot of the summer school. In 1916 Fred C. Graham, who had presented a popular recital in Cedar the year before, came from Salt Lake City with a staff of instructors to establish the Southern Utah School of Music.

More than 150 people enrolled, many of them townspeople. Growing out of this, or perhaps contemporary with it, was the Lyceum program. In 1917 accomplished artists began to come to Cedar, by rail to Lund and the rest of the way on a primitive 50 mile road. Some early events enthusiastically received by the little town, which refused to consider itself isolated from the rest of the world, included the Cherniavsky Trio, the Means-Anderson Trio and the Homeland Male Quartet.

The Lyceum program became the Chautauqua and finally, in 1925-26, developed into the Cedar City Music Arts Association, usually chaired by a citizen of the town, with general management of events directed by a member of the college music faculty.

An ambitious project, the Lyceum has

brought some of the world's greatest performers to Cedar City. An example is a performance by Isaac Stern, renowned violinist. The Utah Symphony and Utah Ballet West traditionally make annual appearances.

Orien Dalley appeared as director of orchestra music in 1924. His contribution laid the foundation for the orchestra program that, later, would be at the heart of the music program for six decades to follow. Professor Dalley left the college in 1926, ultimately to become the director of the Interlochen School of Music, a part of the University of Michigan. The students that Orien Dalley developed were not numerous, but this was the beginning of the great string tradition. His affection for the school benefitted young students for generations hence, when after it had become a university, he gifted the school with numerous small-scale string instruments to be used by beginning musicians.

The middle 1920s saw the BAC rapidly shaking off its status as a part-high-school and part-teacher-training school and emerging into a full fledged collegiate institution. The enrollment of students up to this time had been limited, and this had prevented the expansion of physical facilities and numbers of faculty members. With the emphasis on more college work came the necessity for more specialists on the faculty. J. Howard Maughan, director from 1922 to 1929, set the stage in the music department for this era of specialization by employing a band director, faculty in string and voice and a pianist.

Great characters came and went in the music department of BAC, from 1915 to the time of William H. Manning in 1924, including Kenneth Roylance in instrumental music; H. LeRoy Frisby in vocal music; Gustave Soderland, piano; and Orien Dalley in orchestral music. But of all the people who came and left BAC, none was more colorful than William H. Manning. With his arrival fresh from studying with Herbert Witherspoon, leading basso of the Metropolitan Opera Company and performing with the San Carlo Opera and other opera companies, the music program took a giant leap onward and upward.

With Manning were Ralph N. Hansen in violin, Ernest F. Osborn, piano and Walter S. Berryessa, band instructor.

There was never any question about the extraordinary musicianship of Manning or his kindly interest in the individual student, which earned him the affectionate sobriquet of "Pa," by which he was known to students, faculty and citizens. He was an amazing teacher of

voice; he was an amazing teacher of human values. His motto, somewhat paraphrased was: *"Let's get these kids into a higher realm of music than they ever knew and even higher than they are capable of."* Nothing was impossible; everything was available, regardless of difficulty.

Manning's charisma motivated students to want to excel. Alice Williams, Lorenzo "Ren" Luke, and Annette Betensen all went on to study with Herbert Witherspoon, director of the Metropolitan Opera in New York. Other students excelled under Manning's tutelage. Hazel Dalley Granger, Otto Fife, Ann Jones Gardner, Ralph Perkins, Myles Walker, Idona Jackson, and Maude Macfarlane Halversen all became fine singers. Later there were Janice Merryweather Whitehead, Emma Lou Warren, Norma Edwards and Wallace Adams.

"Pa" Manning could be irascible and hot-tempered, but he was a loving and caring father to

LADIES
CHORUS AND
O.C.
ANDERSON

EARLY
ORCHESTRA

WILLIAM H.
"PA"
MANNING

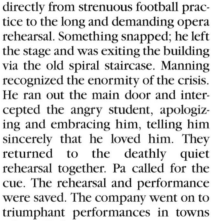

KENT
MYERS,
1950

NORMA EDWARDS

his own children and the students he nurtured. Pa Manning stories are legion. A very few examples must suffice here; the complete history of the department by Blaine Johnson is a must-read.

In the production of Gounod's *Faust,* Manning had cast Kent Myers, a prime football talent, as Siebel, brother of Marguerite. In a crucial rehearsal, very near the performance, everything fell apart. The orchestra was goofing off; the star, Marguerite, could do nothing right and the chorus was ragged. Myers made a small mistake and may have made a smart remark. Pa "took him apart" before the entire company, leaving everyone breathless.

Kent was exhausted. As usual he had come directly from strenuous football practice to the long and demanding opera rehearsal. Something snapped; he left the stage and was exiting the building via the old spiral staircase. Manning recognized the enormity of the crisis. He ran out the main door and intercepted the angry student, apologizing and embracing him, telling him sincerely that he loved him. They returned to the deathly quiet rehearsal together. Pa called for the cue. The rehearsal and performance were saved. The company went on to triumphant performances in towns all over southern Utah.

Many immature high school singers developed under Pa's tutelage and went on to distinguished vocal careers. One was Norma Edwards, who began studying with Manning her first year in high school. At BAC she understudied Janice Merryweather as Marguerite, went on to attend Oberlin College and became a professor at a conservatory in Tennessee.

Pa's wife Elda joined with him in nurturing the string of students who came and went out of their home, receiving food, comfort and encouragement. Roene Bigler DeFiore was one whose potential was discovered and developed by Manning. Roene scrubbed and ironed for her vocal lessons. (The Mannings were one of many loving faculty members at the college who nurtured students, of course.) Roene was later scouted by a Metropolitan Opera agent and offered the chance to audition. She declined the opportunity because she felt that her mother needed her at home.

Manning's spirit was contagious; he influenced all aspects of college life, composing the school song and helping to instigate the Order of the Ladle, a fun faculty tradition, but nowhere was his contagion so apparent as in his musical productions.

Cedar City received some of the music from *Il Trovatore* so enthusiastically in 1925 that he began to prepare for the complete opera the next year. The orchestra was not yet at symphony level, so Bernella Jones accompanied the cast in rehearsal and for the production.

BAC Director Howard J. Maughan was so proud of *The Bohemian Girl* that same year, that he suggested that the production should tour the towns of southern Utah. It was an ambitious notion - transporting 50 singers, along with the stage set! Several men of the town stepped up to the challenge, offering to drive their automobiles to Parowan, Beaver, Hurricane, Kanab, Orderville, Acton, Panguitch, Tropic, Escalante, Circleville, Junction and St. George. An abridged version of *Carmen* and *La Traviata* followed.

In the fall Herbert Witherspoon, after making a stop in Salt Lake City for a nation-wide lecture tour, came to BAC out of friendship for his former student, William Manning, to lecture (waiving his $500 fee) and to conduct auditions for southern Utah singers. As he left Cedar City, Witherspoon invited Manning to assist him the next summer in teaching at the Chicago Musical College. The school and the town basked in reflected glory.

At Christmas time *The Messiah* was presented, accompanied by a small orchestra. What a year for BAC! It was followed by many others during this golden era.

William Manning participated during several summers as a visiting professor to schools of music and universities, producing operas and directing choruses. In the summer of 1937 while at the University of Wisconsin, Professor Manning trained a large music clinic of 300 voices from throughout America, which sang at a closing concert, with a 100-piece orchestra, singing the scene and prayer from *Cavalleria Rusticana.* Because of his work at the University of Wisconsin, over three summers, Manning was listed in *Who's Who in American*

Music.

Pa's compassion for students extended toward the wider community. He worked his magic among the LDS church branch of the Paiute Indian tribe, encouraging them to preserve their old traditions and putting together a show that toured from Ogden to Las Vegas to raise money for a chapel. One incident on that tour demonstrates his characteristic warmth. As he began the tour he was sleeping in a hotel at night. Then one of the Paiutes said to him, "You make us a camp outside of town, you go eat with the white people, you no sleep and eat with us." Pa Manning mended his ways. For the rest of the tour he slept and ate with his Indian friends, and the tour went forward.

Roy L. Halversen came in 1927 to replace Orien Dalley, who went on to teach at the University of Michigan. Halversen had studied trumpet as a youngster, playing in town, high school and college bands. Although active in bands, he had also been a serious student of violin from age seven. Ultimately a product of the Julliard School of Music in New York and a year's teaching of English at Box Elder High, Halversen was also a professional musician.

The year Halversen enrolled as an undergraduate at USAC, he was also hired to play violin in the pit orchestra at the Lyric Theater in Logan. This was a fine professional orchestra which played seven nights a week for silent pictures and for traveling road shows and vaudeville presentations. The experience proved to be a great gift to Cedar City.

In 1927 Mr. Halversen came to BAC to teach band, orchestra, theory and English. Two years later he married Maude Macfarlane, a fine singer and native of Cedar City, and they left for Berlin, Germany for a year's study of violin, theory and the German language. He followed up the year abroad by finishing another full year's program of study at Julliard, concurrently studying woodwinds at Teachers College, Columbia University, and organizing a string quartet there.

His return to BAC saw a period of renewed interest in instrumental music and a marked expansion in ensemble work. A higher plateau was reached at the school as Halversen picked the fruits of the BNS orchestral program and cultivated a fertile bed for significant growth in that area. Dr. Blaine Johnson later recorded in his journal:

My sharpest memories of Roy are bound up in rehearsals. Roy would play the oboe part if we had no oboe; he would know when the bas-

soon passage was critical and would play that - in the proper register; he would play even the trombone part, if needed. He had an intimate and complete knowledge of the score. Of course, he would rehearse the orchestra for any major production bringing them to a stage of development where the opera cast, chorus and orchestra could begin to weld together into a musical cohesiveness. He would then turn the conducting chores over to me, or, in earlier years, to Manning. His generosity in this regard was remarkable.

JANICE
MERRYWEATHER

Halversen nurtured associates with love and patience, including children whom he was eager to include in any production as early as possible, thereby building a great program. A brief memory of Carol Ann Nyman is one of hundreds of examples. She writes:

I think Mr. Halversen must have been pretty desperate to invite an inexperienced high school student to tackle such a difficult undertaking. I was always grateful to him for giving me this opportunity and for his patience with my immaturity. The music was difficult, but so incredibly beautiful that from that time on I was "hooked" on opera. Sitting in the pit, playing for operas and musicals, accompanying the college chorus or the Manning-Halversen Oratorio Society, or playing symphonic music gave all of us a priceless education and appreciation for the great music of the world.

PROFESSOR
ROY
HALVERSEN

We were expected to participate in long hours of practice and rehearsal, sacrificing other interests and activities dear to the heart of teenagers. I guess the most important lesson we learned was a strong sense of responsibility.

Many times when we began a project, we would be very discouraged because of the difficulty of the music. We just knew we could never even begin to play it, because much of the time the music was really way beyond our capabilities. Then a miracle would occur. We were pushed and prodded to rise to the occasion, learning as we went.

Mr. Halversen took a personal interest in me. Of course, I found out later that I was not unique. He treated all his students with the same caring interest.

Floyd Rigby, an accomplished product of the department, draws a sharp visual image:

When Roy Halversen took a violin into his hands, removed a hankie from his pocket and placed it gently under his chin and took a moment to cradle that violin, there was a certain expression that came over his face before he would begin to play, as though all of the music was going through his mind and each note was a personal friend.

Halversen's genius combined with that of Pa Manning to round out the miracle of the Manning-Halversen team. The two worked together for years serving the fortunate college and town. On the death of Pa Manning, Hazen Cooley, financial director of BAC, wrote in a letter to Elda Manning:

Bill and Roy were like two arms working in harmony together. This closeness with one another brought great results. President Daryl Chase, at one time, commented that it was hard to conceive that two great artists, competing, so to speak, for plaudits and recogni-

tion could be so generous with praise and credit for one another. This love and respect and generosity kept them truly together, and together they did great things.

A brief description of the physical facilities in which the team produced some landmark offerings will highlight their production challenges. While the facilities were meager, they were infinitely better than they had been in the founding days.

The auditorium-theater of this era was on the second floor of the administration building. The meager hall seated about 185 people. The stage proscenium width was 23 feet, while the depth from lip of stage to back wall was 32 feet.

Special remodeling of the small stage (installation of a new lighting system and re-installing the audience seating on a newly sloped floor) enhanced the technical quality of productions during this golden era. Still, it would be an almost inconceivable feat to stage performances such as *Carmen, Il Trovatore, Faust, Rigoletto* and *Martha* on such a small stage, but they did it! Somehow, in 1926, the music department presented four world-class grand operas.

In 1927-28 five grand operas played on consecutive nights in a single week!

The Bohemian Girl, Il Trovatore, La Traviata, Martha, and *Cavalleria Rusticana*

September of 1924 blew in with a puff of north wind, leaving a trail of red, yellow and orange, with a little purple and gold added. The campus was ankle-deep in leaves. School had a special meaning , as it was to be my last year at Branch Agricultural College.

There was a new violin instructor at school. Orien Dalley was a handsome local boy just two years older than I, from Summit, Utah who had gone away on his own to Ann Arbor, Michigan. He had been real successful there and came home to teach. He persuaded me that I could do the same, and that he would do everything he could to help me. He said the school of music was much better in Ann Arbor than in Chicago, Illinois, which had rejected my application earlier. From then on I worked with renewed enthusiasm, with my focus on a definite goal. I was more conscious of scholarships than ever before.

Months flew by. I graduated from BAC and I wanted to go to Ann Arbor and become a concert violinist. My dad said, "We can't afford to send her away. I won't have a girl of mine among strangers."

Mother had a different philosophy, "You can do anything you want to in this world, if you want it badly enough."

My good friend, Professor Dalley had written to his benefactors in Ann Arbor, and they promised me employment. He told me about his first trip to Michigan, when thieves stole everything he had while he slept in a railroad depot in Chicago. All he had left was his train ticket and a 25 cent piece that he had carried for luck ever since. He tossed that coin in my lap and said he hoped it would bring me as much luck.

My venture was a success. I graduated from the school of music and became a pioneer instructor in the schools throughout the west. I taught music for 40 years and am now retired. I am 90 years old (1994) and I still have Mr. Dalley's lucky coin.

From the journal of Alice Higbee Krause, Panaca, Nevada

played to full houses. From a printed program of the opera *Rigoletto,* reviewing this week of operas:

No other college in America has ever developed and produced so many operas in one week. This remarkable feat was made possible by three complete casts of principals who had sung the operas in previous years, and two choruses. It was also an example of remarkable cooperation between school and town. Those responsible for the production of the Opera Week were W. H. Manning, R. L. Halversen, Bernella Jones, Virginia Larson and Ira Hayward.

The year of 1927-28 was indeed one of heroic proportion. Professor Manning also assisted a community effort to produce *HMS Pinafore,* besides performing the *Messiah* at Christmas time. All this in spite of the flu epidemic in the late fall of 1927 and early 1928.

How in the world, one must ask, could they have accomplished such achievements? A simplified answer to such a question contains at least four elements: There had to be adequate talent—a pool of voices of operatic capacity from which to cast the productions; a drastic reduction in the scale of the settings, costuming and props, as compared to single productions; Cedar City had to have been prepared over the history of the college and community, to be so opera-minded that they would attend the nightly offerings in droves and most importantly the school had to have the blending of genius of the two men, Manning and Halversen, who began the tradition that was carried on until their deaths.

In '29-30 Melvin Done joined the department to head the band, orchestra and vocal department under Mr. Manning. The glee clubs gave a minstrel show, and the department presented *The Jolly Musketeers,* a light opera.

In 1931-32 the orchestra had a better string section with more mature players. A violin choir of 15 violins performed the classics. Mr. Halversen organized a string quartet. Some doubt was expressed as to the reaction of the public to such music, but the ever loving public of Cedar City took this organization to its bosom with even greater pride than anything heretofore presented.

While the department presented operas every year, the Cedar City Choral Society presented *The Messiah* and the oratorio *Elijah* by Mendelssohn. Another week of opera was presented at BAC in 1933-34. In 1935-36 the opera

was *The Bos'n's Bride.* The department also was nurturing the college orchestra, a dance orchestra, a college band and a high school band, a boys' glee club and a girls' glee club.

WILLIAM H. MANNING CONDUCTING, ROY L. HALVERSEN ON VIOLIN IN BACK, WITH EUGENE HOLMAN, LOUISE MARSDEN AND MARIAN BRADSHAW

During the directorship of Henry Oberhansley, who replaced Dr. Howard Maughan, financial stress was felt throughout the state. Oberhansley came with instructions to keep the ship afloat, whatever measures he had to employ. At his first faculty meeting, Director Oberhansley quoted colleagues at the mother institution who had laughingly said that he was going to a music conservatory instead of an agricultural college. The comments of his colleagues made the new director wary of too great an emphasis on music, placing the department in danger of curtailment. The music department, however, helped to save the very life source of the school.

Five years later, in the legislative session of 1935, there was agitation to cut appropriations to BAC, or even discontinue the college. Fortunately, that season, some state legislators who visited the BNS campus witnessed a grand Manning-Halversen presentation of Handel's *Messiah* in the tabernacle. They were familiar with the work, having seen it produced elsewhere; they sat near the door for a possible early exit. But they stayed, enthralled. On the strength of the extraordinarily professional presentation, they threw their influence behind a proposal to save the appropriation for the school. The department had a new champion in Director Oberhansley.

The first sunrise Easter program in Zion National Park had been performed by Dixie College in 1936. It had included a

THE
ZION
PAGEANT

chorus of 200 voices from St. George and Cedar City under the able direction of Joseph McCallister.

On a December Sunday of that year, Henry Petersen, a citizen of Cedar City; Grant Redford, newly appointed to the drama department at Bac; Wm. H. Manning and Roy L. Halversen drove to Zion National Park. There they visualized together a great drama depicting the closing days of Christ's life. Not only was it to be a great drama, but a musical setting was also envisioned, with a large chorus and symphony orchestra to set the background for each of the scenes depicted.

Manning and Halversen, who had collaborated for years in the production of Handel's *Messiah,* had dreamed of producing a similar spectacle in Zion Canyon. Roy Halversen had been the inspired director of the instrumental accompaniment for the *Messiah* productions. Grant Redford had come to southern Utah with the actual experience of having been a member of a stock company which had traveled over the United States producing a passion play. Henry Petersen, who had just returned from an army

school in Oklahoma, had witnessed a short pageant on the life of Christ, which had been produced out-of-doors.

The idea became a reality. The musical team planned the episodes and accompaniment, Grant Redford wrote the continuity, LaVeve Petty (Whetten) choreographed and trained the dancers and Henry Petersen served as general chairman. After exhaustive planning, deft hurdling of administrative barriers with the United States Park Service and marathon rehearsals, the first Zion Pageant was produced March 29, 1937.

The pageant grew for the next three years, performing in the spring of 1941 to an audience of 12,500 people. The overwhelming response had become too much for the capacity of the park personnel and had had a disruptive effect upon the normal conduct of church services in southern Utah communities, so it was not continued.

Later, in the school year of 1937-38, when Professor Halversen was on leave of absence, Donald Olsen directed the orchestra, band and the Chamber Music Association. The band devoted much of its time to the music of Richard Wagner. In January the band performed an entire radio program from the works of Wagner. The Chamber Music Association also presented a cycle of 12 recitals over KSUB, with music presented in its developmental order from Purcell to Beethoven.

In October of 1939 the Cedar City Choral Society responded to an invitation to sing at the morning and afternoon sessions of the general conference of the Church of Jesus Christ of Latter-day Saints in the tabernacle in Salt Lake City. The chorus had attained recognition by its singing in the Zion Easter Pageant for three

---

When I was a very young girl I watched Mr. Roy Halversen play the violin, and I longed to learn to play. I received my violin for my eleventh birthday and was thrilled. From the time I was fourteen years of age I played for the Messiah, the operas, and with Mr. Halversen in his string ensemble and the BAC orchestra. Mother paid for my lessons with eggs, butter and cream.

When I graduated from high school, I determined that I didn't want to ever go to another school as long as I lived, and this in spite of the fact that I had been a good student. I was adamant in my feelings and made no plans to continue my education

In early September of 1946 a letter came from Mr. Halversen. He didn't write a note, but just enclosed a scholarship award. Having been taught about thrift and the value of the dollar, I realized that I could not waste this valuable opportunity. I went on to obtain degrees in music and elementary education, and I taught school for twenty-four years.

Thank goodness for a very wise teacher, who knew better than I did what was best for me. I will always be grateful to Mr. Halversen, because he not only encouraged my appreciation for music but shaped the direction of my entire life.

Madelon Jones Payne

years. William Manning directed the chorus of 225 voices, 160 of which were students at BAC.

The year that the band acquired 49 classy new blue and white uniforms was 1939-40. Once again business and civic clubs pitched in with funds for new uniforms, as did the classes of the student body. But it was the dance orchestra, Kollegiate Swing Kats, that was in constant demand throughout the surrounding towns and counties, playing at several junior proms. February 7th was the beginning of a weekly college radio program entitled "College Time," featuring the Kats. On April 10th they were starred on a program originated in the college auditorium over college-owned equipment and by direct wire to radio station KSUB.

In 1940-41 the BAC Symphony Orchestra, under the direction of Roy Halversen, embarked on the most vigorous schedule in its history. The mid-winter concert listed Beethoven's *Fifth Symphony*, Grieg's *Piano Concerto*, with Eual Lawrence as soloist, and Tchaikovsky's *Nutcracker Suite*. Shortly afterward they accompanied the chorus in Handel's *The Messiah, Pink Lady* and *Carmen*.

Pa Manning's BAC Chorus offered the heaviest music program of any school in the state, large or small - the above three choral productions, topped off by a music festival featuring 80 voices, 40 of which took principal or solo parts. The band was smaller, but active at ball games and pep rallies, doing maneuvers at the BAC-Dixie games. The Kollegiate Swing Kats were still swinging.

*T*he catastrophe of World War II changed all the world, including the hamlet of Cedar City and especially BAC. The distinguished service of the Manning-Halversen team came to an abrupt end. In 1943 Professor Manning, department chair, was transferred to the Logan campus to head the vocal department there during the war years while Professor Walter Welti was in the service.

Although Professor Halversen met the challenge and preserved the great traditions, including *The Messiah*, new directions had to be established. Local college-age males left BAC to go into the military, but a unit of the United States Air Force brought hundreds of other men to the campus to prepare them to become officers in the Army Air Corps. This training was primary; all elective subjects were limited by military demands.

Roy L. Halversen was appointed academic coordinator of the cadet program, in addition to his becoming chair of the music department.

His expertise in orchestral music and his ability to involve the community literally preserved the musical traditions of Cedar City.

Halversen needed someone to replace Professor Manning. Edward Sandgren came to the department. His greatest accomplishment was the establishment of the Mastersingers, a male choir that thrived until 1978. Frank Van Cott joined the faculty in 1942 as instructor of piano until 1949-50, when he was replaced by Virginia Larson.

Halversen created a program for strings which became a performing chamber organization with its own integrity, not confined to accompanying the opera and oratorio program, which also continued. The community continued to be enriched by annual orchestra concerts as well as the periodic chamber programs.

The end of the war brought Pa Manning back to BAC in 1945. The "Roy and Bill" team was reunited, working miracles for five more years. The Utah centennial year of 1947 provided, among other centennial events in Cedar City, a perfect showcase for the BAC production of Puccini's *La Boheme*. The State Centennial Committee awarded the college $500 to assist in its staging. The opera, double-cast, was warmly acclaimed by the community. *La Boheme* was followed by *Il Trovatore* in 1948 and in 1949, *La Traviata*. These productions, as attested by many, were highly professional in their presentation.

After 30 years of service, William H. Manning left BAC in 1950 to serve an L.D.S. mission in Germany with his sweetheart, Elda.

Blaine H. Johnson of Dixie College was appointed to take Manning's place. Military disruption due to the Korean War caused some confusion in the personnel of the department. After being called back

BLAINE H. JOHNSON, 1950

THE NEW TEAM, BLAINE AND ROY

CHRISTINE
HOUCHEN
WINTERROSE

to active military service for a year, Johnson was re-appointed assistant professor of music at the college, serving along with Wallace Adams, who had been newly hired as vocal teacher. Reed Berrett and Loa M. Johnson were conscripted to aid in the crisis during 1950-1951.

A new team emerged in the blending of the talents and energies of Blaine Johnson with those of Roy Halversen. Old traditions were rescued and preserved. For the next thirty years great music would be at the heart of the music department's efforts. Halversen and Johnson were committed to exposing not only the student body of the college but the young people of Cedar City and the surrounding area to the very best of the musical arts. Opportunities were provided at a very young age for children to play in the orchestra for the annual production of *Messiah*, one of the city's most treasured traditions. Roy told the beginning violinists just to play what they could and stop when the music surpassed their expertise. The youngsters stretched as far as they could. The experiences increased their ability as they grew and developed. Young singers also participated in operas, oratorios and masses.

Blaine Johnson took up where Pa Manning left off in nurturing the talents of youngsters, who thrived under his instruction. Christine Winterrose was one who developed into a fine artist with the benefit of a vocal scholarship, hard work and the opportunity to perform demanding operatic arias.

Dr. Johnson remembers:

An interesting story of 1952-53 concerns Christine Winterrose. I had offered her a vocal scholarship—that is an offer of free vocal instruction provided she would come prepared. Well, she did this for the next three or four years! Aided by her friend Alan Seegmiller, a talented piano student of Bernella Jones, she sang strenuously every day, growing by leaps and bounds. That year she sang the 'Bird Aria' in 'Pagliacci (Leoncavallo) in an amazing performance. From then on there was not an operatic role too daunting for her." [3]

The team collaborated in producing *Cavalleria Rusticana* in 1951 followed by

Pagliacci in 1952. When the new auditorium opened in 1955, Romberg's *The Student Prince* and *The New Moon* initiated the new facility.

During an interlude in which Manning returned to the college as replacement for Johnson, who was away completing his doctorate in 1954-55, the department produced Verdi's *Il Trovatore*. By autumn of 1956 the Halversen-Johnson team was reunited.

The merging of these talents produced great accomplishments in the department and the community. They agreed that the *Messiah* must continue to provide an opportunity each year for people of all ages for religious expression. They worked together to select other religious music in the common belief that spiritual preparation, as well as the works of the great masters, should be at the heart of the program of instruction, whether in private instruction or in the rehearsal hall. Honest preparation for classroom instruction was a given. They never asked, "Is this too difficult for us?" They only asked themselves, "Will the cost in time, effort and money justify it?" They didn't worry much about the facilities, or lack of them. The team produced *La Traviata* followed by *Rigoletto,* then *Faust, and Carmen.*

The team branched out from grand opera to the masses of Beethoven and the requiems of Mozart, Verdi and Faure and to Bach cantatas. All were performed by the whole ensemble of orchestra and choir, and involved the talents of the community as well as students. The Verdi *Requiem* took a chorus of about 150 voices, split into two choirs, an offstage brass choir and a full-scored symphony. That year they also produced *Amahl and the Night Visitors* and the *Messiah,* as well as the orchestra concert and two string quartet programs.

The Mozart *Requiem* not only enthralled the town, but nourished the spirits of the performers and producers. Johnson and Halversen loved the finale, "Agnus Dei." They went home from rehearsals with their spirits soaring in the beauty of the magnificent music. One memory of the piece was less than reassuring. Dr. Johnson relates that moment:

Each year the chorus and orchestra were invited to do one number in the commencement exercises. Both Roy and I loved the "Agnus Dei," and we longed to do it one more time. It took twelve and a half minutes to perform, and we worried that it might be too long. We decided to do it after all. Sitting directly behind my wife was a southern Utah farmer, parent of a graduating senior. As the

Mozart number went on and on, the man leaned near to his wife, and in a voice audible for several rows around said, 'My hell, they've had plenty of chances to quit before now.' Perhaps we should have considered more carefully.

With the somewhat later advent of David Nyman to the faculty, the team had also expanded joint productions with the drama department. One notable production was *Fiddler on the Roof*, a Broadway musical, which had not yet been released for public presentation.

This musical became available through the magic machinations of Professor Fred Adams of the drama department. How did he do it? Who knows? An example of what Fred could do was "Fiddler On The Roof." "Fiddler" had some great moments for us in the music department. Who can forget the beautiful "Sabbath Prayer?" And the sweet nostalgia it wrought in all of us. An unforgettable moment was played by Tevye and Golda, the old peasant couple whose stultifying life style had all but smothered normal expressions of love. When Tevye asked Golda, "Do you love me?" it was both hilarious and deeply touching, and we remember Kent Myers and Sue Turner playing these parts.

So it was in all the productions that were cooperatively produced and conducted by music and drama department people. One memorable moment in "The Mikado," found the Lord High Executioner climbing out of the orchestra pit with a mellophone, (French Horn) wrapped around his foot. It was a real spoof, connecting fantasy and reality all dreamed up by the genius of Scott Phillips. Other productions - "Camelot"; "Once Upon A Mattress;" "Pirates of Penzance;" which was notable for Fred Adams' depiction of the major general, provided unforgettable moments. We in the music department were uplifted and inspired by our participation. Certainly our horizons were broadened.

The harmonious teamwork of Halversen and Johnson was typical of the wonderful linking with other faculty members and students. Johnson quoted Theron Ashcroft as saying one day, "...We could sure get a lot done around here if it weren't for the students." The wisecrack referred to the unique relationships among teachers and students. In 1965 the team presented both *Rigoletto* and the *Requiem* again, using the same soloists as in the early produc-

tion. The unalloyed joy was not to continue long. The Johnsons' daughter, little Sybil D., was dying of leukemia. She died in 1966.

Three years later Roy Halversen was dying of cancer, confiding his condition to no one in the department. He proposed that the team produce one last opera. They chose *Rigoletto*. This time they hired Roy King from the University of Indiana to come out and sing the Duke. "It was a good performance," Johnson remembers, "but not in any way as exciting and thrilling as the first one. Mostly, the clouds of Roy's condition hung over us. In fact, on March 16th, the date of our last performance, Roy was in the hospital, having been operated on for the ninth time." In December of 1969, after rehearsing for one last *Messiah,* it became clear that Professor Halversen would not be able to continue with the rehearsals, nor would he be present at the performance. From his bed he addressed a letter to Blaine, Harold Boyce and *Messiah* cast and orchestra, in which he wrote:

To the entire cast of the Messiah:
There is no use dwelling on the heart-breaking disappointment I feel in not being able to participate in this great undertaking... My hope and prayer is that this night will be a soul-warming joy for each and all of you. My gratitude comes in the knowledge that each of you will sacrifice to have and to give this experience to other. This is something that warms my heart. That Blaine and Harold would bring this project to a successful conclusion earns the respect and love of each of you. That each member of the Orchestra would rally to the call and acquit himself professionally, completes my joy.

I'll be with you in the performance of every note and may God bless you in your devotion to such a cause as the Messiah.

Roy Halversen died in March of 1970, and the school and the town that had rejoiced together in his service, now mourned together as he left them.

RONALD ADEN, 1985

*I*n 1951, Frank A. and Sage Thorley donated their family home and the property on which it sat to BAC to be used as a music building. The college received the gift with gratitude; the legislature was enthusiastic about the difference in cost of the $52,000 renovation as compared to the $225,000 which had been appropriated for a music building.

The home was one of the jewels of Cedar City with its striking whiteness, standing out against the background of tall, beautiful pines and spacious lawns," Johnson observes. *"The Thorley Music Building was our home for the next 14 years. It was a lovely, homey place with a reception room complete with fireplace. There was a large open area where the choir rehearsed and where operatic productions were blocked out. String quartet programs were given there since there was room for a small audience. Those programs had a flavor that, perhaps, was not too unlike the intimate musicals of Haydn's and Mozart's time. The Hall gave impetus to the kind of music and the response to it that a planned formal music building could not have done. It was a popular place for piano students to appear in recital. A beautiful, antique Schiller grand piano had been purchased by the college upon the opening of the hall. Sometimes as many as 30 students presented recital solos of various levels of difficulty, one dimension of the college philosophy being to reach out to the smallest children.*

Thorley Hall was also a germinating spot where whole families working together made significant contributions. All three of Roy and Maude Halversen's children performed there. Parson and Evelyn Webster had three sons who participated in nearly everything. The two Bradshaw families were fine and faithful musicians. Professor Johnson's wife Loa and their children were a prominent part of the music scene. Robert and Mae Potter came from Parowan to add their talents. Mary Macfarlane McDonald, the daughter of Lillian Higbee, the first person to present a recital at the college, gave many years of service joined by her daughter, Lauren, representing a third generation.

By 1964 the department had outgrown Thorley Hall. The legislature granted a modest budget for a new building to be located on the southeast edge of the old football field. Halversen and Johnson made careful plans and multiple trips to Salt Lake City to meet with the architect, Glenn Lloyd. Frustrating delays lead

to inflation's eating at the amount of space planned. The appropriation included monies for the purchase of five Steinway grand pianos, 12 upright practice pianos and an assortment of wind, stringed and percussion instruments. The department moved into the beautiful building during the Christmas holidays of 1966.

During this same period the music department expanded its program to meet the requirements of the Northwest Association of Secondary Schools, Colleges and Universities for full accreditation to offer a music major; the college would now graduate students with a baccalaureate degree in music. Additional faculty had to be appointed to fill in areas of expertise in music history, theory, musicology, instrumental and sound skills to prepare prospective high school teachers. The new music building and several new faculty enabled the department to meet the challenge. Harold Boyce, the high school band director, had taught part-time at the college, but was now ready for a full-time assignment at CSU. Hal K. Campbell joined the faculty in 1966.

Hal K. Campbell had taught at the Stewart School, a subsidiary of the college of education at the University of Utah for 13 years when the school was terminated in 1966. He joined the music faculty of the College of Southern Utah as the fourth full-time faculty member, the others being Roy Halversen, Blaine Johnson and Harold Boyce, new director of bands. This was the last year that the department was housed in Thorley Hall.

With the acquisition of Dr. Campbell, the four-year program was sure of success. He came with a program of theory that was all-inclusive, including and integrating all the courses that related to music structures into one course of instruction including scales, arpeggio, both written and keyboard harmony, notes and thematic structure. In addition to his classes in music history, theory and group and individual piano, the department was required to offer basic theory, such as music fundamentals, methods of teaching, band and orchestra instruments, instrument repair, even piano repair and tuning. The limited department staff committed the heroic effort and time to bring it all about. Campbell was, himself, the embodiment of music principles, as demonstrated by his compositions, for which he had received national attention. The Manning-Halversen Choral and Orchestral Society had performed his *Book of Mormon Cantata*. His loyalty to family and church endeared him to the community; he proved to be a great source of strength in preserving the musical traditions of Cedar City. Ultimately Campbell became the department chair and later the dean of Fine Arts of the college.

C. David Nyman replaced Roy Halversen as orchestra director. He had developed an outstanding program of string instruction in the Box Elder County schools, which was also a priority in Iron County schools.

Nyman teamed with Harold Boyce (who one year after finishing his doctorate, left to supervise music in the schools of Clark County, Nevada) in the music department to produce a series of successful musical productions. His appointment also bolstered the production of musicals under the drama department. The noted Fred Adams required a competent conductor in the pit; Dave was that man. He conducted the summer musicals related to the Utah Shakespearean Festival, which Fred had almost single-handedly brought into national acclaim.

A fter 30 brilliant years in the department of music, at the turn of the decade, Dr. Blaine Johnson retired in 1980. Hal Campbell writes, in his history of the department 1980-1996:

Dr. Johnson has left a legacy of vocal/choral opera training and performance that has affected the southern end of the state - and likely well beyond this area. Those of us who have known him will be indebted to him, and his influence will have affected at least the next generation through us. He told me that he was invited on more than one occasion to accept more 'prestigious' positions at better-known institutions, but he chose to remain here. Blaine's wife and partner, Loa, left a powerful legacy in piano teaching as well. She will be long-praised for her contributions.

Floyd Rigby has warmly acknowledged the great impact on his life of Dr. Blaine Johnson in a piece called "Fond Memories." He writes:

Nothing was out of Dr. Johnson's reach musically. We performed the opera "Il Trovatore" that year. I remember being in that private studio as we studied the part of Count DeLuna. It was the first time I had ever had the true feeling of reaching a covered tone on a high F. To this day, whenever I try to develop a covered tone, I think back on that lesson and that great moment of achievement in my life as I experienced a new feeling and a new sound within myself. Dr. Johnson always had a way of making one feel important and successful during the course of a lesson, and I looked forward to those lessons with eagerness.

DR. HAL CAMPBELL, 1966

A band was always a necessity to The Iron Mission. The early settlers were an upbeat, positive, enthusiastic group of people and they had to have a band, singing societies, dances, and drama productions right from the very beginning.

These organizations served the community well. How else would they properly greet a visiting dignitary than to meet the traveler a mile or two outside of town with a brass band, and sometimes with young girls dressed up in pretty costumes.

John Haslam was the first band director. There were roughly a dozen players of various instruments including a tin whistle played by 15 year-old John Lee Jones, who later became a fair violinist and singer. He married too many times to suit the federal government and was thrown into jail for a short time for his plural marriages. However, he turned his imprisonment to advantage by serenading the warden and his family, along with other prison officials with his prison band.

The band program at the college rose and fell with budgeting and instructional requirements. From 1927 until 1958 Roy Halversen *was* the band. He conducted the band on parade, at games or half-time shows.

Harold Boyce, director of the high school band, at first devoted part-time work to the college and then was appointed full-time as assistant professor of music to establish a band program.

PROFESSOR DAVID NYMAN

Dr. Steve Allen replaced Boyce in 1975. In six weeks from the date of hiring he managed a miracle. A full-sounding marching band of 27 musicians and a few baton twirlers and flag girls filled the football field the first home football game in September. Within five years he had established a band worthy to appear in Washington, D.C. in the Kennedy Center and at the Music Educators National Convention.

The college could not long support such an aggressive program, and Dr. Allen moved on to schools with bigger programs. Joseph Lamoreaux, Dennis Bacon and Bruce Walker, in succession, worked to revive the status of the organization.

C. David Nyman took on the job of getting the

READYING FOR A FACULTY RECITAL IN THE LATE '80S WERE (LEFT TO RIGHT) FRONT, DR. VIRGINIA STITT, DR. MARK L. MECHAM, NANCY LAMB GUYMON, JAN HARRISON; BACK, SARA PENNY, AMANDA MORTENSEN.

THE SCARLET AND BLACK

band back on its feet. The British-style Scarlet and Black Ceremonial Band was born, along with a complementary complete bagpipe corps.

In March of 1986 all of southern Utah took pride in watching on television as the Scarlet and Black marching band performed with 13 other college bands at the Coca-Cola Centennial in Georgia. The Scarlet and Black gained national recognition and was constantly in demand. The showpiece of the music department, the famous organization participated in major festivals and put on quarterly concerts in Cedar.

Until 1955 the department had engaged outstanding choruses in the performances of great operas. When Professor Johnson returned to the college from Korea, he determined to establish a more comprehensive program of choir music. Johnson expanded the choral library and organized an a cappella and chamber choir. A formal choral concert was presented once each year and then once each quarter. The choirs made tours of Utah, Nevada and Arizona and performed for churches and important local functions.

The department branched out to perform the demanding requiems and Bach cantatas. The choral program was extended to the communi-

ty for the performance of orchestral/choral compositions. These performances included gifted townspeople, along with students, and were always received appreciatively by the greater community. Guest conductors were sometimes invited to lend excitement.

After the death of Roy Halversen the golden era of orchestral music waned, although the department moved boldly on with Dr. Johnson and his colleagues. The college choir program continued to succeed. At age 78 retired professor Johnson returned to sing a tenor role in the *Messiah* under the direction of Floyd Rigby, his former student. Never in 30 years of conducting the annual presentation had he given up the baton to participate in the chorus.

Any musical effort by a college has to be based on a solid program of the symphony orchestra. Albert Tollestrup and Orien Dalley built such a base. Roy Halversen began the "feeder" program that provided a pipeline of players for the joint college/community string program and developed the symphony orchestra into the truly fine organization that was the accompanying instrument for the great productions that were always the tradition of the school. The orchestra provided a watershed experience for countless students.

The art of piano performance was ever a part of the music program at the college, beginning with Annie Spencer, O.C. Anderson and Albert Tollestrup, who instigated a strong program of piano instruction.

As any honest and respectable conductor of choral music will tell you, the accompanist is his salvation in a very real sense.

Bernella Gardner Jones became "Pa" Manning's right hand, playing for his chorus classes and also for all the *Messiah* and opera rehearsals. Much of the success of the famous Week of Opera in 1927 is due to her efforts. Numerous other accompanists and piano teachers, too many to mention here, contributed substantively to the development and reputation of the music programs.

Worthy of mention is the story of the piano ensemble festival. Loa Johnson and Bernella Jones organized a piano festival calling for twelve pianos on the stage, each one to be played by two students. All of the piano teachers of Cedar City participated. Each one conducted the ensemble in at least one selection. Over 400 students experienced this marvel of organized routine, marching onto the stage and off without confusion or loss of time. It was an amazing demonstration and was repeated over a period of four years. It is impossible to evaluate

how the horizons of piano students were thereby expanded.

By 1980 Hal Campbell had been at SUSC for 14 years. He had been assigned to take the place of Blaine Johnson as department chair in 1977. After two years, in 1979, upon the release of Dean Eugene Woolf, he was asked to serve as dean of Arts and Letters, in which position he remained until 1984.

During Campbell's tenure as dean of Arts and Letters, David Nyman assumed the 'acting' chairmanship of the department of music until he moved to full chairmanship in 1984. Dr. Steve Brandon was selected as the new chair. Brandon, an experienced music administrator, served until 1991, when he accepted an offer to chair a music department at a college nearer to his ancestral home.

Knowing that Campbell would be retiring at the end of 1992, the administration asked him to again serve as department head while they searched for a replacement for Brandon. Bart Shanklin, who had been serving as the principal vocal/choral director was selected as the new chair.

Following 1980 the department entered a period which included a great deal more turnover of faculty than occurred in earlier decades. There were, of course, many contributing factors. Rarely was incompetence the chief factor; a few teachers were geared to a more intense focus on smaller facets of music than toward the more generalized approach, which had been a source of strength in the earlier eras of the history.

Hal K. Campbell's early contributions, specifically to the four-year baccalaureate program, have been outlined. His contributions spilled over into the '80s. His love has always been working with students in areas of theory, history, and composition and piano performance. As every music major was required to take two years of theory and all majors and minors needed some music history, Dr. Campbell personally influenced the development of virtually all the students of the department. They responded warmly to his expertise and dedication, awarding him the Distinguished Educator Award for 1980, the Outstanding Educator Award for 1984-85 and the Teacher of the Year Award for 1985. Three other informal awards were given him by students: the Groovy Guy Award in 1970 from a group of theory and piano students; a sketch of a comic figure with big ears playing a saxophone, labeled "Like...I

Dig ALL Kinda Sounds;" and a metallic mosquito with a spark plug body to memorialize "The Year of the Bee."

Campbell was invited to compose music upon different occasions before his retirement: a brass quintet performed at BYU under the direction of a doctoral candidate in conducting: *The Year of the Bee*, an orchestral/choral work; *The Book of Mormon Cantata;* an *Old Testament Suite;* musical setting of several poems by Walter de la Mare; children's songs; hymn settings and several piano works. Dr. Campbell retired in 1992.

CAST OF
LA TRAVIATA,
1927

As a replacement for Dr. Steve Allen as Band director, Dr. Johnson was able to secure the services of Joseph Lamoreaux, a trumpeter and band man with some significant high school teaching experience. The band program was in a state of disarray. A few of the band students had left the school to join Dr. Allen. Others felt that no one could take his place, and therefore were negative to any new person. A few left music entirely, "turned off" by the problems that had arisen. So Professor Lamoreaux was given an assignment to re-form the band as best he could. He served from 1977 through the school year of 1983. He quietly brought the band from an almost non-organization to a fairly substantial one, although not reaching the level it had been before.

SUSC
SYMPHONY,
1973

DR. BART SHANKLIN

DR. VIRGINIA STITT

JOSEPH LAMOREAUX

Dr. Johnson also hired a woodwind specialist at the time that Lamoreaux joined the faculty. Dr. Virginia Stitt is the only pre-1980 full-time faculty member still teaching in the music department of SUU (1997). Called by her department chair a human dynamo, Dr. Stitt taught nearly every musical subject in the curriculum, became the full-time orchestra director, worked with David Nyman in collaborations with the drama department, set the pace for faculty recitals as well as devoting hours to consultations with graduates, being twice nominated for the Teacher of the Year award. Dr. Stitt miraculously found time to work with community events and to be active in the Southwest Symphony Orchestra.

At the retirement of Dr. Blaine Johnson in 1980, the department was blessed with an able replacement so that transition for the college students was not difficult. During his three years at SUSC, Ellison Glattly brought to the department his experience with the Roger Wagner Chorale and an excellent knowledge of voice production in solo and opera, as well. He was able to keep the interest in opera theater alive as he produced and participated in *Gianni Schicchi* and *Trial by Jury* with an enthusiastic cast of students.

Professor Ron Aden replaced Glattly, serving from 1982 to 1986. While not neglecting the choral tradition established at the school, he brought a slightly different direction for voice programs. His experience with "show choruses" led to a greater emphasis upon high quality jazz/pop arrangements. Using this new emphasis, he developed a small mobile madrigal choir called "Opus." Additionally, by encouraging arrangements by choral members he influenced a number of young students toward a vocal teaching career.

For a brief time Dennis Bacon replaced Joseph Lamoreaux as director of bands. A highly successful high school band director, he brought an increase in band emphasis and upgrading of the concert band and marching band sides of the curriculum. Performances and morale improved.

David Feller, a single-reed specialist with a new doctorate under his belt, came to the music department in 1986, for one year, to help with orchestra and small ensembles. A one-year, part-time appointment was also given to Bruce Walker, who taught simultaneously in the college and high school band programs. When Dr. Stitt took a brief leave, Julia Quick, a fine violinist, was hired in 1985 to work with the orchestra and teach beginning theory.

The department hoped that they had found a new Blaine Johnson successor in the person of Dr. Mark Mecham, a fine counter-tenor, who replaced Ron Aden, but he was destined to leave the West after four years, 1986-1990. He brought skill and artistry, particularly in the full choral sound. His excellent background gave the program a broad repertoire and in-depth experience.

Dr. Steve Brandon came from the east as department chair in 1987 and stayed until 1990. He was a quiet but skilled administrator and, a tuba player, brought a new dimension of low brass to the area. Dr. Brandon's most significant contribution was in laying the groundwork for the department's goal of membership in the prestigious National Association of Schools of Music, steering the way through evaluations, visitations, summaries and responses to questions posed by NASM.

In 1989 Dr. Suzanne Collier (later Drayer) came as a full-time assistant vocal specialist. She worked with the women's choruses, trained female vocalists and worked with elementary music education students. As the pressure on choral work and small vocal groups had absorbed the full time of Dr. Mecham, Dr. Collier made a significant contribution in taking steps to bring opera back into the curriculum. Since the Theatre Arts people were using every available stage, Suzanne adapted her opera productions to the confining spaces of Thorley Hall.

Dr. Brandon's departure left the department without a band director and head, and Dr. Mecham's leaving necessitated the acquisition of a choral director. An announcement for a part-time string person was made at the same time. Hal Campbell put in another temporary stint as chairperson; Bart Shanklin was hired to fill the choral position; Dr. Paul Garrison was selected to replace Steve Brandon as band director and Dr. Thomas Stillman was employed to fill the string slot.

Professor Shanklin's impressive choral productions and his programming evidenced maturity, thoughtfulness and a good background. He became department chair upon the retirement of Hal Campbell, serving in that capacity until the present (1997). Under Shanklin's administration the music department has grown considerably, the number of majors doubling, resulting in additional faculty personnel.

Dr. Paul Garrison came from working with massive bands belonging to large eastern universities. He came with the dream of expanding the band program at SUU and had the backing of the department and the college, even to an expansion of the band budget. However, after two years Garrison returned to work in a program, in the east, with a large concert band.

Dr. Thomas Silliman, a cellist of high caliber, was a member of the faculty from 1990 to 1993. He taught music history, music appreciation and orchestration. He strengthened the string programs in the college and the community, working well with string ensembles.

The work of the department has been enhanced and magnified by a number of adjunct instructors. They have been influential, and often crucial, to the success of the department. They have given service (frequently unnoticed by the public) that has strengthened programs and, in some cases, has added facets and areas of focus that the full-time faculty could not include in their work loads.

Four, who have especially impacted the university and the community, are: Evelyn Jones, who has been influential in cello, organ and piano for many years; Jan Harrison, who probably did more for organ playing, to make it an integral part of the SUU music curriculum than anyone else since 1980; Dr. James Harrison who has been an adjunct instructor in percussion and has taught such classes as music appreciation and history and Sarah Nelson Penny, an adjunct in the music department from 1982 to 1990.

*I*n the spring of 1991 the music faculty met with the administration of SUU to determine the direction of music programs and to set goals. It was determined that an eventual enrollment of 100 music majors would provide the student leadership necessary for orchestra, band and choir to develop into first-rate performing groups as well as elevating the level of the music program so that it could compete with other universities in the state for the best talent. Increasing the number of talented students would result in raising the caliber of music education to all students in the music program because of their exposure to diverse talents and abilities.

By the following year the faculty had developed a bold five-year plan: setting the fall of 1996 as the target date for having raised the number of music majors to 100; increasing the number of faculty; expanding the opera, jazz and electronic music programs; and adding to computer equipment and instrument collections, including the purchase of a new nine-foot Steinway concert grand piano for Thorley Hall.

The music department, through the hard work of an incredibly talented and dedicated faculty and the support of the administration and community, exceeded its goals each of the years of the five-year plan. The number of majors increased to 118 by the fall of 1995, an increase of 151 percent. Full time faculty increased in the strings and woodwind areas and part-time faculty in voice, piano, organ, horn, woodwinds and guitar. Opera expansion included major operatic productions, musical theater, programs of opera scenes and one-act operas. The SUU Jazz Band progressed and the electronic music program purchased, in 1996, state of the art computer and electronic music equipment. The department, in six years, invested $80,000 in new instruments and in 1996 acquired two Steinway grand pianos, a nine-foot concert grand for Thorley Hall and a seven-foot grand for the piano studio, the first such acquisitions in 30 years.

In addition to meeting the specific goals of the five-year plan, the department also made substantive gains in the choral activities program, under the direction of Bart Shanklin. The concert choir grew to a group of 80-90 members, performing major choral literature including Mendelssohn's *Elijah, The Mystic Trumpeter* by Norman Dello Joio, *Laud to the Nativity* by Respighi, Faure's *Requiem*, Vivaldi's *Gloria, Christmas Cantata* by Daniel Pinkham and Mozart's *Vespers.*

Opus, the chamber choir, provided an opportunity for the more advanced vocal students to participate in a select performing ensemble. The choir performed extensively in the western United States, as well as in a concert tour in

PROFESSOR
DAVID COLE

England in May of 1996. The two groups presented over 100 performances in the six-year period. The choral program also sponsored a high school choral festival each year.

Dr. Don Massengale replaced Hal Campbell in 1992 in piano and theory. His piano students won high honors in competitions and performed with Orchestra of Southern Utah, the Southwest Symphony and the Utah Symphony. In 1993 Dr. Massengale began a piano competition known as the Maurice Hinson Piano Competition, which in 1996 drew some of the finest pianists in the United States.

Dr. Gary Reeves and his wife, Dr. Deborah Reeves, came to SUU in 1992 and began to establish the SUU band program into a solid college-level program. They were able to recruit and teach and build the band to a group of 50 students who played at a high performance level.

Dr. James Williamson, who replaced Dr. Reeves in 1995 built on this base, an outstanding bands and brass program. The marching band approached 100 members, the largest in SUU history. An honor band for high school musicians grew from 50 to 200 participants. The SUU concert band performed a work by Texas composer Greg Sanders, commissioned by SUU stu-

'LA BOHEME,'
1995

dent government, for the celebration of the University's Centennial.

Dr. Michael Dean replaced Dr. Deborah Reeves in woodwinds and music theory. Dean taught in two colleges before coming to SUU. An excellent performer in single-reeds, his youthful enthusiasm and dedication to his students created new interest in clarinet and saxophone.

In 1993 Professor David Cole was hired as director of orchestral activities in 1993, joining Dr. Virginia Stitt, a fine specialist in double reeds and the backbone of the program. The impact of Dr. Cole's influence on the orchestra could perhaps be summed up by a comment made by an audience member: " I haven't heard the college orchestra sound that good since the days of Roy Halversen." Professor Cole's enthusiastic leadership has created the largest all-student orchestra in the history of the department. In addition to performing with the opera program, the orchestra has performed such major works as *Clarinet Concerto No. 2, Op. 115* by Sir Malcolm Arnold," Four Dance Episodes" from *Rodeo* by Aaron Copland, *Symphony No. 8 in b minor, Unfinished,* by Schubert, *Symphony No. 8 in F Major, Op. 93* by Beethoven and P*iano Concerto No. 2 in C minor* by Rachmaninoff.

An opera workshop class has been offered every quarter since 1993 when Professor Carol Modesitt, replacing Dr. Suzanne Drayer, hit the ground running that year. The opportunity for operatic training and for performing in productions at SUU now rivals that of programs at universities three times SUU's size. Opera productions have included *La Boheme* by Pucinni, *Guys and Dolls* by Frank Loesser, *Gianni Schicchi* by Puccini and many one-act operas and opera scenes. The SUU Opera Company performed *Carmen,* by Bizet in February of 1997 as part of the SUU Centennial Celebration.

Many talented students have graduated from SUU and gone forth to distinguish themselves in the music profession. A student survey undertaken in 1994 supported the fact that the department had been able to reach its goals because of personal contact and interest by faculty in the individual student—the same element that has been the strength of the music department throughout the 100-year history of the school.

The future of the music department is bright because of the continuing tradition of great teaching by caring professors and of the enthusiasm of talented and motivated students—all willing to dream their vision of excellence in the art of music—and of the unfailing support of the administration and community.

CHAPTER XIV
Social Sciences

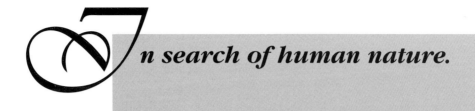

In search of human nature.

The study of the social sciences, a discipline of a university which is the examination of human behavior and which focuses upon salient issues in the lives of people–past, present and future–is as subject to change as the people and institutions it examines and as the faculty and students which create its programs.[1]

The settlers of Cedar City wanted teachers who could train their children to read and write and do sums, yes, but they wanted teachers who would also teach their children, by precept and example, to value the lessons of history and to behave as civilized and ethical citizens. They wanted teachers who could equip their children to understand themselves and their fellow beings, so as to help build better individuals and stronger communities for the future. Those settlers, and the succeeding generations of southern Utahns–who wanted the very same things for their children - got what they wanted, because they were willing to pay the price. And they were blessed, from the beginnings of "their school," with brilliant and experienced educators who had caught the vision of the founders and who left a rich legacy for their successors.

There were no departments in the Branch Normal School in 1897, but Milton Bennion, the principal, taught two courses entitled history and civics and psychology. History and civics was offered every other year. When J. Reuben Clark replaced Milton Bennion as principal in 1901, he taught the social science classes.

By 1902 the catalogue listed an additional class–educational and physiological psycho-

logy. Just one year later child psychology was offered. By this time Elias Hansen taught at BNS from 1904 to 1908, and Charles Mosley shared the teaching loads of the social science classes in the expanded curriculum.

In 1907, when J. Wesley Barton joined the faculty, educational psychology became a requirement for those training to become teachers. All psychology classes were offered as part of the teacher education curriculum, within the Division of Education, until the late 1960s.

During the early years the social science courses reflected the special interests of the social science teachers; specific classes were offered and dropped with changes in faculty. John S. Woodbury, a member of the faculty from 1907 to 1911, and J. Wesley Barton, who taught for four years from 1909 to 1913, shared responsibility for the history classes that were offered during this period. The history and civics class had become United States history and civics. They added European, ancient, mod-

CAMPUS
BUILDINGS,
CIRCA 1920S

THE "A" DAY COMMITTEE IN 1957 WAS ROYCE CHAMBERLAIN, VIC DAVIS, V.R. MAGLEBY AND RICHARD GILLES.

ern and medieval history to the schedule. Geography was taught on an intermittent schedule. Later, history of the American west split off from the general U.S. history offering.

George W. Decker (1897-1913), George Lunt (1914-1924), Claud Lewis (1899-1904), Elias Hansen (1904-1908) and Charles Mabey (1904-1906) were also listed, teachers who had laid the foundation of the social science and other related departments. All of the early faculty relied upon their passion for their subjects and their own creative methods, in the era where few and inadequate text books, maps and visual aids and meager library holdings limited the depth of study. Lean budgets and the difficulty of transportation precluded field trips.

However, there were distinct advantages on the positive side of the ledger of the times. Since it was before the advent of big government and special interest intervention, teachers' paper work and record-keeping were simple in comparison. Distractions competing for the attention of students were at a minimum—the term 'media' could be translated as the *Iron County Record*, "Amos and Andy" and their equivalents on the radio, and offerings of the local movie theatre for those who had an extra nickel. "A trip" usually meant a ride to Parowan. School activities were well-attended by those who could get their farm work done.

Political science had been taught as part of the education and business curricula. In the early 1930s Gilbert L. Janson (1914-1936), George H. Lunt and Hazel West (1929-1931) added classes like state government, United States government and two courses which surveyed the governing systems of key nations in Europe and Asia.

Henry Oberhansley, director of BAC from the early '30s until 1946, was the teacher of record for educational psychology during those years. The college added several new faculty members later in the decade, among them Burns Finlinson (1935-1947) and Gilbert L. Janson, who joined Zoe Palmer (1924-1940) with classes in sociology, economics, psychology, history and political science. Burns Finlinson became dean of men, and Zoe Palmer was dean of women, in addition to their teaching assignments. Palmer served first as department head, replaced by Finlinson. There was still no restriction of a teacher to a particular division of the college. Most faculty belonged to two or three disciplines, determined chiefly by where their teaching skills were needed.

Edwin L. Peterson (1937-1947) and William l. Wanlass joined the others teaching social studies. Soon Rex F. Daly (1941-1943) also joined the faculty, teaching economics.

By 1937 specialization began to play a more significant role in the organization of the departments and was reflected in the curriculum. Henry Oberhansley still taught educational psychology, but he also taught the first class called statistics, as a preparation for those majoring in business, education and the social disciplines. Experience in the field of statistics enabled students to profit by the research reported in scholarly articles, which were beginning to appear in professional journals and other publications.

Harold Bissell (1943-1944) came aboard, along with J. G. Van Zandt (1943-1944), to teach geography, and Lewis B. Lesley (1943-1944) was teaching history when the campus was invaded by Army Air Corps cadets during World War II. Geography was now given special attention to these students in their pre-cadet status. The Air Corps brought in many of its own instructors, but BAC faculty had to stretch to meet the challenge of the transition.

In 1945 Henry Oberhansley died, and H. Wayne Driggs replaced him as director of BAC. Edwin Peterson, who had taken leave to serve in the army, returned to the college to teach history. When Burns Finlinson left BAC to accept a position in California, Vern K. Kupfer (1947-1989) joined the faculty to take his place. Kupfer's major field was psychology, but the pattern still required a teacher to fill in where needed. New faculty moved into whatever space was available. Kupfer shared a walk-in and back-out office under the staircase of Old Main with George LeBaron, who taught chemistry and physics.

The faculty of that era enjoyed a wonderful

esprit de corps. Parties included all teachers, staff and administrators in congenial socialization. Director Driggs, Hazen Cooley and Ward Robb, who made up the core of the administration, took their turns, along with faculty, in the planning and preparation of food for the get-togethers. The setting for the socials was a frame structure which had been recycled from the Topaz Japanese Relocation facility. This make-shift cafeteria had a room which accommodated the parties, even dancing afterward. Occasionally the gatherings were dress-up affairs with the ladies wearing long dresses. Those days make up the beautiful memories of the social science staff of that day, who enjoyed a particularly close association with those of the education department.

Stringent funding has always been a critical issue in the history of the college in Cedar City, but the days of the small, close faculty were also days of proud austerity. Many faculty meetings included a demonstration on how to use a piece of chalk a quarter of an inch in length and a lecture about the importance of establishing a habit of turning off lights when exiting a room. Dr. Driggs was especially proud one year because he was able to return $5,000 to the state. Eddie Peterson was one of the few faculty members in the social sciences who had the services of a part-time secretary, a rare luxury for the time.

When Old Main was destroyed by fire in 1948 the social science and education departments, along with others, were literally out in the cold. Classes were held in every conceivable space. Vern Kupfer remembers teaching psychology from the pulpit in the chapel of the L.D.S. Institute, as kindly arranged by Gustive Larson, Institute director.

At the same time that funding provided for the refurbishing of the burned out structure, the structuring of the disciplines was also being refurbished. The social science faculty moved into new offices on the second floor. Education settled in to offices on the third floor. Dr. Reese Maughan was chairman of the education department, which at that time included psychology. This encouraged the easy and productive relationship of the two disciplines with combined efforts in the growth of majors in elementary education. Each spring elementary school teachers of southern Utah attended a two-day workshop sponsored by the education department with the participation of social science staff.

When Director Wayne Driggs died suddenly

in 1951, Dr. Daryl Chase was appointed to fill the void. At this same juncture, Vern K. Kupfer and Glenn Wahlquist accepted two-year appointments, by the national department of state, to work in Iran. There was a scramble to fill vacancies. At the end of the foreign assignments, when the two professors returned to BAC, there began an influx of Iranian students who had followed their mentors. The college took on an international look. Many of these students finished their work at BAC and then transferred to Utah State University.

BURNS FINLINSON

At this point the BAC was following the departmental pattern established at Utah State University: the social sciences belonged to the business department, and psychology remained with education. The school had become College of Southern Utah, and Director Chase was selected to become president of USU. He was replaced by Royden C. Braithwaite. Edwin Peterson also left to go to the Logan campus. Richard Gillies was appointed to teach history in 1956. He would remain at the college until 1963. Gerald Hansen had been appointed in 1960 to teach political science, which was another small increment in specialization.

Reese P. Maughan's departure for a position in California resulted in Joseph Fillerup's appointment as head of the education department. Richard A. Thompson (1960-1986) joined the social science faculty, teaching history along with Professor Gillies.

In 1960 Vern K. Kupfer was assigned to head the health and counseling unit at CSU; he continued to teach all of the psychology classes, still being offered under the aegis of education. After two years, in 1962, Kupfer took a contract leave with Brigham Young University. Bruce Howard took over the counseling unit and shared the psychology class load with McRay Cloward, who took over some of the general psychology courses. Craig Jones (1963-present) replaced Gerald Hansen, and Rodney Decker (1965-present) was hired; both taught in political science.

VERN K. KUPFER

Still early in the '60s Morris Shirts became head of the education department when Professor Fillerup left CSU for a position in Arizona. Leonard Witt (1965-1977) joined the faculty to teach sociology, and Kupfer returned to his previous position.

MCRAY
CLOWARD

Late in the decade Professor Kupfer, with the help of Leonard Witt, secured a series of grants that eventually brought in more than a million dollars to the college. The first was a survey, funded by the United States Department of Aging, designed to determine the current needs of older residents in a rural setting. The innovative patterns of the grants captured the imagination of social scientists throughout Utah.

McRay Cloward's introduction of a summer program called Group Dynamics brought adult participants from all over the western states to CSU. The group leaders of the program were specialists in this relatively new approach to counseling. Professor Cloward's concurrent responsibility as teacher in the education/psychology disciplines along with director of the summer school program serves as another demonstration of how many faculty members carried on a three-man assignment with no overtime compensation.

When BAC was approved for a four-year curriculum in the social sciences, long a part of the business department, the timing was right to pursue independent status as a department. Psychology, faced with a possible cut in budget under the education umbrella, obtained quick approval for a natural alignment with the social sciences.

The new behavioral and social sciences department included the natural cluster of courses treating anthropology, history, political science, psychology and sociology. Economics stayed with the business department.

RICHARD
THOMPSON

The new department spawned many innovative movements and positive relationships that would have been impossible otherwise. "Team teaching" was a term being used nationwide on all levels of education to describe cooperation between faculty members in the teaching of specific courses. It often designated an arrangement in which different teachers would simply show up for presentations on scheduled days. In some universities where the element of true cooperation was lacking in the teams, serious animosity hung heavy among department personnel.

The manner in which team teaching was employed in the new department at CSU proved startlingly synergistic for faculty as well as students. Two, sometimes three, teachers, present in the classroom at the same time, would share the podium for an exchange of facts, as well as articulating the philosophies of their own disciplines. The format encouraged the cooperation of faculty, not only in the classroom but in conducting special studies and surveys where the content overlapped disciplines.

Behavioral and social sciences settled into the former student center and book store, which had been remodeled. The department offices and reception area, which were located in a small portion of one side, occupied the cramped quarters for several years.

Richard Thompson's office and the anthropology laboratory occupied about 1,800 square feet of the complex, which included a museum. Displays, encased in glass window exhibits with individual lighting, enticed many visitors, especially elementary school children, to the University. The lifestyles of ancient native inhabitants of southern Utah came alive for the children in this setting, where the stories were told by the thousands of rocks and bones.

Some faculty members acknowledged battles inherent in the occupation of war-surplus quarters. Professor Craig Jones wrote:

Among the not-so-fond memories of the old museum were the leaks in the roof, several floods through the south door, an occasional mouse scooting across the office and a dead skunk and a cat found under the floor.

The talented and dedicated faculty did whatever was necessary to make the facilities and the system work. In 1968 Wayne Hinton joined the social sciences faculty, followed by Corrin Nielsen (1969-1973) and Robert Young (1975-1991), replacing Ron Walker and Jon Hammond in history and political science, and Neil A. Davidson (1967-1969) and Leslie Jones (1969-present) were appointed to positions in psychology.

When Professor Kupfer learned that there was a pot of gold available in the field of social work, the department, which did not have a social work program at the time, wrote an ambitious grant proposal which was accepted in Washington. Ken Hennefer and James Chapman took responsibility for initiating a program with the grant of more than $100,000, a large sum at that time. Although it was a continuing grant, the program was challenged each year by social work personnel in metropolitan areas, who questioned the ability of the small southern Utah school to accommodate the offering. Each year the department presented a case for the progress of the fledgling program that was solid enough to override all objections.

In the meantime, Morgan Williams (1968-1986) joined the faculty in sociology. Professor Witt and Kenneth Henefer had taken leaves; Jack Stokes in 1970 and Keith Anderson in 1971 were brought in to take over the social work program. CSU social work students met all expectations, rating at the top in summer field placements, of all students representing participating schools in the state. It took about four years before the battle for acceptance of CSU's social work program was finally won.

One of the primary strengths of the department was the successful meshing of the diverse offerings of the disciplines in a central focus on superior preparation of social science majors. In 1972 Allen Turner was brought into the anthropology area, with grant money, to work closely for three years with the minority population in the area to tie them into social programs.

Professor Kupfer met with representatives from four state institutions to begin what was to be known as the Rocky Mountain Gerontology Center. The sole purpose of the center was to give support and training to the program on aging in the region. The University of Utah offered a four-year certificate; Brigham Young University, Southern Utah State College, Utah State University and Weber State University concentrated on a two-year certificate.

A rigorous program was offered to those who had interest in gerontology. SUSC, the smallest of the member institutions, usually was second or third in the state, in terms of numbers of participants. Substantive input of teaching was made by Morgan Williams, sociology; Wesley Larsen, physiology; Jack Stokes, social work and Vern Kupfer, psychology. Many of the students who were involved in the training were, in 1997, active professionals in programs related to the aging. The department realized over a half-million dollars as a result of the grant. Utah's aging population has benefitted, in a ripple effect, from the training of professionals in gerontology.

Social sciences faculty were always looking for ways to assist their students in their professional training and in graduate school. They ulti-

LESLIE
JONES

mately established a psychological laboratory in Hawthorne Hall, formerly the girls' dormitory, which provided ample space, if somewhat questionable compliance with fire codes. Some financial support came from the college, but most of the equipment was obtained through grants. Although the equipment was very expensive, multiple use made the purchases cost-effective.

Leslie Jones, Vern Kupfer and a student laboratory manager supervised the operation of a rat colony in the laboratory, sometimes even feeding animals and cleaning the animal rooms. The laboratory was moderate in size at the beginning, but some over-zealous lab assistants allowed too many to get together; soon they had more rats than space.

The laboratory also housed the only monkey colony in southern Utah. Most of the animals were of the Rhesus line, but a monkey named Emma was the favorite of the lab staff. She was about two feet tall and too strong to trust very far. Participants conducted reaction studies, some of which were presented at state science conferences by the psychology majors. The laboratory moved temporarily to the old Cedar Hospital on 200 West and 200 South, and eventually to the new Life Science Building.

In the late 1960s representatives of the Utah Social Services Department proposed cooperation between the state department and CSU in establishing a program for training children with disabilities. As yet there was no program in effect in any Utah schools. Paul Sagers, the superintendent of the State Training School, was very supportive of the plan to start a satellite program for the training.

The intent of the proposal was to have the children participate in a program in a "live in" arrangement five days of the week, with the children returning to their parents on the weekend. A special grant funded the refurbishment of the nurses' building south of the old hospital for the program. Professors Kupfer and Leslie Jones travelled the five-county area to find children for the program. The recruitment process was discouraging, as few families acknowledged that they had children with disabilities, but the necessary number of participants was finally reached.

The program was launched in Hawthorne Hall with a teacher, a married couple as dormitory parents and the volunteer help of psychol-

RODNEY
DECKER,
1996

ogy majors. The plan worked. The growth that came to many of these disabled children was truly astonishing, and everyone who was involved in the program reaped rewards of satisfaction.

The Trainable Mentally Retarded (TMR) program was viable for many years, although the public school system did not give support because of its low profile and lack of funding. At length, after a great deal of persuasion, the public schools offered a janitorial supply room in the old Elementary Education Building with the stipulation that the program staff would clean the proposed quarters. Tom Walker, who was the teacher in the beginning, was paid in grant money, but was ultimately paid by the school district. With increasing pressure from state and national advocate groups, the Iron County School System gradually accepted the program, incorporating it into the regular training cycle.

Another grant which enriched the experience of students, was provided by the Regional Department of Social Services. It funded contracts for the presentation of lectures or workshops to social service personnel and other interested individuals. The four-year grant offered a series of bi-monthly events. A good working relationship between the department personnel and social service personnel resulted in stimulating programs. Participating behavioral sciences students received broad insights into a wide variety of new and critical theories, techniques and practices. Many distinguished guests came to the campus as a result of the program.

The department of behavioral science was also enriched by professionals like Sheldon Prestwich and Jim Piacitelli, who taught classes in psychology. President Royden Braithwaite taught a class centering on creativity, which was a great addition to the psychology curriculum. Dr. Floyd Holm (1974-1978), former president of Snow College, joined the faculty, teaching a variety of psychology classes until his sudden and unexpected death.

OAKLEY
GORDON

In 1968 Dr. Richard Thompson of the department's archaeological discipline, initiated a summer training program in the Little Creek Mountain area, close to the Utah/Arizona border. The program, although under different

leadership, was still alive in 1997. It was a rugged camp, though well prepared, which one accessed by a rough three-hour drive from Cedar City. The training offered on site brought advanced students from throughout the United States and from other countries. The students uncovered thousands of significant artifacts over the years, each requiring identification and proper indexing. As a result, the drawers and cabinets of SUU's Natural History Museum hold a wealth of information.

The department faculty, on an excursion, traveled over the bumpy roads to the site on the uncelebrated rim of the Grand Canyon, where only the very hearty ever ventured. Once in camp, air conditioning was never an option, although temperatures often rise in that area to more than 100 degrees. Sleeping on the hard ground was part of the program; a cool drink of water was more important than water to wash your face. The real pay- off was a delicious steak grilled over an open fire.

Professor Thompson's dedication to southwestern archeology was well recognized and respected. Studies under his direction covered a wide area of southern Utah, from Parowan/Fremont, south to the Mohavi and Coconino land mass of Arizona. Much of this work was done under separate contracts with land developers and for legal clearance preceding the placement of utilities. The artifacts retrieved from these studies also added significantly to the holdings of the museum.

Over the years the department of behavioral and social sciences had grand dreams of a home of its own. The inadequate frame building where the department had been housed, hot in the summer and cold in the winter, had been condemned by the State Fire Marshal before they finally moved to better quarters. It was almost legendary, the number of building plans that were submitted to the administration and then the State Building Board. Hopes soared with each submission, but the bubble always burst. Finally, in 1987, the staff moved into new space at the Centrum. It was not ideal, but was much better than anything in the long history of the department.

Students in the department had multiple opportunities for work. Social work, psychology, political science and anthropology students had a variety of placements in related field work. In psychology only those that desired the experience utilized the placements. On-the-job training was required for a degree or certification in social work and gerontology.

The job placements were mainly in Utah, though some went as far as Sun City in Arizona and to the office of Carl Rogers, the noted psychologist, in La Jolla, Calif. Many of the political science majors, through the efforts of Rodney Decker, joined the Washington office staff of U.S. Sen. Orrin Hatch, where they became acquainted with the workings of politics in the capitol. Anthropology students had myriad opportunities for field work with Dr. Thompson.

Since the 'no department' status of 1897, the social sciences had seen many wonderful increments of progress over the century: from the pioneering BNS period, when the principal of the school and a very few others taught a very few classes; to the days of BAC, when a small faculty taught social science classes along with other subjects from diverse disciplines and course offerings fluctuated yearly, according to the interest and background of the teachers; to the days of SUSC, when social science professors' course assignments still depended more upon where they were needed than upon their chosen emphasis, or even discipline, and faculty members still sometimes carried major administrative assignments along with staggering teaching loads; to university status as SUU, when the faculty had grown to a respectable size, their gifts and skills honed in specialties within a structured department.

Growth in the department, after the victory of university status, was steady and productive. New faculty were added: Dr. Oakley Gordon in 1986, Dr. Mark Winter and Dr. John Ault in 1989, Dr. Christina Frederick in 1993, and Dr. J. Michael Crawley in 1996 all joined Dr. Leslie Jones in psychology. Sociology acquired Richard Roper, Dan Pence and Linda Silber in 1994, and Robert Biggert and Michael Stathis were new in 1991 to the political sciences. Jim Vlasich in 1981, Larry Ping in 1989, Earl Mulderink and Curtis Bostick in 1995 assisted Wayne Hinton in history. Geography was welcomed back to the behavioral and social science department, with Fred Lohrengel (who joined the geology faculty in 1986 but taught geography courses in the social science department), Michael Stathis (1991), Stan Hatfield (1993) and Paul Larson (1994) sharing the teaching assignments.

By 1994 the behavioral and social science faculty had become highly specialized within a very complex department. Dr. Wayne K. Hinton, head of the department since 1983, reported the offerings of the program: a major and minor in history, a geography minor, a major and minor in political science with a pre-law emphasis, a certificate of public administration, a certificate of international relations in political science, majors and minors in sociology, a social science composite major for secondary education majors, a social science composite emphasis for elementary education majors and a statistics and computer lab for all students.

Dr. Hinton, who had joined the SUU faculty in 1968, had earned his masters degree from Utah State University, doctorate from Brigham Young University and completed post-doctoral work in environmental history at the University of California at Davis. Hinton was the author of numerous books and professional journal articles, as well as a member of the Utah State Board of History. He also created a board and computer game in 1995 called "The Spirit of Utah," which was adopted by the Utah Board of Education for use in the public schools.

Dr. Hinton assessed the social science faculty at SUU to be excellent and stated that students were being well educated in their chosen fields:

WAYNE HINTON, 1996

Our students are successful in the job market — in counseling, teaching, government employment opportunities and also in the law profession. Our students also report that they're well-prepared for graduate school. We have one of the highest success ratios in the country for getting our pre-law students admitted into law school. In general, we have a high success rate for all of our students who apply to graduate school... About 20 % of the department's graduates choose to pursue a master's degree...Our student teachers are said to be among the best they [cooperating teachers] ever see.

SUU's social science department has well-qualified professors. They stay abreast by researching and writing in their fields. Four have authored books, and all have published articles in professional journals, which is a good indication that our teachers know their stuff... And all of our faculty members have presented papers at professional conferences.[2]

MARK WINTER

Psychology became SUU's newest department in 1994. Dr. Mark Winter, newly-named head of the free-standing department,

JOHN AULT

PROFESSOR
W. CRAIG
JONES

had gained his doctorate at the University of Utah and taught for three years at Utah Valley State College before joining the faculty of SUSC in 1988. Other faculty members of the new department were Dr. Leslie Jones, Dr. Oakley Gordon, Dr. Christina Frederick and Dr. John Ault. New offices in the recently-renovated general classroom building accompanied the change to new department status for psychology.

By 1997 the faculty had grown to six members, several of whom were working on research projects. For example, Christina Frederick was researching sports psychology, while Karen Kopera-Frye, who was at the university for only one year, was studying depression and aging. Both were involving students in their research.

Dr. John Ault, director of a practicum course which offered opportunities for hands-on experience in social service organizations, reported that SUU students were also doing 15,000 hours of volunteer service in practicum settings, a great service to Cedar City and other communities.

The department tallied more than 200 majors and pre-majors in 1995, psychology becoming the third most popular major on campus. Graduates competed very well for social services jobs or went on to graduate school programs such as law and medicine as well as psychology.

By 1997 the department's sociology program included offerings covering a wide range of issues from social relations to ethnic and gender relations to crime and to mental illness and health. Sociology classes complemented several career choices, including counseling and relations, corrections, law enforcement, drug and alcohol education, mental health and race relations. The SUU General Catalog of 1995 assured students that:

"Research methods, including statistical analysis, are essential aspects of each area in sociology."

According to Associate Professor W. Craig Jones, who had been teaching political science at SUU since 1963, political science courses at SUU were constantly expanding the curriculum in an effort to keep up with the times. He explained that political science is the study of governments, analyzing how they work, what political ideologies failed in the past and which applications may flourish in the future. Jones reiterated that both justice and domestic tranquillity are also important aspects of the general study, as well as the influences that affect the political process, including the role of the media, which can alter the entire political process.

Dr. Hinton reported that an amazing 90% of the department's graduates who had applied to law school had been accepted during the decade of the 1990s. Graduates with a bachelors degree in political science in 1997 were finding jobs in governmental and foreign service fields, as well as filling positions as administrators and officials in city, county and federal government. In order to help ensure that its political science graduates were able to get jobs after they left SUU, the behavioral and social science department arranged for internships in both Washington, D.C. and Salt Lake City for students who desired hands-on experience and an opportunity to establish contacts.[3]

Dr. Hinton credited the skilled and professional faculty as one factor in what he termed a vibrant and energetic focus of study. Three professors were added to the department in 1995: Earl F. Mulderink, assistant professor of history; Robert Biggert, assistant professor of sociology; and Curtis Bostick, assistant professor of history.

The history curriculum in the late 90's was "writing intensive," meaning that students were learning the communications skills necessary to be successful in a competitive job market. Many history graduates were certifying to teach, others to go on to graduate school - to prepare to teach history at college level or to prepare for law school. Professor Jim Vlasich stressed:

History is a lot more than just names, dates, and places...History helps people make value judgments...We should look at the roles of everybody in society, not just those who dominate society.[4]

In 100 years the social sciences program at the University has expanded in size and expertise to meet the needs of social science students in succeeding eras. Each new generation of faculty and students has brought gifts and energy to the evolution, building upon the traditions of predecessors. Even with all the change, basic goals have not varied considerably from the course set by the founders of the Branch Normal School.

CHAPTER XV

Theatre Arts & Dance

This town is unique, unusual, — with a tradition of classic culture— Cedar City and southern Utah know great theatre when it happens.

When the Utah Shakespearean Festival crew arrives each year for their first meeting they are told that they must create excellent theatre in this community, because good theatre has been produced in Cedar City from its beginning[1] and Cedar City and southern Utah know great theatre when it happens.[2]

The settlers of Cedar City were bright and resourceful people who, beleaguered with the problems of pioneering, delighted in every shred of cultural enrichment that they could find for themselves and share with their families and associates. Even before families had fashioned dugouts or made more permanent coverings for their wagon boxes, they found refreshment in modest musical or dramatic offerings, after days of labor in plowing or planting. Histories of southern Utah describe both the casts and the eager audiences of early community theatres, the first of which was the Parowan Dramatic Association, which was already performing in the log council house in the winter of 1850-51. Cedar City followed with the Cedar Dramatic Society organized in 1854. The list of members includes the names of prominent settlers and their assignments in the society:

J. M. Higbee, pres.
Hezekiah Simpkins, prompter
Wardman Holmes, stage manager
John P. Jones , asst. stage mgr.
John Jones, call boy
James Haslam, chairman of music

James Whitaker, musician
John Chatterley musician
John Memmott, musician
Joseph Hunter, musician
Christopher Jacobs, musician
William Ridges, musician
Joseph Pugmire
John Stoddard
Benjamin Arthur
James Bosnell
John Bradshaw
John Adams
William Davidson
Eliezar Edwards
I.C. Haight
John S. Humphries
Daniel S. Macfarlane
John M. Macfarlane
David Muir
Samuel Jewks
George Hunter
Thomas Thorley

EARLY DRAMA
PRODUCTION
WAY
DOWN
EAST,

VOICE
TEACHER
LILLIAN
WALKER,
1906

The first theatre production in Cedar City occurred in 1855, when *Priestcraft Revisited* was presented.[3] During the period of professional traveling plays, which ended at the close of the nineteenth century, many townspeople of Cedar City, Enoch and Parowan would memorize scripts in anticipation of the productions that were coming to the region, because they wished to be among the extras that were hired from the local communities.

From its beginnings, the Branch Normal School formed a framework around which the citizens of Cedar City and the nearby towns could be organized to participate in wonderful cultural activities. It is the rich tradition of the school and the town, through a hundred years, that the college and the citizens not only hungered for fine music, great literature and ambitious theatrical productions, but somehow were blessed with teachers and mentors of sufficient talent to serve up veritable cultural feasts.

The emergence and extraordinary success of the Utah Shakespearean Festival has allied, in the public mind, the very identity of the college and of Cedar City with fine theatre. The fallout to the school and the town, of the increased state and nation-wide visibility of the Shakespearean Festival, has included giant leaps forward for the theatre department of the college.

Nevada Watson Driggs offered some recollections which provide the first documentation of theatrical productions at BNS:

The drama director before 1910 was a man named Du Poncet... He directed several plays. Miss Walker, the singing instructor and I were in She Stoops to Conquer. *He directed other plays, but I can't remember any except* Trilby, *which I was not in. In 1910 Professor Hussong directed a parody on* The Merchant of Venice, *and besides myself there were Lillian Higbee and Hazel Dalley in the cast.*[4]

Wonderful old photographs fill in other documentation for early BNS dramatic productions.

Cedar City and the surrounding towns had several local theatre groups from 1850 to 1911. The Parowan and Cedar City Dramatic Societies were succeeded by the Mutual Improvement Dramatic Society. Individual church theatricals also offered entertainment for the public. By 1911 local dramatic organizations were on the decline. The desire of faculty and students of BNS, and then BAC, to present their own plays fueled the efforts of the college to continue to fill in the gap in theatricals for the school and the towns.

Dramatic productions were, apparently, the responsibility of the dramatics committee of the English department, consisting in 1911-12 of Mr. Clifford Ashley and Miss Myrtle Decker. Members of the dramatic club, in 1912-13, were chosen by tryouts.

The first recorded production at BNS was the two-act comedy, *Mr. Bob,* by Rachel E. Gale, presented March 14, 1911. Clifford Ashley and Roswell C. Belnap, instructors in the English department, co-directed the play. It must have been well received, because Clifford Ashley soon began to prepare for the second production, *The Amazons,* also presented in 1911.

Two years later in 1913, Clifford Ashley and Myrtle Decker directed another comedy, *One of the Eight* by Norman Lee Swartout. This time the cast and crew took the production on the road, presenting the play in Parowan and Milford as well as at BNS.

NEVADA
WATSON, LEFT,
AND WALTER
LUNT, BNS
DRAMA,
1909

Another two years passed without a theatrical production by the college, but an item in the *Iron County Record* for Friday, January 15, 1915, under "BAC Notes," manifests student interest: *A great many students are interested in dramatics this year. The College intends to put on two plays, and with such a large number to choose from, for the characters, it will undoubtedly produce plays of worth.*

The English department actually put on only one play that year, in the spring, but it was a more ambitious comedy of four acts, *The Perplexed Husband,* by Alfred Sutro, directed by John C. Christensen. It is noteworthy that John C. Christensen was also the athletic coach and taught in the agriculture department. The cast included Lafe Jolley, Willard Canfield, Vera Pace, Martha Langford, Zelma Jones and Cloris Lunt.

Four plays were produced on the mainstage at BAC during 1917, the first of which, a three-act comedy called *All of a Sudden Peggy,* was directed by John C. Christensen. After a lapse in dramatics of four years, John Christensen was joined by a co-director, Hattie H. Esplin, for *Tony the Convict* in 1921. John Christensen's last production for the college was called *Safety First.* In most cases, he had selected scripts that had appeared on New York stages.

Hattie B. Maughan, who became the wife of Director J. Howard Maughan and was an instructor in the English department, directed the drama program, producing a series of three theatricals at BAC in 1922-23 and 1923-24: *Officer 666, Letters 'n Letters* and *Cappy Ricks.*

In 1923 King Hendricks began teaching at the college, immediately upon his graduation from Utah Agricultural College with a B.S. degree. Hendricks took leave from BAC after two years to earn his master's degree at Stanford, but he is credited with the development of a dramatics club in 1924-25 and for the introduction of the study of dramatics in the English curriculum. He directed four productions that same year. In the late fall the cast and crew tried their hand at Oscar Wilde's comedy *The Importance of Being Earnest.* The winter production, *The Grand Old Man,* traveled from December 17 to January 10 to nine towns from Hurricane on the south to Beaver on the north. The traveling productions continued to foster the dramatic arts and entertain the townspeople of southern Utah.

In 1926 the name of Miss Aulier Dixon appears briefly on the list of English faculty members who directed theatricals during this period. When she left teaching to get married,

Hattie B. Maughan came back for a year to finish the production *The Goose Hangs High,* begun by Ms. Dixon.

Ira N. Hayward really rescued dramatics at the school, when he joined the BAC faculty in 1927 to teach dramatics, English and speech; he was the first permanent stage director for the college. Under his leadership, drama and mysteries were added to the traditional fare of comedies. Hayward had come to Cedar City from Logan, where he had served as head of the speech department of Logan High school directly after his graduation from the Utah State Agricultural College. At the end of the 1927-28 school year he attended the summer quarter of the Sam Hume School of Drama in Berkeley.

The BAC English department averaged two productions a year under the direction of Ira Hayward. Many of the shows traveled to outlying areas. A comment in the 1929-30 *Agricola* records a resurgence of vitality in BAC theatre:

For the first time in many years, the BAC has had an active dramatic club this year. The organization was effected during the fall

CAST FROM *THE AMAZONS,* 1911, CLIFFORD ASHBY, COACH

BALLET GIRLS, DRAMATICS SECTION, 1920 YEARBOOK

DRAMA
CLUB,
1912

quarter and took the name of 'The Peruke Club.'

*I*ra Hayward's success on the main stage of BAC inspired him to present Shakespeare in southern Utah. He directed *Much Ado About Nothing,* the first Shakespearean play ever produced on campus, in 1933, followed by *Twelfth Night* in the spring of 1935.

The effects of the depression on school funding may have been the cause of a cutback to one play per year for the next two years. The last production by Ira Hayward was *New Fires,* in the fall of 1935. Hayward transferred to USAC at the end of that school year, where he had a distinguished career.

Grant Redford, the second permanent stage director at the college, replaced Ira Hayward in 1936. He was able to reinstitute the pattern of two productions per year, in winter and early spring. Enrollment during the fall quarter was meager, as many young people stayed at home to help with the harvest of crops. He also maintained at the college a wider selection of productions during the four school years of 1936-37 to 1939-40. Records show that the casts were of ambitious size for the small school.

Redford's productions included *The Enemy;*, a drama; *Night of January 16th* , a courtroom drama by Ayn Rand; a murder mystery, *The Perfect Alibi,* by A. A. Milne; Sinclair Lewis' drama, *It Can't Happen Here* ; another drama, *Chalk Dust,* by Harold Clarke and Maxwell Nurnberg and a final comedy, *Spring Dance* by Phillip Barry.

After a year's leave, during which Alice (Mrs. Ianthus) Wright directed the one mainstage production in November of 1940, *Ah Wilderness*

by Eugene O'Neill, Redford returned and stayed an additional two years, renewing the practice of producing original scripts for the college stage. As writer, director and actor, Redford was not only a driving force in the development of the Zion Canyon Easter Pageant, but also re-kindled interest in theatre in all of southern Utah.

In the decade between 1940 to 1950 the mainstage director for the college changed seven times. Each director faced the challenges of maintaining interest in drama with few students from which to cast productions. During the war years, 1940-1945, the number of BAC's theatrical productions declined along with the male college enrollment, the average enrollment of this period being 242 students. The selection of scripts, however, reflected the desire to present good theatre. After World War II the college enrollment steadily increased, which brought with it an increase in student interest and in theatre offerings.

Grant Redford returned in 1941 to direct his original dramatic script, *Pattern for Action* and a second show, the Kaufman and Hart comedy *The Man Who Came to Dinner,* in conjunction with the Music Arts Association of Cedar City. The cast for this show included faculty members and townspeople, including William H. Manning, Ianthus Wright, Carma Leigh, Clyde Dixon, Parlcy Dalley, Mrs. Nelson Tydings, Leora Petty, Homer Ogden, Nedra Neilsen, Lowell Whitaker, Walter Lunt, Ruth Jenson, Keith Bushman, Zeke Zimmerman, Donald Nelson, Terry Neilson and Gordon Christiansen.

The *Iron County Record* of November 11, 1943 announced that Grant H. Redford had accepted a position with the University of Montana. His last production was a comedy, *The Great Big Doorstep.* J. H. Plummer, also of the English department, produced *Arsenic and Old Lace* in 1944.

Preston R. Gledhill became mainstage director in 1944-45, but his teaching assignments also included modern languages and English, along with theatre. In order to produce a quality play, Gledhill used faculty and community thespians to assume the mature roles in his cast. His first production was the drama, *Our Town,* by Thornton Wilder. The second play was an all-girl comedy called *Nine Girls,* which reflected the dearth of male students.

Twain Tippetts joined the BAC faculty in 1945 to teach English and dramatics. He had been educated at Snow College, received his B.A. and M.A. at Brigham Young University, taught high school in Salina and Springville and served in World War II before coming to Cedar City. His philosophy, similar to that of Preston Gledhill, was that drama was a serious discipline, that all productions should be of the finest possible quality and that students should not be thrust into roles that they could not portray well. He used faculty and community players for the mature roles, selecting his productions around the actors he had available in the school and community.

Tippetts produced one play, the comedy *My Sister Eileen,* in the spring of 1946 and *Dear Ruth*, another comedy, in November of that year. The next school year, 1947-48, the department went back to two productions: *State of the Union* and *Kiss and Tell.* It is recorded that not everything ran smoothly all of the time. *State of the Union* ran four and-a-half hours on opening night, elongated by the necessity to patch together scenery between the scenes. In 1948 and in 1949 Tippetts shared the assignment of directing the productions, one each year, with J. Harry Plummer, instructor in the English department and Donald K. Nelson, librarian. In 1949 Tippetts *directed I Remember Mama;* Nelson produced *John Loves Mary*. In 1950 Plummer presented *Death Takes a Holiday*.

That same year Twain Tippetts directed *Hamlet*, the third Shakespearean production in the history of the college. The production of Hamlet combined talents of townspeople and students, but even more amazing, the imposing figure of the director of the school, Dr. H. Wayne Driggs, walking the battlements as the ghost of Hamlet's father. Women of the town sewed the costumes for the production. The armor presented a challenge until Lucretia Ashcroft creatively designed and crocheted the mail from heavy thread, spray-painting it silver.

Twain Tippetts' philosophy of casting local actors from the citizenry of Cedar City developed into the Rainbow Arts Guild. The Guild helped to foster dramatic arts in the entire southern part of the state.

Twain Tippetts continued in primary responsibility for the mainstage theatrical productions until 1954, still under the aegis of the English department. Tippetts did not stage his first production of 1950-51, a comedy, *The Hasty Heart*, until February. It was quickly followed by Gilbert and Sullivan's comic opera *HMS Pinafore,* directed by Reed Berrett and Donald Knight. Berrett was filling a slot in the music department, during Blaine Johnson's stint in the Korean war.

The offerings of the next year were interesting. Tippetts directed both productions; he put on a World War II drama, *Command Decision*, which was notable because it featured an all male cast, and the ambitious *Joan of Lorraine* in the spring. The productions typically included students, faculty members and prominent townspeople. This time Lucretia Ashcroft was expert at fashioning armor, which was especially fortunate since her daughter Anne, portrayed a memorable Joan.

In 1953 Tippetts directed *What a Life*. The second production, Noel Coward's *Blithe Spirit,* was directed by Richard Rowley, who at that time represented the speech area of the department of English. Twain Tippett's final production at BAC was Tennessee Williams' drama *The Glass Menagerie*. It was the sole dramatic offering of the 1954 season. Tippetts left Cedar City to pursue his doctorate degree at UCLA, returning to Utah State Agricultural College to finish his career.

Richard M. Rowley served as mainstage director at the college from 1954-55 to 1958-59, which included the transition from BAC to College of Southern Utah. A native of Parowan, Rowley was the first native son to serve as director of theatre offerings. He had earned his bachelors degree at BYU and masters at Stanford University.

Rowley brought an expanded perspective to CSU's theatre. He believed that theatrical productions in an educational setting should place primary emphasis on the student. Therefore, he involved students backstage, as well as onstage, in set construction, painting, lighting, box office and publicity. Interest in the theatre as a discipline increased under his direction. Rowley also re-introduced the production of original scripts, including some he had authored himself; the practice had been dropped after Grant Redford's era.

The addition of the Auditorium to the campus in 1955 gave theatre another boost. Students celebrated the move from the theatre in Old Main, thriving on the opportunity to work in a more modern plant. For the first time college productions sprawled out in the larger stage of the new facility. Directing two to three productions a year, Rowley sparked interest in drama at the college and kept college theatre before the public.

Rowley's offerings, over a five-year period, were widely varied. He showed courage in producing Sophocles' classical tragedies *Antigone* and *Oedipus Rex* as the first productions at the time of the dedication of the new auditorium.

Some of my best memories are the times we spent decorating the Hall of Enchanted Trees at Christmastime. When I was a theatre student, we decorated the trees in the foyer of the old auditorium. The sacrifices were worth it as we opened the doors and saw so many people who had come to enjoy the trees. I remember several sleepless nights as we worked long into the evening to meet the deadline. It was the one time that no matter how talented you were, if you were willing to spend the time, you were part of what was happening. It was sort of a great equalizer of those of us in a very competitive department. It was a time when your energy and dedication were really put to a test. I know I ate enough royal icing while working on the edible tree to never want to eat cake again. I truly cherish the friendships that were made during that time.

I also remember my time spent in the student government offices. Bessie Dover and Ken Benson were surrogate parents for so many of us. There were doors always open for advice or to share the triumphs and that are part of the college experience. Bessie toured with us on the program bureau and always made sure we had a good breakfast and a great time. She always reminded us that we represented the student body, and the reputation of the school was in our hands.

Nancy Wilson Head

The next year he directed his own script, a fantasy called *Man on the Mezzanine*. That same year the third production was a murder thriller, *Night Must Fall*. Another Rowley original script, based on the Utah Parks' tradition of the employees singing farewell to departing guests, was called *Sing Away*. In stark contrast to that bit of fluff, Rowley chose to produce Shakespeare in a group of 15 scenes from *Macbeth*, *A Midsummer Night's Dream*, *Othello*, *Julius Caesar*, *Romeo and Juliet* and *King Henry IV*.

However, comedy remained the main diet of the college theatre. Comedies included: *The Male Animal* by Thurber and Nugent; *Arsenic and Old Lace* by Kesselring; *The Solid Gold Cadillac by* Teilman and Kaufman; *The Staring Match* by Jerry McNeely, originally written for television; *The Matchmaker* by Thornton Wilder; Noel Coward's *Hay Fever* and Rowley's last production at the college, James M. Barrie's *The Admirable Chrichton*.

Fred Adams came to the campus in 1959 to join the communication and theatre department. The program, consisting of a composite major with emphases in each of the two components—performance and production, had been basically designed for certification in secondary education. The prevailing climate of the department became "Yes, you can

have a career in the theatre," but the focus in the early '60s was two-fold: sending out the best secondary school teachers and building an audience for the future. He describes his first year in the theatre program:

My first year at CSU was filled with surprises and a lot of highs and lows. I was taking over a program for which the equipment consisted of four poorly made flats that had been wallpapered ! There was also a set of four-by-twelve foot flats built by the music department that they no longer wanted, seven working lighting instruments and a dimmer board that had been installed wrong...I had four committed theatre arts students, Gaylynn Sherratt, Stephen Foster, Gary M. McIntyre and Janet Hofheins...We scoured the community selling season tickets; very few had any faith in us and only a handful took a chance on a whole year's subscription.

Administrative policy limited teacher certification for about a decade during the late sixties and early seventies, the department being authorized to certify only nine graduates per year. Straining against limitations, the department began to expand its focus by developing a professional theatre approach, the goal being to place students in graduate schools where they could work at the university level and in professional theatre.

This approach began the articulation of the slow development of three emphases in the theatre major program: acting/directing, design/technical and theory/history.

Adams directed all the plays in the '60s and was a one-man operation, teaching both acting and directing.

The mainstage shows included musicals, comedies and dramatic plays. They produced *Bells Are Ringing, Pirates of Penzance, Diary of Anne Frank, Taming of the Shrew, Barretts of Wimpole Street* and *Anne of a Thousand Days.*

The audiences responded, and attendance swelled from meager to marvelous; from an average of 70 when they had begun, to a high of 900 on their best nights.

Paul Vorkink of the education department lent his talent to directing smaller-cast and less-design plays, often in the round, and utilized the considerable talents of the faculty. They delighted audiences with *Harvey, Arsenic and Old Lace,* and *The Importance of Being Earnest.*

Gary McIntyre joined the program in 1968. Teamed with Adams, the two gave each other courage and began to attempt things neither would have dared to do alone.

Adams remembers their first Shakespearean production, *Taming of the Shrew:*

We had not nearly enough men to do a Shakespearean play so I visited with Coach Cleo Petty, who took me to the scrimmage on the old football field. He introduced me to his players and explained that I needed some volunteers. I spoke passionately to the guys and almost a dozen came forward and volunteered to try out. Norm Childs, one of Cleo's star players, got the role of Petruchio, loved the work and stayed in theatre most of his life. Norm married his Kate (Gaylynn Sherratt) and, looking back, I still feel that their work in this production equalled any performances in the ensuing Festival years. And we sold out ! Not a Broadway musical, not a famous current comedy, but a Shakespeare play ! We had to run two extra nights to accommodate the demand. I realized then that this adopted community of Cedar City was unique, unusual, strange. I realized that this town had a tradition of classic culture.

The '70s were a period of 'isms.' The department experimented in avant garde theatre with the production of *Godspell*, which often excit-

HARVEY,
1960s

ed the audience but was very controversial. Negative reaction in the community to the Broadway production *Jesus Christ, Superstar* had led to a general perception that the two plays were anti-Christian. The theme of *Godspell* is taken from the Book of Luke. The Christ character, in the college production, portrayed a teacher, wearing a superman-symbol tee shirt, sharing the beatitudes with his student disciples. The sound effects employed electronic music. The final scene depicted the teacher being crucified against a chain link fence.

When Adams invited clergymen to attend a dress rehearsal he got some positive reactions. The department's great satisfaction was in a standing ovation on opening night and the audible weeping of men and women in the audience during the scene of the last supper, at the sorrow of the young disciples bidding farewell to their teacher.

Terral S. Lewis, a graduate of CSU, returned with a masters degree from Brigham Young University to teach acting, theatre dance and to direct. Lewis founded the Red Cliff Repertory in Kanab, a summer event that gave stu-

MEDEA,
1970

dents repertory experience and summer income. Joseph Gilg was hired in 1974 to replace Gary McIntyre, who took a year-long sabbatical leave at Brigham Young University.

During the eighties decade the department moved substantively toward professional theater, the primary thrust of which was to place students in graduate programs, making sure that they were prepared to survive in the professional world of theatre. Actors now had to be well-qualified in order to participate in the college's dramatic productions. The audition process simulated this element in professional theatre.

The eighties was also an era of commercial success. The box office became a very important factor. SUU President Sherratt authorized the policy of the department's keeping gate receipts from its productions, which resulted in the improvement of all phases of the university drama experience. Ticket sales in the first part of the decade averaged $7,000 a year, in sharp contrast to the average intake of $45,000 at the time of this writing.

Former student standout R. Scott Phillips arrived from Idaho State University. He taught, directed and assisted with the Shakespearean Festival.

Doug Baker brought a wonderful skill to the the classroom as acting instructor and he also directed one show each year. His training included several years with the Ringling Brothers training center in Sarasota, Fla., so he introduced clown and juggling techniques, a unique aspect of the program at SUU. He was lured away from the university to a significant career opportunity to write, direct and star in a spectacular production at the Hotel Excalibur in Las Vegas.

Richard Bugg, a young acting coach and director, who had been trained at Brigham Young University, replaced Baker as head of the acting program. Bugg, assisted by Valeen Ogzewalla and Laurie Birmingham, has built the program using the latest techniques to provide wonderful training.

The department's current (1997) theatre goal is to provide an understanding of theatre's potential as an expressive medium and as a collaborative art form. The theatre emphasis now had three areas of focus: acting/directing, design/technical, and theory/history.

The SUU theatre arts and dance department continued to mature in its professional and technical approach and in the commercial success that is the hallmark of the '90s. The themes of the plays moved toward women's issues and original scripts, a reflection of societal trends of the decade. The department continued to focus on the successes of its students.

G. McClain McIntyre, department head of theatre arts and financial director for the Shakespearean Festival, gave an evaluation of the status of the department in the nineties:

Our philosophy is that the only thing we market is the success of the student. If our students can't go to a graduate school on an assistantship or get into commercial theatre or commercial dance we feel that we have failed. So when our students are able to knock out all the major schools—Harvard, Cornell, Yale, Berkeley—and do a little bit better, that makes us even more excited.

I wish there were a way to measure these statistics: a university of 5,000 students in a city of 18,000 people with a theatre production organization like the Utah Shakespearean Festival, doing regional theatre that is hosted by the theatre arts department... I don't think you'd find anywhere in the world that combination of excellence... There's something unique about this university; there's something unique about the community itself.[5]

SUU has graduated many extraordinarily talented thespians, drama teachers and theatrical technicians over the hundred-year history of productions at the school.[6] By 1997 there were 97 majors with more than 40 minors in theatre and dance. Theatre arts had a faculty/staff of ten and a half people, with an additional five faculty/staff in dance. Approximately 14 graduates receive bachelor degrees each year, and of that number, an average of nine are accepted in major graduate and conservatory programs. From the SUU theatre arts/dance department have come members of faculties of prestigious universities, including Rutgers, the University of Florida, Juilliard, University of Nevada at Las Vegas, the University of Indiana, Weber State University and Utah State University. Graduates from the department were, in 1997, teaching in most of the school districts of the state and in several schools in surrounding states. Graduates of the SUU theatre arts program were also working in some of the nation's most prestigious theatres.

The history of the technical theatre emphasis at SUU commenced in 1968, when G. McClain McIntyre joined the faculty as the scenic designer and technical director. Drama buffs will be interested to learn that when McIntyre, affectionately known as Mac, came to the department, the complete inventory of lighting equipment listed only 13 cannon lekos and seven fresnels–in contrast to the 811 lighting instruments employed in 1996 in the Shakespearean Festival facility and Randall L. Jones Theatre.

In the early days of the technical program, the faculty taught students to build scenery using cardboard, inexpensive paints, canvas and plywood. Initial budgets of about $50 per show required that crews exercise extreme frugality in purchasing and in the recycling of items whenever possible. They stored one set of professional flats in the auditorium, which functioned as a sound baffle, and occasionally as backdrops, for the music arts department. However, for most productions, the crews fashioned sets made up of profile cutouts, attached to flats, that gave a painterly, two-dimensional design. College President Royden Braithwaite was happily surprised when the crew created the entire *Medea* set of formalistic stairs and platforms. The administration was very proud of what was happening in the technical theatre program.

In 1974, when Mr. McIntyre took a one-year leave to teach at BYU, Professor Joseph Gilg joined the faculty to take his place. His forte was lighting design, but he also had background in scenic design and construction. Gilg was retained for a time after Mac returned, which rounded out the faculty to two experts–a scenic designer and a lighting designer–working together to build technical theatre at the school.

The technical theatre area is a burn-out field, but SUU has profited from the contributions of a succession of gifted directors. When Joseph Gilg left to get another masters degree, this one in directing, Tim Bryson replaced him. Bryson came to the SUSC campus with experience at both BYU and the University of Utah. His expertise, along with a bit more budget, gave the department a major step forward in scenery construction.

Michael Sicotte replaced Bryson, when Bryson left for Arizona State University. Michael brought a dry sense of humor and a unique background to the department. He had completed his B.S. degree in chemistry, studied technical theatre at the master's level and worked in the assembly of computers for a time before he came to the department as technical director. He was actually the first technical director in the department who did not design

ROYAL HUNT OF THE SUN, 1968

scenery. His computer experience was invaluable, as the theatre arts department was the first, after the central administration of the college, to utilize computers in the program. When Sicotte left Cedar City, it was for the Virgin Islands to work in the oil industry, a reconnection with his training in chemistry.

Becky White, who was hired in 1986, replaced Mike Sicotte. Becky was hired as the scenic designer/technical director, bringing new techniques in styles of design and scene painting from her training at the University of California, Irvine, campus. She worked for the theatre arts department and, in the summer, for the Utah Shakespearean Festival in grounds and display.

While the foregoing designers and technical directors were developing the program of the department, the Shakespearean Festival had matured to the point that they needed a full-time technical director. The university hired Roger Sherman as the first year-round director for the theatre facilities. Sherman's responsibility included construction of the scenery of the winter program, maintenance of all the technical equipment and technical director for the Festival in the summer. Roger Sherman left, after a productive stint at SUU, to return to his roots in Colorado.

Bob Goss, formerly a professional technical director of the Sante Fe Opera Company, replaced Sherman, introducing to the department the use of metals and master carpentry skills. Goss is credited with advancing the technical theatre program to a level of professional theatre that compares with Broadway or Hollywood, but when an opportunity to man-

MARY STUART, 1965

Borrowed Time, Bells are Ringing, Ondine, Taming of the Shrew and *Diary of Anne Frank.* During these years she also played such roles as Kate and Aunt Demetria, and served as an associate costumer for the first two seasons of the Utah Shakespearean Festival. Gaylynn is married to her Petruchio, Norm Childs.

In 1962 Lee Thompson, wife of Rick Thompson of the SUU faculty, became designer, shop supervisor and head stitcher for the theatre department. Previous to this assignment Lee, a tailor, had become interested in fabric composition and costume design and created costumes in the home economics department. She assisted Gaylynn Sherratt for a year before replacing her as costume designer of the theatre department.

Fred Adams, founder and prime mover of the Shakespearean Festival, has a strong background in costuming, as well as directing and acting. He tells of this experience:

... Lee and Gaylynn had worked together on the winter season's Romeo and Juliet, *so they worked together on making those costumes serve the production of* The Merchant of Venice, *and Lee designed and supervised all of the costumes for* Hamlet. *I went on my daily rounds to see how all was going in the costume area, only to find Lee frozen in motion. She had an exquisite fabric of black silk with a metallic floral pattern we had obtained from Shike Frankel at The Yardstick fabric store in Salt Lake City. It was a very expensive fabric, and Lee was scared to death of ruining it by cutting it wrong. I watched for several minutes as she agonized over it.*

"We haven't the luxury of time to waste on this," I declared, took the scissors out of her hands and cut a huge chunk of the cloth. Lee screamed, looked at the damage I had done and then went blissfully on her way cutting out the costume. It was the principle of the "first dent in a new car"...we just had to get her started. Costumes were a big job, since the bulk of the show's look had to be supplied by the costumes. Yes, it was a big job, but the full company spent time in the shop, carpenters, electricians alike. Ladies in the community added a real bonus, as they would take cut goods home and assemble them (Alice Caine, Mary Anker and others). So the Festival was truly becoming a community-wide project.[7]

age a roadhouse in northern Utah arose, he left the university.

Phil Haslam replaced Bob Goss in 1995. Phil had literally grown up in the discipline, as he had worked as a youngster in Ephraim in the scene shop at Snow College, where his father was developing the technical theatre program. Phil built upon his early experience by graduating and then teaching at Brigham Young University before he was hired at Utah State University. Haslam was looking for a professional career in theatre when he decided to join the program at SUU as a master carpenter; he brought new skills in metals and plastics and training equal to that of any college technical director in the country. During the school year of 1996-97 Haslam became the full technical director. His professional attitude and experience resulted in a substantive boost to the department.

As SUU theatre arts students have been superbly trained in scenic design, painting, sound and construction, they have, in the last decade, been picked up by graduate programs on assistantships and have been sought after for summer theater.

Gaylynn Sherratt was a student at SUU from 1959-1962, but she literally handled both the design and execution of the costuming for all of the department's productions during those years, including *On*

Mary Judd, who began designing as a student at the university, followed Lee Thompson as costume designer from 1964 to 1972. Mary was a quiet woman with an amazing skill with fabric. She could literally make a 'silk purse of a sow's ear.' She costumed all of the department productions of the winter seasons during these years and did several Festival shows in the summertime as well, among them *Romeo and Juliet*. Her tour de force, however, was the design and creation of 'the monster,' the gown of Elizabeth I in the production of Mary Stuart. This masterpiece, which is still (1997) in the collection drawing praise from audiences, is an accurate 75-pound re-creation, crafted from more than 300 yards of fabric. Mary Judd arranged hundreds of yards of lined silk from one end to the other of the Auditorium foyer; eight students at a time followed her pattern, smocking the silk and lining together.

Susan Memmott (Allred) did a superb job of costume design for the department, also as a student, for *The Boyfriend* and *Follies*, 1971-73. Her dreamland costumes for Follies were exceptional, made of hundreds of yards of cut and crushed velvets in various shades of pink. They featured towering headdresses of spun glass, lacquered and studded with jewels. Susan had such wonderful skills that, upon graduation, she was hired as costumer by the Utah Opera Company in Salt Lake City. She became their designer and shop supervisor, winning accolades from the entire opera world for her work.

In 1974-75 Leslie Robinson (Mrs. Guran Greene), also a student, brought a fresh outlook to costumes of department productions. She could do an entire show with a single palette and had great skills in fabric distressing, dyeing and painting, as well as draping. She used a wonderful new fabric called polyester for her designs, all in black, for *Spoon River Anthology*.

Leslie also acted in an extensive range of roles in winter productions, and mothered the entire department. One late night, as the story goes, Leslie reported seeing the "ghost" who purportedly frequented the tunnel area of the auditorium; she quickly stopped her sewing and ran.

M. L. Baker (1976-78) came to the department via the Shakespearean Festival in 1976. One of the best craftsmen and tailors in theatre, with years of experience at Iowa State University, she had been hired by the Festival for the summers of 1975 through 1977. When Leslie Robinson graduated from SUSC, M. L. Baker applied for, and was hired to take the winter design slot in the department, with the intent that she could not only provide excellent design and supervision for the winter program, but could have the

OEDIPUS THE KING

shops and equipment ready for the Festival each spring. The costumes, including undergarments, now took on the silhouette of the period, being constructed to be sturdy enough to be worn for many months on the road.

Her last year at SUSC, when the department produced *Jacques Brel is Alive and Well*, costume funds had run out. M. L. obtained old sheets from motels, died them various shades of red and made all the dresses and shirts for less than $20. Tired of small budget and long hours, she left for greener pastures at the University of Florida in Tallahassee.

The department conducted a nation-wide search to replace M. L. Baker in 1978. Sandra Stiglinski had been a staff designer for California State University, Bernardino. The first full-time department designer/costumer, Sandra still is a faculty member at SUU at this writing (1997), as well free-lance designer for a Las Vegas and regional clientele.

Ms. Stiglinski has contributed to the success of the department on many levels, besides the design of costumes for shows over the seasons, including creation of eight of Elizabeth I's portrait gowns. When the department was looking for creative ideas to build an audience, she founded the Peanut Butter Players, a childrens' production theatre. She has developed the costume design curriculum into a complete program geared for the success of each individual theatre student. Her graduates find placement directly in the industry or in major master of fine arts programs throughout the nation. During her tenure, she has also designed many of the Shakespearean Festival's Greenshows, Royal Teas and Feastes.

Carol Wells-Day (1988-1991) joined Sandra Stiglinski on the SUSC faculty to coordinate the

FIDDLER ON THE ROOF, 1969

winter season and Festival programs. A native of southern Utah, Carol had worked at the University of Utah. Her principal responsibilities were to upgrade the costume shop and teach design to costume majors; she sent many promising graduates on their career track from SUU before returning to Pioneer Theater at the U of U. She also organized the Festival storage and brought the costume cavalcade (a touring program of the department which featured various Shakespearean-era costumes) stock into excellent condition.

When Carol Wells-Day left in 1991, Sharon Mayfield Cullimore joined Sandra Stiglinski in the department to provide construction of Sandra's designs and supervision of the costume shop in the winter season, as well as year-round supervision of shop space and maintenance of the Festival's stock and costume cavalcade. Sharon received her experience in costume rental in Waterloo, Iowa, where she had worked in community theater and managed costume rental at the Waterloo Community Playhouse.

With the theatre arts and dance departments presenting as many as seven or eight productions a year, it is impossible to comment on all of them. The following sampler provides some of the excitement and innovations that each production provided.

Diary of Anne Frank

During the rehearsal process, while the director was working for naturalism, he gave the cast extensive background on the plight of Jewish people in Germany during the Nazi regime. He asked his players to spend as much time as possible confined to the stage, so that they could sense the feeling of confinement experienced by the characters of the play. In keeping with this assignment, cast members often slept on the stage. On several occasions school children,

visiting the set for an introduction to the story of Anne Frank, caught college students napping.

The cast was made up of faculty and students to provide the age range of the Van Dam family. Harry Plummer, an English professor, played the role of Anne's father. He was a great thespian who brought genuine fatherly concern, love and tenderness to the play. As he delivered his final lines in the last scene, his eyes filled with tears, moving an audience to standing ovations.

Fiddler on the Roof

The first off-Broadway production of *Fiddler on the Roof* occurred under the direction of Fred Adams who battled to secure production rights for the first amateur production. Since the rights belonged to the people of Israel, Adams wrote to Golda Meir, comparing the persecution of the Jews by the Nazis to the experience of the Mormons in Illinois, which must have been effective, since the rights were granted. The entire music and theatre departments participated in this production. Some of the audience in Cedar City who had also seen the musical in New York City, expressed the opinion that the SUU rendition was the more poignant of the two productions. The close relationship between faculty and students at the university, and the opportunity to collaborate in the great script, made for a notably satisfying production. Dr. Kent Myers, dean of the School of Education, played the role of Tevye. Local people who had seen the professional show in New York claimed that Dr. Myers' portrayal was more genuine, bringing reality to the play.

As *Fiddler* was Gary McIntyre's master's thesis, his graduate committee came to Cedar City to evaluate his work. They paid the production the ultimate compliment by commenting that they had become so caught up in the play, with its wonderful cardboard sets, that they completely forgot the critique until the end of the play.

Nicholas Nickleby

Nicholas Nickleby presented a real challenge to the theatre department. Many times they had risked the commercial success of a play for artistic goals, but this play is produced in two successive evenings. Would the audience be able to organize busy schedules and be willing to commit the time and money for attending the eight-hour, two-day performance? They came; participating students have called it their most rewarding theatre experience, although many have gone on to graduate school and are working professionals in theatre. Years later, people reminisce about two stunning nights of poetry.

Arsenic and Old Lace

Kent Myers also played the leading role in this classic, which combined faculty along with the student cast. He wanted to bring extra suspense to the role of Jonathan, the malicious brother of two sweet little old ladies. The department produced the play 'in the arena.' In the scene where Jonathan was preparing to carve up his younger brother's face, Dr. Myers handed out medical instruments to audience members, as if asking them to assist him in the surgery. On one particular night, as Myers pulled on his surgical gloves and reached for an instrument to cut up his brother, a youngster in the audience yelled out, "I don't like this!" The comic relief only dispelled the suspense momentarily, and Dr. Myers began to work his magic again.

Gaslight/Angel Street

This play was one of a series of mysteries, which was also produced in the intimacy of the arena setting. McIntyre did not want to close the play with the typical ending where the heroine would surmount all the difficulties with serenity. He wanted the audience to suffer some uncertainty about the outcome. In the final scene, where the young inspector enters and asks the heroine if she is 'okay,' the director instructed the ingenue to look out over the audience as though she were looking at a butterfly, as she replied, "Oh yes, I believe I will be okay."

For three years, whenever one of the secretaries in SUU administration bumped into Mr. McIntyre, she begged for reassurance that the heroine was really all right, that she did not have to be taken away by people in white coats.

Working

Steven Schwartz, the playwright of *Working,* visited Cedar City to spend two days with SUU drama students. The original Broadway production of the play had been short-lived, and Schwartz was reworking the script. Fred Adams, in his inimitable fashion, saw the opportunity to provide a wonderful experience for his students, whom he prepared carefully in class for Schwartz' coming. For 48 hours the cast worked almost around the clock with the author, rehearsing and refining their own production. *Working* later returned to Broadway.

The Boyfriend

The theatre department has historically toured the region with productions. The *Boyfriend* was to tour Utah and northern

WORKING, 1980

Arizona, the first time the cast would be traveling with supervision other than faculty. The production starred Jacalyn Smith, future wife of Utah's governor, Michael O. Leavitt. Carson Henry, who would become the lighting designer for the MGM Grand Hotel's theatre in Las Vegas, was SUU's head technician. After the finale, when the cast was waiting for their curtain call, standing behind a cut-away set with four-foot high walls, Carson sneaked back on hands and knees and tied the men's shoe laces together. The cast and the audience dissolved in hysterics over the resulting contortions. It is amazing that students who pull such stunts, in their joy of creating theatre and sharing experiences with their peers, somehow mature to become some of the greatest designers, teachers, and theatre practitioners in the profession.

*I*n 1962 Fred Adams hatched the idea of taking 48 drama students to New York City. Can you imagine the reaction of these

THE BOYFRIEND, 1971

youngsters, three-fourths of whom had not been out of Utah, to *Camelot, My Fair Lady, Molly Brown, The Miracle Worker* and a performance at the Metropolitan? The projected cost of the 13-day trip was $128, a great deal of money, so the students created bake sales and car washes to generate the cash. If parents could afford $128, they donated it to the general fund.

President Royden Braithwaite, who helped tremendously in building enthusiasm for the trek, brought his car in to be washed several times. He hid money in various places in the car so that the crew would find paper dollars and coins for the fund. Prior to the fourth washing the President said, "I want you to wash under the mats and really clean everything." There was a $100 bill under a floor mat.

The trip included a three-day, two-night drive each way in a Greyhound bus. At the beginning of each day in New York, Mr. Adams meted out $1.50 for the day, 50 cents per meal. Adams was determined to have equality among his ranks. Some female students, whose parents could afford their trip had felt less than committed to the fund-raising. Mr. Adams, observing this, carefully removed from the prepared and waiting luggage in the auditorium, the fancy ball gowns these girls had planned to wear to the theater, knowing that some suitcases held no gowns.

The group had advance tickets for the plays, but had a special experience at *The Miracle Worker* with Anne Bancroft and Patty Duke. In the lobby, ushers kept saying, "Wait, wait just a minute." They held the group until the lights began to dim and then hospitable lady ushers, who had been told that this was the students' first Broadway experience, guided them to front orchestra seats.

Another little miracle occurred at the Ed Sullivan television show. Because fog prevented the Sullivan crew from flying out to Florida, where they were to have initiated the broadcast, they came back to the theatre expecting to play without a live audience. Unaware of the mix-up, the 48 students from Utah arrived at the studio door, to the delight of the management, who also recruited all cast and crew members, not on stage, to complement the small audience. A tribute to Lerner and Loewe, the climax of the show included scenes from *Camelot* that had been panned by critics. Robert Goulet, Julie Andrews and Richard Burton joined the southern Utah kids in the orchestrated applause.

At the Metropolitan Opera one SUU student experienced vertigo when she accompanied the group to seats on the very last row in the theatre, 13 stories above the main floor. To get to their seats they had to climb seven stories and then take an elevator to the very top, where seating was so steep that the person's head in front of you was at the level of your knees. The view below, through the bars of a metal fire escape, terrified her but the fresh air revived her.

On the way home from New York, United States Sen. Frank Moss, of Utah, arranged for the little group to visit the White House, (then occupied by John F. Kennedy) first treating the meat-starved group to hamburgers. He also treated the drama students to a dramatic surprise audience with President Kennedy and his cabinet. After a wait in line, Sen. Moss led the youngsters to an obscure hallway where they were immediately surrounded by secret service officers. When the door to a meeting room opened, the entire president's cabinet invited the little group in. It was the morning of the Bay of Pigs incident, and many government leaders were present, including Lyndon B. Johnson and Mike Mansfield. President Kennedy gave a little speech about how the White House belonged to all Americans, and that he hoped to be able to be a tenant there for a few more years. Later, it was arranged for the students to meet Mrs. Kennedy and the children. A few months later President Kennedy was assassinated.

The history of drama at SUU and of the Utah Shakespearean Festival merge in the year 1961. Not only the people of Cedar City, but all of Utah take pride in the reputation of the Festival, which ranks, with a few others, near the zenith.[8]

Fred and Barbara Adams began tying the dream of a future Shakespearean festival to reality by making notes on a yellow pad during a time they were engaged to be married in 1960. Adams had spent time with Angus Bowmer, founder of the famous Oregon Shakespearean Festival in Ashland, two summers before, noting the similarities of Ashland to Cedar City—small college town, isolated from metropolitan cities and surrounded by breathtaking scenery with a struggling ski resort.

They reasoned that, while it required a stretch of imagination, the necessary elements were indeed within reach for a full-blown summer festival of the Bard's works in Cedar City: a potentially wide audience, built around the people of the little town, who had historically thirsted for good theatre and had flocked to the winter season before; a site, near national

After almost a decade of bedazzling the College of Southern Utah and the community of Cedar City with charming dramatic productions, mostly comedies, Fred Adams dared to do Shakespeare. *Taming of the Shrew* was a smash hit! Cedar City loved it! Was he surprised? Not really. The warm response affirmed what he had already discovered. As he recorded:

"This town had a long history of classic culture - nearly forty years of producing the *Messiah*, complete with orchestra, chorus and brilliant soloists - and the longest running invitational art exhibit in the state, meaning that more original art hung on the walls of Cedar's homes and businesses than could be counted. And opera! More opera had been produced in Cedar City than in Salt Lake! Cedar City was a cultural oasis, and Shakespeare truly belonged here."

And how it belongs! Southern Utah University and Cedar City are identified nation-wide with the Utah Shakespearean Festival, of which Fred C. Adams is the founder and executive producer.

Under Adams' direction, the Festival has grown from a budget of $1,000 in the founding year of 1961 and 3,176 paid admissions, to a 1995 attendance of 129,472 paid admissions and a $3.3 million annual budget in 1997, the 36th season.

The recipient of myriad distinguished service awards and honors, Adams began his long association as a professor at Southern Utah University in 1959, managing the University's theatre season while he taught directing and theatre history courses. He received his BA and MA Degrees from Brigham Young University in theatre arts and Russian. The author of many articles appearing in professional magazines, Mr. Adams is also a favorite lecturer throughout the United States and Europe. He conducts at least one annual tour to Europe.

Fred Adams is the Festival. He watches over every detail, from safeguarding the Festival's standards, choosing the right combination of directors and designers, selecting upcoming seasons, to greeting the thousands of theatre patrons that flock each season to relish the product of his genius.

He was born to the stage. His sister Martha observed, "As a child Fred would create original plays for his childhood friends to present. But my acting time was limited since Fred would kill me off early in the first act, and I would spend the remainder of the play lying under a sheet."

tourist attractions, on the campus of CSU in summertime, when the dorms and the auditorium were vacant; encouragement of the college president, Royden C. Braithwaite, who had said, "I think it will work."

Adams gathered an eager cadre of students to brainstorm how they could cut costs to arrive at a realistic budget proposal of $1,000. Discouraged by the initial reaction of the Chamber of Commerce, the group nervously approached the Lions Club, armed with their creative ideas, and came away with the promise that the Lions would underwrite the festival for any amount up to $1,000 which could not be garnered by ticket sales. Dr. Braithwaite, whom Adams credits as the true angel of the ambitious dream, offered housing in the old married students' complex, which had originally been barracks at Topaz and now were called "the lambing sheds;" utilities; use of the Auditorium; released time of college staff George Barrus and Bessie Dover for promotion and approval to proceed without outside funding, based on the Lions' Club pledge to cover the deficit at the end

of the initial season.

Elated with prospects but needing answers to a list of questions they had generated, Adams, his mother, future bride and two drama students made a tour in 1961 to educate themselves. They picked the brains of Dr. Bowmer at Ashland, Oregon; worked with Dr. Harold I. Hansen at the Hill Cumorah Pageant; saw Tyrone Guthrie at Stratford, Ontario; received helpful warnings from Langer and Reed in Stratford, Connecticut; soaked up Broadway shows in New York City and arrived back in Cedar City to find a letter full of advice from Craig Noel of the Old Globe Festival in San Diego.

By the spring of 1962 the first season was set. Performance dates were to be July 1 through 14, 1962. George Barrus and Bessie Dover had generated a wonderful four-color brochure and sent out newspaper releases. Governor George D. Clyde, receptive to the positive look of the process, claimed the project as the 'Utah Shakespearean Festival," and suggested the formation of an advisory board of directors. The

THE SHAKESPEARE THEATRE AND SUU AUDITORIUM

first board consisted of giants, including Governor Clyde; actor Richard Burton; LDS Apostle Sterling W. Sill; lt. governor of Stratford-Upon-Avon A. J .R. Master; senators Wallace Bennett and Frank E. Moss; USU President Daryl Chase; CSU Director Royden C. Braithwaite; drama directors Harold I. Hansen (BYU), C. Lowell Lees (U of U) and Floyd T. Morgan (USU) and Cedar City's Chamber of Commerce director, Maurice Crichton.

The core of the casts of the first season, 1962, was about the same size company as the one used by William Shakespeare himself. Twenty-one volunteer students who had developed a keen taste for Shakespeare in the previous two winter productions of *Taming of the Shrew* and *Romeo* and *Juliet* formed the nucleus. Julie Ann Farrer played a very exciting Nurse, Burnett Baldwin was her servant, Howard Jensen made an excellent Capulet and Marian Wadsworth played Lady Capulet.

Adams fleshed out the company with local citizens: Walt Lunt as the gravedigger, Venna Johnson and Tom Challis as the player Queen and King and Boyd Redington as old Vincentio. These additions added a wonderful sense of maturity to the student company which played *Hamlet, The Taming of the Shrew* and *The Merchant of Venice.*

Along with the talented corps, the first Festival depended on a committed staff comprised of Norma Jean Benson, box office; Lee Thompson and Gaylynn Sherratt, costumes; Gary McIntyre, stage and scenery; Barry Ford, lighting; LaVeve Whetten, dancers; Blaine Johnson, Madrigals; and Adams' fiancee, Barbara Gaddis, the greenshow. The greenshow, which was wonderful from the begin-

ning, became the signature of the Festival. Whetten's dancers were local kids who used a maypole, hoops and garlands, accompanied by the live recorder music of an authentic Englishwoman, Ena Heap, and LaVeve Whetten's taped Elizabethan airs.

One of the most recognizable features of the current Festival is the tarts and other refreshments. The tradition began with Mary and Ray Anker stirring up punch powder and water in a big aluminum pot in the makeshift kitchen downstairs. Mabel Syrett, a wholesaler of restaurant supplies, after tasting the awful concoction, loaded up the Ankers with punch syrups, pineapple juice and lemons, with a delicious result. Judy Ashcroft, one of LaVeve Whetten's dancers, recruited a handful of girls to roll out pastry for fresh-baked tarts every day of the first season. The Festival, 35 years later, now sells over 600 pastries every evening.

G. McClain McIntyre, then a student who ran the department's scenery shop, had built an Elizabethan tiring house, used inside the proscenium arch of the auditorium, two years before for *Taming of the Shrew.* He now designed the platform, to be used outside on the lawn, on which to erect the tiring house for the Festival.

The platform consisted of plywood over joists of 2x4s placed on two-foot centers. The lawn in those days was watered by flooding. Every other day, after the lawns had been watered, the technicians would have to climb under the stage, lying on their backs on the wet lawn with their feet in the air. While one technician lifted joists in the air, another would drive shingles under the sinking legs to keep the stage level. Sheldon Grant, the grounds supervisor for the campus, was livid, as the lawn turned yellow and seemingly died.

It took everyone in the company to raise the balcony level of the Tiring House. Fred Adams describes the experience:

The floor unit for the balcony weighed a lot, and it took all of us lifting and supporting it with pipes and 4x4's to hold it in place while Mac and Barry Ford scrambled onto it and inserted the bolts and nuts to hold the entire structure in place. You can't imagine the organized confusion of all these 'actor types' huffing and yelling, trying to out-do one another as we tried to lift this monster and at the same time keep it level. Once the floor was up and the escape steps bolted to stabilize the level, it was just a few hours to see walls and columns and arches all in place. We had all retired to the front of the Auditorium to take a break and have a late lunch, when a heavy wind came up, and we sat on the lawn and watched walls of the recently-erected tiring house sail over the building and out into the street. Then it was back to the shop to repair and place cuts in the canvas walls to let the wind through. Even the Cedar City winds did not discourage us...[9]

The lighting was fairly simple, composed of two tall, weighted pipe trees at either side of the seating, fresnels atop, with amber, pink and blue gels. The lights were powered by a small portable Ariel Davis dimmer with slides. The sound system comprised a reel-to-reel tape recorder and live sound effects: thunder was a sheet of tin; a cock crowing was Venna Johnson standing out behind the stage on the quad; rain was made by beans dropping onto a tin pie plate and ghostly sounds were made by the full offstage cast humming or oohing.

Volunteer hostesses Ruth Challis and Clara Wheelwright seated a small but excited audience. Petruchio's servant grabbed torches and escorted the players from the Auditorium to the back of the stage, a processional that was a tradition for years, until a tunnel was built. Director Braithwaite and Fred Adams welcomed the audience, reading two wonderful telegrams from Senator Bennett and Senator Moss, and then Mr. Adams declared the Utah Shakespearean Festival theatre open!

Closing night was an emotional time for the small but talented troupe who had shared something special and had taken a great gamble and won. Patrons from 27 states, numbering 3,149, had bought tickets. The $1,000 pledged by the Lions was never required; the Festival had a bank reserve of $1,500.

History records that steadily expanding successes followed the meager beginnings of the festival. By 1975 the set had evolved from its rudimentary form to a full-fledged theatre in the manner of the original Globe Theatre. From all over the nation people have come to participate in the realization of the dream.

SUU boasts a University dance program that is unique among schools. Expansion of the discipline to its prestigious position came primarily because of the influence of Burch Mann, founder, director and choreographer of the American Folk Ballet. But dance at the school in Cedar City began early and has had a delightful progression.

The first recorded dance review was presented in May of 1913, under the direction of Isabelle Jackson. This was the year the Branch Normal School became Branch Agricultural College, and a dance review served to reinforce the determination that becoming an agricultural college would not diminish the cultural mission of the school. Miss Jackson was a substitute teacher of physical culture and added dancing to the curriculum. Dance, at that juncture, depended upon the availability of a teacher. Dancing scenes in operas and plays made use of whatever talent the school or the town had to offer at the moment.

Significant offerings in dance really began with the arrival in 1939 of Lois LaVeve Petty (Whetten), an exuberant and gifted teacher. When Miss Petty joined the faculty the student body numbered less than 200 students, but they were an active and enthusiastic group. The assignments given to the new teacher did not leave much time for a single emphasis on dance. Her duties included working in the registrar's office, teaching classes in physical education and in secretarial science—typing, shorthand, filing and business English—as well as dance.

Dance was LaVeve's first love, and her enthusiasm infused her students with the excitement necessary for the development of an active program in tandem with the other requirements. A dance class yielded only one credit hour for hours of work and preparation, so the students came because they loved the activity.

Whetten remembers:

We were fortunate to have some of the very best pianists accompany our classes and performances. They played to earn money to go to school at 25 cents an hour. Some of them

ISABELLE JACKSON, 1910

FOLK
DANCER,
1942

LaVeve Petty
(Whetten)

were Mary Jane Seaman, Carlisle Marsden, Michael Houchen and Irene Hyatt, Eula Lawrence and Emily Spencer. When tape recorders came into being, we first had a large reel-to-reel one that had to be carried by one of the larger boys because it was too heavy for most of us.

The dancers learned all the varieties of their art, including folk dances, modern, adagio and tap. In the 1940s, when the nation was consumed with the war effort of World War II, they made creative adjustments, but still they danced:

During the war there was no material to be purchased and no money to buy with, so each girl (there were six or eight) went through the rag bags at their homes and their neighbors, and brought all the pieces they could get and all were placed in a pile on the gym floor. Each one selected the color she wanted such as reds and matching pieces, greens, etc. We sewed the pieces together and made the most attractive patchwork skirts and boleros. These skirts were used for several years for different folk dances. On one trip to Salt Lake, I happened on a terrific sale. The material was embroidered linen in several colors. The store told me if I would take all the material I could have it for an extremely low price. The skirts were also very beautiful and used many times. For many of the folk costumes, both boys and girls needed ribbons and braids of all kinds. Gertrude Walker in the Stevens store would go to the basement, get all the old spools of rickrack, bias tape, and any other tapes that had been discarded because they did not sell, and give them to us for our costumes. Hours were spent sewing designs to liven up the vests and skirts. The cost of the Broncettes (later Thunderettes) outfits never exceeded thirty dollars each, which included the white knee-high boots, that were ordered from Sears. One year, artificial wigs were popular and each girl had one for a specialty num-

ber. Dawn Hunter gave us instructions how to mix the dye to color our shoes to match. The 16 pairs of white keds were placed in the washing machine and dyed to match the dress.

The program became another innovative recruitment method for the school. The dancers toured high schools in southern Utah and Nevada:

At Henderson, Nevada, the entire gym was filled with spectators who gave the students a standing ovation. One disaster did happen with Mary Ann Palmer and Walter Price. They became a bit confused, and Walter dropped her during an adagio number. They continued, but at two o'clock in the morning, Mary Ann awoke and was rushed to Emergency to find out that she had a broken thumb. The unfortunate thing was she had made arrangements to play a violin concerto with the orchestra the next week. Mr. Halversen was most unhappy when he had to reschedule the concert for three weeks later. Fortunately, the break was on the right hand so that her wrist healed so she could play.

Historically, dance at SUU had been supported under two departments, theatre arts and dance and physical education, servicing their programs as areas of emphasis to avoid duplication of course offerings. The physical education department took a broad approach with recreational dance, lower division technique classes, theoretical-academic course work and teaching methods. The theatre arts department had devoted its curriculum to developing dance competencies with advanced courses in a variety of technical disciplines in dance and, with the production assistance of the department, provided a broad range of performance opportunities necessary for the performing arts.

In September of 1985, Teri Lauterbach joined the faculty of the physical education department and became the director of the dance education program. Miss Lauterbach, as the adviser of the drill team, chose to give the team a new emphasis by creating a dance/drill team. The name Thunderettes was changed to the Waukeenyans, which is Sioux for Thunderbirds. The 16-member troupe became well known for their precision dance and were invited to perform at the University of California at Santa Barbara, San Diego State, Weber State and Northridge. In 1990 the Waukeenyans were invited to perform at the UNLV basketball half-

I was in high school when I first became aware of the power of LaVeve Whetten. She was a beautiful, long, willowy woman who had a great love of and enthusiasm for dance. She taught at the high school as well as at Branch Agricultural College, as it was then called. I remember the great Friday afternoon dances in which she and coach LaMont Bailey would have all of the girls in the school line up on one side of the gym and the boys on the other. We would pair off by marching down the middle of the gym, to learn the popular social dances of the day. LaVeve also organized a small company of four to six couples of us high school kids to perform the dances of the '20s—the black bottom, one-step, charleston etc.—for special events in the community. It was great fun, and our love for dance blossomed.

When, in 1945, I enrolled at two-year Branch Agricultural College, my life, and that of all of my classmates, became intimately tied to LaVeve's dreams for us. Along with her physical education classes, LaVeve taught all sorts of dancing - social dancing, folk dancing, square dancing and "Apache" dancing (like night club dancing), which we all loved because it was a couples dance, a chance for the men to throw the women around in arcs and spirals. We took her modern dance classes, wearing black leotards, in a small studio in what was the gym building (now the Haze Hunter Conference Center) at least three times a week - stretching, learning movement, and creating dances for our yearly dance concerts. None of us had much technical or choreographic skill, but her encouragement and positive spirit helped all of us to feel that we were not only remarkable dancers, but very special performers.

It was LaVeve who encouraged many of us to go on to complete our University studies. In my case it was after she returned from a summer dance workshop in Madison, Wisconsin, that she convinced me, and my parents (which was the more difficult of the tasks), that I should enroll in the dance department at the University of Wisconsin and make dance my life's work. I went off to my powerful calling as a little hayseed from Cedar City, Utah, joining seasoned New York dancers in my studies. It was this encouragement and prodding from LaVeve which entirely changed the course of my life, and I shall forever be grateful to her for her insight, her caring, her vision and her faith in all of us. Her efforts have made dance a strong and integral part of the educational fabric at Southern Utah University.

Joan Jones Woodbury

time for a crowd of 19,000 fans.

The dance program continued to grow and by 1987, a major in physical education with a dance emphasis was established.

Miss Lauterbach, realizing the importance of offering students the opportunity to perform and also to choreograph their own pieces, directed a full length dance concert in April of 1987 entitled "Discover Dance." This concert showcased dancers from both the physical education and theatre arts departments, as well as choreography from the faculty of both programs. In the spring of 1989, a similar concert was presented entitled, "On With The Show."

In 1986, the dance education program along with the Convocation Series hosted dancer/choreographer Bill Evans to do a performance and teach master classes to the dancers. This was the beginning of an ongoing alliance between dance education and Convocations in hosting at least one modern dance company annually. Both Repertory Dance Theatre and Ririe Woodbury came to perform and offer classes at SUSC. In 1990 the New York based company, Garth Fagan Bucket Dance came for a three-day residency.

In 1991 Miss Lauterback wrote a course proposal for a modern dance company class which would be called Orchesis. Through participation in the company dancers would learn choreographic skills, costume design, lighting design, and help make decisions in program design and order. The first Orchesis concert featured 16 dancers and was named "Orchesis Unfolding." Other SUU dancers were also invited to participate in this concert.

In 1992, for the first time, SUU dancers traveled to the regional dance conference which was held at Cal Poly, Pomona. The dancers performed a piece choreographed by Orchesis member, Ryan Turner. During the same year, the SUU student government made Orchesis a line item thus providing them with ongoing funding to travel and produce concerts.

The 1992 Orchesis concert, "Kaleidoscope of Dance" was presented at Scottsdale Community College, and the Scottsdale dance company traveled to Cedar City to perform in the Orchesis concert.

The final orchestra concert, under the direction of Ms. Lauterback-Cotts, was entitled "Breaking Bounds" and featured the entire com-

BURCH
MANN

pany with special guests Acclamation.

In 1993 SUU dancers once again traveled to the regional dance conference held at Weber State University and performed two student pieces choreographed by Neesha Zollinger and Camille Bulloch.

During the year of 1992-1993 the university administration, along with the dance professors, agreed that for the growth of the dance program at SUU it was necessary to combine the two programs. In the spring of 1993, dance education was moved to the theatre arts department.

The fortunate union between Burch Mann and SUU added impetus to the expansion of the dance program.

Burch Mann, the founder and choreographer of the American Folk Ballet, began her training as a young dance student in New York City under a succcssion of ballet masters then coming out of Russia. She became a fine ballerina and was among the first classical ballet performers to tour America. As other dance forms, except for classical ballet being imported from Europe, were held in low repute at the time, Burch was forced to "bootleg" lessons in jazz and tap dancing from Jack Manning's studio, which was in a hotel near the theatre where Mann performed as a ballet dancer.

The new types of dance excited her, especially those idiomatic to America. During the

years between her early career as a ballerina and the American Folk Ballet era, she traveled throughout the nation to study dance types ranging from old-style clogging in South Carolina to ragtime jazz in Louisiana. To each of the different disciplines she brought the understanding of line and the hard discipline of classical ballet. As her expertise placed her in great demand in the dance world, she became a widely-acclaimed choreographer, on the east and west coasts, including the early productions of the Mousketeers in Hollywood.

Mann realized her dream to create a professional dance company, which would "remove the frills from the sleeves of dance," with the formation of the Burch Mann Dancers in 1960. They performed the distinctive choreography that won her admirers the world over and later became the hallmark of the American Folk Ballet, which originally performed under the aegis of the American National Theatre Association.

Ever the teacher, Burch was persuaded by Gerald R. Sherratt, then assistant to the president at Utah State University, to come to Logan, Utah, to teach summer dance workshops and to bring her troupe of dancers to perform in the Festival of the American West, which Sherratt was in the process of writing and producing. For 10 summers she came, bringing the exuberant spirit of the frontier to the festival through the performance of her American Folk Ballet, and adding the excellence of her teaching to the summer dance program of Utah State University. When Dr. Sherratt became president of Southern Utah University in Cedar City, Utah, he invited her to establish her company headquarters here. In 1982 she became the distinguished artist in residence, and Southern Utah University became the official dance school of the American Folk Ballet.

Mann found the red soil of southern Utah a fertile place in which to put down the American Folk Ballet's roots. Using the dance program at Southern Utah University as her training school, she saw to it that dancers, prepared to meet her exacting standards, were finally being trained to the performance level she expected. And the rural, small-town atmosphere of Cedar City served to reinforce the company's frontier roots. It was a mutual love affair between Mann and the community. She admired and respected the Cedar City people for their openness and lack of guile. They were enamored of her individualism and strong will.

Since the death of Burch Mann in 1996, the company has been directed by a cadre of admir-

THE AMERICAN
FOLK BALLET

ers of the famed choreographer, a group of distinguished educators and established artists, who are determined that her demand for disciplined training and performance be maintained, and that her unique and elevating style of choreography not be lost to a nation that desperately needs the inspiration her dances so skillfully provided.

To establish the dance program in the department of theatre arts and dance, Mann brought several of the lead dancers in the American Folk Ballet, as well as her daughter, San Christopher, to form the program's dance faculty.

San Christopher brought years of professional dance experience coupled with singular success in the professional theatre. Mann and Christopher provided the department with an exceptional range of dance experience covering ballet, modern, jazz, folk and character dance. Vibrant, exciting teachers, they quickly attracted a cadre of students from Utah and suurounding states.

Christopher had initially intended to stay at SUU for just one year and then resume her professional career as an actress. She had achieved much success in theatrical productions in southern California, including a much-acclaimed role in *Who's Afraid of Virginia Woolf?* She had also become a protégé of noted actress Agnes Moorhead and had toured, under Moorhead's direction, in a one-woman show which received excellent reviews. But she enjoyed her teaching assignment at SUU and remained with the University until her death in 1993.

Others from the American Folk Ballet included Gwen Grimes, the company's lead dancer and, later, Shauna Mendini, Lise Mills and Wendy Turner. To those dance performers were added Roy Fitzell and Mitzi McKay.

Gwen Grimes came as an artist in residence. Ms. Grimes had been a soloist performer for both the Wenta Ballet and The American Folk Ballet. Her 24-year performance career with the American Folk Ballet included major national and international tours. She had performed with the Radio City Music Hall Ballet Co. and various television specials including the Academy Awards show. Her direction experience had included a two tour appointment as dance captain for *Annie Get Your Gun* with Debbie Reynolds.

Shauna Mendini, assistant professor of dance also works as an assistant to the department chair on issues related to dance. Prior to her appointment at SUU in 1993, Ms. Mendini was

dance director at New Mexico State University. She received her graduate degree from the University of Arizona, studying with nationally recognized dance educators. Ms. Mendini combined academic study with 17 years of experience as a professional dancer touring both nationally and internationally.

Lise Mills, adjunct instructor of dance, was hired to teach jazz. Originally from southern California, she came with extensive training in all styles of ballet, tap, modern, jazz and character. She had performed with Walt Disney studios, New York City Ballet, the Leningrad-Kirov Ballet and in television and films.

Wendy S. Turner, adjunct instructor, taught modern dance. She received her masters degree from the prestigious department of dance at New York University. Ms. Turner holds a professional trainer certificate from the Martha Graham School of Contemporary Dance, and had taught as a dance specialist for the University of Utah's Children's Dance Theatre.

Roy Fitzell, artist in residence, received training in the major idioms of dance from some of the world's most noted teachers. As a principle performer, he appeared with the San Francisco Ballet, made his debut in New York with American Ballet Theatre and received major roles with the Los Angeles Civic Light Opera. He had many major film and television appearances to his credit and ten years as a faculty member, including serving as chair of the dance department at University of California, Irvine.

Mitzi McKay, adjunct instructor of dance and theatre arts, taught folk dance. Ms. McKay received her Master of Fine Arts degree from Illinois State University. She had been employed as stage manager for the Steppenwolf Theatre and The American Folk Ballet. She is currently director of personnel for the Utah Shakespeare Festival.

In 1993 the SUU administration recognized the significant growth and made the decision to merge the two areas under the umbrella of theatre arts and dance. At that merger, the dance faculty positions and dance course titles that had formerly been physical education came under the heading of the department of theatre arts and dance, increasing the potential of dance as a full academic discipline in the performing arts and in higher education.

Within the rich emphasis upon history, dance at Southern Utah University is looking toward a new and bright future. In June of 1996, the state Board of Regents unanimously approved a proposal submitted by both the department of theatre arts and dance and the University administration to make dance a full academic discipline, offering a major in dance.

With the approval of the new major in dance, the effect upon enrollment, quality of curriculum and national recognition has proven to be significant. The focus of the program from this time forward was in providing the dancer with the concentrated skills necessary to face the challenges unique to the art form. Majors in dance will be better prepared to compete on a national level for places within prestigious graduate programs, performing companies, and institutions hiring dance educators. Dance has achieved its rightful equality among the arts, reflective of Southern Utah University's dedication to all the arts and to the cultural enhancement of the community.

BALLET STUDENTS, 1990s

In the summer of 1990, SUU dance students were invited to perform with the American Folk Ballet in Leningrad and Moscow, Russia, and in Riga, Latvia, for two weeks. As Burch was ill, her daughter San Christopher took over direction, managing the company magnificently through performances to sold-out crowds of over 4,000 in beautiful theatres and concert halls in Russia. Audiences gave standing ovations in the traditional style of applause–rhythmic, unified clapping that sometimes lasts up to 20 minutes.

One of the most memorable performances was in Riga in the Latvian Hall of Culture, which had been turned into a Russian military base. The Latvian people had refused to enter the theatre after the Russian invasion, but when it became known that the American Folk Ballet would be performing there, overflow crowds thronged into the facility each night. Mitzi McKay, stage manager, recalled how even stern-looking Russian soldiers soon smiled and tapped the floor with their feet.

Three years later, in October of 1993, one of the SUU dancers, Alexander Carpenter, while touring Russia, was in the Octyabrsky Concert hall in Leningrad, reminiscing about the SUU tour. He later learned that San Christopher had died that very day, after a battle with cancer.

Burch Mann passed away in June of 1996. Her American Folk Ballet has given SUU a legacy of dance that will be cherished forever. Gwen Grimes, dance faculty member, was appointed as the artistic director of this still-active troupe, which is headquartered in Burch Mann's former Cedar City home, now owned by the university.

At the time of this publication (1997), the Southern Utah University department of theatre arts and dance offers a well-rounded theoretical and practical approach to both the performance and technical components of theatre, designed to provide comprehensive training, along with a strong interrelationship with the nationally recognized Utah Shakespearean Festival.

The curriculum is designed to train the SUU student theatre and dance student, through a diverse program, as a future director, performer, designer, technician and teacher. The curriculum is also intended to provide experience, through course work, lab workshops and full productions, in a broad range, from performance to the production process. The theatre production program, a training lab for students, provides a central part of the cultural life of the campus and a resource for the region.

CHAPTER XVI

From abacus to main frame

remember one accounting teacher who could add 10 columns of five to six digit numbers as fast as he could write down the answer. He must have had a course in "rapid calculation."

The pioneer families who settled in the southern wilderness of Deseret valued the education of their children above all else except basic survival and devotion to their religion. Many had left the comparative security of predictable futures in their professions or trades in Europe or the eastern United States. Their challenge on the frontier was to build a civilized community. The mission of the Branch Normal School was to train teachers who could equip their children to help build, and then flourish in, this new civilization. The skills needed to succeed in trade and business were an essential part of the early school curriculum.[1]

Mr. O. C. Anderson, the first business instructor, had been hired in 1900 by Principal Milton Bennion to assume the primary responsibility for the teaching of music at BNS. Annie Spencer, one of the founding faculty of 1897, along with Howard R. Driggs and George W. Decker, had been teaching some music classes, but her emphasis was in elocution and physical education. Mr. Anderson, a graduate of Brigham Young Academy, was a well-trained musician, who requisitioned the upright piano which was still in use 50 years later, and established classes in piano and organ and a course in the fundamentals of music.

By 1901 the business faculty had expanded, with the addition of Maude Eastman, Claude Lewis and William Ward. In 1901-02 Nathan T. Porter became principal of BNS and, realizing that his music instructor was a person of many gifts, he asked Mr. Anderson to inaugurate a new course of study in business.

Mr. Anderson developed an embryo curriculum and taught the first business courses, which were bookkeeping and penmanship. The course description for bookkeeping reads:

This course is a practical and fairly complete treatment of the subject of bookkeeping, much drill is given in writing business forms. 3 hours per week, either half of the year.

By the following year the curriculum had taken a broad jump to the dimension of a commercial program, which was identified in the 1902-03 catalog:

These [subjects] are intended to prepare students for office work and for positions as businessmen. The foundation is laid for a thorough training in orthography, penmanship, typewriting, stenography, bookkeeping, and commercial law.
No extra charge for these subjects.

The term orthography designated the teaching of spelling in accord with accepted usage. Journals of that time attest to the need for including this subject in the program. The department had acquired a typewriting lab.

FIRST BUSINESS GRADUATES WARNER MITCHELL, JANET ROLLO AND RAYMOND CUTTER

ELTON JONES'
TYPING CLASS,
1920's

Penmanship is now a lost art; even with the advent of the typewriter, skill in handwriting was still highly valued by 1910, when the catalog description for penmanship read:

The student is trained in a round, smooth, plain style of muscular movement writing. Speed, legibility, and ease are the principles upon which the work is based. A standard equivalent to that required for an 'American Penman' certificate is required for completing the course.

That same year, 1910, a course in "rapid calculation" was offered. The following was the course description for this course:

The work in rapid calculation makes the student able to add and multiply as rapidly as he can read figures, and to solve problems in interest, discount, bills, and prices with rapidity, accuracy and ease. He learns from experience that 'lighting calculation' is the result of effort and practice.

Dr. Larry A. Olsen, compiler of the centennial history of the business department of 1996, comments on the above course offering:

Thanks to our modern-day calculators, students do not need this type of practice. I can remember one accounting teacher I had in high school who could add a ten columns of five to six digit numbers as fast as he could write down the answer. He must have had a course in "rapid calculation." Another interesting note of this catalog description, that would raise eyebrows in the '90s, is the use of the masculine gender in the catalog description.[1]

In 1913, when the Normal School was changed to Branch Agriculture College (BAC), the commercial program was organized into a Department of Business with a department chairman. James Robb was probably the first department chairman. The catalog mission statement for the department read:

This department [business] aims to meet the needs of two classes of students. First, those who desire such business instruction and training as will qualify them for important positions in the business world; and second, those young men and women of the farm, the home, or in the trade, who realize their need of, at least, a little business training. We believe that practically all of our young people of today would find it quite an advantage to have some knowledge of the common business forms and practices and to keep a simple set of books. The economic management of the household, the farm, or any sort of business demands the keeping of simple but accurate accounts. The school provides a well-equipped business department and competent instructors in commercial subjects. Diploma in Commerce is awarded to those students who complete the program.

Gilbert L. Janson replaced James Robb as department chairman in 1916.

Vocational education had its beginning in 1918 when a vocational education course was added to the curriculum. The course description read:

First a study of individual adaptability to a vocation; Second, analysis of factors that influence choice of vocation; Third, a study of an occupation.

Female business students complied with the 1918 Uniform Dress Code for female students which prescribed:

One piece woolen dress of a dark color; suit (skirt, jacket, and wash waist, conservative in color and texture.); one piece dress of wash material such as gingham, galatea, linen, pique or percale; medium or low walking shoes (low heel) and hose of standard quality cotton lisle or fiber.

Interestingly, dress standards for male students were not included in the catalog. These dress standards extended into the late 1960s, requiring female students to come to class dressed in a dress. No slacks or pantsuits were allowed in the classroom.

The department adopted *The Rowe Accounting System* in 1918, and the accounting curriculum was expanded to include household accounting, farm bookkeeping, bookkeeping techniques, and principles of accounting. The curriculum now also included Commercial Correspondence. The catalog description for this course read:

This course is intended for those who wish to become able to write really creditable and up-to-date business letters in conversational English. The form, style and arrangement of the various types of letters, the development of power of expression, and the fact that there is no difference between 'Business English' and good English, are emphasized. Considerable time is devoted to the elimination of common errors in English. In addition to this the different types of the social letter and the intelligent use of business forms are considered.

In 1920 BAC adopted the quarter system. The 1920 catalog indicates:

The commercial department has been completely remodeled and the office fitted up with new equipment. It has its full quota of desks, typewriters, adding machines, and other office conveniences.

Tuition was still free to students, and the average cost of books was between $5 to $10. Students of later years at SUU would be amazed at such a modest cost for an education.

In 1920 the shorthand system was changed from Gregg to the Graham system. The catalog description of the Graham system was interesting:

The Graham system, which needs no explanation, is taught. Its popularity among the experts of the country, and the endorsement by the National Shorthand Reporters' Association are evidences of its superiority. Though many office appliances are coming into use, there will always be a demand for efficient stenographers.

The course was taught for three consecutive quarters. The perception of "superiority" of the Graham system was short-lived, as the department soon went back to the Gregg system. An

GILBERT
JANSEN

interesting nuance of the catalog description gives the first implication that dictating machines may replace the practice of dictation to a stenographer. This statement has led to debate for over 70 years, but the during the '90s shorthand has experienced a definite decline, even annihilation in the curriculum of many schools.

Machine bookkeeping entered the curriculum in 1921. This course used adding machines, where accuracy, speed, and neatness were emphasized.

In 1923 the college and high school curriculums were integrated at BAC.

J. Howard Maughan was the director, and Gilbert L. Janson was the business department head. The social science curriculum was combined with the business curriculum.

In 1929 the first tuition fees were announced in the catalog–by modern standards a real bargain of $27 a year. However, inflation raised the tuition in 1931-32 to $55 a year, marking the beginning of fairly regular increases in tuition to accommodate increasing costs .

Requirements for a diploma in commercial training in 1931-32 included: 15 hours of business credit; nine hours of biological science, 12 hours of English, nine hours of exact science, nine hours of social science, nine hours of special group, and 27 hours of electives.

It is the 27 hours of electives that will be interesting to professors working with curriculum development in the "modern era." In expanded curriculums, since the development of the computer, a student would never find a business program with the allowance of 27 credits of electives.

During 1933, Scott Matheson taught business law at BAC. He had been a student at BNS and was later better known as the father of Gov. Scott Matheson of the State of Utah.

The year of 1936 in the business department was notable for several reasons: Wayne L. Bennion became the department head when Gilbert L. Janson became the Cedar City postmaster; business and secretarial science curriculums were separated; the Gregg shorthand system replaced the Graham system of shorthand.

The earliest news release concerning Vocational Day for high school students is also dated 1936. After 60 years Vocational Day continues to be an annual event at the time of this history (1997).

The Headline in the *Iron County Record* announced:

A.W.
STEPHENSON

PROFESSOR A.W.
STEPHENSON,
CLYDE HEATH,
"KHAY" SMITH
AND VIRGIL NAY
AND AN AM
1200 PRINTING
PRESS.

*BUSINESS VISITORS TO SEE
LATEST IN OFFICE EQUIPMENT;
FULL DAY PLANNED
Students Registered from 12
Schools*

*A full day's program is being
arranged for business visitors on
Vocational Day. This year, for the
first time, the business department
brings to BAC for display and
demonstration, the latest in machines
and equipment. Demonstrations
will be given on the dictaphone,
mimeograph, multigraph, calculator, addres-
sograph, and late-model typewriters. An added
feature of the show will be the commercial
textbook displays arranged by the Gregg and
Southwestern Publishing companies, of espe-
cial interest to teacher, superintendents and
principals. Another attraction in the day's program will be the commercial contests. Twelve
schools in southern Utah and Nevada have
registered students in the competition.*

*Teachers will be guests of the BAC at lun-
cheon, after which Mr. Leonard S. Ralph, state
coordinator of distributive occupations, will
conduct a special commercial teachers' conference. Problems in the teaching of commercial subjects will be discussed...*

*Last, but not least, contest results will be
announced in the gymnasium.*

Rotary and key driven calculators were used
in the business calculating machine courses
through the '40s and '50s. These business
machines are museum pieces in the modern
era. The rotary calculators chugged and whirled
away after the figures were entered, and if the

problem were not too complicated, the answer
would appear on the rotary wheels about 30
seconds later. Key-driven calculators were operated with the first and second fingers of each
hand over a full keyboard.

Electronic calculators replaced the rotary and
key-driven calculators, but at a very high intro-
ductory price. The first electronic calculators
cost from $1,000 to $1,500 in the early 60s; the
cost of the model with a square root key added
an extra $150. In 1996 a pocket-sized calculator
with a square root key could cost as little as $5.

During the Second World War, the business department had fewer faculty
members but a strong will to help the
war effort, as demonstrated by this statement
from the 1942 catalog:

*The business department is the doorway to
trained personnel in this National Emergency.
It offers vocational training in accounting,
business administration, and secretarial science for those who want immediate employment, and in addition to preparatory work in
these fields, for students desiring to continue
their education.*

In 1942 accounting and clerical programs
were offered to those students who wanted a
vocational program. The vocational business
courses were designed for students in business
who were not planning to continue their college training beyond two years. By completing
the prescribed coursework, these students
would graduate with a certificate in business
training.

In 1944 Anthony W. Stephenson replaced
Wayne L. Bennion as department head. During
the war years, the mission statement of the catalog read:

*Appraisal of both direct and indirect contri-
butions toward the waging of total war is difficult to ascertain. Yet those who are affiliated
with the college believe that it has in its way
aided, significantly, a cause which shall be victorious.*

The entire college had 20 full-time faculty
members in 1945. Because of the small number
of faculty members, they were like a unified
family, participating together in making the
decisions impacting the destiny of the institution. At the time of this chronicle many of the
emeriti faculty speak of "the good old days"
when all faculty members knew one another

more intimately than in later years.

In 1948 the BAC four-year elementary education program was authorized. This revitalized the dream for a four-year college.

In 1949 the business curriculum constituted six areas–accounting, business administration, merchandising, economics, secretarial science, and vocational business.

The title of Branch Agriculture College (BAC) prevailed from 1913 to 1953. A new dawn broke over Cedar City in 1954. The removal of the stigma, in the minds of many, of the designation 'agricultural college' gave way to a widely held dream of an institution of higher learning which would offer a full curriculum in all academic areas. The new name, College of Southern Utah (CSU), aroused great expectations of expanding the facilities and mission of the college.

In 1956 the social science department merged with the department of business with A. W. Stephenson as department head. In 1957 the total college faculty had grown to 44 faculty members.

That year the department refined the vocational programs to the format that is still being offered in 1997. The one-year clerical program and the two-year secretarial science program were initiated. The catalog reads:

In these office occupations more than two and a half times as many people are employed in the clerical positions as the bookkeeping, secretarial, or managerial positions.

In 1963 the business education and office administration department was organized, with Larry A. Olsen appointed as department head.

During this year the college was given permission to develop curriculum for junior class status. However, students would still have to attend another institution to complete their senior year. Faculty members and students strained somewhat against circumstances preventing a four-year status for the College. The elementary education four-year program was already in place; natural bridging to the four-year program would be to also offer a secondary education four-year program.

In this climate, the business education and office administration department focused on the addition to the business curriculum of two courses to prepare prospective secondary education business instructors: Methods of Teaching Business–(Nonskilled) and Methods of Teaching Typewriting and Shorthand.

The catalog course prefixes were OA for office administration courses and BE for business education courses.

While four-year business accreditation at CSU was still a year away, students of the business department were not deprived of enriching experiences. In 1963 the department instituted an annual trip to California, where students toured large businesses including the Bank of America. The students were allowed to tour the electrical recording and machine accounting division. They were introduced to the Bank of America training program.

LARRY A. OLSEN

Major specialties in the 1964-1965 catalog were identified as accounting, business education, office administration, business management, and industrial management. Vocational programs were one-year clerical, two-year secretarial, and two-year vocational business.

Finally the banner year! In 1965-1966 CSU became, in reality, a four-year state college. The catalog indicated:

Under terms of legislation passed by the 1965 Utah State Legislature, the College of Southern Utah began the 1965-1966 academic year as a four-year state college operating under its own Board of Trustees. The College of Southern Utah is a school with vision and with great promise for the future. As such, the College offers unrivaled opportunities to students at all levels of undergraduate college education.

The Division of Business and Social Science was organized into three departments: department of business administration, department of

TYPING CLASS, CIRCA 1920s

MRS. JOHNSON'S TYPEWRITING CLASS, 1956

business education and office administration, and department of economics. The mission statement of the Division read: " To provide an education that is practical and realistic, preparing men and women to take an active part in the main stream of our society."

The department of business administration indicated that the goal of its program would be "to provide a broad understanding of the world in which we live, as well as to develop basic communication skills."

The department of business education and office administration viewed the academic degree in business education as an advantage of having a stable, degree-certified business teacher in each of the high schools in southern Utah. Many of the rural high schools had uncertified teachers teaching the business curriculum. The high turnover of business teachers in the high schools was attributed to too many urban business teachers trying to adjust to the small southern Utah community life.

The hope of the department was to build the high school business programs by providing our rural students as prospective business teachers, with the ultimate result of getting better qualified students entering the college business programs. These hopes had been fulfilled by 1997, as nearly every high school in the southern part of the state has a business teacher who had been trained at SUU.

A composite major in business education was instituted with two emphases: Emphasis A was a non-stenographic major and Emphasis B was a stenographic major. The major required 60 credits, 33 credits in secondary education. The interesting historical point here is that preparing for the high school curriculum at this stage included accounting, typewriting, and shorthand as the "bread and butter"

GARY N. GILES, 1982

courses. After the technology explosion with the computer, the curriculum expanded to include a core of more than 90 credits of business.

While not designated as being separate degrees by diploma, the programs of business administration and accounting had different degree requirements and career expectations. Building on the previous junior-year programs as taught by James Watson and LeRay McAllister, accounting became an entry-level, professional preparation into public, private and governmental accounting careers. Of the nine accounting students graduating in 1965-66, six are known to have become certified public accountants (CPAs) and of seven accounting graduates in 1966-67, four are known to be CPAs.

Thus, the growth and recognition of the business administration and accounting programs began rapidly and successfully even in their infant years. Gary N. Giles was hired out of Phoenix, Arizona, in 1965 to teach accounting in the new baccalaureate degree program. Of the class of 10 accounting majors in 1967-68, Giles remembers a recruiter from Los Angeles commenting "there are such strong graduates, I want to pay for seven of the 10 to visit our office in Los Angeles. I can just hear my boss now saying how he sent me to this little, cow-town college in Southern Utah and that I lost my head up there."

*I*n 1966, a separation of the social sciences from the business area was made, resulting in the Division of Social Sciences and Division of Business.

This same year teaching minors were added to the business education and office administration department: office administration, accounting, and economics.

The department also added the executive secretary major as a four-year program. The program was instituted in response to the need for capable, mature administrative assistants.

Foreseeing a new demand in the market, the department also offered, for the first time, a composite major in office administration and family life. This curriculum was designed "for women who desire sufficient secretarial training to provide professional opportunities outside the home as well as a basic training for family living." The program required 72 credits. Program requirements were divided into four groups—two in office administration and two in family living. Students were given the option of completing three of the four groups by taking

20 unrepeated credits in each of the three opted groups.

Business education and office administration department responded to student needs by offering an interesting course called personal development and charm.

This course is designed to help the student make the most of her potential so that she can achieve success and happiness both in her work and in her personal life. Instructions and demonstration show the career girl how to bring out the best in herself and how to be admired and liked by the people with whom she comes in contact.

On-lookers quietly snickered as they watched the students practice walking up the three flights of stairs of Old Main with books on their heads.

A reorganization of CSU took place in 1968. The college was divided into four schools, with internal academic departments. The catalog gives a discrepancy on the name of the business school. One place in the catalog the name is business and technical education and in another place it is business and technology. The latter name probably is the correct title. As the title suggests, the industrial technology area was merged with the business area.

The mission statement of the catalog for the School of Business and Technology indicated,

The American economy provides an unusual opportunity for enterprising managers and businessmen. In a free enterprise economy, the decisions of the business and industrial world are made by individual managers and owners of business. The course of national progress and prosperity is determined by the decisions and actions of business, government, and industry. If the American system is to survive and grow, imaginative leadership is needed in the business and industrial world; and great rewards await those who can provide this leadership.

The first business teacher education class graduated in 1968. Nine graduates included Nanette Savage, Janean Lyman, Shannon Bryant, Lois Linford, Van Bushnell, Eugene Morris, Stan Brown, Ralph Riggs and Heber Lund.

After nearly 16 years as College of Southern Utah, the legislature approved a change in name to Southern Utah State College in 1969.

In 1970 the division chairman title was elevated to the title "dean." A. W. Stephenson was the first dean of the School of Business and Technology. Department heads were: A. W. Stephenson, business administration, Gary N. Giles, accounting, and Larry A. Olsen, business education.

The 1970 accounting mission statement read:

To acquire the business prospective which often leads him into administrative positions.

CONNIE W. NYMAN

The gender bias of the masculine pronouns was soon to hit education. Faculty members learned to take care, in their writing and teaching, to avoid the masculine pronouns for both genders.

That year business education developed a major independent of the business composite major in business-teacher education to satisfy both Utah and adjacent state certification requirements. The department also added the executive secretary minor to the program in 1970.

The first Business Cooperative Education class was added to the curriculum during 1972. This program gave students the opportunity of apprenticeship training in downtown business offices. Connie W. Nyman, the first coordinator of the program, found businesses that were willing to train students in the skills of their offices. Students made formal application, went through the interview process and, when hired, were paid the minimum wage for the hours they worked. Mrs. Nyman made on-site visits to evaluate the progress of the apprentices. The course was a capstone to the training they received at the College.

HAROLD H. HISKEY

In 1972 the student-teaching credit was split between the secondary education department and the other academic departments which were training secondary teachers. The education department received nine of the 15 credits and the business education department received six credits. Fairness in supervision of student teachers from the academic departments occasioned the split.

In 1973 A. W. Stephenson retired from teaching and administration after

ROBERT A. MOORE

DEDICATION OF
DIXIE LEAVITT
BUSINESS
BUILDING,
MAY 8, 1981

a very productive career in helping to forge the business area of the college. Harold H. Hiskey was appointed dean of the School of Business and Technology. Dr. Hiskey also served the 1974 year as head of the business administration department.

Dean Harold H. Hiskey reorganized the School of Business in 1975 by combining the three business departments into one department that was called department of business. Robert A. Moore was appointed department head.

The program objective for the School of Business and Technology was to prepare students for courses in private business, government service, teacher education, graduate studies, and job-entry positions in vocational education. Unique teaching techniques, including individualized instruction, cooperative education placements, and office simulation provided learning experiences to help students acquire knowledge, materials, competence, insight, and a desire for excellence in their selected programs of study.

During the mid-'70s, a trend was signalled when the department dropped the second year of training in shorthand, Shorthand V and VI, leaving only four quarters of shorthand. The shorthand system was changed in 1976 from Gregg Shorthand to Century 21 Shorthand, which was developed at BYU and published by South-Western Publishing Company. The Century 21 Shorthand reduced the memory load for the learner, and the theory made the outlines easier to join.

A new program, initiated through federal and state funding, began in 1975 and ran until 1993, when it was dissolved.

The Manpower Training Program was designed to provide short-term training for secretaries, assisting low-income women to get an education and enter the work force. These students were paid while they attended a six-hour training block. The program eventually evolved into the Career Education Training Act and then into the Job Partnership Training Act as the federal legislation was upgraded. Connie W. Nyman was hired to direct this program, which was first housed in the ROTC-Art Building until it moved into the Dixie Leavitt Business Building in 1980s. The program was an individualized, open entry-open exit curriculum.

The rationale of the manpower training program was adopted into a program of individualized instruction for regular college students. Students had the option of enrolling in self-paced study or traditional classes of business English, business math, keyboarding, secretarial accounting, medical and legal specialization, and records management.

Another innovation throughout the state was called The Model Office, using simulated office experiences. Two of the rooms on the first floor of Old Main were attractively remodeled with wood paneling, carpeted, and decorated with draperies on the windows. Office L-shaped desks and upholstered office chairs in bright yellow, purple, and blue gave the area a splash of color. New IBM electric typewriters and electronic calculators were added to each of the 20 stations. The Bell Telephone company donated a self-contained telephone system, which provided a telephone at each station. Wallace Levere had designed the office simulation program, which integrated skills that the students were acquiring in accounting, secretarial procedures, shorthand, machine transcription, business communication, and records management. As students rotated through different positions of the "company," they received a better prospective of an office experience. The model office facility was housed in Old Main for about two years before it was moved to the Old Administration Building and then to the new Dixie Leavitt Business Building.

In 1977 the business department and School of Education vacated their space in Old Main for a major renovation. Plans were underway for a new business building, but the department moved temporarily into the recently remodeled Old Administration Building (Braithwaite Center), which they shared with the English department. The building, remodeled to restore the feeling of the old pioneer period, was placed on the Historical Register. The plaster was removed from the walls to expose the old pioneer facing-bricks that were made in Cedar City; windows of the period were installed. Perhaps due to inadequate insulation, the building was drafty in the winter. After one blizzard, Dean Hiskey gathered enough snow in his inside window sill to make a sizeable snowball.

Faculty members watched with excitement the construction of the new business building directly south of the new administration building. Officially dedicated May 8, 1981, the new three-story, 25,000 square foot structure was built by Carter Enterprises of Cedar City at a cost of $1,349,000. Boyd A. Blackner, architect of Salt Lake City, included the design for the solar heating system that was to be used as a backup for the campus heating system.

Later the business building received its official name, Dixie Leavitt Business Building in honor of State Sen. Dixie Leavitt, who was largely responsible for the legislative appropriation for the building.

Driven by a national effort to require five years or 225 quarter hours of accounting education for candidates to sit for the CPA exam, Utah passed its version of a five-year regulation in 1991 (becoming only the third of the 50 states to do so). Having no such post baccalaureate program of study and possessing minimal resources, SUSC's accounting department faced a do-or-die situation: should we try to defeat the new law or attempt to secure permission for the awarding of a masters degree? After numerous trips to Salt Lake City for meetings with other accounting program chairs and with the Associate Commissioner of Higher Education, and after two years of planning, designing, and some special lobbying by President Sherratt, SUSC was granted a master's degree in accounting, the first interdependent, stand-alone master's degree on campus. That award virtually saved a heretofore successful program and gave new impetus to our placement of graduates in professional careers.

*I*n 1986 the microcomputer was causing the information revolution in business, just as the industrial revolution changed business in the 1860s. Teachers were caught off guard with the rapidly moving technology in the classroom; they expended hours of blood, sweat, and tears in inservice classes, conferences and workshops to learn the applications of software for these marvelous machines. Faculty members were frustrated by the challenge of keeping current with the software changes required by upgrading of the hardware. Often some stu-

dents, who were more knowledgeable about computers than the teacher, were happy to teach a teacher a thing or two.

ROGER
HILLYARD

Credit for developing the first computerized lab should go to Roger Hillyard who, on a shoestring budget, wired the lab himself and taught the first computer classes. Mr. Hillyard was the pioneer who introduced computer classes to the business department and helped to train many of the faculty members to teach the computer classes. Credit should also go to Dean Hiskey, who had earlier anticipated correctly the real potential of Roger Hillyard, who interviewed in high-topped leather boots, after he piloted his single-engine plane into Cedar City to seek work at SUSC.

Hillyard was a free-spirited dairy farmer from Star Valley, Wyoming, whose resourceful nature, excellent mind and zeal for discovery made him a boon to the growing and underfinanced program. Roger could fix anything, even without prior experience. He was self-trained and continued always to educate himself whenever technology or curriculum changed.

In order that the first computer lab room be ready for fall classes, Roger spent the summer wiring the room through walls, ceiling, and floor and running multiple-colored strands to stations and servers. His grasp was quick, and he did the job that had to be done. And he "mellowed" some with the years, recognizing the great needs of students for time, encouragement, and love. His curiosity, thoroughness, logic, and sense of humor were always appreciated.

Roger served as department head for business from 1984 up until his death from pancreatic cancer in June of 1991. The department has missed his skill and his personality.

At this point it may be interesting to reminisce about an old friend called the typewriter. This machine was for years the work horse of business offices, and especially important in business education. In the 1950s, the electric typewriter was just beginning to replace the manual typewriter. Many people assumed that typists could work much faster with the electric typewriter because of the carriage return process. However, the champion typists could still return a manual carriage faster than an electric carriage. The electric typewriter replaced most manual typewriters in the classroom. In the 1970s IBM came out with the Selectric typewriters with a round ball element and later the correcting Selectric which could lift off the error with what was called lift-off tape. Then the typist could type the correct letter over the space erased by the tape.

In the 1980s IBM developed the Magnetic Card Typewriter, which had the ability to store information that could be recalled at a later time. This machine was soon replaced by the IBM Display Writer, which could perform the same operations as an early personal computer. Personal computers soon became less expensive and more practical.

In 1986 the department offered the first courses in the Management Information Systems (MIS) area. The catalog listed the following courses: secretarial data processing, microcomputer applications in business, business programming (COBOL), advanced microcomputer applications in business, operations research, management information systems, advanced systems analysis and design.

WordStar was the first word-processing software used, replaced by WordPerfect in 1988. This system was developed in Orem, Utah, and soon became a dominant software system throughout the world.

Twice in the 1980s, SUU senior students excelled at the highest level on the GMAT exam. Students seeking admission to graduate schools of business are usually required to take the Graduate Management Admissions Test and to send proof of successful passing results. Brent Hall of St. George, Utah, and Danny Riggs of Kanab, Utah, achieved at the 99th percentile, thus ranking in the top 1 percent of the nation's business college applicants. Big results for a small, Southern Utah University, but these scores are truly symbolic of the fine students enrolled in the business programs over these many years.

Nearly a hundred years had passed; the dreams of many of the educators throughout these years came to fruition in 1991 when the College became Southern Utah University.

The accounting composite major was developed for students who wish to pursue professional careers in public, industrial, governmental and tax accounting.

The master of accountancy program provided flexibility by offering either a four-quarter or a two-year program of study. The four-quarter program was designed for those students who

had received a bachelors degree in accounting with an emphasis in business. The two-year program was primarily for students majoring in accounting who were beginning their senior year and at that time decided to pursue studies leading to a masters degree in accounting. Students had a choice of completing either the CPA (Certified Public Accountant) track or the CMA (Certified Managerial Accountant) track.

Advanced standing status was instituted in the department in 1988, offering a core of classes to ensure that students had sufficient background to enter 300 and 400 level business courses. The objective of the program was to provide sufficient specialized business training to prepare the student for successful entry into the business world, as well as providing a business education which developed the attitude, analytical ability, and social conscience required for future professional advancement. Requirements included the completion of the prebusiness core and a minimum of 72 quarter hours in business, general education, basic skills and elective hours, with a GPA of 2.3 or better.

The business administration composite major program was developed with specialty options in accounting, economics, finance, marketing, small business or management information systems.

The name change from business education to business information management and education signalled the combination of the MIS area with business education. The course prefixes were changed from BE to BIM. The catalog description of this area read:

Business Information Management and Education is a comprehensive program in the latest technology and its applications in business and education. The program is based on a core of prebusiness and business coursework, after which students may pursue teaching specialty options with emphases in administrative support, business management, or microcomputer systems. A non-teaching specialty option is offered in management information systems. This program of study is designed for students desiring to enter the corporate workforce, as well as for those desiring to teach.

Speedwriting shorthand replaced the Forkner and Century 21 shorthand systems.

Vocational programs became applied technology programs. The department of business expanded the number of technology programs to include the following programs: clerical technology, secretarial technology, small business management technology, office management technology and management information systems technology.

In 1991 the business department contracted with Novell to offer the certification courses for licensing both Computer Network Engineer (CNE) and Computer Network Instructor (CNI). This program enhanced the offerings in the MIS area and gained the interest of many of the students interested in MIS.

Economics became a specialty option for the business administration degree. A minor program was also developed in economics. The interdisciplinary degree was designed to provide students a broader education in economic applications and theory, including the areas of political economy, international economics, environmental economics; quantitative economics and financial economics.

In 1992 the State Board of Regents mandated that SUU provide a four-year business program for Dixie College that is referred to as the SUU St. George Center program. SUU currently offers majors in accounting and business administration, with an emphasis in marketing or accounting, taught at the Dixie campus in the daytime and evenings. Students are required to take their general education classes and the prebusiness core courses prior to taking the SUU Center upper-division course work. The general education and prebusiness core courses may be taken at any of the accredited junior colleges or universities throughout the state. If students transfer from out of state, transferable credits may also prove acceptable. The St. George Center classes on the Dixie College Campus are structured to allow students to complete the bachelor's degree in six sequential quarters.

Dean Harold H. Hiskey resigned as dean of the School of Business, Technology and Communication in 1992, to be appointed as vice president of regional services at the University. Robert O. Salmon was appointed dean, replacing Dr. Hiskey. Arthur Porter was appointed department head of the business department after the untimely death of Roger Hillyard from cancer in June of 1992.

The same year, the University designated academic areas as colleges, replacing the term schools. Thus the new name of the business academic area was changed to College of Business, Technology and Communication. It was soon after Dean Salmon received his appointment that the department of business received its accreditation with the Association of Colleges,

Business Schools and Programs (ACBSP) in 1993.

Dean Harold Hiskey had begun the accreditation process earlier with a bid to an older organization, the American Assembly of Collegiate Schools of Business, which designed accreditation for research institutions. In 1991 the department started to gear up for ACBSP accreditation, which primarily focuses on fostering excellence in teaching. The grueling process required meeting high standards of instruction, faculty, research, and assessment of student performance.

The seven-member ACBSP review team, drawn from around the nation, reported that SUU's business computer network was the finest they had seen on any campus in the country; the quality of instruction was rated as "superlative." Two reviewers marveled at the unity, dedication, cooperation, and student orientation of the entire business faculty.

As of December, 1996, the department began its pursuit of accreditation with the American Assembly of Collegiate Schools of Business, or AACSB. The decision to pursue the higher accreditation is a direct result of improvements in the business programs at SUU, and the change in the mission of AACSB, which now actively seeks to include teaching institutions under its umbrella.

Since 1993, Ednet courses have been offered quarterly to assist students at various locations to earn a college degree. These locations have been in St. George, Richfield, Delta, and at Snow College. Business faculty have been required to be trained in Ednet delivery prior to teaching a course over television.

The SUU St. George Center program at Dixie College was restructured during 1996-97 to increase Ednet course offerings from one per quarter to three per quarter, two Ednet courses offered in the evening and one during the day. Students who have completed the prebusiness and general education prerequisites can now obtain a degree over Ednet by taking two courses per quarter for 12 quarters to complete the degree.

*T*he decade of the 1990s brought the global economy concept to the business curriculum. The department found itself in a shrinking world, with American business expanding to many foreign countries. SUU graduates were finding jobs in the international market. Because of the complexity of the world's cultures, the need for courses in international business became essential for SUU students.

DORIS WILLIAMSON

To help meet this demand SUU added the new emphasis of international business to its business department in 1993. The program developed into a specialty for the business administration composite major and also a minor. Because the language department was unable to develop courses in Russian and Japanese, the business department added these courses to the business curriculum. Brad Duerson was hired to teach the new classes in international business. This new emphasis combines business techniques, language and ethics.

After the American and Russian "Cold War" came to an end, and the Communist party was replaced with a democratic form of government, SUU was among the first to assist in the training for free enterprise among the Russian people. President Gerald Sherratt paved the way of SUU's connection with the International University of Moscow. He developed an acquaintance and friendship with Gavriil Popov, then the mayor of Moscow. Popov was so impressed with the University and the intellectual environment that he sent his son to be educated at SUU. From this simple beginning, a connection was made between Southern Utah University and the International University of Moscow. An exchange of students and faculty was made, tying the two campuses into sister institutions.

A great humanitarian effort was attempted and completed in 1992, when SUU Professor Tim Lewis delivered 1,000 volumes of textbooks to the former Soviet Union. Arranging for gifts of recently discontinued texts from various publishing companies, and securing free air freight from WordPerfect Corp., Professor Lewis flew from Cedar City to Rutgers University in New Jersey. After personally packing the books and renting a truck, he made deliveries to shipping docks in New York City and Washington, D.C., and the books made their way to two separate former Soviet Union countries. The docks in New York City helped him appreciate the beauty and peaceful nature

*F*rom the time I was knee-high to a grasshopper my Dad often told me: "When you get old enough, you will get to go to school in Cedar." (He was wise in not telling me that I had to!) Family tradition dictated that when the time came, I would enroll at College of Southern Utah, as the Williamson family history has wonderful connections to this school from Branch Normal School to Southern Utah University, and all stages in between.

My grandparents, Dena and Frank Williamson, met for the first time, when they literally ran into each other on the stairs of the Domestic Science Building at Branch Normal School, where they had both entered in preparation for teaching careers. Grandma said, "It was love at first fall." They ultimately left teaching and established a family farm in Paragonah, their home for the next 60 plus years, but they hoped that their children would want to go to their alma mater. Grandma was honored as the Outstanding Alumna in 1959.

Their children followed the pattern. Frank (my Dad), and Lester attended Branch Agricultural College during the great depression. In drafting classes during his second year, Frank drew most of the blueprints for the director's cottage, and was involved with most of the actual carpentry the following year. Dorothy attended BAC for one year. Two of Lester's sons, Joe and Paul, and at least two of Dorothy's children attended SUSC.

As Frank's only child, there was no question that I would go to Cedar City to school, then the College of Southern Utah, where I entered on a four-year elementary education scholarship and completed an associates degree. After changing majors and transferring to BYU and then teaching for several years in public schools of Salt Lake valley and at Idaho State University, I returned to Southern Utah State College as a member of the business education faculty. Coming to SUSC was like coming home!

I came back because I like teaching in this size of school; the energy of the students; the community support of the University, and the university involvement in the community. I have enjoyed acting as adviser to Phi Beta Lambda for 21 years. The fact that we have done well in state and national competition means that we have a good program on campus.

Looking back fondly through the generations, from my vantage point at Southern Utah University, it is nice to see the family thread through the long history of the school from its humble one-building status to the beautiful and vibrant academic community which is now enjoyed by thousands.

Doris Williamson, department head of business education/computer information systems.

of Cedar City. Tim also served as the first SUU faculty member to teach at the sister institution. After Tim's contribution to the Russian connection, Professors Andy Madsen, David Rees, Denise Woodbury, Jerry Horgesheimer, Joe Merrill and Steven Evans also taught at the Russian institution and supervised exchange students.

One important result of this connection was obtaining Dr. Alla Paroaiatnikova and her husband, Dr. Mikhail Bouniaev, as members of the SUU faculty. Alla teaches courses in Russian language and culture; Mikhail teaches math classes. These two faculty members help to develop an international flavor in the SUU faculty.

So many effective faculty members have worked in the SUU business department since SUU's transition into a four-year institution. Some have left or retired—a few more remain and continue to provide leadership and teaching excellence for a growing and demanding student body. Past instructors include, but are not limited to: Harold Hiskey, Mont Crosland, Garn Huskinson, LaMont Blackham, Robert Lewis, Victor Ishoy,Floris Olson, Stella Johnson, Robert Moore, DeVon Deppe, Ben Bean, Vic Isbell, Clayton Huntsman, Glen Barker, Katherine Queen, Marena Prestwich, Dale Hatch, Roger Hillyard, Van Bushnell, Mary Kruse, Steve Gardner, Tom Williams, Andy Madsen, Scott Clark, Pauline Nelson, Arta Brough, Roseanna Felstead, Barbara Cowley Tollison, Janine Jolley, Steve McQueen.

The successes of the business department would have been slowed and minimized were it not for the efforts of loyal and talented departmental secretaries. Dorthella Smith and Laurie Harris have plugged the holes and made the program stronger and caused unpolished results to look fine and complete. Secretaries of the department in recent years also include Jean Adams, Cheryl Porter, Paula Porter, Lolene Adams, Lois Whetman, Paula Lambeth and Cassie Varga.

During 1993 the area of business information management and education was separated from the department of business and given departmental status. The new department was named business education/computer information systems (BE/CIS). The new department chairman was a reappointment for Larry A. Olsen. Faculty members working in this department were Doris Williamson, Connie Nyman, Coralie Rawlinson, Jean Adams, Janine Jolley, Neil Gailey and Edward Harris.

In 1994 the department of business education/computer information systems made a proposal for a paralegal program. The department had conducted a study among the legal community of southern Utah, concluding that a need for paralegals was sufficient for a successful program at SUU. The study found that 72 percent of the lawyers have had difficulty finding trained applicants to work as legal assistants. During 1995 the Board of Regents approved the program, which will commence as a two-year program with plans to extend it to a four-year program.

CORALIE
RAWLINSON

In 1995 Larry Olsen opted to take an early retirement, and Doris Williamson was appointed as the BE/CIS department head.

In June of 1996 Dean Robert O. Salmon resigned as dean of the College of Business; Frain Pearson from the communication department was appointed interim dean until a new dean could be appointed. At the same time, Jerry Horgesheimer resigned as head of the department of business and John D. Groesbeck, from the economics area, was appointed department head.

Significant to the success of the business programs at SUU has been the departments' ability to place students in meaningful employment upon graduation. Beginning early in 1965, professors invited accounting firms, national, regional and local, to interview on campus and at firm offices, the year's graduates. The business environment has changed over time, and placement results have fluctuated some—but one thing has remained constant, and that is SUU's recognized and proven quality of graduates.

National CPA firms come to Cedar City to interview graduates on our campus. Calls from prospective employers began years ago and continue today, seeking for the same quality of employee that SUU provided in years past. Cooperation with the SUU Placement Service is excellent. Efforts to expand our placement influence to new regions and new employers continues with increased vigor. Accounting students have enjoyed their greatest placement successes in Las Vegas, St. George, Phoenix, and San Diego. Graduates work in all of the western states and as far away as Washington D.C.; Heidelberg, Germany; Garmisch-Partenkirchen, near the Germany/Austria border and Liberia.

At the time of this writing (1997) the busi-

PHI BETA
LAMBDA
FRATERNITY,
1979

ness programs of the University include seven major emphases:

The accounting program provides conceptual and practical knowledge to graduates who will prepare, report, and analyze economic and financial information used for making managerial decisions. Ethics, communications, tax research, legal liability, corporate financial management and professional maturity add breadth and flavor to the advanced course in the masters program.

Business administration offers a broad professional education in business. Founded on a core of pre-business and business coursework, students may pursue specialty options or emphases in accounting, economics, finance, international business, marketing, small business management, and computer information systems. The program of study is designed for students who desire careers in business and industry.

The department of business education/computer education systems has a dual role of (1) offering training to those students planning to teach business and marketing education subjects in secondary education, and (2) providing training to those students planning to utilize computer skills in business and industry. In addition, the department has applied technology programs that lead to an associate of science degree. These programs may be used toward the completion of the four-year degree.

Economics is the study of factors that determine employment and price levels, the distribution of income, and long-term economic growth. It analyzes the role or impact of such things as innovation, competition, conflict, and government in our economy and global economy.

The bachelor's degree program in interdisciplinary studies emphasizing economics is designed to provide students access to coursework in business and government that require the ability to think creatively, as well as a higher level of technical competence in quantitative methods of analysis, planning, and forecasting.

The finance program emphasizes corporate finance. Students also gain specific skills required in the banking and finance industry.

The marketing program emphasizes a conceptual appreciation of the function of marketing and consumer research in our society. Specific skills and perspectives as sales, advertising brand management, and research are discussed.

Work is proceeding on a degree in hospitality and tourism, but had not been approved at the time of publication.

Over the years, recognition has been received for teaching excellence by faculty members in the business and business education departments. Some of these awards are: Gary N. Giles, Outstanding Accounting Teacher for the State of Utah; Larry A. Olsen and Doris Williamson as Outstanding Business Educators for the state; Connie Nyman in the "Feature a Teacher" recognition by the Utah Business Education Association; Gary Giles as Outstanding Educator and Larry A. Olsen, Doris Williamson and Jean Adams as Distinguished Educators at SUU; Doris Williamson as the Outstanding Business Educator at the University level by the Western Region of the National Business Education Association.

*T*hree student organizations for business students have been an integral part of the business curriculum at Southern Utah University. These three clubs are Phi Beta Lambda (PBL), Students in Free Enterprise (SIFE), and Delta Epsilon Chi (DEX).

The Chi Alpha Chapter of Phi Beta Lambda (PBL) was chartered in 1971. During the early years of the chapter, the organization comprised only business education majors. Later the membership was expanded to include accounting and business administration majors.

The Chi Alpha Chapter has been one of the leaders in the state organization. Almost every year there has been at least one state officer from the SUU chapter. State presidents from SUU have been: Stanna Pymm, Betty Ann Bender (Rember), Gary Williams, Roger Olcott, and Darren Adair. State vice presidents have been Frank Mezek, Cal Huber, Betty Ann Bender, Gary Williams, Stuart Bowler, and Jamie Shaw. State secretaries have been Joan Christensen, Trudy Hansen (Knight), and Kim Horsley. State treasurers have been Jeff Maxwell and Tad Wright. State Public Relations chair was Corri Keele, and as State parliamentarian Troy Olsen, and Tad Wright, and Jamie Shaw

Jeff Maxwell served as PBL National treasurer. He is the only national officer SUU has had, although Tad Wright ran for National treasurer and lost by a slim 30 votes.

The Chi Alpha Chapter of SUU has been one of the largest organizations on campus and largest in the State PBL chapter several times. Membership has ranged from 20 to 107 members per year. Members are involved in the business of the chapter, as each member is assigned to a standing committee through which all projects and activities are planned, organized, and carried out.

A tradition of 20 years has been decorating for Christmas the Valley View Medical Center, which is one of the highlights each fall quarter. Other community service projects included several clean-up campaigns for the city. Campus service projects included raising the most money for the SUU Library during a special fundraising drive. The chapter has also participated each year in the SUUSA Sub-for-Santa project. When the East Canyon Park was developed in Cedar City, PBL founded the arboretum and tree planting project. The chapter has been involved with the book brigade in moving books from the old library to the new library. Each year the chapter participates in the Wild West Week, Snow Carnival, and Club Carnival.

PBL has also served the student body over the years by sponsoring a book exchange where students can sell their books and buy other books at a greater saving than through the regular channels of the bookstore. The chapter has made a very small profit from handling the books, but the main purpose of the book exchange was to assist the students.

As a special "thank you" to the Cedar City business community, each year the chapter recognizes an outstanding businessperson who exemplified the goals of PBL. Those businesspersons who have been honored are: James Hoyle, Kent Corry, Evan Jolley, Eldon Schmutz, Dixie Leavitt, Haze Hunter, Kelly Esplin, Calvin and Jack Carter, Adele Evans, Sandra Maxwell, Met Johnson, Wayne Clark, Don Marchant, Cyndi Gilbert, Douglas Knell, and David Carter.

Serving as faculty advisers to PBL have been Pauline Nelson, Larry Olsen, Connie Nyman, Jean Adams, and Doris Williamson. Doris Williamson has had the opportunity to stay young with the students for 21 years.

Each year members have had the opportunity to compete at the state and national levels. Historically, the chapter members have received an average of 30 awards (top 10) at the state level; at the national level approximately three of every four participants have placed in the top ten. Among those receiving national recognition as first place winners were Cal Huber and Philip Lee in Future Business Teacher, Brent Bills in Accounting I, Ken Knudsen in Accounting II, Melanie Ware in Administrative Secretary, Ken Harvey in Future Business Executive, Keilani Lindsey in Business Communication, Jamie Shaw in Human Resource Management.

Students in Free Enterprise (SIFE) was organized in 1992 with 16 members, with the purpose of promoting business entrepreneurship and free enterprise. Dean Robert Salmon was instrumental in organizing this student organization and was its first adviser. SIFE has been been a prime mover in developing free enterprise contests and projects among the high schools of the state. The SIFE chapter at SUU, one of 460 international chapters, was the first to be organized in the state of Utah. During the first four years of its existence, SIFE brought in over $30,000 in scholarships to the SUU campus.

The SUU SIFE chapter has excelled in national competitions, which are held at Crown Center at Kansas City, Mo., where students compete in group presentations before national business leaders, who act as judges. The presentations consist of a multi-media production of the activities and projects the chapter has completed during the past year. The international presentation is given before a panel of about 100 corporate executive officers of Fortune 500 companies. SUU's SIFE has competed in the international competition every year of its four-year existence.

As a special project, SIFE has been involved with teaching English and cultural survival skills in America to foreign students. These skills ranged from helping students to obtain a driver's license, managing a checking account, filling out forms, voting, reading warning signs and danger signals, reading instructions and want ads.

Other projects SIFE has been involved with are providing career information, learning how to find jobs on the Internet, and tutoring math and science in the local public schools.

SIFE has been self-supporting in its programs and competitions. Through prizes garnered at the regional and national levels, SIFE has earned $45,000 within a three-year period.

In 1996 SIFE sponsored a 15-minute TV program "About Your Business" that aired over SUTV. The program started as a weekly column in *The Spectrum*, in which business owners and professors of business informed others about their own businesses and gave guidance on good business management.

Delta Epislon Chi (DEX) is the most recent business student organization to be organized on the Southern Utah Campus. DEX is a post-secondary organization affiliated with Distributive Education Clubs of America. This organization serves students who are interested in marketing.

Students gear up for state, regional, and national contests in the marketing area. Some of the contests in which SUU students have excelled, are management decision making, industrial marketing plan, financial and credit services, food marketing, human resource management, retail merchandising, general marketing, and hospitality and tourism marketing.

Dennis Vredenburg, SUU marketing professor, was instrumental in organizing the DEX chapter on the campus and served as its first adviser.

As coursework in business has been a vibrant, changing process throughout the University's first 100 years, so it will continue to be in SUU's second century. The evolving nature of America's commerce dictated an ever—evolving business curriculum at the college. The advent of the computer and information systems in the way business is conducted has also changed the way instruction is delivered on a college campus. The business faculties will most certainly build on this foundation as they move forward into the new millennium.

DIXIE LEAVITT BUSINESS BUILDING

CHAPTER XVII

Communication

Winning isn't everything, but it's what we do best.

ommunication as a department at Southern Utah University had its origins in 1961[1] when a division of humanities was created with J. H. Plummer as chair. Courses in speech and drama were included within the division. In 1964, the division was reorganized and a separate unit established the division of English and language arts, again with J. H. Plummer as chair, and speech and drama as a division unit.

In the fall of 1965, the College of Southern Utah was authorized by the Utah State Legislature to grant bachelor's degrees in a variety of academic disciplines, speech being one of them. The academic division of English and language arts acquired a new chair that year with Richard M. Rowley succeeding J. H. Plummer. With full four-year status, there was a marked increase in enrollment, coupled with additional course offerings. Classes in reading and television broadcasting were added. Journalism courses, then taught as part of the English curriculum, were also expanded.

In 1968, the academic divisions at CSU were organized into schools, with communications assigned to the newly-organized School of Arts and Letters. The communication discipline was housed in a department of communication with Richard Rowley as its chair. The new department gave communication an enhanced image within the college and set the stage for the advancements that were to follow.

Four years later, 1972, another reorganization took place when communication and drama were combined in one department, Richard Rowley continuing as chair of the merged disci-

plines for two more years. Fred Adams replaced Rowley as department chair in 1974 and was in turn succeeded in 1976 by Frain Pearson. Gary McIntyre assumed the department chair responsibilities in 1979 and served in the capacity for two academic years until drama and communication were separated into two individual departments. Drama remained within the School of Arts and Letters, while communication became a part of the newly designated School of Business, Technology and Communication, where it has since remained.

With the restoration of a separate department for communication, something the discipline had not enjoyed since 1962, and a new school alignment, communication began a period of steady growth. Frain Pearson again assumed the mantle of department head, an assignment he was not to vacate except for a period in 1996-97 while he served as interim dean of the College of Business, Technology and Communication, and Suzanne Larson served as interim department head during Pearson's absence.

While the organization of communication as an academic unit of the university traces its antecedents to 1961, courses in speech were being offered from the time Annie Spencer taught elocution at the beginning of Branch Normal School in 1897. The debating club was organized as one of the first

J. H. PLUMMER

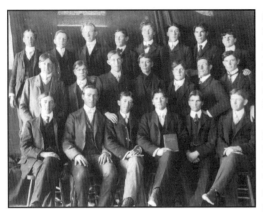

FORENSICS, 1903

student organizations. The earliest clubs included the Debating Club for men and the Literary and Domestic Art Society for women.

By 1907 debate was an important extracurricular activity, which now allowed young women to participate, and the debating team was as enthusiastically hailed as were the athletic teams for their successful competitions with teams from surrounding schools.

A 1915 article in the *Iron County Record* lauded the debate team for winning second place in the state debate tournament:

" The debate teams won their meets with Murdoch Academy and made a trip north where honors were showered upon them."

The debate teams were competing with both Dixie Academy in St. George and Murdoch Academy in Beaver on the resolution: "That the Monroe Doctrine should be abandoned." That year, 1915-1916, the prize debaters were Scott Matheson, Marion Wooley, Leonard Bowen and Bonner Lambson.

In the 20's forensics students experienced limited travel. Meets were scheduled with Dixie College, and students participated in the State High School Debating Contest. The high school contest question: "Resolved that the state legislature should make further appropriation to be used by a commission for the building of good roads."

The school newspaper, *The Student*, reported a debate held on December 2, 1927, pitting two BAC classes against each other in the topic "Resolved that the President of the United States should be elected for a single six-year term." Klive Barney and Wayne Hinton debated the negative position as representatives of the college class. Lloyd Heaton and Elvis Corry represented the second year class by supporting the affirmative side. The college class won.

THE BAC DEBATING TEAM CIRCA 1915, SCOTT MATHESON AT LEFT, OTHERS UNIDENTIFIED

In 1938 Ray B. West, a Cedar City attorney, agreed to coach the college's debate team, with the assistance of Grant Redford. Coach West generally traveled with three teams to a competition and students had to compete in order to travel. In addition to debate, team members could participate in extemporaneous speaking (a limited preparation speech on national and international topics) and in oratory (a prepared persuasive speech.)

James Hoyle, who participated on the team from 1938 to 1940, recalls that the team traveled to Dixie, Snow, and Carbon (now College of Eastern Utah) colleges, to the University of Utah, and on a 10-day trip to California where they debated in a tournament of teams from California, Utah, and Arizona, the Snow College debaters having joined them on the trip.

Forty-two of the best debating teams participated in the tournament. Glenna Esplin and Carmen Leigh took the women's division first place honors and Rodney Palmer and Raymond Kimball won a fourth place award in the men's division. Others attending the tournament were George Armstrong, Howard Knight, Homer Stephenson, and Arthur Evans.

In 1941 Grant Redford assumed coaching responsibilities and on April 14 of that year, the BAC debaters scored a stunning victory at the Utah-Idaho Junior College Debate Competition held at the USAC in Logan. Both the men's and women's teams took first-place victories, and BAC walked off with the sweepstakes award. Max Lunt and Forrest Parry (who would later invent the world's first magnetic card, the forerunner of today's credit cards) took top honors in the men's division without a single defeat. Winona Hunter and Carmen Carpenter won seven debates and first place honors in the women's division. Max Lunt also won the impromptu speaking contest.

Travel often proved arduous since much of it was done at night, and the risk of bad weather challenged many a forensics coach. "I well remember a trip to Redlands, California, in a bus we called 'Blue Boy,' " recalls James Hoyle. "We could see the ground under the bus floor boards." The first national championship for the university occurred on that trip at Redlands University where a debate team of Raymond Kimball, the BAC student body president, and Rodney Palmer won the national debate portion of the Phi Rho Pi (the junior college national) tournament.

Operating with a limited budget, travel to meets in Utah and other states was usually by car, van, or bus, and the history of debate and forensics at SUU in replete with tales of hard-ships encountered on the trips.

One such memorable trip occurred in 1949 when the BAC squad traveled to Denver, Colo., for the Phi Rho Pi nationals in a carry-all containing eight passengers and their baggage. It had been planned to use the trip as a means of also visiting scenic sites in Arizona and New Mexico but, as Velma Williams, a student on the squad, recounts, it was ill-fated almost from the beginning.

In Winslow, Arizona, the carry-all's transmission went out, requiring a six-hour delay while it was repaired. The van ran out of gas between Santa Fe and Albuquerque, N.M. Returning home the carry-all lost the use of its gear shift and the right rear wheel. The van's headlights went out at Beaver, Utah, and the party traveled the remaining 50 miles in the dark.

The squad turned car tragedy into fun by making up new verses to the tune "America." They entitled the song "Serenade to a Carry-All."

My auto 'tis of thee'
Sad place of misery,
Of thee we sing.
Your top is all but torn,
But, joy, we have a horn!
Our carry-all.

Your generator's gone
Your passengers are worn,
But we shall carry on,
Our carry-all.

She may run out of gas,
She may no others pass,
But we'll not cry, alas!
Our carry-all.

We were in bad condition,
Spent funds without permission,
To fix that "damn" transmission,
Our carry-all.

We wired the floorboards down,
We then wired our home town,
Oh, Hazen,[2] please don't frown,
We need the dough!

O, Director, what a gyp.
We pay for it on every trip,
How long will this go on?
We'll never know.

Before the 1970s, forensics tournaments

divided competition between men and women, based upon the assumption that men were better debaters than women. If a school entered a split team—one man and one woman—the team was required to compete in the men's division.[3]

In the early 1980s, the amount of travel increased to accommodate an expanded competitive schedule. Since the squad could not afford to spend a week or two away from campus, overnight trips to and from tournaments were scheduled. Students learned to sleep and study where they could. One student, Karen Reeves, perfected the ability to fall sleep while lying down, sitting or even standing.

1940 DEBATE TEAM DEPARTS FOR CALIFORNIA IN "BLUE BOY"

*I*n 1948, Twain Tippetts assumed coaching responsibilities for the BAC forensics team, assisted by Elva Hatch. The next year BAC hosted the junior college national competition, Tippetts having successfully secured a more adequate budget for forensics. Besides debate, students could enter extemporaneous speaking, public discussion, oratory, impromptu speaking, radio news analysis, extemporaneous poetry, a 15-minute radio play, progressive group discussions and after dinner speaking. BAC students who participated in the nationals that year were Ann Ashcroft and Colleen

1949 DEBATE TRIP TO DENVER. LEFT TO RIGHT: ANNE ASHCROFT (JUDD), ELVA HATCH (ADVISOR), VELMA WILLIAMS (SKIDMORE), JEAN MARIE HEYWOOD (TUELLER), LEROY SKIDMORE, GORDON BETHERS, BLAINE TUELLER AND CARRY-ALL (PHOTO COURTESY OF VELMA WILLIAMS SKIDMORE.)

TROPHY TIME

Neilson, John Brown and Don Whittaker, Walter Gibson and Blaine Tueller and Kent Myers and Andrew Mitchell. Representing BAC as individual debaters were Earl Grotto, LaKay Matheson and Rhea Staples. Interestingly, the group of debaters that year included a future SUSC dean (Myers), U. S. diplomat (Tueller), and a renowned scientist (Gibson).

Forensics, which, like debate, had been interrupted by World War II, also returned to campus in 1950. The college hosted a two-day forensics tournament in February, the dates coinciding with a college production of *Hamlet* on one night and a basketball game between BAC and Dixie College on the other. Tournament participants would thus compete during the day and find entertainment in the evening.

Richard M. Rowley became coach of the college team in 1955 when the school began offering a course titled argumentation and debate. Students who enrolled in the class received three credits of either upper or lower division and instruction in debate, oratory, extemporaneous speaking, impromptu speaking and group discussion. The courses provided the students with more in-depth instruction on the construction of arguments, the development of debate cases, and the preparation of well-reasoned speeches.

From the 1950s, through to 1997, the debate and forensics teams have had nine different coaches: Richard Rowley, Frain Pearson, Larry Wintersteen, Reed Haslam, Stephen Van Dyke, M. L. Smith, John DeBross, Suzanne Larson, Tom Murphy, and Terry West. Serving as assistant coaches have been Steve Schwartz, Neil Gardner, Sage Platt, John DeBross, Mike Olson, David Klope, Mark Mormon, Peter Tagg, Shannon Lane, Marta Walz and Aimee Anderson.

In 1978, M. L. Smith, a successful high school forensics coach in northern Utah, assumed the reins of the SUSC forensics program. With his assistant, Sage Platt, the duo was able to improve the success of the forensics program exponentially.

Headlines in the student newspaper, reflected the squad's improving reputation: "Debaters Do It," "Debaters Win National Award," "Forensic Squad's Power Shown at All Levels," "Forensics Squad Strong, as Usual," "Forensics, 'Sings' Sky High," "Debaters Firm in Saddle," and "Debate Tyros Take Scalps."

Smith's six years as director of forensics at SUSC marked the beginning of nearly two

With a handful of other youths, all graduates of Sewanhaka High School of Floral Park N.Y., I had departed the east for southern Utah, drawn by a teacher, Roscoe Grover, leaving his post at Sewanhaka for his native Utah. "Uncle Roscoe" was more than a teacher. He was a painter, children's radio program producer and station manager of KSUB, Cedar City.

It had always been necessary for me to earn my own way. My parents had never been able to give me financial support. So you can imagine how gratifying it was for me to be given a job as a deejay and announcer at KSUB, which enabled me to pay the bills, to gain broadcast experience in my chosen profession, and to attend Branch Agricultural College on the path to my first college degree.

But the crowning event was Hamlet. Here I was, a novice 20-year old in the middle of a dream cast who hailed from different parts of the country. Peter Ostroff, a marvelous raconteur from New York, played Polonius; William Lundmark, a Hollywood actor visiting with his parents in Cedar City, played Horatio; Walt Lunt, a remarkable grave digger, was a local citizen and Anne Okerlund, a beautiful and talented Ophelia, was a BAC fellow student. Hamlet was a "killer" role for me in terms of length of lines and its demand of energy. But we brought it off splendidly, if plaudits by our audience were to be believed, as well as relished.

Major credit goes to Twain Tippetts, our director, and, of course, William Shakespeare. The perennial instruction proved true for us: "Say the words distinctly enough, and the bard will take care of the rest."

BAC and townspeople gave me many opportunities. The college found a position for me as instructor of a radio broadcasting class, which was something unprecedented, becoming an adjunct faculty member, while still an undergraduate. Now may I express gratitude from Victor Seymour (nee Seymour Salmanowitz) for so many kindnesses, so many years ago.

Victor Seymour, Brooklyn, N.Y.

decades of remarkable successes by the student participants in debate and forensics. With Smith's departure as director in 1983, John DeBross took over the squad for a one-year stint in 1984, followed by Suzanne Larson from 1985 to 1994 (Tom Murphy served for the 1988 year while Suzanne Larson completed her Ph. D.), and Terry L. West from 1995 to the present (1997).

The awards accumulated by the squads during the past 18 years are too numerous to list but the national champions include Philip Shelboure, dramatic interpretations, 1983; Kent Tasso, individual speaking, 1994; Marie Chanley, extemporaneous speaking, 1985; Marty Harris, dramatic interpretation, 1986, poetry interpretation, 1987; and with Kevin Lewis, duo interpretation, 1987; Patrick Posada, dramatic interpretation, 1987; and poetry interpretation, 1987; Jay Lane, informative speaking, 1987; Page Petrucka, dramatic interpretation, 1990; and with Erin Walkman, duo interpretation, 1991; Peter Tagg, overall individual events sweepstakes, 1990; Erin Waldman, prose interpretation, 1992; David Stevens, after dinner speaking, 1993 and John Geertsen, impromptu speaking, 1995.

Three students have been named to the Cross Examination Debate Association's "All American Debate Team." Receiving the highly coveted honor were Aimee Anderson in 1992, Gary Mullenaux in 1994 and Gavin Williams in both 1995 and 1996.

In 1990 Gerald R. Sherratt, SUSC president, boasted of the school's excellent forensics program. *"The college's forensics team recently returned from the national competition in Alabama where it placed fourth in the nation,"* he reported. *"Peter Tagg, a senior student from London, England, won the national championship in speaking, a first in the history of Utah. Normally this would be a matter of great excitement on campus, but at SUSC we have become so accustomed to our forensics team's shining, that reports that it has garnered yet another trophy have become routine. It's news only when they don't win a trophy."*

In 1992 Steve Hunt, director of forensics at Lewis and Clark College, and Ed Inch, director of forensics at Pacific Lutheran University, published a study of the top forensics programs during a 20-year period. Their study's results demonstrated that only 13 schools in the nation placed higher than SUU. It is a record of achievement that is cause for pride to all associated with the University.

A short time after the college received permission to award the bachelors degree, classes in radio broadcasting were added to the communication department's curriculum. Don Blanchard had joined the faculty in 1964; Frain Pearson arrived the following fall. Together they began developing plans for a campus radio station.

FORENSICS TEAM, 1990s

Both Blanchard and Pearson had been involved in professional radio prior to their faculty appointments at CSU. With Blanchard's experience in electronics and Pearson's background in communication, they set out to bring radio to the college.

In 1966 radio station KCDR-FM went on the air. It was housed in two rooms behind the electronics lab in the old museum building, a wooden facility obtained by the college as war surplus and located near where the current Science Center is located. The station consisted of a used ten watt transmitter with a used antenna system, a control board, built by Professor Blanchard, and a few donated albums of music. It was an inauspicious beginning, but the radio station quickly became a popular part of campus and has remained so for all the years since.

Improvements in the broadcast capability of the station have been made through the years. The station's power was increased from ten to 250 watts, and then 1,000 watts. Finally a 10,000 watt stereo transmitter and antenna system were installed on a large hill south of Cedar City in 1985. Lance Jackson was the broadcast engineer who did the planning for the facility and directed the installation of the equipment.

The radio station has had three changes in its call letters. It began as KCDR-FM in 1966. Then in 1976 the call letters were changed to KGSU-FM and, after the school had achieved university status, to KSUU-FM in 1995.

Satellite broadcasts of the Metropolitan Opera, introduced shortly after the station went on the air, remain the longest continuing program on the station,

FRAIN PEARSON

1949
RADIO
CLASS

but from its earliest days, students were anxious to be involved in all phases of broadcasting, including on-air time. From time to time, the possessiveness of students as to who and what should be broadcast has led to controversy between the faculty, who considered the facility as a teaching laboratory, and students who wanted to make it the broadcasting arm of the student body.

In 1970 an enterprising student, Art Challis, was eager to get experience in sports broadcasting. He consulted with Professor Pearson and together they devised a plan whereby Challis would do the play-by play broadcast of a college baseball game. The fact that the radio station at that time did not have any remote broadcasting equipment to get the radio signal from the baseball field back to the transmitter was a major problem. A solution was devised in which Challis took a large tape recorder to the baseball field and recorded the game on sixty-minute audio tapes. When the tape was full, it was shuttled back to the radio station where it was broadcast. In so doing, KCDR produced its first sports broadcast and few, if any, of the listeners were aware that the actual baseball game had ended 60 minutes earlier than did the game broadcast on the radio.

Challis was later to join the university faculty and his sports broadcasts, as the "Voice of the Thunderbirds," has earned him an enthusiastic following among fans of SUU athletics.

In 1988 the radio station was moved from the museum building, which was demolished to accommodate the construction of the science center, to new studios in South Hall (the old manual arts facility), where it remains in 1997. The move dramatically increased the radio station's broadcasting capabilities, as well as enrollment in broadcasting classes.

Television as a viable dimension of the department of communication really came into its own in 1982, when SUSC participated with other Utah colleges and universities in a federal grant program. That year, and again in 1983, the department obtained funds from the grant to purchase cameras, switches, portable recorders, editing machines and audio equipment for television production. The equipment was later to be augmented by additional equipment donated to the department by station KUTV, the NBC outlet at the time in Salt Lake City (now an affiliate of CBS). With its new equipment, television joined radio as a prominent campus entity.

In 1987 construction was completed on the Centrum, the largest building yet to be constructed on campus, combining academic space with a special events center and arena. Included in the building were offices for the communication department faculty, as well as a specially built televison studio, production control room, offices and other support areas for the television program, which had previously been inadequately housed in the old library building. In 1985 Professor Don Godfrey had begun broadcasting university-produced television programs on channel nine of the local cable company. The new facilities greatly enhanced the department's broadcasting efforts and made television production much easier. Students and faculty produced programs were broadcast on channel nine, which the department named SUTV, and Cedar City cable subscribers were able to get area news broadcasts, delayed athletic events and convocation's speakers, as well as other special broadcasts.

A satellite dish was purchased in 1995 which made it possible for SUTV to begin broadcasting the offerings of the arts channel and its 24-hour television programming devoted to the visual and performing arts, as well as the student and faculty produced fare.

At the time this history is written, the communication department consists of more than 200 students who are studying in radio and television, print journalism, public relations and advertising or interpersonal communication. Students from these majors have been eminently successful in their careers. Graduates of the television course work have found jobs in reporting and anchoring newscasts, some at top-ten television stations. Print journalists work at the major Utah newspapers, on national magazine staffs and as writers in industry. Advertising and public relations graduates are working in firms in Utah and on the west coast. Interpersonal graduates are pursuing careers in industry, predominately in human resource fields. The success of its graduates is but one measurement of the progress of the department since its origins in 1965.

CHAPTER XVIII

Technology

The Internet connection seems almost symbolic of the progress of the department in 100 years.

The first catalog of the Branch Normal School listed a course of " manual training." It was intended to prepare teachers in the use of wood, light metal and cardboard in the conduct of their teaching.[1] The course description reads:

This course is designed especially for those who expect to teach in the common schools. It will include constructive work relating to subjects of school curriculum as well as the mechanical principles of construction, involving the use of many materials and tools and methods of construction.[2]

The frontier folks of the fledgling 20th century were practical people. Not everyone could be teachers, and as much as they coveted reading, writing and the elevating effects of art and philosophy for their children, the realities of their society required people who were prepared to fix and build things. With that understanding, the "manual training" curriculum quickly broadened to include the preparations of students in blacksmithing and carpentry, which required the addition of woodworking shops and a mechanical drawing room.

When Nathan Tanner Porter became principal of the school in 1902, he instigated an ingenious educational process wherein the students, under the direction of their teacher, John Tipton, erected a frame structure at the north end of the building which they called "the forge room." Here an iron-working forge was installed along with workbenches and tools, and students were instructed in light blacksmithing and carpentry.

MR. TIPTON'S MANUAL TRAINING CLASS

The catalog of 1903 declares that Maude Eastwood would teach the manual training classes concerned with cardboard cutting and paper work, while Howard Claude Lewis was listed as offering mathematics and shop work, open to both men and women students. The catalog says of the manual training course:

The three years work in the shop is planned to give young men a working knowledge of home and farm mechanics. At the same time a foundation is laid for advanced work in the mechanic arts.[3]

When Charles R. Mabey came to teach manual training during the year 1904-1905, the courses emphasized carpentry, woodworking and blacksmithing. Mabey was followed by K .K. Steffensen, whose tenure was just one year.

In 1907 a new shop

WOODWORKING LAB

MANUAL TRAINING STUDENTS, IN THE 'FORGE ROOM,' BNS

MACHINE SHOP, 1912

JOHN WOODBURY'S MECHANICAL DRAWING CLASS, 1908

was on the horizon. Built in the summer of 1908, the shop would replace the "homemade" forge room, add office space and classrooms on the main floor, and provide a gymnasium on the top floor.

John Woodbury joined the faculty to teach mechanical drawing and shop work. He remained at the school until 1911. Robert Wright replaced Woodbury as shop instructor, teaching until 1917.

When Robert S. Gardner began teaching, also in 1911, interestingly, he taught German as well as manual training. His woodworking courses in manual training. included the making of doors, sashes, frames, cabinets and wood-turning. He also taught a class in blacksmithing and one in machine shop.

A generation later Gardner's son, Robert L. Gardner, would become a prominent Cedar City architect who would design several of the buildings on the campus.

The course name was changed to mechanical arts in 1913-1914, and Randall Jones joined Robert S. Gardner in teaching the classes, which included carpentry, machine work, blacksmithing and mechanical drawing.

It is fascinating to note that in 1916, a woman named Laura E. Peters joined the mechanical arts staff. She taught woodwork, as well as mathematics, until 1924.

Robert S. Gardner remained on the faculty until 1918, continuing to teach mechanical arts and courses in German. When he left to work for the newly-organized Dixie Power Company, Randall Jones was joined by John H. Pendleton. Blacksmithing was now

called "iron work" and times were changing, so that automotive repairs were about to become a more necessary skill than the welding of wagons.

When George Croft arrived in 1919, he brought expertise in tractors and automobiles. While he had been hired to expand the offerings in automotive expertise, the automotive shop was not quite completed. It was being built just south of the shop/gymnasium building.

On a trip to Ogden for the Thanksgiving holiday Croft stopped in Salt Lake City to purchase tools and equipment for the auto shop. Most of his purchases arrived in Cedar City in time for the mid-year season. However, the large portable floor crane and some other equipment were not shipped until the new year. All freighting to Cedar City from the station at Lund was by horse-drawn wagon and a man named "Nat" Gardner did most of the hauling. When this shipment arrived at Lund, Gardner loaded it on his wagon and started for Cedar City. A "January thaw" occurred and the road became soft with mud. The wagon mired down so deep that Gardner had to abandon it about halfway to town, and there it remained, out on the desert, until the roads dried out in the spring.

Young men now learned to repair tractors and automobiles, and often brought their family vehicles to repair or overhaul. In the beginning, the local car dealers were nervous about what they considered to be competition from the automotive classes.

Before long they began to realize that the training provided a hiring pool of qualified mechanics. The dealers became strong supporters of the department, later contributing damaged automobiles for the students to repair.

Thomas H. Porter taught mechanical arts during the year of 1927-28.

In 1930 Charles Bennett Cooley succeeded George Croft as head of the mechanics art department, teaching woodwork and drafting, and Howard Gunderson came, in 1931, as an instructor in auto mechanics and machine works.

Wood working and carpentry had been offered throughout the early years, but with the arrival of "Ben" Cooley came a whole new world of education in the skills of the building trades. He developed a teaching method composed of classroom instruction supplemented by apprenticeship on an actual construction project. He began the practice of building a house each year, auctioning off the house, and using the money to fund the building of another the next year. Students who came to work with him were serious about the construction business, and most of them made careers in some aspect of the trade.

That same year, 1930, the shop building, with its top floor converted to a women's dormitory, burned down. Fortunately the young women salvaged most of their belongings, but there was no hope to salvage the tools and machinery of the mechanical arts department. So the administration acted quickly to plan and build a new facility just south of the building, using brick salvaged from the walls of the shop building in the construction of the new walls. Hyrum Kunz, a local contractor, won the bid to build the replacement, which he was miraculously able to complete by the beginning of school the following year.

In 1936-1938 Ernest C. Jeppsen replaced Howard Gunderson as instructor in auto mechanics, machine shop and welding. In 1939-1940 Clyde M. Decker took Ernest C. Jeppsen's post as instructor of auto mechanics and machine shop.

The enrollment in building trades classes swelled as more and more young men sought to acquire the marketable skills the classes provided.

One of the first of the project houses was the Director's Cottage, initially occupied by Director and Mrs. Oberhansley. Both the men's and women's dormitories were the products of these budding builders. Prominent Cedar City families purchased homes built by the students, under the direction of Mr. Cooley. They were eagerly sought because of the careful workmanship. Cooley was the department chair and sole faculty member in the building construction and drafting program for the thirty years of his service to the department. Despite the unusual weight of his teaching load, he managed it in a manner that brought accolades from admiring students, year after year. His courses provided southern Utah with trained builders to construct a full generation of homes and buildings.

Francis LeRoy Walters, 1940-1944, came to the college as an instructor in auto mechanics in 1940. In 1943 Walters became an assistant professor and expanded his class load to include aeronautics. It was wartime, and aeronautics had become a pertinent need. One of Roy Walter's students was young Vic Davis, who came and stayed for 43 years. Vic wrote of his earliest experience at the school:

I took my first automotive classes from Roy Walters in 1940. The next year, 1941, Eugene

Hardy came and that was my second year. At that time I also took the job of driving and maintaining the college bus which took trips for football, basketball and debate programs to various high schools, and geology trips with Parley Dalley. In January of 1942, Eugene Hardy went to Fort Warren, Wyoming, to teach at the army base. Ben Cooley asked if I would finish teaching Eugene's classes. I taught until Eugene came back in September, 1942.

After a stint in the military, Davis returned to Branch Agricultural College. In September of 1946 he became an instructor in the automotive department. These were the days when war surplus buildings had begun to dot the campus. Buildings were not the only surplus items. The school also found transportation from the stockpiles of used wartime trucks and buses, and hauled furniture for offices and dormitories back to the campus. Davis remembers:

We obtained an old Mack Truck and a Bus Semi, which were used on the military bases to transfer military personnel to different locations on the base. We obtained two army half-track engines which were of White manufacture. We installed one of those engines in the Mack truck, replacing the worn out original. Eugene Hardy, Vic Davis, Joe Roberts, Ed Matheson and Mel Matthews hauled furniture from the army air base in Wendover, Utah, to the college. We made four trips. The furniture in each room contained one single bed, springs and a

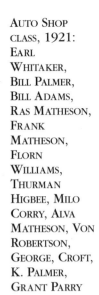

AUTO SHOP CLASS, 1921: EARL WHITAKER, BILL PALMER, BILL ADAMS, RAS MATHESON, FRANK MATHESON, FLORN WILLIAMS, THURMAN HIGBEE, MILO CORRY, ALVA MATHESON, VON ROBERTSON, GEORGE, CROFT, K. PALMER, GRANT PARRY

WOODSHOP, LOWER LEVEL OLD MAIN, EARLY 1900s

SHOP/GYMNASIUM/DORMITORY, 1908-1930

VIC DAVIS,
1940s

BAC BUS, 1939 VINTAGE,
"MODERNIZED" IN THE
1940s

do this we had to remove the ring gear and pinion, which we replaced with a higher ratio. And we had to go into the inside of the differential to drill lubricating holes in different places to lubricate the moving parts. When this was all finished, I had some of my best students remove all the wiring from inside the bus. Then I took them into the classroom where, on the blackboard, I drew one circuit, which they were to install back into the bus, as I had instructed them to do. We repeated this by my making a drawing of other circuits on the black board and giving them a copy, so that the complete wiring job could be finished. This had to be done, because the original engine was different. We had to build adapters on top of the transmission, which was a 5-speed with 5th gear overdrive. The shifting rods to the transmission ran up to the front to the shift control, which was taken from the top of the transmission to the front. We had three shift rods and one clutch operating rod, running back to the rear of the bus. My job was to teach automotive classes and drive the bus on all class trips, sporting activities, geology trips, debate and assembly programs, and to various high schools.

Eugene Hardy, Ben Cooley and Vic Davis made up the faculty of the industrial arts department. They visited post-war industries and farms to ascertain which skills were most needed and most marketable; then they framed the programs in their department to meet the demand.

E ugene Hardy, a quiet, gentle man, was renowned for his ability to build anything of metal. He began teaching in 1941, and taught machine tool operation, acetylene and arc welding, and body repair. It was a time of severely-limited budgets, and the industrial arts faculty spent much of their time building the tools they needed to facilitate their teaching. During one summer, Eugene built a welding table and stands, with a divider in the middle, lined with brick on the base and a seat made to swing out for the students to sit on.

During World War II, Hardy taught an aeronautics class of mostly girl students, since the majority of the student body were young women. Students from his auto mechanics classes over the years remember his patience and good humor, even when they "messed up."

Lyman Munford, a student in 1956, remembered the pattern of the faculty:

mattress; one desk and chair; and a chest of drawers, plus sheets, blankets and pillows.

The duties of the young faculty member were varied, true to the tradition of generations of faculty before him. He applied his genius to building the vehicle, then loaded it with parts in case of trouble, boarded the students and drove them to activities all over the west.

In 1946 the college obtained a bus through the military, which was powered by a Ford 100 horsepower V8 engine. After two years of operation we had to replace the engine every year. In the fall of 1948 we replaced the engine in the bus and converted it with the engine in the rear, along with the luggage compartment. To do so, we had to build the frame out to the back of the bus and put an air scoop on top to take the air in to cool the engine, which was cooled by a large fan mounted and driven by belts from the engine, which was facing towards the rear on the bus. After the engine was installed, we loaded the bus with students and then lined up the drive shaft so that we had a straight line from the engine crankshaft through the driveshaft and the pinion shaft, and differential. To

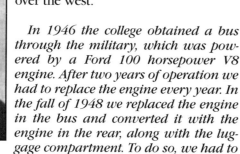

The faculty taught a full day of classes and then had other college responsibilities. For example, Vic Davis was not only the professor in the automotive program, but he was in charge of servicing all of the vehicles for the college motor pool and drove the athletic bus when the football and basketball teams traveled on their road trips. This went on for many years. Mr. Davis would also drive a flat bed semi-truck to Geneva Steel in Orem, Utah, to pick up plate-steel for the welding and machine tools courses. After it was used, the instructors and students would load the semi with used metal, and Mr. Davis and Mr. Hardy would return to Geneva Steel for another load of new steel.

Those were tough times for the faculty, because the budget was limited and they never had all the finances they needed to build the programs as fast as they wanted. Yet, because of the challenges and shortages the faculty faced each year, it helped to strengthen and build a bond among the faculty. Since they all worked together, they felt they had ownership in the college, to build and shape it, to become the university that it is. The faculty bought into the college with their energies, time and sometimes personal finances, because they wanted the college to succeed. The college was founded under adversity, and it has never really been free from adversity even to this day.[4]

Davis and Hardy were innovative in devising ways to obtain needed materials within their meager budgets:

The metal which was used for the welding shop was obtained from Geneva Steel - ends of material cut off from the various sizes of metal. We would take a load of scrap metal into Geneva on the semi, from ten to twelve ton per trip. With a large electromagnet on a crane, they would unload the scrap metal and exchange it for goods of various size and thickness. This was at no cost to the college, because we would do this each year in the fall, exchanging weight for weight. We made containers for the students to put the scrap metal into after they were through learning to weld. The containers were built so that we could lift and empty them into the semi trailer until we went to Geneva.

The classes were made up of students who wanted to find work in welding and auto mechanics, but also of young farmers who

AUTO CLASS

wanted to save money by making repairs on their family farms. They brought their family cars to work on.

When the legislature appropriated $200,000 for the construction of a new trades and industries building, it was a dream realized. In the fall of 1957, Eugene Hardy and Vic Davis moved into the new building, located immediately west of the fieldhouse. The new building was to facilitate auto-body repair, painting, general and farm mechanics, machine tooling and arc and acetylene welding. Davis remembers the move:

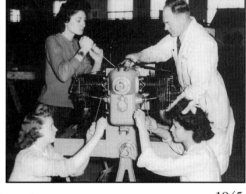

1945 AERONAUTICS CLASS, WITH TEACHER EUGENE HARDY

We moved our heavy equipment from the old shop on a sled, pulled by two horses. We had to get all set up for fall quarter of 1957. This was a big improvement, as the space in which we taught the machine tool operation, welding and the automotive classes was about five times bigger than we had in the past. In this shop we had an oxy-acetylene generator, which was away from the main shop. We used carbide that automatically fed into the generator to produce our own acetylene, which was piped into

FACULTY AND STUDENTS

BUILDING
TRADES CLASS
AT WORK ON A
YEARLY PRO-
JECT HOUSE.
NOTE BEN
COOLEY AT
LEFT.

the welding shop. The welding shop had twenty stalls, ten on each side. Each stall had its own adjustment for regulating the oxygen and acetylene supply to the torches.

Though it was a great improvement, not everything was new. They were still using an old drill press, which had been salvaged from the shop that had burned in 1930. It was hand-operated, but in good working condition. Even though it was a bit outmoded, they could make it fill their needs. From an old fork lift, purchased as part of the the war surplus bounty a decade earlier, they took a hydraulic lift and installed it in the basement of their new building to bring up heavy items.

To save money, they built their own equipment. The engine stands for the auto mechanics division were a prime example. Vic Davis remembers:

I talked with Hazen Cooley and explained to him how much money we could save by building our own engine stands and that I would purchase the materials and design and build them after school. Hazen said, "Go ahead and build them, and I will get the money some way." Thus, our first engine stands were built. Hazen asked how many I planned to make. I told him we could start out with six, which we did. As time went on, I built

BUILDING
TRADES CLASS
WITH BEN
COOLEY, RIGHT

twenty engine stands and parts racks which were on casters, measuring four feet by four feet and three levels high, on which we could put three engines, completely disassembled. Then, with the use of the hydraulic lift, we raised and lowered this equipment to and from the basement. I spent all this time building the equipment, because money was not available at this time in our budgets. Most of the time, after five o'clock, when classes were finished, till ten or eleven o'clock at night, I would work on these stands and racks.

Suddenly, on October 21 1959, as he was beginning his 31st year of teaching, Ben Cooley died of a heart attack. For 30 years, he had been the department chair and the only faculty member in the building construction and drafting program. It was a loss that stunned the school and the citizens of the town. His influence had extended into many communities throughout the state, as he had been actively involved in planning, building and advising.

Young men who learned at his side became the building contractors and skilled craftsmen of the next generation. For a time it seemed that no one could replace his profound influence.

In 1961 the college had found the right man to take up the department. Melvin Roper of Oak City, Utah, was hired as department chair and to teach building construction, residential wiring, plumbing and architectural drafting.

Trauma followed close on the heels of trauma when, on December 15, 1962, Eugene Hardy died of a sudden heart attack—another shocking loss sustained by the department and the town.

The two remaining teachers, Roper and Davis, shouldered the load and moved forward, exerting extra effort to cover the necessary requirements for a time. Paul W. Peterson was hired in 1963 to take the place of Eugene Hardy

The first year I enrolled at CSU I became acquainted with Ben Cooley. He was my advisor in the industrial arts course I was pursuing. He explained that in his course we built a house every year. He was one of the best teachers I have ever met. He encouraged us by allowing us to solve our own problems. Mr. Cooley built character and integrity. He helped students to accomplish their goals, and he helped them in their personal lives.

Ben's knowledge of construction was vast. Under his guidance, we were able to do all steps of construction. This included electrical, plumbing, drywall, concrete, cabinets, and even painting. His classroom instruction included the math and engineering problems that we would need in our construction careers.

He was a very dedicated man - to the teaching profession, to the community and to his family. The association of the students with Ben Cooley prepared us for the building profession and for life.

Gib Mitchell

in the metals area and Anton Lambert came into the department to teach police science. In the fall of 1964, they added another new dimension when Don Blanchard came to create an electronics program. Lyman Munford was hired to teach drafting in 1965.

The department had doubled. From the three teachers who had carried the teaching load for so many years, it now expanded to consist of Melvin J. Roper, department head, woods, building construction and drafting; J. Vic Davis, automotive; Don L. Blanchard, electronics; Paul Peterson, metals; Lyman Munford, drafting and Tony Lambert, police science.

Lambert had served as chief of police for Cedar City and was hired to start the first law enforcement training program in the state of Utah. The program was at first called police science, but was later changed to criminal justice. Don L. Blanchard was hired to implement an associate degree program in electronics.

Both of these were new programs, and there were neither classrooms nor offices in which to fit them. The metals department cleared out a classroom in the trades and industries building and made it into an electronics classroom/laboratory. Blanchard shared a 100 square-foot office with Paul Peterson. Fortunately they were seldom in the office at the same time. Tony Lambert's office was in the student center, and he taught in various corners of the campus, wherever a classroom could be found.

Lyman Munford's drafting class occupied a corner of the tiny arts and crafts building, while the wood shop was tucked into another corner. Since Munford held a Utah contractor's license, he also assisted in the building construction classes.

Steve Taylor was hired, in 1967, as a temporary replacement for Munford, when Munford left to pursue a master's degree. Taylor, just completing his master's at Brigham Young University, brought valuable skills to the department and was hired permanently upon Munford's return.

By 1969, Mel Roper, still serving as department head, had decided to retire and return to Oak City to establish a private cabinet business. His retirement necessitated reorganization of the growing department. Lyman Munford was reassigned to oversee the building construction program; Steve Taylor assumed responsibility to teach drafting; and Ross Hilton, just finishing a doctorate at University of Northern Colorado, was hired as the new department head. Hilton also taught some basic electricity/electronics courses, some of the teacher education courses,

and started the graphics arts program.

The department was expanding rapidly. Roger Chidester, who had completed a degree in industrial arts at the college, was hired, in 1969, to assist in the metals area. Stephen R. Adams was hired, in 1970, to teach woods and to strengthen the industrial arts teacher education program. Adams, also an alumnus, had served as student body president during his student years.

In 1970 Don Blanchard took sabbatical leave to work on his doctorate. As he left to attend Arizona State University, Kenneth S. Munford, an earlier graduate of the school's electronics program, was hired as Blanchard's replacement. After Blanchard returned, Ken Munford completed his master's degree and was hired full-time to teach electronics, drafting and math.

The dilemma of a rapidly growing department, with little space to work in, was becoming more acute. Some of the offices and classrooms were located in the old wooden museum building, and when that became scheduled for demolition, the only solution seemed to be Hawthorne Hall, the aged and vacant women's dormitory, also on the demolition list.

The school had a new name. It had become, by this time, SUSC. The department designation was also new - the industrial arts and technology department. Part of the new School of Business and Technology, it was to have a new chair, but it was located in the abandoned women's dormitory. Ross Hilton describes his beginning experience:

On April 25, 1969, I was hired at SUSC as head of the industrial arts and technology department and assistant dean of the School of Business and Technology. Our department consisted of seven of us. I arrived in Cedar City in August of 1968 to start my work here. Our building was Hawthorne Hall, an old girls' dormitory. I

CB COOLEY

EUGENE HARDY, 1957

WAR MEMORIAL SIGN, MADE BY EUGENE HARDY

DON
BLANCHARD,
1996

LYMAN
MUNFORD,
1996

found the desk piled high with envelopes, all addressed to Mel Roper, the former department head. It took quite a while to get things ready, and I hired Nellie Rae Corry as my secretary. The building housed the industrial arts classes, the electronics classes, crafts classes, police science, and there were offices for each of the faculty. The wood-working was in part of the art building, and automotive and metals were in the T & I building. We were quite separated in location of classes but very united as a faculty.[5]

By April of 1972, plans were being formulated for a new building. It was a roller coaster ride for the beleaguered department. The school was edging nearer to demolishing Hawthorne Hall and considered putting the department in a temporary metal building by the heat plant. The department faculty panicked at the thought. The state building board twice reversed its position on granting the money for a new building. Finally, in March of 1973, the department received authorization to begin planning.[6]

In February of 1974, the state legislature finally appropriated all the money for our building. On March 22, 1974, a groundbreaking ceremony was held out on the old baseball field, and construction actually got started. That was quite an experience.

The gold shovel that was used for the groundbreaking had a lot of significance to all of us in the department.

They still occupied Hawthorne Hall, while they watched the progress of the new building. Unfortunately, someone had failed to coordinate with the demolition crew assigned to dispose of their temporary quarters. Hilton recounts:

One afternoon in the early summer of 1974, Tony Lambert was teaching a police science course, and Nellie Rae and I were in the office. All at once the building began to shake. We thought surely it was an earthquake. Tony came running up the hall into the office, and we all ran outside to see what was happening. A man on a backhoe was starting to tear the roof off Tony's classroom to begin the demo-

MEL ROPER

lition of the Hawthorne building. We managed to persuade him to wait a week until we could get everything moved out into another place.

Another time when we were in the building teaching our classes, we heard a loud and alarming thumping sound coming from outside, and then the lights and power went off. We ran out to see a backhoe, which had been digging a trench, being blown upward about two feet and then falling back to the ground. When the shovel came down into the trench, sparks would fly and up the backhoe would go again. Fortunately, the driver managed to jump off while the machine was in the air and roll to safety. He had hit a 44,000 volt power line.

It was clear that the department would have to find a new location. The college had been given the old Iron County Hospital building, which sat a few hundred yards from the campus, in poor repair but vacant. In July of 1974 faculty members brought their pickup trucks to move all the equipment to the old hospital. The rooms were large enough to accommodate a bed, a chair and a patient, but hardly large enough for classes. They adapted by placing chairs in the tiny rooms and in the hallways next to the rooms, with the instructor standing at the doorway in view of both.

Hilton, department head, used the maternity delivery room for his office. Other faculty members found less prestigious places. Ken Munford's office was in the room where he had been born. Don Blanchard's office was in the baby nursery; Steve Taylor's was in the morgue. Somehow throughout that year and into the fall quarter of 1975, they managed with that makeshift arrangement..

Final inspection came on March 14, 1976. The beautiful new building was finished, and they gladly moved to new offices, new teaching spaces and what would be, for decades to come, their final home. It had been a long and winding journey to permanency.

Permanent location did not mean that the dynamic department stagnated. Unlike the long period when the department had been composed of only three—Ben Cooley, Vic Davis and Eugene Hardy—changes became frequent.

Ross Hilton's retirement in 1981 left the department without expertise in graphic arts, and there was need to find help in the electronics area, as well. After a nationwide search, Benny O'Neill was hired as a temporary replacement.

When Anton Lambert retired in 1983, Jean Newville, a veteran of 20 years service with the Washington D.C. police department, replaced him. The criminal justice program became one of the fastest-growing academic areas. By the time Newville retired in 1996, he had helped to establish a four-year bachelor of science degree in criminal justice and a crime laboratory to serve the law enforcement agencies of southern Utah.

Shortly before Newville's retirement, Lamar Jordan was hired to provide continuity in the program. Lamar came to SUU following a 20-year career with the Federal Bureau of Investigation. With the large growth in the program and the addition of the bachelor's degree, it became necessary to add another faculty member, which resulted in the hiring of John Walser in 1996. Walser also had retired from the FBI. The crime lab, established in 1991, required larger staff, and John Gerlits directed the operation of the lab as well as instructing several classes for the criminal justice program in forensics.

When Vic Davis retired in 1984, after 41 years, he left his automotive program in the charge of Jonathan Young, who taught until 1987. Richard Wittwer joined the faculty in 1987. In 1994 Wittwer moved the automotive program from the old trades and industries location into the previous plant operations headquarters, just east of the Technology Building. The old place was demolished to make room for the new student center addition. The automotive program, under the direction of Richard Wittwer, became certified by the prestigious Automotive Service Excellence designation.

David Ward joined the faculty in the fall of 1986, to teach electronics, graphics and other technology courses required for the technology/teacher education.

*I*n 1986 the state underwent an economic crisis, and Gov. Norman Bangerter. mandated state-wide cuts. Higher education was profoundly affected. In the necessary trimming process, a decision was made to discontinue the welding and machine shop programs at Southern Utah State College. The metals area had experienced declining enrollments for several years, which appeared to be a state-wide trend. To comply with the mandate, every school in the state that offered metals classes closed at least one metals area. Closing the programs led to early retirement for Paul Peterson and Roger Chidester. Chidester took a teaching

position at a high school in Salt Lake City; Peterson continued to teach on a part-time contract for the next year and a half, then retired.

In 1986 Lyman Munford requested that the department hire another building construction teacher to allow him to return to full-time teaching in the drafting program. In accordance with that request, Jerry Lawrence was hired to teach building construction, teaching through the end of the 1991-92 school year.

ROGER
CHIDESTER

The department had been moving toward the area of computer-aided manufacturing (CAM) under the leadership of Steve Taylor. In November of 1989 the University was awarded a $148,960 grant to establish a CNC (Computer Numerical Control) operator training program. This was one of four grants funded by the Utah Department of Community and Economic Development and the High Technology Advisory Council, which had projected the need for at least 2,000 machinists for the aerospace industry within the next five years.

Roger Greener, a machinist of more than 10 years experience with Thiokol Corporation, was hired to head the program. Joe Luke, state director of applied technology from the Utah State Office of Education, awarded the college a grant of $15,066 to convert the jewelry lab into a CNC machining lab. Dr. Ralph Andersen, state specialist for trades and industries, came to the college to draw the plans for the renovation. In the fall of 1990, SUU offered the first computer aided manufacturing class. The new CAM program was located in the northeast part of the Technology Building.

ROSS HILTON

In October of 1989 the State Custom-Fit program was split off from Dixie College. This program was designed to assist industries that were moving into a new area with start-up funds for training, expanding and upgrading the skills of their employees. Tex Asay, former plant manager for Morton Metalcraft, was hired as the coordinator for Custom-Fit and STIT (Short-Term and Intensive Training). His responsibility was to cover Beaver, Garfield and Iron counties. In January of 1991, Danny Shakespear, former manager for Cedar City Products, a division of Hallmark Cards, was hired to replace Tex Asay.

Van Bushnell was appointed as the

ANTON
LAMBERT

VAN
BUSHNELL

FRANCIS LEROY
WALTERS,
1942

vocational director for SUSC in July of 1978 and later was made assistant provost for applied technology. Originally the position was half-time, with Bushnell continuing to teach half-time for the business department. In the fall of 1993, with the business department expansion, the applied technology offices were moved to the technology building.

Jerry Lawrence left building construction in 1992, and the program was not offered during the 1992-93 school year. In 1993 Boyd Fife, who had operated Fife Building Construction Company for several years, was hired to re-establish the construction program.

In the spring of 1995, a decision was made to tear down the technology plant southwest of the campus. The former plant operations building became available for the automotive classes, and progress demanded more space .

During the summer of 1995, Steve Adams was diagnosed with pancreatic cancer. He passed away on October 18, 1995. His death had a profound impact upon the university, as well as people in the surrounding communities. Adams had touched the lives of many students and townspeople, who came to take his woods classes because of his loving, kind, willing disposition and the expertise he was willing to share, as he tutored them in the art of making furniture and cabinets for their homes. His departure was a loss to all who associated with him.

Adams' teaching load was distributed among the technology faculty during fall quarter and a search began to find a replacement. The administration selected Michael McGarvey, who was just completing a Ph.D. at Spalding University, in January of 1996. McGarvey's background was in woods, drafting, and curriculum development, with an emphasis in computers.

McGarvey's coming to the university was unusual. Many of the teachers hired by the department had been, figuratively speaking, reared in the department, but McGarvey was living in his hometown of Bardsville, near Louisville, Kentucky, when he had found the notice of the vacancy on the Internet. He commented later that the job announcement virtually jumped off the page at him. He said it was as though someone had used his resume to write the job description. During the interview, McGarvey's keen sense of humor gave rise to his comment that he wanted the position so much

that he even wore shoes for the occasion.

The Internet connection seemed almost symbolic of the distance traveled over 100 years.

One of the major contributions of the SUU technology department over the years has been its annual "Technology Fair" or "Vocational Day." This fair is held the first Tuesday in May each year. No one knows exactly when it was started, but it has been running as long as anyone can remember, and at least dates back to the days of Ben Cooley and Gene Hardy. It is perhaps the longest-running technology show in the western United States. Thousands of students from Utah, Arizona, Nevada, and even Wyoming, gather to compete in skills contests and participate in project competitions. Many participants have won scholarships and recognition awards, which have shown up in student portfolios and Sterling Scholar applications for years. Another purpose for the fair is the opportunity for secondary teachers to be recognized by the community for excellence in teaching, as their students demonstrate what they have learned.

Four department members have received recognition by the university students and faculty as distinguished educators. These include Stephen R. Adams (twice), Lyman Munford, Jean Newville and Kenneth Munford. Three have received awards as the Outstanding Technical/Vocation Educators in the State of Utah. Don Blanchard was recognized twice— once as Technology Educator of the Year and once as Vocational Educator of the Year; Lyman Munford won the honor of being named Vocational Educator of the Year, and Stephen Adams as Technology Educator of the Year. Kenneth Munford was designated Utah Adviser of the Year by The National Vocational Industrial Clubs of America for 21 years of service. Both Don Blanchard and Lyman Munford have been listed in the top 50 vocational teachers in the United States.

The technology department also sponsors the VICA (Vocational Industrial Clubs of America) Club. Ken Munford served as the first adviser to the club and held that position for 21 years. David Ward assumed the leadership of the club from 1992 to 1995 and Dick Wittwer in 1995. Over the years the club has received many prestigious awards, including numerous bronze, silver and gold medals from state competition. State gold medalists compete at the national level and, as of 1996, the school had garnered four bronze, five silver and seven gold medals from national competition.

CHAPTER XIX
Agriculture

*T*here were those of us who knew that if it were to be an agricultural college, it couldn't be built on a rocky knoll, it had to have land. We went out and secured more land.

*A*t the founding of Branch Normal School, the curriculum courses led to a normal or teaching certificate, and classes were directed to that end. The only departure into what might be considered "practical" courses were the classes offered young women students in various homemaking arts and classes for young men students in "manual training," which included instruction in the use of tools relating both to woods and metal.

The catalog of 1911-12 announced an expansion of direction, because a course in agriculture had been provided by legislative action:

Provisions were made by the Legislature of 1911 for a course in elementary agriculture. Our land where we shall put into practice the principles of agronomy is adjacent to our campus: the athletic field joins the agricultural land. In this course young men will be given courses in agronomy, soil testing, etc., and stock judging, care and feeding of a few first - class swine, sheep, cows, and horses. The course as to be given will fill a long-felt want of the young men of southwestern Utah. Careful attention will be given to the needs of the various communities located in the sphere of the school's influence. The great resources of this section will undoubtedly make this one of the very important departments of the school in a very short time.[1]

R.L. Wrigley, who held a bachelor of science degree in horticulture and had served one year as principal of the school at Lewiston, Utah, was hired and given responsibility to teach the new course, along with forge and mathematics. Principal George Decker, an agriculturalist himself, would have welcomed the expansion of curriculum. But no one expected just how quickly the catalog declaration would be realized, nor how soon agriculture would become a very important department of the school.

When the transfer from the University of Utah to Utah State Agricultural College occurred in 1913, the Branch Normal School became the Branch Agricultural College. Changes in the direction of expanded agricultural emphasis were both swift and sure.

The people of the community were accustomed to being called upon for support, and no one seemed to equivocate this time. Lehi Willard Jones, a founder of the school, is quoted as having said,

...there were those of us who knew that if it were to be an agricultural college, it couldn't

A TYPICAL VIEW FROM THE EARLY CAMPUS

AG BARN,
1915

BRANCH
AGRICULTURAL
COLLEGE
DRAFT
HORSES

together with sheds and yards, the arrangement of which is seldom equaled in the entire state. They are being used as models for farm layouts in southern Utah.

The college owns a number of pure-bred horses, cattle, sheep, hogs and chickens to be used for the purpose of practical instruction in the various courses of animal husbandry. There are Percheron mares, Shorthorn, Holstein, Hereford and Jersey cattle. Rambouillet, Hampshire and Cotswold sheep. Berkshire, Poland China and Duroc Jersey Hogs.

By the year 1918-19 there were two faculty members, Stanley Ivins and John Christensen. The range of classes offered by two teachers is astonishing, especially given the fact that John Christensen was also the athletic coach. V.R. Magleby details the agriculture curriculum and his own incredulity at the accomplishment:

The agriculture course of study included the following subjects: Cereal Crops, Forage Crops, Root and Miscellaneous Crops, Soils, Dry Farming, Irrigation Practice, Farm Management, Farm Machinery, Animal Husbandry, Market types and Breed Types of farm animals. It also included Practical Feeding, Elements of Dairying, Dairy Farm Management, General Poultry, Pomology, Vegetable Gardening and Veterinary Science. How they could offer this many classes with only two faculty members is a mystery to me.[4]

Some of the help came from William Flanigan who, along with being in charge of the heat plant and the grounds, had also been, in the earliest days of the agriculture courses, the farm supervisor.

By 1921-22 the catalog declared the intention of the school: "This year the BAC aims to meet another of the varied demands of an agricultural school. A modern fully-equipped dairy will be ready for operation at the opening of fall quarter..."

The young head of the department was David L. Sargent,[5] and he was searching out and hiring teachers to cover every aspect. Irvin Nelson taught agronomy; Arthur Morris, animal husbandry and dairying; Arthur Fife, irrigation and Ray Lyman taught sheep and wool.

Darrell Matthews describes the effort:

A primary enterprise was the development of a prize herd of Holstein dairy cows, many of which were donated to the school by dairy

be built on a rocky knoll, it had to have land. We went out and secured more land.[2]

The requirement was that there be provided an experimental farm of eighty acres, as well as livestock supplied. Accordingly, thirty acres of the most valuable land in the valley and adjoining the school campus was purchased by citizens and given to the school. The purchase came at a time of high land prices and, in some respects, seemed a more difficult task than the founding of the original school.

In addition to the property near the main campus, eighty acres located five miles west of Cedar City was donated by Henry Lunt. The two farms complemented each other. The Campus Farm, as the first was known, was used as a demonstration farm for both students and farmers. The Lunt property, along with others purchased later, became known as the State Well Farm and furnished pasture and feed for the livestock at the main farm.[3]

Agricultural buildings were constructed as quickly as possible. Sheds and barns were built to house the animals being donated to the new entity. By 1916 the school had been designated a junior college and the catalog read:

The college has a modern up to date barn

farmers. This dairy enterprise demonstrated up-to-date management, nutrition and production for farmers of the southern Utah area. It also furnished fresh milk and later butter and cheese for the campus and the community. A creamery, after being planned for several years, was established in 1921 to furnish a complete dairy production enterprise. The original creamery was located in the southwest corner of the basement of Old Main. A.J. Morris was the faculty member responsible for establishing this creamery and the teaching program associated with it. A new dairy manufacturing building with processing equipment fully installed and functioning was completed in 1938. Students trained in elementary dairy manufacturing operated the creamery. These students were later employed in many creameries in southern Utah and operated the Cedar City creamery which eventually replaced the college creamery.

The dairy cows were top producers and were placed on production testing in early years. One cow, *Korndyke Popular Feldspar*, became a record producer of 23,267.4 pounds of milk and 1,127.75 pounds of butter in 1924. She was purchased from Ben Eldredge, a local farmer, and was the main foundation cow to produce daughters for the school herd. The early dairy testing and production demonstration work was also supervised by A.J. Morris, who later became a top dairy scientist at Utah State Agriculture College.

The aim of the department was stated in the 1928 catalog:

The aim of the Agriculture Department is primarily to train boys in the art and science of production. The school farm is equipped with the best buildings, machinery, and animals. It serves as a laboratory for all courses in agriculture. A modern creamery, a wool laboratory and a soils and botanical laboratory also provide places in which to connect theory and practice.

It is clear that the people at the school made every effort to provide both theory and practice in their effort to train boys. The adventure of young V.R. Magleby, who arrived fresh from a small town in Sevier County, illustrates that point and offers an outline of the operations of the department, and the superb nature of the faculty:

The time was September 1934—a fall of

MAKING BUTTER

excitement and anticipation. I came to Cedar City to enroll at BAC in order to study agriculture, an undertaking that would change my life. Being a country boy from a small town I was overwhelmed by the city - especially the grocery store. It was the first time I had seen a grapefruit. I jumped right into my new life. It didn't take long to get registered, and I even got a job on the college farm to pay my tuition.

The agricultural faculty were such wonderful people. D.L. Sargent was the one that I held in awe. John Loosli taught the animal science classes. He was a small, refined man, always neat; his pants pressed, his shirt white. He was my ideal. He later went on to head the Animal Science at Cornell University. The agronomy classes and the economics classes were taught by Ianthus Wright. I also had half a dozen classes in chemistry, physics and geology from Parley Dalley. A more dedicated teacher could not be found.

In addition to the teachers, the part of the agriculture department that really impressed me was the Old Red Barn. The horse stables were on one side and the milking area on the other. It was the first time I had milked cows in such a clean barn. I couldn't imagine washing down the area with water - both night and morning. I had always milked cows at home under an old straw shed, with manure all around.

I graduated from BAC in May 1936 with a two year certificate. This was the year the Board of Trustees decided to let BAC offer a third year in agriculture. I was most happy to be able to stay another year because I had a good job at the college farm. During the summer of

V. R. MAGLEBY

BAC POULTRY PROJECT

1936 I was the farm manager and operator. I did the irrigating, milked the cows, etc. For this I received the amazing wage of $60 per month.

During the time school was in session I got $25 a month to supervise the other students who did the work. I hoped that after I finished my third year in agriculture I could get the manager job full time—and I would be set for life.

In 1936 a new man took over the agriculture department. He was Sumner Hatch, a superb teacher. I took every class he taught.

At the beginning of spring quarter of 1937, Mr. Hatch called me into his office to tell me that I no longer had a job. They had decided to hire a full-time manager of the farm. I thought my world had come to an end—I had planned on getting that position. However, Mr. Hatch went on to explain that he had found me a job running Parley Dalley's farm. It would pay $50 a month and room and board. He said he was afraid if he didn't fire me I would just stay at the farm and never amount to much.

I was permitted to stay enrolled for the

SHEEP ON CAMPUS, 1915

spring quarter while at my new job—I just had to hand in my assignments and take the exams. I worked for Mr. Dalley for six months and had $300 coming, but he never did get around to paying me. I was in the National Guard as well though, and received 75 cents for each weekly drill plus time off for summer camp, so I did have plenty of spending money.

September came and I told Mr. Dalley I was planning to attend Utah State Agricultural College in Logan. He wrote me a check for $100 and said that would cover my fall quarter tuition and book fees. About a week before winter quarter was to begin, I suddenly received another $100 check in the mail from Mr. Dalley. The same thing happened spring quarter as well. Mr. Dalley wanted to make sure that I stayed in school, so he rationed my pay out to me. I tell this story because it illustrates how teachers had the interest of their students at heart. Some even looked after them after they have gone on to other places.[6]

A thriving poultry operation provided some income, practical experience and eggs for the housewives of the community, eager to purchase fresh, "scientifically grown" poultry products.

Another primary enterprise developed by the campus farm was an outstanding flock of sheep.[7] In the early years the flock consisted of a select group of Rambouillet ewes, many of which were again donated to the school by Utah breeders. A faculty member, E.R. Lyman, supervised the establishment of this flock, which introduced purebred Rambouillet sheep to southern Utah producers. Through good selection and management this Rambouillet flock became one of the leading flocks in the west. Excellent herd sires were purchased from leading breeders and stood at the head of the flock for many years. One ram, Count Utah, raised by J.K. Madsen of Mount Pleasant, Utah, was purchased by the school after he was grand champion ram at the Parowan Rambouillet Days. He became famous throughout the west, especially in Texas and Utah, and many of his progeny were sold as herd sires to producers from many states. Some animals eventually were included in exportations to Russia.

A flock of Hampshire sheep was added to the sheep enterprise in 1940 with a purchase of yearling ewes from David Sharp, Jr., a former faculty member. Other breeds of sheep, including Suffolks, Columbias, Targhees, Polypays, and others were later added to the experimental herds.

Following the establishment of the school farms, under the direction of the dean of the School of Agriculture at USAC, experimental work in crops, soils and irrigation was established. Crop experimental work in 1940 consisted of variety testing of 31 varieties of field corn, 21 small grains, 11 soybeans and 10 varieties of potatoes. These crops were tested for date of maturity, yield, and adaptability to southern Utah conditions.

In addition to the experimental breeding and management with dairy cows and sheep, lamb feeding trials took place during the 1930's.

The campus farm, campus buildings and fields were used as the center for the Southwest Livestock Show for many years. Some of the show animals were housed in the farm buildings and the War Memorial Fieldhouse. Cattle and horses were tied to a tie rack located along the south end of the old football field and the pasture area south of the field house. The animals were shown on the old football field, and the auction sales were conducted in the south end of the Memorial Field House. The Southern Utah Ram Sale and the Utah Hereford Association Sale in Cedar City both originated in these facilities.

In 1936 the school was authorized to teach a 3-year course in agriculture. The legislative decree was issued along with the authorization to offer a four-year degree in elementary education. With this additional year in agricultural courses, the farm played an even larger part in furnishing practical reinforcement for the agricultural curriculum. Many students were also assigned work with the experimental projects and the livestock management. William A. Wood, a student from Minersville, milked the production-tested cows by hand, four times each day. Classes in agricultural practicum were conducted at the farm and in the fields.

The following list of the faculty and farm workers at the school during the early years reveals a group of dedicated men. Many of these men became distinguished scientists in the agricultural field: Leland Dalley, Alma Esplin, Walker Finlinson, Sumner Hatch, D.T. Hoffman, Stanley Ivins, John K. Loosli, Ray Lyman, A.J. Morris, Irvin T. Nelson, Gronway Parry, Eldro Rigby, Dell J. Robins, David L. Sargent, David Sharp Jr., D. Garn Stevens, Elihu Whatcott, William G. Woolley and Robert L. Wrigley.

The sheep flock was moved to the valley farm in 1943, and the dairy herd was moved to new dairy facilities at the valley farm in 1960.

*T*he man who was hired to replace the aspiring young Magleby as manager of the BAC Farm was Eldro Rigby. In the spring of 1937 Eldro moved, with his wife Zina and their growing young family, into the farm-manager's home located on 200 South Street at the end of 700 West. It should be remembered that the barns and sheds, indeed the main farm operation was still located just west of the main campus at the time.

D. L. SARGENT AND FIELD CROPS

In addition to the rent-free home, Eldro received $80 a month for his work with the Cooperative Experimental Crop and Livestock program sponsored by Utah State Agricultural College. He worked long, hard hours in this assignment and had to keep detailed records on all aspects of the extensive program. Many of his duties involved working with various breeds of milk cows and beef cattle as well as purebred sheep. He was also responsible for the corn and soybean crops, from planting to harvesting.

Eldro continued in his work on the campus farm for 22 years. When the farm operations were moved to the valley west of Cedar City, Eldro then worked both places and even longer and harder hours until he was transferred into plant operations with responsibility for custodial duties in Thorley Hall, the Trades and Industry building, the War Memorial

ELDRO RIGBY, 1942

SHEEP SHEARING

Fieldhouse, and the Science building.[8]

*I*ncreased enrollment at the school required an expansion of teaching facilities. New buildings were needed to care for the new students. The campus farm land was the logical place to construct these needed buildings. This conversion required the removal of the dairy cattle and remaining farm buildings. The dairy cattle were removed from the campus farm in 1958 and placed with a dairy operator in Newcastle, Utah, until new facilities could be constructed. Some of the sheds and the old bus garage were moved to the valley farm and used as sheds for the beef cattle and sheep. The farm house was sold and removed by the new owner. Other buildings were torn down.

A new dairy unit was constructed at the Valley Farm in 1960; the dairy cows were brought back to this unit in 1961. The construction included modern dairy unit designs. It incorporated many facilities for up-to-date management and nutrition in dairy cattle and was a valuable demonstration unit for southern Utah. A house located on property later purchased for construction of student dormitories was moved to the Valley Farm and became the dairy management residence. This house belonged to D.L. (Dutch) and LaRue Schmutz. Dutch was later the department head of biology and agriculture.

*E*very department placed the burden of recruitment upon their faculty, and teachers pondered ways to appeal to students; agriculture was no exception. Glenn

Wahlquist, who arrived in 1947, began with the basics:

The faculty was asked to go out to various surrounding communities to let them know when school was starting and about the kind of programs to be offered. The thought kept coming to my mind - if the campus could be more attractive the students would want to come and stay here. I thought about this for a long time. I needed someone to talk to regarding my ideas. The logical place to go was the Director. Dr. Driggs was in favor of my ideas, and he immediately put me in charge, with the entire faculty helping, to produce an attractive campus environment. Our first interest was to get the cows and sheep off the campus. Second, we would need a couple of lawn mowers to do the work the cows and sheep had been doing. Next our aim was to get rid of all trees that were unattractive. I look at it all today and marvel at the beauty.[9]

During the 1930s range sheep problems were a concern of livestock men. Lambing rates were low and management problems were plaguing these sheep producers. The local sheep association members had requested for several years that a permanent research project be established at Branch Agricultural College to study these problems. It was always the aim of the agricultural department to assist the local stockmen in any way possible, just as the stockmen had always come to the aid of the school.

In 1940 a project was initiated to study factors affecting sheep production. This involved observations of privately-owned flocks in the area and some experimental work initiated at the Desert Experimental Range west of Milford. These early studies indicated that more definitive work be done, and the sheep men increased their efforts for a permanent research project.

It was quickly realized that such an extensive research project would require expanded physical facilities. Summer and winter grazing properties and a much larger farm and base headquarters would be required. Discussions were held by the Utah State Agricultural Experiment Station staff with the BAC administration and faculty. It was decided to proceed with such a project if adequate summer grazing range and farm facilities could be purchased. A winter grazing allotment near Modena was obtained from the U.S. Bureau of Land Management.

All local mountain property was privately owned and difficult to obtain, so this was a lim-

DARRELL MATTHEWS
HERDING SHEEP.

iting factor in livestock production in the area. Suitable tracts of mountain land were located, and the possibilities of purchase were pursued. At this point Mr. Kumen Jones offered, although somewhat hesitatingly, his property in Cedar Canyon. Several groups toured this property in the spring of 1943. A group composed of Director Oberhansley; Hazen Cooley, business manager; Dr. Walker, director of the Utah State Agricultural Experiment Station; Dr. L. A. Stoddart of the USAC range management department and Mr. Jones evaluated the property. The boundary lines with the forest service and other property owners were located and noted. The group toured the property on horseback, at considerable distress to the riders, several of whom had not ridden horses for some time. Hazen Cooley admitted that he had not been on horseback for 35 years.

After thorough discussion it was decided to purchase the Jones' property of 2,017.71 acres and an agreement was duly signed on June 24, 1943. Other lands were purchased from surrounding landowners in 1945, bringing the total acreage to 2,542.94 acres. The lands were purchased from funds which were designated as the BAC land purchase account. This account was accumulated when BAC faculty were paid by the World War II wartime "air crew" training program at the school. The teachers were paid from military funds, and regular salary funds were placed in this special account. With the approval of the governor these funds were used for the land purchase of the Jones property, as

COWS ON
CAMPUS

well as the valley farm properties in Cedar Valley.[10]

These ranges supported a very productive animal experimental program, and the sheep men of the area worked closely with and supported the program.

The ewes and lambs were trailed up U-14 to the mountain in late June. This trek of herders and flocks up the Cedar Canyon was a historic tradition followed by all private flocks and

*M*y family moved to Cedar City in the summer of 1936, when I was nine years old. My father, Ianthus Wright, had accepted a position on the BAC teaching staff in the science department. The beautiful campus, with its great old trees and rolling fields of grass, became my playground. We played hide and seek and football and had rubber gun battles on the unfenced grounds that were like a big beautiful park.

BAC was really an agricultural school. At that time there were three main buildings, a couple of shop buildings, a big old barn, corrals, and the rest was grass. There was a small herd of cows, about ten as I recall, and the college ran a small dairy operation. Since those cows had to be fed and the grass needed to be cut, what better way to cut and fertilize the grass than to use the cows?

Well, that's where I came into the picture. One summer when I was about 12, I became the BAC cowboy and milkmaid. I don't know how I got the job, but probably my Dad had something to do with it. Every day I was off at the crack of dawn to the barn to milk those cows and then herd them onto the campus to feed. We had no milking machines, so I had to milk each cow by hand. My pay was ten cents an hour, or $1.00 a day, and I got paid once a month.

I would ride bareback on a horse named Tarzan. I had made a whip out of a stick and an old leather boot lace, and I would crack the whip behind the cows to move them out. I stayed out on the campus all day, and then herded them back to the barn for the evening milking. One day when the whip got caught in a tumble weed and hit Tarzan on the side, he took off running and scared me so bad that from then on I herded the cows on my bike.

Looking back now I realize that those summers, which taught me about responsibility, are part of my fondest childhood memories.

Grant S. Wright

*I*t is impossible to overstate the value of what happened to me at BAC. That experience helped a small town boy from Hurricane, Utah to prepare for the transition from the life that was known to the life that was to be. I came into an educational process much more demanding than anything I had experienced before. Conrad Hatch, Parley Dalley, D.C. Schmutz and V.R. Magleby all took a very personal interest in helping me make that transition. I became the national president of FFA, and serving in that office kept me away from the campus a good deal. Those four men were always there, giving hours and hours of their own time to help me keep abreast of my studies.

At BAC I had the opporunity to participate in athletics, and from that I learned about the competitive side of life. ROTC added another significant dimension. My involvement in drama and the opera stretched my cultural side. These things opened up my vision of what is possible.

All these interrelationships were the beginning of the making of the man. I got my doctorate at the University of Illinois, but it could never have happened if I had started there. Those "beginnings" prepared me for a life and a profession that has taken me to virtually every part of the world. It is not possible to measure what it means to thousands of us who have passed through the school. We form a living memorial to those men and women who built it for us.

Donald L. Staheli.
(As president and CEO of Continental Grain Co.
Staheli deals with more than 100 countries around the world.)

herds grazing in the area. The flocks would leave the old Cedar City stock yard long before daylight, travel up 200 North in Cedar City before traffic was moving and on up the canyon to cover the 12 miles to the mountain ranch by noon. This became a warm tradition of camaraderie and united effort.

*T*he new college farm located in Cedar Valley came into being in 1943 at the time the extensive sheep research project was approved and started. The farm was needed as headquarters for the project and as a location for many of the management practices,

which would constitute the new experimental project. It was soon realized that there were time constraints between the time the sheep left the mountain ranch and the time that animals could be grazed on the federal grazing permits arranged with the Bureau of Land Management. This has always been a problem with local ranchers. Much of this problem has been alleviated by seeded rangelands to introduced forage species. The breeding of the ewes, shearing, and lambing of the experimental ewes were some of the practices that had to be accomplished under very controlled conditions so that accurate data could be taken. The Valley Farm provided such controlled conditions and made the research successful.

The research project involving the experimental herd of sheep was mainly concerned with the crossbreeding of the sheep and the intensive evaluation of the lambs. This large herd of sheep required more summer range than was available at the mountain ranch, so additional property was leased from the Jay Thorley family at Miners Peak on Cedar Mountain. Farm land was also leased from the Thorley family, in order to meet the large hay demands of the livestock. The main responsibility of the Cedar City facilities therefore, was to support the sheep breeding project. Funding for this project was by informal cooperative agreement between the UAES, 60 percent, and BAC, 40 percent.

*A*new BAC beef cattle program was also initiated at the Valley Farm.[11] As was mentioned earlier, most of the BAC sheep

ANIMAL SHOWING
CLASS

flock and some land were donated by supporters of the college. Again, as had happened before, the citizens provided their generous help and support for the school. Twenty-two purebred two-year-old Hereford heifers were given to the college by Ross Gardner of Pine Valley, Winterton Brothers of Kamas, Holly's Farm of Sigurd, John Beal Farm in Cedar City and others. Dr. J.S. Prestwich, a trustee at USAC, in an interview taken by Katherine Adams on June 16, 1982, reported that "this donation of outstanding quality animals were the foundation of some of the top purebred Hereford herds in Utah."

The Advance Domino III bull was donated to the Utah State Agricultural College by Sears Roebuck and Co. and was brought to BAC on loan for several years to breed the cows in the college herd.

The beef unit at the college has provided an important hands-on experience for the animal science students. In addition it has provided many bulls for Utah producers. Many top bulls from the unit have been sold as sires to other purebred breeders.

As participants in the Utah Hereford Association sales and the Utah Herd Improvement Association, the college bulls have won top honors. These include champion and reserve champion bulls at the association show and sales. These honors include the top selling bull in 1983 in the Improvement Association sale which sold for $4,500. The beef unit at the college has also undergone up-to-date changes in housing and management during the years since its beginning. Buildings, yards, and handling equipment were installed and used to demonstrate proper breeding and management to both students and farmers. The cows and many of the bulls produced were performance tested in local and national testing programs.

Other breeds of cattle were introduced in the 1970's. A herd of crossbred cows were produced by using Simmental and Limousin semen to artificially inseminate about one-third of the cows. The Simmental heifers were maintained and upgraded to a herd of about 12 cows. The Limousin calves were sold. The herd of cows in 1980 was composed of about 15 Simmental and 40 Herefords. The Simmental breeding program was eliminated in 1985.

In 1988 a Gelbvieh bull was introduced as a clean up bull after artificial insemination. Plans now include the development of a small herd of Gelbvieh cows, a larger herd of Hereford cows improved through A.I., and a third unit of cross-

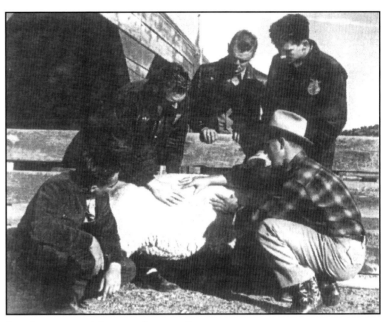

bred commercial cows for maximum commercial beef production.

DARRELL MATTHEWS AND FFA MEMBERS

*I*n about 1970 with a special ruling within the Utah System of Higher Education, special roles and programs were assigned to various colleges and the universities. The dairy units at SUSC and Snow College were considered to be very small and hard to maintain. The recommendation was made to eliminate them and maintain the major dairy teaching and research at Utah State University. After discussions with the SUSC administration, the agriculture department made the decision to drop the dairy program. The cows were sold, and the dairy barns and sheds became part of the beef cattle program and classroom facility at the Valley Farm.

The Valley Farm land was primarily used to produce pasture and feed for the sheep and beef cattle; however, field production records were kept and agronomic information compiled for various crops. Some of the agronomic research conducted at the farm consisted of variety trials of field corn, wheat grasses, and alfalfa and fertilizer evaluations. A specimen garden of most forage plant species was maintained. Detailed experiments in land preparation and seeding wheat grasses were conducted.

The valley farm land was irrigated primarily from deep pump wells with supplementary water from the Coal Creek Irrigation Company in early spring. These pump wells were constantly in need of repair and were a source of continuing problems in maintaining forage pro-

JAMES E.
BOWNS

RAY HALL
TEACHES
STUDENTS
PROPER
HORSE CARE.

duction. New wells have been drilled several times. A Perkins federal grant provided funds to purchase a new computerized center pivot irrigation system in 1994.

The primary farmstead has been improved over the many years of the project. The sheep facilities have been developed and are now practical demonstration facilities in sheep management. The new beef cattle facilities have greatly facilitated the management and instructional value of beef cattle production. Experiment Station Field Days, where results of both livestock and range experiments were discussed, were held semi-annually. These field days were well attended by ranchers of the area. All high school agricultural students of the area attend the annual Vocational Day where animal selection and management are demonstrated and soils and rangeland judging are conducted. Many farmers and students have attended short training courses conducted at the school. These courses included wool selection and grading, sheep shearing school, livestock judging (short course), ram selection for health and fertility, ram performance testing and beef cattle selection for red meat production. Many 4-H clubs and F.F.A. chapters have used the farm facilities and livestock for individual training in agricultural subjects.

In 1989 a State of Utah appropriation of $50,000 was received for emergency repairs and to prepare a master plan for the farmstead. The plan was developed and included the new beef cattle center, now completed, a new classroom area, and a horse unit.

The Valley Farm has undergone a change to a more balanced unit. Under the management of Kirt Bussio the production of the farm has changed to intensive production of alfalfa and barley, while still maintaining pasture for the livestock. The agronomic resources are now in balance with the livestock feed needs. Production now has reached a level where some commercial sales of alfalfa and other crops are realized. The main purpose remains the educational nucleus for a growing agricultural program.

Many faculty and staff members of the school have contributed much to the Valley Farm operation and management as well as the summer and winter ranges. A list of employees of BAC, CSU, SUSC, and SUU includes the following contributors in alphabetical order:

T. Donald Bell, James E. Bowns, Jan M. Burr, Kirt Bussio, Eli Clark, C. Wayne Cook, Carl T. Cox, Daniel R. Dail, James D. Docksteader, Gail Evans, Warren C. Foote, Eugene Halterman, Wallace R. Hanson, William Hill, Jay W. Lee, V.R. Magleby, Don Mathews, Darrell Matthews, Edward S. Nelson, Phil R. Ogden, Delyn C. Olds, Twenty Orton, C. Brad Reeves, Max E. Robinson, T. Gordon Smith, Gary Snowder, John Stephenson, Frank T. Stevens, Fred Tolbert, Verl Tolbert, Glenn R. Wahlquist, Ronald R. Williams, Dean L. Winward.

*I*t is true that the history of Southern Utah University is an agricultural history - from the farmers who mortgaged their property to finance the University, to the once-named Branch Agricultural College. However, agriculture studies at the SUU are far from being a thing of the past. Agribusiness is reported to generate over 100,000 jobs in the state of Utah, originating mostly from the rural counties, which are moderately to heavily dependent upon agricultural activity for a tax base. Southern Utah University continues to draw over 75 percent of its students from the rural counties of the state, and 85 percent of the agriculture students are from these areas. Rural economic development in the SUU service region, coupled with changes in traditional agriculture, is creating an employment need for people who are agriculturally literate. New agriculture industries and changes in existing production demand a skilled workforce and, at the same time, provide opportunities for motivated, well-trained young people to stay and rear their families in southern Utah. It is estimated that over 90 percent of SUU agriculture graduates who actively seek employment in agriculture find jobs related to their field of training. SUU grad-

uates hold a number of positions of responsibility in agriculture and related occupations in the region.

The SUU agriculture program currently serves 120 students and continues to grow at a rate in keeping with, and possibly exceeding, the growth rate of the university as a whole. The most popular degree is the four-year Bachelor of Interdisciplinary Studies degree in agricultural science and industry. From within this program, students can emphasize agribusiness, animal industries, plant industries, or general agriculture. Students who wish to receive a degree or certificate with less than four years of study may enroll in the livestock farm management program and receive a one-year certificate or two-year AAS degree. While a broad and general core is required, there is some opportunity to focus on horses, swine, or range animals. Unique to these programs is that they can either be terminal or apply with full credit to a four-year program. A number of students graduate with two degrees and a certificate, all approximately within the same four years of study. Many SUU students majoring in other disciplines find the agriculture minor to be an excellent complement to their own course of study. While modest in number, SUU students have an excellent acceptance rate into colleges of veterinary medicine. More importantly, over the past nine years, 100 percent of SUU graduates who have attended veterinary schools have completed the degree. Because of our role and responsibility as a regional services university, we plan to enhance instruction in the areas of horticulture, horses, and swine.

The Southern Utah University chapter of the National Block and Bridle Club provides opportunities for leadership, service and social activities for all agriculture students.

The Southern Utah University Valley Farm is the teaching laboratory for students who take agriculture courses. Facilities and equipment include a classroom for pre-lab demonstrations, a beef cattle center and a sheep operational unit. Small grains, alfalfa and pasture grasses are grown on dry and irrigated land, including a modern, computerized, center-pivot irrigation system and demonstration plots. Students are exposed to traditional practices as well as modern technology, such as neutron probe hydrology and ultrasound animal soft tissue analysis.

Because many courses have an information management component, the program does have some computers for student access. To meet the increased demand for equine-related instruction, a horse operational unit is in the initial phases.

The academic home of the agriculture program is the college of science. Agriculture lectures, general education-agriculture classes and some labs are taught in the new 77,000 square-foot science center as well as the adjacent life science building and greenhouse. These facilities have electronic classrooms, modern laboratories, and advanced technology, such as electron microscopy.

The University Ranch, 11 miles up Cedar Canyon, is fenced into allotments for deferred rotational grazing of the university sheep herd. In addition to the Mountain Conference Center, the ranch property provides an excellent range demonstration area.

The SUU agriculture program is one of the most active academic departments on campus in terms of hosting off-campus visitors. Last year, the agriculture program brought nearly 2,000 people to campus. This included leadership conferences, in-service workshops, land, livestock and range judging contests, and the Utah State FFA Convention, which is the largest single event of its type at SUU. Area farmers and ranchers continue to represent most of the purchases of SUU-raised crops and livestock. Agriculture personnel have successfully offered travel-study courses, summer vo-tech courses, and one of the larger concurrent enrollment classes over the EDNET System.

BAC
POULTRY
CLASS

COOKING
CLASS,
1930

FASHION SHOW, FRANCIS ELVA
KNOTT, INSTRUCTOR,
LATE 1930S

CHAPTER XX

Home Economics - More than just cooking & sewing

ork in this department is intended to enable a woman to apply the principles of science to the problems of daily life.

Cedar City settlers came with a resolute determination to bring civilization to the arid wilderness. From the earliest days families bent every effort toward establishing homes and farms in which they could rear children who would be productive and happy. Many fathers and mothers were educated people who wanted a life of culture for their children; all fathers and mothers had a burning desire to provide, for their children, opportunities for an even richer life than the one they had left to come to Zion.[1]

No study is more basic to meeting the needs and enriching the lives of families than the field which has most often been called some version of the term "home economics." The home economics department at Southern Utah University has undergone numerous name changes, each change an attempt to describe the ever-widening scope of the curriculum.

In 1902 the study of domestic science was added to the curriculum of Branch Normal School. Classes were taught by one teacher. When student enrollment increased, a second teacher was hired, and the curriculum was split: the domestic science teacher taught foods; the domestic art teacher taught clothing construction. For two years, 1922-1924, the department was known as household science and household art.

From 1929 until 1955 the discipline was designated the department of home economics. When Dr. Royden Braithwaite became the college director in 1956, the name was officially changed to department of home and family living, but more often called family life department. When permission to train secondary

home economics teachers was granted in 1984, the department re-adopted the name department of home economics.

In the most recent catalog courses are listed under the heading "Home Economics and Family Life." Southern Utah University has kept abreast of national trends in the title of the discipline as well as the actual development and expansion of curriculum. In 1994 the National Home Economics Association adopted the name American Association of Family and Consumer Sciences (AAFCS). In keeping with this designation, SUU's department in 1997 adopted the name of department of family and consumer sciences.

The real history of the curriculum expansion signaled by these name changes is, at heart, the stories of the teachers and their pupils and of the buildings in which they honed and shared their skills.

The Branch Normal School added domestic science classes to the curriculum in 1902. Maude F. Eastwood (1902-08) taught all classes in a "Model Department," where students practiced cooking skills on a wood and coal-burning stove and sewing on treadle machines. The course description in the catalog outlined the goals and facilities for the department:

Domestic Science:
Work in this department is intended to enable a woman to apply the principles of science to the problems of daily life. Housekeeping and garment making are studied and practiced as occupations worthy of the best efforts and of the brightest minds.
The Domestic Science department is provid-

SEWING CLASS, CIRCA 1908

ed with a model kitchen and all accessories, a dining room, a sewing room with the necessary machines etc., required for thorough and practical work.

Student expenses: Among other laboratories, students are charged an incidental fee to cover costs of materials used by them in their exercises (cooking rooms).

The 1902-03 catalog also offered an ambitious list of classes:

Cooking and Home Sanitation:
The course will consist of lecture work and laboratory practice, which will include a study of foods, their sources, composition, preparation, digestibility and function in the body. The work taken up in the second half of the year will include the combining and serving of food, the care of the dining room and its furnishings, arrangement of the dining table and the planning, preparation and serving of breakfast, luncheon and dinner.

The work in Home Sanitation will treat such subjects as the site and construction of the home, including materials used, plumbing, heating, lighting, ventilating and cleaning.
Four hours per week through the year.
Sewing:
This work will consist of plain sewing, plain and fancy stitches, drafting of patterns, designing and making of garments. This course also includes lectures upon the making and the use of various stitches and upon the process of manufacture of the fabrics used.
Four hours per week throughout the year.

In the early 1900's, dressmaking and tailoring were absolutely essential skills. Every homemaker spent many of her available daylight hours, and often strained to see by coal oil lamp into the evenings, creating wardrobes for herself and her husband and children. Wise purchase of the best affordable fabric for each article of clothing was as important as the skill of turning the precious yardage into attractive dresses, suits and "layettes."

Embroidery was also a very useful skill. It was customary in most homes to decorate household linens with embroidery and handmade lace. In the domestic art course at least one class required samples or "models"of hand sewing, such as buttonholes, basting, blanket stitch, chain stitch, satin stitch, french knots, eyelets and other more complicated embroidery.

The final project was often an embroidered centerpiece, such as a tablecloth, or an embroidered "waist," as blouses were called. Students learned to make baby clothes, or layettes. Baby girls wore dresses only; they learned to crawl wearing dresses. Petticoats and dresses were made of sheer cotton batiste with the neck, sleeve and hem finished by a fine crocheted edge. Women were proud of the delicate embroidery at the neck front and hem. Some had lace insertions.

Boys' rompers of cotton percale had a waist-length shirt buttoned up the front with very small buttons and short pants buttoned to the shirt. Some rompers had as many as sixteen handmade buttonholes. The pants were unbuttoned from the shirt every time the diaper was changed. No one had thought of a placket at the crotch.

For several years, the catalogue listed a class in "basketry and cardboard work." The description was as follows:

This course offers instruction in the weav-

CARDBOARD CLASS PROJECTS, CIRCA 1900

ing of plain and fancy baskets in rattan and splint, the use of raffia in making various articles, and the cutting and folding and making of cardboard wall pockets, picture frames, cones, lampshades, plain and fancy baskets.

In that era in Cedar City, purchase of decorative objects to enrich the interiors of homes was limited and expensive. Baskets and cardboard pieces would add interest to living areas in these homes. These skills would also be useful for BNS students who became teachers, particularly if the high schools in which they worked had a very limited number of sewing machines; students would need a second project.

In 1903-04 the domestic science department moved, temporarily, into a two-story home of native brick at 97 South 300 West, east of the school. This building was one of two homes on 300 West which had been built by three brothers - Lehi, Uriah T., and Thomas Jed Jones.

Milton Bennion, the first principal of Branch Normal School, lived in the neighboring home at 107 South 300 West, and his daughter, Claire, was born there. In 1922 Claire returned to Cedar City as an instructor in the household science department at BAC. Two years later she married Lehi Jones' son William. Principal Bennion's home was later owned by Albert N. Tollestrup, instructor of music at BNS and is now on the Historic Register.

As the school had outgrown Old Main, the original BNS building, the 1903 legislature appropriated $35,000 for a new science building and necessary equipment. The 1904-05 catalog includes a sketch of the new science building, which shows curtains at the windows of the first floor room on the southeast corner. The detail of the curtains suggest that the department moved into that area of the new science building, now the Braithwaite Fine Arts Center, in 1904[2], occupying that area until 1961.

After three years Mary Harriet Miller, B.Pd. (1905-06) joined Maude F. Eastwood in the department.[3] Miss Miller also taught drawing and physical culture, which had been the province, along with elocution and music, of Annie Spencer, one of the founding faculty members of BNS when it was established.

Inez Powell joined the Branch Normal School faculty in 1909. She is the only domestic science teacher listed in the catalog for 1909-11. Powell, a graduate of domestic science at Utah State Agricultural College, had joined the USAC faculty for five years before completing her graduate work at Columbia University in New York City.

Jen Leigh (1911-14) was one of the best-known teachers of the early years and a noted contributor to the community. Christened Amy Jane Leigh, she had been born in Cedar City and educated in the local public schools. At 19, Jen graduated from BNS when it was a high school. After one year at the University of Utah she transferred to USAC in Logan and graduated there with a B.S. degree. Ms. Leigh also did graduate work at Columbia University, Oregon State University and Johns Hopkins.

Ms. Leigh taught domestic science at BNS for three years, when the school was in transition from high school to a combination high school and two-year college. Before and after her stint as an instructor in the BNS domestic science department, Jen had a widely-varied and interesting career - she served as dietitian at Latter-day Saints Hospital in Salt Lake City; domestic science, vocal expression and English teacher at Ricks Academy at Rexburg, Idaho; home demonstration agent in Cache County and later

FIRST HOME OF DOMESTIC SCIENCE DEPARTMENT, 97 S. 300 W.

HOME ECONOMICS CLUB, CIRCA 1900

MAUDE
EASTWOOD
TEACHES
IN THE
KITCHEN,
1907

in Utah County and Iron County nurse.

Of special interest in this history is Leigh's partnership with Margaret Williams, the Iron County primary education supervisor, during the summers of 1927 and 1928. These two women built the Canyon Crest Inn in Cedar Canyon, where they served chicken dinners to tourists as well as a local clientele. The site of this business venture is now the SUU Mountain Center. Miss Leigh became Mrs. Kumen Jones, in 1931, at age 47.

The federal government had established funding for the training of young women as domestics in response to a general need for hired girls; new mothers were expected to do very little work for at least two weeks. During the depression Jen Jones set up this training program for hired girls in her home.[4]

Under each faculty picture in several yearbooks of these years was a jingle or humorous comment, which is all that is known about some of these women, including Effie B. Warnick, Sarah Huttleball and Eva Thomas.

Rozina Skidmore taught at the Cedar City school, by this time BAC, for two years (1915-17). In Joel Ricks' *History of Utah State Agricultural College* she is listed as assistant professor of domestic arts in the extension service, 1918-20. Miss Skidmore also had a long and distinguished career as professor of textiles and clothing at the University of Utah.

When BNS became a branch of the Utah State Agricultural College all home economics classes were coordinated with the courses at the mother school, which not only encouraged, but made it very easy to

transfer to the Logan school with no adjustment or loss of credits.

Inez Cooper, writing in *The Daily Spectrum* supplement in the summer of 1980, gives an account of how the home economics department was used by the community during the severe flu epidemic of 1918-19:

...BAC, which was closed during the siege, was maintained as an auxiliary hospital. Beds were set up in the home economics sewing department. The kitchen was used to prepare food for the patients. The patients were cared for by doctors and trained nurses.

Students in 1918, during World War I, were actively involved in Red Cross work. The domestic art classrooms were open two days a week for projects. Girls bought material and made layettes for women in Belgium and France.

Beginning in 1918, and extending into the 1920s, BAC, in cooperation with the USAC Extension Service, sponsored a week-long BAC Farmers Roundup and Housekeepers Conference. The purpose was to improve the farms and the homes in the area by disseminating current information. The home economics classes were based on the specialty of the visiting extension personnel. When Rozina Skidmore and Victoria B. Christensen were scheduled, the classes were on dressmaking and millinery, home health and home nursing. When Hettie White and Rena B. Maycock were guest instructors, the lectures and demonstrations were on foods and nutrition and improving the cleanliness of the home and the town. Local instructors were also included in the program. It is easy to picture the conferees in the 1918 gathering, knitting for the Red Cross while they listened to the lectures. Women were encouraged to conserve for the war effort; instructions and demonstrations were given on cooking beans.

The 1920 yearbook pictures Mary M. Urie (1919-22) both as a senior student and a faculty member in domestic art. A Cedar City native, Mary taught beginning students to "darn and patch articles of clothing" as part of the first course. The athletic department expected Mary to mend uniforms, along with her duties as an advisor for the Girls Welfare Club, an organization open to all girls to "promote school loyalty and through social activities promote companionship."[5]

The 1921-22 BAC catalog proudly described the new home economics department. During the tenure of Christine B. Clayton (1919-22) the department had been remodeled: old work desks were replaced with new modern ones; new and additional utensils had been purchased for "compounding, mixing and cooking," and an up-to-date demonstration area added; a modern laundry room, "carefully planned and fully equipped," was to be made available to all students who had no access to laundry facilities. A course in laundering was added to the curriculum.

Ms. Clayton had taught at Jordan High School and worked in the Extension Service at USAC before she joined the faculty at BAC to teach domestic science. She served concurrently as head of the home economics department at USAC and BAC from 1923 to 1938.

On May 20, 1922, it was decided that in order to furnish power to the Branch Normal School, it would be necessary to run the electric plant for day service on Tuesday and Saturday for the entire day and on Wednesday and Friday for half a day.[6]

Electric power was first produced and used in Cedar City in 1907. For the first four years it was generated for special occasions and for a few hours at night— not a steady, reliable power source. Private citizens organized and financed the company, working against difficult circumstances. There is no available record of when electric stoves were installed in the home economics department or when treadle machines were retro-fitted with electric motors. As late as 1936, some of these machines were still in use.

For many years the students in foods classes worked in their remodeled space to plan, prepare and serve dinners and banquets in the department dining room to college visitors. The students gained practical experience serving the Board of Trustees, conference guests, and student groups. The remodeled space did not, however, include electric stoves.

From the journal of Afton Parrish Parry (1922-23), we get an inkling of the minor irritations teachers faced during these years:

When I was married, I came [to Cedar City] to live. I taught foods classes at the college. We cooked on a large hotel-sized coal and wood stove with two ovens. I always had to look for kindling to start the fire. It was beneath the dignity of the janitor to chop kindling for me, or so it seemed. Imagine preparing the Founder's Day banquet on that stove!

Afton Parrish Parry was not formally listed as a domestic science teacher because she was

hired too late in the year. Late in the summer her fiancé, Gronway Parry, a teacher at BAC, heard it announced at a faculty meeting that the domestic science teacher had resigned, and did anyone know of a teacher who could fill the position? Afton, who had already resigned her home economics teaching position at Snow College, signed a contract to teach at BAC. The couple were married at Thanksgiving time.

We get an idea of how limited women's wardrobes were during this period when we read a 1921-22 catalog suggestion:

Uniform Dress for Girls.
The committee on the standardization of school dress recommended the following costume as suitable for school wear:
  I. School dress - One piece woolen dress of a dark color
  II. Suit (skirt, jacket and wash waist) - Conservative in color and texture

CORA McBRIDE'S SEWING CLASS, MID 1920S

CLAIRE BENNION'S MEAL PREPARATION CLASS, EARLY 1920S

III. One piece dress of wash material such as gingham, galatea, linen, pique, percale
IV. Medium or low-heel walking shoe
V. Hose of standard quality cotton, lisle, or fibre
VI. That a permanent committee be selected with powers to decide on questions of propriety.

The dress code does not appear in subsequent catalogs.

A benchmark in the hiring policy of BAC faculty apparently occurred in 1924. Claire Bennion (1922-24) had taught at BAC for two years. She was a graduate of the University of Utah and had a summer session at Berkeley and a year's teaching experience in Morgan County before she came to BAC. Ms. Bennion married in 1924, planning to continue teaching home economics at BAC. The reason that her contract was not renewed, according to her daughter, Janet Jones Gilbert, was that she had become a married woman. The irony is that Rose J. Thompson, a married woman, was hired the following year.

Rose J. Thompson taught at BAC for nine years, until 1933. She innovated the practice of having college students help in the supervision and grading of high school students in their sewing classes, which was an excellent learning experience. She is remembered for interesting personality traits - she loved to entertain and was known for giving unique parties, but is perhaps best remembered by former students for her vehement dislike of the practice of chewing gum. According to Arr Nita Urie Webb and Winnie Parry Rosenburg, Ms. Thompson would stop in the middle of a lecture, when she spotted a student who was chewing gum, to turn to the board and write:

The gum chewing girl and the
cud chewing cow
What is the difference?
I have it now. It's the intelligent look on
the face of the cow.

The foods laboratory in the late 1920s, during Lillian Wight's tenure (1925-29), had electric lights, but there were still no electric stoves. Lydia Matheson Harter, a student of that time, remembers individual gas burners at each cooking station. The students had to pump the gas to each unit before they could light the burners. They did all their baking in two large coal stoves. Each student made her own white cot-

ton uniform and an apron to wear over the uniform. The girls walked down the hill to the BAC barns to bring back baskets of fresh eggs for the class. Lydia Harter also recalls that Parley Dalley taught a special chemistry class for the four home economics majors, which was required for graduation. She remembers fondly his patience and the individual attention he gave them.

The cooking class prepared the food for all the faculty banquets and some student parties. Lydia recalls one student party especially. When the boys brought in some turkeys they had "borrowed" from someone's farm in the valley, the girls plucked the feathers, cleaned the turkeys, roasted and served them.

Budgets for foods classes were very limited by today's standards. Arr Nita Webb remembers two interesting examples from Lillian Wight's class. The individual student recipe for cream sauce called for one teaspoon of flour. Other ingredients, in proportion, would result in the amount of one-third cup of light cream sauce. In a class demonstration on salad making, Ms. Wight had arranged all ingredients for the salads on a table at the back of the room. Arr Nita Webb and Sylvia Adams Bryant were seated at the back of the room, and during the lecture, sampled a few of the marshmallows. When the time came for the demonstration, Miss Wight did not have the number of marshmallows she had counted out for one of the salads. Arr Nita remembers the scolding Miss Wight gave the two of them.

Arr Nita and Lydia both vividly remember the experience of setting up banquet tables in the basement dining room of the El Escalante Hotel on the south-west corner of 200 North and Main Street. The Union Pacific Railroad brought tours into Cedar City. Tourists had dinner at the hotel, then boarded buses to tour the southern Utah national parks. As part of class assignments, the girls set up the tables and served the "dudes." They remember standing at the end of each table and sighting along the silverware, glasses and napkins to be sure they were in perfectly aligned rows. Neither remembers being paid.

In 1928 High School Day was initiated and continued for several years. The home economics department participated in many programs in which the college invited high school students to the campus to introduce them to programs and facilities. Vocational Day, the most successful recruiting program, was started in 1937. The home economics, business, industrial arts and agriculture departments planned workshops, contests, and demonstrations, geared to attract and interest high school students. Thousands of high schools students have come, through the years, from southern Utah, northern Arizona and eastern Nevada.

Sometime before 1929, while still at BAC, Lillian Wight published a recipe book entitled *Favorite Recipes.* She was assisted by Thora Esplin, Dona Houchen, Roma Higbee, Ruth Leigh, Virginia Macfarlane, Rebecca Platt, Minnie Platt and Dagma Seaman. A second revised edition was published in 1987 by the SUSC Faculty and Staff Associated Women. The foreword reads as follows:

This is not an attempt to exhaust the supply of recipes that one might use in the home, but rather to bring together in one collection those which years of scientific study and practical application have proved most excellent... Practically every recipe listed herein has first been proved in the laboratory of the college before being given its place in this publication. Best results will be obtained only when these recipes are used with the greatest accuracy and care.

This was no small undertaking, considering the limited resources and concern about whether the sales would cover the costs. It would be interesting to know whether she converted old recipes calling for butter the size of a walnut, a pinch of salt, and so many tumblers (glasses) of flour, to standard measurements. How did she measure the temperature of the oven of a coal stove, and how did she keep it constant?

In the revised edition there is a picture of the recipe testers–Lydia Matheson, Arvilla Bauer, Lillian Wight Lunt, Ann Cox, and Virginia Knell. Lydia Harter remembers supervising high school classes testing the recipes, and that all girls preparing to cook were required to wash hands thoroughly and clean their fingernails with a tooth pick. All measurements had to be exact. This may well have been the first locally available recipe book with temperatures and cake recipes adjusted to high altitudes. High school and college cooking classes used it in foods classes, and many copies were purchased in the community.

The first record of a cafeteria is during the tenure of Laura E. Peters (1930-32), foods instructor. Virginia Parrish Chamberlain (1931-33) continued the cafeteria and taught a class in cafeteria management. Only one meal was served, and it was prepared by a foods class as a practical laboratory experience. Chamberlain

FOODS CLASS
CIRCA 1920s

also taught a class in large-quantity cooking.

The great depression fell upon the nation, and unique needs arose. In January of 1932 the State Department of Education, in conjunction with BAC, designed courses to meet the needs of the unemployed. Virginia Chamberlain taught home economics classes in renovation and care of clothing, economic meal preparation and training pre-school children. The classes were also conducted in Beaver, Parowan and Hurricane.

Chamberlain had come to BAC with a masters degree from Columbia University and, after leaving BAC, taught at UCLA in food science.

During the 1933-35 school years when Rhea Johnson was the only instructor in the department, the cafeteria may not have been in operation. Johnson (1933-36) was the only home economics teacher during these depression years. She taught a full teaching load at the college and three years of high school students as well. Rhea had come to BAC with impressive credentials and experience, including a degree from USAC, graduate work at Merrill Palmer School of Child Development in Detroit, practical nursing at Cottonwood Maternity Hospital, assistant at the nursery school level for Michigan State Public Schools and adult education specialist for the State of Utah.

It is a matter of record that the cafeteria program was in full swing in 1935 under Lydia Jennings, later Finlinson (1935-37), who replaced Rhea Johnson. The menu included soup, salad, sandwich, dessert and a drink for 25 cents. Meal preparation students who prepared the food were required to take the class for three quarters.

Frances Elva Knott (1935-42), an outstanding teacher, brought a new excitement to the home economics department. She introduced her students in isolated southern Utah to the outside world. Frances acquainted students with the Paris fashion designers and made high fashion magazines available for the department. She made contact with a fabric shop in New York City which dealt in dress length fabric remnants from fashion design studios. Her students looked forward each year to the exotic fabrics that came from the big city—silk velvets, cashmeres, brocades, Harris tweeds, linens, etc. It was an education to see and feel the materials, and some were priced within the students' reach. Ms. Knott, a mentor to many students who continued their education, teaching home economics or achieving in other related fields, was demanding in her expectations, and at the same time, encouraging and helpful.

The year that the BAC chorus sang in LDS general conference in the tabernacle in Salt Lake City Frances supervised the construction of two hundred robes. Mary Ewing Anker remembers helping in the overwhelming process. The men's robes were black with white collars; the women's robes were white with black collars.

For a few years Frances Knott and Lydia Jennings gave each home economics graduate a demitasse cup in Wedgewood china, another lesson in quality.

Mildred Bowers Hunter taught only one year, 1939-40, in foods and nutrition. She remembers what good times the faculty enjoyed. At one dinner, in particular, each member had an assignment. William "Pa" Manning was in charge of clean-up. He organized the crew so that each person drying the dishes would pick up a dish to be dried and walk around the work tables, at the same time singing a round. Mildred said there was more laughing than singing. Mildred was later head of food service

at University of Utah during World War II.

*T*here is a story in the annals of the home economics department which illustrates the influence of faculty members in the lives of their students, as well as reflecting the gender bias that prevailed during that era. Winona Hunter Cowan, a senior of the 1941 BAC graduating class, had achieved the highest scholastic grades of her class, qualifing her to be designated as valedictorian. BAC Director Oberhansley reportedly called Winona into his office and suggested that the honor should go to a male student, Darrell Christian Ronnow, who was second in grade points. (Ronnow was later to become a district judge in Cedar City). Winona didn't respond immediately, but went to her home economics teacher, Frances Knott, for advice as to what she should do. Ms. Knott reassured Winona that she had earned the honor, which should not be taken away from the qualified student or her department. She also persuaded Director Oberhansley that Winona should be the valedictorian.

In the early '40s there were no dressing rooms in the clothing department to assure the girls some privacy for fittings, so Frances Knott kept the classroom door locked during sewing classes. Director Oberhansley, concerned about fire safety, insisted that the door be left unlocked. One day he walked into the classroom to the accompaniment of screams and hasty cover-ups. There were no more locked door problems.

The '40s marked the beginnings of the outstanding weaving studio. With the cooperation of Prudence Croft, weaver, the department purchased a 20" four-harness table loom.

During World War II the domestic science department published government bulletins on food conservation in the *Iron County Record*. One directive encouraged women to conserve wheat by cutting down on the amount used, substituting corn meal, rice, oats, barley or potatoes, and to reduce the amount of sugar in recipes by half, substituting honey, molasses, syrup, dates, figs and raisins where possible. The publication appealed to the patriotism of homemakers by explaining that the saving was part of "your war service." Fats were especially needed in the war effort; the suggestion was to cut fat by one-third in recipes, but mothers were warned not to cut down on butter and cream for children.

In 1944-45, during the tenure of C. Aileen Erickson, the need for an expanded cafeteria resulted in moving the sewing laboratory to the

FASHION SHOW,
FRANCIS ELVA
KNOTT,
INSTRUCTOR,
LATE 1930S

second floor. A combined bookstore and eating area for the cafeteria occupied the former sewing lab space. The bookstore was located at the north end, tables and chairs filling the south end. Miss Erickson later was head of home economics education for the state of Utah.

Hazel Parks Urie (1945-47, 1963-74) came to BAC well qualified to teach foods and nutrition and to manage the cafeteria. After graduating from USAC in home economics, she had taught at Monroe High School and had served as supervisor in the food service department at University of Utah. Carrie Leigh assisted Hazel in the cafeteria at BAC. Lunch was the only meal served. The foods department was also frequently called upon to prepare and serve banquets for special occasions, for college visitors and faculty parties. Hazel left the college when she married and returned to teach again in 1963.[7]

*I*n the 1950s the home economics department was not still not aligned with any other department, administering the program within rules, expectations of and responsibilities given by the college administration.[8]

In 1957, when Ada Carpenter and Marie Nelson Kreugar began teaching at BAC, Dr. Royden C. Braithwaite, who had a particular fondness for family living disciplines from his days at Brigham Young University, gave marching orders for the department to upgrade the curriculum, promising full support of the administration. Each teacher was expected to add an additional class to already-full teaching and/or administrative loads, since funding was available to build a new science building but none for additional teachers' salaries.

Carpenter and Kreuger began to work with architect Robert L. Gardner for the department's "spot" in the new building on 300 West, even though they feared that the prevailing attitude of the planning committee was that the home economics department should not be included in the new building. At one point in the planning stage, after much discussion, Hazen Cooley, a constant supporter, stood and calmly announced, "This building will not be constructed unless the home economics department is included."[9]

That ended the discussion. Carpenter and Kreuger visited other colleges in order to effect the best planning for the new south wing, which eventually included a large living room, child development laboratory (preschool), clothing and textile laboratory, a foods laboratory, two classrooms, a large outdoor patio for

ADA CARPENTER IN THE CHILD DEVELOPMENT LAB WITH ANN URIE

classes and preschool playground, laundry storage rooms and rest rooms.

In the early '60s the home economics department became a part of the School of Arts and Letters under the leadership of Dr. Eugene Woolf and Dr. Hal Campbell, who were very supportive of efforts to expand the curriculum. Ada Carpenter began serving CSU in a dual capacity when she became Dean of Women, an assignment that was to utilize her gifts and commitment for over a decade, until her retirement in 1982.

The new science building was "ready" for occupancy in the summer of 1961. The building maintenance crew, who moved the department out of the old science building into the wonderful new quarters, didn't miss a thing. Some of the big pans from the old pantry still held dead cockroaches! The great challenge of that first year was successfully holding classes in rooms that were half-finished and half-furnished. Most of the cooking in a food preparation class was done outside on a grill on the patio or taken home to be baked in ovens at the dormitory. Faculty members improvised as they taught full-capacity classes, which continued to grow. Eventually, the growth forced the move of some classes to amphitheater classrooms on the third floor.

The faculty had, as an ultimate goal, a four-year home economics program. However, Dean Phyllis Snow of USU had not encouraged the CSU home economics department to expect independence or expansion to a four-year program, pointing to the state's traditional commitment to the northern universities, the

ADA DALLEY CARPENTER, HEAD OF FAMILY LIFE DEPARTMENT, 1957-1981

CARMEN CROFT JONES IN THE WEAVING STUDIO, TOP FLOOR OF THORLEY HALL, CIRCA 1960s

reliance of USU on transfers from the junior colleges, the lack of funding for a duplicate program at CSU and to the lower division status of the CSU curriculum. This last negative argument was being eroded by a very real movement toward expansion in CSU's home economics program, based on plans for a live-in home management program, a preschool program they would call the Creativity Lab and groundwork being laid for upper division classes.

The same year the department moved to a brand new facility, 1961, negotiations were being made for acquiring the Bradshaw home on 300 West for the setting of the home management laboratory. Alida Van Groningen organized the program, which brought the department one step closer to a four-year status, and gave many girls valuable, real-life experience in homemaking.

At this same time the Creativity Lab opened the door for enrichment of the child development program. Under the direction of Bonnie Magleby Bishop, the preschool offered a practical laboratory in which college students could observe and work with young children. The lab began its history in one room in the Science Building. Within five years Rea Gubler and others joined Bonnie Bishop; they moved the lab to a permanent home across the street in 1967.

THE CHILD DEVELOPMENT LAB

It was an accepted fact that if CSU were to grow into a four-year, degree-granting school, there must be enrichment of the upper division curriculum, but the faculty had to defend the addition of each new class. For example, the sociology department was not immediately persuaded that home economics should offer an upper division family relationship class when they were already teaching one in their department.

By 1963 planning included the addition of upper division classes in home management, child development, consumer education, foods, and clothing and textiles. Carmen Croft Jones developed the weaving department from one hand loom into a program that had no equal in the country. Students often brought their own looms in order to register for the weaving class, now being held in a classroom filled with 17 looms. Ms. Jones, who had joined the faculty as a part-time teacher, gave full-time service, also working magic in the advanced and creative sewing and tailoring class. Other faculty members also gave more than the required amount of time and effort to build the curriculum, which has been the secret to the success of the programs.

The department and the home economics club continued to handle all the cafeteria and food services on the campus, working closely with the food service managers, who taught quantity food classes, all types of food and table service and table setting for the department. Early in the planning toward building a viable, four-year teaching program it was clear that home economics needed the wonderful cooperation and help of other departments, including elementary and secondary education, chemistry and other sciences, business education, technical education, the art department and social sciences.

The year of independence from USU came in 1967 and with it four-year status for CSU. This did not give every department the power to grant four-year teaching degrees, but it made the move to do so much less complicated. The department finally was able to offer a non-teaching degree in family life, which was heavily weighted with child development and family relations classes. Students were also encouraged to enroll in education classes, and during the decades of the '60s and '70s CSU sent well-qualified students to USU, U of U and BYU to become certified teachers.

When Ada Carpenter retired as head of the department, Alida J. Van Groningen assumed leadership, with the daunting challenge of con-

tinuing the forward momentum and maintaining the remarkable esprit de corps of the faculty. The hiring of new faculty bolstered the teaching staff - Cindy Wright assigned to foods and nutrition and Elisabeth Barker (1981-82) and Sandra Smith to child development and clothing and textiles.

In 1982 the new home economics leadership focused on the goal of teacher certification for their graduates. Certification was another uphill battle for the department. Fortunately the faculty were made of the same stuff of the pioneers of every era of the school. Dr. Terry Alger polished the documents that bore the thrust of the proposal to the Board of Regents. Dr. James Miller was instrumental in establishing the teacher education major program, as well as the home economics minor.

The victory was won in 1983. The Board of Regents voted favorably on the CSU home economics certification proposal at their March meeting. New challenges followed victory as the night the day. The faculty studied the curricula of other institutions, scrutinized their own program and made changes during the 80's, which resulted in substantive progress:

A class, "Problems in Home Management" replaced the experiential home management program, which had suffered from the loss of the home it had been using as a classroom/lab.

Faculty successfully grappled with mastering the fabulous new tool of the computer and made it standard equipment in the department.

State vocational funding fostered the upgrading of equipment in the preschool and sewing labs. The two-year child development program, graduating 15 to 20 students per year, produced many elementary education and home economics graduates.

The department responded to a request in 1985, by the coordinator of the Home Health organization, which had received a Utah state grant for teaching nurses, to provide classes in home management. Beth Bergesen taught the added classes.

In 1985 Lenore Johnson Rasmussen replaced Sandra Smith as director of the home economics education program and supervisor for student teachers. She assumed these responsibilities until she began work on her doctorate at USU, as requested by the administration, in 1987.

In 1986 the CSU administration passed along a budget cut from the Board of Regents to the college departments. Home economics was asked to eliminate a one-half faculty position. After much deliberation, Alida Van Groningen,

department chair, solved the problem by her decision to retire in 1988. This made it possible for Rea Gubler to become a full-time instructor.

The department expanded emphasis in interior design by hiring a part-time teacher and requesting authority, in 1987, to award a two-year interior design degree. Kay Alger actually taught in this area without pay for several years because of the lean budget.

In 1988 Lenore Rasmussen assumed the responsibility of the department of family life upon the retirement of Alida Van Groningen, who had begun her career as an instructor in 1963. She served until 1991, when Bonnie Magelby Bishop took the reins.

When Bonnie Bishop became department head, the department expected to be housed in the new science building that was on the drawing boards. Again, a lean budget altered plans. Concerns about the inaccessibility and inconvenience of being situated on the third floor of the new building gave way to worries about where to hold classes during the remodeling of the existing quarters in the general classroom building. The solution lay in effecting the transformation of the old facility during the spring and summer quarters of 1992-93 to meet earthquake and fire codes, as well as modernization and aesthetics. This plan allowed for the teaching of foods classes during the fall and winter. The temporary move of department offices to the third floor of the old science building was acceptable; the transfer of the sewing lab to a dusty old science lab on the first floor presented more of a challenge.

The remodeled quarters proved an enormous improvement (although the space did not allow for future growth), and housed the entire department in one location. The refurbished family living room became one of the loveliest rooms in the state. The classrooms now boasted ample storage space. A new office complex included an interior design workroom. A new dishwasher and four different kinds of ranges offered modern convenience and a variety of cooking experience to the foods students. The Management Center became the Resource Center. The kitchen itself, left intact because it was still

ALIDA J. VAN GRONINGEN, HEAD OF THE HOME ECONOMICS DEPARTMENT, 1981-88

BONNIE BISHOP, HEAD OF THE HOME ECONOMICS DEPARTMENT, 1991-95

new and attractive, continued to be used by students for catering projects. The sewing lab could not be enlarged but was fitted out with new cabinets, cutting tables, state-of-the-art sewing machines, including computerized machines with computer hardware and a private dressing room.

Meanwhile, the curriculum continued to expand: Kay Killpack Alger continued to teach the new interior design class.

Artis Grady, foods and nutrition, joined the faculty. New classes were added: nutrition of the infant and child, a class for child development and nutrition minors and home economics majors with a nutrition emphasis; fitness and sports nutrition, which met with instant positive response; nutrition in the lifecycle, from prenatal to geriatrics.

Marilynn Brown joined the faculty, replacing Lenore Rasmussen, to oversee teacher education and teach sewing and textiles. A beginning sewing class was added. Flat pattern design was changed to an upper division class; clothing selection and consumption, a new name, was changed dramatically to meet the needs of the new secondary curriculum class, fashion strategies.

Neil Mecham, the first male faculty member in the department, came to teach child development and to be head teacher in the preschool laboratory.

Beverly Anderson joined the staff as department secretary, a boon to the department.

Adjunct professors in foods and nutrition and interior design added depth to the faculty.

*I*n 1990-1995 the home economics department experienced a growth spurt, which occasioned the establishment of overload classes every quarter. All child development courses, including summer school, increased by one-third to one-half. The home economics education classes increased dramatically; the department developed a reputation of producing excellent home economics teachers, almost all graduates finding jobs. Foods and nutrition classes and sewing classes experienced comparable growth.

Department administration of the period credited the hard-working, dedicated teachers, who give 110 percent to their teaching, as a leading factor in the extension of the program. The five years were difficult in terms of coping with the challenges of the remodeling and growth. Expansion of the curriculum and the improvement in the physical facility were singularly gratifying, but the marked growth sig-

naled the need for even more additions to classrooms space and faculty.

The growth in enrollment has continued until the time of this document. Expansion of programs, faculty, and additional classroom space continues to be an ongoing challenge. The physical facilities are wonderful, and esprit de corps is evident in faculty and students. Keeping pace with increased technology and equipment presents a welcome challenge. Home economics is committed to the SUU philosophy of excellence.

During 1995-96 the department initiated a five-year plan for renovation of the preschool, including new paint for the outside and systematic improvement of the interior.

Perhaps the greatest achievement of the year was the approval and establishment of a long-awaited program, the SUU Child Care Center. This facility was founded in connection with the Shakespearean Festival and Student Government and is located at 43 So. 200 W. For nine months of the year it functions as a day care center for the children of students, faculty, and staff, with the festival providing day care during the summers. The self-supporting facility is designed for infants (0-24 months) and children (2-6 years) and will be an invaluable tool for the child development curriculum. The center provides an additional facility for students to complete the traditional required preschool lab hours and also provide lab experience in the area of infant care. Beverly McGarvey was hired as the director of the facility, with Dolly Roy serving as her assistant.

And what about the future?

According to department head Rea Gubler:

We are excited about the future. We face the uncertainty of maintaining technological advancements, converting to the semester system and the continuing influx of students with already over-crowded classes. But we know we will be able to continue our quest for excellence and look forward to working with the high caliber of students who are finding their way to SUU.

Marilynn Brown is hopeful that the name change to family and consumer sciences will help eliminate the stereotype of cooking and sewing in the public mind. She expresses a political concern:

...the 1995 Congress voted to rescind the Carl Perkins Bill which automatically funded money to states (specifically to consumer

homemaking). In the past, our state has used these funds to develop great curriculum and provide inservice to secondary home economics teachers. This money is now gone. The federal government has moved to the block grants for states. This will severely put a damper on possibilities for the consumer homemaking areas to keep up-to-date with inservice and curriculum.

... extension services are being cut drastically. The extension home economists are a big part of our futures. We will have to be certain our voices are heard nationally and on the state level to be sure the home and family programs stay viable and supported. This is critical to keep the home economics department as an integral part of Southern Utah University.

Artis Grady expresses a positive outlook, articulating one concern:

We are seeing growth in the nutrition/foods area, both in terms of offerings and in numbers of students. We see quite a few students majoring in Home Ec non-teaching with an emphasis in nutrition, many more nutrition minors than ever before, and (unfortunately), we provide the prerequisites and then send many terrific students off elsewhere to complete their degrees in dietetics.

At about midpoint in the hundred year history of Southern Utah University, in 1958, the faculty of the BAC home economics department realized that in order to expand the program, they needed to have a "home." A home would function as the setting in which students majoring in home economics could experience, firsthand, what it takes to care for a home and family, using the skills and attitudes they had gained in prerequisite classes. All home economics programs within and outside the state of Utah were facing this same challenge.

When the Stanley Bradshaw home, located next to the campus at 331 West 200 South, became available, Ada Carpenter, the chairperson of the home economics department, pursued the opportunity and started negotiation in the early part of 1958-59. The Bradshaw family offered the home to the college for the sum of $45,000, although the house had been appraised at $67,762. The family stipulated that the house would be used only for students approved by the faculty of the family life department.

In September of 1963 a new teacher, Alida

Van Groningen, was hired to begin the establishment of the new program, home management experiences. Plans included her living in the upstairs apartment of the home. Because of the scarcity of housing available to BAC students, the house was used as a dormitory during the fall quarter of 1963. Winter quarter would be spent in furnishing and equipping the home for the students who would occupy it during the spring quarter.

Furnishing the home was an enormous project. Townspeople responded enthusiastically to requests for help. Cedar Home Furnishing and Leigh Furniture stores donated living room furniture. The Halterman family donated a dining room set that is still being used, at the time of this writing, in the home economics department. Hunter Cowan Hardware store added generously to the housewares inventory, including a lovely dinner service for eight of Lenox china. The gray and white dinner service, used in the home for many years, was still complete and in use in 1996.

The home economics faculty (Ada Carpenter, Carmen Jones and Ella Van Groningen) were happy to use some of the furniture left in the garage by the Bradshaws. The trio refinished some chairs and a buffet, which became the pride and joy of the management house and later a showpiece in the family living room of the home economics department.

In the spring of 1964 the first seven home management students moved into the home, which had become a laboratory for students of the department, including majors and non-majors. The program was open to junior or senior students who had successfully passed required classes in home management, foods

REA RICHINS
GUBLER, CHAIR
OF THE HOME
ECONOMICS
DEPARTMENT,
1995

DINNER AT
THE HOME
MANAGMENT
RESIDENCE,
CIRCA 1960S

and nutrition and meal management.

Graduation requirements for home economics majors included residence for one quarter in the management home. The experience offered valuable practice in handling money, time, and energy and the opportunity for the students to apply principles, acquired in the classroom, in practical situations; make managerial decisions and evaluate their consequences; achieve good relationships with group members; learn how to budget money and learn how to be a graceful hostess.

Students who took this course realized that they had gained more than the mere memorization of theory. They had gained confidence in their ability to make decisions and to supervise others. Students evaluations included these comments:

Our relationships deepened and grew. We learned from each other's mistakes and successes.[10] *The management process is a beneficial and profitable learning circle. The rich experiences of the CSU Management Home will, I am certain, color every aspect of my life.*[11]

It was probably my most enjoyable and learning quarter in college. I only wish that the Management Home could still be there to help teach my daughters when they are old enough. It was a good training for the real world.[12]

During the following 16 years the management home, at full capacity most quarters, successfully fulfilled the goals outlined by faculty and students. But it was not to last.

Ella Van Groningen, who had actually lived in an upstairs apartment of the home during its entire 17-year history, has, in retrospect, made her own evaluation:

In evaluating the program I can see that it was time-consuming for the students to be living at the house for a full quarter, especially for those that had to work to pay their college expenses. Other universities and colleges had begun to change and to eliminate the requirements of a living management home for a full quarter. They started to replace it with a seminar course. This is done now at Southern Utah University as a regular part of the curriculum." However, she recalls this period as ..."*a most productive, but also as a fun and challenging time...When we moved out in 1980, we left with many good memories and the knowledge that the program had been success-*ful for many of our students.*[13]

In 1979 SUSC President Orville Carnahan determined that the house was to become a home for presidents of the college. The department negotiated to have the old child development center remodeled to become a Management Center. In July of 1980 the house was vacated; everything which could be used in a Management Center went to the family life department. The students no longer lived together as a family, but occupied the center during lunch and dinner hours. This format continued for three years. In 1984 the class continued as a seminar.

After the migration of the department across campus in 1962 into the new Science building on 300 West, the early child development program, called the Creativity Laboratory, was about to be born. The lab was the brainchild of Director Braithwaite and department chair Ada D. Carpenter. In fact, it was a dream come true for the director. The infant program was located in the south wing of the new SUSC science center in an attractive room decorated and furnished to suit the needs of four-year old occupants. A special two-way mirror enabled college students to observe their subjects without disturbing any activity.

A large, fenced-in patio area adjacent to the indoor facility completed the preschool setting. The patio featured a circulating water fountain, the sculpture of a young child holding a large frog with water pouring from his mouth. One of the children told his mother, *"I know where the water comes from—the boy just squeezes the frog."*

At the earliest stage of the lab a live fox occupied a very secure pen on the patio under the trees, but when Chris Cooley announced to her mother that *"the fox is a pretty bit stinky,"* the fox was expelled from the preschool. Another year the lively scene included a monkey, but when the fire department had to be called a few times to bring their ladder and rescue the truant monkey from a tree, the monkey went too.

Townspeople donated a few toys for the new program, but due to a short budget, much of the play centered on a big sand pile, a few logs, a pond and the forest of trees. When the children brought things from home for sharing, they learned as they interacted with each other, and especially loved walking trips where they experienced the larger world of the campus.

Genevieve Gardner donated her services as a

nurse, checking the "little students" each morning. She walked to the lab each day, with her dog, to see if each child had clean hands, teeth, and germ-free throats. This had a positive effect on their health and cleanliness and offered fun and valuable experiences.

In 1966 Bonnie Bishop became a "permanent fixture" in the SUSC preschool; this was the last year for just one lab, as in 1967 the program added a second location. In 1971 the department acquired Miss Wanda's Day Care building. Then the preschool moved across the street on 300 West. "Miss Bonnie" was the prime mover in developing the finest college laboratory preschool in the state.

Bonnie Bishop describes the program:

It was a dream come true. [The room] was so large. We were able to paint it nice bright colors and make it a really great room. The only bad part was that we lost the observation room. We still do not have one but it is large enough that students can come in and observe and the children don't even notice them.

Several years after we moved into the new building, we were able to put in a new playground. We also put in the new fence which made it a lot safer, although hard on the teacher that locked herself out of the building. We received a shed built by high school students for our outside toys. It has been a wonderful school over the years. We, as teachers and students, have helped keep it that way by cleaning and/or painting the school and equipment at the end of each quarter.

When we moved into the new building we had to get a new teacher for the afternoon lab. For several years that teacher was a college student. Several were student teachers..

In 1973 Karen Clark took my place as head teacher (I took a year off to have a baby). She was right out of college but was an excellent teacher who brought new ideas. She stayed two years. It was great to have a real teacher in both labs. At the end of the second year (1975) Karen left for Oregon. In 1975-76 Rea Gubler became the teacher for the afternoon preschool.

In 1994 we hired our first male preschool teacher. It has been nice to have a male teacher for children to interact with. His name is Neil Mecham. We are hoping that by having a male teacher, we might encourage more male students to seek a degree in child development.

It has been an exciting 30 years at SUU. The lab has seen a lot of changes, but some things remain the same, like oatmeal in the water

table, dolls in the playhouse, clay on the table and lots of excited and creative college students ready and willing to try to be the best teacher ever.*

During the school year 1982-83 the Board of Regents granted the home economics department the authority to award the four-year certification of home economics teachers at the secondary level.

The first meeting for discussion of the request for four-year certification was in January of 1983. This was not the first time that the department had made the proposal, but it appeared to be the best year for success. The home economics faculty had total support from the administration and the education department with President Gerald Sherratt and Provost Terry Alger lending their efforts to find the right strategy to approach the Regents. The fact that Dr. Eugene Woolf had been employed for two years at the office of the Board of Regents certainly helped to clarify the process. The school districts of southern Utah made their own request for the proposal, since they felt that home economics teachers trained at the northern universities were not staying to teach long enough to make their programs successful and, therefore, not giving stability to their programs.

In March of that year, at their next meeting, the Board of Regents voted in favor of four-year certification of CSU home economics students. The department properly celebrated this important milestone, but the success signalled new challenges. The faculty went to work to analyze the curriculum in order to make possible revisions and reforms, according to the needs of the students and to the requirements of the state.

Ella Van Groningen records:

I felt very fortunate to have the help of Title III during the summer of 1983. This made it possible for me to make on-campus visitations to several colleges and universities in the state of Utah and surrounding states to compare, do research, and analyze their home economics programs and curricula."[14]

HOME ECONOMICS FACULTY, CIRCA 1970. L TO R: BONNIE MAGLEBY BISHOP, ADA CARPENTER DALLEY, ALIDA VAN GRONINGEN, CARMEN CROFT JONES, HAZEL PARKS URIE

In l984 the first four students received their certification in home economics: Juanita Esplin, Matthew Kreitzer, Janice Larsen, and Joan Plat.

In 1985 the department certified six students; six in 1986; five in 1987; and in 1988 seven students were certified. From 1988 to 1996 the home economics education program continued to meet the needs of a number of students at SUSC/SUU. Those certifying during those years include two students in 1989; one student in 1990; 10 students in 1991; six students in 1992; six students in 1993; two students in 1994; six students in 1995 and eight students in 1996.

Some former graduates of the department returned for certification. Cedar City residents were happy to be able to graduate and certify at SUSC, remaining at home with their families. Four-year certification had certainly added to the stability of the home economics programs at the secondary level in the southern part of the state. The department had worked well with other institutions who accepted certification for SUSC home economics majors.

As the department needed an additional teacher to teach home economics education classes and supervise the student teachers, and since no money was available yet, Ada Carpenter came back, without pay, to do the supervising for the first year, 1984-85. Sandra Smith then took over, teaching the home economics education classes and supervising the student teachers in 1985-86.

The next year Lenore Rasmussen replaced Ms. Smith, teaching for two years at SUU before beginning her doctorate at USU in Logan. She returned to head the department for one year, leaving in 1990 to become an extension agent for Iron County.

Marilynn Brown oversees the home economics education program at the time of this history in 1997. The program has steadily grown to an average of eight to ten students. This number, of course, does not include students who graduate in general home economics or in the two-year programs of child development and interior design. She summarizes recent developments:

During 1992 two new courses were added to the required curriculum for majors. They are Computer applications in home economics and residential housing and interiors. Students have continued to find employment. Three graduates are currently teaching in Nevada, and others teach throughout the state of Utah. One graduate is teaching in Hawaii.

At the 1994 national American Home Economics Association (AHEA) meeting held in San Diego, California, the AHEA voted to change its name to the American Association of Family and Consumer Sciences (AAFCS). The state association voted in 1995 to change its name to coincide with the national; thus, it became the Utah Association of Family and Consumer Sciences (UAFCS). The secondary schools now have changed their department names to family and consumer sciences.

The SUU home economics department voted to change both the department and the teaching major name to family and consumer sciences.

Our majors are active in the pre-professional state student association of UAFCS. They hold state offices and we continue to have an active student club on campus. Our graduates are sought after by principals and have made a good reputation for SUU and our department.

During the late 1970s and 1980s the Utah Department of Vocational Education supplied grant monies to the home economics department for classes to enrich the lives of women whose husbands were attending SUSC. These classes were held in the evening and were always popular, especially to the young women who needed to "get away" from children for a few hours. Classes were non-credit, and if they did not fill up with student wives, others were allowed to attend. The outstanding feature of the classes was that they reached Native American women along with wives from other cultures. In fact, the most enthusiastic learner was Hazel Staheli, a senior citizen who took every class offered in the program.

The first club organized under the title Home Economics Club in the early 1900's gave added evidence of the deep commitment of the community to the school. The women of the town were intimately acquainted with the students, for they lived in their homes. The trials and vicissitudes of young people living away from home or struggling with difficulty did not go unnoticed. When young people could not meet the meager requirements of fees and expenses, townswomen were the first to become aware. Very early they organized themselves into a club to raise funds for the assistance of worthy students, to do other good works and to provide cultural advancement for themselves and the young women students. This was the purpose for the organization. Almost at once they established "The College Loan Fund" which loaned money to students who might otherwise have had to leave school.

The women were generally concerned for the welfare of the students, especially the young women of the school. They were active in counseling young women students and kept a watchful eye over their well-being.

At first the club of townswomen was a separate entity, the membership made up of the matrons of the community. Later it evolved into a joint association of women students and townswomen. From 1914 until the late '30s the group evidently included students and the women of Cedar City interested in promoting the general welfare of the students and enjoying activities together.

In 1914-15 the membership was 50. In 1916-17 the club had only 17 members. The advisor to the club, Jean Cox, was chosen by the members and called "Guardian." They had a "Creed of Home Economics" which read:

Home Economics Club stands for dignity, truth and right living, and every girl who joins the club pledges herself to live up to this standard.

In December of 1921, an article appeared in the *Iron County Record* to the women of Cedar City. An excerpt of the article reads as follows:

To the Women of Cedar City
The Presidency of the Home Economics Club desires to send a good wish to all its members, past and present, at this Yule Tide - a wish that much good and happiness will come to you in this and all the coming years.

We have existed as an organization for many years and have striven always to be an asset to our community. . . We have lived and grown strong. Just that everyone may know, I want to tell you that in the bazaar held last winter, the sum of $500 was raised for a College Loan fund for deserving students. We do appreciate the splendid response we received on every hand in the raising of so fine an amount. This year we want to add to that fund.

The club is proud, too, to have had a hand in the getting of that splendid apparatus for the children's playground, both in committee work and by money contributed. Now, we have in mind some good work we want to do

that will be fine for our home town, and we invite every woman who is interested in her home, schools and town to join us.

In addition to our outside activities we have an excellent program mapped out. A short course in citizenship, including discussions on subjects designed to make us better citizens, will be given. Supplementing this will be some miscellaneous topics of special interest to women and an occasional literary lesson. These, with music and refreshments, will give both profit and pleasure.

Mrs. Nellie T. Pace, Pres.

The following year, in another article in the *Iron County Record*, the leadership of the club invited townswomen to participate in bolstering the interest-free College Loan Fund, designed to prevent students from having to leave school to go to work. The BAC faculty joined forces with the club in holding a spring festival of music, dancing and a review of the book, *Enoch Arden,* featuring the sale of flowers, refreshments and homemade candies. BAC students canvassed the town for tickets to the event, at the cost of 50 cents.

After 1922 there was no mention, in yearbooks, of the home economics club until the spring of 1932, which proclaimed that the home economics club had been organized in the fall of 1931. There must have been a ten-year gap. The club had twenty-three members, and the advisor was Virginia Chamberlain. The outstanding event was a formal tea in honor of the girls' mothers. The "Creed of Home Economics," as printed in the yearbook of 1932, read as follows:

Membership in the club includes all people at the school interested in the field of home economics. Its purpose is to promote the interest and activities of the girls along this line.

The next year an announcement of the loan fund appeared in the 1933-34 yearbook, and in 1934-35 was also included in the school's catalog:

The Home Economics club of Cedar City has created for the benefit of BAC students who need financial aid while at school, a rather substantial fund. It is generally reserved for advanced students who would be compelled to leave school for financial reasons. Since it is an emergency measure, large amounts are not lent to any one student. Any worthy and needy

HOME
ECONOMICS
CLUB, CIRCA
1970s

student whose school record indicates a seriousness of purpose may apply for a loan from this fund. Students who desire to make use of the fund should consult Mrs. S. J. Foster or Miss Rhea Johnson, instructor in the department of home economics.

Another note in the catalog explained other activities of the club:

The Cedar City Home Economics club, many of the members of which are B.N.S. - BAC Alumni, has the welfare of the BAC students at heart. This club is doing much to make the student's life pleasant and homelike. Its members eagerly co-operate with the school on all questions of student welfare. There is also a standing committee of the faculty, the welfare committee, whose duty it is to look after the social phases of the students' school life both on and off the campus. They counsel and advise by means of individual meetings with students whenever they deem it necessary.

Perhaps, by this time, the membership of the club was largely made up of home economics graduates who stayed interested in the welfare of BAC students and in coordinating activities with the college and the domestic science department. In 1936 there were 34 members and in 1937 only six. After that time the home economics club members were students and associated faculty.[15]

For the next two decades the club was open

to any girls interested in home economics. Annual journeys to state conventions and places of educational interest enriched the experience of women students. They were bound by their enthusiasm for good works, much the same as the early members who had organized the club. In 1945 they sold cookies and hot dogs at ball games to fund their project of sending Christmas gifts to children in war-torn Europe. Through many years the group was a center of elevating and social activity for young women students.

By 1964 the membership of 15 had adopted a new policy: "The Home Economics Club is for girls on campus who are majors or minors in Home Economics." In 1966 the club changed its name to Sigma Delta Omicron, the name used by the national club, which sounded more prestigious. They engaged in state and national activities. The yearbook of 1967 printed the following paragraph:

Sigma Delta Omicron is College of Southern Utah's Home Economics Club designed for majors and minors in this field and girls with an interest in family life. Being connected with the National Home Economics Association, it is the only nationally affiliated organization on campus. Sigma Delta Omicron is also associated with the Utah State Home Economics Association and enjoys many of the privileges.

Sigma Delta Omicron members routinely attended the winter student conferences as well as home economics conventions in the spring, usually held in the northern part of the state. Sigma Delta Omicron hosted winter conferences at BAC in 1975, 1983, and again in 1990.

Beginning in 1970 the club began to undertake a great variety of catering projects in order to finance convention travel.[16] The legacy of ambitious projects, begun by concerned women almost a century before the publication of this history, has been amply preserved in the traditions of the club.

Rea Gubler projects the future:

Delta Sigma Omicron has continued many traditions. . . Delta Sigma Omicron is growing and will probably undergo a few changes as the department converts to the semester format and makes the transition to the new name of family and consumer sciences.

One may hope that anticipated transition will not diminish the values of the tradition.

CHAPTER XXI

Science & Mathematics

"*Well, pull out the equipment from the stock room and let's find out how it works.*"

George LeBaron

From its 1897 beginning, a science tradition was established at Branch Normal School.[1] Under the influence of George W. Decker, science and mathematics became a major thrust of the curriculum. The first graduates of BNS had studied across a broad spectrum of science courses, completing required classes in botany, physiology, zoology, physics, chemistry, geology, mineralogy, physical geography, plane geometry and algebra.

Mr. Decker, as he was called by colleagues and students, taught most of the natural science courses. During the first decade a number of science and mathematics teachers came for short periods. In 1900, BNS hired John H. Tipton as its first physics teacher. A student later described him as a "sedate, loveable little Englishman with a glossy black beard."[2] That same year, H. Claude Lewis became the school's first teacher hired specifically to teach mathematics. Mr. Decker had taught the mathematics classes until that time. In keeping with the practice of duties expanded to fill whatever need arose, Mr. Lewis also served as school registrar. In 1902 William T. Ward became the first chemistry teacher. All were gone by 1905, replaced by others with similar short tenure. When Mr. Decker became principal of the school in 1904, he still remained the primary science teacher. By 1909 his duties as principal required all his time and energy, but he was the person most responsible for the establishment of the science tradition during SUU's formative years. He was also the key individual in establishing a building for the sciences.

Science classes were first held in Old Main, along with all other classes. In 1903 the Utah State Legislature appropriated $70,000 for the next school year's maintenance budget. Half of that money was to be used to construct a new science building and to purchase new equipment for it. The new building, which was completed by the fall of 1904, became the center of science activity at the school for the next 57 years. The building, which still stands, is now called the Braithwaite Liberal Arts Center. It was called the science building from 1904 to 1961; after 1961 it was referred to as the Old Administration building.

In 1913, when Branch Normal School became Branch Agricultural College, Mr. Decker left his post at the school.[3] Though he left teaching, he had been instrumental in the preparation of Parley Dalley, the young man who would become the driving force behind the science tradition.

In the fall of 1909 BNS hired Parley Dalley, a 1905 BNS graduate, to become the full-time science teacher. Dalley had just graduated from the University of Utah in chemistry that spring. He became "Mr. Science" at BNS and BAC for the next 45 years. The physical science department still honors his name by awarding a worthy student with the Parley Dalley Scholarship each spring.

Mr. Dalley was a solo player for his first few years, as he worked to establish the sciences at

GEORGE W.
DECKER,
1904

Branch Agricultural College. In the fall of 1920 David L. Sargent was hired to teach agriculture and biology. Professor Sargent, an energetic young man of superb intellect and character, was a graduate of Utah State University in agriculture. He quickly joined his efforts with those of Mr. Dalley, expanding the offerings in biology. He became "Mr. Biology" at BAC and remained until his retirement in 1953. In 1922 Arthur Fife joined the BAC faculty in agricultural engineering and mathematics. He stayed at the school until 1934 when he left to pursue a distinguished career in New Mexico.[4]

In 1938 Theron Ashcroft joined the science faculty. Again the school was the beneficiary of an outstanding mind and character. Ashcroft had obtained a degree in civil engineering at Utah State just two years before. He was an innovative and creative contributor, serving with distinction for more than thirty years. Ashcroft retired in 1970. In the first 50 years of the school's history there were only five faculty members who served ten years or longer, all of these from the sciences: Decker, Dalley,

Sargent, Fife and Ashcroft.

Professors Dalley and Sargent served as division chairs in the physical and biological sciences from 1924 until their retirements. Both realized that they needed further schooling to keep abreast of new developments in the sciences. Dalley obtained a masters degree from the University of California in 1925, and Sargent obtained his masters degree from Utah State in 1927. Their advanced degrees enabled the offering of junior and senior level courses at BAC.

Beginning with the 1936-37 school year, the sciences were authorized to offer senior division courses in agronomy, animal husbandry, and agricultural economics. The change made it possible for BAC agricultural students to obtain a degree in these areas with one additional year at Utah State Agricultural College at Logan, Utah. The 1936-37 school year was also the first year a full-year calculus sequence was offered at BAC, Parley Dalley being its first teacher.

When BAC Director Henry E. Oberhansley died of a heart attack in April 1945, President E. G. Peterson of Utah State Agricultural College asked Parley Dalley to serve as acting director until a new director could be appointed. He served as both director and division chair until July 1945.

After 20 years with just two divisions in the sciences, a new structure was instituted and three new divisions added. This was a significant broadening of the sciences. T. Donald Bell was to chair the division of agriculture, David L. Sargent chaired the biological sciences, Theron Ashcroft chaired engineering, C. Wayne Cook chaired forestry and physical science was chaired by Parley Dalley.

These five divisions remained at the school until the 1959-60 school year when engineering and physical science were combined.

In 1945 World War II was at an end. Dr. Daryl Chase had become director of the school. A new era in science at BAC was about to begin.

The conclusion of World War II, in 1945, brought thousands back to the classroom throughout the country. At BAC it was no different; enrollments surged and the need for additional faculty was evident. The college was fortunate to attract dedicated and capable new teachers. In 1946, George LeBaron was hired to teach radio classes and physics. That same year,

D.C. (Dutch) Schmutz arrived to teach agricultural economics. The next year BAC added Glenn Wahlquist in agriculture and biology. In 1948, V.R. Magleby brought more expertise in agriculture, and Conrad Hatch was hired to teach chemistry and mathematics. In 1949 Max Robinson became part of the science faculty, further strengthening agriculture and biology. In 1950 Darrell Matthews was hired to replace Wayne Cook who left the college after six years. He brought expertise in sheep production and management. All but Max Robinson would remain through their entire careers at the college.

Some new courses were added, including theory of equations and differential equations in mathematics, (both essential for transfer students to USU) mathematics in engineering; radio circuits, radio electronics, and receivers and transmitters in physics. The radio emphasis resulted from demands arising from the experiences of a nation at war.

The war may have influenced the rather unsophisticated scholars in other ways. Professor Blair Maxfield, who was a student in the late 1940s, recalls an interesting experiment in George LeBaron's physics class:

The physics room was on the bottom floor of the science building (Old Administration) in the south east corner. Just above was the chemistry lecture, taught by Prof. Dalley. In the same building were the administration offices and the office of Director Driggs.

The physics class was taught by Prof. George LeBaron. It was a rather small class consisting of John Brown, Walter Gibson, Neil Rawlinson, Howard Bardwell, Gerald Heppler, Thomas Olds and I. Whenever we questioned anything, Prof. LeBaron would just say, "Well, pull out the equipment from the stock room and let's find out how it works."

This particular day we were talking about muzzle velocity of guns, and how it could be measured. We thought the measurement method was rather simple and questioned that it could be measured

that easily. Prof. LeBaron said, "Well, who has a gun? We'll set up an experiment and see if we can measure it and how close we can come to the advertised measurement." I announced that I had my deer rifle back at my apartment, and so was advised to bring it and the next day we would try the experiment.

My rifle was a 250-300 savage, a rifle with a rather high muzzle velocity. We rigged up the pendulum with a 4x4 block of wood about six inches long suspended on a string and a ruler set up vertically so that we could measure the height of the arc that the pendulum would swing. We then dismantled one of the bullets, so that we could measure very carefully the weight of the lead. I was to fire the bullet into the the end of the wood block, and the others in the class were to watch for the measurement of the height of the arc.

I laid on the floor and fired the rifle into the block. We had not anticipated the tremendous roar that the rifle would make in a closed room. All of Prof. Dalley's chemistry class above, stood up and looked out the south windows toward the chemistry lab building to see if that had been blown up. I think Director Driggs must have been standing outside the door, because he was in our room before the smoke had a chance to clear the barrel of the gun.

We got a talking to and were instructed that we could not perform that kind of experiment again. But the experiment did work, our figures for muzzle velocity came out very nearly the same as that advertised. I know we will not soon forget that experiment.[5]

After that year Professor LeBaron duplicated the experiment using .22 caliber rifles which did not generate such a large noise in a closed room.

In 1952 Parley Dalley officially retired after 43 years at the institution. The next year, Professor David Sargent retired, having taught for 33 years. Both men would continue to teach on a part-time basis for

GLENN
WAHLQUIST

HURRICANE
MESA
PROJECT

more than a decade. Parley Dalley taught his last class winter quarter of 1962 and David Sargent taught his last class spring quarter of 1967.

Both professors were very involved in the celebration of the school's 50th birthday anniversary in 1947. They served on the celebration committee, and Professor Sargent was chair of the pageant committee. Professors Dalley and Sargent also continued with their administrative duties as division chairs in the physical science and biological sciences until June 1954. Both professors had a profound impact on the development of the sciences at the college. As Professor Dalley's family had before, the Sargent family established an endowment for a scholarship in the name of Professor Sargent. The life science department continues to award the scholarship to a worthy student each year. Professors Glenn Wahlquist and Conrad Hatch became division chairs upon the retirements of Sargent and Dalley.

The late 1950s brought another wave of new science faculty and significant administrative changes. In 1957 Harl Judd (engineering) joined the physical science faculty. The next year, Phil Ogden (forestry)and Lawrence Cooper (geology) were added to the science faculty. In 1959 Ron Doney and Don Blue (geology) were added to the CSU science faculty, followed in 1960 by Franklin Faux (chemistry) and Steve Moss (mathematics). Professor Moss was the first professor with a master's degree in mathematics on the staff. Most of these new teachers remained less than five years, but Harl Judd and Lawrence Cooper gave the school their working lives and made wonderful contributions for the rest of their academic careers.

Early in the 1960s a project was offered to the mathematics department at Branch Agricultural College, enlisting their involvement with the United States government. On a flat mesa high above the desert floor and near the tiny town of Virgin, Utah, the government had established a

testing site to measure the effects upon pilots, of high speed ejection from jet aircraft. It involved a sled, in which was strapped a dummy. The sled and dummy were propelled several miles along a track at high velocity. The track ended at the edge of the mesa, the sled came to an abrupt halt , the parachuted dummy was hurled out over the edge of the mesa, the chute opened, gently lowering the dummy to the desert below. When the dummy was retrieved it was tested for various physiological effects.

A number of cameras placed along the track provided time and distance data on film, from which the students made calculations. Students, supervised by Professor Theron Ashcroft used numerical analysis to solve three-dimensional partial differential to determine the trajectory of the dummy. No computers, just a dedicated teacher leading students through a remarkable adventure.

While the long-range results of the testing was never quite clear to the department personnel, it provided a memorable experience for young mathematicians.

In 1959 the divisions of engineering and physical science were merged. Professors Ashcroft and Hatch were appointed as co-chairs, where they served in tandem until 1966. The next year, 1960, the divisions of agriculture, forestry and biological science were combined, and Professor D.C. Schmutz was appointed chair. Professor Phil Ogden left the college and Professor Wahlquist went on leave. Wahlquist had brought rich experience to the college from his two-year appointment by the U. S. government as an agronomy specialist in Iran in 1952-1954.

The year 1960 brought the first Ph.D. to a professor in the science department, Conrad Hatch having completed his doctorate in chemistry from Oregon State University that spring. In the fall CSU hired Professor Wesley Larsen, who became the first Ph.D.-educated professor at the school in biology.

Dr. Larsen gives a picture of the department in 1960:

The biology-physiology classroom was located in the northwest corner of the building where the Braithwaite Art Gallery was later established. It was on ground level so that when the class bell sounded, students were likely to enter or exit through the tall, open windows on the west side. A wonderful room, light, airy, with that pungent smell of formaldehyde from

Teaching at the University has been a love affair for me, especially during the sixties and early seventies. In those days people that served here were like family. Buildings and departmental affiliations didn't separate us from each other. We felt so much ownership, and it caused us to give of ourselves in ways that would be laughed at today—faculty plays and assemblies and work days on campus or at the college farm. We even liked faculty meetings. The Christmas parties and the spring breakfasts were the social highlights of my life. There is a bond among so many of us that have been involved here for these many years. It feels both strong and tender and involves so much respect. I fill with love when I think of people like Blaine Johnson, Kent Myers, Con Hatch, Harl and Anne Judd. Gary Giles, Al Tait, Craig Jones and all the others. I would buy a ticket and drive for miles to hear Cleo Petty play the piano. I honor these people for their devotion, for their talented service and for their traits of character. But I love them because they understood that education has as much to do with love and humanity as it does with facts, figures and skills.

I feel this especially about Royden Braithwaite. He taught me about love and appreciation as no other person I have known. He knew how to make us feel wanted, and it carried over into our classroom teaching and preparation. The evening after I learned of his death, I spent an hour just strolling about the campus, wrapped in my memories, feelings, respect and tears.

There have been discouraging times along with the richness. During the seventies and early eighties salary increases did not come close to keeping up with inflation, and for a nineteen-year span we had no increase in mathematics faculty, during which time the enrollment doubled. Large classes and heavy teaching loads were routine, and sometimes the paper-grading burden was almost overwhelming. There were times when we weren't sure that anybody knew or that anybody appreciated.

Conditions have improved greatly over the last seven or eight years, and I find joy in reflecting upon this place that is so very dear to me.

Dr. Kimball Jones

---

many generations of animal dissections.

My first anatomy-embryology class of nine students made up in quality for lack of quantity. Among the students were Roger Lewis, Chad Halversen, Kent Farnsworth, Roger Halterman and George Manning, all to become prominent medical doctors. The class also included Duane Gubler, now a research scientist and official with the Center for Disease Control. Duane took his doctorate at Johns Hopkins and has saved thousands, if not millions, from the ravages of tropical diseases in Indonesia, Puerto Rico and other tropical regions.[6]

In 1961 L. Kimball Jones came on board to teach mathematics. He was the first professionally trained mathematician at the school, and his coming to the campus was the advent of a distinguished teaching career. Jones developed into a legend among the mathematicians of the state and the nation. Known as an advocate for his students, he also kept them alert. He is noted for impromptu enlivenment to otherwise staid subjects. Writing formulas across his black-

board, one day, he ran out of space. Without a pause, he wrote all the way across the adjoining painted door and into the corner of the wall.

When, in 1965, the four-year liberal arts status was assured, Kim Jones became the author of the math curriculum, which was then reviewed by other members of the department. His expertise in math education has placed him in a position of respect among his colleagues.

With the surge of new and enthusiastic faculty members, three of them with doctorates, there was little question that the sciences were on an upward thrust, but the most significant event came with the construction of a new science building.

After all the years of teaching in the 1904 facility, with students entering and exiting informally through windows, they left the endearing odor of formaldehyde and moved to a wonderful new building, devoted to the sciences. There would be, in the next decade, significant changes.

The new building and the expanded faculty enlarged the possibilities, but the move to obtain four-year status was exhilarating and

CSU
Physics
Lab

Richard
Dotson

challenging. The authorization that had come from the Coordinating Council on Higher Education and the USU Board of Trustees had included a qualifying phrase: "...as soon as enrollment justifies and the availability of funds will permit." The department scurried to do all they could to aid the effort.

Three major issues needed to be addressed by the college: development of four-year bachelor degree programs, development and recruitment of qualified faculty, and funding for these changes.

Dr. Richard Thompson, then serving as academic vice president, sent an encouraging missive through the ranks of his faculty colleagues:

All of us know that significant budget increases result only from significant increases in enrollment...not from plans for future progress, however well-laid those plans may be. Thus we must work to the end of holding as many students as we can for as long as we can do that student any good. We must dig deeply into our own resources, and we must do everything humanly possible to increase the instructional efficiency of the existing staff. This is not a hopeless task. We have begun to move. . . time and effort will, whatever the handicaps under which we may labor, keep our students here for upper division work when the necessary classes are offered.[7]

The CSU science faculty chose to develop four-year degree programs in botany, zoology, chemistry, and mathematics. In addition, and without much additional expense, they included composite teacher education programs in the biological and physical sciences. They also decided to establish minors in physics and earth science. This was in addition to the minors that go with those four majors. Biology added two faculty: Professor Brent Palmer in 1963 and Dr. Russell Anderson in 1964. Doctors Larsen and Anderson were primarily responsible for writing the curriculum for the botany and zoology programs. Dr. Hatch was the principal author of the new chemistry program, and Professors Jones and Moss for the mathematics program. Professors LeBaron and Cooper designed the minor programs in physics and earth sciences. Professors Judd and Ashcroft revised the engineering program and Professors Schmutz, Wahlquist, Magleby and Mathews revised the agriculture program.

By 1965 not only was CSU authorized to proceed with the four-year programs, but it was funded by the Utah State Legislature for the necessary faculty expansion. Five new professors joined the science faculty in 1965. They included Jo Ann Sessions (biology), James Bowns (forestry), Richard Kimball (engineering), Joseph Comp (chemistry) and Richard Tebbs (mathematics). The next year an additional five science faculty were added. They included David Braegger (genetics), Paul Burgoyne (zoology), Merrill R. Jones (physics), Lee Morrell (chemistry) and B. Al Tait (botany). The ten additions brought the total science faculty to 23. Interestingly, all ten would stay at the institution for the rest of their academic careers. Four of the new faculty (Sessions, Comp, Jones, and Morrell) came with the Ph.D. degree. In the next decade or so, Wahlquist, Bowns, Palmer, Burgoyne, Tait, and Kimball completed terminal degrees.

Following this dramatic faculty expansion, there were eight appointments in the next five years. Most came as replacements for departing faculty or for faculty on leave. They included: Preston Leonard (mathematics) in 1967, Willis Werner (mathematics) in 1968, Blair Maxfield (geology) in 1969, Dean Vest (environmental biology) in 1969, Max Rose (mathematics) in 1969, James Cotts (mathematics) in 1970, Steven Heath (mathematics) in 1970 and Richard Dotson (zoology) in 1971. Only Cotts, Dotson, Heath and Maxfield would make a career at the school.

The departments were significantly altered with the retirements of two men who had been institutions at the institution. The year 1970 brought the retirement of Clarence "Dutch" Schmutz after 24 years, and Theron Ashcroft who had been a tradition of 32 years. Both men served with distinction and provided leadership in science at the school for many years. In 1980 a new observatory on the west side of Cedar City was named the Ashcroft Observatory. It was the first college structure to be named after one of its faculty.

One of the significant events of the 1960s in science at CSU was the appointment in January 1966, of Dr. Wes Larsen as director of the Pre-College Course Content Improvement Program at the National Science Foundation in Washington D.C. Professor Larsen's twenty-month experience in the nation's capitol brought an important opportunity to the CSU science faculty. Dr. Larsen wrote:

Taking advantage of what was learned in Washington D.C., I had science faculty trained in learning projects —V.R. Magleby in elementary science; Lawrence Cooper and Blair Maxfield, the Earth Science Project; Russell Anderson, Science, A Process Approach; Richard Tebbs, Minimast Project; and David Braegger, Elementary School Science. Each was sent during the summer to training institutes. For example, LeBaron and Morrell taught black students in the ghettos of New York City.

For about four or five years we held on-campus training and field institutes for teachers in Clark and Lincoln Counties in Nevada, and all counties of southern Utah and northern Arizona. Leadership schools accompanied the Institutes involving principals and superintendents as well as their science teachers. All the training had follow-up assessments for success. With government budget-cutting, the Institutes gradually dwindled. However, there was another spin-off. Jim Bowns and Blair Maxfield held on-site field seminars for elementary and secondary teachers in rural Utah counties. There they learned the geology and botany of their own specific locality.[8]

Enrollment was, and always had been, a challenge. Since the beginning of the school, faculty members assumed as much responsibility as administrators for finding ways to keep students coming. Dr. Harl Judd remembers some innovative methods used by science faculty:

During the formative years of the four-year status, we needed students. We needed students in the worst way. The administrations of the high schools of the state were not eager to have recruiting teams from the colleges interrupting their classes, and rightly so. However, high school students needed to know what programs were offered at the colleges so they could choose which institution they would attend. The teachers were not opposed to using college expertise to improve their programs, and so we came up with a variety of ways that we could accomplish that,which would allow us contact with students.[9]

The Science Fair was an excellent program that brought high school students to the campus. It was initially begun by Theron Ashcroft, later expanded by Joe Comp. The first Science Fair planning meeting was December 6, 1960, at Bulloch's Cafe. Six high school teachers were invited to meet with the science faculty, who stretched their budget to buy lunch at a cost of $25.95 for the 13 participants.

Dr. Judd remembers even more innovative programs:

The Bridge Breaking Contest was another program designed to allow us contact with the high school students. Students were required to purchase a bridge kit which included balsa wood struts, two base boards cut from screen door moulding, a tube of glue, a cardboard deck, the dimensions of the testing machine and the rules of the contest. The testing machine was taken to the high schools and the bridges were weighed and tested to failure. The highest breaking load was declared the winner. The students who were on the ball would have their bridges finished in sufficient time for the glue to dry. Some students waited until the last minute to build their bridges and then tried many different ways to dry them rapidly. One student built his bridge late and put it in his mother's oven to dry, where it caught fire and burned. These bridge-breaking sessions were usually conducted in front of the whole student body. Cash prizes were offered at each school and the over-all winner received a scholarship to the college.[10]

RICHARD TEBBS (TOP) AND DAVID BRAEGGER

Professor Wesley Larsen introduced the Visiting Scientist program in 1968. Each of the

PHYSICAL
SCIENCES
FACULTY,
1972

science faculty were asked to prepare one or two lectures which could be presented to school science and mathematics classes. Letters were sent to schools throughout Utah, southern Nevada and northern Arizona with the topics which the faculty were willing to present. This program also allowed science faculty an opportunity to recruit new students and get acquainted with science and mathematics teachers in the region surrounding the college. The program operated into the mid-1970s and brought a number of superb students to the institution.

BIOLOGY SCIENCES
FACULTY, 1972

That same year, Dr. Ken Cook from the University of Utah approached Dr. Judd about establishing a seismograph station on campus. The University of Utah provided $10,000 for the finishing of a basement room in the new library then under construction. The installation included x, y, and vertical seismonitors. The recording device paper had to be changed every 24 hours. Professors Judd, Jones and Morrell, and their families on occasion, were responsible for the daily task. The new instrument provided earth science students with first-hand experience in the study of seismology. In addition, many secondary and elementary students came to visit the station and received instruction in earthquake detection. The system was active on campus for almost 20 years. It was abandoned when the University of Utah installed a new network in the late 1980s.[11]

The establishment of the four programs in science also led to the formation of the first student clubs. In the fall of 1966, the Physical Science and Engineering Club was organized for science and other interested students. The first president of the new club was Don Smith. The club functioned for about 10 years and was eventually replaced by the Geology Club which was organized in 1979. [12]

The new role as a four-year bachelor's degree institution and the retirements of senior faculty led to a number of administrative changes. At the May 12, 1966 Board of Trustees meeting, the first of these major changes occurred. Dr. Conrad Hatch, who had served with Professor Ashcroft as co-chair of the physical science department, was appointed administrative assistant for academic affairs to CSU's president Royden Braithwaite. He replaced Dr. Richard Thompson, who had been serving in that capacity. At the same meeting Dr. Harl E. Judd was appointed head of the physical science department. The changes were to take effect on July 1, 1966.

The next major administrative change at the institution and in science came in July 1967. At the Board of Trustees' meeting on July 25, President Royden Braithwaite announced the creation of five new "schools" with five deans. Dr. McRay Cloward was appointed dean of the School of Continuing Education and Public Service, Dr. Eugene T. Woolf was appointed dean of the School of Arts and Letters, Professor A.W. Stephenson was appointed dean of the School of Business and Technology, Dr. Morris A. Shirts was appointed dean of the School of Education, and Dr. Wesley P. Larsen was appointed the dean of the School of Science.

Professor Larsen was in Washington D.C. and did not arrive in Cedar City to assume his new duties until September. In addition to his duties as dean, Dr. Larsen acted as chairman of the biology department, replacing Professor D.C. Schmutz. In 1969, because of his increased work load due primarily to involvement in National Science Foundation projects in the area, approval was given for Professor Wahlquist to be chair of the biology department.

With the change of the name of the school from College of Southern Utah to Southern Utah State College, the titles of the administrators also were changed. Dr. Hatch's title of director of academic affairs was changed to vice president for academic affairs. These changes took effect July 1, 1970.

*I*n the spring of 1971, Dr. Wesley P. Larsen stepped down as dean of science and Dr. Harl E. Judd was appointed to replace him. Professor Judd was a capable administrator, who achieved many significant things in science at SUSC. Three of the most significant programs established early in his administration as dean were the Southern Utah Regional Science Fair, the Weber State-SUSC-Dixie cooperative nursing program and the SUSC Water Lab.

Students who had competed in science fairs sponsored by the college over the many years, had been advanced to compete with students in northern Utah, but none had advanced beyond the state competition. In 1972 Dr. Joe Comp discovered that the college could sponsor a regional science fair, whereby winning science fair students and their projects might progress directly to the International Science and Engineering Fair (ISEF). Working with Dr. Judd to establish a budget, the first Southern Utah Regional Science Fair was held in the spring of 1973. The two winning students, Earl Butts and Terrell Sandberg, and their projects, were sent to the 24th ISEF in San Diego. Since that time the fair has expanded greatly, and hundreds of students and their science teachers have been able to attend an ISEF. The quality of the science fair projects and science education in southern Utah has dramatically improved. Southern Utah students have won national awards consistently since 1974, demonstrating that they can compete nationally and internationally. In 1997 Southern Utah University will sponsor its 25th annual regional fair and send 10 students and their teachers to the 50th ISEF in Louisville, Kentucky.[13]

A shortage of nurses in rural southwest Utah

was becoming a serious problem in the early 1970s. The communities of Cedar City and St. George were particularly concerned. By the fall of 1973, a cooperative agreement between Weber State, SUSC and Dixie College was established. Weber State, with an already existing nursing program, would administer the program, and first and second year classes would be taught at SUSC and Dixie. The initial meetings were held on the SUSC campus on October 3-5, 1973.

In the spring of 1974, Dean Judd was able to report that approval had been given to finish the basement of the science building to house the nursing program and to provide for a geology/engineering lab and facilities for a campus computer center. Construction on the basement began on July 1, 1974.

On October 31, 1974, representatives from the college, Washington County and Iron County commissions, nursing representatives, local medical professionals, and local hospitals met as an advisory board to discuss directions and implementation of the cooperative nursing program. Dean Judd was elected chairman of the group and served in that capacity through 1986. Fay Frahske became the first director of the nursing program.

The creation of a water lab at SUSC came as a result of the closing of the Cedar Branch of the Utah State Laboratory in 1974. Because water samples are perishable, and since testing in Salt

RICHARD KENNEDY AND STUDENT

LEE MORRELL

ASHCROFT
OBSERVATORY

Lake City or Denver, Colo., was not always satisfactory, a local testing lab was perceived to be necessary. Dr. Judd, in cooperation with Professor Joe Comp, the lab's first director, were able to get funding to begin a laboratory in the spring of 1975. SUSC participated with the United States government in the "208 Water Quality Program." This participation helped significantly with the funding of the lab and it was a great benefit for the chemistry department. It brought professional-quality equipment to the school and provided important part-time employment for chemistry majors. Because of the downturn in the local and state economy in the early 1980s, serious consideration for discontinuing the lab was contemplated. But with innovative budget cuts and increased charges for lab services, the lab survived and has become one of the essential services in southwest Utah.

With the increasing complexity of the School of Science, the need arose for more administrative assistance. At a physical science faculty meeting on April 23, 1973, Dean Judd announced that approval had been given for the creation of a physical science department with a chair. Dr. Robert M. (Bob) Jones was selected and commenced his duties shortly afterward. Professor Jones turned a measure of his attention toward the establishment of a computer center for the college and the department. In addition to his department duties, he served as the first computer center director.

In 1975, Dr. Jones learned that a 10-acre parcel of land near the College Farm had been given to the School of Science, provided a permanent structure was placed on it within ten years. Professor Jones proposed an astronomi-

cal observatory. A year earlier a 14-inch Schmidt Cassagrain telescope for observing, was donated by Eulalia B. Jones (a member of the SUSC library staff and the mother of Professor Jones). The new observatory met the approval of all parties, but there was one major problem: SUSC had no financial means to undertake the project. After some budget considerations and planning, Professor Jones submitted a formal proposal on October 29, 1976, to the College Development Board Director, Dennis Agle. He asked the Board to raise $23,000 for building costs, an observatory dome, and a road to the site.

The Board, under the leadership of Cedar City civic leader Clayton Frehner, agreed to undertake the project. By January 1977, Raymond Gardner, a Cedar City architect, donated his time and expertise to prepare plans for the observatory. Professor Lyman Munford agreed to construct the structure with his building construction students. Ground breaking ceremonies were held on October 10, 1977. Later, Cedar City Corporation donated equipment and labor to rough-out a road to the building. Elloyd Marchant, chairman of the special projects committee of the Development Board, donated plumbing and electrical supplies. Carter Brothers donated a concrete septic tank. In 1980, science faculty and SUSC maintenance staff put the finishing touches on the interior. Steve Heath and Richard Kimball still remember sheet-rocking the round ceiling under the main observatory deck. The summer of 1980 brought Professor David Menke to SUSC. His expertise in astronomy brought an even greater vision of the role and potential of the observatory. He made it possible for the observatory to be featured in the February 1982 issue of *Sky and Telescope*. The building was dedicated before 200 guests on September 26, 1980, and named the Ashcroft Observatory. Emeritus President Royden Braithwaite, in the early stages of observatory planning, remarked that this project more closely paralleled the construction of "Old Main" in 1898, than any other college project in SUU's then 82 year history, since the project was a college, community, staff and faculty combined effort. The observatory is a monument to a noble cause, a great man, and a continuing heritage.

To attend to the expanding role of agriculture at SUSC, Dr. Darrell Matthews was appointed director of a newly-created division of agriculture. Professor Matthews who enjoyed an international reputation in sheep culture and management, administered the operation of the

Valley Farm, the Mountain Ranch and the new agriculture minor. One of the first assignments presented to Dr. Matthews was the needed capital improvements at the farm. The legislature had appropriated $50,000 to accomplish the needed improvements. But traditional donated labor was also called upon, as science faculty members rallied round to offer tangible support to the new division and its director. During the fall of 1975, "work projects" were Saturday activities for the united faculty.

The pressing need for improved biological laboratories and a greenhouse were never far from the consciousness of Dr. Glenn Wahlquist. Working with Dr. Judd, the two prepared plans and written requests for such a structure. Their diligence was rewarded, when the new building was approved in early 1975. Dr. Wahlquist's able leadership was followed by B. Al Tait, who became biology department chair on July 1, 1975. Professor Tait gave his attention to the details of the new building, which was constructed directly south of the science building. Several faculty members, including Tait, moved into the building in the fall of 1977. The building was dedicated with a number of new campus buildings on April 28, 1978.

When Parley Dalley first came to teach at the Branch Normal School in 1909, there was no geology course, but as soon as the possibility opened, he began expanding the science offerings and included geology. By the time young Blair Maxfield came as a student to Branch Agricultural College, Prof. Dalley's geology courses were long-established and eagerly attended. Maxfield describes the adventure:

I came to Branch Agricultural College in the fall of 1949. It was at this time that I met Professor Parley Dalley. Here was a master teacher. He had a great interest in all his students and a great enthusiasm for the subject. I will never forget the picture I have of him in my mind. A short, rather stocky, silver-haired person leading a group of students up a difficult trail on the side of a cinder cone. He would pause, turning around to look at the string of young students puffing up the trail and say, "Now don't over-do yourselves." Here he was, a man in his sixties leading the group.[14]

It was a nice re-connection when Maxfield returned to Cedar City with a master's degree in geology, employed by Shell Oil Company as an exploration geologist. He came on assignment in the summers of 1959 and 1960, to map the area east of the town. His old professor came along to help him and to enjoy a visit. When later, Maxfield learned that the four-year liberal arts status had been achieved, he contacted Mr. Dalley to reveal that his dream had been to return to teach at what was now CSU. With the help of Mr. Dalley, he persuaded Conrad Hatch and President Royden Braithwaite that he would be the man for the job when the geology program began to expand.

Five years later, in the fall of 1969, Maxfield arrived to join Lawrence Cooper in the geology program. As Maxfield remembers:

Lawrence Cooper was teaching geology at the time. We got along very well. His background was geochemistry, and he loved to teach mineralogy. My strengths were historical geology, sedimentology, paleontology and field mapping. With those backgrounds, we complimented each other instead of competing.

Professor Cooper loved to offer, for both students and townspeople who liked to come along, field trips out through the canyonlands and monument valley areas. We then added a yearly hike into the bottom of Grand Canyon, Death Valley and several shorter field trips.[15]

Blair Maxfield succeeded Bob Jones as chair of physical science on July 1, 1977, so that Professor Jones could devote full-time to the computer center operations and his teaching. Within a month of his appointment, he had the sad task of seeking a replacement for Professor Lawrence Cooper, who was killed in a traffic accident in northeastern Utah. He had the good fortune to secure the services of Dr. Richard Kennedy, who had recently returned to Utah

1927
GEOLOGY TRIP
IN THE FIRST
BAC BUS,
PHOTO
COURTESY
OF HILDA
FOY
GARDNER

PROFESSOR
PARLEY
DALLEY AND
STUDENTS,
GOOSENECKS
AT CAPITOL
REEF.

came from Weber State College. The head of their department even went so far as to write to the Board of Regents stating that neither man (referring to Kennedy and myself) was qualified to teach upper division geology courses. Again Dr. Rigby, along with Dr. Hintze of the BYU, came to our aid. Both Dr. Kennedy and I, as well as several of the Weber State professors, had been educated at Brigham Young University. So Rigby and Hintze were well aware of the qualifications of most of us, and were able to assure the Regents that the claim was not valid.[16]

Through extensive research of the strongest programs in the nation, Maxfield and Kennedy formed their course requirements for the major. They visited other universities, they conferred and asked for evaluations of their plans. They were sure, by the time they finalized their program, that a graduate from CSU could be accepted in the most prestigious graduate programs. Over the years since, students have gone to the finest graduate schools in the nation, not one has been declined, and all have done well.

They met the knotty problem of a summer field school by linking with the University of Missouri, who ran an already-established field school in the southern Utah area. When the CSU program had grown to sufficient numbers, they established their own summer field school and advertised for students from other universities. In 1994 the geology summer field school at Southern Utah University had drawn such enthusiastic response that students were being turned away because of the upper numerical limit.

Implementation of the degree was delayed because of budget shortages in the late 1970s and early 1980s, but it has become one of the strong areas of expertise at the University. Professor Maxfield also organized one of the most successful student clubs on campus. In the fall of 1978, the Geology Club was organized. It has since provided some exciting and educational experiences for students and local citizens alike. The success of the geology program has honored Lawrence Cooper and Parley Dalley, who looked forward to the day that the geology program could become a major thrust of a thriving College of Science.

after several years at the University of Missouri at Rolla. Maxfield and his new colleague worked hard over the next several years to establish a first-rate geology major at SUSC. Their initial proposals met with resistance from Weber State, but when their credentials were questioned, respected geologists at Brigham Young University came to their defense. Maxfield writes of the predictable struggle:

With the addition of Dr. Kennedy to the staff, we now had two Ph.D.'s in geology so the struggle to offer a major in geology began. This was not an easy task. First, the Board of Regents had to be convinced that a two-man staff was capable of offering the necessary courses. We received a great assist in this matter by a study that had just been completed by the Geological Society of America, in which they had been making a survey of the quality of teaching in the universities throughout the USA. A good friend, Dr. Keith Rigby of Brigham Young University, was the chairman of this study group. He noted to the Board of Regents that some of the finest teaching they had found in the nation was in small two and three man departments. This was a great help to us.

The next problem was the opposition we began to receive from other geology departments in the state. The University of Utah had no objection, but Utah State University made a considerable protest. The biggest objection

A science program that is living and vital, requires constant review. In July, 1980, Professor Steven Heath succeeded Dr. Maxfield as the head of physical science, and a year later Dr. Russell Anderson assumed the bio-

arley Pratt Dalley was a legend on the campus for the 43 years that he served as a faculty member of Southern Utah University. Parley had been one of Branch Normal School's earliest students in 1902, at age 16. He was a product of the one-room school in his native Summit, followed by a year at Parowan Stake Academy and another in his sister Amelia's class in the newly-opened public school in Cedar City. Upon his graduation from BNS in 1905, he enrolled at the University of Utah, where he earned his chemical engineering degree in1909, and later his masters' degree.

In the fall, after his summer graduation from the U of U, Parley Dalley joined the faculty of BNS as head of the physical science department. From that time until his retirement in1952, he served the school during four of its eras: Branch Normal School, Branch Agricultural College, College of Southern Utah and the beginnings of Southern Utah State College. And after retirement, to the year of his death in 1970, he taught science classes, part-time as needed.

Dalley was a superlative teacher. One of his students during the BAC era, Nelda Clark Jones, wrote in 1996:

To this day I never see a wonder or marvel of the earth - towering volcanic mountain tops, the fantastic arches of southeastern Utah, faultlines where eons of history are laid bare - without thinking of Parley Dalley. Living in southern Utah was like living in a geology laboratory. He knew his subject and taught it with such enthusiasm, that his students gained a deep reverence for the wonders of this marvelous earth on which we reside.

His other contributions to the school were manifold - he once served as interim director, in leadership of standing committees, professional organizations and the alumni council. He served the community as superintendent of schools and as mayor and was active in his political party, as well as lifetime member of the Chamber of Commerce. He owned and operated a farm specializing in pure-bred sheep and dairy cattle and mentored young students as he employed them on his farm.

But it was for his gifts as a master teacher, his bequest to the school of his indexed collections of fossils and grasses from all over the world and of his manuscripts, programs, brochures, catalogues and photographs that he is best remembered. The name of Parley Dalley will always be beloved by the people who love Southern Utah University.

logical science chair from Professor Tait. They began a study which resulted in curriculum reform and implementation of new core programs in their areas. The effort was greatly aided by a grant achieved by Pauline Nelson, college grants officer. In 1981, she obtained a $950,000 Title III curriculum grant. In physical sciences, leaves were granted to professors Blair Maxfield to study geology curriculum, Bob Jones to design a computer/mathematics curriculum, and to Richard Dotson to design a computers-in-education course. In biology, professors Paul Burgoyne and Joann Bowns studied and reformed the biology curriculum and Eli Clark studied the agriculture curriculum. The projects were the first significant revision of the science curriculum since the establishment of the four-year program in 1965.

Professor Heath was responsible for obtaining the first major National Science Foundation teacher inservice grant in science and mathematics since Dean Larsen's work in the late 1960s. Over a six-year period, Professor Heath received more than $250,000 for inservice projects.

Dr. Russell Anderson was instrumental in establishing a strong pre-medical committee. His work has aided many SUU students in getting admitted to medical schools and other professional schools.

Dr. Chandler Whitelaw was appointed Computer Center director in the fall of 1982. Under his direction, the computer became an integral part of almost all departments on campus. Dr. Whitelaw's goal in 1982 was to get every building wired to a computer and to have terminals in every classroom and office on campus. The accomplishment of that goal has brought significant enhancement to the offerings and the operation of the university.

The family life department was transferred to the School of Science from the School of Business and Technology in 1973.

Perhaps the most trying time in Dean Judd's tenure at the University came in the summer of 1981. Professor Conrad Hatch stepped down as academic affairs vice president to return to the classroom. Since the new vice president, Dr. Terry Alger, was not due on campus until fall, Professor Judd was appointed acting academic

1985 FIELD
TRIP TO
PHANTOM
RANCH

vice president. This action was followed almost immediately by the sudden resignation of President Orville Carnahan. The Utah State Board of Regents, knowing of Dr. Judd's good work, appointed him acting president, a position he would hold for the next six months. For a few days, he was dean of science, actingacademic vice president and acting president. Shortly, Dr. Al Tait was appointed acting dean of science and Dr. Alger was on campus in August to assume his duties as academic vice president. Professor Judd kept the college together during a very trying time. He resumed his duties as dean in January 1982, when President Gerald Sherratt arrived.

During the budget duress of the 1985-86 school year, Dean Judd was faced with the difficult responsibility of making recommendations and implementing mandated cuts in faculty and programs in science. The unpleasant task also took some toll on his health. After a remarkable and very productive 15 years, Dean Judd decided to return to full-time teaching. Dr. Al Tait was appointed dean effective July 1, 1986. After a one-quarter leave, Dr. Judd returned to the classroom in March, 1987. He also retained his position as campus space inventory coordinator. He retired in the spring of 1993. At the 1994 commencement activities, he was presented with the Distinguished Service Award. Colleagues and students applauded the choice.

Perhaps the words "growth, growth, and more growth" best describe the last decade of

the school's first century. Nearly all the major events in science, during these 10 years, came as a result of dramatic growth. By 1988 it was clear that increased enrollment in science classes, and the deteriorating conditions in the science building justified the request for renewal of the science building. There were serious settling problems in the eastern wing of the old building. and the 30-year-old plumbing caused significant stress. In 1988 several science faculty were moved from the science building to other office locations on campus to allow for some stop-gap measure repairs in the building. Under the leadership of Harl Judd, Dean Tait, Paul Burgoyne and Richard Kennedy, plans were proposed that would enable the sciences to offer state of the art electronics with classroom TV monitors, computers and other electronic teaching devices.

Eventually, in concert with Utah Division of Facilities Construction and Management (DFCM), it was determined that renewal of the old building was impractical, if not impossible, and in 1990 the Board of Regents and the Utah State Legislature gave approval for construction of a new facility.

The science faculty moved into the new building during the Christmas break of 1992. They rejoiced in the modern arrangement of office furniture and adequate book-shelf space, as well as a special conference room set aside for department meetings. From the deck on the third floor of the building, there is a grand view of the entire campus. Classes for winter quarter were taught in the new facility beginning January 1993.

Because of the rapid growth and the fact that the funding had to be held in line with the appropriation that would have been made had the old building been renewed, limitations were placed upon the building, and it seemed small from the beginning.

The extraordinary growth was due in part to the school's name change from Southern Utah State College to Southern Utah University on January 1, 1991. To reflect the name change, the School of Science changed its name to College of Science.

The number of science graduates from 1966 to 1996 illustrates the incredible changes in science. In the five-year period from 1966 to 1971, 152 students graduated in science. In a similar five years, from 1992 to 1996, the number of science graduates rose to 396. In the 30 years from 1966 to 1996, 1,402 students received science degrees. Interestingly, nearly one-third (463) of the 1,402 science bachelors degrees were awarded since the school received university status in 1991, and 48 percent (667) were awarded in the last 10 years.

One of the first tasks Dean Tait faced was the appointment of a new department head in life sciences. Dr. Russell Anderson felt that the budget cuts implemented in the mid-1980s were too severe. He resigned as head, in protest, effective October 1, 1986. Dr. Paul Burgoyne was appointed as the new department head. In the spring of 1988, Professor Burgoyne was granted a faculty exchange with Professor Otto Aasdal from Norway, from July 1988 to July 1989. Dr. Michael Donovan was appointed acting head of the department. Upon his return, Dr. Burgoyne resumed his duties.

Since the faculty exchange program was implemented in the mid-1980s, two other exchanges have taken place. Professor Jim Cotts went to Australia for the 1983 calendar year, and professor Ian Ogle brought the sciences some of his "down under" culture. In the 1990-91 school year, Professor Fred Lohrengel exchanged positions with Professor Fred Larsen from Vermont. Dr. Larsen brought cold stories of his Alaskan adventures in geology.

After seven and-a-half years as physical science department head, Professor Steven Heath stepped aside to give others an opportunity and to devote more time to managing science in-service grants. Dr. Richard Kennedy was selected as the new head and began service January 1, 1988.

One of the major events in Dr. Kennedy's

At first when I enrolled at CSU, I was only interested in learning the building trade. Then as I continued to have success there, I told Mr. Cooley I wanted to get an Associate Degree in Building Construction. He said, "You will have to take Biology and Algebra." I told him "Not this kid." He said, "Well, do you want the Associate Degree?" I said "Yes." He again said, "You will have to take those classes and other general education courses, if you want the degree." He helped me with a schedule and I started with Biology from Glenn Wahlquist and Algebra from Phil Ogden.

Mr. Wahlquist's Biology 1A class was at 7:00 a.m., in the basement of the old Administration Building. I was scared to death of the word "biology." Mr. Wahlquist soon removed that fear, and biology began to come alive. He was a master teacher, and it ended up being a wonderful experience. I enjoyed that biology class on plants so much that I enrolled in his Biology 1B on animals. Mr. Wahlquist made the animals biology class so interesting and enjoyable. Yes, I passed both classes.

Mr. Wahlquist helped to build my self-confidence so much that over the next two years, I took all of the botany and zoology classes, along with the labs, at CSU. It was in the biology labs that I had an opportunity to help some of the students with their lab assignments that I decided I wanted to become a teacher. By the time I graduated from CSU, I had something like 35 hours of botany and zoology credits.

Algebra 1 was taught by Phil Ogden, a new math teacher, and again I was scared to death of algebra. I did not want to fail the class, so some of the other students and I would get together at night and study as much as four to six hours a night just to pass the class. I passed the class and then had to take Algebra 2 and then Spring quarter Trigonometry. Trig was taught by Harl Judd. He was another master teacher and I really enjoyed his class. Again I would study four to six hours to learn trig and pass the tests.

I am so grateful for the patience, kindness and gentleness the CSU faculty extended to me in all of the different courses I took. This was the beginning of my education, and the faculty was there to help me become successful in accomplishing my goals.

I first started with a desire to just pass the classes that first quarter, try another quarter until I had an Associate Degree, and then go on to Utah State University for a Bachelor's Degree in Industrial Arts Teacher Education.

There were so many master teachers and mentors at CSU. They include Eugene Woolf and Richard Rowley in English and communication, George Manning in geology, Blaine Johnson and Roy Halversen in music, and David L. Sargent in human physiology. This was a very demanding course, but he had the ability to help students and make a very difficult subject become easy and fun to learn. These were just some of the many great faculty that were the pioneers who helped carve and build the foundation for the college to become the great teaching university it is today. The faculty cared, encouraged, motivated and nurtured the students in a positive way. Their goal was for the students to achieve excellence.

Lyman Munford

THE
GREENHOUSE

administration was the division of the physical science department, which by 1992 was the largest on campus. Effective July 1, 1992, the department became two: the physical science department with chemistry, engineering, geology and physics programs and faculty, and the mathematical science department, with programs and faculty in computer science and mathematics. Professor Richard Tebbs was appointed head of the new department.

Another major development was the establishment of geology field camp centered at SUU. Dr. Fred Lohrengel designed the camp, and it has developed into a first-rate program with graduate students and geology majors from throughout the United States participating. After 16 years on the science faculty and five-and-a-half years as chair, Professor Kennedy retired. He was replaced by Professor Richard Dotson, who had moved into chemistry and computer science since his appointment in zoology in 1971. Professor Dotson's appointment was made effective July 1, 1993.

In the spring of 1994, Dr. Paul Burgoyne retired, after 28 years on the faculty. Professor Donovan assumed the permanent chairmanship of life sciences July 1, 1994. Dr. Donovan, like several of his science colleagues, had served as Faculty Senate president the year prior to his new appointment.

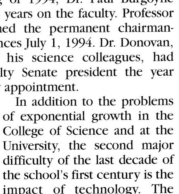

In addition to the problems of exponential growth in the College of Science and at the University, the second major difficulty of the last decade of the school's first century is the impact of technology. The advent of the microcomputer and the hand-held calculator has revolutionized science

RICHARD KIMBALL

throughout the United States and the world. It has been an exacting task for the computer science faculty to keep up with the new technologies. The maintenance and upgrade of computer systems has been a monumental undertaking for the computer science faculty. The impact was felt by faculty in other departments too. Some of the mathematics faculty refer to the period before 1974 as "BC," before calculator. Much of the travel budget is used for faculty to attend conferences which teach new technologies. Several faculty members have taken academic leaves to update themselves and re-write their course curricula. Nearly all of the equipment budget for the past decade in the entire University has been to purchase computers for the classroom, the laboratories, and for faculty.

In the centennial year, 1996-97, science faculty have spent much of their time and energy on changing the curriculum from the quarter system which they have used since the school's founding to the semester system. The conversion, which was dictated by the Board of Regents, was a lively topic of discussion for most of the decade. Physical science and mathematical science faculty have felt that it was a proper move, since it allows them to make significant and needed curriculum changes effectively. Life science faculty were, on the other hand, opposed to the change, since it is difficult to do field work in biology under the semester calendar. The biology curriculum is not as sequential as that in the mathematics and physical science, and so designing a new program has proven more challenging.

*I*n the last decade of the first century, many of the pioneers of the university's advance to four-year status have retired. In the spring of 1988, Dr. Conrad Hatch retired after 40 years of distinguished service. Only Parley Dalley had served longer as a member of the science faculty. During his last year, he donated his salary to an endowment to establish scholarships in his and his wife's name. His wife Elva taught English at the school for over 30 years. He also set aside some of the endowment for a science faculty development fund. Dr. Darrell Matthews, after returning from South America for a second time on a special U.S. government agriculture assignment, retired. At the time of his retirement in 1988, he had been on the faculty for 38 years. The next year, Dr. Joe Comp retired after 24 years. Joe had been instrumental in getting the chemistry program and the SUU Water Lab established.

In January of 1991, Colleen Jones retired as secretary of the physical science department. She had been secretary in the department and Dean Judd's secretary since 1969. She kept minutes of most of the many meetings that were held in the department and school during that 22-year period. They were crucial in re-constructing the history of the sciences in the past quarter century. Her service as secretary has only been exceeded by the extraordinary work of Jeanette Slack. Jeanette began as secretary to Dr. Wesley Larsen in 1968. She was life science secretary from 1972 to 1986 when she became Dean Tait's secretary. She is still serving in that capacity during this centennial year. One of the major responsibilities for Jeanette and Colleen was the keeping of financial records for the department heads and the deans. They have been as important as faculty in their service to the College of Science.

In 1991 Dr. Russell Anderson retired after 27 years of service. In addition to his administrative service, he was instrumental in establishing an excellent pre-professional program at the school. The spring of 1993 brought the retirement of Dr. Harl Judd, who had been at the institution for 36 years. Dr. Richard Kennedy also retired in 1993. He was a master teacher and also brought great success to the SUU Elderhostel program. He spent the last 16 years of his professional career at SUU. In 1995 Dr. Paul Burgoyne, who brought expertise in science education, retired after 29 years. The next year Dr. Brent Palmer, a former BAC student, retired after 33 years at the institution. Brent worked on numerous biology projects with local government agencies and brought scholarly recognition to the sciences at the school.

CONRAD HATCH

Growth in the last 10 years at the university is also reflected in the number of new faculty in the sciences. During Dean Tait's administration, 22 new faculty members were added in life science, physical science, and mathematical science. In addition, a dozen or so one-year appointments were made for faculty on leave. The new appointments and their expertise insure that the sciences will play an important part in the beginnings of the school's next century.

THE SCIENCE CENTER, 1997

TOP: THE STAINED GLASS WINDOWS IN THE GREAT HALL OF THE CONFERENCE CENTER.
ABOVE: THE HUNTER CONFERENCE CENTER, HOME OF CONTINUING EDUCATION, WAS ONCE THE GYMNASIUM.

CHAPTER XXII
Continuing Education

*R**eaching out**

*T*he beginnings[1] of continuing education can be traced back to the years when Professor Ben Cooley was in charge of arranging night classes taught at the college. Eventually President Daryl Chase appointed Dr. McRay Cloward, chairman of the Division of Continuing Education, with responsibility for night classes and extension classes. Most of these were in the business and industrial arts areas. Evening School was considered an appendix to the academic programs on campus.

In 1965, when Southern Utah State College (SUSC) became an independent institution under Gov. Calvin Rampton, the school of Continuing Education and Public Service was created. This was unique in the state because academic ranking was given to the school equal to the other academic areas.

The inclusion of Public Service within the Division of Continuing Education was an important decision at the time because it enabled the school to get a Title I grant to do community development consulting work for governmental entities as well as private industry. Dr. Cloward hired Lynn Ubell to do community development work, using Title I grant money for half the position and college funds for the other half. Lynn did design work for the development of the Brian Head ski resort. He also designed the preschool at Beryl and the renovated offices in the Old Administration Building (now the Braithwaite Center).

Under the community development grant the Division of Continuing Education ran a number of management workshops for organizations such as Utah Power, Utah Construction, and the Soil Conservation Service.

Several research studies were funded including a study of environmental problems at Mammoth Creek, a history of the Navajos in Arizona, and the redesign of the Old Rock Church in Parowan. These and a number of other projects were used as training research projects for students, who received a stipend out of the grant for their work. Lynn Ubell was replaced by David Conine, a community development specialist. David Conine was later replaced by Dr. Ralph Starr.

*O*ne of the biggest programs conducted by the Division of Continuing Education was the National Training Laboratories (NTL) under the direction of the U.S. Department of Education. People came from all over the world to SUSC to participate in the program. For a 14-15 year period the SUSC campus was one of three major centers in the United States where NTL workshops were held. Participants from South America, Europe, and all parts of the United States utilized the entire campus and its classrooms during the month of August. The workshops were designed to teach people to communicate effectively and to explore feelings. Four lab groups were funded simultaneously in community development, higher education leadership, social and psychological development and student leadership.

The NTL program brought national exposure to the campus. The Continuing Education Department of Conferences and Workshops was able to use the money that came through NTL to assist other programs on campus. With the growth of the Utah Shakespearean Festival housing and classroom space was no longer available for NTL.

Many other programs were either coordinated or sponsored by the school. One was a national Educational Leadership Training program involving principals, superintendents, and deans from all over the country. This ran for 34 years on the campus. SUSC was also a site for the State of Utah Police Training Center. SUSC was funded to sponsor the Volunteers in Service to America (VISTA) program, teaching kids to read, teaching Navajos on the reservation to drive safely, doing health work in Arizona with the Navajo people, and helping them to establish businesses.

In addition to these special programs, the school of Continuing Education conducted Evening School and Summer School. Off campus classes were also administered by the Division of Continuing Education. Outreach classes were held in Richfield, Delta, Fillmore, Beaver, Panguitch, Tropic, Kanab, and St. George. The Division of Continuing Education was the center for the outreach graduate program for Utah State University in Education.

*I*n 1979 Dr. Cloward returned to full-time teaching in the department of behavioral and social sciences.[2] Dr. Ralph Starr was appointed assistant vice president of academic affairs over the Division of Continuing Education and Public Service. Boydine Daniels continued as secretary, Virginia Higbee directed Community Support Services, Carolyn White was hired to direct the Upward Bound Program and Daphne Dalley was hired as coordinator of conferences and workshops.

For many years, summer on the campus began with Girls State, sponsored by the American Legion Auxiliary to teach a select group of outstanding high school girls patriotism and the workings of local and state government. Youth Conferences for LDS church groups were also popular on college campuses.

Dr. Ralph Starr left the campus in 1980 to work with the MX Missile Project, and Pauline Nelson was appointed to replace him. In 1982 Dr. Phillip Carter became assistant vice president of academic affairs, and a reorganization of responsibilities occurred. Dr. Carter took responsibility for the Division of Continuing Education including Summer School,

VIRGINIA HIGBEE, 1996

Evening School, the Outreach Program, Community Support Services, and Conferences and Workshops. Dr. Carter assigned Daphne Dalley responsibility for all non-credit programs, and he maintained responsibility for the credit programs. Dr. Carter was a creative educator and administrator and the beginning of his administration marked a turning point not only in summer conference planning, but in expansion of year-round conferences, the development of many new programs for audiences of all ages, and expansion of Summer School and Evening School.

New programs with a unique educational emphasis were added. The Color Country Forensics Institute under the direction of M.L. Smith provided training in debate and individual speaking events to high school students statewide. Working with coaches from the athletic department, a number of summer sports camps were started. Jack Bishop worked with the Football Camp, and Ren Hoopes from Cedar High School worked with the Wrestling Camp. United Spirit Association was brought to the campus with workshops for teens in Utah and Nevada in cheerleading and drill team. The Gifted and Talented Institute was started by Dr. Carter and Jack Stokes.

Several programs for adults were also begun. A program for training Emergency Medical Technicians (EMT) was added under the direction of Robert Tuckett. The Creative Writing Workshop was started by David Lee and has continued to inspire participants through their contact with distinguished presenters with experience in the field of writing and the teaching of writing. The Elderhostel Program for senior citizens was begun and grew to be one of the largest Elderhostel programs in the nation. A Summer Lecture Series and Summer Concert Series were piloted in 1982 and were the prototype for the Convocations Lecture Series and the Summer Concert Series today.

In 1985 Daphne Dalley wrote a grant to begin Turning Point, a federally funded program, to address the feminization of poverty in America by assisting single parents and displaced homemakers in becoming self sufficient. The Turning Point program sponsored training in assertive communication, job seeking/keeping skills, and confidence building.

With Dr. Carter's encouragement several creative programs were pioneered within the Division. The Renaissance Fair was started, with Doug Baker, Dr. Phil Carter, Daphne Dalley, and a work study student doing most of the planning the first two years. The Medieval Feast in the Great Hall was initially developed, with Kathy

McIntyre writing the script, Dr. Carter and Daphne Dalley as program administrators, and Doug Baker as artistic director and Lord of the Feaste. After two years in the initial development, the decision was made to turn the Renaissance Faire over to the Cedar City Chamber of Commerce and to locate it in the city park rather than on the campus. There it has grown and flourished. The Feast was given to the Utah Shakespearean Festival, where it would have the artistic support needed, and has become a popular event in connection with the Utah Shakespearean Festival.

One of Dr. Carter's favorite projects was the renovation of the College Cabin. The cabin had always been an enjoyable place to take groups for a dutch oven cook out or charcoal broiled steaks. Many professional groups, youth groups, and community groups enjoyed the mountain air and the rustic ambiance of the cabin. However, as the years went by the cabin needed repairs and was a little too small and rustic for some events. Dr. Carter had a vision of what the expansion and renovation of the cabin could do for the campus and continuing education programming.

I remember going to the cabin with Dr. Carter in the middle of the winter to enlist President Gerald Sherratt and a couple of other key people on campus into the possibilities for the renovation and expansion of the building. With boots on we hiked through the snow, unlocked the cabin and prepared to serve a lunch of canned chili warmed in a crock pot. All went well until we discovered there was no electrical power in the cabin in the winter, and we had failed to bring a can opener. While the possibilities for the cabin were discussed, we lunched on red licorice, cold rolls and butter.

Through creative planning Dr. Carter did accomplish the renovation, and the cabin, now called the SUU Mountain Center, is available year round for all kinds of Continuing Education and community events.

As the Conferences and Workshops department grew, it was more work than one person could handle. For two or three years the coordination of summer conferences was turned over to a part-time person who worked full time in the summer. In 1989 David Nyman was moved from head of the music department to director of conferences and institutes with Jill Dail as his summer programming assistant. In 1990, Daphne Dalley was made full-time director of

the Turning Point Program. Jane Nelson (Comp) was taken from the Head Start Program and made coordinator of Elderhostel.

With the renovation of the old Student Center into the Haze Hunter Conference Center, Continuing Education has continued to grow and expand, with David Nyman and Lana Johnson as assistant deans, and Jill Dail as director of Conferences Services assisted by Jane Comp. Marla Bingham works with Lana on the Convocations Series and the Summer Concert Series. Jack Hill and Martha Minnick work with the Distance Learning program. Dr. Carter retired in 1996, and the campus is currently seeking a new dean of Continuing Education.

*I*n 1997, the Division of Continuing Education offers more than 377 courses, seminars, workshops, and conferences each year to more than 7,966 students.[2] This office has the double task of 1) supporting colleges within the university through supplemental curriculum development and administration, and 2) responding directly to community requests and student needs not met by existing courses through independent offerings.

• Evening School offers a wide variety of courses to meet the needs of many types of individuals. The schedule includes extended day classes, outreach courses taught in St. George and Richfield, EdNet classes taught via television at locations throughout southern Utah, self-support, and noncredit classes. The popularity of Evening School is growing, as it offers educational opportunities to the students of the University and the community which regular daytime classes do not. Continued growth is anticipated through increased enrollments and the addition of desired courses.

• Summer school includes regular graduate and undergraduate classes, credit workshops, seminars, speciality programs, festivals, and conferences. These classes are targeted to meet the needs of full-time students pursuing an undergraduate degree, part-time students seeking degrees, job-related course work, academic enrichment, graduate students in accounting and education, early entry freshmen, and concurrent enrollment high school students. Summer school enrollments have grown at a rate equal to, or greater than, the University generally. Summer School offerings are adjusted to reflect growth in enrollment, trends in the market place, and student needs.

• Lecture and Performing Arts Programs: President Gerald Sherratt hired Lana Johnson in 1983 to direct the Convocation Lecture Series, and the program was moved under the administration of the Division of Continuing Education in 1989. This program has earned national recognition and continues to generate considerable visibility for the University. An average of 600 students and community members attend the lecture each Thursday. The list of guest lecturers includes some impressive names in politics, journalism, science, social issues, entertainment, justice, and the arts. In 1986 the National Association for Campus Activities presented the SUU Convocations program with its Distinguished Lecture Program Award for in-depth exploration of issues, concerns, and ideas. The Convocation Series significantly enhances the academic experience at SUU. Lana Johnson says "The primary value of this lecture series is that of offering perspectives and points of view of contemporary interest that may be outside of the content area, to which the students are exposed. The series is designed to expose students to ideas outside the areas they are studying."

The Lectures/Special Projects office provides students and faculty on campus with an experienced staff to assist with arrangements for visiting scholars, speakers, and performers. Collaborative efforts will continue to enable the university to expand and enhance lecture and performing arts programming.

• Office of Distance Learning: Organization of the Office of Distance Learning was accomplished in 1993. The impetus behind the effort was an awareness of the academic needs of a growing market of nontraditional students entering higher education. The department was initially divided into programs designated as: Teacher Inservice, Self Study, Independent Study, Concurrent Enrollment and Contract Classes. The majority of enrollments are in the areas of In-service and Independent Study.

Southern Utah University is recognized nationally as a teacher training institution which contributes significantly to the pool of professional teachers in Utah and throughout the nation. Distance Learning has taken to heart the necessity to provide quality education to teachers in the classroom and offers courses across the state of Utah.

Part of the mission of the Division of Continuing Education at SUU is to provide life-long learners with high-quality educational courses at a time and in a place most convenient for them. Inservice enrollments have increased from 700 in 1992-93 to a projected 3,307 for the 1996-97 year. Popular course work is generally those courses which teachers can immediately apply to instructional efforts in the classroom. Examples of course titles are: Current Developments in Instructional Technology, Interpersonal Relationships, Reading Methodology, Computer Science, Computer Programming, Math Methodology, Gifted Education, Management for Local Government Administrators, and Teaching English as a Second Language.

Distance learners in an independent study environment are tied closely to the professor for advisement and supervision. Independent study is a concept often popular with the non-traditional student who cannot take advantage of instruction on the campus. Telecommunication, the computer, and the utilization of the Internet for exchange of materials can enhance the programs of Independent Study. Student enrollment in Independent Study has increased from 150 during the 1991-92 academic year to 326 during the 1996-97 academic year.

In a 1993 address to educators across the State of Utah, Gov. Mike Leavitt spoke of increasing the learning opportunities to citizens via technology. The governor stated, "We can double or triple concurrent enrollment through technology delivered education providing motivated high school students with countless college options..." In 1997, the Office of Distance Learning increased the courses available via technology, from high school students in their schools, to all adults who have access to a computer and a need or a desire for learning. These courses have an extended syllabus provided electronically and the instructor is just a short distance away via the keyboard and the Internet. The need for educational programs for the nontraditional student has increased tremendously over the past several years. Projections for the next five years indicate that the demands will increase and not diminish.

When James Condie accepted the position of dean of students at Southern Utah University in 1968, he had been involved with the federally funded program Upward Bound at Weber State University.[3] Shortly after coming he wrote a grant for an Upward Bound project for Southern Utah University, and the project was funded. Upward Bound, a program conducted out of the United States Department of Education, is an educational program geared to high-school-age students who may be from low income families and are first generation college students. First generation student means that neither parent has completed a bachelor's degree in higher education. One of the main thrusts of the project is to encourage high school students to complete their diplomas and to pursue a degree in higher education.

Mr. Condie hired Wayne Mifflin as assistant director of the new program in April, 1968. The project was funded to serve 60 students, and the initial high schools involved were in Millard, Beaver, Iron, Washington, Kane, Sevier and Garfield counties in Utah, and two Arizona high schools—Tuba City and Monument Valley or Kayenta High School. After Mr. Condie left the University in 1969, the project directorship was assigned to R. Kenneth Benson, then director of Student Activities.

Subsequent directors included Yvonne Parkinson, Celeste Denton, Carolyn White, Peter Emerson, Kirk Lewandowski, Georgia Beth Thompson (1986), William O'Neill (1988), David Hyatt (1991), and Leanne Maxwell (1995). During her tenure Ms. White also submitted a grant for a Special Services program which was funded. Special Services (which became Student Support Services in 1987) is also a federally funded program managed within the U.S. Department of Education. This program serves low-income, first generation college students who may need developmental classes, tutoring and other support to succeed in higher education. It also serves students with disabilities. The project serves 150 students.

Over the years, the enrollment in Upward Bound has been about 50-60 percent Native American. The Upward Bound and Student Support services graduates have moved on to a number of professional careers including education, law enforcement and medical fields.

After reading an article about a unique and innovative educational program for senior citizens called Elderhostel,[4] Daphne Dalley, Coordinator of Conferences and Workshops for the Division of Continuing Education decided that with the Utah Shakespearean Festival, the availability of the National Parks, and the spectacular and unique geology of the area, Cedar City was an ideal location for such a program. The program offered senior citizens across the United States the opportunity to spend a week on a college campus where they were offered three college-level courses taught by college instructors. Two weeks of the program were planned for the summer of 1983, and 60 participants attended. In the summers of 1984 and 1985, additional weeks of the program were advertised. Enrollment in the second year of the program

was 188 participants, and in the third year enrollment reached 355 participants. All of these programs were campus based, using dormitory housing.

Three college-level classes with professors as instructors were taught each week, giving participants the opportunity to learn about the "Geology of Southern Utah" with Dr. Blair Maxfield and Dr. Richard Kennedy, "Trees, Flowers and Shrubs of Southern Utah" with Dr. Al Tait and the "Utah Shakespearean Festival" Seminars with Gwen Sandberg as instructor. The program included tickets to a Shakespearean play, and field trips to areas of Southern Utah where participants could experience hands-on the geology and botany of the area in a way few tourists have the time or opportunity to do. In addition to a class on "Southern Utah History" taught by retired Professor Wes Larsen, these classes remained the core of the program for the next eleven years.

Two unique educational theme weeks were offered and were very popular. One was a program designed around an astronomy class taught by Professor Brent Sorensen the year Haley's Comet was visible in the skies of Southern Utah. Another theme week featured the popular play *Nicholas Nickleby* produced by the SUU theatre department. These programs were fully enrolled months in advance with participants from across the United States.

Dr. Phil Carter, SUU dean of Continuing Education, encouraged the expansion of the Elderhostel program. It was Dr. Carter's opinion that teaching an Elderhostel class was the best in-service training the faculty on the campus could get, as these bright and enthusiastic adult learners stretched the faculty to deliver their best.

Between 1983 and 1990, enrollments doubled every year as additional off-campus sites were added to those offered on-campus. In 1985-86 Brian Head was added as a program site. Cross country skiing was offered with Ann Smith as instructor. Most of the participants were beginners and were told, "If you can walk you can cross country ski." Programs at Zion National Park and Grand Canyon North Rim became very popular.

Dr. Richard Kennedy taught a geology class as the Elderhostelers watched the fog and clouds filling the Grand Canyon through large windows. He received a standing ovation from the group of 100 people at the end of the lecture. Many Elderhostelers over the years were influenced to attend SUU's program because of the word-of-mouth reputation Dr. Kennedy enjoyed nationwide.

In 1988-89, Daphne Dalley's assignment changed, and she began spending full-time working with the Turning Point Program. Jane Nelson Comp was assigned the role of Elderhostel coordinator, working with Jill Dail and David Nyman, with Martha Minnick as secretary.

In 1994, declining enrollment, budget constraints, and lack of availability of faculty to teach the courses precipitated the decision to stop sponsoring the Elderhostel program and to increase those summer programs which would be more advantageous to SUU's current needs.

In the 11 years the Elderhostel Program was sponsored on the SUU campus, a total of 7,614 participants from all parts of the United States, Canada and England visited the campus and the Southern Utah area. Gwen Sandberg reports that until her retirement many returned annually to the Utah Shakespearean Festival, recognized old faces and talked about fond memories of the weeks with Elderhostel here.

As CSU was evolving into a four-year school, it became more evident than ever that the college had a responsibility to the communities in its southwestern Utah service area.[5] As early as 1962, night classes were being taught in several communities.

By 1970, Dr. McRay Cloward, then dean of the School of Continuing Education had arranged for two sets of VISTA (Volunteers in Service to America) volunteers to be housed at what was then Southern Utah State College. One of these sets established a day-care center at the newly built Migrant Housing complex in the Escalante Valley near Beryl. Before the establishment of the day-care center, the children were in the fields as their parents harvested potatoes and other crops, or were kept all day long in the cab of a pickup. Nearly every year, children were injured in accidents as they got in the way of cars or harvesting equipment. The VISTA volunteers also established a preschool in the space previously used by the CSU preschool in the home economics part of the science building.

By 1973, the VISTA volunteers had moved on. Dr. Cloward secured a Title XX mini-grant from the State to continue operation of the two established programs. The Division of Continuing Education advertised for a Coordinator of Volunteers and hired Virginia Bruhn Higbee, a recent SUSC graduate, for the half-time position. She recruited volunteers for the Escalante Valley Head Start/Day Care Center and managed the Campus Nursery School.

By the mid 1970s, community awareness for activities to help children and adults with disabilities was growing. Staff of Division of Continuing Education obtained a small grant to provide summer activities for students and adults with disabilities. Many people helped with this program, including Les Jones and Vern Kupfer of the psychology department, SUSC graduate Tom Walker, and many parents. For the first two years, Virginia Higbee and Tom Walker managed the summer program. Later, Marsha Perkins was hired to manage both the summer program and an evening program for adults. The group named themselves the American Eagles and was very involved in activities such as Special Olympics and crafts. Many campus student organizations worked with the American Eagles.

A favorite event each year was the Prom. Students from the LDS Institute would leave up the decorations from their Spring Formal. The next night, students and adults with disabilities from Cedar City and St. George would have their own Prom. Twenty years later, former American Eagles such as Laurie Jill Stephens and Danny Lister still recall these times with fondness.

In 1979, the State Department of Handicapped Services asked SUSC to establish an Early Intervention Preschool for children aged 0-5 years of age with disabilities in Beaver, Garfield, Kane, Iron and Washington Counties. It was decided that Early Intervention Centers would be established in St. George and Cedar City and that children in the other counties would be served through a homebased program. Sue Ollerton and Loy Ann MacArthur were the teachers.

SUSC contracted with the State Division of Handicapped Services to provide a sheltered workshop for adults with disabilities in Iron, Beaver and Garfield counties. This center, named first the SUSC Beehive Center, was housed for several years at South Elementary School. Marsha Perkins and Jan Parke were the mainstays of the Beehive Center staff. The sheltered workshop, later renamed the SUSC Vocational Opportunities Center (VOC), moved to Renaissance Square and added programs such as supported employment, transportation, transition services, recreation and aging services. Marlene Riddle, an SUSC social work graduate, became director of the program. Others who were instrumental in the VOC Centers success included Randy Hoyt, Shane Swensen, DeVon Childs, Myrna Bowles, Agnes Helquist, and Mary Winn. Many SUSC staff and faculty members served on advisory committees for the Center. SUSC student volunteers in vocational education, nursing, education, psychology, social work and other areas worked in the VOC center to gain practicum experience. The VOC and the St. George Early Intervention programs were eventually passed on to other providers.

The Nursery School program became Head Start in 1984. Dori Kanesta-Crouch and Jane S. Nelson (Comp) served 20 children in Cedar City and 12 children in each of the rural communities of Escalante, Tropic, and Hurricane.

By November 1994, 260 families were being served through 16 SUU Head Start classrooms in Iron, Washington, Garfield, Millard, Beaver, and Kane counties. Also in 1994, Community Support Services programs were moved from SUU Continuing Education Services to the Office of Regional Services. In 1997, SUU

Head Start serves 287 children and families in 17 classrooms throughout southwestern Utah.

The SUU Office of Community Support Services is much more than 24 years of programs and statistics. The programs have become a reality because of the vision of staff and the support of families, communities and Southern Utah University. The programs in the Office of Community Support Services are designed to assist disadvantaged or special needs community groups. These programs do not offer two-year or four-year degrees. Yet they fill a role at SUU. SUU students receive hands-on experience and practicum credit for early childhood, special education, nursing and other classes through their work with the Head Start and Early Intervention programs.

The presence of Community Support Services as part of the SUU Office of Regional Services also reflects Southern Utah University's support of public and regional service programs in southwestern Utah communities.

THE FLAGPOLES, BETWEEN THE HUNTER CONFERENCE CENTER AND OLD MAIN

THE HOUSE OF LDS FRATERNITY, DELTA PHI KAPPA, CIRCA 1960S

CHAPEL EXERCISES, 1906

CHAPTER XXIII

Religious Education

"When I'm feeling down, I know I can go to the Institute and somebody will be there who cares. There's a certain peace there..."

Gloria Nelson, student 1997

When B.N.S was born in 1897, the issue of church and state in education was very much on the minds of Utahns. A bill before the state legislature in 1890 proposed tax-supported denominational schools. It did not pass. The first tax-supported public high school came in 1890, and this seemed the way of the future. Yet in the decade from 1888-1897, the Church of Jesus Christ of Latter-day Saints established more than thirty stake academies. These were private, tuition-supported schools in which the day opened with singing and prayer, and the student body attended a weekly theology class in addition to one period per day of L.D.S. theology.[1]

As a state school, the Branch Normal could not advocate the tenets of any religious sect, but the majority of the people of Cedar City, and the faculty as well, were strong in their Mormon faith, and their zeal for education was part and parcel with their religion.

The first year's circular for the Southern Branch of the State Normal School announced:

Chapel exercises will be held at the beginning of each day. Attendance upon these exercises will be optional, but all students are cordially invited to be present regularly.[2]

Chapel exercises were held "to bring students and teachers more closely together, and to instruct along lines of morality."[3] Though outwardly non-sectarian, these devotionals were shaped by their Latter-day Saint participants, and their "lines of morality" usually took the

form of sermons that would have been just as comfortable in local Sunday Schools.

Chapel, in some form, was part of the college for more than 35 years. Its evolution is a fascinating revelation of the gradual secularization of the school itself. In the nation as a whole, the early decades of the twentieth century brought strong challenges to the sacred and replaced concern for values education with "modern" thought.

In 1908, its 11th year, BNS announced that formerly daily chapel services would now be held "each week." The announcement in the circular for that year reflected the dichotomy of the times:

The necessity of ethical instruction is recognized and regular chapel exercises are conducted each week by the teachers and students. While theological creeds cannot be taught in these meetings, the necessity of honesty, virtue, temperance, and upright attitude in all walks of life is inculcated and emphasized as the fundamentals to success in life. Besides the ethical training received, the students have numerous opportunities in these exercises for developing power in public speaking and reciting.[4]

In actual practice, "chapel" was becoming "assembly." The retrospective school calendar for 1915-16, included such chapel subjects as Mr. Homer's December 7 talk on "Ragging" and a January 4 presentation on New Year's resolutions. Also listed were: October 21, "Special chapel: completion of the plans for the building of the 'A'"; October 26, "Court in chapel for those who did not help build the 'A'"; January 18, "The B. B. club entertains in chapel"; February 1, "Freshies entertain in chapel"; and April 11, "Seniors entertain in chapel (lots of fun)."[5]

The proliferation of secular thought in state schools peaked nationwide after the First World War. In Cedar City, the trend was slower, but "weekly" chapel quietly became "frequent" chapel in the 1918-19 catalog, and the 1924-25 catalog made chapel attendance mandatory, revealing concern from the administration, but lagging voluntary attendance on the part of students, who were becoming caught up in the "New Education."

The response on the part of the churches led to the development of a marvelous new partnership which largely replaced competition between church schools and state schools. It also replaced the original intent of chapel. Having discovered that education for all members from elementary through college levels was beyond their financial means, churches undertook the more limited role of providing religious education, trusting that educators in state schools would properly fulfill the complementary role. In the words of one LDS educator in 1928:

My judgment leads me to the conclusion that finally and inevitably we shall withdraw from the academic field and center upon religious education. It is only a question of when we may best do that.. I look forward to the time when we shall have no fears. In the main, the men in the state universities are seeking the truth, and I think it somewhat a foolish idea to believe that they are willfully perverting the truth.[6]

What the BAC couldn't do legally on campus, strengthen students' faith in God, the local churches began to do for the students who worshiped in their separate congregations. Citizens of faith built facilities for religious education and for student worship off campus. The BAC, in turn, befriended campus ministers, offered credit toward graduation for general theology courses when taught by ministers with sufficient academic credentials, and recognized religious clubs as an important part of the extracurricular campus milieu.

In our overview of religious activities, we will first consider the student programs of the Latter-day Saints, then those of other denominations.

*I*n some ways, the founding of the Cedar City LDS Seminary mirrors the founding of the school itself. In January of 1925, William R. Palmer, president of the Parowan Stake, initiated a seminary building project. Thomas J. Jones was appointed chairman, with Hillman Dalley as secretary and treasurer. Speaking in stake conference, President Palmer gave a charge to the building committee and encouraged church members to contribute generously toward the completion of the project. He reminded them, "All we have is on the altar."[7]

The original estimated cost of the building was $15,260 to be raised by members of the stake. The Presiding Bishop's Office contributed $2,600 over and above the original estimate after deciding to include a combined stake presidency office and bishops' tithing vault in the building, but the entire cost of the seminary itself was borne by the local people without any assistance from the central building committee. The Church agreed to pay the teacher's salary from general church funds.

The Latter-day Saints soon got behind the seminary project, and donations were not long in coming. On June 2, 1925, property was acquired from Pete B. Fife and George W. Hunter at an ideal location on west Center Street, which led from the Tabernacle to the BAC, in close proximity to Cedar City's educational facilities.[8]

On June 20, 1925, President Palmer spoke about the on-going project in the monthly meeting of the stake presidency, high council, and bishoprics. At that time, he set apart and blessed, as members of the fund-raising committee, President Jones, his counselor in the stake presidency, plus Elias M. Corry and Frank B. Wood.

Excavation began July 19, with the school year fast approaching. Arrangement was made to begin the year in "temporary quarters," but the Iron County Record of October 9, 1925 reported that classes had already moved into the still uncompleted building. The walls and roof were up, one coat of plaster was on, and the sub-floor was laid, so why not teach there? Brother Anderson[9] and his students occupied one room while the construction continued around them. When later completed, the seminary building was dedicated by Adam S. Bennion.

A front-page article in the Record for September 11, 1925, announced the fall course schedule. Under the tutelage of Andrew M. Anderson, the first principal, a course for high school students in Old Testament History was to be offered at 8:00 a.m. and one at 10:40 a.m., with others to be arranged "according to requirements and convenience of students." The text was the Bible, plus an outline that could be purchased at the seminary. No tuition was charged.

Participants were released from the BAC during their seminary period. One-half unit of credit was transferred to their school record after successful completion of a seminary course. While intended primarily for students in school, the seminary was also open to those who were not in school, and "students of any religious belief are also welcome to enroll." Students in 9th grade, attending the junior high school, were not included until several years later.

The first year response was enthusiastic. Two classes became three, with the third period added at 8:40 a.m. The total enrollment was 117 by October 9[10] and 121 by the Christmas break, when non-students from the community were again invited to enroll, provided classes didn't get too crowded.[11]

Cedar City townspeople continued their donations in money and in kind. Their contributions paid the $200 per year building maintenance. Mayhew H. Dalley donated a large American flag. Bishop E. M. Corry, Charles Heyborne, William H. Leigh, and Herbert Webster donated religious pictures, and Mrs. Francelle Corry donated a bust of President Brigham Young.[12]

Since the BAC included college freshman and sophomores as well as high school students, Brother Anderson also offered a college seminary course. This 1925 class was aptly described by the Iron County Record as "the first college Seminary class in the church school system."[13] Indeed, the title "LDS Institutes," which now identifies such college programs, was not adopted until April 17, 1928, having been suggested earlier that year by Jay G. Eldridge, Dean of Faculty at the University of Idaho.[14]

First announced as Bible Literature, Cedar City's college seminary course was retitled New Testament Ethics. With no prior curriculum for such a course, Brother Anderson obtained permission from Dean Milton Bennion to use an outline Bennion had created for his classes in Ethics at the University of Utah. Hence, the first principal of the Branch Normal in 1897 developed the curriculum used in 1925 by the first principal of the BAC's seminary!

From the first year on, college students

received credit toward graduation for completion of certain religion courses. In this way, their study of religious and moral values became part of their college training. This pattern continued for 64 years.[15]

FIRST SEMINARY BUILDING

The college seminary class met temporarily in the bishop's office, but later moved into the new seminary building with the high school students. In October, there were 34 enrolled in the college course, which increased to 41 by the Christmas break.[16]

After one year at the seminary, Andy Anderson accepted employment in the fall of 1926 at the junior high school, where he later served as principal.[17] His replacement at the seminary was Gustive O. Larson.

What a tribute of gratitude Brother Larson deserves! Building on Brother Anderson's initial foundations, Gus Larson gave lasting shape to every aspect of LDS religious education in Cedar City. With the exception of one three-year leave, he guided the program through nearly three decades. The only individual ever to serve church education longer in Cedar City was Garry Graf.

During 1926-36, Brother Larson taught primarily high school students at the seminary, since they predominated at the BAC, but his work with the college students was particularly stimulating for him. His college seminary classes, reported as "institute of religion" after that term was introduced in Idaho,[18] benefited from the pedagogical skills developed in his pre-Cedar years. He pioneered new courses and applied his own innovative methodologies, including illustrated lectures. His appetite for

ANDREWS AND THE FIRST COLLEGE SEMINARY CLASS

Gustive O. Larson taught the students of the BAC from 1926 to 1954 with time out to preside over the Swedish Mission from 1936 to 1939. He came from the Richfield Seminary with his new wife, Virginia Bean Larson. Sister Larson contributed to the musical community at the college, teaching piano, chorus, and opera, accompanying and assisting in concerts and programs. She was also hostess for many student activities. Brother Larson taught Bible Study, Comparative World Religions, and Courtship and Marriage, and had charge of the "Institute Ward" for out-of-town students. In addition to developing the seminary and institute, Brother Larson taught history and sociology at the college and was elected in the fall of 1941 as vice president of the faculty association. While in Cedar City, he also gave his energy to community affairs. He became a leader in the Red Cross, the Democratic Party, the Heart Association, the library board, the Utah Heritage Foundation, and Rotary International. More than eight academic and historical societies counted him a member. In 1954 Gus Larson accepted a position at Brigham Young University as associate professor, first in the College of Religion and later in the History Department. His publications include about sixty-five articles and three books: *Prelude to the Kingdom* (1947), *Outline History of Utah and the Mormons* (1958), and *The "Americanization" of Utah for Statehood* (1971). At commencement May 31, 1974, SUSC recognized his scholarship and vast influence as a teacher historian with an honorary doctorate.

knowledge and his desire to present challenging perspectives to college level minds led him to pursue advanced theology study during the summers.

From 1936 to 1939, while Brother Larson was out of the country, H. Alvah Fitzgerald took his place. Brother Fitzgerald's term of service is most remembered for the construction of the first institute building.

When ninth grade students were brought into the seminary, Joy F. Dunyon and Garland W. Puzey served as seminary teachers to help with the increased student load. Most of the high school students were still at the BAC, but as the new Cedar City High School was proposed, then begun, seminary and institute responsibilities were divided. Brother Dunyon became seminary principal, and plans were undertaken for the new institute building.

The change was none too soon. Brother Fitzgerald recalled that before the institute building was constructed, the hall, basement,

and office of the seminary building were in use as "classrooms."[19]

Stake president William R. Palmer, whose presidency was headquartered in the said office, spearheaded the construction drive. Property was acquired on the corner of 300 West and Center Street, just west of the seminary building, where a home formerly occupied by Dod Hunter had stood. The *Iron County Record* for July 6, 1939, announced:

Work was started Wednesday morning on the construction of a new LDS Institute building in Cedar City. The contract for the construction of the building was let last week to George A. Wood. President Palmer reports that the new building will provide a very modern, complete and beautiful institute for college students who study in Cedar City.

The *Record* for July 13 announced that E. M. Corry would chair a committee composed of himself, I. E. Riddle, and Wm. B. Adams to gather funds. The total cost of the building was $30,000, but policies had changed since the construction of the seminary. This time, general church funds generously paid for all but $4,100, which was raised locally by donations of cash, time, and labor.

The new building was much to be admired. It was faced with yellow brick above a red sandstone base and included a classroom furnished in solid oak, a kitchen, a recreation room, a large social hall and a chapel for religious services."[20]

On Sunday, March 31, 1940, Elder John A. Widtsoe of the Quorum of the Twelve Apostles

1940 INSTITUTE BUILDING (NOW THE J. REUBEN CLARK ALUMNI HOUSE)

gave the dedicatory prayer. President Heber J. Grant, who had planned to be there, was unable to attend because of a recent illness, but Franklin L. West, LDS Commissioner of Education and Elmer G. Peterson, President of the Utah State Agricultural College, came for the dedication.[21]

When Gus Larson returned in 1939, the new building was already nearing completion. With separate buildings and an independent seminary faculty, he was now designated director of the Institute of Religion. Excepting the war years, 1943-46, when reduced enrollments again coalesced seminary and institute responsibilities, Brother Larson's primary focus became the college students at the BAC. In fact, during all of his twenty-five years in Cedar City, he alone taught every college level LDS religion class.

But not quite alone. He often avowed that the best decision of his life was his marriage to Virginia Bean. She became his steady companion in the work, volunteering countless hours as hostess, adviser, pianist, chorus director, and as mother-away-from-home to his students. The students saw Brother and Sister Larson as a team.

Though church employed, Brother Larson established what was to become a longstanding pattern of close knit relationships between LDS religious educators and the college faculty. His scholastic credentials, his historical research and publications, and his community leadership earned him well deserved respect. He and his wife were always considered peers and colleagues by the faculty and directors of the BAC.

His students, however, saw his role as different from that of their other teachers. A tribute in the 1942 *Agricola* is typical of their feelings:

While the faculty up on the hill sees to it that

our minds are developed as much as possible, G. O. Larson, director of the Institute, takes care of our souls.[22]

Some of Brother Larson's success came with the times. A post-war yearbook reports:

Mr. Larson proved his adeptness as a teacher in his Courtship and Marriage Class by getting 30 percent of the class engaged before the first quarter was over.[23]

In a 1943 personal letter to Commissioner Frank L. West, Brother Larson estimated that in the previous three years, his classes and activities had touched the lives of from 80 to 85 percent of the BAC students.[24]

From the end of the Larson era through 1997, seven men served as directors of the Cedar City Institute of Religion. Each will be listed here, along with the full-time instructors whose service in Cedar City began during his administration. Many secretaries, librarians, custodians, and part-time instructors, unnamed here, greatly enhanced the functions of the Institute. In the 1990s, when rapid growth in the student population at Southern Utah University brought a tremendous flood of new students to institute classrooms, the service of part-time faculty was

*B*rother Garry W. Graf represents the dedication of the LDS institute "brethren" to the welfare of students. He was born in Escalante in 1936 and raised in southern Utah. In 1964, he came to Cedar City with a fresh M.A. from Brigham Young University to take over as seminary principal in the first year of the new high school. After two years he transferred to the institute. While Brother Graf taught most of the courses in the curriculum, he specialized in teaching the doctrines of salvation: Teachings of the Prophet Joseph Smith, Doctrines of the Gospel, and Doctrine and Covenants. He served students as advisor to Lambda Delta Sigma, Sigma Gamma Chi, and various activity committees. Then he gave himself for eleven years to service in the college stake, on the high council and as bishop of the Sixth Ward (for married students). In more than 30 years of teaching, advising, loving, and caring, Brother Graf has directly influenced the lives of more than 12,000 students. With his wife, the former Donna Chamberlain, he is the father of nine children and the grandfather of 20.

1972
INSTITUTE
BUILDING

especially needed and appreciated.

When Brother Larson left to join the Brigham Young University faculty, Paul E. Felt took over the directorship. He served from 1954 to 1957. College expansion during his administration necessitated the use of seminary personnel to teach institute classes part time. Remodeling was already necessary in the institute building, where the basement was divided into a gameroom, a new classroom, and other facilities.

Paul E. Dahl, one of Brother Felt's part-time teachers, became full-time institute director for 1957-61. He was assisted by Franklin D. Day, who was also Seminary Coordinator of the Southern Utah District.

Brother Day became institute director in 1961 and served for three years. He was joined by full-time faculty member Ray H. Gleave starting in 1961 and by Leland H. Gentry in 1962.

Joseph C. Felix guided the institute as director from 1964 to 1977, serving longer in that position than anyone except Gus Larson. On February 26, 1964, a new Cedar City High School was dedicated to the south of town, and a seminary building was constructed to accommodate high school students at that location. The second seminary building, built on 300 West at the time of the construction of the first Cedar City High School, became the main institute classroom building. Brother Felix maintained his director's office in the first institute building, but institute classes actually met simultaneously in three locations: the first seminary building, the first institute building, and the second seminary building.

During Brother Felix's service, George L. Strebel joined the faculty in 1965, and Garry W. Graf, Gilbert W. Hull, Rex L. Christensen, and Boyd Beagley in 1966. Brother Graf must be singled out for his long service to religious education in Cedar City. He still continues as a valued faculty member in 1997, anticipating yet another five years of teaching before retirement. At that time he will have personally witnessed nearly half of the seventy-one year history of LDS church education at the college.

Brother Felix welcomed J. Phillip Hanks in 1969 and Michael W. Bawden in 1972. Brother Hanks' musical talents resulted in the organiza-

tion of hundreds of institute students into performing choirs that travelled extensively.

During Brother Felix's administration, enrollment growth justified another new building to be used as the institute of religion and the SUSC Stake Center. Ground was broken on July 3, 1970, and on February 13, 1972, LeGrand Richards of the Quorum of the Twelve Apostles dedicated the new facility at 650 West Center Street.[25] Designed by architect John Rowley and built by General Contractors Blackburn and Gower at a cost of $633,000 plus furnishings,[26] it was bigger by far than former church education buildings, occupying 25,255 square feet.[27]

No longer needed, the former buildings eventually passed into other uses. The first seminary building had been razed. The first institute building became office space for other church services until it was offered by the LDS Church to Southern Utah University. Taking title on January 1, 1996, the university remodeled the structure to become the J. Reuben Clark, Jr. Alumni House. The second seminary building was sold to private entities.

C. Kent Hugh served as institute director from 1977 to 1986. In his first year, Doyl N. Ipson and Neil C. Petty joined the faculty, and in the next year, A. Burnell Hunt. Mervin W. Adair came in 1984.

Kent Hugh was replaced by Richard S. Williams, who served as director from 1986 until his retirement in 1995. During his administration, Robert A. Cloward joined the faculty in 1990, James R. Carver in 1991, and Dan L. Dedrickson in 1993. Much of the 1992-93 year was occupied with the expansion of the institute building to provide approximately 10,000 square feet of additional space for offices, classrooms, and worship services.[28]

Brent R. Esplin took over as director in 1995, welcoming Ralph McAffee and W. Sidney Young a year later. Brother McAffee brought with him years of experience organizing show choirs and expanded the choral program at the institute to include a travelling group. Brother Esplin continued to serve in 1997, with a faculty that year consisting of eight full-time employees, including himself, plus eight part-time instructors drawn from Utah South Area Office personnel and from community volunteers.

As early as the 1960s, additional faculty members offered pre-service training at the institute to potential seminary teachers, a parallel to the strong college program in education.

Over the years, the institute of religion faculties have left a significant mark on the culture of the university and of Cedar City. Always men of academic standing, many holding doctoral degrees, they have included some with formal training in religious education, but many others trained in such fields as educational administration, law, history, counseling and psychotherapy, family science, and linguistics. Their willingness and dedication to the challenging profession of bringing students to God is to be commended. In addition to their daily work with students, they have made time for ecclesiastical assignments both in the campus community and in local LDS congregations, for a multitude of speaking engagements, for guiding historical tours, for scouting and other youth programs, as well as involvement in many local community service organizations. They are also family men, committed to nurturing strong, godly homes.

During his years as institute director, Gus Larson oversaw student leaders of the Mutual Improvement Association and Sunday School, who organized Sabbath worship and mid-week services. The institute became a "student ward" with a limited ecclesiastical program for out-of-town students, while local students were supposed to worship with their town wards. The lure of association with others their age was too strong for some locals, however, and Brother Larson's "ward" got a reputation for stealing them away! A jovial toast to him at an institute social was patterned after the 23rd Psalm. It began:

*I leadeth them in the paths of righteousness
Away from the wards.
Yea, though the Institute is my dominion
I shall fear no bishop,
For the crowd is with me.*[29]

This dilemma was resolved during Paul Felt's term as institute director. In the fall of 1956, full church programs, including women's Relief Society, were made available with the organization of a student-staffed branch. This paved the way for the organization of the first college ward in 1957. On Sunday morning of the February 23-24 Cedar Stake Quarterly Conference, Elder Henry D. Moyle of the Quorum of the Twelve Apostles held a special meeting for all college students at the institute chapel. He presented the name of Joseph Fillerup, a professor on campus, to be sustained as bishop of a student ward, to be called the Cedar Ninth Ward.

With the growth of CSU, the Ninth Ward was divided into two wards on February 12, 1961, one for single students and one for married students. By the end of that school year, a third stu-

dent ward (the second for single students), was created.

From this beginning, successive growth led to further ward divisions and to the creation of a CSU College Stake on January 5, 1966, and a second stake on April 30, 1995.

By 1997, 18 student wards were divided between two meeting locations: the institute building, serving the Cedar City University Second Stake, and a stake center constructed just north of the institute building on 600 West for the Cedar City University First Stake. Plans had also been announced to remodel the nearby Cedar City North Stake Center as a third meetinghouse for campus wards.[30]

The availability of strong programs for Latter-day Saint students has long been a major enticement for many to attend college in Cedar City. Parents and students planning their educational futures hope to find friendships with others who share their same love for God and desires for a life of faith. Institute director Brent Esplin reported that an SUU coach who was not LDS came to visit him at the institute, saying, "Tell me all about your program. A lot of athletes I'm trying to recruit want to know how your church is doing here!"

Devotion to their religion causes a significant percentage of 19-year-old LDS men on campus as well as a few women to volunteer one and-one-half or two years for missionary service. The institute provides missionary training courses and encouragement for them to serve. When they return, they enrich the college environment with their leadership and people skills, and some with their intimate acquaintance with international languages and cultures.

In addition to offering courses in religion and a place for student worship, the LDS institute of religion has always been a center for social activities. Some were planned, some ad hoc, but there was always something going on. If nobody else was around, the institute faculty were good for a rousing game of ping pong.

Dances and other social gatherings after Tuesday MIA meetings were well attended, except during the war years, when the men were sorely missed. Preparation for weekly institute broadcasts at a local radio station, float building for the Homecoming Parade, volunteer service for local charities, practicing for the live Nativity Scene enactment at Christmas time, there was no lack for involvement.

Lambda Delta Sigma, a co-educational fraternity, was organized at the BAC when the Cedar High School divided off the high school students in the early 1940's. Inevitably the largest social club on campus, Lambda Delta Sigma met weekly and divided into chapters for men and chapters for women, each with its own officers and advisors.

In 1966, Cedar City was chosen as a pilot area for the LDS Student Association. The new organization was highly successful in its first year and was approved for world-wide implementation wherever Church members were found on college campuses. From that time, LDSSA, with its student-staffed council, served as a coordinating body for all institute activities.

Under LDSSA, the Lambda Delta Sigma sorority, bearing the same name as the previous church club, but now just for women, began to function during the 1966-67 school year.[31] The same year, a separate men's fraternity, Pi Beta, took the place of the former Lambda Delta Sigma men's chapters. Kenneth Cox, local president of Pi Beta, suggested a new name, Sigma Gamma Chi, meaning "Service to God and Country." The name was adopted by the fraternity.[32]

Several clubs for LDS returned missionaries have functioned on campus. Friars Club began in 1949-50, affiliating late in its first year with a national returned-missionary fraternity, Delta Phi. After this fraternity lapsed, Kolob Club organized in 1958-59, and lasted three years. Delta Phi revived and was rechartered during the 1965-66 year with the new name of Delta Phi Kappa. It was active and well respected at CSU/SUSC for 10 years, but dissolved in deference to Sigma Gamma Chi when Church leaders saw a need for just one LDS fraternity.[33]

One of the most significant contributions of the institute to campus general education was the weekly forum. For many years, typical weekly audiences of 250-300 students and faculty heard invited speakers from many fields of expertise present lectures at the institute. The series switched from Friday to Tuesday to Thursday and finally to a Sunday night fireside format. Visiting speakers included: Karl Brooks, Mayor of St. George; J. Elliott Cameron, Dean of Students at BYU; Dixie Leavitt, Utah State Senator; Philo Farnsworth, inventor of television; Robert J. Matthews, authority on the Joseph Smith Translation of the Bible; David Yarn, philosopher; Royden C. Braithwaite, President of SUSC; and a host of others. Occasionally, as with visiting general authorities and Church presidents, gatherings were held in the auditorium and attended by many more. The visit of President Gordon B. Hinckley on February 11, 1997 attracted 4,200 students and faculty to a gathering in the Centrum.

Formal organization of the Community Presbyterian Church (sometimes early referred to as the Union Presbyterian Church) took place in Cedar City on May 9, 1926. There were 35 members in the congregation. The church building on the corner of First East and Second North, dedicated May 26 of that same year, was the first Protestant house of worship in Southern Utah. It served not only Presbyterians, but other area Protestants as well.[34] A 1926 BAC activities booklet shows a photograph of the building and its congregation with this caption: "Presbyterian Chapel - This new chapel was dedicated in May. Its pastor, Reverend Elmer P. Gieser, is a real friend to the students of the college."[35]

As other Protestant denominations established themselves in Cedar City, caring pastors ministered to students of their own faiths. Small numbers hampered full organization, but they did what they could. For example, the Rev. John Manweiler, pastor of Trinity Lutheran Church, arranged for Tina Clark, the only university student attending his church in 1996-97, to attend a Lutheran student retreat in Alamosa, Colo., in the fall of the year.[36]

Officially chartered Protestant and interfaith clubs appeared at SUSC in the 1970s. In 1970-71, Christian Youth Fellowship organized "to meet the needs and wants of the many different religions." Professor Jim Cotts was the adviser. In 1972-73 they were called Thunderbird Christian Fellowship.[37] In 1973-74, Maranatha! Christian Fellowship appeared, also non-denominational, promoting "the importance of the Bible for spiritual guidance" and "spiritual growth in the knowledge of the love, grace, and power of the Almighty God and our savior Jesus Christ."[38] SUSC yearbooks chronicle the club for three years. The Baptist Student Union was officially recognized on campus beginning in 1975-76. This group sponsored Bible studies and planned activities. Membership was not limited to Baptists, but was open to everyone.[39] During this period, these clubs ranged from six to 16 active members, plus guests and visitors, but their outreach and service touched many lives.

In the 1990s, Protestant students desiring campus affiliation participated in United Campus Ministry, an interdenominational club. UCM respected "the richness of our varied traditions" and invited representation on their board of directors from each community church in town.[40] The club was officially listed as a social/service organization, and met on Thursdays in the Centrum. Their records with the University list Lynne (Finton) Brown as adviser. Membership in 1993 was 25.[41] United Campus Ministry taught Christian service with such projects as painting walls and stacking supplies at the Cedar City Care and Share on March 10, 1994, and visitation at the Cedar Care Center on January 14, 1995. The latter activity was evaluated by Jay Spillers, UCM president, as "a major success! It made both the elderly people and our group feel really good." UCM also sponsored films and devotionals on campus that were open to the student population at large.[42]

Although Catholics had lived in Cedar City much earlier, the first Roman Catholic parish was established in town in June, 1936. Father Alphonse A. LeMay, who had first come to the area in 1935, served as pastor until 1943 and again from 1946 to 1950. A remodeled home on property purchased from the Leigh estate became Christ the King Catholic Church.[43]

The Newman Club, the Catholic Church identity on non-Catholic campuses, was first sponsored by the parish at CSU under the direction of the third pastor, Rev. Everett R. Harman, who served in Cedar City 1955-65. Father Harman had extensive education, experience as an educator, and was a licensed architect, having attended Massachusetts Institute of Technology in Cambridge in 1920-21. He was ordained in 1949.

In a letter to Bishop Federal of the Salt Lake City Diocese in 1960, Father Harman reported:

...the college called me to say that I had been approved for three courses, one in philosophy; one in history, ecumenical councils; one for psychology, personality problems for credit. One course in Religion will be without credit, all on the same basis as the LDS Institute. I am calling them the Newman Hall Courses, given at our new "Newman Hall" recently christened![44]

"Newman Hall" was an addition to the church building, constructed specifically for the purpose of conducting regular religion classes for college students.[45] Father Harman was a man of energy and vision, but his responsibilities kept him spread thin. In 1961, he reported:

The college teaching courses keep me busy, and a talk I gave on Communism yesterday at the college. The college... women's

group here kept me busy.[46]

Father Harman focused on religious education as long as he served in Cedar City. In 1963, he suggested the establishment by monks or nuns of a monastery in the area. Noting that "the present parish site and Newman Center is near the College of Southern Utah," he recommended the build-

NEWMAN CLUB

ing up of a "complete religious and education program at every level."[47] Although this plan did not unfold as he had hoped, one part of it did—the later assignment of Patricia Riley and Eileen Dewsnup, two Holy Cross Sisters, to parish duties, including Catholic campus ministry at SUSC, but this had to wait until the 1980s.[48]

After the time of Father Harman, the next identification of Newman Club on campus occurred late in the 1979-80 school year. The SUSC yearbook for 1980 showed 16 student members, listing Joe Lamoreaux as adviser.[49]

The club organized in April 1980 at the Church Hall, with a visiting priest from Salt Lake City to help them. The next year, Eric Houle and Pat Czarny, members of Newman Club, were SUSC student body president and vice president, respectively. The club's candidate for Homecoming Queen won "Miss Talent SUSC." The club was one of the top fund-raisers for the March of Dimes, raising more than $4,000. Meetings were held monthly at students' apartments. One member of the club recalled, "We developed life-long friendships and grew in spirituality."[50]

After this, activity of the Newman Club fluctuated from year to year. Even though it was not always chartered on campus it continued to be part of the functioning parish.

In his first months as new pastor, Father Michael J. Winterer scheduled a separate mass for students each Sunday at the church at 7:00 p.m., followed by social activities. Weekly attendance at his student masses and socials in spring 1997 averaged 20 to 30.[51]

(This chapter was written by Dr. Robert A. Cloward, Instructor LDS Institute, Cedar City)

TREE PLANTING,
ARBOR DAY, 1905

RODDY COX, EARLY
MANAGER OF THE
HEAT PLANT

FACULTY STAFF ASSOCIATION PLAY,
ARSENIC AND OLD LACE, 1962

CHAPTER XXIV

The Staff, Faculty Staff Associated Women, Emeriti

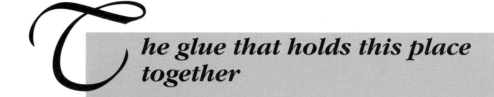

he glue that holds this place together

The terms "faculty" and "staff" have been used interchangeably at SUU since its founding. But as the University has grown and a diversity of duties developed, the two expressions have come to signify a division of responsibilities. Faculty is generally defined to mean those people who fill full-time teaching positions in the academic sense, and staff describes the workers who serve as support to faculty, students, and administrators as well as to the public.[1]

At the Branch Normal School, teachers performed tasks that would now fit into the staff category, never questioning that their "extra-mile" efforts were simply part of their duties. They managed custodial chores, room preparation and equipment management. When a principal assumed responsibility to keep the lawns mowed, he also assumed that his faculty could sweep their own floors, paint their own offices or perform any of the jobs necessary to keep the place running smoothly.

Budget constraints and expediency demanded that everyone on campus should do whatever had to be done to meet the needs of the institution. This was merely an extension of the philosophy which brought about the establishment of the college in the first place. A teacher of home economics or a groundskeeper had the common goal of fulfilling the founding edict of survival. And they survived through sheer determination and willingness to do what needed to be done, when it needed to be done.

The early catalogs declare the existence of two janitors and a custodian, but list no names. Whether or not there was a person who swept the floors, it is clear that the heating plant would need a caretaker, and an early photo of Roddy Cox, shovel in hand, verifies his position. The coal was hauled from the mine and delivered to the school by the Ashdown Brothers.

As the rocky harshness of the hill was of special concern to George Decker, he began to enlist the efforts of faculty, staff and students. Some of the tall trees of the campus are tangible evidence that faculty, staff and students responded.

When William Flanigan was hired in 1909, his job description included management of the farm, the heat plant, janitorial care of the buildings and responsibility for the campus grounds. He remembered:

I never did like farming and if it hadn't been for my desire to work on the campus, I don't believe I'd have stuck. After nine years of running from one place to the other, I asked if I couldn't be given only the heat plant and the campus. . . There had been 12 evergreens put out on the campus before I came, but I wanted to see more—lots more.[2]

By the time George W. Decker had retired to manage his own farm, Branch Normal School had become Branch Agricultural College, and Roy F. Homer had become director. Mr. Homer

SHELDON
GRANT

thought Flanigan's preoccupation with trees was less than practical:

One of the first things I did was to win over Roy F. Homer. Mr. Homer thought it would be a waste of time, but I kept at him until finally he said, 'Well, if you think you can make them grow, go and get them.' So I did! I took a team and went up to Dave C. Bulloch's place. I'd go every spring to get a few trees. I got a lot from Dave Haight's, Milt Urie's, Mrs. Tom Urie's, Kumen Jones' and the Forest Reserve. I always cut strictly according to the rules. Sometimes I'd trade trees for the use of a team and wagon. I used all sorts of hooks and crooks, but I got them... The tree that became the traditional Christmas tree, we brought down and planted on June 7, 1919.

And did he confer with his employers about where to place the trees? Did he have a blueprint or a plan ?

Well, no, you never see two people who think they know landscaping agree. . . and it's good they don't. You get a better variety that way. God is the best landscaper I know, so I patterned after Him.

ELDRO
RIGBY,
1940's

Will Flanigan became a symbol to generations of staff people. Those who followed him and worked to create a world of beauty on the campus were no less dedicated than he. Sheldon Grant, Verl Kelsey, Wilmer Anderson, Gary Davis, Joyce Messer and Chris Gale, to name a notable few, were inspired by their own love of the campus as well as the tradition of earlier days.

The early emphasis upon agricultural, livestock, and industrial studies provided the opportunity for farm specialists, dairymen, and herdsmen to teach students through actual work experience. Auto mechanics and machine shop were taught by doing the maintenance work on college vehicles and equipment. Homebuilding involved construction of residences as large as the home of the college president. Many staff duties now carried out by paid professionals were performed by students, and although the student work force has remained the basic group of hourly-wage workers, their staff supervisors usually have classified titles and serve as planners and efficiency experts in assuring the smooth operation of the infrastructure of

ED
MATHESON

the campus. They also instruct the students, as they work with them, forming a long-standing source of camaraderie and friendship.

The world of work was also the world of sociality for staff and faculty, because all their lives intertwined with the students, and they shared a common focus upon the well-being of the school. Faculty friendships were remembered for their characteristic disregard for division of labor. Ben Cooley, Ianthus Wright, Ed Matheson and Eldro Rigby were a foursome. Cooley taught industrial arts and Ianthus Wright, teacher education, Matheson's responsibility was the heat plant and Rigby's the farm, but each offered assistance to the other when more hands were needed. Then, when the work was done, they gathered other campus comrades and camped and hunted together.

When Eldro Rigby became the manager of the BAC farm in 1937, he moved his wife Zina and their growing family into the farm manager's home on 200 South Street at 700 West. His salary was $80 a month and rent-free residence in the home. Long, hard days included working with purebred sheep, milk cows and beef cattle; with corn and soy bean crops, from planting to harvesting; and with detailed record-keeping on the extensive experimental program. It was made possible, he remembered, because of his student helpers:

I never could have done it all except for my good helpers. I had boys like Conrad Hatch and Gail Duncan and all those Stewart boys, who were expert cow milkers. V.R. Magleby was one of the student workers, always diligent in his duties.

After 22 years on the campus farm, the operation was moved to the valley west of Cedar City. For a time Rigby worked both on campus and at the farm, eventually returning to supervise the campus custodial program. This was a definite career change, which brought with it the advantage of close association with Joe Roberts, legendary for his kindess, his hard work and generosity.

Students who had left chemistry notes in classrooms now darkened, co-eds who had been locked out of the dorm because they arrived a few seconds late for dorm curfew, or nervous performers who needed an early morning practice could always find Joe Roberts, divert him from his constant watchcare and prevail upon him to rummage in his small tin bucket of keys or his large round key-ring to let them in. There were no master keys. Security of the students, the campus and the buildings rested in the capable hands of Joe Roberts. He was the first to arrive and the last to leave, no matter what the function, and whether or not he had official responsibility.

Reid Cox, superintendent of maintenance, and his staff, were expert at fixing whatever was out of commission, at as little cost as possible. Yet, despite the never-ending series of emergencies, Mr. Cox always found time and patience to see that each need was met by his staff or himself, and that the work was the best that could be done. He concerned himself with the most minute of details, from finding the right paint for the beds in the women's dormitory to innovative counsel and help with student projects. Cox worked with the students early and late to insure the success of their activities, whether they were building floats for the homecoming parade or hanging crepe paper for the prom.

Effective ministering extended beyond the grounds and physical facilities. Registrations, credits, accounts and correspondence also had to be managed with diligence and dispatch. Faculty members had filled multiple assignments from the founding of the school. Howard R. Driggs had fulfilled the positions of secretary and registrar while he taught English language and literature. Later, Gilbert Jansen doubled in those duties along with his teaching assignments. When Hazen Cooley arrived to be the financial officer, he juggled public relations, purchasing, financial affairs, calendaring and countless miscellaneous details. He was famous for keeping his finger on the pulse of every aspect of the school; he was invaluable to the directors. The tradition of the financial office inspired constancy. Paul Daniels, Tebbs Adams and Paul Southwick each assumed aspects of the financial tasks, and each left a legacy of superb service.

Ward Robb, who served for more than 40 years as registrar, kept in his head a running tally of students he had allowed to start classes while they were still in the process of coming up with full tuition. Robb's accounts balanced when students ultimately paid, and the students reaped lasting benefits:

I was in the "Ugly Duckling" stage of my learning, but the college personnel, the professors and townspeople seemed to see beyond what I was at

that time; they pulled together to help me plow through...One quarter I was $50 short of being able to register. Mr. Robb said to me, "Go ahead and start your classes. I know you'll pay me when you can." And I did![5]

Secretaries were administrative assistants in the broadest sense of the term. Audrey Duncan, Setsuko Nakamura, Mary Lunt, and Ruth Challis kept their bosses organized. Whether they were called "director" or "president," the chief executives would have struggled without these remarkable ladies.

Many of the miracles resulted from the unity that flourished between faculty and staff. When the survival of the school depended upon rapid expansion of the physical campus and the solution was found in war-surplus buildings, both staff and faculty rolled up their collective sleeves, bringing expertise, manpower and muscle to the challenge. Both groups joined in the college cabin project. Together they cut logs and peeled them, faculty and staff men working together to lay them up; faculty and staff wives prepared tasty meals for their husbands and then made the draperies for the windows in the new cabin.

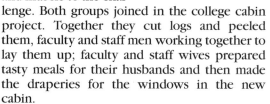

JOSEPH ROBERTS,
PROTECTOR,
WATCHMAN
EXTRAORDINAIRE

When the work was done, they socialized together. A campus activities committee, composed of faculty, staff, students and townspeople, planned and

REID COX,
1943

DOUG
JACKSON

REGISTRAR
WARD
ROBB

organized joint social events. The fall social, Christmas party, and spring breakfast were examples. The fall social often consisted of a venison potluck dinner contributed by successful deer hunters and good cooks who brought side dishes of all kinds. Programs featuring faculty-staff talent often served as the core for assemblies presented for students and Cedar City residents. The famous spring outing to Zion Canyon was a faculty, staff, student party. LaVeve Whetten's description of Senior Sluff Day at Zion Canyon demonstrates the inclusive nature of the society:[4]

It was an annual affair that everyone, students, staff and faculty–looked forward to with great anticipation. The Mulligan stew was prepared in the BAC kitchen under the watchful eye of Mildred Bowers or Grace Hawks. I can't remember the instructor of that year. The stew was then taken down to the Arden Dairy for safekeeping until the next day. On Friday just after noon, Eldro Rigby and I were to transport the food, ahead of the crowd, down to Zion. After everything was loaded, we started for the outing with high spirits for a fun weekend in Zion.

We had traveled to the south end of Cedar, which in those days was just barren terrain. All of a sudden we heard a powerful explosion and stopped to see which of the tires had blown to find that the top of the milk can had shot into the air. The fresh air was filled with a most horrible odor, and the stew had fermented and was a spoiled mess. Luckily, Eldro had his shovel in the back of the truck. He dug a hole and disposed of the stew in short order, the delicious meal gone.

This escapade was during World War II, and so we had to come back to town and find enough food stamps to buy hot dogs and buns–to the very great disappointment of the guests. The big ladle that was always used to stir the stew in the ritual by Pa Manning before partaking of the meal, was unused. Pa Manning made up another original ritual for hot dogs and buns. We all learned a lesson about cooling hot Mulligan stew. Everyone sang, danced, and had a glorious time in spite of the disappointment!

Faculty and staff pooled creative energies and considerable talent in the annual faculty/staff play, always eagerly anticipated by community and campus alike. They produced classic favorites like Harvey, Arsenic and Old Lace, and the Agatha Christie mysteries. Whatever the offering, the plays were sell-outs, for staid and dignified academics became nine-feet tall rabbits or dotty old spinsters, and the town and college-community loved it.

Often presented as theatre-in-the-round, directed by Dr. Paul Vorkink of the eduction department, the productions included the audience in hilarious ways.

Every year singers and musicians representing all ranks of SUU from students to administrators, joined with devotees from the community to perform the annual Christmas presentation of Handel's *Messiah*.

A yearly spring event that brought all elements of the school together was B-Day or Beautification Day. Teachers, students, administrators, and all staff employees dressed in work clothes to clean every nook and cranny of the ever-expanding campus. This annual activity was supervised by the plant operations and grounds personnel, and their guidance and directives were highly respected. Cedar City often coordinated a community-wide clean-up day with the beautification day of the University. One young student, Harl Judd of Kanab, Utah, remembered years later the associations spawned by "B" Day efforts:

I remember with fondness the "B" Days. On these designated days we trimmed trees and shrubs, painted, washed windows, put in concrete sidewalks - anything to keep the campus looking nice and clean. The first project I helped with was painting a giant BAC on the roof of the old fieldhouse. The faculty advisor working alongside me on the project was Theron Ashcroft. Little did I know that a couple of years down the road he would become

HAULING LOGS FOR
COLLEGE CABIN

my father-in-law. The point here is that there was real camaraderie among the students, the staff and the faculty. They really cared.

In the 100th year of its existence, in 1997, the University staff had grown from meager numbers in 1897-98 until the staff force exceeded the faculty in actual count, with its influence notably felt in every department on campus and in the town.

*T*he SUU Staff Association was organized in the early 1960s as a group to formally conduct staff business and to pursue advantages relating to benefits and recognition, just as the Faculty Senate served the same purposes for teachers. However it was not until 1977, that comprehensive guidelines for staff employees' policies and procedures were approved and published. Until that time about four pages of guidelines for non-academic (non-teaching) personnel had sufficed.

In 1990 the Southern Utah University Staff Association Constitution and By-laws were included in the institutional *Policies and Procedures Manual.* The purpose of the Constitution was stated as follows: The non-teaching employees of Southern Utah University, in order to effectively foster a program of mutual helpfulness to ourselves and to Southern Utah University, do hereby unite ourselves and establish this Constitution of the Southern Utah University Staff Association. Excerpts follow:

1. To further the interests of Southern Utah University.
2. To promote high professional standards.
3. To serve as a means of representing the Association with the administration, governing boards and the legislature.
4. To create a spirit of fellowship among the staff, the faculty, the administration, and the students.
5. To foster cooperation with all other employee organizations.

A Utah Higher Education Staff Association Constitution was ratified in August of 1994 for UHESA, the official staff employees' state of Utah organization. The objective of this document is to serve all staff employees in Utah higher education and to better serve the institutions

*O*fficial titles for Bessie Dover evolved, changed and compounded over the years, but involvement with students was perpetual. First assigned to the staff in 1962, she accepted responsibility for information services, including publicity for the Shakespearean Festival. When George Barrus became director of public relations, she remained as assistant, taking the task alone while he left on leave, and resuming full responsiblity when he resigned to accept employment at BYU. For two years she managed the task by herself, including sports reporting. Relief came when Jim Robinson was hired to cover the sports beat.

Dover taught journalism and English, advised student publications and, while juggling those jobs, accepted responsibility as foreign student advisor. She recalls the day she received the assignment:

In 1969, Dr. Braithwaite called me into his office and said to me, "You're the new foreign student adviser. I just had a woman from Samoa in here, and I couldn't understand a word she said."

Realizing that the student was actually from Nigeria, she understood the need to assist the interface process, took up the task and kept it almost 20 years until her retirement in 1988. The foreign student organization became one of the most active on campus, sponsoring International Week, with entertainment and food-fests from the cultures of her charges.

A new designation, in 1972, as assistant director of student activities, required her to get a chauffeur's license to drive the college van filled with students to workshops, conferences and traveling assemblies. Though her title was director of student services, most students called her "Mom." Kenneth Benson, the director, wondered if the appellation carried sufficient dignity, but affectionate relationships prompted the title, and the students were difficult to dissuade.

A masters degree, earned during summers, secured a multi-faceted assignment in 1979, as the institution's career counselor. She no longer chauffeured in the van, but still was surrounded with students of every variety who called her "Mom" in a dozen different tongues.

of higher education and the state of Utah. The UHESA Council consists of two representatives from the staff association of each institution. SUU staff leaders were instrumental in the formation of this new statewide organization. Lois Bulloch, immediate past president of the SUU staff association, served in 1996 as president of UHESA.

In October of 1994, President Gerald R. Sherratt pledged his support by annually allocating budget monies from institutional funds to the SUU Staff Association. With that change each staff member qualified as an official member of the association without payment of dues. Lois Bulloch and Rex Michie represented all SUU staff members in effecting the change, which was approved by President Sherratt.

Although separate in function and organization, the staff association and faculty senate at SUU have remained closely connected as to spirit and mission. Both call upon the other for cooperation, support, and friendship. Students have benefited from this alliance, as has the community in general.

One unifying activity that continues at SUU is a long-held practice of holding departmental open houses during holiday times and to send off, with best wishes, those who retire or move away. SUU presidents have always paralleled this tradition with their own socials at the beginning and ending of each year, during the Christmas season, Homecoming, Founders Day and other special occasions. Retirement dinners for all faculty and staff who have completed their service at SUU are now important years end activities. Retiring employees are immediately invited to join the Emeriti SUU to continue their association with one another and with the institution.

A tradition which has specifically honored staff employees since 1978-79, is the awarding of the Outstanding Staff Member title and an accompanying monetary grant to individuals who have been selected by a committee of campus and community participants to receive this honor. During its initial year, Shirley Cowan was the recipient followed by Ward Robb, Jean Morrison, Ken Benson, Bessie Dover, Zelma Alger, Sandy Gillies, Maxine Stolk, Lorraine Warren and Mary Leone Foley. Since 1988-89, both a male and female recipient were named including Nolan Truman and Eva Deen Milne, R. Scott Phillips and Sheila Johnson, Dale Orton and Treva Peg Thorley, Gary Dunford and Betty Kingsford, Dan McClanahan and Valynne Nicholes, Cal Rollins and Daphne Dalley, Harman Bonniksen and Marlynn Smith, and

Luann Briggs and Chris Gale.

Those who have served as staff association presidents from 1964-65 include Paul Daniels (two terms), Vern Winter, Sheldon Grant, Jack Cannon, James Robinson, Ken Benson, Max Payne, James Piacitelli, Dale Brinkerhoff, Gary Davis, Shirley Cowan, Rex Michie (two terms), Phil Robison, David Taylor, Luann Briggs, Dorian Page, Mary Leone Foley, Dale Orton, Kris Orton, Eric Schmutz, Mitch Bealer, Sandy Gillies, Carlene Holm, Rhea Tuft, Sue Stratton, Jim Stevenson, Lois Bulloch, Sherri Batt (two terms) and Peter Heilquist.

"Inside observers" are surely best-qualified to assess the remarkable manner in which the tradition of unity and loyalty, beginning with Branch Normal School, has carried through the years and through the ranks of those who serve. A cross-section of SUU employees have offered comments about some of the colleagues with whom they have worked as well as a few others who became central to campus history. The accolades offered these staff members are representative of countless others who could receive equal praise.

Paul Southwick, former executive vice president for financial affairs and now a member of the Emeriti SUU, was cited by Jack Cannon, retired director of placement and formerly director of financial aid, as "an administrator who managed the fiscal affairs of the institution most capably from 1967, until his retirement in 1995. He served meticulously with presidents Royden C. Braithwaite, Orville D. Carnahan, and Gerald R. Sherratt during decades of significant growth and increased visibility for SUU. Jack also stated that during his tenure, Paul was often the key liaison to staff personnel in communicating the status of University plans and decisions affecting salaries and other policy matters. "In preparation," Jack said, "Paul Southwick always did his homework well."

Tebbs Adams, another administrator whom Jack Cannon admired, "was a leader who the University was most fortunate to have working in behalf of students and employees." First appointed to the position of controller on July 25, 1972, Tebbs endeared himself to all of his colleagues and gained their respect. In November of 1980, he was hired by the University of Utah to serve as assistant treasurer and chief investment and banking officer. All at SUU were very pleased when Tebbs returned to the local University on August 14, 1984, to fill the position of assistant vice president for financial affairs. He retired on July 1, 1996.

Tebbs not only had the trust of those around him, Cannon said, *but he gave others confidence in doing the right thing at the right time. His integrity was unswerving.*

As with all employee groups in competitive employment, staff salaries were always a concern. Most staff association presidents were active in salary matters and negotiations, especially for those employees on the lower end of the salary scale. Jack Cannon recalled that as far back as the late 1960s, one staff association president was concerned enough to recommend a different approach to salary negotiations. He suggested a flat dollar increase for all employees to negate the fact that "the rich get richer and the poor get poorer," when the same salary percentage increase is applied to all contract personnel. He further suggested that a small percentage increase be added to the flat dollar amount. His was not an original idea, but it was innovative in that situation. Mr. Cannon reported that staff association representatives have found that the SUU administration has always been willing to listen to ideas and has steadily worked to upgrade salaries whenever possible, within the guidelines of the Utah system of higher education. Staff members have generally remained loyal and appreciative of efforts in their behalf by numerous leaders.

Sterling Church, whose association with the University began with his enrollment as a student in September of 1960, graduated and went on to BYU for a master's degree before he returned to the University in 1965 as coordinator of student activities. He became dean of students in 1972, and progressed to his current position in 1997, as vice president for student services. Church offered an insight into the continuing tradition: "University staff employees continue to serve students with remarkable dedication, which is exciting." He said that there are new contingents of "miracle workers" such as the crews of Chris Gale, grounds superintendent, and Nolan Truman, supervisor of construction and repairs. He cited work with the Summer Games and the planting and maintenance of acres of grounds as examples of these miracles.

Vice President Church singled out Ruth Challis as a prime example of perseverance and dedication.

Whereas most presidents' offices have several professional secretaries, we have one, and her role is uniquely hers.

He also spoke of the late Ward Robb, who served for more than 40 years as registrar of the University:

Ward and his staff have been truly irreplaceable workers during their long tenure. Our staff employees are people who love students and are dedicated to their success.

The University is fortunate not to have had a high turnover of staff employees and a group who have cooperated so well with the faculty and administration as joint partners in the institution's development. It is also significant that a large number of active emeriti are former SUU staff employees.

PAUL
SOUTHWICK

Staff and faculty observers have commented on many staff supervisors, who have performed heroically, with small crews, to produce great volumes of work. In the late 1960s and early 1970s Jim Robinson, Sandy Gillies, Boyd Redington, and Barbara Morgan created the text and photography for all publications, which included the catalogue, press releases detailing all of the campus activities from sports to the Utah Shakespearean Festival, and brochures and recruitment materials. They were also responsible as advisers to student publications such as the student newspaper and yearbook. The information services department also initiated recruiting and public relations visits on campus as well as in high schools and junior colleges. The growing needs of the University have required an expanded staff, composed mainly of specialists who concentrate on one area of activity of production, and who also do their work exceptionally well.

REX
MICHIE

Workers in the grounds and plant operations departments have experienced similar transitions in going from minimal staffs on extremely stringent budgets to an increase in personnel in both administration and work forces. Growth and realistic accommodation have brought this about.

Scott Chamberlain,

BOYD
REDINGTON

who worked for the physical plant at the school from 1964 to 1994, recalled that he always considered SUU to be a beautiful place to work, and that he has seen tremendous growth take place under sometimes difficult circumstances. "You are always working with dedicated people," Scott said. He too mentioned Joe Roberts, who was revered by his fellow employees for his exceptional kindness and his harmonious relations with his staff.

Scott spoke of Ed Matheson, Reid Cox, and Eldro Rigby in this same vein, and of Vern Winter, Frank Jex, Merrill (Bud) Kunz, Gordon Slack, and Dale Brinkerhoff.

With all of their capable staffs, they have succeeded with limited resources and incredible demands as buildings were added and plant operations were expanded.

Another employee cited was Max Payne, who followed in the footsteps of Joe Roberts in taking care of security of keys and became an expert locksmith.

Sheldon Grant, superintendent of grounds from the 1960s to the 1980s, typified the spirit of the school's founders, as did Wilmer Anderson, Verl Kelsey, and Dale DeMille and Gary Davis. All were superb and dedicated workers, who often pushed around the clock to preserve and enhance the beauty of the campus.

A recurrent theme of those who have had long association with SUU is their regard for students and for each other. Many faculty members were exceptionally close to staff employees when the campus population was small. Roy Walters, Eugene Hardy, Vic Davis, C.B. Cooley, Tony Lambert were especially noted for the relationships they fostered with students.

Paul Daniels, a native of Annabella, Utah, was hired in 1962 as the school's bookkeeper. "P.D.," as he is affectionately known, was an individual unique, in part, in his handling of serious health challenges from birth. He retired from SUU in

GORDON
SLACK

1994, as director of personnel with a campus-wide reputation for fairness, approachability, and a great sense of humor and balance. Jack Cannon extolled Paul's ability to move from one position to another, even though the duties were not closely related, as typical of the versatility of staff employees. Many have been hired to fill a particular position, but have had the opportunity to move into other situations in which they had an interest and for which they were qualified. Dale Orton, Maxine Stolk, and Luann Briggs are examples of this, as are others, including Rex Michie, who filled such major assignments as director of housing, director of placement, and later director of financial aid. He has also served as an expert instructor and workshop participant for various "how to" classes.

R. Kenneth Benson, coordinator of student activities, filled many positions during his tenure at SUU from 1968, until his retirement in 1982, and coped with tremendous physical challenges. Before his appointment to student activities, he directed the school's Upward Bound program and supervised all of the non-academic space scheduling. He also taught a number of classes. As a student in the 1950s he was a formidable threat on the football field. Bessie Dover, who served for five years of her 28-year SUU affiliation as assistant to Ken in student activities, remembers that during his term as president of the staff association, Ken called a general meeting of the association every month to keep the membership fully informed of all that was taking place on the campus. He held the meetings in a different department each time to acquaint all members, first-hand, with the functions of the departments. Refreshments added to the sociability of these meetings. Ken was a great dutch-oven cook and often personally catered meals on and off campus for various groups. Especially concerned with recruitment and retention, he exhorted staff members to make this a high priority. Ken was very proud of his staff colleagues, students, and all SUU personnel. He invited the Dixie College staff association to visit SUU and meet with SUU association members. He was well known and well loved, not only at SUU, but throughout the area.

The latest scoop about staff employees has been communicated in a variety of bulletins and newsletters throughout the years. Since October of 1994, *SUU Staff Stuff* has been published quarterly in a catchy format by veteran staff member and editor, Eleen Evans, with assistance from staff personnel Stacia Thomas,

Mylen Roth, and Carolyn Wyndham. This publication is highly praised by those who look forward to it each quarter. The activity also illustrates the diversity of skills that can be brought into use by employees.

Jim Stevenson, an SUU alumnus-turned-staff member, president of the staff association in 1993-94, by nature accessible and open, enabled staff members to readily express their views to him. He was responsible for producing the "Hope Calendar," which has contained a myriad of informational items and anecdotes.

Eric Schmutz headed the staff association in 1987-88, succeeded by Mitch Bealer as president the next year. Both individuals brought financial expertise to the position and were highly regarded for their professionalism and service to the institution and its employees. During their tenures, staff employees were granted special ticket rates to campus theatre productions and athletic events by the administration. Staff members have appreciated the SUU administration and their own officer advocates for these and other benefits.

Rodney and Sharon Batt are one of several staff employee couples at SUU who are noted for their helpfulness. Rod began employment with SUU in 1981, and is currently in 1997, a custodian in the physical plant. Sharon, who started at SUU in 1982, is the catering manager for food services. Both extend themselves to accommodate those who need their help. They are friends to students and all who work at SUU as well as to townspeople and others in the public who use University facilities.

Phyllis Davis began as a staff member with the Utah Shakespearean Festival in 1963. After her marriage to John Taylor, the two served well together for 13 years, until his early death on January 12, 1988. The two were another example of the kind of valiant service that has helped SUU to endure for so many years.

In addition to executing their jobs very well and being exceptional representatives for SUU, staff employees have also funded an annual scholarship for worthy students, provided book grants, and responded generously to the many development projects which gain a large share of their resources from University personnel and community supporters. Staff members have enthusiastically supported all of the campus events, including athletic competition, cultural presentations, convocations, lectures and academic programs that the public may attend. Many staff people actively participate in these events, as well as preparing the rooms, setting up the equipment and working with techni-

cians, program directors, traveling show personnel and all of the other people sponsoring on-campus activities. After each event, it is also the duty of staff employees to clean up and restore all of the facilities to their normally good condition. The full complement of food service employees must be involved with the dozens of luncheons, dinners, open houses and other events involving the serving of food. In addition to this service to special groups, Garth Jones, director of food services, and his workers and supervisors, have served all of the meals provided almost every day and evening in the Thunderbird Circle cafeteria.

BUD
KUNZ

A crowning achievement of the Staff Association, in terms of visibility and enjoyment for the campus and community, was the Parterre, planted in the spring of 1996 by the grounds staff and funded by the staff association. The staff association board members, led by President Lois Bulloch, involved as many staff members as possible in projects celebrating the founding of the University.

The idea for the Parterre came to full fruition as the thousands of beautiful flowers bloomed through the summer and well into autumn of 1996. The garden is a glorious spectacle that centennial participants will enjoy in 1997, which date is observed in a special planting featuring the numerals 1897-1997. Located south of the Harris Pavilion, the Parterre was formally dedicated on August 29, 1996, as the first event of the centennial year.

Joyce Messer, a talented and indefatigable

PRESIDENT
SHERRATT,
VAUGHN
MCDONALD
AND NOLAN
TRUMAN LOOK
OVER STADIUM
EXPANSION
WORK.

staff groundskeeper, spearheaded the work on the Parterre. Schematics of the planting design, with names of flowers and shrubs and information relating to their times and seasons, were made available in a miniature replica of the Harris Center built by Nolan Truman.

Dedicated service to students, a deep love for the school and its traditions, and a sense of pride in the quality of their work has characterized staff employees at Southern Utah University for the past one hundred years. Their example will serve those who follow them into the next century and far beyond.

One most enduring extension of the faculty senate and staff association is the organization known as Southern Utah University Faculty-Staff Associated Women. Originally organized as a way for faculty and staff wives to socialize with each other, enlarge their own horizons and nourish young women students, it quickly became a group oriented to service as well as to socialization. As Bessie Dover has noted:

The organization began in September of

1932 as an affiliation of Branch Agricultural College faculty and wives of faculty. Twelve women met at BAC to found an association that would help them to maintain closer contact with one another and with women students at BAC. Present at that meeting were Mary Bastow, Lita Cooley, Mabel Dalley, Maude Halversen, Dora Hayward, Barbara Hendricks, Virginia Larsen, Elda Manning, Adele Matheson, Salome Oberhansley, Zoe Palmer and Mildred Sargent.

Minutes of the first meeting read: "Mildred Sargent occupied the chair. Nominations for president, vice-president, secretary and treasurer, also corresponding secretary were called for. By standing vote Mrs. Sargent was elected president; Mrs. Oberhansley, vice-president; Mrs. Halversen, secretary and treasurer, and Mrs. Larsen, corresponding secretary."

All policy and procedure decisions were made through Robert's Rules of Order. During the first meeting it was agreed by the founding members that the organization should be a literary one, that it should meet twice monthly on the second and fourth Thursdays of each

Will you allow me to reminisce for awhile , so that you can see why the Parterre was such a labor of love for me? My father attended school here in the mid 1940s when I was a little second and third grader. We lived in the trailer village and then in the old dorm that was about where the administration building and parking lot stand today. So this campus, and particularly the area east of Old Main and the Braithwaite Center, was my own special place. This was where I played in the dirt and climbed trees and played dodge ball. I learned to ride my very first bike on the tennis courts, where I also spent hours rollerskating. I played house and played hide-and-seek here. This is where I dreamed all my childhood dreams and acted out my fantasies of becoming a movie star or a ballerina or just being all grown up.

The trees were so wonderful. In the twinkling of an eye, I could imagine myself in a forest away from the whole world. We moved away for a few years to Logan while my father attended school there, but that was not the end of my love of this campus. We moved back to Cedar City when I was in sixth grade, and we lived adjacent to the campus, where I spent many lazy summer afternoons playing in the trees and daydreaming. And in the winters it was such fun to make angels in the snow by lying on my back and waving my arms up and down and playing fox and geese in a big open space of the untrammeled white stuff.

I also had the privilege of living next door to William Flanigan. At that time I didn't know that William was responsible for the beauty of this campus and that he personally planted so many of the trees that are here today. I just knew that he was a neat neighbor for a young girl, and I honestly believed that he might be Santa Claus. After all, he always decorated his house for Christmas and made lots of wooden figures in a workshop behind his house that looked like Santa's workshop.

He had a wonderful rock garden, and I used to spend many hours just looking at everything in his yard. I have had many tender experiences in relation to the Parterre, but something that happened one day was the culmination. Nellie Flanigan called me and said they would like to donate a rock to the rock garden. Isn't that neat! The rock gardens have special meaning to me because I personally placed rocks from all my favorite places and having a rock from William Flanigan's rock garden is wonderful.

Lois Lindsay Bulloch

month, and that the primary purpose of the club should be "to make the influence of the BAC felt in the outlying districts, probably through closer contact with the girls of the institution." In keeping with this resolution, it was decided that an annual reception be given the girls as a welcome to BAC.[5]

From a modest beginning, they evolved into an entity to be reckoned with. Not only were they active in promoting good works, but the group became a beacon of fashion and good-taste. The annual faculty ladies luncheon became "the" occasion when each spring the women of the town gathered wearing new hats and their most fashionable frocks. They enjoyed an afternoon of chamber music, a book review or the reading of a new play. Maude Halversen remembers:

Though none of the faculty staff women would think of appearing at our social events unless attired from head to toe in the latest fashion, complete with hat and gloves, some of the group's leaders mandated this strict dress code for all of the club's meetings.[6]

Some small affectations notwithstanding, the group became a positive force on the campus and in the town. The annual tea for women students welcomed young women, introduced them to faculty and staff wives, and was an event eagerly anticipated every year. The scholarships presented to worthy but struggling young women students provided education for scores of girls. The group contributed funds for badly-needed equipment in various academic departments, aided in the drive to replenish the library collection and remained an influence that furthered the cultural life in the community.

"Fantasy In Frost," a cherished annual Christmas tradition, began in 1983. A wonderland of beautifully-decorated Christmas trees greeted families of the community each evening of the holidays, providing a festive backdrop for delightful programs.

The long-standing loyalty of the members is part of the magic of the organization. As the university approaches the century mark, and the Faculty/Staff Associated Women nears its 64th anniversary as an active club, the good works, the sociality, and the positive cultural influence promises to continue undiminished.

Emeriti SUU has effectively brought faculty and staff members together as an active group of retirees, thus perpetuating pleasurable asso-

A "SPOOF ON HATS," FACULTY-STAFF WOMEN

ciation and bonds of friendship established among the staff and faculty over the years.

Emeriti SUSC was established on May 10, 1982 at the home of SUU President Gerald R. Sherratt, who considered such an organization to be a high priority at the college, then SUSC. He had obtained emeriti constitutions from other universities and invited all SUSC retirees and spouses, as of that date, to attend the May dinner. President Sherratt had held a reception for retirees in January of 1982 in order to renew his friendship with many whom he had known and to meet new emeriti friends. He termed this group as "some of SUSC's most valued supporters."

On the evening of organization, an Emeriti SUSC constitution was approved by the more than 50 guests present. The constitution stated that the purposes of the organization were to promote the interests of retired employees of Southern Utah University and to promote the advancement of the College.

Officers were elected to head the organization: D.C. Schmutz, president; Gwyn Clark, vice president; and Ada Carpenter, secretary and historian. It was stipulated that the vice president would also be the president—elect. Later, in accordance with the constitution, George LeBaron and Wilmer Anderson were appointed to serve on the executive committee. George was requested to serve as treasurer (which he did for seven years), and Anderson represented the SUU staff. Presidents would remain on the board for one year after their term of office was completed. After the meeting was over, Ada Carpenter wrote in big letters on her first set of minutes, "EMERITI SUSC IS ALIVE AND GOING!"

Spouses of all retired faculty and staff and board of trustees (then called the institutional council) presidents and their spouses were eligible for membership under the constitution, which itemized the benefits to be accorded to

ADA
CARPENTER,
ALMA KUNZ,
LOIS ROWLEY
AND GENEVE
PLUMMER WITH
EMERITI QUILT

emeriti. Included were free campus parking, library and recreation privileges, free education benefits for on campus classes, honorary membership in the faculty, subscription to campus publications made available to employees, special rates for athletic and cultural events and first-class mailing for emeriti announcements.

Expenses to be covered by dues of $10 per year included costs for publications, mailing and operating expenses. It was suggested that expenditures for activities and projects be voluntary and on a pay-as-you-go basis.

In 1993 the constitution was amended to change the name of the organization to SUU Emeriti and to add more benefits, including one-half tuition waiver for dependent children of emeriti under age 27, invitations to all faculty-staff social gatherings, participation in the SUU death benefit plan, invitation to the President's annual Christmas dinner, invitation to the Baccalaureate buffet (at no charge) and a ten percent discount on purchases from the SUU Bookstore.

In addition to the emeriti organizational dinner, President Sherratt inaugurated in May of 1982, annual dinners to honor faculty and staff at the time of their retirement. At these ceremonies, each person receives a gold watch (necklace watches for ladies) and plaques inscribed with citations of service and expressions of appreciation. President Sherratt personally read the declarations and invited close colleagues of each honoree to represent their departments in paying tribute to retirees. The new retirees were congratulated at the dinner and invited, with their spouses, to join SUU Emeriti by the president of the organization. A special program of music by campus and community groups is provided, at President Sherratt's invitation, to make these evenings as memorable as possible. In the emeri-

ti minutes, as well as by personal letters to him, the president's ongoing consideration of University employees and his gracious expressions of appreciation to them were gratefully acknowledged.

After the establishment of Emeriti SUSC in May 1982, President D.C. Schmutz organized committees to oversee activities, with President Emeritus Royden C. Braithwaite as chair, and membership relations headed by LaVeve Whetten. Fourteen emeriti served on the two committees, which President Schmutz exhorted to respond quickly and willingly when called by their chairmen so that "we can get quickly from home plate to first base!"

President Sherratt hosted the first Christmas dinner for emeriti in his home on December 10, 1982. This has since become a most enjoyable tradition during the Christmas season, and is now held in the Gilbert Great Hall due to the growth of the emeriti association.

The energetic and devoted members formed committees to enhance the social interaction and establish goals for projects to benefit the university.

Several traditional social events have resulted, in addition to President Sherratt's annual invitations. The spring breakfast held each year by combined faculty and staff on campus welcomes the participation of the emeriti. The annual hot soup supper is an event that traditionally warms the group with superb programs and excellent food.

Significant financial contributions to the Centrum, the Old Sorrel Monument and an ongoing list of good causes have emanated from the efforts of the Emeriti. Creative fund-raising projects include "Trash and Treasures" sales, bake sales and quilt raffles, with the quilts produced by energetic women of the group.

One of the major goals of the organization was to fund an annual full-tuition scholarship for at least one worthy student through an interest-generating endowment. In 1986 Wilmer Anderson, as emeriti president, and a committee of emeriti members met with administrators of the institution's development office. Funding provisions were discussed, and the emeriti made a commitment to establish the scholarship endowment. The fund grew each year until the principal was more than enough to draw interest sufficient to fund the scholarship. Other areas of need received assistance through the surplus.

The philosophy and spirit of Emeriti SUU remains alive in 1997, insuring a continuation of unity and service to the University in the years ahead. One could still write in large letters: "Emeriti SUU is Alive and Going!"

CHAPTER XXV

Alumni

t is the goal of the Alumni Association to stand as a bridge linking the history and tradition of the past to the challenges and ideas of the present.

The earliest records of the Alumni Association indicate that the officers for the 1911-12 year were Parley Dalley, president; Kate Palmer, vice-president; Hattie Mackelprang, secretary; Annette Webster, assistant secretary; and Rass Macfarlane, treasurer; with E. B. Dalley, Mamie Jones, and Myrtle Decker as members of the executive committee. Also, the BNS Alumni Day program dated June 2, 1914, includes a list of the 1913-14 alumni association officers. Rufus Leigh served as president, with John Fife, vice president, Herbert Haight, treasurer, Mrs. Rass Macfarlane, secretary, and Rass Macfarlane as assistant secretary. This program also includes a list of all former students of the BNS.

Throughout the written histories and recollections of SUU, there are several references made to an alumni association, as well as mentions of the many projects with which the group was involved. For example, a reference is made to an association in 1913 and again in 1927, when the group pledged $6,000 toward the construction of a gymnasium and was actively involved in raising other funds for campus improvements. In 1940, the alumni association felt compelled, in their words, to make a "definite step toward the preservation of the historical incidents connected with the founding of the Branch Agricultural College, formerly known as the Branch Normal School." They formed a general committee to publish a record of the founding of the institution. The committee was comprised of Lehi W. Jones, chairman, with Edward J. Palmer as secretary and John S.

Woodbury as a general committeeman. Others involved in gathering historical information were Randle W. Lunt and George W. Decker. This work, titled *BNS-BAC Alumni Historical Booklet*, details the institution's founding, the history of the school until 1940, and represents a very accurate and compelling history of the school.

When Dr. Daryl Chase was appointed director of Southern Utah University (then Branch Agricultural College) in 1951, he authorized Dr. Edwin L. Peterson to prepare a list of the school's alumni. This effort revitalized the focus and direction of what was to become the modern SUU Alumni Association. A student, Barbara Albertson, was hired to serve as secretary and to assist in the research. Peterson and Albertson obtained the old student grade files and, with close cooperation of Professor Parley Dalley, a long-time faculty member who personally knew many of the former students, a rudimentary list of alumni was compiled. It was probably the most comprehensive alumni list the school had ever compiled, and it is from this list that BAC began to mail out material and questionnaires to its college alumni. The arduous and on-going task of identifying and locating the institution's former students continues to be one of the

PARLEY
DALLEY

EDWIN L.
PETERSON,
1950s

alumni association's most vital efforts, and one that has seen thousands of the University's former students and graduates renewing their friendship and association, not only with the institution itself, but with the many classmates with whom they shared the educational experience.

Dr. Peterson remembers the group's first efforts to locate all former alums as being a very difficult task. The first comprehensive list of alumni was recorded on 3x5 cards, he recalls, which were stored in a simple cardboard box. Later, with the advent of the first computers, the records were transferred onto punch cards, which could be fed into a computer and a hard-copy report of the entire data base generated on paper.

It was a tedious task to key punch the individual cards with the correct information listing, among other notes of interest, each alumnus' name, degree, current address and occupation. Further advances in computer technology have dramatically improved the alumni association's ability to record and retrieve such information; and current efforts find all alumni files stored electronically and accessed through a personal computer. The task certainly seems much easier today than it must have been in the 1940s—but at the same time, our modern, mobile society and the blossoming numbers of University students and graduates have combined to make this a task that needs constant attention, especially as SUU strives to meet the challenges and opportunities of its second century.

Following on the heels of Dr. Peterson and Barbara Albertson, Naomi Platt became the secretary of the Alumni Association, and served for many years in maintaining records and implementing the plans of the association. So dedicated was Mrs. Platt to the cause of the Alumni Association that her name will be listed among those few who have been responsible for the success of the Alumni Association. Naomi Platt was also the editor of the *CSU Alumnus* magazine.

Treva Peg Bulloch Thorley became involved in the efforts of the Alumni Association in the mid-1970s, when she served as a part-time executive director. She was

NAOMI
FORDHAM
PLATT,
1960s

the logical choice when the organization was ready to hire a full-time director in 1983. Over the years, with extraordinary dedication of staff and officers, the association increased its records from 1,500 alumni names to nearly 30,000. Records have become much more complete, now including spouses' names, and the ability to cross-reference families through a new computerized data base. This information has proven invaluable as the University has come of age in finding lost alums and updating and maintaining existing records. In 1991 the institution's first issue of the *Alumni Directory* was published. Peg Thorley researched and published the valuable document.

When the legislature provided only half enough money to build the badly-needed gymnasium in 1927, loyal alumni pledged $6,000 toward the construction. The alumni association has proven a valuable asset as they have organized programs to assist students by providing scholarships and grants. Additionally, the alumni association or groups of alumni have participated in nearly every endeavor toward the betterment of the institution's campus. They have contributed to several building projects, including the construction of a new University library

That sense of activity, loyalty and participation in campus events has been extended to the University's annual Homecoming festivities, which SUU alumni have supported over the years. They have assisted in organizing the parade, building a float each year, and in participating in the events of the week.

The alumni association has also played a major role in several significant campus events and has organized, supported and developed other notable activities in the history of the University.

On December 12, 1948, the historic Old Main building caught fire. During the fire, the bell (which had been cast using iron from the Cedar City iron mines), fell from the tower through all the floors of the building, coming to a final rest in the basement. As a result of the fall and the heat of the fire, the bell was irreparably cracked and had to be replaced. It was the alumni association which led the effort to raise the money to replace the bell. The tower was reconstructed and a carillon with amplified chimes installed. It is reported that the old bell was hauled off and remelted for salvage.

Of particular interest and significance, the alumni association also led the petition drive to grant the University the right to offer four-year programs of study. Under the direction of Van Bushnell, who was president of the alumni association, and Naomi Platt, the association circulated petitions throughout the communities of southern Utah, northern Arizona and southern Nevada in 1964. The University's alumni and friends also petitioned the legislature and the Board of Regents to grant the school full four-year status. The petition effort was successful, and the school became Southern Utah State College in 1965.

The fiftieth anniversary of the graduation of the first class from the Branch Normal School provided an opportunity to present a program in honor of these first graduates. Organized under the direction of Gail Duncan, president of the alumni association, the alumni banquet of May 18, 1950 was the setting for this historic moment. All five living graduates of 1900 were in attendance. Mr. Joseph T. Wilkinson had died prior to 1950. The following evening, the Fifty Year Club was organized with Julius S.Dalley, president; Alice Redd Rich, vice president; Ella Berry Leigh, secretary-treasurer; and Amelia Dalley Green and Emma Gardner Abbott, board members. *The History of the Fifty Year Club* records that no reunion was held in 1951, because Ada Bryant Leigh was the only class member who survived the 1901 small pox epidemic. Professor Parley Dalley, a graduate of 1905, wrote the club constitution, which was adopted in 1953, and the club began holding its reunions on campus in 1955. Professor Dalley was recognized as the driving force behind this organization and was key to identifying the early graduates of the University and assisting in gathering these former students together for reunions. Spending countless hours researching former alums, Professor Dalley was in many cases the definitive expert on who and where people were located during the early years of the institution, because he had both attended the school and been a member of the faculty for so many years.

The Fifty Year Club continues to be an active and vibrant organization on the University campus today. Each year, members of this club assemble on the campus for a reunion and luncheon, where new members are welcomed into the club on the anniversary of the 50th year after their graduation. In 1994, the Fifty Year Club became the Anniversary Club in order to accommodate the small numbers of students due to virtually all the men being called to World War II. For the past three years, members of the Anniversary Club have been honored on the 45th anniversary of their graduation and

invited to join members of the Fifty Year Club.

Activities enjoyed by club members each year include attending the annual alumni banquet, where the alumni association honors outstanding former alums, and, of course, visiting one another and renewing old friendships.

Southern Utah University's Alumni Distinguished Service Award was first presented in 1968. Past recipients of this prestigious award include:

TREVA
PEG
THORLEY

1968–*Hazen J. Cooley*
1969–*Stanley H. Bradshaw*
1970–*Blaine H. Johnson*
1971–*Grace Adams Tanner*
1972–*John L. Seymour, Elda R. Manning*
1973–*Cedar City Chamber of Commerce*
1974–*Ella Berry Leigh*
1975–*Max J. Thorley, Robert J. Thorley*
1976–*Reed W. Farnsworth, Dixie Leavitt*
1977–*Warren H. Bulloch, Henry A. Jones, A.W. Stevenson*
1978–*J. S. Prestwich*
1979–*Sheldon B. Grant*
1980–*H. Grant Seaman, R. Kenneth Benson*
1981–*Wanda Tollestrup*
1982–*Clayton Frehner*
1983–*Royden C. Braithwaite*
1984–*Frank J. Petty, Jr.*
1985–*Maude M. Halversen, Elda R. Manning*
1986–*Cedar City Lions Club*
1987–*Lanell N. Lunt*
1988–*Calvin Carter, Jack H. Carter*
1989–*Mary E. Anker*
1990–*Wayne K. Heppler*
1991–*Fred C. Adams*
1992–*Roger Hillyard*
1993–*LuAnne Brown, Evelynn Jones, Mary M. MacDonald, Carol Ann Nyman, June D. Thorley*
1994–*Jeanne Ahern*
1995–*Conrad V. Hatch*
1996–*Treva Peg B. Thorley*

Instituted in 1984, the Outstanding Alumnus/NAE Award is presented to individuals who have distinguished themselves in their chosen professions. The following individuals have received the award:

1984–*Ellis L. Armstrong '32*
1985–*Fredrick C. Esplin '71*

THE FIRST
ALUMNI
HOUSE

1986–*RaNae N. Morris '49*
1987–*James M. Miller '59*
1988–*Robert A. Anderson, Jr. '65*
1989–*Hans Q. Chamberlain '65*
1990–*Gerald R. Sherratt '51*
1991–*Michael O. Leavitt '78*
1992–*Darrell W. Krueger '67*
1993–*Joan D. Woodbury '47*
1994–*J. Elliott Cameron '42*
1995–*Gayle F. McKeachnie '67*
1996–*E. Val Clark '51*

*T*he alumni association office has been located in several places over the years, but only two locations have enjoyed the distinction of being known as Alumni House. The institution's first alumni house was located on the corner of 200 South and 500 West streets. When the third-floor addition to the Administration Building was completed in 1985, the alumni association moved into the new space and the house became the offices of the *Thunderbird* newspaper. The house was demolished in 1988 to make room for campus housing.

In January of 1996, the Church of Jesus Christ of Latter-day Saints made a gift of the old Institute of Religion building, located on the corner of Center and 300 West streets, to SUU to be used as an alumni house. Named the J. Reuben Clark, Jr. Alumni House, after a former president of the BNS and a prominent LDS church leader, the alumni association now has a permanent home that will become a gathering place for former students and friends of the institution. Following several months of upgrading and installing phone systems and fiber optic

cable for computer capability, replacing the sprinkler system and the lawn, and installing a ramp to make the building accessible for disabled persons, the alumni association moved into the building in October of 1996. The final plans for the renovation of the building are nearing completion, and fundraising efforts have begun. During the next several months, the rest room section of the building will be completely redone and the kitchen will be expanded. The building's hardwood floors will be restored to their original state, the windows will be replaced, the fireplace will be restored, the furnace will be replaced and some minor modifications will be completed in the basement, which currently houses the University's annual fund and telethon operations.

*S*ince the institution became a four–year college in 1965, the president of the alumni association has represented all former and current alums on the Board of Trustees. A comprehensive list of alumni association presidents who served prior to 1965 is unavailable. Although we are unable to publish every name here, it is safe to say that each president played a vital role in the growth and development of the association through the years. Without these dedicated men and women, surely, today's alumni association would be woefully disadvantaged.

Known former presidents of the Alumni Association include:

1911-12 - Parley Dalley
1913-14 - Rufus Leigh
1915-16 - J. A. Widtsoe
1940-41 - Lorin Hirschi
1946-47 - Kumen Gardner
1949-50 - Gail Duncan
1954-55 - Willard Jones
1959-60 - Dixie Leavitt
1960-61 - J. Clair Morris
1963-64 - Frank J. Petty
1964-65 - Van Bushnell
1965-67 - J. Clair Morris
1967-68 - R. J. Potter
1968-69 - Elden J. Yergensen
1969-72 - Frank J. Petty
1972-73 - Rex Harris
1973-75 - Ralph Platt
1975-77 - Grant Seaman
1977-78 - Ann Jones
1978-79 - James Hoyle
1979-81 - Don Marchant
1981-82 - Loraine Warren
1982-83 - Brent White

1983-85 - Mildred Cardon
1985-87 - Juanita Esplin
1987-88 - Hans Chamberlain
1988-89 - Carol Ann Jones
1989-90 - Celestia Nichols
1990-91 - Joyce Sherratt
1991-92 - Alan Jones
1992-93 - Gerald Bybee
1993-95 - Cyndi Gilbert
1995-present -Vaughn MacDonald

In 1994, the alumni organization underwent significant change with the organization of a National Alumni Board of Directors. This was done to address the ever–expanding numbers of alumni, and also to provide representation to those who had moved away from the Cedar City area. As our graduates have begun to live in all parts of the country, it was determined that the association should be represented by those in other areas as well. The change in organization not only helps the association to keep track of far–flung alums, but also provides a pool of ambassadors to represent the University in these many and distant cities and towns. Since initiating the effort, the alumni association has established committees in nearly every county

in Utah, and will be establishing committees in other areas of the United States where the University enjoys active, supportive groups of alumni and friends.

It is the goal of the alumni association to stand as a bridge linking the history and tradition of the past to the challenges and ideas of the present. In this way, both past and present will share in upholding and building upon the cherished traditions of academic achievement, social exchange, athletic prowess and personal growth and traditions which foster a sense of loyalty and belonging to the institution.

These goals cannot, of themselves, be achieved; it is only through the efforts of people who have vision and dedication that anything of significance will be achieved. We desire to attain and maintain productive relationships with the people of the region, state and nation that will stand as an energetic and valuable extension of the University's overall educational quest. For this reason, it is vital that we recognize the contributions of SUU's alumni, so that we may encourage future students and graduates of the school to continue in this grand tradition of sacrifice and dedication to the University and its educational programs.

THE J. REUBEN CLARK ALUMNI HOUSE

Appendix

THE FOUNDERS SPEAK

By Rhoda Matheson Wood, 1947

Foreword

There has now come the time in this 100th year of Utah's existence that stories of achievement are needed in the history books of her many localities, that the children and grandchildren of brave hardy pioneering women and men who have made tolerable living conditions in Utah's many cities and towns, may know of the struggle in their behalf.

Who did break the land, put in the dams, plant the trees, kill the snakes and grizzlies, the mountain lions, the rabbits, build the libraries, schools, churches, homes and log roads? We are still building, yes, but not in the manner nor without the conveniences as they did. Rugged men with a splendid ideal made it possible for you and me to go on better equipped from here.

My purpose in this brief paper is to throw new light on an old story. The men who gave me these brief personal statements are now Cedar City's older citizens. They are few in number.

This thing should have been done many years ago while each man who participated could have had the chance to speak for himself. The few men still remaining are dependent upon memory after 50 years, yet, without an exception, those weeks so full, so intensely lived, in the ruggedness of keen young manhood have left no apparent trace of failing memory.

These things are being given now, not to discredit nor belittle the versions of those who have already spoken or written, but to revive interest and belatedly acknowledge a debt of gratitude and appreciation that has been too-long delayed.

It is somewhat like speaking our sweet thoughts and loving words into dead ears, yet not quite, for in each of these people there live hundreds of posterity who are proud to claim credit for the honest work and effort that has given to the masses a more abundant life.

A brief statement follows from each of the remaining men, who did the hard cruel task of lumbering in and over some of the most rugged of Southern Utah's highest mountains in the dead of winter, and in an exceptionally cruel winter.

"We avoided our mountains in winter, 50 years ago."

"Our weather man never followed a pattern of stability."

"The 50 years that lie between the 'then' and the 'now' have been fifty years of steady and continuous mechanized progress. The 'then' mountain roads, as compared to the present ones, were only cow trails. Some oxen were still in use in some parts of the West."

Richard Benson told me once that oxen were much better than horses for logging. He said, "A pair, but better a double span of oxen can wallow a heavily loaded wagon with ease, where horses could not begin to go at all."

Well, in 1898 we had progressed from slow moving oxen to faster moving horses. The road from Cedar to Jensen's Mill, never measured, is thought now to be about 30 miles, a drive of four full winter days with team and wagon. The planes that fly over our valley I am sure could cover the distance in five minutes or less. An automobile driven over our Cedar Breaks highway on a summer picnic would take not more than one hour.

Our recent war years have shown us that no country or place or climate on earth is beyond man's reach. The human mind grasps the 'mighty' only from the built-up miniature and all the mechanization on earth cannot be accomplished without human hands and brains.

Strange it is that the credit due for notable accomplishments is often steered far from its natural course, but eventually truth proves where the mistake has been made, the originator shares with the benefactor and there is no great permanent loss.

In the effort to secure for Cedar City a school of higher learning, perhaps more than any other individual, the Honorable John Parry, then serving in the first State legislature, fought longest and most intensely with his tongue and his pen, to bring to pass this school. He was always jealous for Cedar's successes, for anything and everything that gave her precedence over her sister towns. Sometimes to the point of boredom he would boost her location, her advantages and her superiority, especially when his listener happened to think such thoughts concerning his own home spot.

Francis Webster was more than attentive to duty. His sudden appearance spelled failure to one's own plans, or the fulfillment of one's own personal desires. If he asked for some donation of material, and he seemed to always know if you had anything to spare, you might as well say "Yes" immediately, for he always got what he went for. And they all give him credit for not asking something unless you were able to spare and share.

Jed Jones was untiring in his determination to win for Cedar this school.

Though the other members of the committee, Bladen and Dover, seem to not have been quite so aggressive, they were all more far-sighted than the general run of the people in pursuing that ideal to its splendid conclusion.

There are few institutions that train their people and then take them back into their faculties for a lifetime of steady teaching service, but such is our school, and Parley Dalley is such a teacher. His wisdom, understanding and conscientious help to the young people who come under his influence, makes him one of the best loved of all the teachers who have taught within its walls.

At this date, May 1947, of the general committee, J. S. Woodbury and L. W. Jones still are with us. The five members of the building committee have all passed on. There are four of those who made the first trail through the snow to the Jensen Mill. They are Randall W. Lunt, John Perry, Jim Hunter and Orson Tyler; of the immediate follow-up groups, there are Sam Heyborne, D. D. Sherratt (died April 2, 1947), Frank Adams, R. B. Sherratt and R. W. Bulloch. There are two blacksmiths, J. H. Walker and Fred Ashdown; of rock and brick masons, Herbert Adams, only.

There are statements of a few other men given here. They are men who did some kinds of work which helped the project and represent personal knowledge of what was going on.

Dozens of men and boys worked out assessments, on brickmaking, burning lime, excavation, leveling and graveling the grounds, carpentering, plastering, plumbing, planting shade trees and such other jobs as has made college hill the interesting and lovely spot it is today. If all these names were mentioned the male population of Cedar City would largely be listed. In the main the majority of them were never students of the school but the work they did was unselfish giving of themselves toward a project that has benefited thousands who followed.

During the 50 years of its continuous existence, first as the Branch Normal School, then as the Branch Agricultural College, many of Utah's outstanding educators have partaken of its influence and scattered its ideals abroad, always for good. What greater credit could one ask than to have been such means of benefit to humanity. May the coming fifty years of our school show a tything of the progress of the rugged strength and idealism, of clean fine manhood and womanhood and an increasing number of such directors as G. W. Decker, some of his predecessors and some of his successors.

In contacting these men, Orson Tyler is the only one I have not been able to see personally. His home is now in Thatcher, Arizona.

THE FOUNDERS SPEAK

Founders - men both tried and brave
You had the courage it needed, to save
From doom, a people's dream.
Yours are the hands that grasped the tools,
You forced king-winter to loosen his hold
From the treasures that would build our school.
Yours is the courage that reaches out
To shove aside the stumbling block
And change predicted failure to achievement.
Though the years have brought infirmity
Though vital manhood is but a memory now,
As founders you have the world's acclaim
For the determination you had and won.
Now that history has been written, all there is to tell,
And the fiction has been sifted from the truth, right well,
You men, FOUNDERS, will not be found wanting.

RHODA M. WOOD

D. DUNN SHERRATT

On the afternoon of February 7, 1947, I had a delightful visit with D. D. Sherratt and his good wife. He sat in his lovely living room in stocking feet, relaxed comfortably. He told me many interesting items of his younger days, of his mother, her emigration to Utah, of his Uncle Dave Bulloch and his cousins, Rob-Will, and John T., of his horses (beautiful teams and good saddlers), and of my father and other neighbors. I asked about his connection with the lumbering expedition of the early Branch Normal School. He spoke freely and confidently of his part in the affair. There was no hesitancy or half-remembered statements. He knew what he was talking about.

I was one of the mill crew. We were all rugged, hard-working men, used to rough weather. The sissy-men who came onto the job soon left it.

With the exception of the night when Neil, Randall, Richard Bryant and myself were caught and had to sit by the fire all night at Bryant's Hotel, I never missed a meal, and I ate much better than I usually ate at home. On this night we weren't too bad off. We had one of John Perry's clean flour sacks of the dry bread that was being sent back to town. What did make us sore was that in the morning we saw less than a block or so away, one of the supply wagons loaded with food, bedding and horse feed.

No sir, that job was no harder than many others I have done. I had the time of my life. We were a bunch of a kind down there at the Mill. Along with the work there was fun. John had his fiddle. There was plenty of good food that the women of Cedar sent us in a constant stream, and not only food, but mittens, caps, wool-sox, and we were furnished with good tobacco if we wanted it. They sent warm clothing, underwear, felts and rubbers, overalls and jumpers.

If anyone felt like stressing the hardship end of it, I would laugh at them, but then, I had a good warm camp at night and some of the haulers didn't enjoy such a privilege.

I cut logs with Billy Daugherty, Sim Simkins and Jim Bryant and I always felt like I had the choice job, and certainly I wouldn't have traded jobs with any one of the committee who did the begging.

One night Jule took one of John's hard round loaves, drilled a hole in the center and made a hobby horse out of it. Most of our bread was sent up baked, but John did make it in emergencies and Jule had to always be up to some prank.

A month after Dave Dunn Sherratt told me these things he had passed away. My paper wasn't finished and I regret that I didn't have another session with him. He was born November 13, 1874, was 73 years old, and died April 3, 1947.

JIM HUNTER
(77 years old)

It was February 17, 1947 when Will and I called on Jim Hunter and his wife. I must give you the picture we saw there. His youngest daughter had him propped back in a big easy chair giving him a shave and a facial massage. Her little boy was helping, sitting on his Grandad's lap, brushing the lather. Jim said, "This is when I get my face washed clean."

Unannounced visitors would not be permitted to see such an intimate picture of home life 'posed' for an occasion, but it showed me a very ordinary occurrence and I felt privileged to see it for it showed love, respect and good-will among his big family, and as he and his wife spoke lovingly of the absent ones, I couldn't help but wish there was more of such home-life in our community.

I wasn't married, but living at home with Mother on the property where the El Escalante Hotel now stands, in January 1897. I had just driven into the lot from weeks of freighting between Milford and the Nevada mining camps. I had two good teams and a new Bain wagon, and wanted a rest from the dog's life of freighting, when Francis Webster came to where I was unhitching. 'Jim, we need you and your outfits to go into the mountains to help get the lumber out for the new building to house the high school.'

He talked and argued. I had been out camping in the weather all I wanted for that winter, and his talk didn't convince me. Mother told me she thought I ought to go. Anyway, the next day another of the committee came, Jed Jones, I think. They kept coming until all five had been there and I felt compelled to go, so I told them I'd go on that trip, and that mostly to get rid of them.

I knew that a mountain assignment in January could not mean a summer vacation. I had been out for weeks in the cold and had good clothing, woolen sox and underwear, German sox, gum boots, and didn't suffer severely with cold as some of the men not so well prepared.

With 10 other men, let me give you their names, Heber Jensen, Jack Webster, Neil Bladen, Renz Adams, Jim Bryant, Orson Tyler, John Perry, Sim Simkins, Dan Perkins and Randall Lunt, we left town early on the morning of January 5th to work through about a foot of old snow. The first day we made it to the Summit Sheep Corral in the head of Maple Canyon, turning off our main canyon to the left from Martin's Flat. The second day we made it to the Old Settin' on Bear Flat, and the third day to Jensen's Mill. There were two men to each wagon and two teams. John Perry was with me. I intended to bring out a load of already sawed lumber and be through.

We were camped at the Mill when it began snowing. When it kept on with no break, we all agreed the only thing to do was to get out while we could, so we turned right around and began pulling back up the road. Neil had 600 or so, feet of lumber on his sleigh and I had 840 feet on my wagon. The rest of the wagons were empty except for beds and grub boxes. There was not even a faint trace of the road we had made the day before and it kept on snowing. At night we pulled into a thick grove of pines on the Mammoth to make camp. I had to unhitch my leaders so I could swing the wagon into position where I wanted it, for the front was dragging snow.

After an uncomfortable snowy night we got out of bed from under an extra cover of fresh snow to throw our beds on the horses, take a little food, and string out single file, heading for home, each man on a horse.

As we came at night down into the Old Settin' in this manner, there were Rob-Will Bullock, Byron Carrigan, Spence Coburt and Uriah Leigh from below. Rob-Will said that his party of four were there and had a good fire going in the big fireplace. Maybe they were. I know that we were mighty glad to get in there and take some of that stiffness out of our tired cold bodies. We had bucked snow on the level three or four feet deep, and drifts double that. The wind, sweeping across the Mammoth and other level areas, was nearly more than we could stand.

Hay for the seven double teams and two extra saddle horses was pretty meager. We rationed it with the best wisdom we had. If some of those tired horses had less than their share, and others more, well,

I often say that the best place on earth to learn a person's true character is in just such a situation.

There was some quarreling, plenty of argument, but most of those 15 men were thankful to have survived that trying day without worse and more serious things happening.

At the very best, the road up the canyon was dangerous. Switch-backs, dugways, narrow shelves, steep pitches, and close timbers, in that constant falling snow, made it hazardous in the extreme for the men coming up, and doubly so for teams going down.

The little cabin would hardly hold us all standing up. We couldn't all sleep there. Most of us went out into the boiler shed where with a little shoveling we could scoop the snow from the dry sawdust and with a fire for light and warmth we got by. The teams were blanketed and most of them sheltered in old sheds. I wished they had been better fed.

Morning saw all but Neil, Spence, Orson, Renz and myself on the way back to town. We stayed to try and break the other side of the road open, back to our camp in the pines so as to get our outfits out. After a few days of tramping trail with our teams, we drove Neil's Bobsleigh out. Sam Heyborne and Dave Urie had come that morning and they stayed with the five of us others to help. After that first day's tramping, Renz drove his "Sorrel" and George Wood's "Doll" on the small sleigh that Sam and Dave brought in, with grub and bedding to the camp in the pines.

My wagon was unloaded and the lumber was put on the Bob. Neil hitched his four to the Bob as it had been brought up from the Mill. The wagons were not moved. Then we too left for town, reaching the camp at the Top of the Cedars to find the mill crew camped at the close of their first day on the way in to the Mill. The men I remember were Gus Mackelprang, John Tait, Al Connell, Dave Dunn Sherratt, Jule Rosenberg, Billy Daugherty, John Perry, Spence Coburt and Sim Simkins.

It was here that we held a memorable little meeting. I was determined to go home and told them so. Neil who was made boss of the party before we ever left town spoke directly to me. 'Jim Hunter, you are not going home. You are going to stay on this job until we get this lumber out.'

The lumber I had brought this far was unloaded for the wagons to pick up and I turned around and went back to the Mill with the other outfits. No one had wagons this time, but there were several Bobs and we knew that more were being made to use on the upper hauls. Neil tentatively assigned all the fellows to their jobs and they worked where they were told to. He kept things moving all down the line and drove first on one, then another of the hauls and changed the men to where he thought they could do the best work. With this set-up food and materials began to come up to us for our greater efficiency. The best hay we got was the grass hay that grew in the old slough on George Wood's farm. We got all the hay he raised.

One day as we drove across the wind-swept blow-hard, it was bitter cold and all the clothing we could put on didn't seem to break it. Suddenly someone shouted, 'There goes a cougar,' as an animal leaped across the road some distance ahead of the teams. Sim Simkins and I grabbed our guns and made for the clump of timber into which it had disappeared. With three shots we got, not a cougar, but a great mountain hare which weighed fifty pounds or more. Everyone enjoyed a treat of unusual meat.

I was put to logging with Steve Walker. We worked together for two months. I had been there two or three weeks when my best horse died. The committee sent a big sorrel mare of Henry Houchen's up to take his place. She was clumsy and awkward. When they were bringing her in she got off the road into the deep snow and the men had such a time getting her out of it that I told them to take her back. I wouldn't be bothered with her so when they got her out of the snow they just led her back to town and she never reached the Mill. I sent my one extra horse back to town, and they brought me Danny Pendleton's team which I drove with my other team until I left to come out.

I had been there just two months when with Tom Urie and Sam Heyborne, I started for town expecting to go to the camp in the pines and trail out my wagon. We drove there and looking around I said, "'Where are the wagons? There are none here.' Tom with that sly grin of his asked if I expected them to be here. Then they told me that mine was hauled out in pieces on the Bobs almost the first trip and that Al Connell had used it on one of the lower hauls and broken it up so badly that it would take a lot of fixing to put it together again. There I was, minus my best horse and a new wagon, and two months of hard work for nothing. I felt that I had donated plenty.

The first job that offered itself for pay I took. A dramatic company playing a week's engagement in the old opera house wanted to be hauled to Milford, so with two teams I took their baggage in my wagon and Will Corry with two teams on the coach took them to Milford. We were away four days and loaded freight back on new wagons. When we pulled into town I was told that the men had all come out of the mountains.

Rone Thompson and Sam (Poots) Walker did my work for the few days that were left. Caleb Haight was cooking then. When I left the mountains my job was done so far as I was concerned. I had kept no time because I understood it was all donation and therefore expected nothing. I and my horses had been well fed and for the most part I had not suffered. I don't remember ever having to eat dried peaches. I never was in any grave danger except maybe my high and handsome ride down the "S" turns which I'll tell you about later. Anyway, a year or more after it was all over, Will Houchen took me into his office on Main Street and gave me a check for $100. The committee also got me a good, nearly new, wagon to replace mine.

For years we never found ourselves in groups but there would be a recalling of funny things that had happened to some of us. For instance, Renz wanted to warm us up when he came up in the cold one day. His joke was played on me first. He had loaded a bottle with cayenne pepper but didn't tell me that when he said, 'Here Jim, take a swallow of this. It will warm you up quick.'

It doubled me up so quick that for a time they all thought I would die, and I was afraid I wouldn't.

When I left that day and started down from the Mammoth, I had the front end of my load lashed securely to the front standard of a half-Bob. Neil had said, "Aren't you going to roughlock Jim?"

'No, I'm not afraid,' I said. 'Let me pass you and get on lead.' (They always double-locked when the road was extra slick, but always half-locked to be safe.)

Orson Tyler was with me. He thought he'd like to ride the tail of that load, but when the weight began pushing the horses, they went faster, swinging the dragging end into a snow bank or a hillside, then into a tree, whipping to first one side then the other. Orson jumped into the snow, and when we got to the bottom he begged me, 'Don't tell the fellows that I was too big a coward to stay with it!'

The fellows watching said they saw nothing but a cloud of snow after I got to moving.

Many months afterward, Jim Bryant, myself and some others were in the Mercantile. One of the fellows was telling of things that had happened to the men in the mountains. He turned around to me and said, 'You didn't get in on that, did you?'

'I'd sure have liked to have been there,' I answered. As I looked at Jim Bryant he winked and a little later remarked, 'Aren't you glad you didn't get in on such a tough deal, Jim?'

It was such as he who did all that job I presume, and then how we did laugh.

I have never before been asked for a sketch of my part in this story. In every detail it is as true a picture of the parts she has written as I could give Mrs. Wood, although it is a very small part of the happenings of those two months.

Jim will be 77 years old in Sept. 1947. John Perry said, "Jim Hunter is one grand guy. I lived and worked with him for weeks, under anything but ordinary circumstances and found him to be happy, reliable, kindly and rugged. He took on the task of going out in the cold every night before going to bed to look over the horses and not only his own but every team on the job. The teams were always, to him, first and last."

Many of the people who walk out on the rim of Cedar Breaks in the summer time grow dizzy looking into that great depthless beautiful vacuum. The heart actually skips a beat at the thought of men in blinding snow trying to keep to a road that skirts so closely that dangerous drop off.

FRANK ADAMS
(Died June 7, 1947)

Frank Adams is within a few months of 80 years old and declares that other than talking over with his companions of those times the things of mutual interest, he has never been asked to tell of his part in this thing for the purpose of public research.

Two separate evenings I spent conversing with Frank Adams and his good wife in their nice home on Third East Street. They have wonderful memories of early days in and around Cedar City. His work took him into the mining camps among the rougher elements. He could do any and all kinds of work wherever a job for pay was offered. Wages were small and the needs of a growing family many. Perhaps the exposure and hardship that attended freighting and such jobs in all kinds of weather is responsible for his failing health at this time.

We talked of many subjects. "There are so many things I would like to do and places I would like to go. It is Hell to have to sit here in the house unable to do any of it." His voice quivered and tears sprung into his eyes as he sought to suppress the feelings that only strong men can feel.

He went on, "In every phase of our community development we were asked for donations of time, money and material. Public buildings, sidewalks, streets, water and lighting systems, field-ditches, flood-control and other things, so it was nothing new to be asked for donations on the new high school. We were pleased to think that our town was chosen for its home, and I was never left out when there was some hard outdoor work to be done."

In February 1898, I had a load of coal on my wagon ready to leave for Delamar, having promised to deliver it at a certain time. I was just back from a long freighting trip and since we didn't make much money I needed all the cash I could get. The evening before I was to leave, Francis Webster and Jed Jones came to my place to tell me that my help was needed in getting out the finish-lumber for the new school building. The rough lumber was pretty much milled and hauled out, at least a good start had been made toward it, but the finish-lumber must be sawed and piled to season and because I was an experienced logger, I should feel it my duty to assume such an assignment without pay, regardless of the needs of my wife and four little children. My wife had already had a hard winter and sickness while I was away but they thought she could manage regardless of the weather.

They won out. I got Albert Nelson to take my outfit and deliver that load of coal. He was glad to get the job and I, riding one of my horses and Levi Walker riding one of Jed Jones's, on our rolls of bedding, left for Jensen's sawmill. We met Gus Mackelprang and Randall Lunt leaving the Mill with their last loads out. Levi's horse couldn't keep on the road. He was floundering most of the time in snow which was fast becoming rotten, so I led him behind mine and Levi walked and held to his tail. Levi and I changed each other off from time to time.

They told us that John Perry had been cooking but that Tom Urie had taken his place. Tom was there on the job when we arrived. We had plenty of good substantial food and many things that were luxuries to me. Our clothing was good and we had a good camping place.

At the Mill, lying as it does on the south-east slope, on the other side of the Mammoth, the lengthening days of February grew milder. The weather wasn't so terribly cold as it had been for the men there earlier and especially the haulers on the high and windy Mammoth, so we didn't suffer with cold as the others had done although it was no summertime vacation.

Levi and I went to work together. In three days we got out 63 logs. Hebe remarked, 'If you fellows had been here earlier we would have been through a lot sooner and at less expense.'

After a week or so of eating Tom Urie's cooking, Rob Burns Sherratt came up with a request from Joe Cummero for Tom to come down and fix up a cattle deal. Then Jim Bryant was taken in from the cutting job to act as cook.

I stayed there until the finish and flooring-lumber was all sawed and piled to season for hauling during the summer, and then all of us left. One outfit went around and out by way of Panguitch, Bear Valley and Parowan. They thought that the long heavy timbers that reached through the center of the building couldn't be brought down our canyon on account of the sharp turns on the road. The melting snow was known to make a dangerous road-bed. Try to imagine what would have happened had a fifteen foot road made of breaking snow, given away under a team and wagon.

From the time Jim Bryant came into the camp he kept track of our working time. He did it for fun because no one then expected to get any pay and those three or four days were on record. Jule and I, and maybe some of the others, were given the extravagant sum of $12 for 30 to 40 days of hard work. Jule had been there for a month or so before me. Now wasn't that generous? They couldn't take our word for our own time although we had plenty of witnesses.

The year 1898 wasn't so far removed from pioneer times but that we felt the shortage of many things. Good iron was one item that had never been plentiful. In my freighting trips I had gathered quite a store of good pieces from the junk around the mining camps. This was all on my lot when the committee began to call for stuff to make Bobsleighs with. All of my iron was taken to the blacksmiths to be made into sleigh runners. John H. Walker, Fred Ashdown and George Urie each got some, and the Bobs were in use a month or more before I went on the job.

I believe that Dave Dunn Sherratt and the other cutters had the meanest jobs of the outfit. They had to dig out a hole in the snow to get down to the ground around each tree, and one big enough so they could use the big cross saws. They would kneel on the wet cold snow a good share of the time to work, besides wallowing down the trails from tree to tree to locate the good ones.

I am happy to look back on the little part I played in bringing to pass the one thing of so great worth in the building of our community. My pay has been had many times over in seeing the advancement of my own children and grandchildren, and of my friends and neighbors. Two of my grandsons, Clemont and Alden Adams are making the most of their opportunities in that school. Their names are now on recent student honor rolls in the Branch Agricultural College.

HERBERT ADAMS
(a cousin of Frank Adams)

I called on Herb Adams at his home today, April 7, 1947, on Fourth West Street in Cedar City. He had been ailing all winter, but on this sunny April day felt pretty good. Someone with flying fingers should have accompanied me on this visit so as to catch the humor, the detailed conversation, and the remarks that brought to mind so many situations and contacts.

I have these few notes from Herb concerning the building of the Branch Normal School.

At the insistence of Francis Webster, I put off an anticipated trip to Delamar to go to my rock quarry out in Dry Canyon on the 8th of January and make a start toward getting out the rock for the foundation, the corners, and the lintels for the new Branch Normal School building.

There were few rock masons in the country. Sometimes I had help and at times I didn't. Tom Bladen, Evan Williams, George H. (Johnar) Walker, Naze Harris, Samuel Bauer, and some others helped me at different times. Herb Webster and L. W. Jones hauled the dressed stone. It was the end of June before we had it all done.

Among the masons I remember Ed Ashton, William Dover, and Bengt Nelson. Richard Palmer, in his blacksmithy on Main Street kept our iron sharp.

The big arch over the front door is from the white ledge on the south side of the Red Hill, near where the first power plant stood in the mouth of Cedar Canyon, and the red stone is from my rock quarry in Dry Canyon.

A year or so later, at the end of six months of hard steady rock dressing, I received $294. Someone had also donated me a small jag of hay.

Herb and his wife and I talked of the old times, the pictures of the cornerstone laying ceremony and the prominent Cedar people in the foreground of the picture. There were Jos. H. Armstrong, John Parry, Aunt Charlotte and Uncle Tom Walker and many other faces that a good magnifying glass brings out, and Herb said, "But I don't see Josh Arthur or the wine bottle. You know, that ceremony was like the launching of a new ship. There has to be a bottle of wine broken over the cornerstone, and he was the man to do the honors."

Amelia, Herb's wife, said that one day George H. Walker (Johnar) came to her home from work with

Herb and scolded her roundly. That day Herb had no custard pudding in his lunch pail. "Well, I broke the little bowl that fitted the bucket," she explained to Johnar who retorted, "Don't you miss it ever again." After weeks of having that custard Herb missed it and he simply must have that custard if he does his best work for the school." Amelia laughingly added, "Of course I knew that was his way of joking over a silly situation."

As I left, Herb, now past 80 years, said, "If my memory was as good as my hearing I could really give you a story."

"How much rock is there in the building?" I asked, to which he replied, "All of the foundation and partitions up to the top of the first big windows."

On my way home, I walked by to see. There are nine tiers of stone above the ground to the top of the windows, the whole front entrance, reaching to the top floor is of stone and the decorative work is all of the white stone he mentioned. All is in very good preservation except the tier at ground level which is shelling off a little. The foundation is about four feet thick and the whole structure looks solid enough to stand until Doom's Day.

R. W. BULLOCH

In Cedar City, there are a few choice building spots, such spots as gives one a view of our most lovely living pictures. Such a view of Lone Tree Mountain is framed in the large south living room window of R. W. Bulloch's modern home on the corner of College Avenue and Third West. The west window frames the pine-tree walk and parts of our first Branch Normal School building that are still visible behind the ever increasing giant pines and lovely grounds of College Hill.

George Decker is responsible for the pine shaded path, William Flanigan for the grassy beautifully landscaped loveliness of the rest of College Hill, where when I was a student in the early 1900's, could be seen nothing but the newly planted pines, the freshly graveled white path and rocky sage covered hill, where springtime showed all varieties of our native wild flowers and feeds, and in winter a brown or white snowy stretch of gently rounded hill topped by a huge new rock-buttressed square building of brick, against the skyline.

Above the well balanced rock-arched entrance, outlined with a narrow band of white stone is this caption for all to see as they approach the building, "Branch Normal School, Established 1897."

Now, the skyline to the North and South outlines other nice buildings but none more substantial, nicer in workmanship, nor dearer to the hearts of the people.

In 1898 Rob Will Bulloch was unmarried, a happy, fine specimen of young vital manhood, when he was asked by the new school committee to go into the mountains with the group in winter to get out lumber with which to build this first school building.

I was living at home. There were five of us boys, all doing our share toward looking after Father's sheep, cattle, and farming interests. If any young fellow could afford to give his time and energy, I could, for the other brothers could take my place. Father was more than willing to have me drive his good teams and try to work out our share in this community project, although there were always other errands and work for the teams and boys of the family.Our situation was somewhat as George Wood used to express it. When his nine were growing up, Cedar's young men were moving into new areas as new lands were being offered for homesteading. One day U. T. Jones said, 'George, why don't you urge your boys to stay home and develop our own section.' George, scratching his head and thinking answered, 'Well, if they make decent citizens they'll be needed wherever they are, but if not, I don't want too damn many of them in one place. I could keep 20 of them at work, but they have to make their own choice.'

I joined the lumbering expedition. The first 11 men had been gone a couple or three days when Oriah (Yi) Leigh, Byron Carrigan, Spencer Coburt and myself left for the mountains on a warmish melting January Day. I was driving two teams on Father's wagon, and Byron hired by and driving two teams of Jed Jones' on a sleigh. Yi was on a saddle horse and the rest were riding on the outfits. We were being sent with extra horse-feed and supplies but I had the bulk of it on the wagon because in the lower canyon and south hillsides the sleigh runners dragged mud.

We were quite late getting away that morning, but drove without mishap to the bare hillside at the Summit Sheep Corral and camped there. We had gone out unconcerned about the weather, ordinarily clothed because warm winter days were no worse than others if you were used to our climate. We could have fire for cold nights, so at midnight when snow began to fall steadily and fast, we began to think we had taken the weather too much for granted.

At what we thought was dawn, one of the group threw off the bed covers and said, 'I'm getting out of here while I can.' Horses were hitched, beds rolled and without breakfast we began traveling, hardly able to keep track of the road ahead. After the first half a mile I unloaded a good share of the hay and stacked it by the side of the road. At the top of the Cedars I unhitched the horses and left the wagon. As we passed the Sugar Loaf we had only three or four bales of hay and one sack of grain and our beds and grub on Carrigan's sleigh, the other five horses breaking road ahead of the sleigh.

At the Old Settin' was the abandoned cabin and sheds from previous years of the Jensen Brothers' sawmilling. The cabin was drifted half-full of snow, anyway, higher than the table. One of the men scooped snow and got a fire going while the rest of us took care of the horses. Next day, instead of trying to go on, we broke trail back with the horses taking turns on the sleigh to try and get the supplies up. We knew that the party ahead would need them and were pretty uncertain what we ourselves would need before we were through the venture. I can see that old sleigh now, crazily riding the snow up and down somewhat as a boat rides the waves.

We were rounding the last turn into the Old Settin', on our third day out, when there on the white hillside above, strung out in single file came winding slowly down the slope 11 men with 21 horses. Both parties let out a whoop of relief, one that echoed and re-echoed on the canyon walls in that world of white. Fifteen stiff, damp, tired men gathered in the cabin that night to argue and talk over their situation and try to plan for tomorrow. Most of the men were determined to get home. They were all too miserable to think of anything else.

I wouldn't have blamed anyone, or all of those men, for an outright refusal to stay under such conditions. Uncle Neil was using every argument and persuasion he could muster to get them to stay. We all recognized Neil Bladen as the boss on that part of the deal, but I don't know now and never have known, who elected him to that office. He took me aside and begged me not to desert the thing before it was begun. I remember saying to him as if it were yesterday, 'Uncle, when we go down and report to the committee as to the depth of this snow and the impossibility of doing this thing, they'll not ask a man of us to face it.' He answered me, 'You could do it if you weren't such damn tenderfeet.' My response to that was 'I'll go today and then you'll have a better road to come down on tomorrow.'

Well, six or eight of us went out into the old boiler shed to sleep. By scooping the fluffy snow back off the sawdust and making a fire, we weren't too uncomfortable, but we talked and heard each other's arguments for and against going home and the majority were for going home.

Morning came, all hustle and bustle. Jim Hunter, Uncle Neil, Renz and one or two others were determined to take their wagons down. They had been left in their camp of the previous night on the Mammoth, so they stayed to break the other side of the road back to get them. We were already to break up and go our opposite directions when here came Sam Heyborne and Dave Urie from below to say that other supplies and outfits with Bobsleighs were on the way and to please stay on the job, but with the exception of four or five who started back up the canyon, we all headed home. I can't remember if we all rode our horses and bedding out or if there was a wagon or sleigh. It had turned bitter cold and we used horse blankets, gunny sacks, blankets and anything we could to break the freezing cold.

It was a sorry looking lumbering expedition that trailed back into town late that night, and the snow, naturally, lessened in depth as we trailed out of the canyon.

In a day or so, another town meeting was called to be held in the Jones Building, Parry, Jones, Webster and others were to talk and consider whether or not we would go through with this project. That meeting is a matter of history now. We younger fellows were loitering around and wondering what they might say or do that could make us face that deep snow and cold again, rather sure that they couldn't put it over.

One and another of us drifted in and out, listening, arguing among ourselves. Who said it, when or how it was said I can't say, but something stirred us to a determination to go back, get to work and see the thing through.

Within three or four days the blacksmiths, J. H. Walker, Fred Ashdown, George Urie, maybe others, working overtime, had home-made Bobsleighs ready for us to go back with. From Thos. Taylor's railroad material and from Frank Adams' accumulated horde came iron that the blacksmiths shop hand-sawed plank runner with. A few miles of icy road brightened the rusty iron and the runners rode the snow as efficiently as much more pretentious looking outfits.

We were much better prepared with clothing for the job when we went back. The work settled down into somewhat of a routine, and we held to our own part of the job. Cooked food came to us in a constant stream from the good women of Cedar. Every other night the men on our haul, which was the second lap of the road out from the Mill, camped at the Old Settin' cabin, and I shall always remember the big slices of good homemade bread toasted by the open fireplace.

I brought a load to town every week or so and cleaned up, then went back. The men who met us and took our loads on the next lap of the road always brought up the supplies to be passed along the line to where they were needed. Among these I remember Ephraim Perkins, Hy Perry, Jack Urie, Al Connell and Dave Hunter.

At an especially bad piece of road, David Haight, Jim Sherratt and one other man had arrived one day to work and fix it when Al Connell and myself drove up with our extra big loads. This bit of bad road had kept some others from loading heavily but we took a chance on its having been fixed and loaded a little higher than usual. When we got there these three men had only just reached the place and nothing had been done. We debated. We had to do one of two things, risk a break and tip-over, or wait. Al said, 'If you break down, Dave Bulloch will fix you up. If I do, Al Connell will have to. You go first and if you make it I'll try.

Well, I went, the others watching. I gave the horses the whip as they struck the steep icy pitch. The wagon began to slide. The hind wheels struck a log that saved me from tipping over, but I made it. Al wouldn't try. I went to town and he waited until the road was done and came in hours later.

Our lower canyon road was a series of steep pitches, short turns and icy crossings. Most of the way it was impossible to pass each other, but according to the direction of the wind one or the other outfits approaching would be warned by the chuckle of wagon and rattle of harness, if your team hadn't already told you. I think it was at one of these bad places that Al busted up Jim Hunter's new wagon.

On days that were sunny and bright we were as happy as any men ever were while working. Driving out onto some of the wind-swept, bleak, open spaces, the wind would seem to cut and sting like needles, cutting the flesh off our faces, and our lungs would burn with the cold air. I sometimes tied a sack over my knees to keep the snow from sifting down into my boots. After that first trip however, I wore German sox and boots over good woolen sox.We had trouble keeping to the road and would sometimes be as much as half a mile off until Hebe came along with us and staked in it with the edgings from the Mill. That gave us all, even the horses, more confidence. It had slowed up our trips and was so annoying to have the horses step clumsily off the packed road down into the fluffy soft snow and then have to dig or tramp a trench to get them back up. The willing, teachable horses learned valuable lessons on those jobs, as did the men. No matter what their color, they were all white at times with the hoar-frost that clung to every hair. Many of the horses could have made it without drivers because they became so cautious.

Jule Rosenberg had the toughest job of all, in my opinion. He was off-bearer, handling all the green, cold, icy slabs from the saw, but he stayed on the job and never complained. Spence Coburt was the saw operator and he was at it steadily until the last log was sawed.

To Ben Carrigan should go the credit of taking the first sleigh on that job. At the head of Sheep Hollow, on what we called the "S" dugway, Jim Hunter decided he would try one trip down without rough-blocking. Orson spoke to ride the tail-end if Jim could drive that way. The load began to push the team. They began to go faster to keep out of its way. Soon they were trotting, then galloping. The back end of the lumber slipped out of the chain and spread out fanwise. Orson was pitched through a cloud of snow to land feet first, rods away, buried in snow to the neck as Jim and his outfit in a cloud of snow slowed up and stopped at the bottom of the hill. Some driving!

After six weeks or so of hauling between Bryant's Hotel on the Mammoth and the Old Settin', I quit and came home. I had been out quite late one night, and it seemed like I had just gotten to bed when there came a loud rapping at the door that roused the whole house. Presently I heard Father's and Francis Webster's voices. 'But Dave, I can't get anybody else and they can't go on with the building without his help.' I knew that I might as well say 'Yes' because that man didn't take turn-down, so I got up and began to get ready.

I worked one stretch of hauling with Ben Gower who was paying off a doctor bill to Doctor Forrester. He was frail and ailing. I told him he shouldn't be trying to do this kind of work, but he was determined. After he got a shot of Renz's cayenned whiskey and we thought he was dying, he seemed to perk out of it and feel much better afterwards.

Shortly after we got started and well on the way, Brother Webster sent up a letter which was passed along to us all with a lot of comment. It said, 'Now next time a big frost comes, don't give up so easy. Stick to your work and you'll never regret it.' Not long after this he and Jed Jones drove up in a small pleasure sleigh to lend encouragement. Brother Webster was heard to remark, 'They really did have a big frost, didn't they?'

We made much of our fun, often at the expense of each other, but it made our situations interesting. One day while I was in town, I thought that since I must put in my time for the school I would try one of the jobs out on the building, so made arrangements to run the windlass that raised the loads of brick and mortar to the masons. One day of it was enough. I was willing to go back into the mountains.

You ask if I got any pay out of it. The pay for anything we do in this life simmers down to the valuable lessons we learn and the good that goes out from us to others. My family of eight boys and girls have had the benefit of the school that I helped to build. I am unable to estimate the value to the thousands of other young people that we have seen passing our house here on College Avenue. If they have received a benefit comparable to that which my own have received, then I have been thousands of times repaid for my part in the establishment of the Branch Normal School, now the Branch Agricultural College.

SAM HEYBORNE

Sam Heyborne and his snowy-haired wife Lizzie, now 71 years old and he 74, welcomed me into their lovely little new home, just recently built on the old Birkbeck property, by the side of his massive older home. His 12 children have all gone out for themselves and now he and Lizzie are enjoying the smaller home with its conveniences.

"Yes, come in. Of course I have time to tell you anything I can. Time is the only thing I have left and that is dull entertainment."

We talked of the development that has come to Cedar City in recent years, of the changes in the city and of times and people past.

In response to my query as to his part in getting out lumber for the school in winter-time, he laughed as he said, "I was there with two teams, even if I was small," and speaking of small men, Sam Heyborne was, a few years ago, one of the most powerful and rugged and biggest, of Cedar's big men. I visited with him first in February 1947.

When I came out of the Mountains that March in 1898, I heaved a sigh of relief and thought, 'Well, I'm thankful that job is behind me.' I'd given about my share, but once in town, again, the air was filled with talk of the school. It was the subject of conversation everywhere and we were not allowed to forget it for a day, that is, not until the building was completed and school was being held in it.

I've made no conscious effort to remember my part in it until now. You and one or two others are asking me to rake back through my memories and tell a connected story of the events. I would like to do that but I'm sure some details would not be the same as another might remember them, so I shall try to give you just my part in it.

My first child was just a month old when at the insistence of the committee I agreed to go. We were living with my Father's family. I was anxious to get started on a place for ourselves but I went."

Lizzie added, "Yes, one stretch lasted six weeks."

The road that I traveled for those weeks in the cold was the top of the circle. From town it was four days to the Mill, three days to the Mammoth and all uphill. Across the Mammoth and down to the Mill on the other side was another days travel. This fourth stretch, across the windswept level Mammoth, down to the Mill one day, from the Mill back to the place that came to be known as Bryant's Hotel, the next. Once in awhile I would drive back the second lap of the road and camp at Old Settin'. It was while I was camped at Old Settin' a week or so after I started to work that I lost one of my team. I was driving my own and my Father's teams. The committee replaced my horse, but when a week or so later one of Father's horses died, he had to stand his own loss.

My first trip into the hills began while the other two parties were struggling in the snow further ahead. Dave Urie and myself, one day behind Rob-Will's party, were urged to push ahead as fast as possible to stop the others from coming back out by promising fresh supplies to them, and the promise that the Mill crew, equipped with Bobsleighs, would follow immediately with more and better supplies.

It snowed all night on us at our camp in Sheep Hollow so that when morning finally came all we could do was straddle a horse and go on. At the Little Red Creek we met those of the other parties who were on their way down. We gave them our message and then went on to join and help the five who had stayed to break the other side of the road back up to the Mammoth. This was a worse task almost than if there had been no trail at all, because in spite of us the horses would slip into the old rut in the deep snow. In places we men had to go first in snow shoulder deep. It was badly drifted. Our safety lay in keeping to the old road-bed as nearly as possible. Night after night we would come into camp wringing wet from perspiration, inside and out. We stayed at this until we had a road broken clear to the Mill. Someone hit upon the idea of uncoupling the sleigh in the middle and dragging and packing the snow down by putting a tongue in each half-Bob, lashing trees or lumber on it, and letting the other end drag.

Those of us who watched Jim and Orson take their snowy ride down the "S" turns that day are still wondering why they weren't killed. It wasn't many years afterwards that Danny Pendleton was killed, in summer weather, on this same road. Jim was a real dare-devil and was always taking unnecessary chances but he had outlived nearly all of us.

Before I went into the mountains, Father had secured a good sturdy sleigh from a man in New Harmony, expecting to haul out some lumber for himself for barn and fences. I had been sent for it to New Harmony. It was already there on the lot, so that sleigh is what I used all the while I was on the job. My companion was R. A. (Al) Thorley. It had been ruled that there should be two men to each load. That was good sense because if anything went wrong, if horses became tangled or went off the road, or if any one of a number of accidents happened, two men would be better able to survive trouble than one.

Sim Simkins lost one of his horses at the Old Settin'. I don't know if he ever got another.

Spencer Coburt, Steve Walker's son-in-law, handled the saw. Jule Rosenberg was off-bearer. John Perry, Tom Urie, Jim Bryant and Caleb Haight were the cooks at different times at the mill. August Mackelprang, John Tait, R.A. (Al) Thorley and myself were haulers on that first lap of the road out from the mill. Other men who worked at the logging and cutting were Dave Dunn Sherratt, Jim Hunter, Billy Daugherty, Sim Simkins, Renz Adams, Rone Thompson, Frank Adams, Sam (Poots) Walker and Steve Walker. William Webster fired the boiler and John or Hebe watched the Mill. There were possibly others that I don't recall now. Rob-Will, Ben Gower and Sam Bauer were usually the men who picked up our loads at Bryant's Hotel and hauled them along the second lap of the road, bringing in the supplies for the mill hands, and the horse feed. We had trouble keeping to the road for awhile, so for several days Hebe came with us. a bunch of lumber edgings were put on each wagon and with these he staked the road. Horses and men felt more confidence then. It was such a nuisance to have the horses get off into the soft snow.

I don't know who hauled on the other end only as I would hear one and another mentioned.

All the lumber was unloaded from the sleighs on the top of the Cedars and put on wagons to go from there to town. The men who drove the wagons didn't have any easy job. The creek had to be crossed seven times in that many miles, with water backed up and filled with broken chunks of sharp ice, or worse, frozen over with ice that would suddenly give way under one wheel or the other, leaving you to chop your way out, or double out if other teams were near, anyway, get out the best you could, working sometimes wet and cold for hours. The steep frozen banks on both sides made your getting in a sudden jerk that would cripple your back if you weren't on guard.

Moderns know nothing of riding a dead "X" wagon, nor the art of handling the wagon-brake and four horses at one and the same time while sitting on top of a bale of hay or a bed-roll on a jerking, bumping running gear. That is something we see very seldom, if ever, now days.

At first we thought the horses would do better sharp-shod but found that they did best barefooted.

In the work at the Mill, we couldn't leave the sleighs or the logs standing still longer than a few minutes without their freezing tight. Some of the horses would pull as long as they could stay on their feet but no amount of straight pulling would break the frozen stuff loose. One day Jule took a cant-hook and gave a hard-set log a little shake. The team then walked away easily. Men and teams too had to learn that a quick side-swing would break loose the tightly frozen down runners or logs.

Neil worked on all parts of the road wherever he could best help to keep a never-ending stream of lumber moving back into town. His team "Hank" and "Rum" were mighty good horses.

It was Ben Carrigan's job to keep parts of the road clear of snow and some of the sidling stretches chopped down to a level. The sleigh runners usually cut grooves enough to keep them from slipping off over the edge on the turns and dugways.

Our children have all had the advantages of that school as their desires and inclinations dictated. They are all honest reliable citizens. I am satisfied that I had a part in the building of it.

Later on I received some cash, but I don't remember now how much it was.

JOHN PERRY

One Sunday afternoon, February 23, 1947, I first saw and visited with John Perry. Two months later I took to him this sketch of the things he had told me for his approval. He said, "That is very good. I am well pleased with what you have there."

As I read it to him he worked re-tying the coils to make the smooth rounded foundation seat of an overstuffed couch. All of this took place in his little furniture shop back of his new home on Center Street in Cedar City. The paper he approved follows:

I was crossing the street near the old Stewart property on January 6, 1898, and as I stepped onto the wagon bridge I met Francis Webster and Jed Jones, face to face. 'Here is a boy we could use on that lumbering expedition for the school.' 'Tell me about it,' I said.

'The group are ready to leave in the morning,' they told me after explaining.

'All right, I can go. I have nothing special to keep me so I'll be ready.'

I had good warm clothes, felts, rubbers, cap with earlaps, heavy overcoat, the tails of which could be wrapped and tied around each leg, and mittens. I understood that I was to donate my time, and there would be no pay. I was paired off with Jim Hunter. He had a fine outfit, two teams and a new wagon. There were 10 other men. Neil Bladen had the only Bobsleigh.

We worked through a foot or more of snow all the way to Jensen's sawmill. Hebe was with us or I doubt if we'd ever have reached there. He seemed to have a sixth sense for pointing out the road under its snowy cover. The hills all looked alike to the rest of us. We reached the Mill at the end of the fourth day, camping out three nights. We could see that the wagon would be useless. It began to snow and snowed all night. The task looked so impossible that we decided to turn back while we could.

We put a little lumber on Jim's wagon, 800 feet or so, and some on Neil's sleigh. After all day of struggling through snow that kept falling and getting deeper by the minute, we pulled into a heavy grove of pines upon the Mammoth to try and make a camp. The snow was dragging across the tongue and against the front standard of Jim's wagon as he swung into place. When morning came we put our bedding and a little food on the horses and left, leaving the rest of our outfits sitting there in the trees. As we strung out single file, 20 horses and 11 men, Neil on lead, he stopped suddenly and yelled, his voice drifting back to the hindmost, 'We're not going to quit and don't get it into your heads that we are. We are going to go down and get Bobsleds and then come back in here and get that lumber out.'

I have often thought of that picture and felt that the man was inspired. Perhaps some of us felt foolish at giving up without more of a try. We went down to the Old Settin' on Bear Flat to camp with the second company, Rob-Will's outfit. That made 26 horses without very much food. Jim and the others saw to their care and divided up the feed.

I think Neil, that first night out of town, had been named boss of the whole expedition by the rest of the men. At any rate we all recognized him as boss.

I went on next day with the majority group to town. I was back a few days later as cook for the Mill hands and haulers on that end.

I went to work never lacking good food to cook or things to cook with, and having charge of all that came into the house. Cheese, butter, honey, jams, sacks of sugar, halves of pork, quarters of beef, beans, rice, raisins, baked bread, cookies, cooked roasts, even cakes and pies, and not only food but clothing, woolen underwear, mittens, overalls, felts and rubbers, shirts, jumpers, horse-blankets, hay and grain, attesting to the fact that the people also took the job seriously.

One time two full boxes of cut plug came up, one of "horse-show" and one of "Battle Ax." I had heard the merits of both brands argued pro and con by those who chewed, so for fun I changed the symbols. "Battle Ax" fans enjoyed "Horse-shoe" and "Horse-shoe" fans enjoyed "Battle Ax" and never knew the difference.

There was no whiskey. Renz thought to warm some of the men up one cold day with a swallow from a bottle into which he had poured a can of cayenne pepper. Jim took one swallow and threw himself across a log suffering with a cramp that nearly killed him. That was all the whiskey I saw.

The horses played no small part in the success of the expedition. They were the best that could be had. Neil's "Hank" and "Rum," Renz's "Sorrel," George Wood's "Doll" worked side by side with "Sorrel." Jim's "Nance," "Jake," "Dick" and "Pat" and many others whose names were familiar at the time but I have since forgotten, were real trail-breakers and where one of a pair was, his team-mate was also doing his level best. Men, without those loyal and conscientious helpers, could have done little.

Jim Hunter was one of the best men of the group. His horses were first and last in his thoughts and they learned to handle themselves in the trying situations of the snow country, feeling their way to keep on the hard packed roads.

The bread that got hard and dry, I put into the clean empty flour sacks and sent back to town where it could be used for feed. It was one of these sacks that had been hung in a tree and proved to be of value to the four hungry tired men who had to sit by the fire all night at what came to be known as Bryant's Hotel.

I had no way of knowing who worked on other parts of the road only as I would hear the talk at meal time. I spent thirty days, mostly indoors, except to rustle wood for the cooking. I know it was cold and unpleasant, especially when the sky was overcast but the men were tough and they didn't complain. They sometimes got wet but they didn't get sick. Evenings were happy and full of fun. When Tom Urie came up ailing, I gave him my place as cook and I cut for a few days.

I am happy and proud to look back to my association with such men and for such a cause. I know it has meant more to our community than any other thing in it. I am proud of the record my family has made through the help of the Branch Normal School.

The little I gave to the establishment of the school is small indeed as compared to the many fine things I and mine have received.

John stated again as I was ready to leave, "I am proud that I was offered the chance to go and work for it."

RANDALL LUNT

In late winter of 1898, I had on my wagon a load of coal and my team was sharp-shod ready to leave for the Washington Factory where the coal would be traded for goods, such as coarse cotton cloth, or linsey woolsey that the factory was making at that time. The evening before I was to leave a town meeting was called to be held in the new tabernacle. This proposition was put to the people:

"Our year of grace is running out and we have a chance to get this school here permanently. This year is showing what it is worth to people of this town and other towns. You know that if we get the building ready for next Fall's beginning we can't wait until farm work begins, until high water closes the canyon, and with the muddy mountain roads from melting snow. Our canyons are nearly impassable until May and June dries the roads and by then it will be too late to start getting out lumber. Disagreeable as a winter lumbering expedition will be, is it not the solution to our problem? We must either grab this season of slack work and make the best of it or give it up entirely." Jedediah Jones was speaking.

Expressions from the group were heard, questions and arguments. Finally Cornelius Bladen volunteered, 'I am willing to try it.'

Other volunteers were asked for. If Bladen would lead out who would follow? Eight or nine others offered their services. Jim Hunter was later persuaded making 11 in all and they agreed, 'If we start we must not turn back.'

Richard Bryant said, "I don't own a team or a part of an outfit and couldn't drive if I did, but if I would be any good anywhere I will go.'

Around the first volunteer centered the planning. We agreed it would be wisdom to use two teams on each wagon, and for one man never to go alone. Thus we began to prepare. I didn't go to Washington. My coal was disposed of. My Mother got a part and my team and wagon with Daniel G. Perkins' team made one outfit.

Neil Bladen's and Sim Simkins' teams on a big Bobsleigh made one outfit. Lorenzo Adams' three good horses, with George Wood's "Doll" on his own wagon, with Orson Tyler for partner made another. Jim Hunter's two teams and wagon with John Perry for partner made a fourth outfit. The fifth was Francis Webster's son John, driving his own outfit with James Bryant for partner. Heber Jensen, co-owner of the Jensen Brothers Sawmill was to ride his saddle horse, scout ahead and point out the road as none of this group of men had hauled over the road since the Mill had been moved to a new setting last summer.

We knew that we must donate our time, teams, feed, food and whatever we used. There would be no pay. We also knew that getting out lumber in winter meant everything connected with it. There was but very little lumber on the ground already sawed. The one thing we could not predict was the weather.

On the 7th of January 1898 we were on the way, breaking through a foot or so of snow on a warmish winter day. We camped three nights and on the fourth without mishap camped at the Mill a distance of perhaps 35 miles, if it could be measured.

After we reached the Mill it began to snow. It snowed all night so that when morning came we turned around and started right back out. We didn't want to be snowed in, especially with no more provisions than we had for 21 horses and 11 men. We made it back up to the Mammoth and pulled into a heavy grove of pines to make an uncomfortable snowy camp. Leaving the wagons we rode our horses and bedding out as far as the Old Settin' by night on the second day, to meet there the second group of four men with nine more horses and very little food or feed. Some stayed to try and break back to the wagons, but most of us were back in town that night, determined to go back better prepared and equipped to work in the snow.

In town again, with Jed Jones and Francis Webster urging us to greater speed, we began to assemble materials with which to make Bobsleighs. I helped George Urie all I could and he worked overtime. We went back four or five days later with four horses all hitched to a good sturdy Bobsleigh, hand-made every inch of it.

It was impossible to load heavy big loads on the up-hill parts of the road, and dangerous to men and teams with big loads on the down-hill, so the idea was to keep a steady run of lumber on the way with such loads as could be easily handled.

If no accident occurred the men usually met on schedule, for instance, three outfits hauling from the

Mill up to the Mammoth, would unload onto two outfits starting down hill on the first drive after leaving the Mammoth.

At first there weren't enough Bobs, and in order to pack the snow and make a better road, we took the king-pin out, put a tongue in the back end, lashed the lumber tightly to the half-Bob letting the other end drag. This packed and hardened the road and built it up as high as 10 and 15 feet. Nowadays we see scarcely any roads that are not hard and smooth with gravel, oil or cement surfacing. We would be surprised to drive on an ice or snow surfaced one.

No, it really makes no difference now who or what men get the credit for this or that. The really important thing is that the job was done on time and that we got the school. It is, and was, the rugged out-of-door workers who do the real work of this world. Methods and equipment have changed. We live in an age of science but grit, determination, courage and ingenuity still count for much in this world, and human beings still get joy from a task well done.

The Legislature after a few years, got around to appropriating 52 cents on the dollar to partially reimburse the men who had worked. At that rate and allowing three dollars per man and team. I received $160. I had been on the job steadily from the 5th of January until the 12th of March 1898.

I am now 82 years old and very grateful for the part I had in getting us the Branch Normal School. My seven children grew up with its culture and ideals in their lives. The hardship end of it was tough at the time, but time has healed even that.

FRED ASHDOWN
(75 years old)

Fred had a serious operation but was feeling some better on Sunday, May 5, 1947, when my husband and I spent an afternoon with him.

Fred has an exceptionally keen mind, but like John S. Woodbury he said, "I remember best the things that happened when I was young." Always active, interested in people, in work and honest endeavor, it is very trying for him to take it easy.

He told us of his father's sawmill, of the dangerous roads that he and his brothers hauled lumber over, of the teams they drove and the blacksmithing they did. He is a happy optimistic older man, his handsome clean-shaven face with the smile wrinkles deeply engraved reflected the ability to laugh off a tough situation and face life smiling.

In connection with the building of the school many times he mentioned Uriah T. Jones. I asked him, "Do you not mean Jed Jones?" for not a single one of the other men had mentioned Uriah T. As we always spoke of him. "No indeed, I mean Uriah. He did as much pushing for the school as Jed did."

He spoke of Rube Walker as having said to Uriah T., "Brother Jones, I've been dodging you all day." "Yes, I know it and I've been dodging right after you all day. I need you. You're the only man for this job. Why shouldn't I dodge after you?" Uriah T. was known for as much persistence as his brother Jed and Francis Webster. Fred said, "You had just as well say 'Yes' at first for anyone of the three didn't know what 'No' meant."

He went on, As a young fellow I went into partnership with Bishop W. H. Corry in his building on Main Street, just where the south drive of the Hotel El Escalante now stands. We shared the proceeds, his being two-thirds and mine one-third. Cash was very scarce. The little we got was precious. Bishop Corry said 'Let all the other jobs that can, wait for the cash jobs.'

For 15 years we worked that way. When I quit, he quit blacksmithing and then for 15 years I worked with Jos. Fife a little further up the street. It was while I was with Bishop Corry that the school was built. When he left the shop or left town, he would say, 'Here are the keys Fred, you be Bishop until I come back.'

Oftentimes I saw to the selling from and the unloading of hay into the tything barns, and to distributing fresh beef and other commodities from the tything office on the corner, besides doing the blacksmith's job. One summer with the help of his sons, Elias M. and Parry, I filled both the big tything barns and made an extra stack of hay. These barns were of from 75 to 100 tons capacity. When Bishop came home he said, 'You do better than if I were here to boss.'

He had given me a little vacation one holiday time. I had taken it by driving Father's brown team to Toquerville. I saw a chance to secure some good iron for the shop. I came back with 2,200 pounds for which I paid $7.50 and the promise of making two cow brands. One was "TX," a well known Dixie brand.

When the committee came asking us to make bobsleighs we didn't try to do it at our shop, but I was sent to help George Urie in his. Some were made of iron-shod plank in two sections, and others were of wagon-length all in one piece, the runners being made of the lighter weight iron railroad rails braced well in three places.

On the down-hill grades rough-locking helped, but often the weight of the loads would crowd the teams. The horses didn't like being bumped with the single-trees, and the weight shifting and hitting rocks, trees and banks as the load swung from side to side, kept a never-ending stream of broken sleighs and chains. We often worked until midnight repairing for the outfit's next day's driving. This we did over a period of two and one-half to three months without pay.

Fred Stump was an expert wheelwright. We had built an extension in back of our shop so that he had a place for his work too. The men hauling in the lower canyon on wagons had helped with the wagon repairs during that time. His work was given willingly. More than any other man however, I would like to pay a tribute to the conscientious efforts of Bishop William H. Corry in promoting and pushing to completion the Branch Normal School with every means in his power.

My job was just on the working end, but what I did I did willingly. Sometimes I think that in days gone by the blacksmith shop held the spotlight of the town. It was the place of exchange. Men from all kinds of jobs gathered there. We knew all the news and what people were saying and thinking. I miss my friendly contacts and good natured exchange.

I am grateful for your visit and the chance to tell you my thoughts and memories concerning this thing of such vital interest to this part of the State.

JETHRO PALMER

Francis Webster came into the harness shop sometime in January 1898, to say to me, 'Jethro, I want all the horse blankets you have or can get. With teams working in the cold high in the mountains, they must have blankets.'

I answered him, 'The horse blanket season is pretty well done, but you can get what we have. I didn't intend to order more and don't think I could get them if I did.' 'Well, you can make some can't you?' he asked. I told him I had no material but if I had some I could try.

He went away and soon came back with a big chunk of heavy canvas. He told me that John M. Higbee had secured it from one of the sugar factories where he had been recently and was donating it for the purpose of making horse blankets.

'Canvas is not enough,' I told him. 'Good blankets have to be lined.' Well, an hour or so later here he came with the lining in the form of several extra-heavy stout bed blankets. 'Now if you need help I'll get that too,' he told me.

My brothers Ted and Will usually helped with extra work so I guess one of them helped me. We were using our first machine for stitching, and at that time we were making complete harnesses with the use of this new machine.

With all of the other jobs of harness repair, getting ready for this school lumbering expedition, I made three pairs of extra large horse blankets, complete with lining, buckles and straps. They lasted the men who got them for many years and proved to be the most remarkable of all horse blankets. It was many years before their notoriety waned, for the stitching done with heavy linen thread outlasted anything previous or since.

When Brother Webster took them he said, 'You understood this was a donation job?' 'Yes,' I answered, 'I expected you would come to that.' 'The Lord will bless you,' he said as he closed the door.

I have been blessed in many ways so I suppose Francis Webster's prophecy came true.

From the time the first men went into the mountains, there came to my hands a continuous stream of stuff to be mended. I have worked far into the night to have harness or other gear ready for another day's driving. I felt sometimes as though some of the men took advantage of the situation to get a lot of free work. If they did I feel that it was worth it. I was glad to do my part.

The school was undoubtedly the best thing that ever came to our community, and I have no regrets that I gave of my time and materials as I did.

Jethro Palmer is now close to 80 years of age. He stood at his cutting bench in his shop, back of the Palmer Dress Shop as I talked with him this morning, May 5, 1947. He didn't seem to be very busy. He is active, his memory keen and he knows and remembers the stories that were told of the situation under which the men worked in the mountains that winter 50 years ago to secure the lumber necessary for the new school building.

J. H. WALKER

It has always been a thrill to me to step into Johnnie Walker's blacksmith shop and watch his big powerful arms and hands in their methodical, sure movements as he did some repair work on farm machinery. He is nearing 80 years but still does smaller repairs that help out his townspeople, in spite of the numerous welding shops that have mushroomed up and down the length of Cedar's Main Street. I like to listen to his homey philosophy and comments for his years are full of wisdom and understanding.

My father came to Cedar City among the first to help in the development of the iron. His specialty, though, was sawmilling and with his seven boys did all the work connected with the sawmill as long as we were with him. I have been in the blacksmith business some 52 years, right here close to our home. Often one of my brothers has helped me when I've been rushed, and my own boys, all of whom are expert help have also helped me. My life has been an open book to the community. I have helped wherever and whenever there have been projects afoot that would add to the pleasure or comfort or the advancement of our town.

My connection with the Branch Normal School began when members of the committee came to me asking if I would donate my time and what material I had, to make Bobsleighs for the men who had gone into the mountains in stormy January weather to try to secure the lumber necessary to build with. It was about the 10th of January. We had had a deep snow storm and the weather had turned bitter cold. I told Brother Webster that such an expedition in this weather looked extremely risky. He answered, 'Well, we must have this school for Cedar City regardless. The men are already in the mountains and we must provide their needs and keep them on the job.' He stressed the point that there would be no pay for the work.

Well, I knew about the size and shape of a Bobsleigh. I fashioned the wood parts from plank, shod the runners with good iron, some of which had been Frank Adams'. I do not remember now how many sleighs I made but I know that keeping them repaired, keeping hooks and rings on the log chains, and the broken wagons repaired, was a job in itself and a full-time one.

At first I shod some of the teams but with shoes on the horses that would go down would cut themselves badly, scrambling to get up, and then we found that they could get along as well barefooted. The calks on the shoes would fast fill with ice or frozen snow so that they were smooth and helped the horses but very little to stay on their feet.

I had no gripe about the work brought to me. I kept no account of time spent or materials used. I sometimes felt that some of the fellows made it an excuse to get their own work done but since I kept no accounts I received none of the money that was later appropriated.

In the light of that winter's work and what it had come to mean to the people of Southern Utah communities, I am proud that I could do my bit to secure the school with all of the opportunities and culture it has provided. It is a great satisfaction to know that my own children and grandchildren are better people through their contacts with the fine men and women who have directed the destiny of the Branch Normal School.

JOHN S. WOODBURY

I would like to write a book on the life of John S. Woodbury, one of the two remaining members of the general committee of the Branch Normal School building project. He was my best school teacher, actually disliked by some of the sixth, seventh and eighth grade pupils with whom he wrestled so conscientiously to give the fundamentals of education according to the newest educational methods of the time. It was not his fault if the method was poor. What education has stayed with me, I absorbed from John S. Woodbury and his companion teachers, George W. Decker and Albert N. Tollestrup. These three, very unalike, had much of the same ideals as to what we should be taught and how we should behave, as well as the procedure by which we should learn. What a pity that some of their discipline could not be projected down the years to reach the disrespectful, undisciplined, devil-may-care attitudes of the majority of the sixth, seventh and eight-grade pupils of today. We were average people of the time but shame and disrespect forbade the expressions of sarcasm, tack-talk and disrespect for authority that we see most everywhere today.

Lehi W. Jones is the other living member of that committee. When I went to him on May 9, 1947, he was so feeble and weak (now in his 93rd year) that he could scarcely speak. He urged me, "Go to John. He can give you a more complete statement of what you want than I can, now." I had asked him for a very brief statement as to the nature of the work that the committee had to perform, so then I went to John, who is 15 or more years younger than Lehi.

We spent the afternoon rehearsing incidents of things and people in common. Aunt May was listening and enjoying with us our laughter and tears, for congenial people must weep as well as smile together.

"Oh," he said, "If I could forget the unkindnesses, the unintentional hurts, the abominable behavior of my youth, it would make me very happy now. To think that from the practical prankster I turned into a staid, sober-sided school teacher, well, I've done other things too, besides teach school.

When I first came to Cedar in 1893, four teachers, Bengt Nelson, Jr., Sadie Wilkinson, Sadie Meeks and myself took care of Cedar's school population. In 1895 I married May Higbee and we built the small neat frame home up on First East Street. George Decker bought that home when I went to Leeds that season to teach. Then I came back to teach in Cedar until 1903.

It was during this period that Cedar had its serious epidemic of typhoid fever. The serious illness of typhoid which my own two children contracted, postponed for a year the contemplated two years of post-graduate work at the University of Utah. I did finally go and when I came back to Cedar from those two years of college work, I taught at the Branch Normal School. During those years I didn't keep a diary or any other system of notes that would have been invaluable to me now.

I was one of the general committee for the building of the school, but the details elude my memory. I know that we thought that if we rushed to completion the already begun Ward Hall building, that it would take care of the housing of the school for a few years. The school was then in progress in its first year.

Just after the turn of the year we found that unless the school could be housed in a State-owned and approved building the opportunity would be given to a city that could fill those requirements. If they meant to find out what we were made of or put the pinchers on us, they surely struck at the proper time.

Rough winter weather, cold snow-filled canyons and mountains, followed by spring floods and impassable muddy, miry roads, would take us well into June before we could make a move toward getting out native lumber from the mountains. Imported lumber had never been heard of. There was no cash to buy with even if we had of heard of it. We had very little cash for anything, so, grabbing the bull by the horns, determined to keep the school if work would do it, the most persistent men of the town were chosen to act as community whips and stir the population out of their complacency and get them moving. The idea took hold gradually but gathered momentum as time passed. Enthusiasm spread with everyone until all were united in the common cause that brought to a completion and into practical use our first Branch Normal School building.

I suppose that I helped to plan and study ways and means, contact men, helped to push the thing all I could, but I can recall little of it now. I do know that the work we did was all donation and that I spent the summer of 1898 carpentering on the building, and that it was ready, although not completed, for the opening of school that September.

Frank Walker, Jabez Benson, Sam T. Leigh, Tom Perry and Will Lunt were the carpenters of the town at the time and I don't think a single one got by without donating some time to the cause.

Our three children have all studied, graduated and grown to manhood and womanhood in the shadow of the school and in its cultural atmosphere. What would this town have been without the school?

The inborn desire for decency and culture has, on the part of the majority, improved the morale of the whole countryside. It has been a great force for betterment. Many have had the chances it offered, where had they been forced to go to some other school that was out of reach, they couldn't have done it.

John S. Woodbury's home is a little south on College Street. His life has been spent with young people, students from all walks of life. He knows Cedar's hope, fears, and desires because he has always had a finger on its pulse. He laughs at the futile efforts and rejoices with our successes.

He helped with the campaign to put good clean spring water into a city water system. He instigated the campaign for a municipal power plant, our telephone system, and has been instrumental in the water adjudication of near revolutionary proportions.

Yes, his life can be classed with the outstanding biographies of Cedar City in each and every move toward the betterment of her citizenry.

RUBE WALKER

Having known Rube all my life but never having known his full name, I still consider him to be one of Cedar's outstanding characters. You cannot be in his presence without feeling his calm kindly, steadying presence. No matter what the occasion or the excitement, he makes you feel that as you go down into the valley of the shadow you would do well to hold such a hand to steady you in your faltering.

"I am so glad you came to visit me," he repeated.

I was not married but a young man of 20 living with my parents on the southeast corner of Center and Third East Streets when the 'school' question was agitated. Of course I could help along with everybody else and I hardly know a person who ever was asked that refused. So, for a week or two maybe, I helped Al Connell haul from somewhere up near Sugar Loaf on into town.

We raised everything we ate. I helped raise it and helped eat it, right along with the rest of Father's family.

After helping Al, they put me on the building itself. The outside foundation rock walls were not all in and I went to work tending mason. William Dover was boss of the rock work while they started the long partition walls through the center of the building. Danny Pendleton was my partner. I wasn't extra big or husky, and because Danny was stout and heavy, he always took the heavy end of the rock, the wagon, or whatever we were handling. We helped put in every stone in those partition walls. There are nine tiers of rock above the ground. I haven't the slightest idea of how many tons of rock went into that building but I do know that we would lift until our tongues would hang out on some of those single stones.

Brother Dover often took us to his home for a meal or for some nice treat after our work. There were about six of us younger fellows, and we would have done anything for that man. There was never a disagreement or dispute among the men who worked under him.

After the foundation was all in we began on the front entrance part. After it got up above where we could roll the rocks onto the wall, we fixed a hoist and used that to lift and place them. Danny and I handled every stone and helped William Dover lay the key-stone in the big arch over the front entrance. Danny and I also carried and set in place every door and window frame that went into those walls. When Danny left to go somewhere for two weeks, Jim Gilbert took his place. Jim handled the horse on the hoist. Instead of steadying the start-up by putting his hand on the chain on the grab-hooks, he would hold to the rope. I would shout down to him, 'Take your hand off that rope. It is too darn close to the pulley!' but he persisted until he let the rope drag his hand into it and ruin his middle finger. It was his fault for I warned him many times.

I stayed on the job until Sam Webster laid the last brick and my little black donkey carried me faithfully to and from work for three full months.

About three days before the south wall was finished (the southwest wall is where the last bricks were laid) there came up a terrific windstorm. You could put a hand on the green wall and feel it sway inward. It looked dangerous so we hauled all of the extra scantling timbers up, toenailed them to the subfloor and braced the whole south wall.

I was given $60 worth of credit in the building when we were through. I couldn't see what good it would ever be to me so I traded it to Sam Webster for five acres of field ground.

John McFarlane did a lot of work in different jobs on the building and Danny McFarlane, John's younger brother, was a dandy errand boy. He was quick, active and willing. He was plenty tough too and what he thought he could do he would do, or bust a gut trying.

At Founders' Day one time I was invited to play my little old accordion and speak if I cared to. I told them of my work on the building, especially of seeing the keystone put in. Roy Halversen chirped in with, 'That all sounds very well Rube, but you aren't old enough to have done that.'

Just once in my lifetime I moved from one home to another. That was when I married Lena Ash and moved from my father's home into my own. I have never paid a day's rent anywhere. I haven't a single regret for the things I have done. There is no doubt that I might have done better than I did at times, but in regretting afterwards there is no comfort. We have always had plenty and we have been happy. I don't care to be worried by the newer conveniences being offered. I have never been sick and will never give up to stop working until I am forced to, because death is the last thing I want to give in to.

ROB BURNS SHERRATT
(71 years of age)

I was a big husky boy when Dod Walker, Dennis Perkins and myself, one holding the handles, the other two pulling with ropes, would take big loads of brick up the long plank ramp to the scaffold on which the men stood to lay the brick that went into the wall of the old Ward Hall, which was being rushed to completion so as to house the first year of the Branch Normal School. I made one of that trio for all of the summer.

Sometime in early February, Jed Jones and Francis Webster came to me saying, 'Robert, there's a telegram here, just came for Tom Urie from Joe Cumero. It has to be sent as soon as possible, Will you ride up to the mill and take it?' I said, 'Yes, I'll go if you will get me a good horse.' This was late in the afternoon. 'Be ready early,' they told me. 'It will be a big days ride.' I had never been over the road, but they told me that I couldn't miss it, that I would meet men and teams all along the way.

The next morning I was on the way in good time riding Tom Urie's black "Kelly." He was a fine horse, grain fed and stout. I rode from early morning until about four o'clock in the afternoon, and reached the Old Settin' without meeting or seeing a single team. I rested and fed the horse from the hay and grain there, expecting someone to come, but no one showed up, so I started out again. At the next stop there was lumber piled up, and they afterwards told me they called the place "Bryant's Hotel." It became dark. There wasn't the least sign of a road. The moon was full and in its brilliance, intensified by the white snow, I saw the first marker, a piece of edging standing in the snow. Several times I had the horse go down into the soft snow and spent time tramping a trail to get him back up. Then I tried walking and leading him, and even after I could see those markers ahead we sometimes went off the road.

I don't remember being unreasonably cold, but I was unreasonably tired and more than thankful to come, at two o'clock in the morning, to the Mill house and tap on the door with my quirt-butt. Tom Urie's voice called "Come in and light the lamp on the table.' No matter how badly I might have needed matches, only then did I realize that I didn't have a single one.

How those men did condemn the men who would send a lone person on such an errand, and one who had never been over the road. Well, someone was ignorant of the condition and at fault. I have never learned why there were no haulers on the road that day but suppose it was a planned condition. I shudder at the unnecessary chances under which I made that trip. Well anyway, the next morning the fellows asked if I would take Tom's place cooking. I told them 'No' but that I would be willing to help with the other work, which I did for three weeks or more, helping to load or log, or roust-about the Mill. They put Jim Bryant in the house to cook and I guess I took his place cutting for awhile.

Dave Urie, Dave Dunn Sherratt, Jule Rosenberg, John and Hebe Jensen, Caleb Haight and Frank Adams were others who were there. It was a glorious happy time for me. I never did anything but outdoor work. We had fun, good food, and good congenial fellowship. The road was still hard when I came out of the mountains.

The next summer, after the snow was gone, I went back. The marks of the single-trees on the close timbers were six and eight feet up the tree trunks, showing how high that packed road-bed of snow had been in the winter.

The school has meant a great deal to my children. Each one has had the chance of a fine education. Three are business people and one is a splendid teacher, but that was yet future when I rode Tom Urie's "Kelly" into the mounts that winter day in 1898.

I have never before this, throughout the 50 years, been asked for a statement or an opinion, or to tell of my part in making possible the Branch Normal School for Cedar City. I am more than satisfied that I had a part in it all.

Ethel, his wife, added, "We could not have sent our children away from home to receive education but with the school here we have managed."

ISAAC HIGBEE

The Isaac Higbee home now stands on North 4th West Street at this time, but at the time of which I write, it was on Main Street between the old J. M. Higbee and the George Wood homes. Aunt May M. answered my knock this afternoon of May 9, 1947.

"We have been married 58 years," she told me as we visited. "My birthday just past. I was 79 and Uncle Ike is three years older."I told her that I would like a statement of their part in the building of

the School. "We didn't keep any account of what we gave. We were asked to donate and we donated again and again, and over again, of food and horsefeed. We had no help. Ike had livestock and farming land to look after and did not feel that he could leave them to the care of others. What our share had been was given in this way and we were happy in doing a small part to put over this worthy project."

Later I learned from May M. Higbee that the Cedar Dramatic Company, with herself, William B. Adams, A. H. Rollo, Lafe McConnell, Florence Lunt Webster, Chauncy McFarlane, Dan Matheson, Ada Wood Webster, Naomi Perkins Urie, Billy J. McConnell and some others put on several plays, and gave many performances under the leadership of Joseph Cosslett with the help of his choir and glee club. The proceeds of all of this went into the school building fund.

WILLIAM CORRY

I am 75 years old but in the pink of health and I consider that a wonderful blessing.

When they began working on the school, I was married. My nice black team, "Dick" and "Prince," the best team that ever walked, were my means of earning a living. Of course they needed teams—teams were as necessary as men.

I and mine hauled rock at first, several days of it, and then we made a trip or so for lumber from town to the top of the Cedars. After that we hauled lime, brick, gravel, sand and whatever had to be moved to the building site. Between times I did my own work.

MARY CORLETT

From Rob-Will and Minta Bullock, Maggie and Winnie Urie, Agnes Wood, John Perry and others, I learn that Mary Corlett in her home on a prominent corner on Main Street, collected and distributed all of the materials that went and came from the lumbering crews.

Home prepared foods and clothing were sent on to the ones who needed it. Containers were checked and returned to the owners. Bread and other ready prepared foods were kept steadily moving in about the proper quantities to men who had no camps where such things could be prepared.

Everyone gives her credit for a job well done and ably accomplished.

SAMUEL B. JONES

"We," speaking of his Father's family, "responded to the committee's request for donation on the school project by giving of our supplies, meat and flour, and help,

William Perry and myself hauled hay from stacks in the North Field to town to a baler where it was baled for the use of the teams working in the mountains. That was what I did toward the good of the cause. I was in Parowan most of the time Cedar was pushing for the school.

MRS. F. W. (SARAH) MIDDLETON, Widow

When I inquired if her husband did any work such as others did she said, "We were newly married and living on the farm at Hamilton's Fort. Dick was unable to leave but we helped by giving hay and grain and other food items that were needed."

MRS. WILL (DESSIE) WEBSTER, Widow

She said, "We had been married just one month when Will went with the Mill crew into the deep snow that January, to tend the boiler for sawing the lumber for the school. I was a stranger in Cedar. We had courted and married while Will worked at one and another various saw mills. I was anything but happy at being left alone, but I stayed on my job, as he did his, through that long winter and on into the spring. Will's work during most of our married life was spent as a boiler-man."

WILLIAM SIMKINS

William Simkins, in his late 70s, is in feeble health. He lay on a bed in a cool clean bedroom in the home of his only daughter, as we visited one July afternoon. "I did not do much on the school building," he began.

It was late in March or early April when my brother Hezekiah (Ki) and myself, each driving our own single teams and wagons, drove to the Summit sheep corral to load what we could haul from piles of lumber there. The canyon road up that far was quite muddy, but we had no trouble at all. The crossings were good. Ki and I made three or four such trips.

The committee furnished us hay and grain for the teams. We drove into John Parry's yard to get that.

Maria and I were dairying at our ranch up in Shurtz Canyon that summer and we sent cheese and butter to help feed those who needed it. Later on in the summer, after we came down from the ranch, I went on the building job and carried mortar. I would carry two candy buckets up a stairway, not much better than a ladder, to where Gomer Cosslett and Uncle Ed Parry and Samuel P. Horsley of Paragonah were laying the brick. Horace Dover was there some of the time that I was. I spent six weeks at it. Sometimes my arms and shoulders would ache until I couldn't sleep and then Maria would rub me with liniment until I would drop off.

William's daughter, Adrean Haight, also told of herself and little brother carrying their daddy's noon lunch to him.

He said, "I received no pay for what I did, didn't expect any, but that is alright and always has been."

DAVID GIBSON

David Gibson, now in his late 70s, is enjoying good health. We visited in the Third Ward Chapel after an interesting Sunday School on June 29, 1947.

Yes I did my bit on the Branch Normal School Building, nothing outstanding, but it amounted to several weeks of work without pay, and I was looking forward to a new addition to my family, which at that time consisted of wife and two small children.

The spring before this I had spent considerable time, hauling lumber for the Ward Hall building. In company with Al Connell and his son Johnnie, Albert Nelson and Sylvester Jones, I made some trips to the Ashdown saw mill, which then was located at Bear Spring, on the head of Deep Creek. Soft roads, long grueling days for the horses, doubling through spongy creek banks and steep pitches, all added up to create tiresome hard trips.

When they asked us to go on the brick making job there was nothing to do but do it. Richard Bryant was boss of this job. My part was to sand the moulds. Joseph Bryant, Jim Hunter, Mr. (Tut) Larson were others who worked at that. The mud was worked into the horsedrawn machine, then, with a crude press, forced into the freshly sanded moulds and carted away to be dried and then stacked in the kiln ready for burning. This operation was carried on the east bank* of the creek near where the Stake Welfare Building now stands.

I received no pay of any kind. In November when I left to go on my mission, I left with $17 cash. I have never felt that my time was wasted and I am very well satisfied that it was put to such good use.

*(Author's note) *This must have been some of the brick that was made for the Ward Hall building because others state definitely that the brick for the School Building was hauled from south of town.*

SAM BAUER

Samuel Bauer, in his 75th year, is in extremely poor health. He is cheerful and expressed himself as very pleased to be able to make a statement concerning his part in the work of building the school. I visited him on June 24, 1947, and with labored breathing he told me that which follows.

I drove the best team that ever walked, "Buck" and "Dan." Ask Arthur Nelson about them for he drove them too. With John Nelson I camped at the Old Settin' and we hauled on sleighs from there to the Top of the Cedars. I cannot remember other men we met or passed, it is too long ago. Sometimes the days were pretty miserable and other times not unpleasant at all. Jon Nelson and his team were never off that job from start to finish. If he was not hauling lumber, he was hauling something else. After several weeks of mountain hauling, I was put to work on the rock quarry, working with Evan Williams, Sr., Thomas Bladen, John Parry, Herb Adams, and others. The 12 boys and girls we have raised have all enjoyed the privileges of the school as they desired. They are mighty good to my wife, and I know that we need them.

DAN (DANNY) McFARLANE

I was a barefoot boy of about ten when my father offered my own and my brother John's services for whatever we could do to help on the building then being started for the prospective Branch Normal School. During the summer of 1897 when the town was trying to finish the Ward Hall, myself and some other boy—any boy who happened to be around—would fasten our little ropes to the wheelbarrow-loads of brick or mortar and with an older boy or man to hold the handles and guide it, spend our days dragging those heavy, hard-running old barrows up the plank ramps to where Edward Parry, William Dover, Gomer Cosslett, Thomas Bladen, Billy J. McConnell, Herb Adams or Bengt Nelson or other masons of that day, worked on the walls.

When the building was begun out on College Hill, I was on Al Conell's horse all the while, although I suppose others sometimes held the handles too, but Al seemed to always be there. None of us boys ever wore shoes even if we had them. Bare feet scarcely ever slipped. We were resourceful and tough and liked to work with the older men, especially those who were possessed of the patience to teach us. I would like to pay tribute to such men. That spirit is so seldom manifest now-a-days.

My brother Glen and I were very young when we were sent to the mill to haul lumber with which to build our home on 2nd East. Usually we tried to go when some older man was going and I've never known one of them to refuse to help by checking our brakes, harness, binding the load and giving us the benefit of what scouting they knew.

I think men generally were more cooperative when we depended on teams than they are now with the faster moving trucks and motor vehicles.

I am in the same condition as others when I try to recall companion workmen and details of fifty years ago. My own attitude of happiness when I was busy, the feeling that I was doing something worthwhile, that my job was as important as that of anyone else, so long as I did it well, are, after all, the things I like to remember concerning the building of our school.

HORACE DOVER

Upon my promise that I would write a very plain, unadorned statement concerning his part on the Branch Normal School building job, I give you the following:

I am a son of William Dover who was one of the building committee, also general mason-work over-seer of the college building that we know as the first Branch Normal building. I never worked in the mountains and I never did work steady. I worked on the school job in between or when not busy at other things. I helped put the last wood on the roof of the Ward Hall which was used for school that first season. I did some hauling of materials other than lumber.

I was present at the ceremony at the laying of the northeast cornerstone and helped to roll it into place. Other than that I was hod-carrier for Bengt Nelson and Ed Parry, who one day in the heat said to me, 'Horace, you do all the grunting and I'll take care of the rest of it.'

Later on, after the beginning of school when they built the heating unit into the southwest base-ment corner, I helped lay that brick.

William (Bill) Dix, Sr., was specialist in sand and lime mortar of the type we used in those days. I remember his being there at work and with one of his four sons,* Bill, Tom, Dave or Dan, who were somewhere near my age.

(Author's note) * Their stepsister Lou Holland confirms this statement. Dave and Dan are both dead and Bill and Tom live near Salt Lake City.

ALEX H. ROLLO

This statement is a part of the typed letter which Mr. Rollo wrote to me in response to the request for his own statement of the part he took, in the work for the school.

It was Jed Jones who was directly responsible for getting the brick-making under way, although Richard Bryant was our boss. The first group of brick-makers were Harry Hunter, mill feeder; Joe and Jule Rosenberg, off-bearers; and myself, molder. The kiln boys, as I remember, were my brother Andrew and Steve Gower. There were also sand-haulers, coal and wood haulers, rackers, those who stacked the adobe to dry, and burners. I cannot remember them all because there were constant replacements. I do know that Harry Hunter as mill tender, and I as molder, stuck to the job until 250,000 bricks were made.

We had a sheep-wagon out at the grounds, south of town. We camped on the bank of the South Field Canal. Here we cooked our own dinner of sow-belly, cooked to a fare-ye-well, with Dixie sorghum poured into the fat. Into this we would dip one-inch thick slices of good old burr-milled-flour bread, which I must say stuck tenaciously to our ribs. The color of that bread was mulatto and when smeared with sorghum was a rich mahogany. We sometimes had a little weak tea to wash it down with, but took care that no bishop was around to see us break the Word of Wisdom. At other times we drank, belly-down, from the rich red or brown water from the canal and sometimes the soil had to settle before we could swallow it. This was before the time of water systems and everyone used creek water. It was full of bacteria but that seemed to fatten us. It is a wonder though, that everyone didn't die of typhoid.

The committee had promised to feed us while we worked since we had no incomes or any others means. I have told you what we ate, and no joking.

At a Founders' Day when I was asked to relate my part in it, the director told everyone there that such conditions could not possibly have existed. Well, what I have written you is the truth. I molded part of the brick that went into the Ward Hall building, also, I believe every brick that went into the first Normal School Building and most, if not all, of the brick that went into the Science Building although the latter was done under a contract taken by a Mr. Dix from Salt Lake many years later.

The boys and men I worked with put in 10, 12 and sometimes 14 hours a day and Sunday without time-and-a-half for overtime, social security or other protection. We were not even exempt from any-thing although at that time we had nothing to pay on.

Two years after the bricks were made, the legislature reimbursed the workers by 52 or 54 percent of what they had earned. At that it was feared that some had shirked or added some extra days. Signed, Alex H. Rollo.

JAMES C. PARRY

In early days my father and Uncle John Parry each owned a lime kiln on the bench hills east of town. Uncle John and his four boys and my father, Edward, with his two boys, burned all the lime that went into nearly all of the masonry of that time. We did not make a great deal of money but had a fair living, mostly by exchanging commodities.

As were other teen-age boys of the time, I was where something was doing. We acted as carpenter's helpers, haulers, hod-carriers and mud-mixers, doing any and every kind of a job that boys could do. Randall Jones, Bill Dix, Paul Poyner and I were often together. Paul was especially good at working wood, and Randall was much more adept than I. I am sure that Paul could give you a write-up of the building because he was the studious type of a boy that liked things orderly and kept notes and records. J.J.G. Webster also did a great deal of carpentering. Samuel P. Horsely of Paragonah did much of the finest brick-work. My father and Bengt Nelson, Sr., Sam Webster and others also worked the brick and we helped on the Ward Hall building as well as the Branch Normal School.

PAUL POYNER

I have been a train dispatcher for the Frisco Railroad for more than 25 years, but getting to the subject you mentioned regarding the first building of the old Branch Normal School, during those days I made a record of most everything, but in moving around it has been lost, so it is of no value to me now. The Legislature had authorized the construction of such a building in southern Utah and most all of the southern towns were bidding for the school. Cedar City secured the authority to construct the building provided the work would be completed by a certain date. To do this volunteers were called for to go in the mountains in the middle of winter to begin getting out lumber. The snow was deep. I can only remember one of those men, Chris Ashdown. However, there was quite a bunch of others. Trails had to be made through the snow and it was a big job to get the timbers out at that time of year, but they did it and did it on time.

I helped to build the old Ward Hall where school was first held until the building was finished. I then went to the building that had just started and was to be the Branch Normal School when finished.

I was a hod carrier from the time the foundation was laid until the building was finished, plastering and all. Dan Dix was with me as another hod carrier and Dan's Father Bill Dix, Sr., mixed the mud.

As to salary, nothing was said about any pay to me or any of the other boys that I know of. I remember Brother Jed Jones did buy me a suit of overalls one time. Brother Jed Jones was head carpenter and I have a bad scar on my right hand today where Brother Jones accidentally hit my hand with his hammer while laying the joists on the second floor.

Frank and David Leigh were serving their apprenticeship as masons at the time and worked on the brick and stone laying under the tutorship of their uncle who was in charge of that work, but I can't remember which uncle it was. No doubt I could think of much more if I could see the statements of some of the other workmen.

I am proud indeed of the work I did on that first building of the Branch Normal School and also the Ward Hall. We even burned the brick for the Ward Hall.

I feel I will be fully rewarded for all of my work in helping to make it possible for the people of Utah to have a good school in the southern part of the State so the young could lay a good foundation for a worthy and useful life.

I can remember by name, more people in Cedar City today than I can here in Jonesboro, Arkansas. Where one is raised from childhood to manhood is the only place that really seems like home. I certainly hope I will hear from you again and will get to see one of the reports when they are finished.

In writing an after-thought to this paper, I would like to add that I have tried to portray faithfully the pictures that the men have helped me to see, reconstructing them in my own words according to my ability. If in some details there are contradictions, I think that is only to be expected after a lapse of fifty years with all involved relying solely on memory.

I feel sure that there are a few other men still living whom I have not known of, who worked and contributed to the founding of the Branch Normal School. I have followed every clue that has been suggested by those whose statements I have given and if any have been omitted their pardon is asked.

THE FOUNDING OF THE B.A.C.

Written by Fae Decker Dix
from Recollections of Randall W. Lunt

*I*n March 1897 the state legislature of Utah passed a bill declaring that an institution of "higher learning" should be established somewhere in Southern Utah, the place to be designated by a committee appointed for the purpose of investigating all proposed sites. This institution was to become a branch of the State University and would be the only such branch in the state. Naturally all southern communities were bidding for it, including Beaver, St. George, Richfield, Parowan, and Cedar City. The committee appointed to make the selection was composed of Dr. Karl Maeser, Dr. John R. Park, and Dr. James E. Talmage.

In May of that year Cedar City was finally selected, and the problem of housing arose. It was concluded that it would be permissible to use the new Ward Hall, then under construction by the Mormon Church, for the first school year, provided the citizenry would promise to have a suitable building ready by the opening of the second year, September 1898. Hence, the institution known as the Branch Normal School opened its first year in the Ward Hall, formerly located where the Armory now stands.

During holiday time of that first year Thomas Jedediah Jones, chairman of the local school committee, called a mass meeting of the people of Cedar City. He explained that time was growing short for beginning construction on a new building to be finished by the next September as they had promised. If the building were not completed on the specified date they would not only have failed to keep their word, but they would lose their new school, already proving itself invaluable to the small communities in this region. He stood before the group to say:

"Boys, we are confronted with a real problem. The ground has been purchased by the community, as you know, and donated to the state. The bricks have already been kilned, but we cannot begin building without lumber. We cannot get lumber unless we go into the mountains for it, and I realize as well as everyone of you do what it means to venture into these mountains in the dead of winter. Nevertheless, we must ask for volunteers from this gathering to work their way through to Jensen's sawmill and procure the lumber we need. Are you willing?"

There was hurried murmuring through the crowd. There were voices that said it couldn't be done, but there were those who said it could be tried.

So at eleven o'clock on the morning of January 5th, 1898 a little band of hardy, determined men set out to brave the rugged mountainous areas that no one tackled in winter time. They could not bear to see the school they had fought for lost.

Members of the main committee saw them off and bade them Godspeed. This committee composed of Mr. Jones, chairman, Frances Webster, John Parry, and later Thomas S. Bladen, and Wm. H. Dover, had for months been untiring in their struggle to establish and keep the school they dreamed of for their community. Now they must call on others for assistance in work they could not achieve unaided.

It is true that hundreds of men all over the frontiers of the West had made and were still making such perilous journeys into the wilderness for some cause, but one wonders if there had ever been such a precedent in the cause of education.

As the little train moved eastward toward the red hills one might count only five outfits, one sleigh and four wagons. Horses numbered twenty-one, or four to each pair of men, and an extra saddle horse for the guide to ride. The wagons were stripped running-gears with a pole on each side onto which were strapped "grub-boxes" and hay for the horses. Carrying enough hay and grain for twenty-one horses was no small problem in itself.

The men were traveling in pairs as follows: Cornelius C. Bladen and Simeon Simkins; Lorenzo Adams and Orson Tyler; John J. G. Webster and James A. Bryant; James Hunter and John H. Perry; Daniel M. Perkins and Randall W. Lunt; and Heber C. Jensen, one of the owners of the mill, who was to act as guide with only the "lay of the trees" to direct him.

This company camped the first night in Maple Canyon at a point about ten miles from Cedar City. Here they selected Mr. Bladen as captain of the company during its entire journey.

The following day they reached "Old Settin'"---original site of the sawmill. This was to be one of the permanent camp sites during the whole winter's job of getting out lumber. Here were left old sheds and cabins that could provide adequate shelter. The largest cabin even boasted a huge fireplace, which was luxurious to men used to sleeping on the ground beside a flickering campfire.

Progress was slow the second day, with the snow getting as deep as two or three feet. The journey was hazardous in many places.

On the third day out the snow was still three feet deep, but there were few drifts, for which the men expressed due gratitude. They made their way that night to just over "Lightning Hill," which is at the intersection of the present road down Parowan Canyon. Upon reaching this spot they determined to tramp a trail into the ravine below where they knew a stream of water ran. They wanted to water their horses there rather than go through the arduous process of melting enough snow for them. The snow was shoulder-deep, and the men pushed it back with their hands, beating, pushing, kicking, and tramping their way to the creek bed. Finally they looked back through a narrow hand-made trail along which they could lead the horses single file to water.

It had been a trying experience to reach "Lightning Hill" through the deep snows, and that night the men gratefully scraped the snow down a few inches, laid their mattresses of hay (which on the morrow would be fed to their horses), and unrolled their bedding to lie down to merciful sleep.

The following morning, noting the depth of the snow, the little company decided to leave one wagon at the hill so they might have four extra horses to help break the road across to the timberline. Stretching before them was the broad plain known as "The Mammoth." Yawning out on their right was a strangely formed amphitheatre of bright-hued bluffs. They did not know it would one day be called "Cedar Breaks" and that all the world would come to worship the beauty of its red bluffs. They glanced at it, saw its majestic cliffs wearing robes of snowdrift on their shoulders, the great pines on its rim bending with the weight of the white gift of winter, but they did not consider it further. They had not time for saluting beauty. They were grimly bent on achieving a certain goal before nightfall.

Finding it almost impossible to break a trail through the heavy drifts across "The Mammoth," they set upon a plan. They drove the loose horses single file ahead of the rest and so discovered an easier route. By noon they had reached the timberline, and from there it was much less difficult to get to the sawmill. By nightfall they had reached their destination, having traveled more distance than on any previous day's journey.

On the morning of January 9th, after spending their first night at the sawmill, they arose to find a steady, quiet snowstorm pouring itself relentlessly down. The flakes were so large it appeared as if they were looking out into a wall of great white sheets flapping themselves rhythmically in the faces of these dauntless men.

The trail they had painstakingly made was to be completely obliterated so soon, and they must stand helplessly by to see it vanish! But no, they would go out at once and fight to keep open the road they had made for the other companies that would soon follow. They must not lose out to a mere snowstorm. These trailblazers were pioneers, sons of pioneers, and it was part of an unspoken creed among pioneers not to give up. They would go back over the trail at once and work all day to keep it open.

By nightfall they had traversed only five miles. It looked hopeless. Drawing their wagons and the sleigh into the sheltering pines, they once more dug holes in the snow for their beds, cooked their homey meal over the campfires, and crept between high quilts to sleep until dawn.

Morning found them waking under thick blankets of snow despite the shelter they received from the towering pine trees. A blanket of snow laid over a bed of camp quilts is truly a blanket, and many of the men were uncomfortably warm.

Crawling out from their primitive shelters, they discovered every wagon buried in snow. Captain Bladen at once called a council of the company to decide whether they should go on with the task set them or quit. A few expressed unwillingness to continue, but the majority agreed to a new plan. They would return to town and get sleighs enough to carry on the work, since the heavy snows made it totally impracticable to consider further use of the wagons.

Consequently, they left their wagons buried in the snow with the hay and grain supplies still strapped on them, and packing their bedding and food upon the twenty-one horses, began to plod their way back over the snows, hoping to reach "Old Settin'" again that night. The clearing where they left their wagons was dubbed "The Wagons" and remains known as such among the older members of the community this day.

At this point in the story of the birth of the school a tribute must be paid to one of the greatest characters that ventured on this journey--an old sorrel horse. Men who later told of his patience and strength have fondly called him "the savior of the expedition." It was on this return trip to "Old Settin'" that they first realized how priceless this animal was going to be to the task set them. He was the greatest trailblazer of all. Strong and quiet, he would go steadily into the drifts, push and snort and strain against the white barriers, step back, throw himself into them again and push until presently they gave way before his persistence. Here he would pause for a rest, sitting down on his haunches as a dog does, and after heaving his great sides in long, deep breaths, he would get up and begin over again.

"Without 'Old Sorrel,' I doubt if the lumber would have ever been brought from those mountains," one of the men said in explaining how this animal gave courage to the other horses through the example of his own steadiness.

The men soon learned not to trust to the high-spirited horses when bucking a snowdrift. Without fail these were the ones to give up. The job of "getting through" was always achieved by the plodders, the quiet level-headed animals that pushed and snorted and rested, and then began over again.

Upon reaching "Old Settin'" at dusk the evening of January 10th, the men were overjoyed to meet another company sent up from Cedar City with fresh supplies, of which they were badly in need. In this second company were Byron Carrigan, Oriah Leigh, Spencer Covert, and Rob Will Bulloch. Survivors still recall how happy these two groups were upon meeting at "Old Settin'" that stormy night and recounting their experiences of the past few days.

The following day it was decided to leave four men at "Old Settin'" for the purpose of tramping the road back to the sawmill and keeping it packed hard. These four were Cornelius C. Bladen, Lorenzo Adams, (owner of 'Old Sorrel'), James A. Bryant, and Spencer Covert. Needless to say, "Old Sorrel" was their light and hope for the trail breaking job ahead of them.

The remaining men returned to Cedar City and at once began lining up workers to make bobsleighs enough to take back to the mountains. This organization was supervised by Randall W. Lunt. George Urie, local blacksmith, worked strenuously day and night to get the sleighs finished. Within three days they were completed, and on the 14th of January, Mr. Lunt and others went back with the first sleighs. They found the road well-packed as far as "Lightning Hill."

Work could now begin in earnest. For greatest convenience, the bobsleighs were cut in two and a wagon tongue placed in each. One end of the load of lumber was allowed to drag which aided in keeping the road packed. By cutting the 'bos' in two they had more sleighs to use, and so could make a more rapid transit from station to station.

Some of the men were set to chopping logs. Some were sawyers. Another crew planed logs into lumber and still others hauled it out from the mill. The haulers would take their load from the mill to "Old Settin'" which was the half-way point and a full day's journey. Here they would camp overnight and resume their trip next morning, going a distance of five miles to the "Top of the Cedars," another station. At this place the loads would be transferred from sleighs to wagons awaiting them from town, and so hauled the remaining miles into Cedar City.

Not a man became ill during all this perilous work, and accidents among the horses were nearly as rare. About the end of January they experienced their first of such accidents when one of the horses died suddenly. At the time two of the school committee members, Mr. Jones and Mr. Webster, had driven up the mountain to lend cheer and encouragement to the workers. They at once proffered one of their team to go on with the work and remained with the men, while Randall Lunt was dispatched to Cedar City for more horses. He was commissioned to 'talk his best' to get enough animals to insure against such losses retarding the work.

Mr. Lunt later recounted the toilsome ride home with a bit of humor. He remembered riding bareback all the way, with only a tie rope for bridle, and worse still, on an animal that was so high-spirited it would lie down at every snowdrift along the way. Leaving "Old Settin'" at ten in the morning, he did not reach his home in Cedar City until eleven o'clock that night.

Early next morning he busied himself securing horses from various loyal citizens. Mr. Caleb Haight volunteered a pair. A horse to replace the dead one was given by Robert Bulloch. Uriah T. Jones gave one to replace the teammate of the two stranded committee men.

Everywhere when good fellows get together there must be something to laugh over, and these men found much merriment in each other's company during the weeks spent together in the mountains. Laughingly they tell of the strange pictures they made bundled in every known item of heavy clothing. Everybody wore mitts instead of gloves. You could keep your fingers closer together in mitts and let them warm each other. To protect their legs from the biting winds, they tied rows and rows of gunny sacks about them from the waist down. These sacks came filled with grain for he horses, but as fast as they were emptied they became wearing apparel for hard working men. It must have made a ridiculous yet brave picture seeing these men tramping through the snow in their ingenious garbs, icicles hanging from their mustaches--icicles that matched those frozen on the noses of their toiling horses. Every man clapped his mittened hands together to keep the feeling in them, drawing closer into his heavy cap and muffler to defy the weather that beset them.

At night time they made their own fun--lots of it--as they gathered in the mill-house for supper. Many a good squaw-wrestle was on the evening's program, and many jokes were told and songs were sung as they passed the short hours away before crawling into their bunks.

About the first of February food supplies ran so low that the men at the sawmill had only dried peaches to eat. Mr. Bladen offered to go to town for supplies, and Lorenzo Adams volunteered to go with him.

On February 6th the fiercest of blizzards swept this region and continued for two full days. Mr. Lunt and D. D. Sherratt were assigned the duty of keeping the road open. They had a single bobsleigh with lumber dragging to pack the road. There had been many days when such blizzards from the north were disturbing and caused the roads to give way under the stress of the horse's weight. This condition was known among the workers as "rotten roads." On this night the roads were not only "rotten," but the snow was falling so fast it soon became impossible to see. At last Lunt and Sherratt were forced to abandon their sleighs, tie their bedding onto the horses and trust the animals to find their way along the trail.

Suddenly, they met Bladen and Richard Bryant who were making their way back with the supplies. Their load consisted of hay and grain for the horses. Following them were Lorenzo Adams and Orson Tyler with foodstuff for the men. But, the latter two had not caught up with their companions. The four sat up all night around the campfire waiting, and very, very hungry. The fire they built was in itself almost a miracle. They had whittled a dry goods box into shreds, added bits of hay, rubbed it to make it fluffy, kicked in the snow to find bits of wood to coax it along, and then struck no less than a dozen matches, all of them to blow out in the mocking blizzard. The last stump of a match worked the miracle and set alight the fire that proved their salvation for the night. To keep it ablazing the men took turns dragging logs from nearby with a horse and chain.

But all the blizzards in the world could not kill the urge for a joke in these men. They merrily named the little clearing where they spent the night, "Bryant's Hotel," honoring Mr. Bryant who was being initiated into the mysteries of "lumbering" in the dead of winter. "Bryant's Hotel" is still pointed out to you if you journey past that region today.

Daylight brought to sight another joke. Hanging in the forks of a tree overhead was a loaf of bread they had tossed there many days before, but starving though they were, the frozen loaf was not delectable enough to eat.

Being very anxious about Adams and Tyler, they started back along the trail in search of them. Presently they detected an abandoned sleigh perched atop a snow-covered hummel. There were strange movements in the snow nearby. Drawing closer the men saw a horse partially buried under the deep snow and making feeble efforts to rise. They began digging to release the benumbed animal, but upon reaching it they found it was too nearly frozen to death to stand up. Immediately they began rubbing the horse with gunny sacks in an effort to revive it. Mr. Adams and Mr. Tyler soon appeared to explain that at that point in the road the previous night this animal (another high-spirited one) had given up and lain down in the snow, and no amount of perseverance could arouse him. They were forced to leave him, making their retreat back to "Old Settin'" on the other team-mate. With them this morning was Samuel Heyborne, who had come to give assistance. The seven men undertook to lift that self-willed animal out of the hole into which it had sunk--eight feet below where the sleigh stood.

They proceeded by tying a heavy rope to the tail of the horse as a "balance" and then all lifting together with a continuous process of rubbing its joints with the aforementioned gunny sacks.

They were successful at last, and reached "old Settin'" at dusk that night, having spent an entire day trying to save the life of the horse. Horses were precious things to this expedition.

One can fancy the joy with which they were again welcomed at the sawmill by the hungry men who had been so long on a diet of dried peaches.

The days moved into March, and the roads began to be nearly impassable due to spring thaws. By the end of the month it was necessary to quit hauling down to the "Top of the Cedars," and the drivers had to go the long route through Panguitch, Bear Valley, and on up to Parowan again before reaching home. In April their work ended for a time, and early in July they could use their wagons on the old route, making the remaining "lumbering" a simple task when compared with the same job in winter.

The building was finished according to agreement, and so ends a tale of achievement in education by men who never attended the school. Hardy men, rough spoken, sometimes swearing through the tough spots. Men of a type without whom the frontiers of the west would have never been conquered.

Historical matter recorded from material given by Randall E. Lunt, a member of the "lumbering" expedition.

WE SALUTE
From the 1973 *Tavi*

We salute the citizens of Cedar City whose dreams, determination, courage, hard work, and sacrifice built this college. If the names of all who worked or contributed were listed, most of the citizens of early-day Cedar City would be mentioned. But, by bringing together the names that have been remembered and recorded we recognize and honor all.

MEMBERS OF COMMITTEES:
Thomas S. Bladen
John Chatterley
William H. Corry
Mayhew H. Dalley
William Dover
William Houchen
Lehi W. Jones
T. Jedediah Jones
Uriah T. Jones
Henry Leigh
Edward J. Palmer
John Parry
Francis Webster
John S. Woodbury

THOSE WHO SIGNED CONTRACTS TO PAY FOR TEACHERS AND SUPPLIES, 1897:
Robert Bulloch
John Chatterley
Joseph S. Hunter
Lehi W. Jones
T. Jedediah Jones
Henry Leigh
John Parry
Francis Webster

THOSE WHO MORT-GAGED SHEEP FOR THE HEATING AND VENTI-LATING SYSTEM:
Catherine Bell
David Bulloch
Henry Leigh
Richard A. Thorley
Francis Webster

THOSE WHO BOR-ROWED FROM THE CEDAR SHEEP ASSOCIA-TION:
Thomas S. Bladen
Thomas J. Jones

Uriah T. Jones
John Parry
Francis Webster

MEN OF THE WINTER LUMBER EXPEDITION:
Frank Adams
Lorenzo Adams
Chris Ashdown
Samuel Bauer
Cornelius Bladen
James Bryant
Richard Bryant
Robert W. Bulloch
Byron Carrigan
Al Connell
William Corry
Spencer Covert
William Daugherty
Ben Gower
Samuel Heyborne
David Hunter
James Hunter
John Jensen
Oriah Leigh
Randle Lunt
August Mackelprang
John Nelson
Daniel G. Perkins
Ephraim Perkins
J. Gold Perkins
Hyrum Perry
John Perry
Julius Rosenberg
David D. Sherratt
James Sherratt
R. B. Sherratt
Hezekiah Simpkins
Simeon Simpkins
William Simpkins
John Tait
Rone Thompson
Orson Tyler
David Urie
John Urie
Thomas Urie
Caleb Walker
Levi Walker
Reuben Walker
Samuel Walker
Stephen Walker
John J. G. Webster
William Webster

BLACKSMITHS:
Fred Ashdown
William H. Corry
Randle Lunt
Richard Palmer
Davie Urie
Thomas Urie
John H. Walker

HARNESS MAKERS:
E. J. Palmer

Jethro Palmer
Ted Palmer
Will Palmer

SHOEMAKERS:
John V. Adams
Timothy Adams

COLLECTED FOOD SUPPLIES:
Mary Corlett
Harry Hunter
Joseph H. Hunter
Bengt Nelson

HAULED LIME, ROCK, BRICK, GRAVEL, SAND, AND SUPPLIES:
C.C. Bladen
Byron Carrigan
William H. Corry
Horace Dover
David Haight
William Middleton
John Parry

BRICKMAKERS:
Joseph Bryant
Richard Bryant
Thomas Dutton
William Fretwell
David Gibson
Stephen Gower
Harry Hunter
James Hunter
Tut Larson
Ed Mackelprang
Andrew Rollo
Alex Rollo

WORKED AT LIME KILN:
Edward Parry and sons
James C. Parry
John Parry and sons

WORKED AT ROCK QUARRY:
Herbert Adams
Samuel Bauer
Thomas Bladen
Edward Parry
George Parry
John Parry
Evan Williams
Richard Williams

ROCK AND BRICK MASONS:
Herbert Adams
Edward Ashton
Samuel Bauer
Thomas Bladen
Gomer Cosslett
William Dover

Naze Harris
Samuel P. Horsley
S. W. Jones
William J. McConnell
Bengt Nelson
Edward Parry
George H. Walker
Herbert Webster
Samuel Webster

HOD CARRIERS:
R. W. Bulloch
Al Connell
David Connell
John Connell
Daniel Dix
David Dix
Thomas Dix
William Dix
Horace Dover
John Elliker
James Gilbert
Daniel Macfarlane
John Macfarlane
Edward Mackelprang
Owen Matheson
Lafayette McConnell
William McConnell
Daniel Pendleton
Paul Poyner
William Sawyer
William Simpkins
John Walker
Reuben Walker
Thomas Walker
William Walker

CARPENTERS:
Jabez Benson
Charles Dover
Lamoni Jones
T. Jedediah Jones
Samuel T. Leigh
William Lunt
Joseph M. Perry
Thomas Perry
Frank Walker
John J. G. Webster
John S. Woodbury

CARPENTERS' HELPERS:
Al Connell
John Connell
William Dix
Horace Dover
David Gibson
Randall Jones
Sylvester Jones
James C. Parry
Dennis Perkins
Paul Poyner
R. B. Sherratt
Dodd Walker

■

NOTES & SOURCES

Chapter One

THE PLACE AND THE PEOPLE

(Author's comments are listed in italics)

1 Leonard Arrington, Cedar City:The Building of a Community (Cedar City: Southern Utah State College, 1978).

2 Gerald R. Sherratt, A History of the College of Southern Utah, 1897 to 1947 (Logan: Utah State Agricultural College, 1954).

3 Andrew Carl Larson, I Was Called To Dixie (Salt Lake City: The Deseret News Press, 1961).

4 Orson Ferguson Whitney, History of Utah (Salt Lake City: G.Q. Cannon, 1892) 1: 420.

5 Parley P. Pratt, Autobiography of Parley P. Pratt (Salt Lake City: Deseret Book Co.,) 1968) 339.

6 Ibid.

7 Parley P. Pratt, "Notes of Parley P. Pratt," rpt. in Gateway to Rainbow Land by Gustive O. Larson (Cedar City: S.N., 1950).

8 Deseret News 27 July 1850.

9 *("The Chatterleys, the Corletts, the Walkers, the Arthurs and the Woods had been wealthy. The Lunts, the Haights, the Simpkins, the Leighs, the Parrys, the Bladens and dozens of others had been well trained in specific skills. All of them put everything they had into the iron experiment." The preceding quote is from Caroline Keturah Parry's "The People Yes The People," CKP Collection.)*

10 Luella Adams Dalton, ed., History of Iron County Mission (Cedar City: S.N., 1962-1967) 16.

11 Henry Lunt, Life of Henry Lunt, Together with a Portion of his Diary, comp. By Vern and Rachel Lunt (Cedar City: S.N., 1970) 36.

12 Ibid.

13 *("Prest. Smith" is an abbreviation for President Smith. George A. Smith was designated to preside over the company, and would have been called by that title as a matter of respect.)*

14 Editors of Doctrine and Covenants 88:118, 90:15.

15 George A. Smith, Journal of George A. Smith (Dec. 1850 - Nov. 1851). SUU Special Collections Doc SM 1-2.

16 Larson 12.

17 Kate B. Carter, Our Pioneer Heritage (Salt Lake City: Daughters of Utah Pioneers, 1975) vol. 18.

18 Gustive O. Larson, Iron County Centennial, 1851-1951 (Cedar City: S.N., 1951) 12.

19 Carter vol. 18.

20 William R. Palmer, Early Utah School History.

21 "Booklet" 23.

22 John Urie, John Urie Diary. *(Courtesy Samuel Urie Leigh.)*

23 William Clayton, "Come Come Ye Saints," rpt. in LDS Hymns (Salt Lake City: LDS Church, 1985) #30.

Chapter Two

THE FOUNDING

(Author's comments are listed in italics)

1 Henry Lunt, "Journal of Henry Lunt," rpt. in Mayors of Cedar City, by York and Evelyn Jones (Cedar City: Southern Utah State College, 1986) 7.

2 William R. Palmer, Early Utah School History.

3 Joseph Fielding Smith, ed., Teachings of the Prophet Joseph Smith (Salt Lake City: The Deseret News Press, 1938) 357.

4 Caroline Keturah Parry Collection, Southern Utah University Special Collections.

5 Palmer, op.cit.

6 Parry, op.cit.

7 Original copy of telegram, CKP Collection, File 11.

8 Editors of Monuments to Courage:A History of Beaver County (Utah: Daughters of Utah Pioneers of Beaver County, 1948) 82-83.

9 Deseret News 6 March 1897: 54:858.

10 Editors of The Revised Statutes of the State of Utah in Force Jan. 1, 1898 (Salt Lake City: Utah State Legislature, 1897) 41.

11 Ibid.

12 Elias Morris, letter to John Parry, CKP Collection, File 11.

13 James E. Talmage, Journal of James E. Talmage.

14 Talmage, 10 May 1897 entry.

15 CKP Collection.

16 Inez Cooper, A Delicate and Tenuous Thread 1973. *(Cooper is an alumna of the institution.)*

17 Talmage.

18 CKP Collection.

19 Caroline Keturah Parry, The First Hurdle. *(This first-person account of the incident, accompanied by the original telegram and letter, is contained in the Collection. Miss Parry was the daughter of Rep. John Parry.)*

20 Waldemar Van Cott, letter to John Parry, Henry Lay, M.H. Dalley and Committee, 22 June 1898, CKP Collection, File 14.

21 "First" op.cit.

22 CKP Collection, File 15.

23 Rhoda M. Wood, The Establishment of the Branch Normal School.

24 CKP Collection, File 22.

25 CKP Collection. *(This is the list most often given, though some accounts vary. Jim Hunter and Randall Lunt, both members of the January 5 contingent, agree on the membership of this group in their separate first-hand accounts.)*

26 Rob Will Bulloch, as told to Gladys McConnell, For Sweet Learning's Sake (Cedar City: Southern Utah State College, 1972). *(See box in Chapter 2 for the entire excerpt of Bulloch's wonderfully clear description of both the road and the route.)*

27 Fae Decker Dix, Recollections of Randall Lunt, and Rhoda Matheson Wood, The Founders Speak (1947). *(Some of the account of the first group's journey is taken from Dix's writing of the first-hand account of*

Randall W. Lunt. Some is taken from the first-hand accounts of Jim Hunter and John Parry, as written by Wood. The accounts sometimes vary slightly in detail. In those instances, I have followed the rule of using the account agreed upon by two of the three, always filled with gratitude for those who recorded them.)

28 Dix.

29 Wood 3.

30 Wood 21.

31 Bulloch. *(McConnell's written account of Bulloch's story is a priceless addition to the history of the founding of the university. Much of it will be quoted in this history, for it offers intimate details and insights that would not otherwise be available.)*

32 *(Spencer Covert had worked as a sawyer at the Jensen Mill for two years, and had experienced the work both at the Old Settin' and the new mill. His knowledge of the trail and of the facilities was probably responsible for the safety of the men of his group in the memorable storm.)*

33 Bulloch.

34 *(See box in Chapter 2 for Charlie Adams' story of Old Sorrel as a colt and an early adventure with snow that may have helped prepare the horse for its later heroic performance during the mountain expedition.)*

35 Sim Simkins, as told to Gladys McConnell, <u>For Sweet Learning's Sake,</u> op. cit.

36 Rob Will Bulloch, as told to Rhoda Matheson Wood, <u>The Founders Speak</u> (Cedar City: 1947) 14.

37 Ibid.

38 *(See Appendix for the full roster of the expedition.)*

39 Wood. *(Mrs. Wood collected these accounts by visiting the homes of the remaining founders over a period from May to November. She walked from house to house, recording the stories in her own hand. Her hand-written accounts were then typed by her daughter, Esther Hankins. See Appendix for the complete excerpt.)*

40 H. Marvin Jones, radio-address interview with Heber Jensen, 5 March 1938.

41 William R. Palmer, excerpt from <u>BNS/BAC Alumni Booklet</u> (1940).

42 Rhoda Matheson Wood, introduction, <u>The Founders Speak</u> (1947).

43 CKP Collection, File 23. *(This account of the cornerstone ceremony and the remarkable list of attending families was included in Mrs. Parry's papers. Any inadvertent deletions were unintended, I feel sure!)*

44 Cooper.

Chapter Three
BRANCH NORMAL SCHOOL

(Author's comments are listed in italics)

1 Editors of <u>Circular of the Southern Branch of the State Normal School</u> (1897-98).

2 L.W. Macfarlane, M.D., <u>Dr. Mac: The Man, His Land, and His People</u> (Cedar City: Southern Utah State College Press, 1985) 24.

3 "Circular."

4 *(These details are taken from <u>Memoirs of Milton Bennion</u>, courtesy of Dr. Craig Jones. It is interesting to note that after the marriage of Cora Lindsay to Milton*

Bennion on June 22, 1898, the Bennions, the Driggs and the Deckers went together to Chicago to study at the University of Chicago. The Bennions and Driggs lived together in a furnished apartment. All of them returned in the fall to teach again at BNS.)

5 Myrtle Decker Janson, <u>Influence of BNS/BAC.</u>

6 *(Details of the early life of Miss Annie Spencer are from a delightful autobiography contained on a series of audio tapes made by Annie Spencer Milne in 1962. The tapes were kindly provided by her son, David Milne, of San Diego, California. I became so enthralled with Annie Spencer that I could not stop writing of her. The excitement of what she brought to the young people of rural southern Utah cannot be overstated. The tapes are located now in SUU Special Collections at the SUU Library. A transcription has been made and is available.)*

7 Caroline Keturah Parry Collection, Southern Utah University Special Collections, File 27.

8 *(The term "old folks" must refer to adults as opposed to children. There still exists a copy of the napkin signed by those present at the banquet, and it is clear that the attendees were adults young and old.)*

9 *(Though Milton Bennion did not get as broad coverage in the <u>Deseret News</u> as the visiting dignitaries, local people recorded that Principal Bennion gave a stirring account of the activities of the people of Cedar City, and praised them for enduring such hardship. He also told how local leaders had taken him through the four southern counties upon his arrival in town to solicit students to enter the school. He praised the people for their desire to conform to the law, and expressed great faith in the future of the school.)*

10 <u>Deseret News</u> 29 Oct. 1898. CKP Collection, File 27.

11 Caroline Keturah Parry, <u>The Transfer.</u> CKP Collection, File 26. *(Participants in the musical groups included Florence Lunt Webster, May Macfarlane Higbee, Chauncey Macfarlane, Gomer Cosslett, Daniel Macfarlane, Belle Macfarlane, Eliza Macfarlane, Florence and Violet Lunt, Joseph Cosslett, Caleb Haight and Ada Wood.)*

12 *(Part of the strategy of John Parry included submitting editorials to the <u>Deseret Evening News</u> that detailed the story of the Cedar City school. He was successful in getting some printed. He always bought copies and distributed them among his fellow legislators as part of his lobbying effort.)*

13 William Houchen, letter to John Parry, 30 Jan. 1899, CKP Collection, File 28. *(The second page of the letter is missing. Original copies of four handwritten letters addressed to John Parry during the 1899 Legislature are found in File 28 of the Carolyn Keturah Parry paper in the Library Special Collections, Southern Utah University. One of these, a cover letter for the transmittal of the heating plant accounts sent by Henry Leigh, Trustee and TJ Jones, General Manager, bears a left-hand corner notation: "Bro. Sherratt passed peacefully away this evening. His wife very poorly.")*

14 <u>Deseret Evening News</u> 15 Dec. 1900. *(This article is not attributed to an author. However, it was written by J. Reuben Clark, who was acting principal of the BNS at the time. It reflects his enthusiasm for the school and dares to approach some ideas that were uniquely his regarding the future of the school. The complete text of the article can be found in Chapter 3, Appendix 1.)*

15 Ivan Decker, <u>Incidents in the Life of George William Decker</u> 2, 13-14. *(By permission of Bruce Decker.)*

16 Parley Dalley and George Wood, personal interview

with Tom Challis and Inez Cooper.

17 Macfarland 27.

18 Janson.

19 Gerald R. Sherratt, <u>A History of the College of Southern Utah 1897 to 1947</u> (Logan: Utah State Agricultural College, 1954).

20 Editors of <u>Annual of the Southern Branch of the State Normal School</u> (1912) 21.

21 Editors of <u>Revised Ordinances, Branch Normal School</u>.

22 Rhoda Matheson Wood, <u>Memories of My Branch Normal Years</u>.

23 Ernest Hungate Burgess, <u>School Days Journal of Ernest Hungate Burgess, 1899-1904</u> (Cedar City: Southern Utah State College, 1989). (*By permission of Ernest Miles Burgess, M.D.*)

24 J. Reuben Clark, Jr., letter to Milton Bennion, 7 Nov. 1900.

25 David H. Yarn, Jr., <u>Young Reuben, the Early Life of J. Reuben Clark, Jr.</u> (Provo: Brigham Young University Press, 1973) 106-107.

26 Ibid.

27 Frank W. Fox, <u>J. Reuben Clark, The Public Years</u> (Provo: Brigham Young University Press, 1980).

28 Yarn 107-109.

29 J. Reuben Clark, Jr., letter to Rebecca Little, 3 May 1901, in Yarn 113.

30 (*J. Reuben Clark, Jr. became a renowned international lawyer, U.S. ambassador to Mexico, and a member of the First Presidency of the Church of Jesus Christ of Latter-day Saints.*)

31 J. Reuben Clark, Jr., letter to Joseph Nelson, 27 April 1901.

32 J. Reuben Clark, Jr., <u>Deseret Evening News</u> 15 Dec. 1900.

33 Sherratt 33.

34 Ibid.

35 Will Flanigan, personal interview with Rhoda Wood, in Rhoda Wood, <u>The Founders Speak</u> (1947) 28.

36 Ibid.

37 Annie Spencer Milne, <u>Autobiographical Tapes</u> (1962), SUU Special Collections. (*Tapes courtesy David Milne, San Diego, California.*)

38 Sherratt 40.

39 Editors of <u>1907-1908 Branch Normal School Catalog</u> 26.

40 William H. and Rhoda Matheson Wood, personal interviews with Inez Cooper, March-Sept. 1968.

41 Sherratt 43.

42 <u>The Student</u> 6 February 1913: 6.

43 Wilford Day, address on KSUB radio, 6 March 1938.

44 Ibid.

45 (*Reference is to a law which prohibited the college from offering courses in liberal arts, pedagogy, the profession of law or medicine or engineering. The law was subsequently changed.*)

46 S. R. Wilkinson, "Do We Want to Change the BNS to a BAC?" <u>The Student</u> March 1913: 1.

47 Editors of <u>Compiled Laws of the State of Utah</u> (1917) 1051.

48 Rhoda and Will Jones, personal interview with Inez Cooper, March 1968.

49 (*In the early 1900s, a teacher named John Scopes was tried and convicted of teaching evolution contrary to Tennessee state law. William Jennings Bryan and Clarence Darrow were the opposing lawyers and the trial gained national attention.*)

50 Parley Dalley, statement to Gerald R. Sherratt, January 1954.

51 John A. Widstoe, letter to Wilford Day, 28 March 1913. (*A copy of the complete text may be found in Special Collections, Utah State University Library.*)

Chapter Four
BRANCH AGRICULTURAL COLLEGE
(Author's comments are listed in italics)

1 <u>Iron County Record</u> 14 Feb. 1913: 1.

2 Ibid.

3 <u>Iron County Record</u> 7 March 1913: 1.

4 <u>Iron County Record</u> 28 March 1913.

5 <u>Iron County Record</u> 4 April 1913.

6 John A. Widstoe, letter to Sen. Henry Lunt, 28 March 1913.

7 Ibid.

8 <u>The Student</u> 13 May 1913: 8.

9 (*In a letter dated September 20, 1913, Principal Homer wrote to Dr. John A. Widstoe: "What reply shall I make to Branch Normal School teachers of last year who inquire about their salaries for the last month of service in that Institution? ...I have advised the teachers to send a letter to the Board of Regents of the University and let them worry a little about the matter."*)

10 John A. Widstoe, "To All Friends of the State School at Cedar City," <u>Iron County Record</u> 21 July 1913.

11 <u>Iron County Record</u> 20 March 1914. (*The land adjoining the campus was paid for by means of a viluntary assessment of one percent on the property of the Cedar City people, a fact supported by this newspaper article.*)

12 <u>Iron County Record</u> 19 Sept. 1913.

13 <u>The Student</u> February, April 1913. (*These titles came from actual students compositions.*)

14 (*The delightful journal of J. Harold Mitchell recalls his experience with the basketball team and records the names of the members of that team: "I made the basketball team at B.A.C. that year [1914]. At first I was on the second team with Orlando Adams, Adam Seegmiller, Albin Brooksby and Wilford Griffin. We had no substitute. We traveled to Kanab and Orderville for games. I played well there and when we returned to Cedar City, Coach Jack Christensen, a very wonderful man, placed me on the main team with John Lunt, Walter Hansen, Clyde Bunker, Rass Jones, Lorin Griffin, and John Gurr. We played St. George soon thereafter and went to the state tournament at Provo. Our team played for the state championship but were beaten by Pleasant Grove."*)

15 Editors of <u>Agricola</u> (1913-1914).

16 (*See references in Chapter 3 to the diary entries of Ernest Hungate Burgess, which describe the student involvements in the elections and the duties of the student city.*)

17 John A. Widstoe, letter to Roy Homer, 19 July 1913.

18 <u>Iron County Record</u> 19 July 1916. (*This restoration did*

not occur until the year 1918-1919, when the normal course relationship was again re-established. See the chapter on the education department.)

19 Iron County Record 16 March 1917.

20 (The January 25, 1918 edition of the Iron County Record notes: "Mr. Rogers, one of the Normal students received word to come home at once in order to be examined for Military service. He left for home yesterday. Mr. Rogers will be greatly missed if he is not allowed to return to the school.")

21 "Liberty Food Requirements, Iron County Record 15 Jan. 1918. (This is a directive from the domestic science department.)

22 Iron County Record 7 Feb. 1919: PAGE.

23 George Croft, George Croft at the B.A.C. (1964) 12. (Used by permission of Carl Croft and Carmen Croft Jones.)

24 (Also arriving were Fred Braithwaite, who came to teach art at BAC, and Miss Matilda Peterson and Miss Eva Buys, both of whom were coming to teach in Iron County Schools.)

25 (The El Escalante Hotel later occupied this site. Built into the front wall of the hotel porch were some stones taken from the old Tithing Office.)

26 Croft 12-13.

27 Croft 15-18.

28 David L. Sargent, autobiographical tapes from a series of personal interviews with Inez Cooper, 1967-1968. (Used by permission of Mildred S. Cardon.)

29 Ibid.

30 Ibid.

31 Personal reminiscences of Orien and Jesse Dalley. (Used by permission of Ada Carpenter.)

32 Iron County Record 3 June 1921.

33 Iron County Record.

34 Iron County Record 11 August 1922.

35 Iron County Record 1 Sept. 1922.

36 (Details of the hoisting of the bell are from George Croft's history. The students most involved with Mr. Croft were Ray Knell and Keith MacFarlane. Charlie Slaughter faithfully rang the bell until the tradition was established.)

37 Papers of Hazen Cooley, SUU Special Collections.

38 Hazen Cooley, The College and The Community (1969). (The reader may want to re-read the last three paragraphs of the quote from Mr. Cooley in order to gain an accurate sense of three things: 1. The difficulty placed upon BAC when the legislature gave the appropriation to the Agricultural College; 2. The narrow escape provided by Walter K. Granger's fortuitous amendment; and 3. The ongoing, cooperative spirit of all community entities, dedicated to furthering the cause of the college.)

39 Edwin L. Peterson, personal interview with Anne O. Leavitt, 27 June 1996.

40 Hazen Cooley, personal interview with Anne O. Leavitt, June 1996.

41 Iron County Record 9 May 1931.

42 Hazen Cooley, personal interviews with Anne O. Leavitt, 1996.

43 Gerald R. Sherratt, A History of the College of Southern Utah, 1897 to 1947 (Logan: Utah State Agricultural College, 1947) 55-56.

44 Ray Baumgartner, personal interview with Anne O. Leavitt. (Mr. Baumgartner was a former cadet who returned to Cedar City to marry Helen Gardner, a local girl.)

45 Robert Avedisian, personal interview with Anne O. Leavitt, 2 June 1996.

46 Sgt. Herb Stone, A/S Danny Gaunt, and A/S John Powers, 1943. (Quote is from a song written by the three and performed at the 316th Follies Sept. 2, 1943. Courtesy Alva Matheson.)

47 Elizabeth Swenson Driggs, speech, 23 May 1994. (The speech was given on the occasion of the presentation of H. Wayne Driggs' portrait to be hung in the Great Hall on the campus of Southern Utah University.)

48 McRay Cloward, And We Built A Cabin: A Story About a Cabin, a Mountain Ranch and a Dedicated Faculty (Cedar City: Division of Continuing Education, Southern Utah University, 1994) 6.

49 Ibid.

50 Ibid. (Other information came from the author's own vivid memory.)

51 Fae Decker Dix and Twain Tippetts, personal interviews with Anne O. Leavitt, 4 Dec. 1996.

52 Souvenir Program from "College Cavalcade: The Golden Jubilee Year," 1947. (Courtesy Bessie Dover.)

53 Iron County Record 12 April 1948.

54 Iron County Record 14 Aug. 1947.

55 Iron County Record 19 Feb. 1948.

56 Iron County Record 16 Dec. 1948.

57 Cooley.

58 Iron County Record 12 May 1949.

59 Luana Nelson Warner, My Experience At B.A.C.. (Mrs. Warner was a member of the BAC Class of 1952.)

60 Hazen Cooley, personal interview with Anne O. Leavitt.

61 Cloward 8.

62 (Recommended reading: And We Built A Cabin, a history of the Southern Utah University Mountain Center, by McRay Cloward.)

Chapter Five

COLLEGE OF SOUTHERN UTAH

(Author's comments are listed in italics)

1 Inez S. Cooper, Story of the Name Changes of the College.

2 Edwin L. Peterson, personal interview with Anne O. Leavitt, July 1996.

3 Ibid.

4 (Each week the Iron County Record reports, with increasingly panicky tone, that no director has been named.)

5 Iron County Record 23 Dec. 1954.

6 Cantus South Utahn 5 April 1955: 48:23.

7 Iron County Record 8 March 1956.

8 Iron County Record 18 Dec. 1958.

9 Ibid.

10 (Barbara Grimshaw Dykstra excerpts her personal history with this detail of student-generated activity that became the first of the traditional "marching

groups." *The group included: Sharon Adair, Kay
Ashcroft, Georg Ann Braegger, Peggy Charlesworth,
Gail Crawford, Katie Fordham, Cora Le Gibson, Helen
Hatch, Varue Holgate, Linda Knell, Marcia Johnson,
Donna Robbins and Geraldine Skougard.)*

11 Iron County Record 14 Jan. 1960.

12 Wesley Larsen, The CSU, SUSC, SUU Years.

13 Iron County Record 8 June 1961.

14 Iron County Record 15 Feb. 1962.

15 Ibid.

16 Iron County Record 31 May 1962.

17 Dixie L. Leavitt, Personal History of Dixie L. Leavitt.

18 *(A notable part of the needed supervision was the
efforts of the little boy pages, who sewed sequins on
their own costumes as they sat on the lawn waiting
for their rehearsal cues.)*

19 Iron County Record 21 June 1962.

20 "Minutes of the Utah State University Board of Trustees
Meeting" (16 May 1964).

21 Iron County Record 21 May 1964.

22 "Minutes of the Utah State Board of Trustees Meeting" (9
Oct. 1964). *(Instruction to prepare the legislation is
included in the minutes of the May 21 meeting.)*

23 *(The very interesting text of Senate Bill 97 and Senate
Bill 209 is available in Southern Utah University
Special Collections.)*

24 *(From a first-hand account given by Arthur T. Challis,
who was present at the Fifty-Year Club meeting. It had
been previously arranged that Parley Dalley, because
he was the person with the longest association with
the college, should be the person to receive the news.)*

25 Iron County Record 11 March 1965.

26 Leavitt op. cit.

27 "Report of the Utah State Board of Trustees Meeting" (9
Dec. 1965), rpt. in Iron County Record 16 Dec. 1965.

28 Leavitt 847.

Chapter Six

SOUTHERN UTAH STATE COLLEGE

(Author's comments are listed in italics)

1 Bruce Osborne, personal interview with Anne O. Leavitt.

2 *(For more extensive information on the career of Lael
Jones, please see Chapter 10.)*

3 *(Of special note is the amazing diligence of the Iron
County Record in reporting the affairs of the college
from the earliest days of its existence. Publisher/editor
Morgan Rollo had loved the college, and though his
affection sometimes caused him to subtly editorialize
in his reporting, he sensed the interests of the people of
the community and kept them abreast of the progress
and problems of the college through its many phases.
His record has been invaluable in preparing this history.)*

4 Iron County Record June 1974.

5 *(This quote from Dr. Kent Myers is found in his centennial history of teacher education at SUU, where is also
found an expanded account of Dr. Gwyn Clark's distinguished contribution to the school.)*

6 Iron County Record 28 Nov. 1974; The Thunderbird 6
Dec. 1974.

7 The Thunderbird DATE.

8 Ruth Challis, personal interview with Anne O. Leavitt.

9 Iron County Record 19 April 1979.

10 The Thunderbird 17 Nov. 1978.

11 Orville C. Carnahan, "Memorandum to Faculty and Staff"
(27 Nov. 1979).

12 Orville C. Carnahan, "Memorandum to Faculty and Staff"
(6 Jan. 1980).

13 *(See Chapter 19 for more information on the fair.)*

14 *{See Chapter 13. The complete text of "A History of the
Music Department," by Dr. Blaine Johnson, is found in
the SUU Special Collections.)*

15 Orville C. Carnahan, "Memorandum to Faculty and Staff"
(2 Jan. 1981).

16 The Thunderbird 22 Jan. 1982.

17 Ibid.

18 *(Here quoting William Ellery Channing.)*

19 *(The complete text of the inaugural address is found
in the SUU Special Collections.)*

20 Iron County Record 29 March 1982.

21 Deseret News 20 Feb. 1983.

22 Ibid.

23 Terry Alger, personal interview with Michael D.
Richards, rpt. in The Thunderbird 24 March 1983.

24 Gerald R. Sherratt, personal interview, rpt. in The
Thunderbird Summer 1983: 14.

25 The Thunderbird 13 Jan. 1983.

26 *(The "inside" story of the saving of the business building is of interest. Dane O. Leavitt, a college freshman
serving as a legislative intern, was assigned to Sen.
Dixie Leavitt, then a majority leader in the state
Senate. Sen. Leavitt had kept a close watch over the
bonding bill, being sure the business building was
safely positioned on the critical list. During the intense
last days of the session, young Leavitt, on an errand to
the House of Representatives unrelated to the building
appropriation, arrived on the floor of the House just
in time to hear two Ogden legislators about to push
through an amendment to remove the SUSC building
from the bonding list. Racing back to the Senate, he
brought his father the nefarious news. The elder Leavitt
appeared forthwith upon the floor of the House, asked
for a committee of the whole and addressed the legislators. He made a strong appeal, outlining the need
while denouncing the lapse of fair play that had
almost happened. The amendment failed. The building
appropriation was intact, and the SUSC business faculty watching from the gallery considered it a miraculous "save.")*

27 *"Project Image" evolved as the Institutional Council
projected future efficiencies that could result from
increased enrollment. They reasoned that if they could
achieve an enrollment of 4,000 students, the efficiencies of scale would greatly benefit the school. A professionally conducted survey revealed that most respon-
dents believed Southern Utah State College to be a
junior college in St. George. It was clear they had to
increase public awareness of the school. They raised
$125,000 from the Cedar City Corporation, Iron
County Commission and Utah Power Company for
their media campaign. The success of their effort is legendary. At the same time, the Council, realizing that
their students were mostly from small Utah towns and
moderate income families, set about to find a source
for employment for their anticipated student body. Their
negotiations with NICE Corporation, which later*

SUU · A Heritage History · 507

became Matrix Marketing, resulted in the establishment of that business in Cedar City, and plenty of part-time employment for students.)

28 (Enrollment had exceeded 5,000 by 1995.)

29 (Enrollment exceeded 5,000 students by 1994.)

30 (Sometimes known as "Cockroach Hall" or "the slums of Cedar City.")

31 (Regent Michael Leavitt had clarified the political realities for WSC by informing the Ogden Regents that if they elected to initiate the process without SUSC, they would not have his vote. They could all count.)

32 "Minutes of the Utah State Board of Regents Meeting" (19 Oct. 1989).

33 "Minutes of the Utah State Board of Regents Meeting" (17 Nov.).

34 Ibid.

35 The Spectrum 24 Jan. 1990:A3.

36 Ibid. (The complete text of his letter is found in this issue, p.A3.)

37 Wm. Rolfe Kerr, "Memorandum to Presidents Gerald R. Sherratt and Stephen D. Nadauld" (5 Dec. 1989).

38 Wm. Rolfe Kerr, "Memorandum to Regents" (8 Dec. 1989). (Formal proposals from SUSC and WSC were attached.)

39 "Minutes of the Utah State Board of Regents Meeting" (15 Dec. 1989).

40 (The full text of Senate Bill 119 is available in the Southern Utah University Special Collections.)

41 (An interesting coincidence connected the proceedings of the Board of Regents with the work going on in the Utah State Senate. The regent most active in driving the name-change engine in the Board of Regents was Michael O. Leavitt, a graduate of SUSC, a Cedar City native and a son of Sen. Dixie Leavitt, who was the driving force behind the SUSC name-change legislation in the Senate. Though each worked independently in his own sphere, it was a fascinating juxtaposition.)

42 "Minutes of Utah State Board of Regents Meeting" (26 Jan. 1990) 106-107.

43 Ibid.

44 (Little wonder that Karen Haight Huntsman became at that moment a heroine in the annals of Weber State University, Southern Utah University, and especially in the legends of the family Leavitt.)

45 "Minutes" (26 Jan. 1990) 107-108.

46 Michael O. Leavitt, personal interview with Anne O. Leavitt, Sept. 1996.

47 "Utah House Approves SUSC's Name Change," The Spectrum 8 Feb. 1990.

48 Michael D. Richards, Background on SUSC Name Change.

Chapter Seven
SOUTHERN UTAH UNIVERSITY
(Author's comments are listed in italics)

1 Harl Judd, Personal History of Dr. Harl Judd.

2 The Thunderbird 14 Feb. 1991: 3.

3 Michael D. Richards, The SUU Years (1996).

4 (Funding for the windows was provided by Mr. Jay Dee and Mrs. Alice C. Harris, and Mr. Dale L. and Mrs. Afton Jolley Peterson.)

5 The Thunderbird 4 Jan. 1993.

6 Richards.

7 Ibid.

8 The Thunderbird 4 Feb. 1994

9 In addition to this list from Caroline Keturrah Parry, the following families are listed on the Founders Monument: Andelin, Anderson, Ashton, Barnhurst, Barnson, Bell, Bringard, Campbell, Cannon, Cobaut, Coswell, Durnford, Esarry, Evan, Ford, Froyd, Givson, Gilbert, Goodfellow, Granger, Hertwell, Horsley, James, Jenson, Jolley, Kingonsmith, Lambeth, Larsen, Lewis, Liston, Mc Donald, Mcnally, Mausdell, Melling, Millett, Mosdell, Muir, Mulliner, Paynon, Pollock Pugson, Reese, Robinson Sheppenson, Schoppman, Simkins, Smith, Snyder, Stapley, Stephens, Stephenson, Stevens, Stewart, Stump, Tate, Talmage, Thompson, Tyler, Walder, Westerhold, Whittaker, Williams, Woodbury.

10 University Journal 3 May 1996.

Chapter 8
TEACHER EDUCATION DEPARTMENT
(Author's comments are listed in italics)

1 (The source of this abbreviated history is Dr. Kent Myers, Teacher Education, The Heart of BNS-SUU Southern Utah University Special Collections.)

2 (Fascinating biographies of the first graduating classes are included in "Teacher Education.")

3 (See Appendix 1 to "Teacher Education" for the text of M.J. Macfarlane's letter to President E.G. Peterson.)

4 (Biographies of the first class of twenty persons who received bachelor of science degrees fulfilling all requirements at Cedar City can be found in the more complete history by Dr. Kent Myers, SUU Special Collections.)

5 (It is not possible to give honor to all students who came and went on to the professional ranks, but individual biographies of the pioneer Class of 1900 and the Class of 1950 appear in "Teacher Education.")

6 (Biographies and photographs of the faculty and staff from 1947 to 1996 are included in "Teacher Education.")

Chapter Nine
PHYSICAL EDUCATION AND ATHLETICS DEPARTMENT
(Author's comments are listed in italics)

1 (This abbreviated history is distilled from a more complete "History of the Department of Men's Athletics" by Bruce Osborne, and "A History of Women's Athletics" by Kathryn Berg. Another prime source was "History of the Junior College Athletic Program of the College of Southern Utah," a master's thesis by C. Stephen Lunt, Utah State University, Logan, Utah, 1967. All three histories can be found in the SUU Library Special Collections.)

2 (The original lyrics were: "There's a dear old place in the mountains high, Where the sunlight always shines, Where the breezes blow, And the pure white snow, The mountain air refines. That place is hallowed by a school, That's where we long to be; And meet with dear old friends we love, At our Grand Old BAC. Oh, BAC is the school we love, For the vigor of her youth. Her blue stands out as the blue of the sky, And the white is the light of truth. All her children thrill at her very name, No matter where they be; She's the school of the blue

*and the white we love, She's our Grand Old BAC. All
hail to our college young and strong, Her children call
her blest; Sing praises to her worthy name, The queen
of all the West. Her strength will grow with the coming
years, Her light we'll always see, And loyal hearts will
ever beat, For our Grand Old BAC."*)

Chapter Ten

THE LIBRARY, BNS-SUU

(Author's comments are listed in italics)

1 (*Information for this chapter was extracted from
Arthur Tom Challis, History of the BNS-BAC-CSU-SUSC-
SUU Library, SUU Library Special Collections. The
chapter also draws extensively from Diana Graff, The
Library 1980-1997, SUU Library Special Collections.
Additional information has been supplied by Sharon
Clark Leigh, Sue Stratton, Matt Nickerson, and Vick
Brown.*)

2 Editors of Circular of the Southern Branch of the State
Normal School (1897-98).

3 Editors of Branch Agricultural College Catalog (1914-15).

4 Editors of Branch Agricultural College Catalog (1918-19)
15.

5 (*See Chapter 4 for more details of the book donations
and the completion of the library / auditorium.*)

6 Deseret News 19 Oct. 1966.

7 Daphne Cooper Dalley, personal interview with Anne O.
Leavitt, February 1997.

Chapter Eleven

ART DEPARTMENT

(Author's comments are listed in italics)

1 (*The material in this chapter is extracted from Mary M.
MacDonald, History of the Art Department, SUU
Special Collections. Mrs. MacDonald included the following note in her preface: "This has been a labor of
love for me. As I perused catalogues and publications
of one hundred years ago I found interesting bits of
information... Pictures and articles about my mother
[who was the first graduate of B.N.S. In music] my
father, uncles, aunts and later priceless friends and relatives who were my contemporaries at B.A.C., C.S.U.,
S.U.S.C., and S.U.U.*)

2 Editors of the BNS Catalog.

3 Mary M. MacDonald, personal note.

4 (*A comprehensive history of the Cedar City Art Exhibit
is included in MMD History, SUU Special Collections.*)

5 Ianthus Wright, Dissertation on the Cedar City Annual Art
Exhibit.

6 Wayne Kimball, letter to Mary MacDonald, 1996.

7 Thomas A. Leek, address at a gallery opening, Oct. 1993.

8 Dr. Royden C. Braithwaite, address at a gallery opening,
1976.

9 Arlene V. Braithwaite, "Prospectus" (1 Nov. 1996).

10 (*The history of the art department contains a comprehensive listing and descriptions of exhibits over the
years, a series of more extensive sketches of art department faculty than can be included here, and some of
the honors and recognitions accorded students and
graduates of the department.*)

Chapter Twelve

LANGUAGE, LITERATURE & HUMANITIES DEPARTMENT

(Author's comments are listed in italics)

1 (*This chapter was prepared by Blanche Cox Clegg,
librarian at SUU Special Collections. Mrs. Clegg and
her staff provided valuable research assistance
through the whole process.*)

Chapter Thirteen

MUSIC DEPARTMENT

(Author's comments are listed in italics)

1 (*The primary source of this abbreviated department
history is Dr. Blaine Johnson, History of the Music
Department, SUU Special Collections. Other sources:
brief historical sketches by Inez Cooper, Roy L.
Halversen, Bernella Gardner Jones, Carol Ann Parry
Nyman, Floyd Rigby and others, all included in the
appendices to Dr. Johnson's history. The history is filled
with warm and delightful details that could not all be
included here. It is recommended reading. Dr. Johnson
drew upon many sources, notably the music history by
Cynthia Williams Dunaway.*)

2 (*Unfortunately, no photograph of William Knudsen is
available.*)

3 (*Space constraints in this volume preclude the mention
of myriad other students who participated in a succession of productions. Johnson's history of the music
department is replete with names, descriptive detail
and heart-warming stories.*)

Chapter Fourteen

SOCIAL SCIENCES DEPARTMENT

(Author's comments are listed in italics)

1 (*This abbreviated history is distilled from the more
complete Dr. Vern Kupfer, History of Behavioral and
Social Science at Southern Utah University, SUU
Special Collections, with additional information pro-
vided by Dr. Wayne Hinton, Prof. Craig Jones and Dr.
Leslie Jones.*)

2 Wayne Hinton, "University Preview," University Journal Fall
1994: 12.

3 W. Craig Jones, University Journal 7 April 1995.

4 Prof. James Vlasich, University Journal 3 Nov. 1995.

Chapter Fifteen

THEATRE ARTS AND DANCE DEPARTMENT

(Author's comments are listed in italics)

1 (*This abbreviated history is distilled from G. MacLain
McIntyre, Theatre Arts and Dance Department History;
Blanche Clegg, History of the SUU English Department;
and Fred Adams, Beginnings of the Utah
Shakespearean Festival, all in SUU Special Collections.
Information for the dance department courtesy of
Shauna Mendini.*)

2 McIntyre.

3 Kate B. Carter, edt., Our Pioneer Heritage (1975) 18:196.

4 Nevada Watson Driggs, letter to Inez Cooper.

5 "Focus on Theatre and Dance," University Journal 6 Oct.
1995.

6 (*Brief biographies of some recent SUU theatre grads are
included in the history of the department, SUU Special*

Collections.)

7 Adams 43.

8 (*The information from this section is gleaned from Adams 32. The entire account is delightful, fascinating and a must read. It may be found as part of "The History of Theatre Arts and Dance" in SUU Special Collections.*)

9 Adams 44.

Chapter Sixteen

BUSINESS DEPARTMENT

(Author's comments are listed in italics)

1 (*Dr. Larry A. Olsen, professor emeritus of business education, 1996, is the compiler of First Century of Business Curriculum Development at Southern Utah University (1897-1997), SUU Special Collections. Dr. Olsen's history is the primary source for this chapter. Doris Williamson, Prof. Gary Giles and Dr. John Groesbeck also contributed valuable information.*)

Chapter Seventeen

COMMUNICATION DEPARTMENT

1 (*The material in this chapter was distilled from Dr. Suzanne Larson, Winning Isn't Everything But It Is What We Do Best: A Chronology of Southern Utah's Forensic Program, and Frain G. Pearson, A Brief History of the Department of Communication. These more complete histories may be found in SUU Special Collections. Faculty lists, competition results and references are included in these documents.*)

2 Hazen Cooley, college financial officer.

3 (*Judicious reading between the lines of the photo caption will suggest that the debate trips were highly productive, since two marriages resulted from the three couples included in the photo.*)

Chapter Eighteen

TECHNOLOGY DEPARTMENT

(Author's comments are listed in italics)

1 (*This chapter has been compiled from materials provided by Vic Davis, Ross Hilton, Don Blanchard, Lyman Munford, and from the journals of George Croft. The compilation of these materials is available as a bound history in SUU Special Collections.*)

2 Editors of Southern Branch of the State Normal School Catalog (1901-02).

3 Editors of Southern Branch of the State Normal School Catalog (1903-04).

4 Lyman Munford, Personal Remembrance of SUU (1997).

5 Ross Hilton, A Brief Overview of The School of Business, Technology and Aerospace (1997).

6 Ibid. (*Only a few of the interesting details of the adventures of planning and building found in Hilton's paper can be included here. The complete piece is available in the compiled history, SUU Special Collections.*)

Chapter Nineteen

AGRICULTURE DEPARTMENT

(Author's comments are listed in italics)

1 Editors of Branch Normal School Circular (1911-1912).

2 Darrell H. Matthews, The History of the Southern Utah University Farms and Mountain Ranch. (*Much of the information for this chapter is gleaned from this history, and is footnoted as faithfully as possible. Further information has been provided by Dr. James Bowns and Dr. Dan Dail.*)

3 Ibid.

4 V.R. Magleby, History of the Agriculture Department at BAC (Cedar City: 1996).

5 V.R. Magleby, The BAC Agricultural Department, As Seen Through the Eyes of a Former Student (1996).

6 Ibid.

7 (*Details of the sheep flock operation are all extracted from Darrell Matthews' history.*)

8 Bessie Dover, Stories of the Staff (1996).

9 Glenn Wahlquist, personal history notes.

10 (*Further details concerning the mountain ranch properties and the extensive sheep experiments and operations can be read in the complete history by Darrell Matthews, SUU Special Collections.*)

11 Matthews.

Chapter Twenty

FAMILY & CONSUMER SCIENCES DEPARTMENT

(Author's comments are listed in italics)

1 (*This history is distilled from the more complete History of the Home Economics Department and includes delightful tales of personalities and programs that wove the tapestry of the department. It consists of three parts by Carmen Croft Jones, Ada Dalley Carpenter and Ella Van Groningen. Additional contributors to the history include Rea Gubler, Artis Grady, Bonnie Bishop and others. The entire history is a bound volume found in SUU Library, Special Collections as well as in the department of family and consumer services.*

2 Catalog, Branch Normal School 1902.

3 (*See History of the Home Economics Department for a comprehensive listing of faculty over the years.*)

4 Henrietta Jones Harris, interview by Carmen Croft Jones.

5 Hazel Parks Urie , interview by Carmen Jones.

6 York and Evelyn Jones, Lehi Willard Jones, 163-71.

7 Hazel Parks Urie, interview by Carmen Jones.

8 (*The primary source for the department history of the era 1950-1970 is Ada Dalley Carpenter , "Personal Reflections and History (1950's - 1970's)" from History of the Home Economics Department, SUU Special Collections, SUU Library.*)

9 Ibid.

10 Annette White, home management student.

11 Ellen DeMille

12 Lucinda Duncan

13 (*This abbreviated outline is a distillation of Ella Van Groningen's " Chapter 3 - Organization and Programs of the Home Economics Department," History of the Home Economics Department, SUU Special Collections,*

SUU Library.)

14 Ibid.

15 (*A more complete history of the Home Economics Club from its early organization through 1997 is included in *The History of the Home Economics Department,*SUU Library Special Collections.*)

16 (*A reading of the more complete history reveals delightfully innovative projects serving campus and community organizations.*)

Chapter Twenty-One

SCIENCE AND MATHEMATICS DEPARTMENT

(*Author's comments are listed in italics*)

1 (*The primary source of the material for this chapter is *Short History of Science and Mathematics At Southern Utah University 1897-1996,* by Steven H. Heath. Other contributors include Dr. Harl Judd, Dr. Wesley Larsen, Dr. Blair Maxfield. Newspaper articles and yearbook entries have also been consulted.*)

2 Parley Dalley, Science Center dedication, 1961.

3 (*Some other details can be found in Chapter 3.*)

4 Iron County Record 7 June, 1962.

5 E. Blair Maxfield, A History of the Geology Department Southern Utah University, SUU Library, Special Collections.

6 Wesley Larsen, The CSU, SUSC, SUU Years, 1996

7 Richard Thompson, "Memo to All Faculty and Staff," Nov. 12, 1962.

8 *Thunderbird,* 11 Jan 1966.

9 Harl Judd, "Personal History," 1996.

10 Ibid.

11 (*Photograph and greater detail on the saga of the seismograph is found in Chapter 5: College of Southern Utah.*)

12 *Thunderbird,* October 3, 1966.

13 (*The Regional Science Fair is treated in more specific detail in *A Short History of Science and Mathematics at Southern Utah University,* by Steven H. Heath , Special Collections, SUU Library.*)

14 E. Blair Maxfield, History of The Geology Department of Southern Utah University, SUU Library, Special Collections.

15 Ibid.

17 Maxfield, op.cit.

Chapter Twenty-Two

CONTINUING EDUCATION

(*Daphne Dalley is the author of this chapter. Her comments are listed in italics*)

1 (This chapter was written by Daphne Dalley with assistance from others in Continuing Education. Sources include interviews, newspaper articles from the 1980's, the author's personal recollection of events between 1979-1990 and information on current Continuing Education programs, provided by Lana Johnson, David Nyman, and Jack Hill. Dalley records the following about the writing of this section:

Short histories of three programs were written by those responsible for them. While they were and are important programs, the writing of these histories was dependent on the willingness of the authors to take

the time and energy required to put the history into manuscript form. Information on the early history of the Division of Continuing Education and Public Service comes from an interview with Dr. McRay Cloward by Daphne Dalley. The interview took place in her office on the SUU campus on February 12, 1997.

2 Daphne Dalley, from information contributed by C. David Nyman, Lana Johnson and Jack Hill.

3 Georgia Beth Thompson, Upward Bound Director 1986-88.

4 Daphne Dalley, Elderhostel Coordinator 1983-1990.

5 This section by Virginia B. Higbee, Executive Director, SUU Office of Community Support Services.

Chapter Twenty-Three

RELIGIOUS EDUCATION

(*Dr. Robert Cloward is the author of this chapter. His comments are listed in italics.*)

1 M. Lynn Bennion, Mormonism and Education, The Department of Education of the Church of Jesus Christ of Latter-day Saints, 1939, 147-174.

2 "Circular of the Southern Branch of the State Normal School of the University of Utah, Cedar City, 1897-98," (Salt Lake City: G. Q. Cannon 1897) 9.

3 "Circular of the Southern Branch of the State Normal School of the University of Utah, Cedar City, 1905-1906," (Cedar City: 1905) 10.

4 "Circular of the Southern Branch of the State Normal School of the University of Utah, Cedar City, 1908-1909," (Cedar City: 1908) 13.

5 Agricola, 1916, 79. *BAC was still using the label "chapel" in 1924-25 for activities like the farce debate topic imposed on Zoe Robinson and Huldah Mitchell in front of the student body for initiation into Phi Alpha Beta: "Resolved: That long hair and short skirts are more expensive than short hair and long skirts"; the same sorority's "Sirkus," with balloons, sideshows, hats, popcorn, a Hula Dancer, etc.; and for Parowan High School faculty members Mr. Ostler and Mr. Hansen's comic one act play "Moonshine," which "amused those present" (Agricola, 1925, 132, 135, 149). Times had changed.*

6 Adam S. Bennion, Church Board of Education Minutes, The Church of Jesus Christ of Latter-day Saints, March 23, 1928, as cited in A. Gary Anderson, A Historical Survey of the fulltime Institutes of Religion of the Church of Jesus Christ of Latter-day Saints, 1926-1966, Ph.D. dissertation, Brigham Young University: 1968, 45.

7 "History of the Cedar LDS Seminary: Historical Data From Inception through School Year 1956-57," Cedar City Seminary historical files.

8 *The first LDS Seminary stood on property that in 1997 was the parking lot just east of the J. Reuben Clark, Jr. Alumni House. The Alumni House occupied the northeast corner of 300 West and Center Street.*

9 *LDS educators are referred to as brother or sister.*

10 Iron County Record, Oct 9, 1925, 1.

11 Iron County Record, Dec 25, 1925, 1.

12 Ibid.

13 Iron County Record, Oct 9, 1925, 1.

15 *J. Wyley Sessions was sent to establish a college seminary at the University of Idaho in 1926, a year after Andrew Anderson had already initiated college seminary in Cedar City. Despite this fact, the Moscow Idaho Institute of Religion is commonly designated the "first" institute in the LDS Church, probably because when*

the terms "seminary" and "institute" later came to designate high school and college religion programs respectively, Sessions was seen to have served a university while Anderson served the Branch Agricultural College, where the majority of the students at the time were in high school.

15 *The practice of offering college credit for selected religion courses was continued by mutual agreement between the LDS system and the college through the 1989-90 school year, after which both institutions deemed it no longer advantageous.*

16 Iron County Record 1925, cited above.

17 Pratt M. Bethers, A History of Schools in Iron County 1851-1970 (Cedar City:1972) 44.

18 *When Dr. Joseph F. Merrill, LDS Commissioner of Education, informed Larson by letter that his college seminary classes were to be called "institute of religion," it was "just a change of title." (From "Excerpt from Gustive O. Larson personal history," holograph in Gustive O. Larson Collection, Special Collections and Manuscripts, Harold B. Lee Library, Brigham Young University [hereafter, Larson Collection], Box 1, Folder 1.)*

19 H. Alvah Fitzgerald, personal interview with A. Gary Anderson, August 16, 1965, Anderson, op. cit.,168.

20 Iron County Record, cited in Joseph C. Felix, "The Church Educational System in Cedar City," (talk given to Iron County Historical Society, 24 March 1982, 6-7.

21 Ibid.

22 Agricola, 1942, 62

23 Agricola, 1947.

24 Gustive O. Larson to Dr. Frank L. West, May 12, 1943, Larson Collection, Box 12.

25 "History of Cedar City LDS Institute of Religion," Dedication Program of the Cedar City Institute of Religion, Feb.13, 1972.

26 "Annual Historical Report, Cedar City LDS Institute 1971-72"; Cedar City Institute of Religion historical files.

27 "Annual Historical Report, Cedar City LDS Institute 1992-93."

28 Ibid.

29 *Copy in Cedar City Institute of Religion historical files. Larson noted in his handwriting on the file copy that this should be dated about 1952.*

30 *The best source for dates and names of LDS ecclesiastical organization for students is a paper by Steven H. Heath, "A History of the Southern Utah University Stake," April 1995.*

31 Lambda Delta Sigma Leader Handbook, LDS Church:1995, 4-5.

33 Sigma Gamma Chi Reference Manual, LDS Church:1995, 3; Robert A. Cloward, personal interview with W. Sidney Young, 1997.

33 William G. Hartley, Delta Phi Kappa Fraternity, A History 1869-1978, Salt Lake City: Delta Phi Kappa Holding Corporation, 1990, passim.

34 Janet B. Seegmiller, A History of Iron County, Iron County Commission 1997.

36 Student Activities 1926, Branch Agricultural College, Southern Utah's State School (Cedar City) 20.

36 Robert A. Cloward, interview with Tina Clark, 20 Feb. 1997.

37 Tavi,1972, 140; 1973, 205.

38 Tavi, 1974; 1975, 144; 1976, 156.

39 Tavi, 1976, 167; 1977, 141; 1978, 176; 1979,147; 1980,

180.

40 "Constitution for United Campus Ministry of Southern Utah University (UCM),"Club Records Fall 1993-Spring 1994,"" (P-Z binder) SUUSA Offices, Valerie Olson, Student Body President, March 5-6, 1997.

41 "Clubs/Organizations Director's Files, Fall 93-Spring 94, SUUSA Offices, Valerie Olson, Student Body President, March 5-6, 1997.

42 UCM Section, "Club Records— Fall 1994-Spring 1995," SUUSA Offices, Valerie Olson, Student Body President, March 5-6, 1997.

43 Seegmiller, op. cit.; Bernice Maher Mooney(with Monsignor Jerome C. Stoffel, ed.), Salt of the Earth: The History of the Catholic Diocese of Salt Lake City, 1976 to 1987,(Diocese, 1987) 203-206.

44 Rev. Everett R. Harman to Bishop Joseph Lennox Federal, 23 September 1960; *original in diocese archive; copy of relevant paragraph kindly provided by Kay Sheehan in the form of a 19 March 1997 fax to her from Bernice Mooney of the diocese office, copy in Cedar City Institute of Religion historical files.*

45 *See also the listing of Father Harman under "Accredited Instructors Cooperating with CSU," College Course Catalog, 1964-65, 1965-66 105.*

46 Harman to Federal, 1961; op. cit.

47 Harman to Federal, 1963; op. cit.

48 Spectrum "Nuns give non-denominational aid throughout Southern Utah," Church Life section, October 29, 1982.

49 Tavi, 1979-1980,181.

50 Cyndi Winfield to Kay Sheehan,14 March 1997, personal fax,(copy Cedar City Institute of Religion files).

51 Father Michael J. Winterer, Pastor, Christ the King Catholic Church, personal interview by Robert A. Cloward (Cedar City; February 13, 1997).

Chapter Twenty-Four

STAFF, FACULTY/STAFF WOMEN ASSOCIATION AND EMERITI

(Author's comments are listed in italics)

1 *Distilled from a more complete history by Bessie Dover in collaboration with Jack Cannon, "SUU Staff Then and Now", Oct-Dec. 1996. Also included are excerpts from "Staff Stories" by Bessie Dover. These documents are bound together and are available from Special Collections, SUU Library. The document also includes many photographs and indexes of staff personnel.*

2 William Flanigan, personal interview by Elaine C. Southwick (Meredith), 1942.

3 Sheryn Dougherty, "Recollections of CSU," 1972.

4 LaVeve Whetten, "Some Historical Recollections," 1996.

5 *A complete history of the Faculty/Staff Associated Women is included with Bessie Dover's history: "SUU Staff Then and Now." This history includes a chronological account of the years of the organization's existence. The document details many of the significant contributions of the organization and gives insight into remarkable personalities behind the faculty and staff men.*

6 Ibid.

Chapter Twenty-Five

THE ALUMNI ASSOCIATION

1 *This chapter was written by Marlo Jensen, director of Alumni Relations.*

INDEX

Cameron, J. Elliott: 456, 474
Campbell, Hal K.: 172, 189, 324-325, 327, 329-330, 413
Campus Nursery School: 446
Campus Placement Office: 254
Canfield, Willard: 79, 341
Cannon, Allen: 305
Cannon, David: 61
Cannon, Jack: 188, 464-466
Cannon and Fetzer: 95
Cantus South Utahn: 127
Canyon Crest Inn: 408
Cardboard: 153, 347, 350, 383, 406-407, 429, 472
Cardon, Guy: 111
Cardon, Mildred: 475
Cardon, P. Vincent: 89-90
Carling, Sen.: 211
Carlisle, John: 135
Carlson, Richard: 309
Carnahan, Orville D.: 172-173, 177, 418, 436, 464
Carpenter, Ada D.: 133, 138, 140, 143-144, 172, 237, 413-414, 417-420, 469-470
Carpenter, Alexander: 360
Carpenter, Carmen: 378, 417
Carpenter, Don A.: 208
Carpenter, Don R.: 179
Carpentry: 132, 293, 347, 372, 383-384
Carr, Jeff: 268
Carrigan, Ben: 484, 486
Carrigan, Byron: 30, 478, 482, 498, 501
Carrigans: 36, 239
Carroll, Geles: 261
Carruthers, Matthew: 8, 14, 243
Carter Brothers: 168, 432
Carter, Calvin: 473
Carter, David: 375
Carter, Phillip: 178, 203, 251, 253, 442-443, 445
Carter, Jack H.: 375, 473
Carter, Rich: 268
Carter Enterprises: 168, 232, 369
Carver, James R.: 454
Castro, Dave: 267
Catholic Church: 3,457
Cazier, Stanford: 178, 210
Cedar Breaks: 28-29, 476, 480, 498
Cedar Canyon: 20, 28, 34, 399, 403, 408, 481
Cedar Cattle Company: 10
Cedar City Annual Art Exhibit: 293
Cedar City Chamber of Commerce: 90, 110, 127, 135, 137, 139, 293, 354, 443, 473
Cedar City Choral Society: 319-320
Cedar City Cooperative Mercantile: 11
Cedar City Cooperative Sheep Association: 10
Cedar City Corporation: 198, 293, 432
Cedar City Dramatic Societies: 340
Cedar City Lions Club: 127, 193, 264, 473
Cedar City Livestock Association: 263
Cedar City Music Arts Association: 314, 342
Cedar City National Competitive Exhibition: 295
Cedar Co-operative Sheep Association: 9
Cedar Dramatic Society: 339, 493
Cedar Ridge Golf Course: 268

Cedars Hotel: 59, 86
Centennial: 137, 202, 231-233, 237-240, 277, 321, 326, 330, 362, 438-439, 467
Center Street, Cedar City: 2
Centrum: 189-190, 192, 194-196, 199-200, 217, 222, 225, 231, 233, 238-239, 264, 296-298, 336, 382, 456, 470
Centurium, The: 231, 233, 239, 288
Certification: 100, 190, 244, 246-248, 250-254, 257, 336, 344, 367, 371, 415, 419-420
Chadwick, Vera: 280
Chaffin, Lavor: 307
Chaffin, Mrs.: 14
Chaffins: 36, 239
Challis, Arthur Tom: 136, 140, 161, 176, 282, 284-285, 354, 382
Challis, Ruth: 282, 355, 461, 465
Chamber Music Association: 320
Chamber of Commerce: 58, 64, 90-91, 98, 109-111, 114, 127, 135, 137, 139, 142, 151, 164, 293, 353-354, 435, 443, 473
Chamberlain, Donna: 453
Chamberlain, Hans Q.: 225-474-475
Chamberlain, Ramona: 169, 282-284
Chamberlain, Royce: 332
Chamberlain, Scott: 465
Chamberlain, Virginia: 411, 421
Chanley, Marie: 381
Chapel: 40, 48-49, 51, 61-62, 64, 81, 93, 219, 304, 314, 317, 333, 448-450, 452, 455-456, 494
Chapman, James: 334
Charlotte, Aunt: 481
Chase, Alice Koffard: 117
Chase, Daryl: 116-119, 127-130, 132, 135, 137-139, 145, 154, 250, 281, 318, 333, 354, 424, 441, 471
Chase, Mary: 164
Chase, Peter: 117
Chatterley, John: 13, 19, 25-26, 243, 311, 339, 501
Chatterley, Joseph: 14, 243, 501
Chatterleys: 36, 239
Chautauqua: 60-61, 94, 314
Cheerleaders: 157, 194, 272
Chemistry Lab: 157
Chi Alpha Chapter of Phi Beta Lambda: 374-375
Chi Theta Iota: 107
Chidester, E. Leon: 308-309
Chidester, Roger: 389, 391
Chidester, Stephanie: 309
Childs, DeVon: 447
Childs, Kenneth W.: 308
Childs, Norm: 345, 348
Choral, Manning-Halversen: 324
Chorus: 100, 109, 119, 132, 175, 312, 314-317, 320-322, 326, 353, 412, 452-453
Christ the King Catholic Church: 457
Christensen, Bruce: 299
Christensen, Doug: 205
Christensen, Joan: 375
Christensen, John C.: 261, 341, 394
Christensen, John S.: 78, 87, 259, 265, 269, 341
Christensen, Randall: 200, 284, 287
Christensen, Rex L.: 454
Christensen, Victoria B.: 408
Christiansen, Gordon: 342
Christiansen, Neil: 266

Christmas, Robert A.: 308
Christopher, San: 230, 232, 235, 359-360, 465
Church, Sterling: 165-166, 183, 465
Church, Troy: 236
Church of Jesus Christ of Latter-day Saints, The: 41-43, 54, 58, 67, 82, 91, 121, 161, 171, 189, 201, 236, 239, 320, 449, 470
Circle of Fame Award: 276
Citizens Committee: 20, 25, 27, 36
City Council: 18, 52, 85
City Hall: 23, 25
Clark, Amasa: 303
Clark, Douglas: 121
Clark, E. Val: 474
Clark, E.L.: 73
Clark, Eli: 402, 435
Clark, Gwyn: 54, 132, 140, 169, 172, 250-252, 255, 257-258, 306, 310, 469
Clark, J. Reuben, Jr.: 39, 50, 53-56, 104, 189, 331, 452, 454, 474-475
Clark, Karen: 419
Clark, Luacine Savage: 54
Clark, Scott: 373
Clark, Tina: 456
Clark, Wayne: 375
Clarke, Harold: 342
Clarks: 36, 239
Clausen, Rene: 236
Clayton, Christine B.: 409
Clinic: 253, 316
Cloward, McRay: 106, 132, 140, 149-150, 172, 204, 255, 333-334, 430, 441, 446
Cloward, Robert A.: 454, 457
Clyde, Aileen M.: 211
Clyde, Gov. George Dewey: 140, 353-354
Co-op: 14, 21, 23, 28-29
Coal Creek: 7, 87, 401
Coal Creek Irrigation Company: 401
Coburt, Spence: 478-479, 484
Coburt, Spencer: 478-479, 482, 484-485
Cohen, Michael: 308-310
Cole, David: 330
Coles, Katherine: 237, 310
Coliseum: 231, 264
College Cabin: 202, 204, 443, 461-462
College Cavalcade: 108, 238, 244
College Development Board: 170, 432
College Hill: 82-83, 100, 116, 477, 482, 494
College of Southern Utah: 119, 121, 127, 129-130, 133-135, 138-139, 141-148, 150-151, 154, 165, 183, 200, 250-251, 254, 258, 281, 299, 324, 333, 343, 353, 365, 367, 372, 377, 422, 431, 435, 446, 457
Collier, Suzanne: 328
Color Country Forensics Institute: 442
Comes Spring: 120
Commencement: 45, 92, 104, 108, 111, 115-116, 121, 131, 136, 139, 149, 154, 162-163, 165, 167-169, 172, 174, 177, 182, 185, 201, 248-249, 283, 312, 322, 436, 452
Commercial Club: 58, 73, 76
Committee on Education: 15, 17, 114, 211
Communication: 45, 135, 144, 178, 185, 189, 197, 222, 226, 297-298, 306-308, 312, 338, 344, 366, 368, 371, 373-375, 377, 381-382, 437, 442

Photo: Arthur C. Porter, 1955